A Critical History of
Doctor Who *on Television*

POLICE BOX

A Critical History of *Doctor Who* on Television

JOHN KENNETH MUIR

McFarland & Company, Inc., Publishers
Jefferson, North Carolina, and London

RECENT WORKS BY JOHN KENNETH MUIR AND FROM MCFARLAND

Horror Films of the 1970s (2002; paper 2008)

A Critical History of Doctor Who *on Television* (1999; paper 2008)

The Encyclopedia of Superheroes on Film and Television, 2d ed. (2008)

Horror Films of the 1980s (2007)

An Analytical Guide to Television's
One Step Beyond, *1959–1961* (2001; paper 2006)

A History and Critical Analysis of Blake's 7, *the 1978–1981 British Television Space Adventure* (2000; paper 2006)

The Films of John Carpenter (2000; paper 2005)

An Analytical Guide to Television's Battlestar Galactica (1999; paper 2005)

Exploring Space: 1999*: An Episode Guide and Complete History of the Mid-1970s Science Fiction Television Series* (1997; paper 2005)

The present work is a reprint of the library bound edition of A Critical History of *Doctor Who* on Television, *first published in 1999 by McFarland.*

Frontispiece: Landfall! The Doctor's old blue Police Box sets down on an alien landscape. Artwork by Mindy Easler.

LIBRARY OF CONGRESS CATALOGUING-IN-PUBLICATION DATA

Muir, John Kenneth, 1969–
A critical history of *Doctor Who* on television / by John Kenneth Muir.
p. cm.
Videography: p.
Includes bibliographical references and index.

ISBN-13: 978-0-7864-3716-0
softcover : 50# alkaline paper ♾

1. Doctor Who (Television program) I. Title.
PN1992.77.D6273M85 2008 791.45'72—dc21 99-38016

British Library cataloguing data are available

On the cover: The 1983 TV movie *Doctor Who: The Five Doctors*—(clockwise from left) Richard Hurndall, Jon Pertwee, Peter Davison, Patrick Troughton and Tom Baker (BBC/Photofest)

Manufactured in the United States of America

McFarland & Company, Inc., Publishers, Box 611, Jefferson, North Carolina 28640
www.mcfarlandpub.com

Acknowledgments

This author thanks the following people for their assistance in the creation of this book: Kathryn Muir, for watching hundreds of hours of *Doctor Who* and proofing the text; Loretta Muir, for scouring the flea markets and bookstores of North Carolina for all *Doctor Who*–related publications; Kenneth Muir, for photographing *Who* collectibles; and Mindy Easler, for her tireless work on the illustrations.

Finally, this author gratefully acknowledges Jean-Marc Lofficier, Terrance Dicks, Jean Airey, John Peel, and all the other *Doctor Who* historians and scholars whose many knowledgeable works provided the foundations on which this text is built.

For Kathryn,
the most supportive and
nurturing character
in canon, alternate, or
parallel space/time dimensions

And
For the incomparable Lulu

Table of Contents

Season 4

Season 5

Season 6

Season 7

Season 8

Season 9

Season 10

Season 11

SEASON 12

SEASON 13

SEASON 14

SEASON 15

SEASON 16

SEASON 17

SEASON 18

SEASON 19

In Great Britain, *Doctor Who* has been beloved by generations of fans not only for its interesting stories, but also for its imaginative alien monsters. Artist Mindy Easler's rendition of *Doctor Who*'s "Rogue's Gallery" reveals why.

Introduction

Doctor Who was a pioneer in the annals of science fiction television and film. Before the dawn of *Star Wars* (1977) and *Star Trek* (1966–69), and even before the day of Irwin Allen's juvenile *Lost in Space* (1965–68), the BBC's *Doctor Who* was merrily traversing the airwaves in Great Britain and delighting children and adults alike with its fanciful outer space fables and sci-fi morality plays. By the time NBC's *Star Trek* made its historic American network debut with George Clayton Johnson's "The Man Trap" on September 8, 1966, *Doctor Who* was quietly but successfully beginning a fourth season with "The Smugglers," a time travel–historical adventure by frequent *Who* contributor Brian Hayles. In this context, and with apologies to Abbott and Costello, it is appropriate to note *Who*'s on first!

Doctor Who's historical position is an important distinction in the universe of visual science fiction imaginings. It is an oft-repeated American pop culture myth, perpetuated now for over 30 years, that *Star Trek* was the "first" science fiction television series to probe continuing characters, adult genre principles and futuristic philosophies in serious terms. This is a singular honor. However, history records that *Doctor Who* was seriously investigating continuing characters, cosmic turbulence, otherworldly societies and moral dilemmas of all varieties while in America *Star Trek* was an embryonic glimmer in Gene Roddenberry's eye.

Doctor Who premiered on British television on November 23, 1963, two months after Leslie Stevens' and Joseph Stefano's seminal science fiction anthology *The Outer Limits* began to control our television sets in America. It is perhaps difficult for the modern sci-fi fan to believe it, but *Doctor Who* was born into this world before all generations of *Star Trek*, before *Star Wars*, before *Planet of the Apes* (1968). Succinctly put, *Doctor Who* began exploring outer space and the darkest corners of time before *every* sci-fi production familiar to Generation X was conceived. Accordingly, many revolutionary aspects of *Doctor Who* serials, such as time travel "law," non-humanoid aliens, alternate dimensions and living machines, had never before been envisioned for the masses, even though today's viewers are so familiar with these inventions that they are considered clichés.

Perhaps of more genuine historical importance, *Doctor Who* arrived on television the day after the Kennedy assassination in Dallas, Texas. So while on November 22, 1963, a real-life Camelot was cut tragically short, on the November 23 a fictional Camelot was beginning an unmatched and mostly unheralded broadcast run. *Doctor Who* finally ceased regular production in 1989 after 26 years on the air.

Doctor Who represents not only a television pioneer but a genuine video anomaly as well. No sci-fi show before it had lasted even four continuous years except Rod Serling's anthology series *The Twilight Zone* (1959–65) and the juvenile *The Adventures of Superman* (1951–57). Even if one were to tally three years of classic *Star Trek*, two years of animated *Star Trek*, seven years of *The Next Generation* (1987–94), seven years of *Deep Space Nine* (1993–99) and five years of *Voyager* (1995–), the total number of Trekker hours would not equal the incredible two-and-a-half-decade span of *Doctor Who*. As of this writing, over 600 hours of *Doctor Who* have been produced — a staggering number. This total does not take into account the record albums, radio presentations, stage shows, comic books, novelizations or other tie-ins.

Despite this longevity, *Doctor Who* remains to many American television watchers an enigma that requires a great deal of explanation. In many parts of the United States, this BBC-produced sci-fi venture has never been run at all. The American exposure it got was usually through local syndication or PBS stations. Unheralded and barely remembered by the U.S., 13 Jon Pertwee–era *Doctor Who* episodes (1970-74) did run in Philadelphia, Chicago and Los Angeles television markets in the mid–'70s.[1]

Yet the only time *Doctor Who* made a significant ripple on American television was late in the '70s and early '80s on the heels of George Lucas' blockbuster *Star Wars*. During this sortie, this author was fortunate enough to catch the entire Tom Baker roster of serials from "Robot" to "The Invasion of Time" (1975–78; Seasons 12–15) on WWOR Channel 9 in New York City, thanks to the efforts of distributor Time-Life Television. Ironically, the program aired at five o'clock on Saturday evenings...just an hour before competing station WPIX offered *Star Trek* reruns.

If *Doctor Who* premiered on United States shores in the late 1970s, why should a book published in 1999 presume a need to "introduce" him to America? For the simple reason that American audiences have never had the opportunity to appreciate him as British audiences have — and the numbers prove it. *Doctor Who*'s largest viewing audience in history was approximately 14.5 million viewers in Great Britain. In America, a new *Doctor Who* movie premiered on May 14, 1996, and was watched by only 8.5 million viewers, a measly number considering the size of the American public. This *Doctor Who* incarnation was trounced in the Nielsen ratings by *Roseanne* and *3rd Rock from the Sun*.

So for those millions of American newcomers to *Doctor Who*, the immediate question is this: Who or what is *Doctor Who*? First, there is no "Doctor Who" at all. The main character of the program is always enigmatically referred to as "The Doctor." He is never called "Doctor Who" except during end credits, in the anomalous serial title "Doctor Who and the Silurians," mistakenly in the early episode "The War Machines" and in two apocryphal *Dalek* films made in the '60s and starring horror film legend Peter Cushing.

Issues of nomenclature aside, the Doctor is an incredibly old alien who has been knocking around the universe for more than 900 years. He is a "Time Lord" from the distant planet Gallifrey in the constellation of Kasterborus. His advanced race has harnessed the energies of black holes and suns. More importantly, the Time Lords have unlocked the mysteries of time travel. Though time travel technology has made the Gallifreyans virtually invincible, the Time Lords believe firmly in remaining neutral and only rarely do they use time travel for any purpose but peaceful observation of developing cultures.

The Doctor does not share this philosophical stance. He is a renegade. He is a mysterious man, an exile with a secret past. He may be a criminal, or perhaps a revolutionary. Because he was bored, because he was tired of seeing the weak overcome by the strong, he abandoned his secure life on Gallifrey and decided to intervene in the fast and furious action of a dangerous universe. He appropriated a Time Lord Type 40 capsule, a space-time vehicle known as a TARDIS (Time And Relative Dimensions In Space). He then set out, like Earth's noble Robin Hood, to right all the wrongs he encountered.

In his long crusade against evil, the Doctor has not stood alone. He has been accompanied by a variety of companions including a loyal robot dog named K-9, a fellow Time Lord named Romana and even the Stone Age woman Leela. With his fellow travelers, he has defeated villains as diverse as the mutated Daleks, the brutal Zygons, the militaristic Sontarans, the Krynoids, the Silurians, the Martian Ice Warriors, the Borg-like Cybermen and the non-corporeal Nestene. He has also grappled with intergalactic terrorists such as Omega, the Master, Scaroth, the Shadow, Magnus Greel, Eldrad, the Black Guardian, Solon and Morbius. He has restored peace on beguiling alien worlds like the war-ravaged Skaro, the swampy moon of Delta Magna and the Zarbi–populated planet Vortis. He has also participated in various heroic quests including the search for the invaluable "Key to Time." The Doctor has even been captured by his own people and tried in Time Lord court for his frequent meddling and contravention of sacred Gallifreyan Law.

With all of his knowledge and galactic experience, the Doctor still has one soft spot in his heart(s). Gentle soul that he is, he holds a special affection for that tiny, insignificant planet called Earth. He harbors this love because he considers human beings terribly vulnerable. Accordingly, he has made a point of witnessing nearly every important historical event in Earth's long and varied history. He was in Rome in 64 A.D. with Emperor Nero when fire swept through the city ("The Romans"). He met Richard the Lionhearted in 1191 A.D. and tried to negotiate a peace with Saladin ("The Crusades"). He traveled with Marco Polo in 1289 and played backgammon with the great Kublai Khan ("Marco Polo"). He even participated in the infamous gunfight at the O.K. Corral in Tombstone, Arizona ("The Gunfighters").

The Doctor has also encountered time loops ("Image of the Fendahl," "The Armageddon Factor," "Carnival of Monsters"), time and space paradoxes ("The Mysterious Planet, "Earthshock") and extraterrestrial opponents so dangerous that they have forced him to "regenerate"— another unique ability of the Time Lords.

The Doctor's species may change or "renew" physical appearance. They may regenerate brand new bodies 12 times in an average life span.

As of this writing, the stalwart Doctor is in his eighth incarnation. To keep the television program fresh and to accommodate the personalities of new actors, each incarnation of this hero highlights different elements of the Doctor's complicated personality. The first incarnation was a white-haired, grandfatherly gentleman prone to fits of crankiness. The second was a sentimental, humorous man and a sort of cosmic Pied Piper. The third incarnation was a logical thinker, fluent with Venusian karate and quicker to resort to physical action. And so on.

Over the years, eight distinguished British actors have portrayed the Doctor on television: William Hartnell, Patrick Troughton, Jon Pertwee, Tom Baker, Peter Davison, Colin Baker, Sylvester McCoy and Paul McGann. Although the face of this alien is constantly changing, his heroism, his dedication to honor, his commitment to truth and his pursuit of justice have remained consistent for 35 years. With characteristics like this, *Doctor Who*'s popularity in America would seem a safe bet, and those Yanks lucky enough to see the show have certainly been taken with it. But persuading television programmers to take a chance on a low-budget, British-made sci-fi series is no easy task, even after three decades.

Perhaps American programmers can be forgiven for their reluctance to spotlight *Doctor Who* in high profile prime time spots in the '90s. *Doctor Who* first became available to U.S. syndication in the '70s and was deemed risky for several reasons. First, television executives found it lacking when compared to the British import *Space: 1999* (1975–77), which had been a bonafide ratings hit in its first year. That series had featured state-of-the-art special effects and familiar American stars Martin Landau and Barbara Bain, late of *Mission: Impossible.* Unlike *Space: 1999* or even the earlier *UFO* (1970), which featured an American air force officer at the center of the action, *Doctor Who* made no concession whatsoever to American viewing sensibilities. Even as late as 1989, *Doctor Who* failed to feature the high quality of special effects seen on *Space: 1999* in 1975. To be certain, the series offered imaginative and well-written sci-fi, but it was sci-fi on a meager budget. Perhaps more than any other thing, this factor has kept the series from enjoying tremendous popularity in America.

In *Doctor Who*, there is no acknowledgment of the American passion for flashy gadgetry and technology. The British, it would seem, prefer solid, dramatic plots well told. As a result, *Doctor Who* might be best described as flagrantly anti-technology. The Doctor travels through time and space not in some souped-up Spielbergian spaceship of enormous technical detail and proportion, but rather in an old, beat-up, blue police box! His TARDIS is equipped with a device called a "chameleon" circuit that should allow it to mimic the appearance of any object. Unfortunately, the chameleon circuit broke down during the first televised adventure, "An Unearthly Child," and the TARDIS has been stuck in the shape of a police box for 35 years. This particular police box has outlived the real police boxes in London, which were replaced in the '70s by hand-held walkie-talkies.

Beyond its appearance, the TARDIS is a bit eccentric in function as well. It is constantly breaking down and sending the Doctor to the wrong location or an incorrect time zone. Would that kind of eccentricity fly in *Star Wars*? In *Doctor Who*, there are no roaring spaceships with bright neon engines that perform barrel rolls or loops. The supposedly "futuristic" sets on *Doctor Who* are seldom incredible to behold either. As late as "Ark in Space" (1975), a serial watched by 14 million people in England at the time, Styrofoam played an important part in set construction.

With these production factors measured against it, *Doctor Who* certainly did not appear to be in the same league as *Space: 1999*. The only other '70s British science fiction import to compare it with was *Star Maidens* (1976), starring Judy Geeson and *Blake's 7*'s Gareth Thomas. *Star Maidens* was a ratings disaster when it aired in the New York market on WNEW Channel 5, and that fact left the Doctor in a tight spot on American shores. Following on the heels of the U.S.–friendly, big-budgeted *Space: 1999* and this *Star Maidens* failure, *Doctor Who* must have seemed like a very long shot.

Today the problem is not necessarily one of production quality but rather, if one forgives the pun, of space. Where are *Doctor Who* reruns to fit in a schedule crowded with syndicated hits like *Hercules*, *Xena*, *Deep Space Nine*, *Babylon 5* and *Highlander*, not to mention endless reruns of sitcom giants *Seinfeld*, *Roseanne*, *Home Improvement*, and so forth? That the early serials are black-and-white and of varying running time does not help matters either.

The perception that *Doctor Who* cannot hack it in the U.S. has been reinforced by the sometimes snobbish attitude of *Doctor Who*'s own creator, the BBC. BBC network executives have always treated *Doctor Who* as if it were a something to be ashamed of, hiding it, ignoring it, cancelling it or even mocking it publicly. This strange "children's program" is not considered highbrow, and the regal BBC, with its expensive costume dramas and accurate period pieces, desires to cater to intellectual audiences around the world. Typical of the BBC's continued mishandling of *Doctor Who* was the revelation in the early '80s that many of the early *Who* serials had been destroyed or taped over to make storage room for other BBC shows in their film and video vaults. Thus, many classic stories of the Hartnell and Troughton eras, including "The Power of the Daleks," "The Tenth Planet" and "The Macra Terror," are gone forever.

Equally incomprehensible was the BBC's ruthless, unjustified 1987 firing of Colin Baker, the sixth actor to portray the Doctor, as well as its decision not to produce a 30th year celebration show. With the BBC slamming the show left and right in this manner, is it any surprise that for decades American programmers have decided to pass on the series in prime time? Nevertheless, *Doctor Who* has had the last laugh on the BBC. This kid's show, this so-called silly little lark, is the most profitable BBC export in history.[2]

Despite these many hardships, *Doctor Who* is a common name for "in the know" American science fiction fans in 1999. Scores of episodes have been released on VHS by BBC/CBS-Fox home video and are currently available around the country. It is rather bewildering, though, that *Doctor Who* has never run on any

American television channel in its entirety (or as much "entirety" as now remains, thanks to the BBC's short-sightedness). It has not even appeared recently on the Sci-Fi Channel, sanctuary of every homeless sci-fi series from *Automan* to *VR.5*.

Perhaps even more perplexing than *Doctor Who*'s lack of exposure on American television sets is that in all of the 1,500-plus books written about this fascinating British teleseries over 35 years, few authors have examined the ideas, philosophies, conceits and morals put forth by the series. Though there are highly detailed technical manuals, behind-the-scenes accounts, the inevitable episode novelizations, and celebratory works of all varieties, an analysis of *Doctor Who*'s thematic concepts and genre antecedents has rarely been attempted — perhaps because *Doctor Who* is still considered by many to be a children's show. To those unenlightened, it may not warrant serious critical attention. Another possibility is that the producers of the "official" books are not permitted to offer anything but toothless propaganda and cheerleading for the series, in fear of angering the big bad BBC. Or perhaps this dearth of critical examination has been caused by the fear that a true exposure of *Doctor Who*'s progressive philosophies and dramatic stories will reveal that sacred American television programs and films such as *Star Trek* and *Star Wars* owe a great debt to this unique program.

Whatever the explanation, *Doctor Who* has never really been placed under the microscope for serious critical and historical examination. It is the goal of this text not only to introduce the unknowing in America to the world of *Doctor Who* and to document the history of its long television adventure, but also to examine the film and video sources from which *Doctor Who* is certainly derived. At the same time, *Doctor Who*'s enormous influence on popular film and later television programs will also be surveyed.

Read on and discover the bedside manner of sci-fi television's most charming and charismatic alien. The Doctor will see you now!

PART I

THE HISTORY

Parturition

To fully understand the long and rather complicated history of *Doctor Who*, it is necessary to first elaborate on the age which spawned it. In 1950s America, science fiction television consisted primarily of programs such as *Captain Video and His Video Rangers* (1949–55), *Space Patrol* (1951-52) and *Tom Corbett, Space Cadet* (1950–52). These were fun adventure programs about larger-than-life futuristic heroes and their sidekicks. The sets and special effects seen in these early outer space efforts are extremely primitive by today's standards, and it has long been rumored that in many cases the props and visual effects budget amounted to less than $50 an episode. Despite the crude nature of these efforts, they served a noble purpose. Since they catered primarily to youthful audiences, *Space Patrol* and the like opened the minds of children to the possibilities of space travel, not to mention the appeal of science.

More literate science fiction series included *Tales of Tomorrow*, a 1951 production which adapted the works of Jules Verne and other authors, as well as the praiseworthy *Science Fiction Theater* (1955–57), host Truman Bradley's attempt to highlight the "science" aspect of science fiction. Still, it is fair to state that these anthologies were isolated examples of quality sci-fi. The epoch of mature science fiction drama did not truly arrive in the United States until Rod Serling's *The Twilight Zone* (1959–65) and John Newland's *One Step Beyond* (1959–61) debuted in the last year of the decade. These series were not set in the action-adventure, "space" military mode of *Space Patrol*; *Tom Corbett*; *Rocky Jones, Space Ranger* (1953) or *Rod Brown of the Rocket Rangers* (1953). Instead, they featured well-acted, tautly scripted flights of imagination about alternate worlds, mental telepathy, voyages into space, etc. Unlike anthology predecessors *Tales of Tomorrow* or *Science Fiction Theater*, these shows enjoyed comparatively long runs and successfully established a beachhead for other science fiction programming. Their "stable" influence prompted genre television to blossom in the '60s. *The Outer Limits* appeared in 1963 and more colorful forays into outer space, *Lost in Space* (1965–68) and *Star Trek* (1966–69) among them, followed quickly. By the end of *Star Trek*'s run, larger budgets, better acting and solid stories were commonplace. The genre had grown up.

In Great Britain, the land where *Doctor Who* was born, the story was not quite the same. English televised sci-fi in the 1950s did have at least one factor in common with its American counterpart: pitifully low budgets. Yet conceptually and dramatically, the British programming of the '50s was far superior to *Captain Video*, *Tom Corbett, Space Cadet* and their ilk. As early as 1953, the BBC presented *The Quatermass Experiment*, a serial written by Nigel Kneale, which concerned the exploits of British professor Bernard Quatermass. In the first *Quatermass* series, astronauts returned to Earth carrying a deadly alien fungus. Quatermass sought to investigate and contain the crisis. This riveting series was such a *coup de maitre* that a second Quatermass installment was produced in 1955, this one also about hostile extraterrestrial life arriving on Earth. A third series, the landmark *Quatermass and the Pit*, aired in 1958. Generally the highest regarded of the three series, it involved the unearthing of ancient alien artifacts near London. *Quatermass and the Pit* examined topics such as psychic forces, believable alien races and society's response to a crisis. All of these noteworthy adventures spotlighted top-flight actors and mature science fiction writing courtesy of the talented Kneale.

The *Quatermass* saga eschewed the action, mock heroics and *Buck Rogers*– style clichés of concurrent American programming, and instead had a thoughtful, intellectual approach to the material. And, significantly, where in America science fiction heroes were always members of unbelievably benevolent military hierarchies like the Space Academy, the Video Rangers, the Rocket Rangers, the United Planets and Starfleet, the lead character in the British *Quatermass* was an eccentric individualist. Quatermass was a man of science, not a soldier or part of "the establishment." Also of importance was the fact that Quatermass was an older gentleman, not a young, handsome American futuristic cowboy like Richard Crane (*Rocky Jones*), Cliff Robertson (*Rod Brown*) or William Shatner (*Star Trek*). *Quatermass* was sterling, contemplative drama, not shallow Hollywood hijinks and gimmickry.

So successful was *Quatermass* and its sequels that other mature science fiction programs cropped up in England soon after the beginning of the saga. *A for Andromeda* (1961), starring Julie Christie, and its sequel *The Andromeda Breakthrough* (1962) concerned genetic instructions transmitted across space, and the birth of a new, superior life form. So forward-thinking was this drama that the same plot was replayed in more malevolent terms in the big-budget feature film *Species* (1995). Also in 1961 and 1962 came the advent of a technique called "Supermarionation," and the miniature special effects breakthroughs of Gerry and Sylvia Anderson in *Supercar* (1961–62) and the space adventure *Fireball XL-5* (1963). Though starring well-detailed puppets, these shows featured not only complex special effects and models but fairly innovative plots and characters as well.

Perhaps of greatest interest to *Doctor Who* fans was a series produced by the head of the BBC Drama Department, *Doctor Who* creator Sydney Newman. Called *Target Luna* (1960), this drama explored the plight of precocious British child

Jimmy Wedgewood when he became trapped in space aboard a runaway rocketship. One of the series' stars was Michael Craze, an actor who would later find greater fame as Patrick Troughton's companion Ben Jackson in *Doctor Who. Target Luna* was Newman's sincere attempt to create an educational and entertaining program about the hazards of space travel. Subjects of various episodes included exposure to cosmic rays, freezing in the vacuum of space, and the perils of re-entry descent. All the *Target Luna* stories were co-written by Malcolm Hulke, later a frequent contributor to *Doctor Who*, and Eric Paice, the creator of *Star Maidens*. *Target Luna* was so successful that Newman followed it up with three sequels: *Pathfinders in Space* (1960), *Pathfinders to Mars* (1960) and *Pathfinders to Venus* (1961). In total, there were 27 episodes concerning the Wedgewood family's adventures in the void, each lasting 30 minutes. The later *Pathfinder* episodes revealed the existence of alien spaceships and cultures, so the follow-ups were more fanciful and less factual than *Target Luna* had been.

Luna and its progeny aired on the BBC during what was in the '60s considered "the Family Hour"— on Saturday afternoons following major sporting events. Although as primitive in production values as their American contemporaries, these early shows were so much more full-grown in concept. Unfortunately, like many *Doctor Who* serials, film prints and videotape originals of *Target Luna*, *A for Andromeda* and the first *Quatermass* serial have all been destroyed by the BBC. Today these landmark programs are rarely honored or even remembered in histories of science fiction television.

Evolution

In the early '60s, Sydney Newman and BBC executive Donald Wilson set out to create another new "children's" science fiction drama which could air on Saturday afternoons, fill the time slot following "The Big Game," and successfully repeat the ratings triumph of *Target Luna* and its offshoots. The series they created was, of course, *Doctor Who*. Despite this achievement, Newman and Wilson have never received the same level of respect accorded other science fiction television auteurs such as Gene Roddenberry, Rod Serling, Joe Stefano, J. Michael Straczynski, Chris Carter, the Andersons and Irwin Allen. This is doubly baffling since Newman's accomplishments range far beyond the world of *Doctor Who*. He also created another pop culture sensation, *The Avengers* (1961–69), before there was a James Bond film series or international spy-film craze. Newman also created the literate science fiction anthology *Out of This World* (1961), which was hosted by Boris Karloff. And, at one time during his illustrious reign, Newman oversaw production on all the BBC's dramas, a whopping 726 programs in all.[1]

Newman and Wilson originally envisioned *Doctor Who* as an educational program which would enlighten children about various historical time periods. The need for historical accuracy was stressed; two of the series' main characters were teachers, people familiar with the mores and personalities of the various time periods they encountered. Newman also devised a format which incorporated the "outer space" angle, so the new series might mine the space science issues that had been the bread and butter of *Target Luna* and *Pathfinders*. He described his premise for the series in *Starlog* #116 (March 1987) more than 20 years after *Doctor Who* first aired:

> I dreamed up this old man of 760 years of age who fled from a distant planet in a time-space machine. Being so old, he is somewhat senile and doesn't know how to operate his machine.... The rest of the series dealt with these Earthlings trying to get back to Earth, the old man trying to get back to where he came from and no one knowing how to operate the machine.[2]

Aiding Newman in his attempt to get the TARDIS off the ground and onto television screens was Verity Lambert, an experienced producer later responsible for the genre series *Adam Adamant Lives!* (1966) and the fourth series of *Quatermass* (1979). Lambert, educated at Roedean and the Sorbonne, was instrumental in the casting of *Doctor Who* series lead William "Bill" Hartnell (1908–1975). The 55-year-old actor was a seasoned performer by 1963, having appeared in nearly 50 films, including *Lure* (1933), *Follow the Lady* (1933), *Headline* (1943), *The Agitator* (1954), *The Pickwick Papers* (1954), *The Mouse That Roared* (1959) and *Heavens Above* (1963). He was most familiar to British viewers for his 1957–61 stint on the popular television sitcom *The Army Game*. In some respects, *The Army Game* could be considered an English version of *The Phil Silvers Show* (1955–59). The main character was a variation on the Sgt. Bilko character whom Silvers had popularized, a con man concerned more with bets, cards and scams than the rituals and regulations of army life. In *The Army Game*, Hartnell essayed the "Colonel Hall"—style role of rigid military taskmaster, in this case called Sgt. Major Bullmore. All the action of the ITV show took place at Hut 29, the surplus Ordnance Depot at Nether Hopping; Hartnell's Bullmore was the straight man and butt of many jokes. The role was a fun but limited one; *Doctor Who* offered the skilled actor a chance to branch out and take center stage.

Hartnell was joined on the set of *Doctor Who* by a group of talented fellow performers. William Russell, known later in the profession as Russell Enoch, became the action lead of the series, schoolteacher Ian Chesterton. In the mid'-50s he had played Sir Lancelot in *The Adventures of Sir Lancelot* (1956-57) and in 1962 he appeared in the film *The Great Escape*. After *Doctor Who*, Russell went on to play in the popular *Coronation Street*. RADA graduate, Joan Collins classmate[3] and top fashion model Jacqueline Hill was chosen to essay the crucial, well-written role of Barbara Wright, the other schoolteacher. The last member of the cast was the experienced Carole Ann Ford, a young actress who had begun her performing career at age eight. Ford, a native of Dagnham, Essex, became the Doctor's granddaughter Susan. Together these four performers created the memorable first team aboard the TARDIS.

Hartnell's Halcyon Days

A pilot film for the new BBC science fiction series *Doctor Who* was shot at Lime Grove Studios in 1963 for a budget of £2000. It was lensed entirely indoors on sets representing Totter's Lane, the Coal Hill Secondary School and the TARDIS interior. Like many early episodes of *Doctor Who*, the four-part serial, known officially as "An Unearthly Child," was exclusively a time travel show. It did not feature aliens, outer space, spaceships or otherworldly civilizations. Instead, the program introduced the main series characters and then went on to chronicle the Doctor's journey to prehistory and his subsequent encounter with the caveman Tribe of Gum. In the historic first 25-minute episode of the four-part serial, the Doctor identified both himself and his grandchild Susan as "exiles" from another civilization. The dimensionally transcendent (bigger on the inside than the outside) TARDIS time-space capsule was also introduced as the product of an alien civilization. Coal Hill schoolteachers Ian and Barbara were dragged along for the wild ride from 1963 to 1,000,000 B.C., and the *Doctor Who* odyssey was off and running.

The completed pilot was aired for the BBC brass and some modifications were made before the network debut was scheduled for late November 1963. In the first version of the pilot, the Doctor and Susan were delineated with harder edges and the Doctor in particular was downright unfriendly at times. Susan also revealed that she and her traveling companion (not yet identified as her grandfather) were from the forty-ninth century. This throwaway line pinned the Doctor's origin down to a specific time, and it was decided by the producers that the best approach would be to leave the Doctor's home, origin and exact nature a mystery. The reference to the forty-ninth century, much of the Doctor's rigid attitude and some unsuitable electronic sound effects were changed. The half-hour introductory program was reshot and the show was deemed ready to go.

The original version of the "An Unearthly Child," complete with original soundtrack and dialogue, finally aired on the BBC on August 26, 1991, almost 30 years after it was produced.[4] As for the edited version, it would become the foundation of a franchise.

One of the most exciting and unusual aspects of "An Unearthly Child" was the strange, rhythmic electronic theme music devised for the series by Ron Grainer and the BBC Radiophonic Workshop. Composer Grainer had recently come off a stint composing the music for *Maigret*, a 1960–63 detective show, and his very different, very unusual *Doctor Who* theme immediately and expertly conveyed the otherworldiness of the series' main character. So effective was the distinct theme music that it served the series, with only minor variations, through the '70s and '80s. Also joining the production team with Sydney Newman and Verity Lambert were story editor David Whitaker and associate producer Mervyn Pinfield. All early indications were that the compelling time travel show would have a grand take-off, but the world of reality threw a nasty curve at the fledgling science fiction series. U.S. President John F. Kennedy was shot and killed on Friday, November 22, 1963.

Doctor Who became the first entertainment program to air on the BBC after a full Saturday of grim assassination news coverage. Understandably, many parents were not in the mood to appreciate the well-directed efforts of Waris Hussein or the charming performances of Hartnell, Ford, Hill and Russell in "An Unearthly Child." Also hindering the show's premiere was the fact that it started at 5:25 P.M., ten minutes later than its scheduled debut. Already the series was on shaky ground in the ratings. Fortunately, the BBC decided not to trash a series which many believed could be immensely popular. The first serial was rerun the following week and it doubled the audience of the former Saturday, drawing six million Brits to the television set.

Fortunately, *Doctor Who*'s fortunes changed dramatically and something occurred which changed the face of science fiction television. Author Terry Nation, a frequent contributor to *The Avengers* (1961–68), *The Saint* (1962), *Out of the Unknown* (1965–71) and later British television programs such as *Survivors* (1975) and *Blake's 7* (1978–81), invented the Daleks. Designed by Raymond Cusick, these terrifying mutant creatures who inhabited mobile, armored suits starred in the second *Doctor Who* serial produced, "The Daleks," in late December 1963. Although Newman's intent had not been to feature evil aliens on *Doctor Who* at all, this directive fell by the wayside due to Verity Lambert's persuasive abilities and persistence.

The seven-part serial "The Daleks" was lensed, complete with the non-humanoid creatures and their nefarious, advanced weaponry. The audience response was immediate, overwhelming and unprecedented. Children all over the country were transfixed to the television by these metallic monsters and their grating, electronic voices. Dalekmania, a full-blown phenomenon not unlike Beatlemania, swept the country. *Doctor Who*'s ratings, which for four weeks had been adequate but not spectacular, went straight through the roof. The series became a bonafide blockbuster courtesy of the efforts of Cusick, Lambert and Nation to bring the Daleks to the screen in a frightening yet believable fashion.

The remainder of the freshman season proved to be as well-written and inventive as both "The Daleks" and "An Unearthly Child." These triumphs were followed by a character-driven bottle show called alternately "The Edge of Destruction" and "Inside the Ship," which had to be produced hastily when *Doctor Who*'s limited budget could not sustain the more expensive serial "Beyond the Sun." Season 1 also saw the epic *Doctor Who* travelogue through the Far East, "Marco Polo." It was a sumptuous, beautiful period production which has been destroyed by the BBC. The remaining photos from "Marco Polo" reflect its high quality: It looks like a feature film.

The popular "quest concept," which would return many times during *Doctor Who*'s long run, most dramatically in the sixteenth season, also appeared first in writer Terry Nation's second contribution to the series: "The Keys of Marinus." John Lucarotti's "The Aztecs" was another well-plotted show filled with tension and highlighted by John Ringham's great performance as the High Priest of Human Sacrifices, Tlotoxl. Friendly aliens were found in the seventh serial, "The Sensorites," and the season ended with another impressive historical chronicle, "The

Reign of Terror." The latter adventure was the first *Doctor Who* to feature location shooting and to be lensed at the new BBC installation, the Television Center in Shepherd's Bush.[5]

By the time *Doctor Who* began its second season in 1964, Dalekmania had increased. There was a Dalek record album from the "Go Joes" spotlighting a rockin' single entitled "I'm Going to Spend My Christmas With a Dalek." Also on the market, and available at Gamage's and everywhere, were Dalek toys, Dalek playing cards, Dalek model kits and other Dalek-related merchandise.

During the third week of the 1964 television season, a *Doctor Who* comic strip replaced *Fireball XL-5* in *TV Comics* #674.[6] Although the black-and-white comic featured both Hartnell's Doctor and the TARDIS, the companions were different from those seen on television. Still, the comic was clear evidence that children could not get enough of the imaginative *Doctor Who* series. Riding high on such successes, *Doctor Who*'s second season was more confident thematically than its first. It opened with the ambitious "Planet of Giants," a tale which found the Doctor and his companions miniaturized! Otherwise, the season continued to offer the same story mix that had succeeded so admirably in its first sortie: a combination of outer space sci-fi and time travel adventure. Significantly, humor was also highlighted in the second season, particularly in witty serials such as "The Romans." The show was growing, finding its way and prospering. In October 1964, the series was sold to television stations in Canada, Australia and New Zealand, beginning *Doctor Who*'s international empire of fans.[7]

The Daleks returned to conquer Earth in November 1964 in the six-part serial "The Dalek Invasion of Earth." Filmed on location in the streets of London, this adventure featured the famous shot of a Dalek rising ominously from the water of the Thames. Predictably, this second appearance was met with even more enthusiasm than the first Daleks serial. People just could not get enough of the evil machines! "The Dalek Invasion of Earth" also heralded the final appearance of actress Carole Ann Ford as Susan. Her character elected to stay behind on the future Earth depicted in that serial, a departure caused in reality by the performer's desire to pursue interests outside of *Doctor Who*:

> As far as I'm concerned, it almost completely finished my career. ...As soon as I finished *Doctor Who*, I was still offered ... work, but it was all the same, and I was being continuously offered teenagers, which I wanted to stop playing, and Science Fiction young ladies along the same lines of what I had been doing...[8]

Ford's exit was a bump in the road for *Doctor Who* but not a major one in the scheme of things because Hartnell, Russell and Hill were still with the series. They were quickly joined in their travels by actress Maureen O'Brien as the companion Vicki in the story "The Rescue." Despite the casting hiccup, *Doctor Who* continued forward boldly.

"The Web Planet" by Bill Strutton was a big-budget extravaganza replete with experimental visual and sound techniques. It introduced a villain which many hoped would surmount the popularity of the Daleks, the ant-like creatures called the Zarbi.

Although "The Web Planet" garnered ratings of over ten million viewers, the Zarbi are not well-remembered villains today, perhaps because these giant bugs lacked the personal malevolence of Nation's Daleks. While "The Web Planet" aired in March 1965, a second comic strip based on *Doctor Who* appeared. This strip, "The Daleks," was created by Terry Nation and David Whitaker for AP Merchandising's *TV Century 21*. It was in full color and did not feature the Doctor, his companions or the TARDIS at all, only the villainous Daleks! The comic strip story progressed from the Dal-Thal war on Skaro and the development of Dalek armor to Dalek invasions of other worlds. Much of this information was later contradicted by the 1975 serial "Genesis of the Daleks."

On television, the Daleks returned in May 1965 for a third adventure, "The Chase." As "The Chase" unfolded on television screens, AARU, later Amicus Productions, unveiled the big-screen event called *Doctor Who and the Daleks*. Produced in Technicolor by Milton Subotsky and Max J. Rosenberg, the picture starred horror legend Peter Cushing as a character named "Doctor Who." The film's screenplay differed from the television series in several important details, including the origin of the lead character and his relationships with his various companions. The film grossed big bucks in the U.K., but it was not the overwhelming critical success which many had hoped for. Grosses in the United States were dismal. Nonetheless, the Daleks remained immensely popular on television and in comics.

"The Chase" was important for other reasons. Jacqueline Hill and William Russell followed Carole Ann Ford's lead and left the series in the last installment of the Terry Nation serial. This was a devastating blow to the series because in the early days of the series *Doctor Who* was an ensemble show which often featured four distinct subplots. Hartnell's character, though important, was not always the primary mover of the narrative. William Russell had in fact carried the lion's share of the action, and Jacqueline Hill provided dramatic moments a-plenty in "The Aztecs" and other adventures. When these two gifted performers left *Doctor Who*, it became obvious that the series had to shift gears. Hartnell became the unequivical lead character and he was surrounded by new companions who were not nearly as well-drawn, three-dimensional or interesting as Ian, Barbara and Susan. Peter Purves' (*Z-Cars, Stopwatch*) Steven Taylor was an astronaut very much in the action-hero mold of Ian, but without the teacher's sense of humor. Vicki, Dodo and even Polly repeated the adolescent charm and naiveté that had made Susan so popular, but for the most part without the captivating personal qualities of Ford. In later years, *Doctor Who* companions would often be completely opposite in personality from the ones they immediately replaced but, in the early days of the show, new characters and performers were selected for familiar qualities rather than unfamiliar ones.

The last show of the second season, "The Time Meddler" was the first program in *Doctor Who* history to introduce another member of the Doctor's mysterious race, a less-than-holy character called "The Meddling Monk" who was played by Peter Butterworth. He was a figure of fun and mild evil rather than of true menace, but he was nonetheless a precursor to "The Master," another representative of the Doctor's race who would appear in the Jon Pertwee era and become a mainstay of the series.

Season 3 progressed much as the first two seasons. Time travel was again the order of the day as the Doctor, Steven, Vicki and later Dodo visited the Trojan War in "The Myth Makers," the St. Bartholomew's Day Massacre in "The Massacre" and the gunfight at the OK Corral in "The Gunfighters." The sci-fi concepts initiated in this season were more mature than previous ones. A dimension existing "outside" time was visited in "The Celestial Toymaker," the lesson that what is beautiful is not necessarily good was explored in "Galaxy Four," a multi-generational space ark was visited in "The Ark" and the advent of artificial intelligence was probed in "The War Machines." Inevitably, the season also saw the return of the Daleks in the massive 12-part adventure "The Dalek Masterplan."

By the end of the third season, Maureen O'Brien's Vicki had left the Doctor to found Rome in "The Myth Makers," and Peter Purves' Steven Taylor had also departed to rule over a newly unified race of aliens in "The Savages." Even Dodo Chaplet returned home to 1966 Earth in "The War Machines." Dodo's last adventure introduced two new companions: Polly and Ben. Played respectively by Anneke Willis and Michael Craze, these characters were perhaps more hip and contemporary than their immediate predecessors.

While "The War Machines" finished its run in July 1966, the second AARU *Doctor Who* movie premiered. *Daleks: Invasion Earth, 2150 A.D.* also starred Peter Cushing, and it was an uninspired, inferior remake of the Season 2 serial "The Dalek Invasion of Earth." The second *Doctor Who* film was less successful financially than the first, and the plans to make a third movie (based on "The Chase") were scrapped. Back on television, the third season of *Doctor Who* also saw the departure of producer Verity Lambert. "The Ark" was the last serial she produced.

Season 4 was another time of unrest for *Doctor Who*. "The Smugglers" opened the year and it was one of the series' last purely time travel (rather than otherworldly) adventures. The series had seen forays to Ancient China, Greece and Rome. It had been to the Old West, and to historic France twice. These stories were mostly good ones, but the historical story formula was becoming repetitive. Inevitably there were mistaken identities, dangerous captures and narrow escapes in each such "history" adventure. Because of the limited nature of these stories, the pure history serials would not survive beyond the season. *Doctor Who* would instead launch itself with full force into outer space.

More significant than the format switch, William Hartnell planned to leave *Doctor Who* early in the year. The actor had been in poor health since early in *Doctor Who*'s first season. In 1966 he became too sick to continue working the arduous hours required of a series lead. At the same time, Hartnell expressed the belief that many of the recent *Doctor Who* stories had perhaps become too mature and filled with violence. Obviously, there were at least two good reasons for the veteran actor to leave the series.

Nevertheless, this departure created a dilemma for new producer Innes Lloyd and series creator Sydney Newman. *Doctor Who* was still an unqualified success on television, but it was clear that the series could not survive in its current format without Hartnell. After all, he was the last of the original four actors remaining with the show. The only options the producers had were to end the series or to recast the role. Of course, recasting Hartnell seemed an incredibly difficult task. In the three years he played the Doctor, he had made the role his own. One part beloved grandfather, one part cranky old man, Hartnell was fluid both with technical jargon and in the more loose, humorous scenes. He seemed an impossible act to beat, and to this day some consider his interpretation of the Doctor to be the series' finest.

The answer to the casting dilemma came unexpectedly in the form of the Doctor's "alien" qualities. It was decided that at the end of Hartnell's last episode, the character would "renew" or "regenerate" into a new, younger body. This would permit a new actor to assume the part. It would also allow a physically different interpretation of the Doctor. He could be anyone, ranging from a young blond man to an older character like Hartnell. It was also decided that when the Doctor changed bodies, he would also undergo a dramatic change in personality. Thus any new performer would not feel pigeonholed into repeating the last interpretation of the character. It was a brilliant idea that gave the series a new life. At the end of the second Season 4 adventure ("The Tenth Planet"), it was decided that the Doctor would undergo this surprising regeneration process.

"The Tenth Planet" also introduced the Cybermen: enhanced humans who had replaced failing limbs and organs with artificial, metal parts. The Cybermen quickly rivalled the Daleks in popularity, and they would become a mainstay of the series' second era. After the Cybermen's first invasion attempt was squashed by the Doctor in "The Tenth Planet," Hartnell regenerated into Patrick Troughton, and fans were flabbergasted. The era of the first Doctor was over.

Troughton's Time in the TARDIS

As it turned out, the producers of *Doctor Who* need not have worried about replacing their lead actor. Newman's selection of a new lead, Patrick Troughton (1920–87), proved to be an inspired choice. Many fans, including this writer, consider him the best of all incarnations of the Time Lord. Unlike his predecessor who had dabbled in drama but remained for the most part a comic actor, Troughton was a serious Shakespearean dramatist who had acted in a variety of films including *Hamlet* (1948), *Treasure Island* (1950), *Richard III* (1956), and *The Moonraker* (1957). He was also a strong presence on British television. Before Troughton assumed the mantle of *Doctor Who*, he appeared in the six-part saga of *Robin Hood* (1953) and *The Adventures of the Scarlet Pimpernel* (1955). Troughton was also a frequent guest star in series such as *Doomwatch* (1970–72), *Survivors* (1975), *The Saint* and *Out of the Unknown*. Almost immediately, Troughton was honest with the producers of *Doctor Who* in his desire not to be typecast. He decided early on that he would remain with the series for only three years. Despite

Patrick Troughton, who became the second incarnation of the Doctor in episode #30, "The Power of the Daleks."

the decision to leave the popular sci-fi series after a limited time, Troughton was nonetheless associated throughout his career with the horror and sci-fi genres. Several of his credits in the field include Hammer films such as *The Phantom of the Opera* (1962), *The Gorgon* (1964), *Scars of Dracula* (1970) and *Frankenstein and the Monster from Hell* (1973). He also appeared in *Jason and the Argonauts* (1963), *The Omen* (1976), *Sinbad and the Eye of the Tiger* (1977) and the *Space: 1999* finale, "The Dorcons."

As the Doctor, Troughton's interpretation was a quantum shift away from Hartnell's gruff portrayal. Troughton was much more overtly friendly, and far more physical in demonstrating affection than Hartnell had been. His Doctor was a jovial figure who would dance his way around the TARDIS control room tooting on his flute-like recorder. He was unpredictable in his mood shifts, childish in his pursuit of leisure and, of course, deadly serious when the situation warranted it. Fortunately for fans of the series, Troughton's Doctor was equally adept as Hartnell's in dispatching villains.

As they had with Hartnell, series writers treated Troughton's Doctor not as an *uber mensch* or as an infallible hero, but as a being with faults. Appropriately, the second Doctor proved as incompetent at flying the TARDIS as the first Doctor had been. He also made mistakes and errors in judgment, as the first Doctor had done in stories such as "The Aztecs." The new Doctor was thus superior to his human companions in intellect and knowledge, but not infallible in his decisions. This is an important distinction because, as *Doctor Who* the series evolved, so did the Doctor himself. In later years, particularly the Sylvester McCoy era, the character became, like the super-astronauts of *Star Trek: The Next Generation*, an infallible being more God than mortal.

Doctor Who fans have long debated which incarnation of the Doctor is the most important to the series. Some believe that Hartnell was *the* crucial performer since he started the series off. Others think Tom Baker was more important because he popularized *Doctor Who* in America and enjoyed the longest reign. There are even those who believe that the era of Sylvester McCoy was the most important since it introduced the character of Ace and presented new mysteries about the

Doctor's origins. It is important to note, however, that Troughton's incarnation is of a singular importance. He was the first actor who had to sell the untested regeneration concept, and were he not successful in doing so, the series would have died in a matter of weeks. By the time Jon Pertwee, Tom Baker, Peter Davison and the rest arrived on the series, the process of regeneration was an accepted part of *Doctor Who* lore. In later years, fans *expected* new incarnations of the Doctor to be different. Had Troughton not made the part of the Doctor his own in the midst of Season 4, *Doctor Who* would surely have not survived. Therefore the actor and his era are worthy of a special respect.

Perhaps worried that their new series lead would not be immediately accepted by diehard fans, the producers hedged their bets and made Troughton's premiere serial a Dalek story, "The Power of the Daleks." Children would watch the show to see their Daleks again, while at the same time they would be introduced to a new Doctor. The ploy worked beautifully, and children came to accept the new series lead as the "same" character who had held them to their television sets for three years.

The second adventure of Troughton's reign, "The Highlanders," is notable historically for two reasons. First, it introduced young Frazer Hines to the series as Scottish piper Jamie McCrimmon. Almost instantly this young actor and Troughton established a funny, unique rapport. Accordingly, Jamie accompanied the Doctor longer than any other companion in *Doctor Who* history. "The Highlanders" was also important because it was the last of *Doctor Who*'s purely historical time travel adventures. By this time, the escapes, captures and mistaken identities of these tales had worn thin. No future *Doctor Who* would be devoid of hard sci-fi concepts.

The remainder of Season 4 saw a second Cyberman adventure called "The Moonbase," an encounter with crustacean-like alien horror in "The Macra Terror," and explorations of new territory (such as the lost city of Atlantis) in "The Underwater Menace." There was even a visit to *Invasion of the Body Snatchers*-type horror in "The Faceless Ones." The latter story also saw the departure of Polly (Anneke Willis) and Ben (Michael Craze) from the format. The final serial of the year was a second Dalek encounter, entitled "The Evil of the Daleks." This adventure introduced Deborah Watling to the series as Victorian innocent Victoria Waterfield. By the last frame of Season 4, Troughton was firmly established as the new Doctor, having vanquished the Daleks twice and the Cybermen once. His freshman outing had been a success.

Doctor Who's fifth season was another historic one. It opened with perhaps the greatest *Doctor Who* serial of all time, "The Tomb of the Cybermen." This well-designed and superbly written adventure was followed by several more sterling stories which introduced classic *Doctor Who* villains and monsters such as the Yeti and the Great Intelligence in "The Abominable Snowmen," and Brian Hayles' Martian conquerors in "The Ice Warriors." Other notable stories included "Fury from the Deep," which saw Deborah Watling's departure from the series. Also of interest was "The Web of Fear," because it welcomed Nicholas Courtney's character,

Alistair Lethbridge-Stewart, to the series. Courtney's witty portrayal of a 1960s military officer captured the attention of *Doctor Who* fans and casual viewers alike, and he returned in the sixth season story "The Invasion." Even more impressively, Brigadier Lethbridge-Stewart graduated to series regular in *Doctor Who*'s seventh season. He is among the most beloved of *Doctor Who*'s companions.

In the final episode of Season 5, yet another young companion was presented. Exuberant Wendy Padbury portrayed a teenage genius from the future, Zoe Herriott. Together with Frazer Hines and Patrick Troughton, Padbury formed an essential part of the prototypical *Doctor Who* triangle. She was the intellect to contrast Hines' action and Troughton's blending of characteristics. With this team firmly in place for Season 6, the series had never been better.

Doctor Who continued to stretch its boundaries in Troughton's momentous last year in the role, the unforgettable Season 6. Another new robotic menace, the Quarks, were introduced in the season premiere "The Dominators," but they proved to be no more popular than the Zarbi had been in "The Web Planet." The Doctor and his friends encountered the surreal Land of Fiction in the stylistic "The Mind Robber," and the rest of the season saw the return of the Cybermen in "The Invasion" and the revenge of the Ice Warriors in "The Seeds of Death." A young writer named Robert Holmes also landed his first teleplay on *Doctor Who*, an adventure called "The Krotons." As the years passed, Holmes would pen many of the best *Doctor Who* adventures in Pertwee, Baker, Davison and Colin Baker eras, as well as episodes of *Blake's 7*.

The last serial of Season 6, however, was the most interesting of all. "The War Games" was a ten-part serial which found Troughton's Doctor in terrible peril. When he was unable to resolve the dilemma at the climax of the story, the Doctor was forced to call upon his own people, the mysterious and frightening "Time Lords." This was the first time in six years that the Doctor's people had been identified by name. In "The War Games," the Time Lords were depicted as a frightening, almost supernatural race with incredible powers. The season concluded in jaw-dropping fashion when companions Jamie and Zoe were forcibly sent back to their own time periods and made to forget their adventures with the Doctor. If that was not traumatic enough for fans, the Doctor was exiled to twentieth century Earth and forced to regenerate. At the conclusion of "The War Games," Troughton's incarnation was seen spinning through a black void, screaming. No new actor was yet cast in the part of the Doctor and the BBC was not even sure it intended to continue with the series, so it was a shocking ending to the season, and perhaps to the series as a whole. Suddenly and rather mercilessly, the Troughton era was ended.

Pertwee's Period of Physical Prowess

In early January 1970, *Doctor Who* returned to television sets across the country in a revised format. The production budget had been substantially increased

In addition to his television work, Jon Pertwee, the third Doctor, had a motion-picture encounter with horror. Here the actor contemplates vampires in *The House That Dripped Blood* (1971).

by the BBC and *Doctor Who* was now shot in color. In addition, the increase in money meant that the science fiction series could afford to shoot on location more frequently. More importantly, the show changed dramatically in concept. Now exiled to twentieth century Earth, the Doctor could no longer visit other worlds regularly. Instead, he would be called on to stave off alien invasions and stop the nefarious plans of mad scientists. It was a fundamental shift in formula. The mid- to late–'60s had been the heyday of superspy shows such as *The Man from U.N.C.L.E.* (1964–68), and *The Prisoner* (1966–67) as well as the James Bond film series. It was decided that *Doctor Who* would benefit by being similar to these other shows. This new approach would highlight fast action and terrestrial adventure rather than alien civilizations on distant planets. Accordingly, the Time Lords also changed considerably from their first appearance in the 1969 serial "The War Games." Instead of being telepathic super-aliens with Draconian laws, the Time Lords became friendlier "superiors" to the Doctor who would frequently send him on top secret missions in stories such as "Colony in Space" and "The Mutants." Essentially, the Doctor became an intergalactic secret agent when he was not fulfilling the role of Bernard Quatermass and saving the Earth from alien invasions.

In accordance with the updated format of *Doctor Who*, a new style of leading man was required to fill out the lead role. Dashing Jon Pertwee (1919–1996), a familiar British comedian, was selected to become the Third Doctor. Pertwee was an experienced performer by the time he landed the part , having appeared in films such as *Mr. Drake's Duck* (1951), *Carry on Cowboy* (1965) and *A Funny Thing Happened on the Way to the Forum* (1966). On television he appeared in *Toad of Toad Hall* (1946), an adaptation of Kenneth Grahame's *The Wind in the Willows*. After *Doctor Who*, Pertwee again found success as the scarecrow *Worzel Gummidge* (1979–81), a character created by Barbara Euphan Todd. An actor with much experience in comedy, Pertwee interestingly opted to downplay all funny elements in *Doctor Who*. Instead, he became a debonair, deadly serious man of action. He reveled in chase scenes, indulged in Venusian fisticuffs, and faced each new threat with tough language and unwavering resolve. He was the first actor to play the Doctor who could prove a legitimate *physical* threat to his opponents. He was part John Steed, part James Bond, and part Quatermass.

Pertwee's first year, the seventh for *Doctor Who*, also made UNIT (United Nations Intelligence Task Force) a primary factor in new stories. This multinational organization was designed to prevent invasions from space and it was run in superb fashion by Nicholas Courtney's Brigadier Lethbridge-Stewart. Upon recovering from his regeneration, Pertwee's Doctor became UNIT's unofficial, unpaid scientific advisor and embarked on many new terrestrial adventures. The Doctor was ably assisted in Season 7 by Caroline John's Liz Shaw, an intellectual Cambridge scientist more than a match for the Doctor's wit and brains. Caroline John (*A Perfect Spy*, *The Hound of the Baskervilles*, *Poirot* and the feature film *Raising a Riot*) sank her teeth into this role and developed a sort of love-hate relationship with the Brigadier. All in all, this was a good team, but it was clear that the new, Earthbound show had several restrictions. "Spearhead from Space" and "Ambassadors of Death" could easily have fit into the *Quatermass* series; in both stories, strange aliens landed on Earth and had to be dealt with by the Doctor. The other two serials of the season, "Doctor Who and the Silurians" and "Inferno," were much more inventive in concept, exploring the vicissitudes of evolution and the sci-fi subgenre of the parallel universe. Still, at seven parts each, all four serials produced in Season 7 seemed a bit long and thematically shallow. It was decided that for Season 8, changes would be made.

Caroline John left the series and was replaced by a more traditional female lead, Katy Manning, who would later appear in the BBC series *Target* opposite Ken Hutchinson. Manning's Jo Grant was a daffy, helpless damsel rather than the brilliant scientist that John had essayed so brilliantly and memorably. It was also decided that for Season 8, the Doctor needed more imposing menaces to face. The scientists and mad military men of "Inferno" and "Ambassadors of Death" were not nearly interesting nor dangerous enough to be a serious challenge to a Time Lord. Thus the Master was created. A renegade Time Lord like the Doctor, Roger Delgado's Master was an evil reflection of the Doctor. He was Prof. Moriarty to Pertwee's Sherlock Holmes; this new villain appeared in all five serials of Season 8. Despite these changes, Season 8 saw ever more invasions from space in "Terror of the Autons" and "The Claws of Axos," more evil scientists in "The Mind of Evil" and more *Quatermass*–style posturing and storytelling in the derivative

"The Daemons." Despite these flaws, the show was still immensely popular, as was Pertwee's swaggering, action-oriented interpretation of the lead role.

Buoyed by this continued popularity, Season 9 began in 1972 and was considerably more ambitious in its narrative attempts. The year opened with "Day of the Daleks," a serial which featured *Terminator*–style time paradoxes more than ten years before there was even a *Terminator* (1984) to compare it with. The season continued strongly with mystery and intrigue in "The Curse of Peladon." There was also a fine sequel to "Doctor Who and the Silurians" called "The Sea Devils," a serial which benefited from great location work and equipment loaned from the Royal Navy. There was even an outer space exploration of racism and exploitation called "The Mutants," and another visit to Atlantis in "The Time Monster." Significantly, four of the five serials in 1972 occurred in worlds or times outside of the twentieth century exile. It was thus obvious to everybody that fans of *Doctor Who* missed the forays to other worlds and times, and the format was molded to accommodate fan preferences. The year 1972 also saw the release of a single from Jon Pertwee called "Who Is the Doctor." Released by Purple Records, the album (PUR 111) featured some groovy lyrics:

> I cross the void beyond the mind
> The empty space that circles time.
> I see where others stumble blind,
> To seek a truth they'll never find.
> Eternal wisdom is my guide.
> I am — the Doctor![9]

Also during 1972, *The Making of Doctor Who* by Malcolm Hulke and Terrance Dicks was published by Piccolo Books.[10] It recounted the history of the series up to that year, interviewed crew members and revealed behind-the-scenes decision making. *Doctor Who* was as popular in its ninth year as it had been in its first and second.

Season 10 was perhaps the best year of Pertwee's age. The season premiere was a story that appropriately paid tribute to the first decade of *Doctor Who*. Entitled "The Three Doctors," the story saw William Hartnell, Patrick Troughton and Pertwee working together to stop the evil Omega from destroying the Time Lords and the universe itself. It was an exciting story and it highlighted the great chemistry between Pertwee and Troughton. Because of his multiple sclerosis, Hartnell was limited to giving advice on the TARDIS viewscreen. Best of all, in the closing moments of "The Three Doctors," the Time Lords gave the dematerializer circuit from the TARDIS back to the Doctor, and his period of exile on Earth was officially over. This celebratory program and formula change seemed to jump-start the series, and the remainder of the year was quite inventive. "Carnival of Monsters" featured great special effects monsters called "Drashigs" and a witty story of alien xenophobes, while the epic, galactic tapestry of "Frontier in Space" led to the return of the Daleks in "Planet of the Daleks." The final show of the season, "The

Green Death," saw the departure of Katy Manning and her character, Jo Grant. "Frontier in Space" was also the last appearance of Roger Delgado's the Master. The talented actor was accidentally killed on June 18, 1973, while working on the set of a feature film, *Bell of Tibet*, in Turkey.

Pertwee's last year, Season 11, introduced Elisabeth Sladen as journalist Sarah Jane Smith. This talented young actress (*K-9 and Company*) brought new wit and humor to the series, and quickly became one of the most popular of modern companions. Sarah's first story was a clever nod to *A Connecticut Yankee in King Arthur's Court* called "The Time Warrior." It involved the Doctor and Sarah's attempt to save medieval England from a futuristic alien. "The Time Warrior" was thus the first *Doctor Who* adventure to feature another popular alien villain, Robert Holmes' race of clones called Sontarans.

The rest of the season saw a return of the Daleks in "Death to the Daleks," a return to Peladon in "The Monster of Peladon" and an invasion of unconvincing dinosaurs in "Invasion of the Dinosaurs." The last serial of Season 11 brought Pertwee's era to an end in style. "Planet of the Spiders" highlighted an extended chase over land, air and sea. It featured the Doctor's yellow roadster (Bessie), the futuristic vehicle dubbed the "Whomobile," a hover craft, an autogyro, a helicopter and a motorboat! It was an appropriately rousing end for Pertwee's third incarnation of the Doctor. In the last moments of "Planet of the Spiders," Pertwee's incarnation successfully faced down his greatest fears and returned to Earth mortally wounded. On the floor of UNIT HQ, before the eyes of the Brigadier and Sarah Jane, Jon Pertwee changed into Tom Baker...

Seven Years with Tom Baker, America's Favorite Doctor!

As legend has it, Tom Baker was performing grueling manual labor on a London construction site when he got the call to play the fourth incarnation of the Doctor. He dropped his task as cement mixer and promptly began a role with which he would become irrevocably associated throughout his career. Like Pertwee before him, Baker was quite an unusual choice to play the Time Lord. Well over six feet tall and with an unkempt mop of curly brown hair, his appearance was distinctive to say the least. His big, round eyes conveyed remarkable intelligence as well as a sly wit. Before joining the ever-changing cast of *Doctor Who*, Baker put these unusual, wild looks to effective use throughout his film career. Appropriately, he played the hypnotic Russian devil Rasputin in *Nicholas and Alexandra* (1971). He also appeared in the off-kilter "Drawn and Quartered" segment of the Amicus horror film *Vault of Horror* (1973). Baker's other weird turns included a stint as Donald Pleasence's freakish assistant in *The Mutations* (1974) and a major role as the evil Prince Khoura in *The Golden Voyage of Sinbad* (1974).

Baker's enormous, Rasputin-like charisma was intoxicating on *Doctor Who*. His intense personal magnetism and screen presence permitted him to fit more

Before signing on to play the fourth incarnation of *Doctor Who*, Tom Baker starred (left) in *Vault of Horror* (1972) and also appeared (right) as a villainous prince in Ray Harryhausen's adventure film *The Golden Voyage of Sinbad* (1974).

rapidly into the universe of *Doctor Who* than any performer who preceded or followed him. More than any other actor to play the Doctor, Baker really seemed like a genuine alien. One minute the fourth Doctor smiled, the next he screamed. One minute he would be spewing a stream of technical jargon, the next he would be staring off into empty space, seeing something not evident to his companions. It was a bold, larger-than-life interpretation of the alien character.

Baker oversaw perhaps the most interesting and eclectic period in *Doctor Who* history. He depicted the Time Lord from the last moments of "Planet of the Spiders" in 1974 until the final sequence of "Logopolis" in March 1981. His first serial was "Robot," a Beauty and the Beast–style story which shared many elements with *King Kong* (1933). Like much of the Pertwee era, this first Baker serial was set on Earth at UNIT HQ. Elisabeth Sladen remained with the series as Sarah Jane Smith and she was joined by actor Ian Marter. A fledgling writer and previous *Doctor Who* guest star in "Carnival of Monsters," Marter became UNIT medico Harry Sullivan and quickly established a friendship with Baker.

In Baker's second episode, "The Ark in Space," Harry, the Doctor and Sarah encountered a race of malevolent alien insectoids who devoured humans in cryosleep. The details of story forecasted *Alien* (1979) and its sequel *Aliens* (1986).

The serial was so riveting that it netted a record 14 million viewers. In his second serial, Baker's Doctor became the most popular Doctor in *Doctor Who*'s 12–year history.

Before the end of his freshman season, Baker also encountered the popular Daleks in "Genesis of the Daleks." The teleplay by Terry Nation forced the new Doctor into some very difficult, morally ambiguous decisions. It was a highpoint amidst a season of highpoints, and the rest of the year depicted the Doctor's dramatic tussles with old nemeses such as the Sontarans ("The Sontaran Experiment") and Cybermen ("Revenge of the Cybermen"). It was a banner year for *Doctor Who*, one that shifted the action away from twentieth century Earth to the endless mysteries of deep space. So successful was Season 12 that Ian Marter and Tom Baker were prompted to co-write a script for a *Doctor Who* feature film entitled *Doctor Who Meets Scratchman*. The movie was never made and Ian Marter departed the series at the close of Season 12.

Although 1975 was a great year for *Doctor Who* as drama and as television sci-fi, it lost one of its founding fathers. William Hartnell lost his long battle with multiple sclerosis and died on April 24, 1975.

Season 13 was equally memorable in terms of story development. During producer Philip Hinchliffe's second year behind-the-scenes, there was a marked shift towards intelligent space horror. Frightening shows such as "Planet of Evil," "The Pyramids of Mars" and "The Android Invasion" dealt with anti matter aliens, ancient gods of destruction and sinister android duplicates. The series had never been more frightening, more witty or more tantalizing in its explorations of the universe. Other stories in the thirteenth year also focused firmly on horror. "The Brain of Morbius" was a reworking of *Frankenstein* by Terrance Dicks, and "The Seeds of Doom" modified the Howard Hawks' film *The Thing from Another World* (1951). There was more physical action in *Doctor Who* than ever before, and better special effects to boot. In many circles, the program was now being favorably compared with *Star Trek*! On an acting note, "The Terror of the Zygons," the opening gambit of the season, highlighted the last performance by Nicholas Courtnery as Brigadier Lethbridge-Stewart until the Peter Davison era adventure "Mawdryn Undead" (1981).

Doctor Who's thirteenth season also saw it going head-to-head for the first time with some rather serious outer space competition. The long-standing BBC drama played against another science fiction masterpiece, Gerry and Sylvia Anderson's *Space: 1999*. Although *1999* featured American stars, bigger budgets and incredible special effects, *Doctor Who* was consistently victorious in the ratings. Of course, audiences were already familiar with *Doctor Who*, and *Space: 1999* was not able to muster in a matter of weeks the equivalent of 13 years of fan devotion. It was during this year of fierce rivalry that Baker loudly and publicly denigrated *Space: 1999* in virtually every interview he granted (in *Starlog* #34 and *Sci Fi Monthly* #5, to name just two). The actor claimed that *Space: 1999* had no right to exist as drama because it lacked humor.

Season 14 represented the culmination of what many *Doctor Who* fans considered Baker's "classic years." It was Philip Hinchcliffe's last season as producer, and so his preference for horror-oriented adventure was again the order of the day. The Doctor faced a formless energy monster in the lavish production "The Masque of Mandragora." Shot at Portmieron, the same locale as Patrick McGoohan's *The Prisoner*, "The Masque of Mandragora" sported authentic Renaissance costumes and brilliant guest performances. Elisabeth Sladen left *Doctor Who* after the second episode of the season, "The Hand of Fear." She had been with the series since Season 11, so her departure was a moment of deep emotion and heartfelt sadness. Sarah was not replaced immediately, and Baker's Doctor was sent alone to Gallifrey to prevent the assassination of the Time Lord President in "The Deadly Assassin." The mastermind behind the attempted assassination proved to be a mutilated, deformed Master, a villain not seen since Roger Delgado's death in 1973.

The next story, "The Face of Evil" by Chris Boucher, introduced Louise Jameson (*The Omega Factor*, *Tenko*) as the savage huntress Leela. Leela was a soldier and she wore only the skimpiest of outfits. Predictably, *Doctor Who*'s ratings peaked as curious fathers returned to the series in droves to ogle this provocative new character. After "The Face of Evil" came "The Robots of Death," another all-time great *Doctor Who* adventure which seemed based in part on the works of Agatha Christie. The season finale was another period piece, "The Talons of Weng Chiang," set in Victorian England.

Graham Williams took over the producer's seat in Season 15. His first story for *Doctor Who*, "The Horror of Fang Rock" was Gothic terror set on an isolated lighthouse. By midseason and a story called "The Sunmakers," however, comedy and satire had taken hold of *Doctor Who* in a significant way. The series would shortly experience a giant shift in style and attitude. "The Sunmakers" was a pointed satire but its thrust was still a serious one, even if the dialogue jabbed at the British government's tax practices. Such would not always be the case.

The fifteenth season was also important in *Doctor Who* history for introducing the lovable cybernetic dog, K-9. (K-9 appeared in late 1977 after the droids of *Star Wars* had made such a powerful impact in the world of sci-fi.) K-9 was both a loyal, cute dog and a brilliant computing device, so he was the perfect assistant for the Doctor. The mechanical critter was ably voiced by actor John Leeson ("The Power of Kroll").

At the end of the 1977 season, the revolving door of companions continued to spin, and Louise Jameson's Leela left the series. Her character remained on Gallifrey at the climax of "The Invasion of Time." Rather implausibly, the fierce, independent Leela settled down for domestic bliss with a Time Lord.

Mary Tamm (*The Odessa File*) became Baker's newest companion in Season 16. The talented actress and frequent television guest star on series such as *Return of the Saint* (1978) and *Not the Nine O'Clock News* essayed the role of Romana, a regal Time Lady of Gallifrey. Tamm's character combined Leela's tough characteristics and the witty aspects of Sarah Jane Smith's personality. Tamm was a delightful, intellectually provocative presence on the TARDIS and she shared wonderful chemistry with Baker. Romana and the Doctor bantered their way through the whole season, casting sarcastic and witty asides at one another with enjoyable regularity. The six adventures of the season were also held together by the "quest" concept which had first appeared during Season 1's "The Keys of Marinus." In "The Ribos Operation," the first story of Season 16, the White Guardian sent the Doctor, Romana and K-9 on a quest to locate the six segments of the all-powerful Key to Time.

Season 16 also saw a shift in format. Horrific space adventures concerning carnivorous aliens, silicon life forms, anti-matter and the like were abandoned for a more satirical, comical interpretation of the universe. Douglas Adams, author of *Hitchhiker's Guide to the Galaxy,* wrote an exceedingly silly segment entitled "The Pirate Planet." The remainder of the year found the intrepid searchers locating disguised Key to Time segments in the unlikeliest of places, including giant squids in "The Power of Kroll" and even a person in "The Armageddon Factor." No villains from past years recurred in Season 16, and *Doctor Who*, for good or bad, seemed like a brand new series. Unfortunately, the wacky new humorous elements managed to alienate a large portion of *Doctor Who*'s loyal audience. Only Baker's personal charm made some of these silly stories endurable.

While Baker and Mary Tamm toiled with the Key to Time saga in 1978, in October of the same year *Doctor Who* arrived in force on American shores. Seasons 12 through 15 of the season were syndicated via Time-Life television. There was a full-color cover story about *Doctor Who* in *Famous Monsters of Filmland* #155, a guarantee that American genre fans would seek out the series. At the same time, Pinnacle Books released a series of ten books from Tom Baker's era (as well as a few from Pertwee's age like "Day of the Daleks" and "Colony in Space"). This penetration into the American market succeeded beyond expectations. Fortunately, they were seeing *Doctor Who* at its absolute best. Stories such as "The Ark in Space," "Genesis of the Daleks," "Terror of the Zygons" and "The Deadly Assassin" were received by *Star Trek* fans with avid interest and much appreciation. The release of *Star Wars* a year earlier also brought many new genre fans to *Doctor Who*. This was the year when American *Doctor Who* fandom was born.

Back in England, Season 17 saw yet another cast change. Mary Tamm left the series, feeling that the Romana character was largely undeveloped and underutilized. She was replaced by Lalla Ward (a guest star in Season 16's finale "The Armageddon Factor") as the second incarnation of Romana. Ward was more girlish and innocent in her approach to the character, and thus much of the acid banter that enlivened the Key to Time quest was gone. Ward and Baker were married in 1981, but their marriage ended after just a year and a half.

Douglas Adams was promoted to story editor for *Doctor Who*'s record-breaking seventeenth season. This appointment resulted in several more absurdist serials and caused some severe damage to old series friends. The Daleks returned in the Season 17 premiere "Destiny of the Daleks," but the villains were not served well by the new, comedic approach. The story by Terry Nation was a good one, but the Doctor teased the Daleks and mocked their creator, Davros, throughout

***Doctor Who*'s 1978 arrival in the United States was heralded by *Famous Monsters* Issue #155 with this cover, a montage of *Doctor Who* aliens.**

the four parts. The Daleks were no longer treated as genuine threats to the safety of the galaxy.

The second story of Season 17 marked *Doctor Who*'s ascent to the big time. "City of Death" was written by Douglas Adams and Graham Williams, and it guest-starred big names John Cleese, Julian Glover and Catherine Schell. Many parts of the serial were shot on location in Paris, giving it a more expensive feel. It was a big-budget success. The story itself was wonderfully inventive and original, a latter-day *Doctor Who* masterpiece. However, the season ended on a down note when Douglas Adams' serial "Shada" was left unfinished. A BBC technical crew strike at Christmas of 1979 prevented the last few days of shooting on the story, which concerned a Time Lord penal planet called Shada. The episode was officially cancelled in January 1980 when it was impossible to coordinate the schedules of the guest cast members, many of whom had moved on to other projects. By 1980, Douglas Adams and Graham Williams had both left the series.

Perhaps the most controversial figure in *Doctor Who* lore assumed the position of producer in 1980. John Nathan-Turner, who had worked as Production Unit Manager on the series since Season 15, replaced outgoing producer Graham Williams. Almost immediately, Nathan-Turner declared his intention to bring *Doctor Who* back to its roots. He had done some serious thinking about *Doctor Who* and determined that the series had come to rely too heavily on gimmicks such as K-9 and the Doctor's all-purpose sonic screwdriver. He also felt that the humorous aspects of the Douglas Adams years gave viewers the impression that the Doctor was infallible and immune to all menace. The humorous aspects of the stories were severely cut back although Baker, as always, improvised many funny moments which survived into the aired serials. Nathan-Turner had also watched "Destiny of the Daleks" with a keen eye and determined that the evil machines had outlived their usefulness. Dalekmania, after all, was 15 years in the past. Nathan-Turner retired the Daleks from the series, but promised to bring them back when he felt that they could be done again in a more respectful, believable fashion.

John-Nathan Turner, seen here at an American *Doctor Who* convention, produced the final nine years of the series.

Season 18 was important not only for the arrival of Nathan-Turner, but also for numerous character and actor departures. K-9 was injured in the line of duty and the character left the series in "Warrior's Gate," along with Lalla Ward's Romana. Although the season introduced three new companions (Matthew Waterhouse as Adric in "Full Circle," Sarah Sutton as Nyssa in "Keeper of Traken" and Janet Fielding as Tegan in "Logopolis"), the shocker of the year was not these introductions, but rather the departure of star Tom Baker. Season 18 was to be his last year on the series. *Doctor Who* fans around the world went into shock when it was announced on November 4, 1980, that Peter Davison would soon be filling Baker's rather large shoes.[11]

When "Logopolis" aired in February and March of 1981, there was a high degree of denial and morbidity in the *Doctor Who* fan community. In the last scene of the serial, Baker regenerated into the young, almost intolerably handsome Peter Davison. To many, this change represented the end of the great *Doctor Who* years. In America especially, Baker was critical to the show's success. All of a sudden, *Doctor Who*'s future seemed uncertain. There had been three regenerations in the past, but no actor had ever held on to the role as long as Baker had. Could his success be repeated?

While fans waited for that burning question to be answered, *Doctor Who*'s first television spin off aired on December 28, 1981. Starring former companion Sarah Jane Smith (Elisabeth Sladen) and a new K-9 (John Leeson), *K-9 and Company* was also produced by Nathan-Turner. There had been a public outcry when K-9 left the series earlier in the year, and this pilot film was a response to the desire to see more of the cybernetic pup. The program was 50 minutes long and it concerned an investigation into the world of black magic. It was a solid, enjoyable hour written by Terence Dudley, but the ratings, unfortunately, were poor, partly because of a regional power outage. No follow-up was ever made. Still, it was delightfully nostalgic to see Sladen and K-9 in action again.

At the end of 1981, 18 new serials (from "The Ribos Operation" through "Keeper of Traken") were made available to syndicators in America. However,

Time-Life's television branch had been dissolved and it was uncertain who would distribute *Who*[12]. And by this time, the bloom was off the rose. *Star Wars* was still popular, but fans had been exposed to films like *Alien* (1979), *Star Trek: The Motion Picture* (1979) and *Flash Gordon* (1980), and the space craze was cooling. Accordingly, the second round of Tom Baker *Who* episodes aired mostly on PBS and did not repeat the immense ratings victories of Seasons 12–15. Whether this decline was due to the cooling of the space craze alone, or the fact that many Americans did not appreciate or enjoy the absurdist tone of Seasons 16–18 after the action-packed horror sci-fi of the earlier package, is hard to determine.

Davison's Day as Doctor

At age 31, Peter Davison was the youngest actor ever to play the role of the Time Lord. A traditionally handsome man with fair features and a baby-faced innocence, Davison had already commenced a distinguished career in television drama by the time he became the fifth incarnation of the Doctor. Before *Doctor Who*, Davison had guest starred on such genre series such as *The Tomorrow People* (1973–79) and *Hitchhiker's Guide to the Galaxy* (1978). He also carried the role of Tristan Farnon in the popular series *All Creatures Great and Small.* It was during the latter experience that Nathan-Turner became familiar with Davison's extraordinary talents. When casting a new Doctor in 1981, Nathan-Turner remembered the gentlemanly young thespian and realized he had found his Time Lord. It was a bold and unusual choice because Davison was so very different in age, appearance and demeanor from his immediate predecessor, Tom Baker. Where Baker was confident and boisterous, Davison seemed timid and contemplative. Where Baker was strange and quixotic, Davison was stolid and dependable. With his good looks and earnest qualities, Davison's Doctor was a traditional romantic leading man, and much less eccentric than all the previous incarnations. His interpretation of the Doctor as kind, soft-spoken gentleman had never been done in the show's long history, so it was as valid a revamp as Troughton's, Pertwee's or Baker's.

To help Davison adjust to his role and escape the large shadow of Tom Baker, the first several episodes of the nineteenth season were shot out of sequence. "Four to Doomsday," "The Visitation" and "Kinda" were all lensed before the premiere adventure of the season, "Castrovalva." By the time "Castrovalva" was produced, Davison's interpretation of the Time Lord as tender innocent was cemented. Garbed in a red-striped cricketer costume and with a celery stalk pinned to his lapel, Davison began to build his legacy. The actor also took to heart the advice he had received from former Doctor Patrick Troughton. The elder statesman of the series had instructed the youth to do only three years as the Doctor so he could avoid typecasting in the future.[13] It was a plan that had worked well for Troughton, who stayed busy in cinema and televised drama throughout his post–*Doctor Who* career. It also worked splendidly for Davison, who after the series went on to star in the film *Black Beauty* (1994) and television series such as *Campion* (1988).

Peter Davison (seen here with Caroline Munro, Stella Starr of *Star Crash* [1978]), played the young, innocent fifth incarnation of the Doctor.

In Season 19, producer Nathan-Turner distributed a memo to series writers putting an end to the silly humor that had dominated many of the later Baker–era adventures. *Doctor Who* was to be serious business again, and all jokes of the Douglas Adams variety were curtailed. Unfortunately, this dictate had the effect of making many new serials seem rather bland in comparison to *Doctor Who*s of the past. Forbidden from expressing his humorous side, Davison had much less room in which to maneuver, and it was doubly difficult for him to create a memorable individual.

While the new leading man took the reins, the *Doctor Who* production team also faced some serious difficulties. The annual budget for *Doctor Who* was cut significantly by the BBC. This financial shortfall resulted in an edict from Nathan-Turner stating that there would be only the most limited location shooting in the 1982 season. Instead, most serials would be shot entirely in-studio. Clearly, it was not going to be an easy year. Then the BBC also made another shocking decision: It booted *Doctor Who* from its Saturday timeslot after 18 consecutive years! The series was moved to the early evening hours during the work week. Additionally, *Doctor Who* would now be required to air two episodes a week, on Monday and Tuesday nights, rather than only one. This shift meant that the series would use up its backlog of episodes faster than ever before. It also meant that the series would now have to compete with soccer practice and homework, among other things.

Thematically, the standouts of Davison's first season were "Black Orchid," a Charlotte Brontë–type mystery of glittering production values and fine performances, and the Cyberman adventure "Earthshock." It was that episode which shocked fans by culminating in the death of companion Adric (Matthew Waterhouse). In the rest of the season, actor Anthony Ainley (*The Land That Time Forgot*) returned as the Master in "Castrovalva" and "Time Flight." He had first assumed the role at the end of the Tom Baker era in stories such as "The Keeper of Traken" and "Logopolis."

The overall ratings for Davison's first season were quite good, and the series regularly captured approximately 10.5 million viewers.[14] Although this number was down somewhat from the banner, early Baker years, there were many reasons for the drop. Besides the time slot shift and the change in lead actors, *Doctor Who* also had to face the advent of home video. This factor alone probably accounted for a significant dip in viewer numbers.

Ignoring these obstacles, Season 20 was designed as a year of celebration. *Doctor Who* had prospered on television for two decades, an amazing feat. Accordingly, the serials produced that year took time to remember villains and friends from the past. "Arc of Infinity" opened the year on planet Gallifrey and featured the return of the deranged Omega from the tenth anniversary special "The Three Doctors." Nicholas Courtney's Brigadier Lethbridge-Stewart also returned to the world of *Doctor Who* in the excellent "Mawdryn Undead." Amidst these nostalgia-driven shows, Sarah Sutton's Nyssa left to nurse a futuristic leper colony in "Terminus." She was replaced in what this author terms "The Turlough Experiment." Mark Strickson (*Angels*, *Bravo*) was presented as a companion named Turlough in "Mawdryn Undead." He was secretly used as the pawn of the evil Black Guardian, and on a mission to kill the Doctor. For his first several episodes, Turlough traveled with the Doctor and attempted to murder him. Because he failed continuously, the character came off as incompetent. This story thread was resolved in "Enlightenment" and Turlough was freed of the evil influence. Turlough promptly became another typical subordinate of the Doctor: constantly in need of rescue and offering little in terms of drama.

The centerpiece of Season 20 was undoubtedly the anniversary special "The Five Doctors," which saw the return of Jon Pertwee and Patrick Troughton. (Since William Hartnell had passed away in 1975, his incarnation was played by Richard Hurndall. Conspicuously absent from the proceedings was Tom Baker. His wild incarnation was represented by clips from the unaired Season 17 finale "Shada." Also coming back for more action were companions Carole Ann Ford, Liz Sladen, Nicholas Courtney, Frazer Hines, Wendy Padbury, Caroline John and Richard Franklin. *Doctor Who* villains were represented by Anthony Ainley's the Master, a Dalek, a troop of Cybermen and even a Yeti. It was a delightful adventure, and a splendid way to celebrate *Doctor Who*'s twentieth birthday.

Season 21 was yet another year of dramatic change. Janet Fielding's Tegan and Mark Strickson's Turlough both left *Doctor Who* before year's end. They were replaced by Nicola Bryant as the American botany student Perpigillium "Peri" Brown. Before these comings and goings, however, the season opened with "Warriors of the Deep," a Johnny Byrne–penned sequel to Season 7's "Doctor Who and the Silurians" and Season 9's "The Sea Devils." The Daleks also came back to life when John Nathan-Turner was granted permission by Terry Nation to revive them. "Resurrection of the Daleks" was buoyed by strong production values and location filming at the Tower Bridge in London. It was an action-packed adventure that restored the Daleks to the status of effective menace.

After some location shooting at the Canary Island of Lanzarotte for "Planet of Fire," *Doctor Who*'s production team experienced another dramatic departure. "The Caves of Androzani" was Peter Davison's last adventure. He had fulfilled his promise and remained with the series for three years. Davison could not have asked for a better send-off. "The Caves of Androzani" was an exciting science-fiction riff on *The Phantom of the Opera*, and the show had an unremitting pace. In the final moments, the Doctor regenerated once again. Davison was out as the Doctor, and Colin Baker was in.

Colin Baker's Bad Breaks with the BBC

At the end of "The Caves of Androzani," the curly-haired Colin Baker bolted up abruptly from a prone position in the TARDIS control room. He made eye contact with the camera, and thus with *Doctor Who*'s television audience. With pure arrogance and disdain etched all over his expressive face, Baker mouthed his first words on the series. Each word rolled from his tongue with a delightful, acidic quality. It was a powerful, defining moment for the new Doctor, and a startling reinterpretation of the Time Lord. The span of the kinder and gentler fifth Doctor was over, and Colin Baker had arrived to reinvigorate and challenge *Doctor Who* precepts with his daring new take on the sci-fi material.

Like each of the actors who preceded him, Colin Baker was an unusual and inspired choice to play the Doctor. Although the actor had appeared on series television in *Brothers* (1974) and guested on *Blake's 7* in "The City at the Edge of the World" as well as in *Doctor Who*'s "Arc of Infinity," he was by no means a household name when he was cast by John Nathan-Turner in *Who*. Nonetheless, this versatile performer played with gusto, and made the sixth incarnation of the Doctor the wildest one yet. At age 42 he was only eight years older than Peter Davison, but Baker's version of the Doctor seemed infinitely more confident in demeanor. He was pompous, strutting, comedic, exciting, unpredictable, sarcastic, physically adept and larger-than-life. He was also daringly theatrical, and arguably as charismatic as Tom Baker's quixotic fourth incarnation. His Doctor also had the distinction of being the worst dressed yet, garbed in a hideous patchwork jacket of clashing colors and fabrics. Unfortunately, Colin Baker's outstanding portrayal of the Time Lord was not to be long *or* popular. During his short reign, *Doctor Who* experienced more trouble than in the past 21 years combined.

Colin Baker was introduced to the British press as the new Doctor on August 20, 1983.[15] At the press conference, he loudly proclaimed his intention to play the Doctor for at least eight years and thus best the duration of Tom Baker's record era. Colin Baker seemed genuinely honored and thrilled to be playing the Doctor, and there were no stereotypically "actorish" reservations about being typecast in the role. His focus was clearly on making the show the best it could be. He also stated his intention to make the Doctor more alien in his responses — in other words less courteous and less polite.

For Colin Baker's first season on *Doctor Who*, things seemed to go very well despite more interference from the BBC. The show's format was changed from multiple-part serials of 25 minutes apiece to two-part episodes of 45 minutes apiece. Understandably, this change threw the series writers for a loop.

Although *Doctor Who*'s ratings were down in Season 22, they were respectable. Almost nine million people tuned in to "Attack of the Cybermen," the premiere of the twenty-second season. The rest of the season averaged between 6.5 and 7.5 million viewers. Considering the inroads made by home video, these ratings were solid, if not spectacular. In dramatic terms, Colin Baker's first serials were quite strong. "Vengeance on Varos" was one of the best *Doctor Who* serials of the 1980s, and "The Mark of the Rani," "Attack of the Cybermen" and "Revelation of the Daleks" were all solid, well-told adventures featuring popular historic *Who* villains. Although "Timelash" was not popular at the time of its airing, or even now with fans, it had an interesting structure that ribbed the works of H.G. Wells. It may not have been brilliant *Doctor Who*, but there was clearly some wit behind it. The most enjoyable program of the season, however, saw Patrick Troughton and Frazer Hines return to the Whoniverse. "The Two Doctors" proved not only that Hines and Troughton were still a great team, but also that new Doctor Colin Baker could effectively play against even the most consummate scene stealers.

In early 1985, even as the last stories of Season 22 were airing, disaster struck the era of the sixth Doctor. New BBC Controller Michael Grade announced to the press that *Doctor Who* would be going on an enforced 18–month hiatus. The first explanation for the cancellation of Season 23 was expense. Grade claimed that *Doctor Who* was simply too expensive a series to produce. Of course, this was a ridiculous assertion as it was far cheaper a series than any number of concurrent BBC dramas which did not have the benefit of a huge fandom in 60 countries. Troughton and other series stars spoke out against this bogus "budget crunch" explanation, suggesting that perhaps the BBC was really using fan devotion to *Doctor Who* as leverage so their compulsory annual levy would be increased. As the drama continued to unfold, Grade began to denigrate the series in interviews. He claimed the series was "overly" violent. He said the producers were lazy and uninventive. He said the show was basically past its prime. In America, an executive would never go to the press and badmouth a popular television series he was overseeing, even if he personally disliked it. Grade's crusade against *Doctor Who* was thus quite unfathomable. Many writers and people in the British entertainment industry also suggested it was unprofessional and economically suicidal as well.

The response to the cancellation was immediate. Thirty thousand letters were sent by fans to the BBC requesting the Time Lord's return.[16] Fans in America offered to send money to help bail the series out. Even more dramatically, producer Ian Levine and songwriter Fiachra Trench produced a single called "Doctor in Distress." This song highlighted the vocal talents of the Moody Blues, Ultravox, Time UK, Colin Baker, Nicola Bryant, Anthony Ainley and Nicholas Courtney. It was an effort to save not only the Doctor's television life, but also to raise money for cancer relief.[17] Despite these efforts, Grade continued to slam the series. In July 1985, Colin Baker, Nicola Bryant and Eric Saward attempted to keep interest in the series alive by participating on a BBC *Doctor Who* radio serial entitled "Slipback." Directed by Paul Spencer, the program aired in six segments of 11 minutes each.[18] It was not as thrilling as the television show, but it helped ease the withdrawal pains of many fans.

Followers of *Doctor Who* mourned the loss of a season that would have seen the return of the Celestial Toymaker in "The Nightmare Fair" by Graham Williams and other dramatic stories. Meanwhile, Michael Grade blissfully presided over a tour of *Who* creatures and spaceships in the U.S. He reassured American fans that the Doctor would soon be back. (Indeed, by that late date, the hiatus was over and the series was gearing up for a new year.) Also present for the U.S. tour was fifth Doctor Peter Davison and representative series bad guys such as Daleks and Cyberman. Even old Bessie, the 1953 English Ford Popular that Pertwee had piloted during the early 1970s, was in evidence. This tour went from Washington D.C., to Philadelphia, to New Jersey, New York and finally to New England. Its goal was to publicize *Doctor Who* in all the major cities where it aired on PBS.[19]

The long-awaited Season 23 finally began airing in September 1986, and it was to consist of just one 14-part story: "The Trial of the Time Lord." For clarity's sake, fans and *Doctor Who* history quickly split the serial into four digestible parts titled "The Mysterious Planet," "Mindwarp," "Terror of the Vervoids" and "The Ultimate Foe." Nicola Bryant's Peri left the troubled series in "Mindwarp" and was replaced by Bonnie Langford's exercisaholic Melanie Bush in "Terror of the Vervoids."

The epic-length serial "The Trial of the Time Lord" was not without its share of problems. Author Robert Holmes, a regular *Doctor Who* writer since "The Krotons" in the Troughton era, passed away before he could finish the final act of the drama. Eric Saward, then story editor, quit the series and refused Nathan-Turner permission to use his version of the finale. At the last minute, Pip and Jane Baker were rushed in to finish the tale before shooting began. Understandably, the overall story suffered from all this authorial confusion. It literally was written as it went along. Not surprisingly, many *Doctor Who* fans felt that the conclusion of "The Trial of the Time Lord" did not justify all the build up. Audiences seemed to agree, and the season as a whole garnered a viewership of only about 4.5 million people.

Whether these low ratings were caused by the fact that viewers had only one story to choose from during the whole season (*à la Murder One*) or the fact that the *Doctor Who* habit had been permanently interrupted by Grade's enforced hiatus, it was difficult to tell. Whatever the reason, *Doctor Who* was actually in worse shape at the end of the twenty-third season than it was during the 18-month hiatus.

In December 1986, BBC handed down another unexpected edict: Colin Baker was to be ousted from the show. This was especially confusing because Baker himself wanted badly to come back. He loved the series and the character. The BBC explained that they felt Baker was unpopular with fans, and that it was good to have a switch in lead performers every three years. Of course, Baker had only played *Doctor Who* in one-and-a-half seasons, not three. With Nathan-Turner negotiating, an accommodation between Baker and the BBC was attempted. In the end, the best the BBC would do was offer Baker one four-part serial, at the end of which his Doctor would regenerate. Baker refused the paltry offer, and the reign of the sixth Doctor ended without a regeneration story. It was an ugly, sad time in *Doctor Who* history.

McCoy's Moment of Magic

The role of the Time Lord from Gallifrey was recast in 1986 for the seventh time in 23 years. Reportedly at the top of John Nathan-Turner's wish list was Michael Keating, Vila, of *Blake's 7*.[20] For whatever reason, this decision was reversed and the role was offered instead to Scottish actor Sylvester McCoy. Diminutive in size (five feet, six inches), McCoy was a talented physical comedian and graduate of such films as *Dracula* (1979). His real name, Patrick Kent Smith, had been supplanted some years earlier when he did a one-man stage show entitled *An Evening with Sylvester McCoy— The Human Time Bomb*. McCoy was a switch from Baker and Davison because he was neither imposing in size, nor young, vigorous and blond. Of all the Doctors, McCoy physically resembled Patrick Troughton the most, although he consciously attempted to evoke all previous incarnations in his performance:

> If there were any moments that I thought were a Patrick Troughton moment ... or a Tom Baker moment ... I would think of that.... That's why my Doctor was comedic ... that was a bit like Patrick Troughton. If he was a bit crabby that was like William Hartnell ... sometimes he was a bit dangerous, like Colin Baker...[21]

McCoy began his age as the Doctor in another time of turbulence. Nathan-Turner had declared his intention to leave the series after the twenty-third season, but then he changed his mind. He remained producer of *Doctor Who* until the bitter end in 1989, and many fans accused him of coasting. Soon after McCoy's first few stories aired, the fans were expressing outrage at the high level of slapstick comedy in evidence. They were also less than thrilled by the continued appearance of Bonnie Langford's Melanie. Though Langford approached the part of Mel with sincerity, many fans had difficulty relating to her ebullient, elfish creation. Facing these problems, *Doctor Who* stumbled through a very weak year. "Time and the Rani" was probably the worst post-regeneration story in the series' long history. The season culminated with two less-than-sterling serials: "Delta and the Bannermen," which featured a guest appearance by American vaudevillian Stubby Kaye, and the cartoonish "Dragonfire." The only standout show was "Paradise Towers," a brilliant, well-conceived satire. However, it was still more funny than dramatic.

Ian Brigg's "Dragonfire" was significant because Bonnie Langford left the series to be replaced by young Sophie Aldred as "Ace." This was the last companion switch in the history of the series. Although it would not be obvious until the start of the twenty-fifth season, Aldred would prove to be the best companion of latter-day *Doctor Who*. She and McCoy made magic together. Before that magic could happen, however, Season 24 finished its lackluster run. The ratings hovered constantly near four million viewers ... the same figure that had triggered the BBC expulsion of Colin Baker.

While 1987 saw the birth of a seventh Doctor, it lost the actor who had portrayed the second. Patrick Troughton died at age 67, just two years after his last appearance as the Doctor in the Colin Baker–era story "The Two Doctors."

It was also during 1987 that a company known as Coast to Coast purchased the film rights to *Doctor Who* from the BBC. Over the next two years, various big-name actors were named as top candidates for the role of the Doctor, and Caroline Munro was reportedly cast in the film as the new companion. Johnny Byrne, writer of "The Keeper of Traken," "Arc of Infinity" and "Warriors of the Deep," was tapped to write the screenplay. Although there were frequent bulletins about the film in genre magazines, no real progress seemed to be made and the picture was never produced.

Shooting on the twenty-fifth season of *Doctor Who* began just after Easter 1988 near Waterloo and the Thames. Almost 24 years after they had invaded London, the Daleks were back in England once again. The Daleks, Davros, Totter's Lane and Coal Hill School were all featured prominently in the first show, "Remembrance of the Daleks." It was a fast-paced adventure filled with *Doctor Who* lore and history, and it had none of the comedic elements which had made the previous season less than well-regarded. The remainder of season was of a moderate, if not sterling, quality. "Silver Nemesis" was saddled with a confusing plot but it also brought back old time villains: the Cybermen. The final show of the season was a great original by author Stephen Wyatt: "The Greatest Show in the Galaxy." *Doctor Who* had regained much of its luster by this time, and the fans responded enthusiastically. Aldred and McCoy had a smooth working relationship, and it showed in the results. There was also a new conceit in the show, courtesy of producer Nathan-Turner and story editor Andrew Cartmel. In stories such as "Silver Nemesis" and "The Greatest Show in the Galaxy," it was suggested that the Doctor was much more than a Time Lord. In fact, he seemed to hide a greater secret. Was he an agent of a higher force? Was he, in fact, a supernatural force himself? These questions raised interest in the series, and McCoy grew into the role. His seemingly "funny" side actually hid the manipulations of a chess master. It was a new take, but it worked.

Doctor Who's last season on the air was a strange one. "Battlefield," "Ghost Light" and "Curse of Fenric" each could have been great shows, but all the stories were ruined to a degree by narrative confusion. Overnight, *Doctor Who* lost the capacity to tell linear, understandable stories. "Ghost Light" and "Curse of Fenric" made very little sense dramatically. The final story, ironically named "Survival," was a thin one that borrowed key ideas from *Planet of the Apes*. The ratings for the series stagnated at approximately four million, and *Doctor Who* did not return for a twenty-seventh season.

Cancellation

Even while *Doctor Who* was finishing its network run in 1989, there were bad omens about the future of the long-lived science fiction series. The BBC Head of Drama Peter Creegan announced his preference to "farm" *Doctor Who* out to an independent television production company.[22] After Season 26, the BBC declared that it intended to sell the series to an independent producer. After loyally buttressing BBC ratings for two-and-a-half decades, *Doctor Who* was unceremoniously put on the auction block. The BBC's decision to sell the series to an autonomous production company was apparently a response to a new government mandate requiring at least a quarter of British programming to be made by independent business.[23] But *Doctor Who* need not have been affected by that ruling. The BBC had many other properties which could have been "farmed out," or sacrificed. Had it wished to, the Corporation could have chosen to continue producing new episodes of *Doctor Who* while simultaneously shopping around for a buyer. This decision appeared to be an underhanded attempt by the BBC to unload a series which they felt had outlived both its appeal and its audience.

Nothing at all happened on the independent market, and the series simply ceased to exist in any form. After 26 years on the air, *Doctor Who* was shelved indefinitely, if not cancelled officially. Understandably, the '90s were to be a gloomy era for the Time Lord. By 1991 it was obvious that Coast to Coast was getting nowhere with its long-planned *Doctor Who* film and that the television series was dead in the water. In response to the outcry from fans, Virgin Books released a series of "New adventures" featuring the seventh Doctor and Ace. These new novels were written by prominent *Doctor Who* historians like John Peel, and the series' own writers such as Marc Platt, Ben Aaronovitch and Terrance Dicks. Unlike the Pocket Book *Star Trek* novels, these new *Doctor Who* adventures were considered "canon" by many *Doctor Who* enthusiasts. The books were overwhelmingly popular; *Doctor Who* was obviously far from dead or forgotten. In fact, videotape releases in America and Great Britain sold extremely well, and many new non-

Even in cancellation, *Doctor Who* continued to spawn mainstream interest, appearing in magazines such as *Epilog* and *TV Zone.*

fiction books about the heyday of the series were written too. Fans did not give up hope that a film or new television series would soon materialize. Unfortunately, the wait was far from over.

The 30th Anniversary

Nineteen ninety-three marked the thirtieth birthday of *Doctor Who*. Sadly, this milestone was celebrated "officially" only with a BBC documentary entitled *More Than 30 Years in the TARDIS*. A special entitled *Dark Dimension* was announced by the BBC but it fell through, apparently due to lack of planning and internal politics. The story, had it been produced, would have seen the fourth incarnation of the Doctor trapped on twentieth century Earth trying to save his future incarnations. The special would presumably have starred Tom Baker and Sophie Aldred. It would have also featured Jon Pertwee, Colin Baker, Peter Davison and Sylvester McCoy in "cameo" roles.

Dark Dimension died a quick death amidst a sea of finger-pointing. The BBC claimed (erroneously) that the surviving *Doctor Who* actors could not get along well enough to perform in a special, and the actors reported, conversely, that they had never even been formally approached to appear in the proposed 30-year celebration. It was a strange, confusing incident that once again demonstrated the

BBC's lack of commitment to their most valuable property. The final result was that the thirtieth anniversary went by without a reunion show. But many *Doctor Who* stars did appear together on November 26 and 27 of 1993 in a 20-minute special called *Dimensions in Time*.[24] The brief production was more a fundraising effort for the "Children in Need" charity program than an authentic *Doctor Who* adventure.

At approximately the same time, Steven Spielberg and Amblin Productions became involved in *Doctor Who*. Rumors began to fly fast and loose that *Baywatch* star David Hasselhoff was going to portray the Time Lord in a new American television series.[25] Negotiations were made in early 1994 for producer Philip Segal (*SeaQuest DSV*, *Earth 2*) to purchase the rights to *Doctor Who* for five years. This deal was cemented by the backing of Spielberg's Amblin Entertainment. For some reason, this deal also fell through and yet another unlikely alliance was formed. Now a pilot for a new *Doctor Who* series was to be made for Fox Television in cooperation with the BBC. Philip Segal was still to be involved as producer but not with Spielberg or with Amblin. Instead, Universal Television was now the backer. In a 1995 interview with *Dreamwatch*, Segal revealed that it was actually his interest in *Doctor Who* that had crushed *Dark Dimension*, the thirtieth anniversary show.

> The reality of it was that we were in the process of negotiating the rights for the show. The problem is, if you are launching a new series, it is confusing to the audience and difficult to deal with if something is sandwiched between the new and the old... It wasn't about in-fighting and about actors who didn't want to do it. ...It wasn't a good script...It was the wrong way to bring the show back.[26]

This revelation was a shocker, but *Doctor Who* fans could hardly express their anger with Segal. After all, he was their savior — the man who would bring *Doctor Who* back to television. To his credit, Segal did manage to do just that.

McGann's Movie Is Made in America

Thanks to Segal's efforts, *Doctor Who* returned to television in 1996, seven years after the BBC's unofficial cancellation of the series. The teleplay for *Doctor Who*, which Segal unofficially renamed *The Enemy Within* for clarity within the Whoniverse, was written by Matthew Jacobs. On January 6, 1996, it was announced that 33-year-old Paul McGann, best known for roles in *The Rainbow* and *Alien^3*, was to be the eighth incarnation of the Time Lord. When production started in Vancouver in February 1996, the remainder of the cast included Eric Roberts (*Star 80*, *Runaway Train*, *Heaven's Prisoners*) as the Master and old friend Sylvester McCoy as the seventh incarnation of the Doctor. The new companion, cardiologist Grace Holloway, was portrayed by Daphne Ashbrook, a beautiful young actress most recognizable for playing Dr. Julian Bashir's physically challenged love interest in the second season *Deep Space Nine* story "Melora." McCoy appeared only in the first few moments of the film and then regenerated into McGann. Ron Grainer's *Doctor Who* theme was revamped by composer John Debney (*SeaQuest DSV*), but the TARDIS remained, in the shape of a London police box.

Doctor Who— the television movie — premiered on the Fox Network at 8:00 P.M., May 14, 1996. The film finished a dismal seventy-fifth for the week out of 98 programs. In numbers of viewers, this equated to roughly eight million people. Though this would have been a decent finish in Great Britain, in America it was ratings death. Segal had already announced to *Doctor Who* fans that the series needed a 15–18 share of the viewing audience if *Doctor Who* were to go to series. The final share was approximately nine percent. It was no surprise when Fox did not pick up its option to pursue a new series. Once more, *Doctor Who*'s future looked to be in grave doubt. Universal was also uninterested in making any further *Doctor Who* films.

In Great Britain, the television movie did considerably better. It was watched by nine million viewers. This was the best rating for *Doctor Who* in England since the Peter Davison era in the early 1980s. Video sales of the program were also quite high, proving that the Doctor had been missed in the half decade since the series cancellation.

Nineteen ninety-six was another sad year for *Doctor Who* fans, however. Although they had seen a new eighth incarnation of their favorite character, they lost another old friend: Jon Pertwee, the third actor to play the Doctor, died in May 1996 of a heart attack. He was on vacation in the United States when he died on May 20, just six days after Paul McGann's premiere adventure.

While in 1997 fans pondered the future of their favorite Time Lord, the BBC found itself in a bit of a pickle. Lumiere Pictures (once Coast to Coast) filed a 1997 lawsuit against the BBC claiming that the British Broadcasting Corporation had entered into negotiations with Philip Segal while Lumiere still owned the rights to make a *Doctor Who* film. Lumiere was seeking significant financial compensation from the BBC for the failure of their project, which at one time had big names like Leonard Nimoy and Alan Rickman associated with it.

At the time of this writing, no new *Doctor Who* projects have been announced but it seems a fairly certain bet that *Doctor Who* will reappear again in some form. There have been rumors that America's Sci-Fi Channel will produce a new show. There has also been persistent talk of a new movie, or a new BBC series. After all, the Doctor still has three regenerations left!

PART II

Curriculum Vitae

Lineage: *Doctor Who*'s Parents

Like most science fiction television programs, *Doctor Who* did not spring from the mind of its creators (Sydney Newman and Donald Wilson) as a completely original, fully developed work of art. On the contrary, its many roots in cinematic, video and literary forebears are fairly obvious to the keen-eyed observer. Just as *Star Trek* transformed the "military in space" and psychological "Monster from the Id" aspects of the classic MGM film *Forbidden Planet* (1956), *Doctor Who* came about first as a kind of cathode tube version of director George Pal's hit movie *The Time Machine* (1960).

Written by David Duncan and based on the classic novel by H.G. Wells, *The Time Machine* starred Rod Taylor, Yvette Mimieux, Sebastian Cabot and Whit Bissell. It spun the tale of two disparate futuristic civilizations, one peaceful and tame (the Eloi), the other menacing and exploitative (the Morlocks). The industrial, powerful Morlocks utilized the Eloi as slaves and fodder until a British time traveler encountered the two races in the Earth's distant future (802,701 A.D.) and interfered to preserve humanity. In *The Time Machine*, the Morlocks were depicted as albino monsters with shaggy white hair and penetrating white eyes. The Eloi were dramatized as trim, sexy humans with golden blond hair.

The Time Machine's central dynamic, that of two unlike cultures trapped in mortal conflict, was a critical one to *Doctor Who*'s foundation. The physical appearance and characteristics of the two peoples (monsters representing the "bad," beautiful young men and women representing the "good") as well the depiction of the central character as a time-traveling crusader or meddler, set the tone for virtually every episode of *Doctor Who*'s 26 years. *The Time Machine* is unquestionably *Doctor Who*'s template because the two races in opposition could just as easily be the evil Daleks and the peace-loving, golden-haired Thals in "The Daleks," the insectoid Zarbi and the elegant Menoptera in "The Web Planet," the life-sucking Elders and the vitality-drained Savages in "The Savages," the Drahvin and the Rill in "Galaxy Four," the Spiders and the human colonists in "Planet of the Spiders," the Usurians and their overtaxed populace in "The Sunmakers," or even the Nimon

Ancestors of the Thals? The peaceful Eloi tribe approaches the Morlock city in *The Time Machine.*

and the Skonnons in "The Horns of Nimon." The specifics do not matter. Yet if one were to name any *Doctor Who* serial, it would certainly center around two races locked in a life-and-death struggle. One race would be seen as the ruthless exploiter, the other as the exploited or oppressed. This conceit comes from *The Time Machine.*

The Doctor's role in *Doctor Who* is also identical to that of Rod Taylor's gentleman in *The Time Machine.* He is morality's avenger; the righter of cosmic wrongs. He arrives on the scene, assesses the situation, and sides with the underdog. Using his superior knowledge of science, time travel, history, politics, etc., he leads the downtrodden to a victory over the oppressor. And he never leaves until the scales of justice are equalized. Just as Taylor's Time Traveler ventured down into the Morlock mines to rescue the Eloi fodder and destroy the bad guys, so does the Doctor tussle with the Daleks, the Cybermen, the Monoids, the Morokians, the Macra, the Oracle and the Ogri. The Doctor's goal is never his own survival or even his escape, it is the complete upheaval of the society he has judged unjust.

The physical and psychological characteristics of the Eloi and the Morlocks also form a critical part of *Doctor Who*'s gestalt. Just as the Eloi are trim beautiful blondes, so are the Thals equally lovely and graceful in "The Daleks." Just as the Morlocks are inhuman beasts, so are the Daleks, the Monoids, Wirrn and the Sontarans totally inhuman in their various appearances and desires. Just as the Eloi have forgotten their human heritage through generations of servitude, likewise

Rod Taylor pilots his time machine in the George Pal film *The Time Machine* (1959), *Doctor Who's* direct antecedent.

have the denizens of Leela's Sevateem in "The Face of Evil," the human guardians aboard the Ark in "The Ark," the awakening humans in "The Ark in Space," the underdwellers in "The Mysterious Planet," the Dulkians in "The Dominators" and the Gonds in "The Krotons." The Doctor's victories, again akin to the Time Traveler's in *The Time Machine*, always rest on his ability to stir within the exploited and oppressed their buried feelings of pride in their forgotten heritage. Only when the fallen reclaim their heritage and history as fighters (the Thals in "The Daleks"), readers (the underdwellers in "The Mysterious Planet"), multi-task builders ("The Ark in Space") and survivors ("The Ark") can they successfully overcome their manipulative opponents.

The oppressors in *Doctor Who* all tend to be variations on the Morlock prototype seen in *The Time Machine*. They are usually physically unattractive (witness the Borad in "Timelash," the Gastropods in "The Twin Dilemma" and Sil in "Vengeance on Varos"), or at the very least non-human (the Daleks, the Cybermen, the Sontarans, the Ice Warriors). Like the Morlocks, who used the Eloi both as slave labor and as food, the villains of *Doctor Who* always exploit the weaker, seemingly less intelligent race. The Elders drain the lifeforce from the vivacious Savages in "The Savages." The Daleks reduce mankind to enslaved, zombified miners in "The Dalek Invasion of Earth." The pattern is always the same: The strong, technical and intelligent race exploits the weaker, less advanced, confused one. Perhaps the greatest evidence of *Doctor Who*'s dependence on *The Time Machine* for its prototypical story is the fact that the Doctor himself (any incarnation) could be dropped into the story of the Eloi and Morlocks with no difficulty whatsoever. He would act in exactly the same manner and with the same purpose as Taylor's Time Traveler. *Doctor Who* itself made some notation of this fact in the 1980s Colin Baker story "Timelash," which featured H.G. Wells, a character named Lena (Weena in *The Time Machine*) and aliens called "Morlox" (Morlocks).

The Time Machine is the not the only source from which *Doctor Who* was derived. The other, equally important sources of inspiration are the first three *Quatermass* teleseries by Nigel Kneale. The first *Quatermass* saga preceded *Doctor Who* on British television by a decade and was described earlier in the History section of this work, but it recounts the adventures of a British man of science, Bernard Quatermass. In the first story, the professor investigates an alien fungus which has attached itself to an astronaut who has returned from a mission in space. In the second story, Quatermass prevents an invasion from space by "body snatcher"-style aliens. In the last series, *Quatermass and the Pit*, Quatermass unearths an ancient spaceship in Hobb's Lane which reveals the truth about the Devil, occult legends and "possession." Each one of these adventures has been put to use by *Doctor Who* at least twice. More importantly, the Doctor himself is a direct descendent of Quatermass. The Doctor is also (usually) an older man of science; he frequently pleads with the military not to destroy an alien force before he can understand it; and he too dreams up scientific solutions to extraterrestrial problems. Like Quatermass, the Doctor also has a healthy dislike of government bureaucracy and the military mentality.

The first *Quatermass* serial, *The Quatermass Experiment*, details the threat of a contaminated astronaut returning to Earth. This scenario was also the plot of *Doctor Who*'s Pertwee–era story "Ambassadors of Death." At the end of *The Quatermass Experiment*, the astronaut Caroon transforms into a giant fungus on the verge of reproducing. Quatermass warned the military to deal with it before that eventuality, lest the world be overcome by spores. This sequence of events was repeated in the Tom Baker–era story "The Seeds of Doom," which saw the Doctor battling the threat of further Krynoid spores should reproduction occur. In addition, the notion of a human being who transforms into something alien and dreadful as a result of alien biology is also seen throughout *Doctor Who* history. It was an important factor in the serials "Inferno," "Planet of Evil," "The Seeds of Doom" and "Terror of the Vervoids."

The second *Quatermass* serial, called simply *Quatermass II*, focuses on a hostile invasion from space. The alien "invasion" theme also runs throughout the Pertwee era of *Doctor Who*, particularly in the stories "Spearhead from Space," "Terror of the Autons" and "The Claws of Axos." Like Quatermass before him, the Doctor successfully defeats the alien invasion before Earth is doomed.

Other than *The Time Machine*, *Quatermass and the Pit* is perhaps the greatest single contributor to typical *Doctor Who* stories and style. Just as Quatermass confronts an ancient, awakening evil in Hobb's Lane, so does the Doctor confront another ancient, awakening evil in Devil's Barrow in the story "The Daemons." This *Doctor Who* serial came straight from *Quatermass and the Pit* not only in revealing that ancient legends were actually written to explain extraterrestrial landings, but also in the suggestion that supernatural "remedies" such as stakes, iron and salt could defeat the opponent.

The "Daemons" template is repeated throughout *Doctor Who* history nearly as frequently as the *Time Machine* scenario. Oriental myth cloaks a futuristic evil in "The Talons of Weng Chiang." Egyptian myth is the source of alien evil in "The Pyramids of Mars," and devil worship is again related to alien life in "Image of the Fendahl." In each case, it is either future beings or alien life forms and alien technology that are revealed to be the source of mankind's superstitions and myth. In *Doctor Who*'s long history, many fans have called this a "homage" to *Quatermass*, but it is actually an out-and-out translation of Kneale's original *Quatermass and the Pit* story into Whovian terms.

Although many *Doctor Who* fans will undoubtedly quibble with this next statement, there is no doubt that the original *Star Trek* also influenced some *Doctor Who* stories. From the late '60s onward, a number of *Star Trek* conceits and ideas appeared on the long-running BBC series. A "warp drive" spaceship powered by a matter-antimatter reaction was referred to in "Earthshock" (1982). It is an important distinction that *Doctor Who* did not name the propulsion method a "time warp drive," a "hyperspace drive" (as in *Star Wars*) or a "jump drive" (as in *Space: 1999*) or any other similar name. Instead, *Doctor Who* repeated verbatim the name and description of the *Enterprise*'s motive power, as if the warp drive *were* a real scientific possibility, not a fabrication of a fellow entertainment.

The Time Lord non-interference directive, introduced in 1969's "The War Games," echoes *Star Trek*'s famous Prime Directive. Both the Federation and the Time Lords have had disastrous contacts helping primitive worlds (with the Klingons and Minyans respectively), and so this edict forbidding interference was pronounced. Both *Doctor Who* and the original *Star Trek* are obsessed not with obeying the non-interference directive but in circumventing it!

Nineteen sixty-nine also saw the advent of a *Doctor Who* device called the transmat in the story "The Seeds of Death." For all intents and purposes, the transmat (or transmaterializer) was identical in function and design to *Star Trek*'s famous transporter. The Transmat grew to become an ongoing conceit throughout *Who* stories such as "The Ark in Space," "Mawdryn Undead" and "Remembrance of the Daleks." Interestingly, however, the transporter concept appeared in *Doctor Who* at least once, pre–*Star Trek*. In "The Dalek Masterplan," the Doctor (Hartnell) was sent through a Molecular Disseminator to the distant planet of Mira.

In 1972, *Doctor Who* aired "The Curse of Peladon," a story about a benevolent Galactic Federation and its divergent peoples. The story's crux was planet Peladon's admission into the grand-sounding Federation and the efforts of anti–Federation agents to prevent said admission. *Star Trek* had already introduced the similarly named United Federation of Planets, an identical organization with an equally disparate alien population. *Star Trek* stories such as D.C. Fontana's "Journey to Babel" were built around new planets seeking admission into the Federation, and alien plots to stop that membership. Tellingly, the possession of a rare mineral found on the unaligned planet was the object of the conspirators' desire in "Journey to Babel" and, later, "The Curse of Peladon."

Also in "The Curse of Peladon," the Ice Warriors inform Katy Manning's Jo Grant that they have evolved beyond violence and grown into logical, reasonable creatures. This evolution to logic mirrors the development of the once-savage Vulcans on *Star Trek*.

The Time Machine, *Quatermass* and *Star Trek* are the three greatest influences throughout *Doctor Who*'s 26-year network run. Over the years, however, the series has plundered numerous other science fiction and horror sources as well. Indeed, one of the greatest joys in watching *Doctor Who* is the discovery of which antecedents it has modified, updated or satirized. In the episode guide section of this book, these influences are noted more thoroughly. However, a brief list includes "Dragonfire," a modification of *Aliens*; "Robot," an ode to *King Kong*; "The Brain of Morbius," a retread of *Frankenstein*; "Tomb of the Cybermen," an outer space variation on *The Mummy*; "Curse of Fenric," which shares elements with the 1979 John Carpenter film *The Fog*; "The Caves of Androzani," a delightful, inspired translation of *Phantom of the Opera*; "Survival," a revisit to the *Planet of the Apes* scenario; and "The Invisible Enemy," a witty continuation of the themes seen in *Fantastic Voyage* (1966).

Even beyond these revamps, *Doctor Who* has offered Charlotte Brontë-esque adventures ("Black Orchid"), a television cop pastiche ("The Twin Dilemma") and even a revenge-of-nature giant bug epic ("The Green Death").

Outside of the sci-fi and horror genres, the literary adventures of Sherlock Holmes are also an important component in *Doctor Who*'s basic set-up. Like Holmes, the Doctor is a brilliant thinker. Like Holmes, he also faces an evil nemesis bent on killing him (the Master instead of Moriarty). And finally, the many time traveling companions of *Doctor Who* serve as the Doctor's sounding boards, just as Watson is Holmes'.

With sources as diverse as these, *Doctor Who* is never dull. If it is true that every science fiction television series builds on the success of filmic and video antecedents, then *Doctor Who*'s success is indeed derived from some very solid, very dependable sources. Elements of *The Time Machine*, *Quatermass* and *Star Trek* all blend beautifully and uniquely in *Doctor Who* and have propagated a science fiction television milestone.

Doctor Who's Children

In the previous section, it was noted how *Doctor Who* as an embryonic television series (and later as a full-scale success in the late '60s and early '70s) erected its universe from the supports of older filmic and video productions. Conversely,

Doctor Who has also found itself occupying the opposite position in the structure of genre programming: It has also been a source of inspiration, and a crucial part of the creative framework of innumerable later sci-fi ventures. *Doctor Who*'s influence on and relevance in the universe of sci-fi television and film can be measured by a survey of various programs and movies. To start, virtually every time travel television series created after the advent of *Doctor Who* in 1963 owes the series some measure of gratitude for initiating time travel concepts and precepts so splendidly on the tube.

When tracking *Doctor Who*'s effect, it is best to start with time travel television. Three years after *Doctor Who* premiered, Irwin Allen presented his big-budget follow-up to *Lost in Space*, a 20th Century-Fox production for ABC-TV called *The Time Tunnel* (1966–67). Like *Doctor Who*, the focus of this new science fiction television series was a haphazard, uncontrolled spiral through Earth's history courtesy of a malfunctioning time machine. The giant Time Tunnel apparatus supplanted the TARDIS, but both devices performed identical functions in terms of performance and plot. And, like *Doctor Who* episodes "The Chase," "Marco Polo," "The Myth Makers" and "The Reign of Terror," *The Time Tunnel* sent its heroes to the Civil War to meet Lincoln in "The Death Trap," to the Far East to meet Marco Polo in "Attack of the Barbarians," to the Trojan War in "Revenge of the Gods" and even to the French Revolution in the identically monikered episode "Reign of Terror"! There were other familiar episodes too. "Idol of Death" dealt with Aztec culture and Cortez, *à la Doctor Who*'s "The Aztecs." There was even a knock-off of *Doctor Who*'s famous chase through time and space (Terry Nation's Dalek serial "The Chase"). On *The Time Tunnel* it was called "Chase Through Time."

Like *Doctor Who*'s creative team, *The Time Tunnel* producers soon realized the limits of a pure time travel series formula. They relied on the same trick as *Doctor Who* had, and began to incorporate aliens and outer space themes into later episodes such as "Visitors from Beyond the Stars" and "Raiders from Outer Space" (both by Wanda and Bob Duncan), and "The Kidnappers" by William Welch. The addition of aliens to *The Time Tunnel* mix did nothing to improve the ratings, and the series disappeared without a trace before a second season could commence. Yet in one season of 30 episodes, *The Time Tunnel* managed to repeat nine story ideas that had already appeared on *Doctor Who*.

In the closing months of 1982, NBC offered the public another time travel series so reminiscent of *Doctor Who* it was startling. The show was *Voyagers!*, starring Meeno Peeluce and Jon-Erik Hexum. Like the doctor, the two central time travelers of *Voyagers!* (Jeffrey Jones and Phineas Bogg) went to ancient Rome in "Created Equal," to the American Civil War in "The Day the Rebs Took Lincoln," and to China and the adventures of Marco Polo in "The Travels of Marco ... and Friends." More interesting than these voyages to the same time periods as *Doctor Who* was the central format of *Voyagers!*. The show was concerned with a race of beings (not Time Lords, but Voyagers) who could control time. Furthermore, the central time traveler (not the Doctor but Phineas Bogg) could not control his machine (not the TARDIS but the OMNI). Additionally, Bogg always traveled with a companion (shades of the Doctor). The time travel effect on *Voyagers!,* which showed Bogg and Jones flying through a kind of brown vortex, also recalled the spinning electronic patterns first broadcast on "An Unearthly Child" in 1963. (Still, *Voyagers!* never added aliens to its formula.) The series was cancelled after only one season. It is interesting to note, however, that *Voyagers!* did beat *Doctor Who* to one intriguing story. In 1983's "The Trial of Phineas Bogg," the central time traveler of *Voyagers!* was put on trial by his own people, just as the Doctor would be similarly tried in the Season 24 epic "The Trial of the Time Lord."

Other time travel series such as *Quantum Leap* (1989–93) and *Time Trax* also owe a debt, though perhaps a smaller one, to *Doctor Who.* In *Quantum Leap*, Sam Beckett, like characters in *Doctor Who*, *The Time Tunnel* and *Voyagers!,* traveled haphazardly or randomly through time (seemingly a requirement for all television time trippers), and in later seasons he opposed an evil Time Lady not unlike the Rani, a character seen in the *Doctor Who* episodes "The Mark of the Rani" (1984) and "Time and the Rani" (1987).

In 1993, Harve Bennett's *Time Trax* introduced the world to Darien Lambert (actor Dale Midkiff), a time traveler from the twenty-first century who traveled to the 1990s not only with extensive knowledge of the future, but also with physical and mental abilities greater than the average humans of the time period ... just like our old friend, the Doctor.

Outside the realm of time travel, *Doctor Who* has spawned many imitators in the arena where it is perhaps most the innovative sci-fi television series in history: the creation of alien villains. The Daleks were introduced in 1963 as mutants encased in armor suits. They screamed "exterminate," and were committed to wiping out the peaceful, humanoid Thals. In "The Daleks," the Daleks lured the Thals into their city with the promise of food and a peace treaty. In fact, the feast was a ruse and the Daleks planned to kill the Thals. In essence, this entire Dalek dynamic was repeated in *Battlestar Galactica* in 1978. The robotic Cylons of Glen Larson's series were defined first as reptile creatures living inside robotic suits (akin to the Daleks), but the concept mysteriously changed and the Cylons become robots in the service of one lizard creature (the Imperious Leader).

The Cylons in "Saga of a Star World," the first episode of *Battlestar Galactica*, also had a word for their goal ... a word that they frequently repeated in electronically enhanced voices: "extermination!" Sound familiar? The Cylons also destroyed the Colonial Fleet by luring them away from their home worlds with a promise of a peace treaty, similar to the Dalek bluff in *Doctor Who*.

Incidentally, *Battlestar Galactica* also featured a robot dog called "Muffit" in 1978, a year after *Doctor Who* introduced its own cybernetic pup, K-9.

It was not *Battlestar Galactica*, however, which succeeded the most by building on concepts first shown on *Doctor Who*. It was *Star Trek: The Next Generation*! The sequel to the original *Star Trek* series really came into its own when it developed a race of cybernetic villains in its second season story "Q-Who." The villains in question, of course, are the Borg! The Borg are enhanced humanoids who have had mechanical limbs and organs built for themselves. The main purpose of the Borg is to assimilate humanoid cultures and use them as the "raw materials" to build more Borg. The notion of mechanically enhanced men had been introduced previously in *Doctor Who* in 1966. The Cybermen, as they were called, had also replaced body parts with mechanical limbs, and they also sought to procure more bodies so they could continue to build more Cybermen. The idea is identical.

The similarities between the Borg and the Cybermen do not stop with superficial race resemblances. In "The Best of Both Worlds," the Borg assimilate the bald Capt. Picard to speak for their race and facilitate the introduction of the Borg into human society. In the Season 6 *Doctor Who* serial "The Tomb of the Cybermen," the Cybermen abduct the bald logician Klieg and prepare to turn him into a Cyberman so he can lead the new Cyberpeople of Earth. In addition, the Borg in *Star Trek: The Next Generation* are seen to hibernate, immobile, in individual sections of their ship. Fear and tension is generated by the fact that these Borg can "come alive" and stagger out of their cubicles at any time. This idea too had seen its foundation in "Tomb of the Cybermen." In that story, humans found the hibernation cubicles of the Cybermen and proceeded to unfreeze the evil warriors. Like the Borg 20 years later, the Cybermen shambled out of their hibernation canisters and began attacking the enemy. Other similarities include the fact that both races can survive in the vacuum of space (as proven in *Star Trek: First Contact* and in "The Moonbase" and "The Wheel in Space" on *Doctor Who*), and that both races have eliminated emotion and individuality to the point where it is considered "irrelevant."

In late 1987, *Star Trek: The Next Generation* also introduced a race of greedy, capitalistic aliens called Ferengi. *Doctor Who* had already dramatized this idea in the 1984 and 1986 stories "Vengeance on Varos" and "Mindwarp." In "Vengeance on Varos," viewers were introduced to Sil, a being of a race called the Mentors. He was a short, physically repulsive creature who seemed like an evolved fish or sea serpent. More interesting than his appearance, however, were his concerns. Sil visited the planet Varos to negotiate a mining contract. He also expressed interest in paying less than a fair price for Zytton ore so he would be assured a "profit." As anyone who has seen the Ferengi on *Star Trek: The Next Generation* can attest, this description is remarkably similar to that alien race. Like Sil, the Ferengi on *Star Trek: The Next Generation* also gesticulate wildly, at least in early episodes such as "The Last Outpost" and "The Battle." The Mentors and the Ferengi also share disgusting eating habits: the Mentors eat a sickly green marshmallow substance and the Ferengi eat grub worms. The characteristics of the race (physical repulsiveness, cutthroat capitalist tendencies and obsession with profit) are also the same. For the record, the Ferengi did not appear on *Star Trek: The Next Generation* until three years after Sil's first appearance on *Doctor Who.*

Doctor Who's children are many. R2-D2 in *Star Wars* (1977) resembles a Dalek in design with his domed head and barrel-shaped mechanical body. *Total Recall* (1990) revisited the notion of alien pyramids on Mars, a subject explored rather fully in the 1976 Tom Baker serial "The Pyramids of Mars." *Independence Day*

(1996) with its penchants for blowing up landmarks such as the White House and the Empire State Building, recalls the "The Dalek Invasion of Earth" with its action on the Thames, its chase through the streets of London, and its reference to Big Ben. Luc Besson's *The Fifth Element* (1997) has much action taking place on a beautiful cruise ship of the future, the same setting as *Doctor Who*'s "Nightmare of Eden" and "Terror of the Vervoids." The *Alien* series with its insect-like drone aliens which communicate with one another and attack humans in hypersleep recalls the similar *Doctor Who* story "The Ark in Space." *Star Trek: Voyager* repeated *Doctor Who*'s notion of intelligent dinosaurs (seen in "Doctor Who and the Silurians") in an episode called "Distant Origins." And *Voyager* also introduced an alien race interested in repeating famous historical battles in "The Killing Ground," a play-by-play repeat of the ten-part *Who* saga "The War Games."

Finally, many episodes of *Star Trek: The Next Generation*, *Deep Space Nine* and *Voyager*, including "Cause and Effect," "All Good Things," "Visionary" and "Coda" have revisited the time loops and paradoxes that have been the mainstay of *Doctor Who* serials, including "The Space Museum," "Image of the Fendahl," "The Claws of Axos," "City of Death" and "Meglos." Though *Doctor Who* may not have specifically been on the minds of anyone involved with these films or television shows, it is still significant that *Doctor Who* dramatized similar if not identical concepts long before these newer productions existed.

Perhaps the silliest and most offbeat reference to *Doctor Who* came in 1988. Excellent surfer dudes Bill and Ted traveled through the corridors of time in an American telephone booth in *Bill & Ted's Excellent Adventure* (1989). Like *Doctor Who*, they also crossed paths with Napoleon ("The Reign of Terror") and Abraham Lincoln ("The Chase").

Doctor Who has also borne some "legitimate" children, not just offshoots which illicitly recycled concepts. In 1965 and 1966 there were two *Doctor Who* feature films produced by AARU. In 1978, Dalek creator Terry Nation left the Whoniverse and created his own science fiction series, *Blake's 7*. Though taking place in a different reality than *Doctor Who*'s, the series nonetheless used some of the same props, covered some of the same ground and offered generous helpings of Nation philosophy, an element clear in serials such as "Destiny of the Daleks," "Genesis of the Daleks" and "The Dalek Invasion of Earth."

In 1981, *Doctor Who* beget its own spin off, the pilot *K-9 and Company* starring John Leeson and Elisabeth Sladen. Then, when *Doctor Who* was cancelled, fan Bill Baggs took it upon himself to create an unofficial *Doctor Who* product starring Colin Baker called *The Stranger*. All of these efforts might genuinely be coined children of *Doctor Who*.

The Elastic Format

How does a television series stay on the air for more than 20 years? More to the point, how does a *sci-fi* television program manage such an impressive feat? In

America, even the very best of sci-fi programming is exceedingly hard to sell to audiences because the genre has never been considered "mainstream." *Star Trek*, perhaps the most popular American genre series ever, stayed on the air for only three years. *The Outer Limits*, an acknowledged classic, survived for two seasons. *Battlestar Galactica*, the highest rated American sci-fi program of the past three decades (before *The X-Files*), died after one season! Even the many series based on hit movies or mini-series, such as *Planet of the Apes*, *Logan's Run* and *V*, have failed after less than a full season on the air.

In Great Britain, the history is similar. *Thunderbirds* (1965–66) and *Space: 1999*, arguably Gerry and Sylvia Anderson's most popular series, flew for just two years. Though *Blake's 7* lasted four years, only 52 episodes were produced in that time, 20 episodes shy of *Star Trek*'s three-year, 79-episode run.

In this light, *Doctor Who*'s extended stint on television is surely nothing short of miraculous. However, there are some very basic, empirical reasons for its longevity. Foremost among these is the elastic format which has served *Doctor Who* so well since 1963. Although many programs feature a format which can encompass many different story styles, none are as elastic as *Doctor Who*'s. It is one-part outer space drama; the writers have sent the Doctor to hundreds of different worlds, from the surreal Vortis in "The Web Planet" to the jungle of Spiridon in "Planet of the Daleks."

Doctor Who is also one part-time travel epic. The renegade Time Lord has traveled everywhere in time, from the Big Bang ("Castrovalva" and "The Edge of Destruction") to the extinction of the dinosaurs ("Earthshock"). He has witnessed many landmark historical events such as the French Revolution ("Reign of Terror"), the Trojan War ("The Myth Makers") and the struggle between the Protestants and Catholics in 1572 France ("The Massacre"). He has also interacted in the Aztec culture of 1490 ("The Aztecs") and seventeenth century Scotland ("The Highlanders").

There is yet another setting frequently utilized in *Doctor Who*, one beyond the "conventional" confines of time and space. Adventures have taken place in locales that can only be described as alternate realities or dimensions. "Inferno" features an alternate Earth replete with an evil version of the Doctor's friend, the Brigadier. Other stories occur in realms such as "E-Space" ("Full Circle," "State of Decay," "Warrior's Gate"), the surreal domain of the evil "Toymaker" ("The Celestial Toymaker") and the remarkable Land of Fiction ("The Mind Robber"). Thus the setting and playground of *Doctor Who* is all of existence itself.

Where *Star Trek* is for the most part confined to 11 percent of the Milky Way galaxy in the twenty-third and twenty-fourth centuries, and *The X Files* is limited to 1990s Earth, *Doctor Who* is a series that can voyage to any place and to any time. No story at all is beyond its purview. Even the interior of the Doctor's unusual Time Lord body has been navigated in detail ("The Invisible Enemy")!

Doctor Who stories incorporate a wide variety of genres within the general sci-fi setting of "any place, any time." "Terror of the Vervoids" is an adventure that unfolds in deep space on an isolated spaceship, the *Hyperion III*. Passengers harbor secret identities and are dying with regularity. Although the denouement involves carnivorous plant monsters not terrestrial murders, its spiritual ancestor is surely the Agatha Christie mystery novel *Murder on the Orient Express.* This source is referenced in the episode itself when the very book shows up in the hands of guest star Honor Blackman!

Other stories are also unique and unpredictable. "The Stones of Blood" begins as an earthbound mystery dealing with Druid cults and silicon life forms who devour human blood. It ends unconventionally with a satirical courtroom "trial" aboard a spaceship with two officious justice machines presiding over the proceedings. Likewise, "City of Death" opens with an art heist and ends not with the capture of the criminals, but at the very point of human creation in prehistory! In *Doctor Who*, multiple genres and story ingredients are thus combined, distorted and lovingly re-invented to produce brilliant, offbeat adventures.

Doctor Who also captures viewers by combining filmic and literary stories in futuristic (or alien) settings. As already noted, Terry Nation's "The Daleks" is a reworking of *The Time Machine.* "The Tomb of the Cybermen" is a "mummy" movie transplanted to an alien world, complete with underground tombs, booby traps and monsters awakening from a long slumber. "The Brain of Morbius" is a rewrite of the *Frankenstein* saga with alien sisterhoods, a grotesque mutant monster and an insane scientist called Solon. "The Time Warrior" is an ingenious reworking of Mark Twain's *A Connecticut Yankee in King Arthur's Court.* And so it goes. No movie, no matter how seemingly unrelated to *Doctor Who*, time travel or outer space, is outside the boundaries of the elastic format. The setting of the series is so wide that it can accommodate scenarios and plots as different from one another as are *Aliens* and *Jane Eyre.*

Popular films and literature aren't just rehashed in *Doctor Who*, they are turned on their heads and dramatized in innovative fashion. "The Invisible Enemy" starts as a retread of the film *Fantastic Voyage* with a miniaturized clone of the Doctor traveling through the Time Lord's own body to eradicate a deadly infection. The story really becomes inventive when the clone Doctor fails his mission and dies. The virus infection, a nasty living creature with crab-like pincers, utilizes the clone's escape route through the tear duct! Hence it is the infection, not the heroic clone, who is finally grown to "human size" after the adventure inside the body! The *Fantastic Voyage* scenario is merely a building block on which to heap new imaginings. Similarly, the early tale "Planet of Giants" would at first blush appear to be a ripoff of the film *The Incredible Shrinking Man* (1957). Instead of focusing on the psychological effects of miniaturization, however, the story concerns how the shrunken Doctor and his companions overcome their handicap not only to save Barbara, but to defeat a madman attempting to poison the world. This same conceit, that "miniature" people can effectively complete a mission, was also utilized on the television spy series *World of Giants* (1958), Irwin Allen's *Land of the Giants* (1968–70) and the Gerry Anderson NBC pilot *The Investigators* (1973).

In addition to these interesting attempts at modifying existing science fiction film and literary themes, the many producers and writers on *Doctor Who* have continually altered the already elastic format to make it even more dynamic. From the beginning of the Jon Pertwee era in 1970, the Doctor is exiled by his people to Earth for a period of time and unable to use his beloved TARDIS. For Seasons 7 and 8, the "advanced" Doctor had to deal with different sorts of scenarios. Frustrated by his entrapment on a primitive, war-like planet, he constantly sought to outsmart his captors and escape by re-learning TARDIS functions. He also developed a love of antique automobiles and served as scientific advisor to UNIT (United Nations Intelligence Task Force). This position, the only pro-establishment position the Doctor ever held in the series, exposed him to a whole universe of new adventures dealing specifically with Earth interests and intrigues. The *Quatermass* series became the overriding template for the series, replacing *The Time Machine* scenario which had served the series since Christmas 1963.

In Season 16, the wily producers decided it was again time for another change. The Doctor was dispatched by a higher life form called "The White Guardian" on a quest for the six segments of the all-important Key to Time. Each of the six adventures featured in that memorable season found the Doctor carrying out this incredible search. After many years of endless and somewhat random wandering in space and time, this new mission brought both a renewed sense of purpose and a heightened sense of tension to the aging series.

Season 23 also reinvigorated the series formula. All four serials produced that year were part of an ongoing saga called "The Trial of the Time Lord." Four different adventures to various worlds and time periods were broadcast as "evidence" in the Doctor's trial. This format adjustment, like the Key to Time saga, brought a new perspective to the middle-aged series and provided it an admirable "umbrella of unity." All three of these format variations occur at approximately seven to eight year intervals, never giving the faithful audience time to tire of the "same old thing," a dilemma that faces other aging shows.

Doctor Who's elastic format has allowed tonal change as well. The most conspicuous change occurred in Tom Baker's era. His span began with some of the best "serious" sci-fi stories ever showcased on *Doctor Who*, including "The Seeds of Doom," "The Hand of Fear," "The Robots of Death" and "Pyramids of Mars." But following the departure of Leela and the first model of K-9 in "The Invasion of Time" and the beginning of Season 16 and the Key to Time saga, the tenor of the program changed dramatically to one of satire and comedy. With Douglas Adams, author of *Hitchhiker's Guide to the Galaxy* in command as story editor and serving as a plot contributor, Baker's penchant for out-and-out comedy came to the forefront. The very nature of the universe itself seemed to change. No longer was the Doctor in constant danger from evil empires and dangerous beings. Instead, he was enmeshed in funny, strange squabbles with comical third-world planets that poked fun at English legal systems, taxation policies and red-tape ridden bureaucracies. "The Pirate Planet," and "The Ribos Operation" are two stories from this era in which alien cultures were treated as objects of the Doctor's derision. This was a massive dislocation from the galactic, important stories of fallen empires, alien resurrections and interstellar warfare that had epitomized the Doctor's world previously. It may not have fit with *Who* tradition, but it was nonetheless a tonal adjustment that injected new elements into the aging series.

The tilt towards the absurd and parody came to an abrupt end when Peter Davison assumed the role of the Doctor after Baker's departure. In fact, so serious was the attempt to take *Doctor Who* back to its dramatic roots that a memorandum was dispatched to writers instructing them to remove all jokes from new stories.[1] This directive explains to some extent why Davison serials seem restrained and lifeless compared to those of other eras.

Later, in the mid–1980s, the tone of the series was modulated again, this time to a deadly, nihilistic one. Colin Baker's era saw the advent of frightening, almost oppressive tales rife with horror and death. This hard-edged version of *Doctor Who* represented a complete departure from the two-decade-old family atmosphere of the show. In fact, the very first episode of Baker's tenure featured a deranged Doctor suffering terribly from the effects of his unplanned regeneration. In "The Twin Dilemma," he tried to strangle his companion Peri after accusing her of sabotage. The planets he visited and the creatures he encountered were also more frightening. In "Vengeance of Varos," the Doctor found a grim world where imagination and independent thought had been replaced by government-sponsored television, where people flocked to violent "snuff" television that featured torture and public executions, and where the corrupt government ruthlessly exploited the people's ignorance and lack of education. During this time, the Doctor also saw Peri possessed by a repulsive alien life form from Thoros-Beta and then ostensibly killed in a brutal massacre in "Mindwarp." Even more distressing, the Doctor himself may have been responsible for genocide in "Terror of the Vervoids." He also faced his future self, a character of pure evil, in "The Ultimate Foe." The program no longer had the "fun" atmosphere of the Tom Baker–era stories, but it was riveting television nonetheless, and an interesting experiment for a 20-year-old series. Many fans despise Colin Baker's era because of this shift to a fatalistic tone, but it was just one more format modification in a long line of similarly bold moves.

Of course, there is one other obvious reasons why the show has stayed fresh: "regeneration." The lead actor of the series has changed no less than eight times. Each actor has brought a new flavor, a new twist to the *Doctor Who* mythos while nonetheless remaining true to the character of the noble Time Lord. If variety is indeed the spice of life, then the shifting lead performers of *Doctor Who* have truly peppered the series with tremendous new energy at regular intervals. The first Doctor, William Hartnell, was a lovable grandfather taken to moments of pure crankiness ("An Unearthly Child") but with heartbreaking moments of tenderness ("The Rescue," "The Chase"). The second Doctor, Patrick Troughton, was much more physical in his affection for his friends, frequently hugging his companions after dangerous situations ("The Mind Robber," The War Games"). He was more childlike than his predecessor, and arguably sweeter as well. The third Doctor, Jon Pertwee, showed considerably less humor and affection than Troughton did but took delight in the action elements of the series ("Planet of Spiders"). The next Doctor, Tom Baker, was a charismatic comedian who could successfully carry weak stories purely by his dynamic screen presence. The fifth Doctor, Peter Davison, was a much younger man who showed some of the old William Hartnell crankiness. Overall, he was much less eccentric than his immediate predecessor. Colin Baker, the most underrated and underappreciated Doctor of all, was another shift. He was pompous, arrogant, mischievous — and a fiendishly bad punster. Successor Sylvester McCoy was a mysterious character whose overt physical humor masked a grave, calculating side. Each one of these interpretations re-invigorated the spirit of the series, much as each new actor playing Shakespeare's *Hamlet* reinterprets that dramatic role.

Of course, the Doctor's companions changed constantly too, and this change also kept the series from stagnating. At first, the original companions Susan, Barbara and Ian were replaced with rather pale imitations (Steven, Vicki, Dodo, Ben and Polly), but then things really got interesting. Teenagers Jamie and Zoe were two of the best companions ever, representing the yin and yang of action and intellect. Their memorable presence skewed the series to a hipper, teenage crowd. Then there was the wonderful Sarah Jane Smith (played by Elizabeth Sladen), a very headstrong female. Leela, a savage warrior who was even more liberated, followed. Romana, a Time Lord companion who was more than a match for the Doctor in intellect, was an even stronger companion, at least in her first incarnation. There have been other notable companions including the robot dog K-9, the shapeshifting robot Kamelion, the turncoat Turlough, the cranky Brigadier and the rough-and-tumble Ace. Each one of these characters added spice to the series.

Doctor Who remained fresh all the way through its run for other reasons as well, because of circumstances that were perhaps more accidental than intentional, but nonetheless insured that the show would survive for many generations. The show began with no back story whatsoever. In "An Unearthly Child," Episode 1, the Doctor states that he and Susan are exiles from another civilization. Few details are given about this civilization, or even about the TARDIS. Thus, the mystery of the series' main character kept viewers watching in weeks to come. Who was this traveler through time and space? Why did he travel? Where had he escaped from? Answers came only after many years, and one suspects they were invented on the way rather than known all along. The Doctor's heritage as a Time Lord was not revealed until after six years, in the climactic episode of the Troughton–era serial "The War Games." Other Time Lord secrets were not revealed for many years after that. The story of Omega, the Time Lord engineer who captured a black hole for the Time Lords, was not revealed until the Pertwee age ("The Three Doctors"). The myth of Rassilon, another Time Lord architect, was not fully expounded upon until the Tom Baker and Davison years.

With all of eternity as a backdrop, the universe of literature and film to draw upon, an ever-changing central face and mutating overall tone, new companions and a healthy dose of mystery, *Doctor Who* is the most versatile sci-fi series in history. If one were to mix the basic ingredients of *Star Trek*, *The X Files*, *Lost in Space*, *Quantum Leap*, *The Time Tunnel*, *Quark* and *The Prisoner*, *Doctor Who* might very well be the result. Amazingly, *Doctor Who* successfully merged all of these divergent elements before any of the aforementioned programs even existed. This makes its unprecedented long run all the more impressive. *Doctor Who* is the epitome of invention and versatility in science fiction television.

Morality and Meaning in the *Doctor Who* Universe

Most modern genre television programs are heavily didactic in nature. They are designed not only to entertain the masses but likewise to impart ethical lessons to audiences looking for a moral compass. The immortal *Star Trek* taught people that there is strength in racial diversity and that man is an evolved, growing creature capable of great good if only he does not succumb to his baser instincts. Accordingly, various stories in *Star Trek* pertained to the evils of racial prejudice ("Let That Be Your Last Battlefield") and the uselessness of war ("A Taste of Armageddon," "Errand of Mercy"). Patrick McGoohan's *The Prisoner* single-mindedly avowed that all people in any modern society are prisoners so long as they tolerate a bureaucracy which files, numbers and catalogues them. The American anthology *The Outer Limits* (1963–65) reminded onlookers that there are times when man reaches too far too fast. "The Bellero Shield" and "The Sixth Finger" were just two episodes in which man tried to gain access to knowledge he was not yet wise enough to possess.

What then is *Doctor Who*'s message? What is its stance on morality? Unfortunately, it is more difficult to find an easy or pat answer to that question because *Doctor Who* has endured so long and transmuted so drastically from the early 1960s to the mid-1990s. *The Prisoner* lasted only 17 episodes and was an exploration of late '60s conundrums and fears. *The Outer Limits* and *Star Trek* both lasted two or three years but they too were products of one era's speculation, the early and late '60s respectively. *Doctor Who* has lasted a weighty two dozen years and has overseen tidal-wave shifts in audience perspectives on morality and virtue. It adjusted its stance on morality in each era that it contended with and perservered throughout.

When *Doctor Who* began in November 1963, its ethical perspective was traditionally didactic. The lessons it taught were firmly aligned with the dogma of Christianity and Western philosophies. The initial episodes of the series could be interpreted as sermons reaffirming these stock beliefs. Such sermons frequently took the form of "life lessons" learned by the series' main characters. Terry Nation's "The Daleks" stated boldly that there are some things in the universe worth fighting for. All of life is a struggle, it said, so why not struggle to survive and fight evil? Why not fight for liberty? "The Keys of Marinus" espoused the tenet that justice resides not in technology, but in a man's heart. Computers like the Conscience Machine on Marinus cannot determine morality or dictate justice for him. "The Aztecs" by John Lucarotti affirmed that a person cannot force change on people who are happy the way they are, even if a person thinks he/she knows better because he/she is more "enlightened." In "The Sensorites" and "Galaxy Four" it was established that looks do not necessarily make the man. Aliens need not be evil just because they look different than humans. In "The Rescue," the Doctor suggests to Vicki that she should not judge Barbara on her actions (killing Vicki's pet) but on her intentions (to save Vicki from a strange beast). This is how it went through the Hartnell and Troughton years of *Doctor Who*. Every episode was characterized by a strong basis in traditional values. Parents could entrust their children to *Doctor Who*, comfortable in the knowledge that it would shape them into decent, moral, upstanding members of Western society.

Surprisingly prominent in the introductory days of *Doctor Who* was the typically American belief that liberty is earned through blood, sweat and tears, not bestowed by others. Of course, Americans had once learned a similar lesson in the Revolutionary War against a repressive, overtaxing British Empire. Yet revolutions of that very class are undeniably the terra firma of the *Doctor Who* series. The quest for liberty and individual freedom sparked adventures in "The Web Planet," "The Dalek Invasion of Earth," "The Space Museum," "The Ark," "The Savages," "Timelash," "Attack of the Cybermen," "The Twin Dilemma" and many others. In this regard, *Doctor Who* was notably anti–Empire and pro-democracy in its approach. As a continuing program it articulated the terrors of oppression, exploitation and even taxation ("The Sunmakers"). It is fair to state that *Doctor Who* revisited the very dynamics that had given rise to the American Revolutionary War. In *Doctor Who*'s vision of the conflict, the Brits were recast as the exploiters, an Empire trying unfairly to hold onto a territory or people that no longer desired their protection or governmental infrastructure. In essence then, the British were the flabby, complacent Morokons facing the end of their galactic superiority in "The Space Museum," or even the power-hungry, conquering Daleks!

Important too in the early days of *Doctor Who* was the stock sci-fi belief that history cannot be changed. The Doctor constantly needled Barbara and Ian about the fact; in "The Aztecs," Barbara asked what the fun of time travel was if people could not change things. The Doctor's insistence that the current of time must remain unchanged was a reiteration of a motif oft-voiced in science fiction films of the 1950s: "Do not tamper in God's domain." The underlying philosophy behind the treatise was that time had an order, a flow and a purpose. Any attempt by an individual (like Barbara in "The Aztecs") or power (like the Cybermen in "Attack of the Cybermen" or the Androgums in "The Two Doctors") to alter that purpose was a doomed, immoral attempt to contravene destiny and God's cosmic plan. Surprisingly, however, the series was not long-sighted enough to keep this dictate in mind during the "futuristic" stories. The Doctor interfered in future societies with considerable verve. The writers of the series neglected to realize that our future (post-twentieth century) is somebody else's past...

In the Troughton epoch, *Doctor Who* continued to be a strong proponent of traditional or Christian moral values. In every serial there was a clear dramatization of right and wrong. The Doctor had to choose which side to champion, even though he could leave via the TARDIS or choose not to become involved in the affairs of others. The choice to help those in need was what really mattered, however. That was the critical piece of *Doctor Who*'s stance on morality as a series. The choice, *a person's willingness to fight for right*, was valued above all else. The prominence of "the choice" and its ramifications never really changed, even when *Doctor Who* changed in the '70s and '80s. During the Troughton era, "the choice" was made easy because the people and races encountered by the Doctor were frequently perceived in absolutes. The Daleks, the Cybermen, the Krotons, the Dominators, the Ice Warriors and the Macra were judged to be "evil" and were destroyed. Their underlying motivations or needs as species were not explored or even acknowledged. As non-human representations of absolute evil, they had to be eliminated before they could annihilate humanity.

Perhaps *Doctor Who*'s ultimate statement on morality came in Patrick Troughton's final serial, "The War Games." The Doctor was put on trial by his own people for interfering in other cultures. Acting as a surrogate voice for the writers and producers of the show, the Doctor declared that it is better to harbor a conviction and help someone than to sit back and watch callously while the weak die. Troughton's Doctor essentially argued that the Time Lords should be the policemen of the galaxy, defending those who could not defend themselves. This too was a surprisingly American stance when one considers American involvement in Vietnam, Kuwait, Haiti, Bosnia and Kosovo.

The 1970s arrived after sweeping societal changes in ideals and morals in the late 1960s. Appropriately, shades of gray were introduced into the *Doctor Who* format along with color film and the third incarnation of the Doctor. In the Jon Pertwee era there were still absolutes, but they were absolutes of a new generation — the hippie generation. The new primary lesson of *Doctor Who* was that Mother Earth had to be saved from environmental rapists and warmongers at all costs, lest the planet have final revenge on mankind. This lesson was the playing field of "The Green Death" and "Inferno." Environmental issues were also at the heart of dramas such as "Colony in Space" and "The Mutants," which depicted imperialistic empires plundering other planets for their valuable natural resources. During this span, the Doctor had been exiled by the Time Lords and seen his existence limited to one planet and one time period. Importantly, he fully understood the importance of preserving the stability of a planet's biosphere. Without his TARDIS, he had no place he could escape to. Just like his television audience, he had a vested interest in preserving the Earth. This realization brought home to millions of viewers the importance of environmental issues.

The shading of moral issues occurred in many *Doctor Who* stories of the time, particularly in "Doctor Who and the Silurians" and "The Sea Devils." In both serials, the Doctor was confronted with the same ethical dilemma. Two races (human and lizard) had an equal claim to the planet Earth and were poised to fight over it. The Doctor, speaking for all those youths around the world who wanted the end of the Vietnam war, espoused peace, cooperation and compromise rather than a war to determine superiority. In the end, he was not able to end the encounters peaceably, yet it was significant that he tried at all. As an outsider, he was able to say to children, "It is better to talk than to fight." Pertwee's Doctor also preached peace while the warmongers in fictional British government officials preached war and hatred in stories such as "The Claws of Axos."

Pertwee's enlightened Doctor even confronted his own racism in "The Curse of Peladon." In that adventure he encountered the Martian Ice Warriors, an old nemesis. He told Jo that he did not trust them based on past personal experience. Well, the Ice Warriors turned out to be trustworthy after all, and the Doctor learned a valuable lesson about himself and his shortcomings, specifically that stereotyping the behavior of a whole race based on the behavior of a few individuals was not fair. Again, he was a role model for the children of England. *Doctor Who* of the early '70s declared that only by challenging one's own perceptions and biases can peace and true understanding be reached. It was a potent message and a sign of the free-thinking '70s.

Despite these forays into liberal thinking, *Doctor Who* did veer back to conservative philosophy occasionally. "Invasion of the Dinosaurs" preached that even the best of instincts (read: liberal instincts) were valueless if they were not instigated in a humanistic, thoughtful fashion. For the most part, however, the *Doctor Who* of the '70s was pro-environment, pro-peace, pro-cooperation and pro-youth. This was also seen in the consistent ribbing of the Brigadier character during this span. Of course, Lethbridge-Stewart was an over-30, rigid military officer, part of the hypocrisy-ridden establishment. *Doctor Who* serials frequently found Lethbridge-Stewart and the Doctor in serious disagreement about how to proceed in morally ambiguous situations, with the Doctor besting the Brigadier in verbal repartee every time.

By the beginning of the Tom Baker era, moral ambiguity was firmly entrenched in *Doctor Who*. The Terrance Dicks teleplay "Robot" treated its title character with surprising sympathy, yet the Doctor destroyed it at the end of the serial with little remorse. Was this right? Was the robot more than a villain? Was he sentient? These questions were raised in the story, but then ignored in an action finale. More thought-provoking was Terry Nation's "Genesis of the Daleks." The teleplay questioned whether it was right for the Doctor to destroy an evil race, the Daleks, in order to save a universe. It wondered what such a decision would make of the Doctor. Would he be a murderer? A mass murderer? Worse? Or, conversely, would he be a hero for interfering in destiny and preserving the weak? "Genesis of the Daleks" represented *Doctor Who* at its most morally complex. The Doctor finally decided that great good could come from great evil. Therefore, he did not destroy his long-time enemies.

Following the early Tom Baker seasons, *Doctor Who* saw a return to black-and-white didacticism, although it still preached liberal social values. "The Power of Kroll" suggested that others should not be treated differently because of differences in skin color or culture. Self-sacrifice was considered a noble act when it was performed to save the lives of friends in "Mawdryn Undead"; "Terminus" preached that the sick should be cared for compassionately, not treated as lepers. Universal decency and tolerance were the order of the day.

Colin Baker's reign as Doctor saw perhaps the grimmest age in *Doctor Who* history, but the dictates of Western values nonetheless prevailed. In "Vengeance of Varos," a world enmeshed in moral quandaries was visited. People were hurting, torturing and executing one another with a gleeful bloodlust. Entertainment was violence-ridden, like *The Jerry Springer Show*, and it took the arrival of the Doctor and Peri to say that this is not the way people should live.

"The Trial of the Time Lord" revealed that the non-interference policy of the Time Lords was a fraud. The Gallifreyans were exposed as hypocrites. The Doctor, the selfsame Time Lord who had so frequently become involved in the affairs of others and revelled in it, saved them. Surprisingly, the Doctor did not win a complete moral victory. The Valeyard, the Doctor's evil final regeneration, reappeared in the courtroom as the Keeper of the Matrix after the Doctor saved the day and departed from the Time Lord space station. The suggestion was that good would not always triumph over evil. That is a standpoint which early *Doctor Who* would never have adopted.

Sylvester McCoy's era as the seventh Doctor is perhaps the hardest to categorize in terms of moral stance. As always, the Doctor was presented as the hero of the series, but he suddenly and frequently committed egregious acts of violence with little hesitation. In "Remembrance of the Daleks," he obliterated Skaro in 1963 with the Hand of Omega. By doing so, he killed millions of people (Daleks and Thals) and wiped out an entire timeline. In "Silver Nemesis," he destroyed 1,000 Cybermen ships without batting an eye. In serials such as "The Greatest Show in the Galaxy" and "The Curse of Fenric," the Doctor kept secrets from friends, hid the truth of his history, and played a chess game to determine the future of mankind. He risked everything on the assumption not only that he could win the game, but that he had the right to interfere in the course of destiny in the first place. The Doctor had come to represent something quite different than a guarantor of liberty. In the McCoy era he intervened *even* when he was not asked to, even when his presence was not requested. The Doctor had finally become every bit as much a meddler as the Master or the Meddling Monk. His intentions were noble, but they were still *his* intentions alone that dictated the interference. Do the races of the universe not have the right to decide for themselves how to proceed? By choosing to intervene in such grand, galactic ways, the Doctor took that essential element of free choice from the citizens of innumerable cultures. He had become the tyrant of time, the controller of destinies, the master manipulator.

All of these acts of destruction were depicted in a matter-of-fact fashion in late-'80s *Doctor Who*. It was perhaps a more realistic, less formalistic approach to morality. Only Ace, a lowly human being, challenged the Doctor's right to act in this cavalier manner. Do the ends justify the means, she asked? Is life and death just a game? These were the questions raised in the final years of the BBC's *Doctor Who*, and they shifted the series into some uncomfortable, ambiguous terrain.

All *Doctor Who* fans know that the Doctor is dedicated to truth, honor, and the defense of the weak, but they do not know why. Is he a hero or a dangerous criminal? Is he a renegade from a society he has denounced or a dangerous exile from a society that would not tolerate him and his meddling? Is he different at all from the Master, or is he the flip side of the same coin? In over 26 years of stories,

Doctor Who intimated all of these fascinating possibilities. After two dozen years on the air, the main question the series still generates in terms of morality is this: *Doctor Who*? Is the Doctor that being who teaches others to fight for their freedom, or is he the one who destroys planets and vanquishes whole races based on his own personal moral compass? *Doctor Who* indeed!

Playing Doctor: Strictly Forbidden!

Despite all the talk about *Doctor Who*'s elastic format, there is one essential element of human behavior that is never discussed or examined openly during the British television series: sex. Sex has always been a taboo subject for *Doctor Who* because the series aired for 18 years on Saturday afternoons and was therefore geared towards children. However, many American sci-fi television series have assured their immortality by examining provocative sexual issues. Indeed, the sexual side of man has been a critical part of literature as far back as classic Greek drama like *Lysistrata* and Homer's *The Odyssey*. Therefore this discussion is by no means a lascivious one, nor a sign of vulgar twentieth century times. Many of the greatest stories throughout mankind's long "entertainment" history, including *Othello*, *Romeo and Juliet*, *Tartuffe*, *Gone With the Wind*, *Taxi Driver*, *Annie Hall* and *Cool Hand Luke*, have been made doubly memorable because of their insights into human sexuality.

Within genre television, the original *Star Trek* was profoundly conscious of and curious about sexuality and romance. Mr. Spock was compelled to return home to Vulcan to mate in "Amok Time," Capt. Kirk exchanged bodies with a woman in "Turnabout Intruder," and he made love to the alien Queen of Scalos for purposes of breeding in "Wink of an Eye."

Star Trek: The Next Generation was even more provocative. Lt. Yar bedded the fully functional Lt. Commander Data in "The Naked Now," Riker made love to aliens in "Angel One," "First Contact," "Up the Long Ladder," "The Game" and "The Outcast." He even had sex with Dr. Crusher in "The Host"! Clearly, *Star Trek*s of all generations have never been afraid to confront sexual issues or present sexually skewed stories. Pure sex appeal may even help to explain *Star Trek*'s ongoing popularity to some degree — just look at Seven of Nine.

Even at a basic, cheesy level, protean sci-fi films in the '50s such as *Abbott and Costello Go to Mars* (1953) and *Queen of Outer Space* (1958) supported adolescent male fantasies with their clichéd stories about planets populated solely by scantily clad females. There is thus a tradition of sexuality and romance in visual imaginings of science fiction. It is not just commonly seen, it is expected.

The *Doctor Who* story is quite a different one. Unlike leading men Riker and Kirk in *Star Trek*, the Doctor has only rarely become involved in relationships that could even remotely be construed as romantic. In 160 television stories he only came "close" to romance twice. He befriended the Aztec woman Cameca in "The Aztecs" early in the run of the series, but there were no signs of physical affection between these two mature adults. Finally, after more than 30 years, Paul McGann's eighth incarnation of the Doctor took the plunge and kissed cardiologist Grace Holloway in the American co-production of the *Doctor Who* 1996 telemovie. This was a historic occasion. The Doctor had never been seen to kiss any person during 26 years on the BBC! Apparently it took his defection to the Fox Network and to America to spur his Time Lord libido.

Because *Doctor Who* is a series that deals with elements of the human condition such as liberty ("The Dalek Invasion of Earth," "The Daleks"), tyranny ("Timelash," "Vengeance on Varos"), self-sacrifice ("The Dalek Masterplan," "The Caves of Androzani," "Earthshock"), racism ("The Mutants," "The Power of Kroll," "Kinda"), emotionalism ("The Evil of the Daleks"), loneliness ("The Three Doctors") and hypocrisy ("The Trial of the Time Lord," "The Happiness Patrol"), sex is a perfectly legitimate "human" theme to explore, and it need not be done in a lewd or inappropriate fashion. Since sex is an essential element in human behavior, any drama that does not choose to acknowledge or explore issues of sex and romance is neglecting reality and missing many interesting character and story possibilities. By ignoring sexual content with such Victorian rigor, the universe of *Doctor Who* can never be interpreted as a "realistic," universe like that of *Star Trek*, *Space: 1999*, or *Babylon 5*. After viewing many *Doctor Who* serials in rapid succession, it becomes increasingly obvious that an important ingredient is missing from the mix. A verisimilitude seen in *Star Trek*, *The X Files* and even in *Battlestar Galactica* is conspicuously absent.

The often used argument that *Doctor Who* is a children's program does not carry weight in regards to the issue of sex. *Doctor Who* stopped being "just" a children's program in 1975, if not earlier. It grew into an adult sci-fi vision capable of supporting graphic violence when necessary ("The Deadly Assassin," "Vengeance on Varos"). Why could it not also support a tastefully executed story concerning, even obliquely, sex and romance?

The only real acknowledgment of sex in *Doctor Who* comes in the costuming and casting departments. Rarely does a television program feature as many lovely young women as this series does. Carole Ann Ford, Jacqueline Hill, Anneke Willis, Deborah Watling, Wendy Padbury, Caroline John, Katy Manning, Elisabeth Sladen, Louise Jameson, Mary Tamm, Lalla Ward, Sarah Sutton, Nicola Bryant and Sophie Aldred are just a few of the beauties who have lit up the screen with their charm. It is probably fair to state that many of the Doctor's female companions were cast not only for their considerable acting skills, but also for their fetching appearances. Companion attire over the years certainly supports this assertion. As Pertwee's companion Jo Grant, Katy Manning frequently donned ultra miniskirts and tight jeans. Louise Jameson, the wonderful Leela, was garbed only in a provocative set of skins! Nicola Bryant's Peri was perhaps the most blatant of companion sex symbols because she was forced to display one tight, elastic leotard top after another. In the film industry, this kind of sexist visual distraction is often referred to as "keeping the fathers interested." In other words, *Doctor Who* attempted to exploit sex without ever exploring sex.

It is especially strange that Leela, a warrior of the savage Sevateem, was allowed to saunter about all sorts of locales in her short jungle outfits, yet her psyche was never studied in a sexual sense. This was a ridiculous oversight since Leela was always a physical rather than an intellectual presence on the show. It is only logical that sex would play an important part in her primitive culture. Such a notion would have proven a powerful contrast to the Doctor's own undoubtedly more civilized attitudes about sex, and consequently spurred several fascinating scenes. Had such a hypothetical conversation been written, its authors would have been forced to decide how the Doctor felt about sex. Do Time Lords have sex? Does the Doctor prefer women? Men? Hermaphroditic Hexapods? Clearly, these are interrogatives no producer or writer wanted to raise. If the door was opened to a mature discussion of sex, then what was to keep television viewers from picturing all kind of carnal activity inside the TARDIS? This was a silly fear, however. Fans have speculated about sex in the TARDIS for years. The series should have taken some stance on the subject. Instead, the producers left a vacuum, a vacuum which has subsequently been filled by the strangest and most perverse of speculations.

As a result of this stringent "no sex" policy, most romantic relationships on *Doctor Who* seem either forced or restrained. Susan, Leela, Vicki, Jo and Peri all leave the series to wed guest stars, but the decisions by these women to marry seem more a result of plot necessity than passion or romance. It is a business decision, not a legitimately dramatic one. The actresses had expressed a desire to leave the series and had to be "gotten rid of" somehow. Marrying them off on another planet or in a different historical era was the easiest way to accomplish that task. But realistically, what *Doctor Who* fan believes for a minute that Leela would choose to marry a docile Time Lord and spend the rest of her life on the sedate world of Gallifrey? Who believes that the spunky Peri, so determined to pursue her career in botany on Earth, would stay behind on the inhospitable homeworld of Sil and marry the overweight blowhard King Yrcanos? These decisions do not match the character, only the requirements of the producer.

On *Doctor Who*, the women who stay behind to marry inevitably act not as if they have succumbed to passion, lust or love. On the contrary, they act as though they have contracted a strange disease that has drained all traces of personality from them. In the context of *Doctor Who*, falling in love and getting married clearly has a negative association because it means leaving the Doctor! Of all the romantic relationships seen on *Doctor Who*, the only that one seems natural, sweet and authentic is the one that develops between early companions Barbara Wright and Ian Chesterton. These two characters talk like lovers, share confidences, and are physically affectionate with one another. One would be hard-pressed to name another positive love relationship in the series.

While watching *Doctor Who*, one will not see stories of alien temptresses stirring the blood of male companions like "Guardian of Piri" in *Space: 1999* or "The Muse" on *Deep Space Nine*. Nor will one see the Doctor exposed to a strange virus that makes him lose his inhibitions and act in romantic fashion like the crew of DS9 did in "Fascination" on *Deep Space Nine* or as the crew of the Enterprise-D did in "The Naked Now" on *The Next Generation.* If a viewer is looking for love and sex on *Doctor Who,* he or she is looking in all the wrong places.

Cinematography and Special Effects

Doctor Who has been a low-budget science fiction vision since its inception in 1963, especially in comparison with other notable genre television productions such as *Space: 1999* ($275,000 an episode in 1976), *Battlestar Galactica* (a million dollars an episode in 1978) and *Star Trek: The Next Generation* ($1.6 million an episode in 1989). By these standards, *Doctor Who* is definitely small potatoes. The special effects budget for "The Daleks" serial in *Doctor Who*'s first year was rumored to be but $800. It was reported that the minuscule budget was later increased to $4,000 an episode during the Tom Baker years.[2] Even that is a ludicrously low figure when one remembers that the cost of just one visual "laser blast" in the 1984 television series *V* cost $1,000. With such a low budget, the visual effects on *Doctor Who* have always been cheap. Not necessarily cheesy, but primitive (to say the least). This was a potential weakness that *Doctor Who* overcame in some beautifully inventive ways during the black-and-white era, from 1963 to 1969. In fact, *Doctor Who* was probably at its most visually distinct during the 1960s, when the black-and-white photography could successfully hide the seams and the strings. The low special effects budget simply led directors to be creative and to attempt new things. Some of the results remain startling today.

The set designers deserve credit too. There were beautifully painted backdrops in "The Aztecs" to give one the impression of a vast Aztec City surrounding the mountaintop temple, and complex miniature cities and installations built for "The Daleks," "The Chase" and "The Dominators." There were also armies of Daleks built on miniature landscapes in "The Power of the Daleks" and "The Evil of the Daleks." All of these effects were competent and interesting, if not expensive or completely "realistic." The only place in which protean *Doctor Who* fell notably short in design was in the representation of spaceships. The space vessels seen in "The Dalek Invasion of Earth" and "The Dominators" were clearly of the flying saucer school which had dominated '50s sci-fi productions. Uninventive in scheme, these ships also had the distinction of hanging from visible wires. The other spaceships in *Doctor Who,* particularly those seen in "The Seeds of Death" and "The Dominators," were needle-nosed rockets reminiscent of the early *Flash Gordon* and *Buck Rogers* serials. Also less-than-satisfying on *Doctor Who* was the practice of using stock footage from other productions any time big effects were needed. The explosion of the Dalek mine in "The Dalek Invasion of Earth" was a badly edited montage of stock footage explosions, and the TARDIS' encounter with crocodiles and undersea monsters in "The War Games" was also from BBC stock. This shift to stock footage was certainly harder to spot in black-and-white than it would have been in color, but it was nonetheless a money-saving ploy that did not always work.

Despite these isolated problems, *Doctor Who*'s directors and editors made their special effects memorable by using cheap but effective film techniques. To simulate time travel in "An Unearthly Child," a weird swirl of electronic images was superimposed over the faces of the main actors. Coupled with otherworldly, electronic sound effects, the inexpensive superimposition effectively captured the feeling of spinning through the time vortex. The blasts of Dalek gunfire in "The Daleks" and other early serials were also accomplished cheaply by turning the image of the collapsing victim into its "negative." This shift to the negative image was accompanied by a lingering "blast" sound. The illusion of a deadly ray was complete. In later shows such as "The Dominators" and "The Seeds of Death," the effects of alien weaponry were dramatized by burning holes in the film and by distorting photographic frames, respectively. All of these "laser" effects cost significantly less than $1,000 apiece, and each successfully suggested the terror of extraterrestrial weaponry.

Hand-held camerawork and extensive location shooting also contributed to the success of early *Doctor Who* shows such as "The Dalek Invasion of Earth." The series did not have the budget to create an alien city the size of London, so they brought their aliens to London instead. Seeing the non-humanoid Daleks ascending from the Thames and marching on the "real" city was a fruitful use of the effects budget. The grainy film stock and hand-held chase footage through London caused the sequences to seem more immediate and urgent. Tight editing of these segments also gave the serial a kind of crazy, frenetic pace. The same editing techniques were later used in "The War Games," one of the series' most stylish serials.

In *Doctor Who*, there are dozens of examples of production ingenuity. Film is reversed to create the effect of a sudden, powerful gravity pull in "The Dominators." "The Chase"'s final sequence sees the artful blending of quick cutting, model work, low and high angle shots, and image superimposition to give the impression of a monumental battle between the Mechanoids and the Daleks. The deliberate use of slow motion in "The War Games" (after the fast-paced, tightly edited climax of the story) reveals the ultimate temporal power of the Time Lords better than any other visual effect ever could. Even the main special effect of *Doctor Who*, the materialization of the TARDIS, is accomplished cheaply by filming an empty landscape, stopping the camera, and fading the TARDIS into the scene. The effect is not only cheap but also believable, especially when coupled with the grinding and wheezing TARDIS motor sound effects.

In its early days, *Doctor Who* proved that sometimes the cheapest effects are also the most dramatic. P.O.V. subjective shots were used in "The Daleks" to express Barbara's entrapment in the Dalek City. In "The Mind Robber," Jamie and Zoe found themselves on a giant empty plain, one completely overexposed with light. On the soundtrack, a strange clicking was heard. The feeling of isolation in an unknown, vast realm was very powerful. The same episode also saw the Doctor, Jamie and Zoe clutching the TARDIS console as it spun into blackest space. All that was required to create this shot was the central control panel on a revolving platform and a black background. When shot in slow motion and from a great distance, it appeared as if the travelers were holding on for dear life, whirling through a time-space eddy. Perhaps all of these special techniques are better described as "tricks" than effects, since there are very few optical effects such as laser blasts or matte paintings seen in *Doctor Who*'s 1960s days. Whatever they are called — effects, gimmicks, or tricks — they are part of *Doctor Who*'s unique visual appeal.

The '70s saw the advent of a new *Doctor Who* in color. It was perhaps too soon for this development, because many of the effects that had squeaked by in black-and-white could simply not pass muster in realistic color. The poorly detailed spaceship miniatures which had barely been acceptable in B&W serials were egregiously fake in stories such as "Death to the Daleks" and "The Ark in Space." Making matters worse, the color series could not hide the jarring transitions from 16mm film (for location shooting) to videotape (for sound stage shooting). Many '70s episodes suffer visually from very distracting cuts which contrast these distinctly different media. The blatant shifts draw attention away from the story.

Color also brought new detail to famous *Doctor Who* creatures like the Daleks. Unfortunately, in many episodes the Daleks were seen to be scuffed and held together in parts by thick black electrician's tape! Not easily detected in black-and-white, such flaws were made painfully obvious by the shift to color. Chroma Key and Blue Screen technologies were also inefficiently applied to many adventures. "Carnival of Monsters" featured a great design for the alien Drashigs, but when filmed in Chroma Key and blended with live-action footage, there was a visible matte line separating the two generations of footage. The size of the Drashigs also seemed to vacillate from shot to shot. The Drashigs were most convincing when seen not in combination with actors, but rather on highly detailed miniature sets that did not require widescale integration with a live-action component.

In the serial "The Claws of Axos," many actions shots were filmed in front of a blue screen and never combined with any background at all! Thus Sgt. Benton and UNIT's best men are seen acting their hearts out not on an authentic English landscape, but against the tell-tale phoniness of a pure blue backdrop.

As late as Colin Baker's era, many special effects and creatures were dramatized in a less than believable fashion. It was possible to see the "hidden" lips of the actors playing the Sontarans in "The Two Doctors" underneath the immobile plastic lips of the Sontaran prosthetic headpieces. More importantly, by the Pertwee era, many directors seemed content that they were filming "just" a television show and not a motion picture. Thus the P.O.V. shots of "An Unearthly Child" and "The Daleks," the slow-motion and cross-cutting of "The War Games," the hand-held camera work of "The Dalek Invasion of Earth" and the still-shot montages of "The Chase" were all gone. Even horror-oriented serials such as "The Brain of Morbius" and "The Pyramids of Mars," both of which cried out for menacing filmic style, were shot in average television fashion: establishing shot, medium shot, two shot, close-up. Conventional television editing also replaced the inspired editing of serials such as "An Unearthly Child" and "The Mind Robber." No longer were there any crazy high angles to suggest doom and destruction or low angles to suggest the menace of villains such as Morbius and Sutekh. When combined with jarring transitions from video to film, poorly detailed miniatures like Nerva in "The Ark in Space" and bad blue-screening composites like those in "The Claws of Axos," this blandness in cinematographic style makes many of the '70s and '80s era *Doctor Who* serials unforgivably dull from visual and stylistic standpoints.

Without inventive camerawork to buttress it, *Doctor Who* of the 1980s came to depend more and more on its set designs and costume designs to portray its visually distinctive world. Some serials were more successful than others. "The Robots of Death" was one of the best designed serials in *Doctor Who* history because it perfectly captured the elegance and decadence of the human society it depicted. "The Curse of Peladon" was another great success from a design standpoint with its evocative painting of a medieval castle and its *John Carter of Mars*–style costumes. "Paradise Towers," which depicted a futuristic apartment complex degraded into a slum by the weight of time, was another classic episode in terms of overall design. Yet there is no denying that had these fantastic vistas been shot with more visual flair, they would be infinitely more memorable today than they already are.

In Colin Baker's last year, there was a return to special effects majesty in the opening moments of "The Trial of the Time Lord." The camera found its way to an ominous space station (a well-detailed miniature) and cruised over its surface while space seemed to spin dizzily in the background. On the soundtrack, a grave-sounding bell rang repeatedly, suggesting that a time of reckoning had arrived. It was a memorable special effects triumph and perhaps the best pure effects moment in the series since the black-and-white days of William Hartnell and Patrick Troughton. Almost immediately, however, that triumph was undone in the opening of Season 24. In the beginning seconds of "Time and the Rani," the TARDIS was seen rolling through space, buffeted by laserblasts, in an early computer animated special effects sequence. It looked like a 1940s Max Fleischer *Superman* cartoon, not the next generation of hi-tech special effects. It was truly awful.

The William Hartnell and Patrick Troughton eras of *Doctor Who* are the most distinct and interesting periods from a purely visual standpoint. The black-and-white photography hid the monster zippers and wires for the most part, and the camera always moved in interesting fashion. More than that, the camerawork revealed information about characters and propelled the story forward. Though many *Doctor Who* fans prefer later generations of the series because they were lensed in color, *Doctor Who*'s earliest days are its most interesting from a special effects and cinematographic viewpoint.

PART III

THE SERIES

Critical Reception

Unlike almost any other popular sci-fi television drama, *Doctor Who* has only rarely in 35 years been reviewed on the basis of its merit and quality. When reviewed by American critics, it is frequently praised for its zany, "British" qualities while simultaneously scoffed at for its primitive visual effects. It is not often the subject of intense critical derision as are *Battlestar Galactica* or *Space: 1999*, but neither is it praised wildly as the greatest television show of all time, as are *The Outer Limits*, *Star Trek* or *The Prisoner*. *Doctor Who* is usually referred to as a "cult series" with a "huge" following, a description which tells potential viewers absolutely nothing about the nature of the series.

Since *Doctor Who* never had an official "premiere" in America but instead arrived via the back door of local syndication, most newspaper or television reviewers have never given it a hearing at all, good or bad. This is a strange situation, and a rather unique one in the valhalla of SF television. Usually, sci-fi shows generate a strong opinion, either positive or negative. *Doctor Who* is critic-proof, it seems, generating no strong reaction either way from the genre community. Below is a sampling of some of *Doctor Who*'s more notable critical reception.

> *Star Wars* is adolescent nonsense; *Close Encounters* is obscurantist drivel; *Star Trek* can turn your brains to puree of bat guano; and the greatest science fiction series of all time is *Doctor Who*! ...This TV viewing will not harm you ... will, in fact, delight and uplift you, stretch your imagination, tickle your risibilities, cleanse your intellect of all lesser visual SF affections ... *Doctor Who* is the apex, the pinnacle, the tops, the Louvre Museum, the tops, the Coliseum, and other et cetera.
>
> —Harlan Ellison, from his 1979 introduction to the *Doctor Who* Pinnacle novelizations

> It exploited (and often mixed) every imaginable SF trope as well as historical adventure and parody, gothic and mad-scientist horror, Ruritanian romance, and Victorian and 1920s murder mystery ... a uniquely popular SF adventure series with a broad audience.
>
> —James Gunn, *The New Encyclopedia of Science Fiction*, Viking Penguin Inc., 1988, pgs. 136–137

You so rarely see anything that really tries to be different, that tries to break out, on television. On that basis alone, *Doctor Who* is a kick. But the strong point of the show is the writing and the imagination that went into it. It was written by people willing to take a flight of imagination — people who didn't look to copy other forms.

— Rick Du Brow, *L.A. Herald Examiner*, *The Best of Science Fiction Television*, Harmony Books, 1987, page 13

The Doctor was always at odds with any establishment going ... from the very start he was a renegade, out of favor and on the run from other Time Lords. In the early years, the companion usually got herself, with "female" irrationality, into hot water, from which she had to be extricated by the Doctor. In later, more politically correct times, she was no longer required to be a certifiable idiot, and the plots of the four- or six-part stories were more involving.

— John Clute, *Science Fiction- The Illustrated Encyclopedia*, Dorling Kindersley, 1995, pgs. 302–303

Doctor Who, after a promising start, degenerated sharply into repetition and clumsy melodrama. One wishes that this program could have held to its original high quality, retaining the brilliance of imagination that produced creatures like the Zarbi, ant-like monsters that preyed on humanoid butterflies in an Aubrey Beardsley catacomb of art nouveau screens. Unfortunately, the success of the Daleks, dustbin robots with cleverly engineered 'mechanical' voices, drew the producers into endless consideration of other corrupt robot societies, and the series collapsed. Despite this, *Doctor Who* remains a good example of what may be done with limited facilities if a producer has imagination.

— John Baxter, *Science Fiction in the Cinema: A Complete Critical Review of SF Films from A Trip to the Moon (1902) to 2001: A Space Odyssey*, Paperback Library, New York, 1970, page 187

Dr. Who, while basically aimed at children ... has nonetheless explored most of science fiction's major themes.... The writing is resolutely middlebrow, but given the fact that the series is aimed at a predominantly juvenile audience, there is surprising sophistication in some of the concepts.... The general level may not be high but the series must have served as a valuable breeding ground for interest in the genre.

— Alan Frank, *Sci Fi Now*, Octopus Books Limited, 1978, page 19

Where else on TV can viewers expect to see something so off the wall? Not on cop shows like *Starsky and Hutch*. Or space operas like *Star Trek*. And it's too silly for a serious anthology like *The Twilight Zone*. That kind of endearing insanity is the exclusive property of *Doctor Who*— which is why fans are still watching it.

— John Javna, *The Best of Science Fiction TV*, Harmony Books, New York, 1987

Perhaps the greatest science fiction series of all time ... all too often U.S. series have spent lavishly on top-notch effects only to fail because of the inane storylines. *Doctor Who* is just the reverse, where much effort has been placed in telling stories, and telling them well — certainly the secret of its 26-year success.

— Richard Kirkpatrick, *Epilog* #11, October 1991, page 29

While the B&W episodes featuring Hartnell and Troughton are spikier and stranger, the show probably hit its peak between the Pertwee and Davison versions, with Tom Baker's long-lived Harpo-Marxish Time Lord the most popular of all and the writers of the 1970s gradually revealing more of the secrets of the Time Lords. In the late 1980s the show lost direction (some say thanks to the tiredness of John Nathan-Turner's regime as producer, begun August 1980). ...The authors have unblushingly pirated hundreds of ideas from pulp-magazine SF, but often make intelligent and sometimes quite complex use of them.... A notably self-confident series juggling expertly with many of the great tropes and images of the genre.... At its worst merely silly, at its best it has been spellbinding."

—John Clute and Peter Nicholls, *The Encyclopedia of Science Fiction*, St. Martin's Press, 1993, page 346

Credits

CAST: *The Doctor:* William Hartnell (Episodes 1–29, 65); Patrick Troughton (Episodes 30–50, 65, 130, 141); John Pertwee (Episodes 51–74, 130); Tom Baker (Episodes 74–116); Peter Davison (Episodes 116–136); Colin Baker (Episodes 135–146); Sylvester McCoy (Episodes 147–158)

CAST (The Companions): *Susan Foreman:* Carole Ann Ford (Episodes 1–10, 130); *Barbara Wright:* Jacqueline Hill (Episodes 1–16); *Ian Chesterton:* William Russell (Episodes 1–16); *Vicki:* Maureen O'Brien (Episodes 11–20); *Steven Taylor:* Peter Purves (Episodes 16–26); *Katarina:* Adrienne Hill (Episodes 20–21); *Sara Kingdom:* Jean Marsh (Episode 21); *Dodo Chaplet:* Jackie Lane (Episodes 22–27); *Polly Lopez:* Anneke Wills (Episodes 27–35); *Ben Jackson:* Michael Craze (Episodes 27–35); *Jamie McCrimmon:* Frazer Hines (Episodes 31–50, 130, 141); *Victoria Waterfield:* Deborah Watling (Episodes 36–42); *Zoe:* Wendy Padbury (Episodes 43–50, 130); *The Brigadier:* Nicholas Courtney (Episodes 46, 51–75, 80, 126, 130, 156); *Sgt. Benton:* John Levene (Episodes 46, 51–75, 80, 83); *Dr. Liz Shaw:* Caroline John (Episodes 51–54, 130); *Jo Grant:* Katy Manning (Episodes 55–69); *Sarah Jane Smith:* Elizabeth Sladen (Episodes 70–87, 130); *Harry Sullivan:* Ian Marter (Episodes 75–80, 83); *Leela:* Louise Jameson (Episodes 89 — 97); *K-9:* John Leeson (Episodes 93–114, 130); *Romanavoratrelunder:* Mary Tamm (Episodes 98–103); *Romanavoratrelunder, Incarnation Two:* Lalla Ward (Episodes 104–114); *Adric:* Matthew Waterhouse (Episodes 112–122) *Nyssa:* Sarah Sutton (Episodes 115–127); *Tegan:* Janet Fielding (Episodes 116–134); *Turlough:* Mark Strickson (Episodes 126–135); *Peri (Perpugilliam Brown):* Nicola Bryant (Episodes 135–148); *Melanie:* Bonnie Langford (Episodes 147–151); *Ace:* Sophie Aldred (Episodes 151–159)

A note about technical credits: *Doctor Who* is different from a standard American television production in that it does not sport a regular technical crew which returns to the series week after week, year after year. Instead, various BBC technicians arrived on *Doctor Who* and stayed only for the four-part serial shooting at the time. Some technicians did return frequently over the years to contribute to further serials, while others worked on but one serial and never came back to *Doctor Who*'s universe. Therefore, the credits listed below do not represent the technical crew of *Doctor Who* during any one particular serial in history. Instead, the credits represent an amalgamation of all the talented people who worked on the series over its incredible 1963–1989 run on BBC-TV.

Crew

Creators: Sydney Newman and Donald Wilson. *Producers*: Verity Lambert (Episodes 1–19); Innes Lloyd (Episodes 23–36, 38–40); John Wiles (Episodes 20–22, 24); Peter Bryant (Episodes 37, 41–49); Derrick Sherwin (Episodes 50–51); Barry Letts (Episodes 52–75); Peter Hinchcliffe (Episodes 76–91); Graham Williams (Episodes 92–109); John Nathan-Turner (Episodes 110–159).

Story/Script Editors: David Whitaker (Episodes 1–10); Dennis Spooner (Episodes 11–16); Donald Tosh (Episodes 17–22); Gerry Davis (Episodes 22–36); Peter Bryant (Episodes 36–40); Victor Pemberton (Episode 37); Derrick Sherwin (Episodes 41–45, 49); Terrance Dicks (Episodes 46–48, 50–74); Robert Holmes (Episodes 75–92); Anthony Read (Episodes 96–109); Christopher H. Bidmead (Episodes 110–116); Antony Root (Episodes 118, 120, 122); Eric Saward (Episodes 117, 119, 121, 123–145) Andrew Cartmel (Episodes 148–159).

Associate Producers: Mervyn Pinfield (Episodes 1–12); Peter Bryant (Episode 35). *Executive Producer*: Barry Letts (Episodes 110–116). *Title Sequences:* Bernard Lodge, Sid Sutton, Terry Handley. *Graphic Designer*: Oliver Elmes. *Computer Animation:* Cal Video.

Theme Music: Ron Grainer and the BBC Radiophonic Workshop. *Incidental Music:* Norman Kay, Tristram Cary, Richard Bennett, Dudley Simpson, Francis Chagrin, Raymond Jones, Charles Botterill, Humphrey Searle, Don Harper, Carey Blyton, Malcolm Clark, Geoffrey Burgon, Peter Howell, Paddy Kingsland, Roger Limb, Jonathan Gibbs, Liz Parker, Dominic Glynn, Richard Hartley, Keff McCulloch, Mark Ayres. *Special Sounds*: Brian Hodgson, Dick Mills and the BBC Radiophonic Workshop.

Production Managers: Margot Hayhoe, Roselyn Parker, Geoffrey Manton, Jim Capper, Jeremy Silberston, Ann Aronsohn, Corinne Hollingworth, Elizabeth Trubridge, Michael A. Treen, Tony Redston, Margot Eavis, Gary Downie, Clare Graham, Kevan Van Thompson, Ian Fraser, Michael McDermott, Valerie Whiston.

Production Assistants: Peter Grimwade, Marion McDougall, Malachy Shaw Johns, Christopher D'Oyly-John, Nicholas Howard John, Ros Anderson, Carole Wiseman, Prue Saenger, Jane Shirley, Michael Owen Morris, Teresa-Mary Winders, Carol Montagu, Kate Nemet, Ann Aronsohn, Rosemary Crawson, Henry Foster, Patricia Greenland, Olivia Cripps, Jane Ashford, Julia Randall, Juley Harding, Jean Davis, Rita Dunn, Valerie Letley, Joy Sinclair, Christine Fawcett, Carolyn Mandsley, Jane Whittaker, Patricia O'Leary, Karen Jones, Jane Wellesley, Frances Graham, Rosemary Parsons, Winifred Hopkins.

Production Unit Managers: George Gallaccio, Janet Rodenkovic, Thea Murray, John Nathan-Turner. *Production Associates:* Angela Smith, June Collins, Sue Anstruther, Jenny Doe, Anji Smith, Ann Faggetteer. *Assistant Floor Managers:* David Tilley, Val McCrimmon, Carol Scott, Renny Tasker, Alison Symington, Nicholas Laughland, Pauline Seager, Maggie Campbell, Ian D. Tootle, Matthew Burge, Susan Hedden, Stephen Jeffery-Poulter, Betth Millward, Penny Williams, Sophie Neville, Ilsa Rowe, Anna Price, Karen Little, Joana Newbery, Christopher Sandeman, Lynn Grant, Jeremy Fry, Stephen Garwood, Judy Corry, Leigh Poole. *Director's Assistants*: Roz Berrystone, James Wellesley.

Costume Designers: Mauree Heneghan, Daphne Dare, Tony Pearce, Pauline Mansfield-Clarke, Sandra Reid, Juanita Robinson, Mary Woods, Martin Baugh, Susan Whee, Bobi Bartlett, Nicholas Bullen, Christine Rawlins, Ken Trew, Barbara Lane, Michael Burdle, Mary Husband, Maggie Fletcher, James Acheson, Barbara Kidd, Hazel Pethig, L. Rowland, Prue Handley, Andrew Rose, Joan Ellacott, John Bloomfield, Elizabeth Waller, Joyce Hawkins, Raymond Hughes, Amy Roberts, Rupert Jarvis, Dee Kelly, June Hudson, James Doreen, Colin Lavers, Odile Dicks-Mireaux, Rosalind Ebbutt, Dinah Collin, Dee Robson, John Peacock, Judy Pepperdine, Jackie Southern, Anushia Nieradzik, Janet Tharby, Pat Godrey, Ann Harding, Jan Wright, Alan Hughes, John Hearne, Shaunna Harrison, Richard Croft.

Makeup Supervisors: Jill Summers, Sonia Markham, Gillian James, Sylvia James, Heather Stewart, Magdalen Gaffney, Jean Steward, Jean McMillan, Ann Briggs, Christine Walmesley-Cotham, Janis Gould, Anne Briggs, Marion Richards, Cynthia Goodwin, Jan Harrison, Anne Rayment, Angela Seyfang, Deanne Turner, Judy Clay, Jenny Shircore, Sylvia

Thornton, Judy Neame, Jeane Williams, Heather Stewart, Pauline Cox, Jill Hagger, Cecile Hay-Arthur, Dorka Nieradzik, Carolyn Perry, Lisa Westcott, Sheelagh Wells, Eileen Mair, Jan Nethercot, Shirley Stallard, Denise Baron, Catherine Davies, Shaunna Harrison, Lesley Rawstorne, Gillian Thomas, Joan Stribling.

Film Cameramen: Peter Hamilton, Charles Parnall, James Court, Stan Speel, John Baker, Fred Hamilton, Bill Matthews, John Baker, Len Newson, Max Samett, Elmer Cossey, John Walker, Martin Patmore, Phil Law, Peter Hall, Peter Chapman, Keith Hopper, Godfrey Johnson, Ian Punter, Kevin Rowley, William Dudman. *Senior Cameramen:* Alec Wheal, Reg Poulter, Robin Barnes. *Camera Supervisors:* Alec Wheal, Spencer Payne. *O.B. Cameramen:* Alastair Mitchell, John Hawes, David Hunter, Robin Sutherland, Barry Chaston, Alan Jessup, Paul Harding.

Film Editors: Gita Zadek, Norman Matthews, Alan Martin, Chris Hayden, Martyn Day, John Griffiths, William Symon, Adam Dawson, Geoffrey Botterill, Michael Sha-Dyan, Jim Walker, Dan Rae, Bob Rymer, M.A.C. Adams, Mike Stoffer, Clare Douglas, Christopher Rowlands, Ian McKendrick, David Lee, John Dunstan, David Yates, John Gregory, Michael Goldsmith, Dick Allen, Paul Humfress, Robin Jackman, Kevin Bilton, Mike Houghton, Chris Woolley, Dan Rae, Roger Guertin, Ray Wingrove, Mike Robotham. *Videotape Editors:* John Turner, Rod Waldron, Alan Goddard, Malcolm Banthorpe, Hugh Parsons, Steve Newnham.

Lighting: Howard King, Brian Sothcott, Sam Neeter, Eric Monk, Clive Thomas, Ralph Watson, Nigel Wright, John Mason, Alan Horne, Brian Clement, Duncan Brown, Dennis Channon, Derek Slee, Brian Clemett, Ron Koplick, Peter Catlett, Duncan Brown, Jim Purdie, Mike Jeffries, Warwick Fielding, John Dixon, Henry Barber, Ron Bristow, Fred Wright, Don Babbage, Dennis Channon, Mark Jeffries. *O.B. Lighting:* John Mason, Hubert Cartwright, Ian Dow.

Sound: Richard Chubb, Ray Angel, Brian Hiles, John Holmes, Jack Brummitt, Colin Dixon, Tony Miller, Bob Roberts, Gordon Mackie, Derek Medus, John Holmes, Trevor Webster, Vic Godrich, John Lloyd, Bill Chisneau, Tony Miller, Alan Machin, Doug Mawson, Hugh Cleverley, Graham Bedwell, John Gatland, Alan Fogg, Bill Meekums, Mike Jones, Stan Nightingale, Clive Gifford, Graham Bedwell, Jim McAlister, Laurie Taylor, Ron Blight, Martin Ridout, Ron Brown, Malcolm Campbell, Scott Talbott, Barrie Tharby, Keith Bowden, Andy Stacey, Colin March, Brian Clark, John Nottage. *O.B. Sound:* Vic Godrich, Doug Whitaker, Les Mowbray.

Technical Managers: John Dean, Terry Brett, Clive Gulliver, Derek Martin, Alan Jeffery, Derek Thompson, Alan Arbuthnott. *Technical Coordinators:* Alan Arbuthnott, Richard Wilson. *Engineering Manager:* Brian Jones. *Vision Mixers:* Nigel Finnis, James Gould, Carol Johnson, Shirley Coward, Paul Wheeler, Dinah Long, Jayne Beckett, Jim Stephens, Sue Thorne, Fred Law, Barbara Gainsley, Susan Brincat. *Paintbox Artist:* Jim McCarthy.

Special Effects: Michael Harris, Peter Day, Ron Oates, Bernard Wilkie, Len Hutton, Bill King, Jack Kline, John Horton, Jim War, Ian Scoones, Peter Pegram, Rhys Jones, Clifford Cully, Richard Conway, Colin Mapson, John Friedlander, Tony Oxley, Ulrich Grossner, Dave Havard, Mat Irvine, Tony Harding, Peter Logan, Steven Lucas, Jim Francis, Andrew Lazell, John Brace, Peter Wragg, Simon McDonald, Mickey Edwards, Tony Auger, Steve Bowman, Christopher Lawson, Stuart Brisdon, Mike Kelt, Jim Francis, Charles Jeans, David Barton, Kevin Molloy, Simon Taylor, Andy McVean, Perry Brahan, David Bezkorowajny, Graham Brown, Malcolm James.

Property Buyers: Robert Fleming, Chris Ferriday, John Charles, Nick Barnett, Yvonne Alfert. *Fight Arrangers:* Derek Ware, Peter Diamond, John Greenwood, Rick Lester, Terry Walsh, Tip Tipping.

The Episodes

Unlike an average hour-long American television drama, each *Doctor Who* serial is not uniformly 48 minutes in length. On the contrary, serials consist of several parts, or episodes, with each segment lasting approximately 25 minutes. Some serials are 10, 12 or even 14 episodes long and have total running times that exceed 250 minutes.

Doctor Who serials are reviewed in this text in broadcast order rather than production order. This list indicates the chronological order of the Doctor's adventures through time in space. In the last few years, a series of novels called "The Missing Adventures" has been released by Virgin Books. These stories effectively make mincemeat of this long-accepted 159-serial sequence. Since this author does not necessarily consider the original novels to be canon, the sequence below should still be considered the official one as far as television history is concerned.

Please note that in the first 25 adventures of *Doctor Who*, each individual chapter, or "part" of a serial, carries an individual title as well as a title for the "whole" story. Following episode 25, "The Gunfighters," *Doctor Who* serials no longer featured individual titles for each 25-minute installment.

Sad to say, many early *Doctor Who* serials have been completely destroyed, taped over or mysteriously lost by the BBC, and are hence unavailable for review in 1999. Much of Patrick Troughton's era, including most of Season 5, has been lost to the ages. To fill in these "historical" story gaps and offer a thorough journal of the Doctor's journeys, this author has in compiling the synopses utilized various secondary sources, including episode adaptations and Jean-Marc Lofficier's landmark 1981 text *The Doctor Who Program Guide Volume 1.* Since it is impossible to critically evaluate a program that no longer exists, each commentary for a lost episode will indicate its status as "missing."

SEASON 1

1. "An Unearthly Child" Written by Anthony Coburn & C.E. Webber; Directed by Waris Hussein; Designed by Barry Newbery and Peter Brachacki; Part I: "An Unearthly Child" Airdate: November 23, 1963; Part II: "The Cave of Skulls" Airdate: November 30, 1963; Part III: "The Forest of Fear" Airdate: December 7, 1963; Part IV: "The Firemaker" Airdate: December 14, 1963

SYNOPSIS: At London's Coal Hill School in 1963, teachers Barbara Wright and Ian Chesterton are suspicious about their young pupil Susan Foreman, who possesses incredible mathematical and scientific knowledge. They follow her home from school and are shocked to discover that she lives inside a police box in a junkyard at 76 Totters Lane! Inside the police box is Susan's white-haired grandfather, an eccentric but brilliant old man who enigmatically refers to himself as "the Doctor." The Doctor and Susan soon reveal that they are exiles from another planet and that this strange booth, the TARDIS (Time And Relative Dimension In Space), is their spaceship-time vessel! Furthermore, the unusual craft is much larger on the inside than the outside because it is dimensionally transcendent.

Only when the TARDIS jumps to another time, and Ian and Barbara step out onto a prehistoric plain, do the teachers realize that the Doctor's amazing story is true. The time travelers explore their new world and face danger from Kal, a vicious prehistoric hunter who believes they can make fire. Now the Doctor must not only extricate himself and his wards from a tribal rivalry between Kal and Za, the son of the dead chief, he must find a way to get the TARDIS back to London.

GUEST CAST: Za (Derek Newark); Hur (Alethea Charlton); Kal (Jeremy Young); Horg (Howard Lang); Old Mother (Eileen Way)

COMMENTARY: *Doctor Who*'s first serial is a startling debut for the new series. It begins small, almost innocuously, with two schoolteachers curious about a strange student. It ends not with a typical explanation, but with an open door to the mysteries of time and space! The plot structure is a brilliant one because it allows the audience to fathom the riddles of Susan, the Doctor, the TARDIS and time travel at the same time as the stunned Ian and Barbara do. Had the program simply opened aboard the TARDIS with the Doctor landing on a new planet, there would be no sense of a journey shared or an enigma solved together. Instead, the audience is invited to investigate Susan's mysterious origins with the Coal Hill instructors, its representatives on screen, and consequently glimpse a whole new world. When the answers finally do come, they are wholly unexpected. Though *Doctor Who* is well-known today as a television series about a time-space traveler, imagine the surprise of the uninitiated audience watching it for the first time in 1963. An interesting little mystery about an eccentric teenage girl leads to the first peek into a larger universe. Because this story structure is so effective and because the mystery leads the viewers into the world of *Doctor Who* so successfully, "An Unearthly Child" is an unqualified success as drama.

Beyond the excellent writing, some interesting cinematic style raises the story above the level of the average television production. The program opens as a policeman navigates his way through an eerie bank of fog. The mist clears as the camera accelerates through it, and the old wooden door to I.M. Foreman's Scrapyard is revealed. Functioning as the audience's point of view, the camera pushes through the doors and focuses on the TARDIS, a London police box. The camera then slowly pans up and down the police box. It pulls back suddenly and the screen fades to black. Even before the mystery of Susan's odd behavior is mentioned, the audience has seen the solution to that mystery — the show's time travel machine. Of course, the significance of the police box in the junkyard is not yet known, but the manner in which the camera lingers on it for a long moment suggests its importance in the episode's events and in the series as a whole.

There are other absorbing conceits in "An Unearthly Child" as well. As Ian and Barbara recount their odd experience with Susan, there is a quick fade to a flashback. The camera again operates as the audience's point of view. It sees through

"An Unearthly Child," episode #1, has been released on videotape so *Doctor Who* fans around the world can remember where the saga began.

Barbara's and Ian's eyes as they question Susan about her unusual behavior. Ford's Susan faces not another cast member, but the camera itself, as she delivers her strange answers. Again, these P.O.V. shots have the effect of pulling the audience directly into the drama. Susan is talking not merely to her teachers, but to all those watching in the living room as well.

Since "An Unearthly Child" also serves as the audience's introduction to the *dramatis personae*, Waris Hussein's camera frequently lingers on long closeups of each character. As Barbara and Ian discuss Susan's eccentric conduct in the car, their expressive faces fill the screen. The message is clear: The audience is supposed to like these people. The teachers are surrogates for the viewer. When the Doctor appears, he is also shown in closeup and the first thing one notices about him are his cunning, intelligent eyes. Perhaps Susan's introduction to the series is strangest of all. Her first scene begins with a closeup of her mouth and neck as she "grooves" to rock music emanating from a hand-held radio. The camera pulls back and looks up and down the beautiful girl's torso in what, for *Doctor Who*, is a surprisingly sensual and natural moment. Carole Ann Ford, the actress portraying Susan, has an erotic, unusual look. With her angular features and penetrating eyes, it is plain to see why this particular student has aroused the curiosity of her teachers. There is something almost hyper-human about her, and the camera captures this otherworldly appeal in its first scan of her.

There are other striking images in "An Unearthly Child" that make it much more stylish than later episodes. When the TARDIS begins to travel through time, the audience gets an aerial view of London. This photograph of the city recedes slowly into a sea of blackness, suggesting with a minimum of optical effects that the TARDIS has withdrawn from Earth and entered the time vortex. Making this departure even more clear, spinning whirlpools of energy and throbbing blobs of light are superimposed over closeups of the unwitting travelers. As the TARDIS lands, these shapes abruptly blur and reform into the barren landscape of the prehistoric past. This is the only time in the series that any effects are used to indicate the effects of time travel on the TARDIS crew. In fact, the crew here falls unconscious during the journey, as if their bodies have experienced an enormous force. Like the optical superimposition, this side effect of time travel is not repeated in later stories.

Perhaps the most striking image in the entire serial is that of the TARDIS perched on a prehistoric cliff. The sky is barren, and dead trees surround the ship. It is an empty, frightening world. The TARDIS leans slightly to one side, its dorsal light flashing like a beacon. The feelings of loneliness and of an alien landscape generated here are unforgettable. They are made more so by the fact because it is all recorded in stark black-and-white.

Beyond the introductions of the characters and central situation of the story, "An Unearthly Child" introduces the series to its first time travel adventure. The prehistoric tribe, depicted here as sun worshippers, makes a fine first culture for the travelers of *Doctor Who* to encounter, but the central adventure at the dawn of time is far less interesting than the mystery at the Coal Hill School and the introduction of the main characters which preceded it. The cavemen are appropriately depicted as primitives, garbed in tattered furs. They also sport smudges of dirt on their faces, with little or no makeup evident. This is a relief from the cavemen frequently portrayed in film, such as the beautiful, perfectly washed and coiffed Raquel Welch in *One Million Years B.C.* (1967). What makes the prehistoric tribe less than believable in "An Unearthly Child" has less to do with appearance than voice. All the prehistoric characters speak nearly perfect English with a refined British accent! That is just a bit hard to swallow. When *Space: 1999*, another British sci-fi series, produced its own "caveman show" (1975's "Full Circle"), it avoided this pitfall by permitting its primitive Neanderthals to communicate only with a series of grunts and guttural hums. Such a solution would have been nearly impossible in this tale, however, since the Doctor and his friends are supposed to communicate verbally with the primitive men and learn of their need for fire.

Mankind's need to possess fire, the central dilemma of this prehistoric tale, is also the motivating plot point in the high-budget feature film *Quest For Fire* (1982) directed by Jean-Jacques Annaud and starring Everett McGill, Rae Dawn Chong and Ron Perlman. In that film, the characters not only speak their own primitive language and master the mysteries of fire, but also discover the joys of the missionary position ... a revelation that would certainly never pass the BBC censors or be acknowledged on a so-called children's program such as *Doctor Who.*

Another engrossing facet of "An Unearthly Child" is the depiction of the Doctor. He is not at all the sympathetic being one might expect of a series lead. He is haughty, paranoid, clever, arrogant and even vicious. At one especially awful moment, he runs by Barbara after she has fallen down in the jungle. He does not stop to assist her, or even hesitate for an instant. He simply runs right on by. This is not the behavior of a gentleman; the Doctor in this story displays some very rough edges. Perhaps the producer's original idea was for the Doctor to operate essentially as a hindrance in each story, in much the same way Dr. Smith would later cause problems on *Lost in Space*. This idea was dropped here, and the Doctor, though still a touchy and arrogant character, became more caring and paternal.

One thing is for certain about the Doctor in "An Unearthly Child": from Event One he is played with extreme confidence by William Hartnell. The symbiosis between character and actor in this case is seamless. Hartnell projects the intelligence, cunning and mystery of this old man perfectly. Though many other actors have played the Doctor since Hartnell, few have been able to cement their style so quickly and so immutably.

It is illuminating to remember that there is an alternate version of "An Unearthly Child," a pilot which dramatizes an even more unfriendly side of the Doctor. The producers reshot portions of the episode to make the central character less mean-spirited and difficult. They also took out references to the forty-ninth century, which would have pinned the Doctor and Susan down to a specific time and place of origin.

While discussing trivia, it is important to acknowledge some contradictions between "An Unearthly Child" and the remainder of the long-lived series. Firstly, Susan reveals that she herself has named the time machine TARDIS, based on the initials Time And Relative Dimension (*singular*) In Space. In most future episodes, the TARDIS is referred to as meaning Time and Relative Dimensions (*plural*) In Space. Throughout the series, TARDIS is also the accepted name of the craft and used by Time Lords, the Master and other characters. It is clear that at some point the premise of the series changed and the TARDIS became a class of time ship (a type 40 to be exact) rather than just a single craft named by the Doctor's granddaughter. Also, the Doctor reveals in "An Unearthly Child" that the chameleon circuit was working prior to this landing in London in 1963. The TARDIS' materialization in prehistory thus represents the first occasion in which the chameleon circuit malfunctions and the ship is stuck in its form as a "police box."

The most fascinating point of all this early information is the Doctor's reference to himself and Susan as "exiles." This description does not jibe with revelations about the Doctor. In "The War Games" (Season 6), the Doctor reveals to Jamie and Zoe that he ran away from his people because he was bored. This is hard to reconcile with the "exile" speech in "An Unearthly Child." However, it is certainly not out of the realm of possibility to believe that in this case, the Doctor is lying. He deceives others and bends the truth many times during his voyages through the cosmos, so his exile speech in "An Unearthly Child" may only be a cover to hide his theft of a time machine. One can justify these discontinuities in any number of ways, and doing so has become the part-time occupation of many *Doctor Who* fans!

"An Unearthly Child" has long been at the center of many fan controversies anyway, and not merely because of discontinuities with later episodes. The title of the episode itself has caused considerable difficulty. Before the advent of videocassette, the episode was often referred to as "The Tribe of Gum" or "1,000,000 B.C." The story has been novelized by Target Books and released on video as "An Unearthly Child," so it is fair to assume that this is the canonical title of the premiere serial.

Waris Hussein, who directed "An Unearthly Child" with such an unwavering, stylistic hand, would return to direct the fourth episode of the fledgling series. His later contribution, "Marco Polo," is the first purely historical, rather than prehistorical, adventure seen on *Doctor Who*. His effort to launch *Doctor Who* successfully can be fully appreciated today since "An Unearthly Child" is currently available in VHS format from BBC/CBS-Fox video.

2. "The Daleks" (a.k.a "The Dead Planet") Written by Terry Nation; Directed by Christopher Barry and Richard Martin; Designed by Raymond Cusick and Jeremy Davies; Part I: "The Dead Planet" Airdate: December 21, 1963; Part II: "The Survivors" Airdate: December 28, 1963; Part III: "The Escape" Airdate: January 4, 1964; Part IV: "The Ambush" Airdate January 11, 1964; Part V: "The Expedition" Airdate: January 18, 1964; Part VI: "The Ordeal" Airdate: January 25, 1964; Part VII "The Rescue" Airdate: February 1, 1964

SYNOPSIS: The TARDIS materializes at the edge of a petrified forest on a dead planet called Thal, and the Doctor theorizes that the surface's condition has been caused by a nuclear war. The Doctor wishes to explore the incredibly advanced city on the horizon, and so sabotages the TARDIS' fluid link so the others cannot force him to leave the planet.

Inside the city, the Doctor and his companions are captured by the denizens of the metropolis, the evil Daleks. Armored beings in pepper-pot-shaped radiation suits, the Daleks are armed with laser tubes, a long thin probe and a cylindrical eyestalk atop their domed heads. Completely mobile, these dangerous creatures are not robots, but small, tentacled mutants who exist inside the highly advanced metal armor. The Daleks are also suspicious, malevolent creatures bent on exterminating all life forms other than their own. Currently, their goal is to destroy a race of friendly humanoids, the Thals. Teaming with the Temmosus, leader of the Thals, the Doctor and his companions launch a daring campaign against the Dalek stronghold.

GUEST CAST: Temmosus (Alan Wheatley) Alydon (John Lee); Gannatus (Philip Bond); Antodus (Marcus Hammond); Dyoni (Virginia Wetherell); Dalek voices (David Graham, Peter Hawkins); Dalek Operators (Robert Jewell, Kevin Manser, Peter Murphy, Michael Summerton, Gerald Taylor); Thals (Gerald Curtis, John Crane, Chris Browning, Vez Delahunt, Kevin Glenny, Ruth Harrison, Lesley Hill, Steve Pokol, Jeanette Rossini, Eric Smith)

COMMENTARY: More so than the late Anthony Coburn's compelling premiere adventure of *Doctor Who*, Terry Nation's "The Daleks" seems to be the prototype from which many future *Doctor Who* episodes were derived. Like later stories "The Dalek Invasion of Earth," "The Web Planet," "The Space Museum, "The Ark," "The Savages," "The Dominators," "The Krotons," "Colony in Space" and "The Mutants," "The Daleks" at its core is about a planetary revolution against an oppressive enemy. This adventure, in addition to being the first of these stories, is also the most direct regurgitation of the future scenario depicted in the George Pal film *The Time Machine* (1960). In this case, the "exterminating" Daleks with their thirst for death fill in for the monstrous, inhuman Morlocks. The pacifist Thals stand in for the simplistic, naive Eloi. The Doctor, who here stirs the Thals to insurrection, fulfills the same function as the Time Traveler in *The Time Machine* by leading the battle against the man-hating enemy. Despite the blatant similarities to *The Time Machine*, "The Daleks" is nonetheless an historic and dramatic *Doctor Who* serial for many reasons.

"The Daleks" details the Doctor's first recorded encounter with a hostile alien species, the Daleks. This represents the course of most subsequent serials. After several historical adventures, the series begins in Season 5 only to visit alien cultures, leaving Earth history as an element of *Who* stories, but not the sole one. The example of "An Unearthly Child," a purely history- (or prehistory-) based adventure, is disregarded in favor of more sci-fi background, as in "The Daleks."

This adventure is historically important for reasons besides its position in the *Doctor Who* story roster. Most notably, it introduces to the world of television its first non-humanoid threat. Although *The Outer Limits* (1963) frequently featured monsters and aliens (referred to as "Bears" by the producers), most of those creatures were based on the human form, with the exception of the stop-motion insects seen in "The Zanti Misfits." Even *Star Trek*, which was produced three years after *Doctor Who* had been on the air, distinguished "otherworldly" creatures only in the most simplistic of humanoid terms. By *Trek*'s vision, aliens were identical to humans but with pointed ears and arched eyebrows ("Balance of Terror") or swarthy skin and beards ("Errand of Mercy"). Or they were human infants ("The Corbomite Maneuver") or beings who adopted human form "so as to be understood" ("Charlie X," "The Squire of Gothos," "Arena," "Errand of Mercy"). The notion of aliens as bearded, swarthy fiends was surely an extension of the racist image painted by '30s serials such as *Flash Gordon* (1936) and *Buck Rogers* (1939), which highlighted alien hordes based on the appearance of Chinese people. For the planet Mongo, read simply "Mongol," and that explains a great deal about the look of early Hollywood extraterrestrials. *Doctor Who*'s creators opted for a more innovative approach and succeeded in creating an unforgettable non-humanoid villain in the Daleks. In 1963, when sci-fi television was still in its infancy, this was a major achievement.

The Daleks were designed by BBC artist Raymond Cusick and created by writer Terry Nation. Although unaware of it at the time, these talents not only created a hostile race of aliens, they created a phenomenon. When the Daleks first appeared in the "flesh" on December 28, 1963, they created a sensation. A Dalek craze swept the country. When the Daleks appeared on the television, children ran away from it screaming in horror. Scores of Dalek toys were soon manufactured. Daleks suddenly started appearing in political cartoons in the newspapers and they even starred in two feature films: *Doctor Who and the Daleks* (1965) and *Daleks: Invasion Earth 2150 A.D.* (1966). Perhaps the height of Dalek "fever" was the release of a Dalek pop song. At appropriate times in the tune, the grating mechanical voice of a Dalek would join the chorus. This phenomenon may be hard for Americans to understand in 1999, but in 1963 it was amazing. Dalek fever was on the scale of Beatlemania. Comparatively it was much bigger than the Power Rangers craze that inexplicably grabbed American children in the early '90s and would not let go for years, so much so that in 1997 parents were still enduring Power Rangers feature films! The end result of all this merchandising is that the Daleks quickly became the most popular villain on *Doctor Who* and the word "Dalek" can be found in the Oxford Dictionary of the English Language.

For *Doctor Who*, the immediate result was quite gratifying. The Daleks not only threatened the good Doctor, they nudged his ratings right into outer space. This boost undoubtedly saved the series from early cancellation.

Today, the Daleks have become somewhat devalued as a serious opponent. After watching them for 36 years, a few things have become obvious. One such factor is that Daleks, with their wide, clunky lower halves, cannot climb stairs or ascend ladders. The second fact about Daleks is that their arms look uncomfortably like toilet plungers and are hardly threatening or efficient. The third point is that the Dalek eyestalk is extremely vulnerable. Over the years, Daleks have been blinded by everything from a dollop of what looks like refried beans (*Doctor Who and the Daleks*) to the Doctor's hat ("Destiny of the Daleks"). These factors have combined to make the Daleks seem less than threatening in the 1990s than they were in the 1960s. With all these design flaws, who could not escape from a Dalek?

Still, this modern assessment is unfair. All monsters have their day, and perhaps the day of the Dalek is over. Movie and television audiences have been treated to three decades of more advanced alien invaders since the Daleks first appeared. The creatures of *Independence Day* (1996), *The Arrival* (1996), *Species* (1995) and the *Predator* films (1987, 1991) have made the villainy of the Daleks seem rather primitive in comparison. But before the Earth was decimated by the aliens of *Independence Day*, the Daleks were sweeping through London in *Doctor Who*. The admission that the appearance of the Daleks is no longer frightening to audiences is in no way a degradation of Terry Nation's and Raymond Cusick's accomplishment. In 1963, before *Star Trek* and *Lost in Space*, a gliding, inhuman entity with a sinister mechanical voice was nothing less than an inspiration.

"The Daleks" is successful not just in the depiction of the villains. The episode works well today as a suspenseful serial because the performers react to the Daleks so believably. Jacqueline Hill established from her first moment on-screen in "An Unearthly Child" that Barbara Wright was a self-confident, intelligent woman. She continues that reading of the character in "The Daleks," and reacts with wholly believable terror as the Daleks first bear down on her. Hartnell is also adept at showing apprehension and dread in the presence of the Daleks. As much as the special effects execution of the Daleks, the performances sell the believability of these creatures. Even if the most expensive special effects had been used to dramatize the Dalek threat, it all would have been meaningless if the cast had not thrown every bit of their talent into their reactions. In this sense, Hill, Hartnell, Ford and Russell deserve as much praise for the success of the Daleks as Cusick and Nation do.

Christopher Barry makes the Daleks ever more believable with stylish camerawork too. When the first Dalek approaches Barbara, the camera adopts the Dalek's perspective. The audience sees only an outstretched mechanical arm reaching for the screaming schoolteacher. This is the shot which ended the first episode, as well as the shot that had viewers all over England wondering what kind of monstrosity was at the other end of that arm. Barry keeps the tension high by frequently shooting the Daleks from a low angle, making them seem large, menacing and powerful. Undoubtedly, he too deserves some of the credit for the Dalek success. Barry would go on to direct many episodes of *Doctor Who* including "The Rescue," "The Romans," "The Savages" and "The Power of the Daleks." Two decades after his excellent work on "The Daleks," he would attempt a second success with another race of evil mechanical creatures: He directed several episodes of the BBC series *The Tripods* (1984-1985). These creations, based on the trilogy by John Christopher, had none of the Dalek "personality" and failed to capture viewer attention as completely as Nation's exterminating machines had. Six years after his work on this episode of *Doctor Who*, Barry also directed an alternate universe story entitled "Random Quest" for the anthology series *Out of the Unknown* (1965-71).

"The Daleks" is Nation's first contribution to *Doctor Who*. He wrote several further serials including "The Dalek Invasion of Earth," "The Chase," "Mission to the Unknown," "The Dalek Masterplan," "Planet of the Daleks," "Death to the Daleks," "Genesis of the Daleks" and "Destiny of the Daleks." On the non–Dalek front, he also wrote the fifth *Doctor Who* adventure "The Keys of Marinus" and the Season 13 story "The Android Invasion." Nation was also a regular contributor to the Roger Moore series *The Saint* (1964–1968), producing six stories ("Jeannine," "Lida," "The Revolution Racket," "Sign of the Claw," "The Inescapable Word" and "The Contract"). He also wrote for *The Avengers*, and dreamed up "The Fox and the Forest" (1965) for the anthology *Out of the Unknown*. He is a cult figure not only for inventing the Daleks, but also for creating British television's other famous outer space sci-fi opus: *Blake's 7*. During the early '80s, Nation made the move to America and co-created the action-adventure series *MacGyver* (1985–89) starring Richard Dean Anderson. With all of this incredible work, Nation was one of the genre's most influential writers and philosophers.

Of philosophical interest in "The Daleks" is Nation's stance on the fight for independence. Though the Doctor is not usually one to advocate warfare, his position here is that some things are worth fighting for, even if "peace" is the victim. This would be a recurring theme not only in *Doctor Who* but also in *Blake's 7*, which featured another band of characters sparking revolution in a corrupt totalitarian society.

Nation passed away on March 9, 1997, after working in the television industry for over 30 years. His contribution to the genre should not be underestimated. The Daleks and *Blake's 7* are surely his greatest legacy. He will be missed, but his work will live on well into the future with the popularity of *Doctor Who* continuing into the twenty-first century. Curious viewers can take a good look at Nation's landmark work for *Doctor Who* since "The Daleks" has been released in a special two-tape edition ("The Dead Planet"/"The Expedition") from BBC/CBS-Fox video.

"The Daleks" teleplay was tweaked and reinterpreted in 1965 to serve as the basis of the AARU feature film *Doctor Who and the Daleks* starring Peter Cushing.

3. "The Edge of Destruction" Written by David Whitaker; Directed by Frank Cox & Richard Martin; Designed by Raymond Cusick; Part I: "The Edge of Destruction" Airdate: February 8, 1964; Part II: "The Brink of Disaster" Airdate: February 15, 1964; a.k.a. "Beyond the Sun"; a.k.a. "Inside the Ship"

SYNOPSIS: After their close encounter with the Daleks, Ian and Barbara are anxious to return to 1963 London, but the Doctor is no help since he seems unable to control the TARDIS. When the TARDIS inexplicably experiences a series of malfunctions, suspicions and fears grow among the shipmates. Convinced that his "guests" have manipulated the TARDIS to break down, the Doctor believes this act of sabotage is an attempt to force him to Earth. In fact, the malfunction is due to a built-in TARDIS self-defense mechanism which activates during emergencies. One of the controls on the main control column has become stuck and the TARDIS is locked on a course for the Big Bang, the very moment of creation!

GUEST CAST: None

COMMENTARY: Story editor David Whitaker's first writing contribution to *Doctor Who*, "The Edge of Destruction" is what is known in the television industry as a "bottle show" because it features only standing sets and regular cast members. Without expensive guest casts, sets and creatures like the Daleks to skyrocket expenses, a production team can frequently find its way back within budget limitations by producing an occasional bottle show. The original serial slated for position three in the *Doctor Who* roster was "Beyond the Sun," but for budgetary reasons that story was abandoned.

"The Edge of Destruction," the first *Doctor Who* serial shorter than five parts, begins what this author calls the "legend" of the TARDIS. Here the TARDIS is discovered to have a self-defense mechanism as well as a psychology. Through the years, the TARDIS would develop more and more into a critical "character," part of the *Doctor Who* ensemble. In future stories it is revealed that the TARDIS aids in the regeneration process of Time Lords ("The Power of the Daleks," "Castrovalva") and can even hear when people are talking about it. It has a distinct personality, and the Doctor frequently calls it "the old girl." Other ship functions include the HADS (Hostile Action Displacement System), seen in "The Krotons," and the automatic recall to Gallifrey, seen in "The War Games" and "Arc of Infinity." It is the jammed Fast Return Switch which precipitates the action inside the space-time capsule in "The Edge of Destruction."

This serial is also important because it brings several early character arcs to a head. The Doctor distrusts Ian and Barbara, Ian distrusts the Doctor, and Barbara is fed up with the Doctor's attitude. All of these problems make for some exciting interaction in the control room. These dynamic relationships would not last long after the departure of Hill and Russell from the series, however. Many of the Doctor's later companions would not be permitted to show the diversity of opinion and the tempers that Ian and Barbara brought to these early days. An attempt was made in the Davison era of the early '80s to bring some "hostility" back to the companions with the temperamental Tegan (Janet Fielding) and the treacherous

Turlough (Mark Strickson). Though Tegan was a moderately successful companion, Turlough's hostility actually hindered stories rather than added to them. In these early days of the Hartnell age, it is the relationship between the Doctor and his teacher friends that raises many stories above average.

Fortunately, both parts of "The Edge of Destruction" still exist in the BBC vaults and perhaps one day this serial will be made available on videocassette.

A final note: Like many early *Doctor Who* serials, "The Edge of Destruction" is often referred to by various titles, in this case, "Inside the Ship" and "Beyond the Sun." Although fan preferences on these things seemingly switch on a day-to-day basis, the "Inside the Ship" title is an unofficial one used before the advent of home video.

4. "Marco Polo" Written by John Lucarotti; Directed by John Crockett & Waris Hussein; Designed by Barry Newbery; Part I: "The Roof of the World" Airdate: February 22, 1964; Part II: "The Singing Sands" Airdate: February 29, 1964; Part III: "Five Hundred Eyes" Airdate: March 7, 1964; Part IV: "The Wall of Lies" Airdate: March 14, 1964; Part V: "Rider from Shang-Tu" Airdate: March 21, 1964; Part VI: "Mighty Kublai Khan" Airdate: March 28, 1964; Part VII: "Assassin at Peking" Airdate: April 4, 1964

SYNOPSIS: The TARDIS lands on Earth in the year 1289 and its crew encounters Tegana, a warlord who favors executing strangers. Tegana is stopped by none other than Marco Polo, the famous Venetian who is still in the service of the great Eastern ruler, Kublai Khan. The Doctor's group is taken to Polo's camp and Susan meets a lovely young girl, Ping Cho, who is traveling to Shang-Tu to marry a 75-year-old man. Susan is disgusted by the principle of arranged marriages, and she befriends Ping Cho.

The Doctor, Susan, Ian and Barbara join the voyage east to the city of Lop on the edge of the Gobi Desert, and finally to Cathay, but they remain suspicious of the war-like Tegana, an emissary from the Tartar ruler Noghai. Polo, however, has more on his mind: He has not been allowed to leave Kublai Khan's service since 1271, and he desires to return to Venice. He believes he has discovered the perfect way to leave Khan's service graciously: He will make a present of the Doctor's "flying caravan," the TARDIS!

During their long trek through the Orient, Ping Cho and Susan are nearly killed during a nocturnal sandstorm, the group almost dies of thirst in the desert, the Doctor challenges the great Khan to a game of backgammon with the TARDIS as the prize, and Tegana plots a nefarious assassination.

GUEST CAST: Marco Polo (Mark Eden); Tegana (Derren Nesbitt); Ping Cho (Zienia Merton); Chen Chu (Jimmy Gardner); Malik (Charles Wadi); Acomat (Philip Voss); Bandit (Philip Crest); Ling-Tau (Paul Carson); Wang-Lo (Gabor Bareker); Kui-Ju (Tutte Lemkow); Vizier (Peter Lawrence); Kublai Khan (Martin Miller); Foreman (Basil Tang); Empress (Claire Davenport)

COMMENTARY: Unfortunately, "Marco Polo" *Doctor Who*'s first historical adventure, has disappeared from the BBC film-video vaults. No episodes of this

A very young Zienia Merton guest-starred in *Doctor Who* episode #4, "Marco Polo," many years before assuming the character shown here, data analyst Sandra Benes in *Space: 1999* (1975–77).

serial exist, and at present it is presumed destroyed. Perhaps with a bit of good fortune, "Marco Polo," like the long-lost Troughton classic "The Tomb of the Cyberman" or the Hartnell mini-epic "The War Machines," will one day resurface and be made available. It is truly unfortunate that this story is lost because the production stills taken during the shooting of the episode reveal very high production standards all around. Not only would "Marco Polo" be an exciting serial for its sets and costumes, but also because it showcases an early performance by popular genre actress Zienia Merton as the betrothed child, Ping Cho. Twelve years after appearing in *Doctor Who*, this young actress achieved cult stardom by portraying Moonbase Alpha's data analyst, Sandra Benes, in two years of the Anderson series *Space: 1999*. It would certainly be interesting, and of note to fans of both series, to see a pre-*1999* Merton playing a role on *Doctor Who*. Merton also appeared in the BBC '70s production *Casanova*, as Cristina.

Mark Eden, Marco Polo in this adventure, has been seen in other genre television, notably in Patrick McGoohan's *The Prisoner* (1966) in the episode "It's Your Funeral." Before appearing on *Doctor Who*, Eden appeared in the third season (1960-61) of John Newland's occult sci-fi series *One Step Beyond* in the haunting episode "Signal Received." He is perhaps most famous for playing villain Alan Bradley in the long-running BBC series *Coronation Street*. Eden was interviewed about his *Doctor Who* experience by *TV Zone* magazine in 1993 and referred to his time on the series as "one of the happiest things I ever did,"[1] mainly because the cast was so friendly and he was familiar with director Waris Hussein.

John Lucarotti, author of "Marco Polo," returned to formulate other historical adventures for *Doctor Who* including one of the best, "The Aztecs." He has written for other sci-fi and fantasy series including the early '80s drama *Into the Labyrinth* (1981-82), for which he penned "Alamo." He also wrote "The Proton Storm," an episode of *Star Maidens* which aired on September 29, 1976.

The NBC time travel series *Voyagers!* (1982) revisited the era of Marco Polo and Kublai Khan to little effect, years after *Doctor Who*. "The Travels of Marco ... and Friends" aired on December 3, 1982 and took place in 1262 and 1275 respectively, almost 15 years before the Doctor's adventures with Marco occurred. In *Voyagers!*, the time travellers had to set time straight when Marco Polo failed to arrive in China. In *Doctor Who*, the mission of the time travelers was to stay alive, prevent the assassination of Kublai Khan by Tegana, and win back the TARDIS after the Doctor loses his backgammon game. Interestingly, in "The Travels of Marco ... and Friends," the time travel device of the Voyagers, the mysterious "Omni," is confiscated ... just as the TARDIS is confiscated in "Marco Polo"! A good lesson for temporal voyagers: If one is to encounter Marco Polo, one must expect the loss of one's time travel machine!

In fairness, *Voyagers!* was not the only American time travel series to explore the battle between Mongol hordes and the Great Khan after *Doctor Who* had already done so. Irwin Allen's *The Time Tunnel* took its travelers, Tony and Doug, to the same time period in "Attack of the Barbarians," a program produced three years after "Marco Polo" on *Doctor Who.*

5. "The Keys of Marinus" Written by Terry Nation; Directed by John Gorrie; Designed by Raymond Cusick; Part I: "The Sea of Death" Airdate: April 11, 1964; Part II: "The Velvet Web" Airdate: April 18, 1964; Part III: "The Screaming Jungle" Airdate: April 25, 1964; Part IV: "The Snows of Terror" Airdate: May 2, 1964; Part V: "Sentence of Death" Airdate: May 9, 1964; Part VI: "The Keys of Marinus" Airdate: May 16, 1964

SYNOPSIS: After the TARDIS lands near a sea of acid on an alien world, the Doctor, Ian, Barbara and Susan investigate torpedoes that have washed ashore on the beach. The travelers discover that these canisters once contained Voord Assault Troops. Inside a fabulous city nearby, the sojourners in time and space encounter a regal man named Arbitan, who informs them that they are on the planet Marinus. Technology on this world reached its peak over 2,000 years ago. Arbitan reveals a machine called "The Conscience of Marinus"; this massive computer, a judge and jury that was never unjust, once decided for the people of Marinus what was morally and legally right and wrong. Over many centuries, evil was eliminated from the planet, and from the thoughts of men altogether. Violence, war, fear, hatred, all negative emotions became virtually unknown on Marinus. This paradise came to an end when a Voord named Yartek invented a device known as an "immunizer." He gave it to his followers, and they were able to rob, cheat, kill and exploit.

Arbitan overcame the immunizer with the Conscience of Marinus machine, and five activation keys were taken from the machine and hidden in places of safety. Arbitan kept one key, but the other four are now hidden all across the planet and must be recovered before Yartek and the Voords get them. Arbitan has sent many people, including his own daughter Sabetha, to recover the keys, but none of the searchers have returned. After trapping the TARDIS in a force field, Yartek demands that the Doctor and his companions undertake a quest to recover the five keys of Marinus that can restore Marinus to a just society.

GUEST CAST: Arbitan (George Coulouris); Voord Soldiers (Martin Cort, Peter Stenson, Gordon Wales); Altos (Robin Philips); Sabetha (Katherine Schofield);

Morphus (Heron Carvie); Darrius (Edmund Warwick); Vasor (Francis de Wolff); Larn (Michael Allaby); Ice Soldier (Anthony Verner); Tarron (Henry Thomas); Senior Judge (Raf de la Torre); Judge (Alan James); Kala (Fiona Walker); Aydan (Martin Cort); Eyesen (Donald Pickering); Yartek (Stephen Dartnell)

COMMENTARY: Terry Nation's second writing effort is almost as historically important as "The Daleks" because "The Keys of Marinus" introduces the "quest" concept to the young series. Here it is the quest for the five keys that drive the plot forward. The idea of sending the Doctor and his companions on a search for an important "relic" or power source would be repeated as the theme for an entire season in *Doctor Who*'s later years. Season 16, known unofficially in fan circles as "The Key to Time," repeated this scenario with little variation. Instead of searching the planet Marinus and the cities of Morphoton and Millennium for the critical keys, however, the Doctor scours the universe with Romana and K-9 for the six segments of the White Guardian's "Key to Time." By the time of this year-long saga, the quest concept had already recurred in *Doctor Who* lore once in the 1974 stage play *Doctor Who and the Daleks in Seven Keys to Doomsday*. Written by *Who* story editor Terrance Dicks, this adventure concerned the Doctor's quest for the Crystal of Power. At the close of the story, when the Daleks arrived to take the crystal, the Doctor scattered the pieces again, just as he would later do to the Key of Time, to prevent it from falling into the hands of the Black Guardian in "The Armageddon Factor." Like "The Daleks," this early "quest" adventure is another template for the embryonic series.

Besides the quest conceit, "The Keys of Marinus" is noteworthy because it is the first time that the Doctor visits a planet with many unrelated cultures. Already he had met the Thals and the Daleks in "The Daleks," but those races were joined by their ancient war. In "The Keys of Marinus," Morphoton, Millennium, Arbitan's city and Vasor's sector all co-exist without being interconnected. They are diverse civilizations. This is an especially believable set-up since it is not at all logical to assume that an entire planet would boast only one culture. One of the critical credibility issues in *Star Trek* is that the *Enterprise* was always encountering worlds with only one culture. In "Patterns of Force" there is a Nazi world; in "Piece of the Action" there is a gangster world; in "The Apple" there are only the servants of Vaal; in "Bread and Circuses" there is a world based on the principles of the Roman Empire, etc. This is an unrealistic and simplistic approach considering the number of varied cultures and peoples that exist here on Earth. Nation deserves credit for recognizing this sci-fi fallacy, and offering a fictional world with the diversity of a "real" one.

The cultures seen in "The Keys of Marinus" are interesting to boot. The land of Morphoton, which is ruled by dictatorial, controlling "brains," is a science fiction notion that goes back to pulp magazines in the '30s. The city of Millennium, with its "backwards" legal system, is more perhaps interesting and less clichéd, although the concept of "guilty until proven innocent" has been seen in many series since this episode of *Doctor Who* first aired. The Cardassian legal system, explored in the Avery Brooks–directed second season *Deep Space Nine* story "Tribunal," is just one example of the same precept.

With "The Keys of Marinus," the *Doctor Who* creative team scored another innovative winner. In just five episodes, the series offered a stylistic introduction to the lead characters in "An Unearthly Child"; changed genre television history by inventing a non-humanoid threat in "The Daleks"; featured a dramatic bottle show in "The Edge of Destruction"; visited Earth's distant past in "Marco Polo" and started the tradition of the "quest" in "The Keys of Marinus." One would be hard-put to name another science fiction series featuring such diversity in plots and settings in its maiden year.

Although "The Keys of Marinus" has not been released on video yet, all six episodes of this serial exist. Perhaps it could be released on a double-tape set with "The Edge of Destruction."

6. "The Aztecs" Written by John Lucarotti; Directed by John Crockett; Designed by Barry Newbery; Part I: "The Temple of Evil" Airdate: May 23, 1964; Part II: "Warriors of Death" Airdate: May 30, 1964; Part III: "The Bride of Sacrifice" Airdate: June 6, 1964; Part IV: "The Day of Darkness" Airdate: June 13, 1964

SYNOPSIS: The TARDIS materializes inside an Aztec temple in the late 1400s. Aztec culture is Barbara's specialty, and she is thrilled with the opportunity to examine the culture, but Susan remembers the Aztecs too, and is horrified to think about the human sacrifices that were so integral a part of the civilization. Barbara believes that there was good in the culture as well as bad, and that it was a tragedy that everything was destroyed by Cortez. Donning an Aztec bracelet found near the body of the dead High Priest, Barbara is mistaken for the reincarnation of the dead High Priest Yitoxa by Autloc, the High Priest of Knowledge.

Tlotoxl, the High Priest of Sacrifice, soon suspects that this new Goddess, Yitoxa, is not what she appears ... especially when Barbara suspends indefinitely all human sacrifices. While the Doctor consults with the wise and lovely Cameca about another entrance to the temple where the TARDIS is locked away, Susan is schooled in Aztec bonding rituals and Ian is made honorary head of the Aztec militia. When the Doctor learns of Barbara's meddling in the society, he warns her that history cannot be rewritten. Barbara does not heed his warning, however, and soon Tlotoxl plans her untimely demise. While Tlotoxl plots bloody deeds, the Doctor must rescue Ian from a death duel, protect Susan from disciplinary action, and find a way back to the TARDIS. All the danger boils over on the Day of Darkness, at a ceremony of the eclipse, as Barbara finds herself presiding over a human sacrifice. The only problem is that the person to be killed is none other than Susan!

GUEST CAST: Autloc, High Priest of Knowledge (Keith Pyott), Tlotoxl, High Priest of Sacrifice (John Ringham); Ixta (Ian Cullen); Cameca (Margot Van Der Burgh); First Victim (Tom Booth); Aztec Captain (David Anderson); Priest Tonila (Walter Randall); Perfect Victim (Andre Boulay)

COMMENTARY: "The Aztecs" is perhaps the best-written of *Doctor Who*'s first-year serials. More than that, John Lucarotti's teleplay is among the best written and best executed stories of the entire 26-year run of the series! It is a tense story full of fine character moments and it espouses an excellent philosophical viewpoint. In addition, it overcomes the clichés inherent in many historical stories. In series such as *The Young Indiana Jones Chronicles* (1992), *The Time Tunnel* and *Voyagers!*, the main characters inevitably interact with "famous" historical characters such as Lawrence of Arabia, Adolf Hitler, General Lee, Lewis and Clark and Albert Einstein. On these shows, it is almost as if a traveler cannot go back in time without bumping into a person of incredible historical significance. Though *Doctor Who* would have its own share of this historical celebrity silliness ("Marco Polo," "The Gunfighters"), "The Aztecs" gains its strength not from highlighting historical characters, but by placing the philosophies of the past, particularly Aztec social mores, in opposition with those of the main characters who represent 1963 London. For that reason alone, "The Aztecs" is one of the most fascinating time travel stories in the history of television. Rarely has a culture clash been so well-delineated or involving.

Lucarotti's teleplay is brilliant in the way that it develops tension and points of view from act to act. Barbara, doubling again as the surrogate for the viewing audience, objects to human sacrifices in Aztec culture. She thus makes informed moral and "Christian" decisions at every critical point in the story. Amazingly, each such "correct" decision on her part leads to an unexpected reversal. Every time Barbara acts in accordance with her upbringing and values (*our* values!), she makes her own position, and that of her friends, weaker. When she attempts to stop human sacrifices, she is named a false goddess. When she tries to convince Autloc, a man whom she respects because of his gentleness and knowledge, that he should rule over Tlotoxl, it is Autloc, *not* Tlotoxl, who suffers. At the end of the story, Autloc leaves the city and his position of influence because he has lost his faith. Barbara tries to bring a better, more humane sensibility to the Aztecs and yet when she leaves, the despicable Tlotoxl is now more firmly in control than ever! Because Barbara meddles in history and makes no attempt to respect the reality or context of Aztec culture, she falls from a position of supreme authority to one of ultimate vulnerability.

The adventure culminates with the fake goddess running for the TARDIS, just feet ahead of crazed Aztecs out to kill her. These dramatic plot reversals make the story a tense and unconventional one. It is not often on television that central characters see how their decisions cause chaos and death. It is also rare that Christian beliefs are shown to be ineffective in the face of a different culture. The message of "The Aztecs" is clear: Christianity cannot be applied to a time and place with different historical traditions. For all these reasons, "The Aztecs" is one of the most thought-provoking and unusual serials in *Doctor Who*.

Another delight of this story is Barbara's central role. It is the female teacher, not the Doctor, who is the focus of all the action, and this makes for a different kind of show. In these early days of the series, the companions were truly three-dimensional people, not just walking, talking props to be rescued by the Doctor. It is fair to say that in "The Aztecs," the viewer learns more about Barbara as a person than one does in a whole season with Bonnie Langford's Melanie Bush or Lalla Ward's second Romana. Beyond the highlighting of Barbara, Lucarotti also provides plenty for the secondary characters to do. The Doctor's interlude with Cameca is a delight, and one of the few times in the entire 26-year history of the series that the Doctor is drawn into anything resembling a romantic relationship. That this relationship between older adults is treated in a mature and respectful fashion is even more unconventional than the story's overturning of Christian mores. Russell's Chesterton gets the lion's share of the action scenes and he proves again that he is up to the task, confidently dueling the Aztecs with his hands and his wits. If any main character is minimally slighted, it is probably Carole Ann Ford's Susan, although she is provided with a marvelous scene wherein she refuses to be married to a man she does not know (a nice carry-over from her relationship with Ping Cho in "Marco Polo"). Still, there are stretches of the episode where Susan is out of sight, locked up in a seminary.

One other factor that cannot be overlooked in the success of "The Aztecs" is John Ringham's performance as the Priest of Sacrifice, Tlotoxl. With his evil eyes, dangerous smile and obsequious attitude in the face of a goddess, Ringham creates one of the greatest *Doctor Who* villains of all time. In his eyes there is more menace than a hundred Daleks or Cybermen. His clashes with Barbara and the other time travelers are aflame with both menace and wit. Ringham would return to *Doctor Who* on two other occasions. The first is in the Hartnell-era fourth season opener "The Smugglers." The second is in the Pertwee story "Colony in Space." Neither appearance would prove to be as intense as this stand-out performance.

"The Aztecs," like many early episodes of *Doctor Who*, allows all of its characters, villains and heroes alike, to make mistakes. The Doctor is shown to be gullible, taken in by the wily warrior Ixta, a man who hopes to kill Ian. Barbara, led on by a feeling of moral superiority, is also revealed to be less than perfect. Sadly, this "human" aspect of the Time Lord and his companions would lessen over the years until everyone who traveled with the Doctor is automatically considered "good" and "wholesome" as an almost *a priori* fact. Even the treacherous Turlough of the Peter Davison era undergoes a complete (unbelievable) rehabilitation and becomes the Doctor's buddy after freeing himself from the influence of the Black Guardian. In these early, halcyon days, the faults of the characters propel the action, move the story forward, and tighten the drama. Should *Doctor Who* return to television, a new producer would be wise to review "The Aztecs." It is a serial alive with both danger and intelligence.

All four parts of "The Aztecs" are available on video cassette, but because "The Aztecs" is in essence an historical rather than sci-fi adventure, it is not among the Doctor's most popular stories. It should be.

7. "The Sensorites" Written by Peter R. Newman; Directed by Mervyn Pinfield & Frank Cox; Designed by Raymond Cusick; Part I: "Strangers in Space" Airdate: June 20,

1964; Part II: "The Unwilling Warriors" Airdate: June 27, 1964; Part III: "Hidden Danger" Airdate: July 11, 1964; Part IV: "A Race Against Death" Airdate: July 18, 1964; Part V: "Kidnap" Airdate: July 25, 1964; Part VI: "A Desperate Venture" Airdate: August 1, 1964

SYNOPSIS: The TARDIS materializes on an Earthship of the 2900s. Investigating their new surroundings, the time travelers realize that the space vessel is high in orbit around a planet known as Sense-Sphere, the world of the xenophobic Sensorites. The Sensorites, humanoid creatures with bulbous heads and unparalleled telepathic abilities, have put the human crew of the ship, including Capt. Maitland and a female officer named Carol, into a state of hypnosis. Unless a peace can be reached with the alien Sensorites, the humans will remain paralyzed forever. The Doctor, who has discovered that the TARDIS has also been sealed off by the psionic Sensorites, quickly sets about freeing the humans.

The Sensorites communicate telepathically with Susan and reveal that their world, Sense-Sphere, is rich in the vital mineral molybdenum. They fear that the Earth ship has arrived to steal the mineral and exploit the resources of the planet. This does not seem like an unrealistic possibility since ten years earlier another group of humans from Earth came to this planet to steal the mineral. During that visit, the Sensorites mysteriously began to die. They suspect that humans beings are responsible for this attempt at genocide, and they have responded by waging war against all new intruders with their mental abilities. The Doctor investigates further and finds that the Sensorites are being truthful. Their water has been poisoned by a deadly chemical known as "nightshade." The Doctor follows the poison back to the human survivors of the first expedition, survivors who even now are hiding beneath the Sensorite city.

GUEST CAST: John (Stephen Dartnell); Carol (Ilona Rodgers); Capt. Maitland (Lorne Cossette); Sensorites (Peter Glaze, Joe Grieg, Arthur Newall, Ken Tyllsen); Elders (Eric Francis, Bartlett Mullins); Commander (John Bailey); Survivors (Martyn Huntley, Giles Phibbs)

COMMENTARY: Like many *Doctor Who* episodes of later years, "The Sensorites" takes the unusual (for television) stance that mankind is the real menace in outer space. Man is depicted as a genocidal being in "The Power of Kroll" and "The Mutants," and as a ruthless exploiter of natural resources in "Colony in Space," "The Power of the Daleks" and "The Caves of Androzani." Indeed, long before the Sean Connery space opera *Outland* (1981) made pertinent points about the corruption of big business and offered the ad line "Even in space, the ultimate enemy is man," *Doctor Who* was exploring the same territory in arguably a more profound manner. In "The Sensorites," like the Pertwee–era "Colony In Space," it is the promise of mineral wealth, here molybdenum, that drives humans to kill innocent aliens. In this case, the human crooks have bitten off more than they can chew because they are faced with powerful, psionic aliens. Still, it is up to the Doctor to stop the exploiters from causing interstellar terrorism.

What is refreshing about this approach is that the aliens are not merely evil because the story demands it of them. On the contrary, the Sensorites have very valid reasons for despising mankind, and the serial's conflict arises from these reasons. The Daleks, on the other hand, have no real motivation for being so destructive and hateful ... they are just "evil." Later in the series, it is established that the Dalek creator, Davros, bred out all feelings of sympathy and genetically engineered aggression into the species, but this was a "retro" explanation for their antisocial behavior, not a natural one. The Sensorites then are justified in their actions, and considerably more well-rounded aliens than the Daleks could ever be.

The Sensorites would not be seen again in *Doctor Who*, although the theme of corporate corruption would recur in several stories, including the superlative Colin Baker adventure "Vengeance on Varos." All six segments of "The Sensorites" exist, but the serial has not been released on video as of August 1999.

8. "Reign of Terror" Written by Dennis Spooner; Directed by Henric Hirsch; Designed by Roderick Laing; Part I: "A Land of Fear" Airdate: August 8, 1964; Part II: "Guests of Madame Guillotine" Airdate: August 15, 1964; Part III: "A Change of Identity" Airdate: August 22, 1964; Part IV: "The Tyrant of France" Airdate: August 29, 1964; Part V: "A Bargain of Necessity" Airdate: September 5, 1964; Part VI: "Prisoners of Concierge" Airdate: September 12, 1964

SYNOPSIS: Ian and Barbara wish to return home to London in 1963. Susan begs them to stay, but they have made their decision. The Doctor is angry at their choice but he testily agrees to set the TARDIS on a trajectory for Earth. The TARDIS does return to Earth ... to France during the French Revolution! Ian, Susan and Barbara are soon captured by the militia and taken to Paris, where they are sentenced to death.

To rescue his friends, the Doctor masquerades as a Provincial Officer, and in that guise he soon meets the Tyrant of France himself, Robespierre! With the help of an English spy named James Stirling and a little-known French military man named Napoleon Bonaparte, the Doctor sets out to rescue his friends and escape this turbulent period in Earth's history.

GUEST CAST: Small Boy (Jean-Pierre) (Peter Walker); Rouvray (Laidlaw Dalling); d'Argenson (Nevill Smith); Sergeant (Robert Hunter); Lieutenant (Ken Lawrence); Soldier (James Hall); Judge (Howard Charlton); Jailer (Jack Cunningham); Webster (Jeffrey Wickham); Overseer (Dallas Cavell); Peasant (Dennis Cleary); LeMaitre (James Cairncross); Jean (Roy Herrick); Renan (Donald Morely); Shopkeeper (John Barrard); Danielle (Caroline Hunt); Colbert (Edward Brayshaw); Robespierre (Keith Anderson); Physician (Ronald Pickup); Soldier (Terry Bale); Barrass (John Law); Napoleon Bonaparte (Tony Wall)

COMMENTARY: "The Reign of Terror," the first season capper, is *Doctor Who*'s third historical adventure. The teleplay is perhaps less interesting than the compelling "The Aztecs," but it nonetheless points to the direction the series would soon head. Several stock formula elements appearing for the first time in "The Reign of Terror" are repeated in later historical adventures. First, the Doctor assumes the identity of an official to gain some authority over the native culture. Here he forges documents. In "The Massacre," he uses the same gambit, and he just happens to be a dead ringer for the villainous Abbot of Amboise. He would also imitate an important figure (a musician) in "The Romans." The companion prison stay, here at the Concierge, would also be repeated in adventures such as "The Highlanders." Indeed, the captured companions quickly became something of a mainstay of the *Doctor Who* series. Whenever there is a need for a quick action scene, the companions are simply captured and then liberated by the Doctor.

It is a shame that "The Reign of Terror" was chosen as the template for further historical adventures instead of the impressive "The Aztecs." In that story, it was a clash of cultures and social mores that provided the tension. In stories such as "The Reign of Terror," "The Highlanders," "The Crusades" and "The Massacre," it is simply the need to stay alive and stay free from the evil governmental authority running things which propels the plot. "The Reign of Terror" is first and foremost about escape, not about people, or even the French Revolution. While the French Revolution is a great era to explore, especially in the context of man's bloody history, this *Doctor Who* takes the travelogue approach to its drama. The era is merely a backdrop for a *Great Escape*–style story.

Doctor Who is not the only series to send time travelers into the French Revolution to face the guillotine. Irwin Allen's one-season series *The Time Tunnel* also told what was substantively the same story, right down to an encounter with Napoleon Bonaparte. *The Time Tunnel* adventure guest-starred David Opatoshu and was written by William Welch. Coincidentally, it was also titled "Reign of Terror." The 1981 feature *Time Bandits* also introduced its temporal explorers to Bonaparte, played with maniacal style by British thespian Ian Holm (*Alien, The Fifth Element, The Sweet Hereafter*).

For trivia buffs, *Doctor Who*'s "The Reign of Terror" does not represent the first time the Doctor and Susan have been to this time period. In Anthony Coburn's "An Unearthly Child," Susan opens a book entitled *The French Revolution*. She takes one look at it and comments that the author got it all wrong. This clearly suggests that the Doctor and his young ward have been to this locale before. Since dialogue in "The Reign of Terror" establishes that the French Revolution is the Doctor's favorite time period, perhaps it is only right that he should visit more than once. However, if he has been to this era before, how does that fact take into account the all-important "Blinovitch Limiting Factor," a time travel physical law mentioned in the Pertwee–era adventure "Day of the Daleks" and the Peter Davison story "Mawdryn Undead"? The "Blinovitch Limiting Factor," for the uninitiated, is a law which indicates that a person *cannot* keep returning to the same time period over and over again to meddle and change things.

Dennis Spooner, writer of "The Reign of Terror," returned to write other episodes of *Doctor Who* including the witty "The Romans" and the quasi-historical "The Time Meddler," about the Doctor's contact with another member of his mysterious time-traveling race. For a time during Season 2 ("The Rescue" through "The Chase"), Spooner served as the series' script editor. He was particularly successful in this capacity, and his era offered everything from tight drama in "The Rescue" to satire in "The Romans" to experimental surrealism in "The Web Planet."

Other than his work on *Doctor Who*, Spooner wrote frequently for many Gerry and Sylvia Anderson series. He penned six episodes from the first year of the Supermarionation hit *Thunderbirds* including "The Mighty Atom," "Vault of Death," "End of the Road," "Day of Disaster," "The Impostors" and "Cry Wolf." In 1963 he contributed eight teleplays to the Andersons' first outer space foray *Fireball XL-5*. These titles are "Space Pen," "Space Vacation," "Robert to the Rescue," "Mystery of the TA-2," "Whistle for Danger," "Invasion of Earth," "Faster than Light" and "Space City Special." Spooner's association with the Andersons also continued on the 1965 underwater spectacular *Stingray* (1964–65). He co-wrote "Treasure Down Below," "The Big Gun, "The Loch Ness Monster," "Stand by for Action," "An Echo of Danger" and "A Christmas to Remember" with Alan Patillo, "Sea of Oil," "The Golden Sea" and "The Ghost Ship" with John Kelly. He also wrote with Desmond Saunders "In Search of Tajmanon" and with David Elliott "The Invaders." All in all, Spooner wrote more than 24 stories in the sci-fi television genre in a span of two years, quite an impressive record!

Today, only four parts (1, 2, 3, 6) exist of the serial "The Reign of Terror." The remaining two parts have been destroyed by the BBC. There have been some rumors about the video release of the four surviving segments of the serial in a format similar to the Patrick Troughton story "The Invasion." The video release of that Season 6 serial is missing two of the eight episodes, but the story gaps are filled in by the narration of Nicholas Courtney, the Brigadier Lethbridge-Stewart. Hopefully "The Reign of Terror" will similarly resurface one day soon.

SEASON 2

9. "Planet of Giants" Written by Louis Marks; Directed by Mervyn Pinfield and Douglas Camfield; Designed by Raymond Cusick; Part I: "Planet of Giants" Airdate: October 31, 1964; Part II: "Dangerous Journey" Airdate: November 7, 1964; Part III: "Crisis" Airdate: November 14, 1964

SYNOPSIS: During a landing attempt, the TARDIS doors swing open. Ian, Barbara and Susan manage to close them while the Doctor completes a safe landing. To the horror of the time travelers, they find that they have been shrunken, along with the TARDIS, to almost microscopic dimensions. The TARDIS itself stands only one inch high! All that makes the situation tolerable is the fact that they have arrived on present-day Earth, Barbara and Ian's home. As the Doctor sets about to discover what has gone awry, Ian and Barbara investigate their surroundings.

The shrunken humans run across a devious plot being perpetrated by a wealthy industrialist named Forester. He plans to release his new insecticide, DN6, on the world market in just a few days. Its purpose is to cause crop stimulation in underdeveloped areas of the world. Unfortunately, the insecticide is poisonous to many forms of life on Earth. If the DN6 is used, worldwide disaster will result. Ian and Barbara watch in horror as Inspector Farrow is murdered by Forester before he can warn the world about this evil plot. Barbara is unwittingly exposed to the dangerous DN6 and Ian must brave the dangers of a giant world to save her life.

GUEST CAST: Forrester (Alan Tilvern); Farrow (Frank Crawshaw); Smithers (Reginald Barrat); Hilda (Rosemary Johnson); Bert (Fred Ferris)

COMMENTARY: "Planet of Giants" is a complete departure from the first season of *Doctor Who,* and a fresh take-off point from which to begin the second year. Instead of drawing on the lore of time travel, outer space or even historical elements, this unique story pulls ingredients from another favorite science fiction trope: the miniaturized human being! This story idea was executed earlier in Ernest B. Schoedesack's *Doctor Cyclops* (1940). In that film, an insane scientist named Dr. Thorkel, portrayed by Albert Dekker, reduced people to doll size and trapped them in his overgrown garden. The same idea was more imaginatively presented in the landmark Jack Arnold-Universal film *The Incredible Shrinking Man* (1957). Like this *Who* serial, that well-regarded film dramatized a miniaturized man struggling with "normal" everyday accoutrements such as telephones, pencils, kitchen sinks, insects, pins and dollhouses suddenly inflated to gigantic, and therefore dangerous, proportions.

Long after *Doctor Who* debuted its second sortie with "Planet of Giants," Irwin Allen introduced his take on the same material to America: *Land of the Giants* (1968-1970). This ABC-TV series starred Don Marshall, Deanna Lund, Gary Conway and others as passengers and crew aboard sub-orbital Flight 612, stranded on a distant planet ruled by giants. Like "Planet of Giants" on *Who*, the tiny people of the *Spindrift* were frequently called upon to stop dastardly giant plots such as bombings ("Doomsday") and assassinations ("The Deadly Dart"). Miniature people acting as "secret agents" also formed the basis of the Ziv series *World of Giants* (1958) and the scarcely seen British Gerry Anderson pilot *The Investigators* (1973).

In many ways "Planet of the Giants" is a bridge between the Arnold 1957 film and the Allen 1968 series as it is among the earliest teleplays to suggest that man can be an effective covert agent in tiny form. That is a very different conclusion than *The Incredible Shrinking Man* and *Doctor Cyclops,* which saw man not only undersized, but constantly under siege from the innumerable dangers of a giant world. The goal was always escape, survival and restoration, not the completion of a seemingly impossible mission. *Doctor Who*'s message is more uplifting in the sense that once the Doctor and Ian accept their handicap (their reduced size), they are able to overcome it and defeat Forester.

The miniaturization theme has recently been used for more comedic effect in the 1989 blockbuster *Honey I Shrunk the Kids* starring Rick Moranis, a movie which is certainly more about fantastic special effects and humor than any deep philosophy of life.

Doctor Who would feature the miniaturization scenario again in the Season 15 story "The Invisible Enemy," but the template there was not *The Incredible Shrinking Man* but *Fantastic Voyage*. The Doctor's nemesis, the Master, would also end up inadvertently miniaturized in the Season 21 tale "Planet of Fire," courtesy of a malfunction in his Tissue Compressor blaster.

Louis Marks, author of "Planet of Giants," wrote "Day of the Daleks" (1972) for Pertwee's third incarnation of the Doctor and "Planet of Evil" (1976) for Tom Baker's fourth. He also contributed two teleplays for the speculative British series *Doomwatch* (1970–72), "The Human Time Bomb" (1971) and "Cause of Death" (1972).

All three episodes of "Planet of Giants" exist, but the serial has not yet been released in VHS format in the United States The story was novelized in 1993 by Terrance Dicks and is #145 in the *Doctor Who* episode adaptation library.

10. "The Dalek Invasion of Earth" Written by Terry Nation; Directed by Richard Martin; Designed by Spencer Chapman; Part I: "World's End" Airdate: November 21, 1964; Part II: "The Daleks" Airdate: November 28, 1964; Part III: "Day of Reckoning" Airdate: December 5, 1964; Part IV: "End of Tomorrow" Airdate: December 12, 1964; Part V: "The Waking Ally" Airdate: December 19, 1964; Part VI: "Flashpoint" Airdate: December 26, 1964

SYNOPSIS: The TARDIS lands on the bank of the Thames River in London. Ian and Barbara are thrilled to be home, but the Doctor is agitated: The city seems ruined and abandoned. The weary time travelers soon learn that they have arrived in the year 2164 and that the nefarious Daleks have conquered the Earth! Worse, the emotionless Daleks have converted much of the human populace into mindless drones called "Robomen." The Doctor, Susan, Barbara and Ian join up with the London resistance, but time is against them. Very soon, the Daleks will complete their project in the mines of Bedfordshire, a project which will result in the total conversion of the Earth into a mammoth Dalek spaceship! While the Doctor, Ian and Barbara attempt to save the Earth and free the enslaved populace, Susan falls in love with a young resistance fighter, David Campbell.

GUEST CAST: Carl Tyler (Bernard Kay); David Campbell (Peter Fraser); Dortmun (Alan Judd); Robomen (Peter Badger, Martyn Bentley); Rebel (Robert Aldous); Daleks (Nick Evans, Robert Jewell, Kevin Manser, Peter Murphy, Gerald Taylor); Voices of Daleks (David Graham, Peter Hawkins); Jenny (Ann Davies); Jack Craddock (Michael Goldie); Thomson (Michael Davis); Baker (Richard McNeef); Larry Madison (Graham Rigby); Wells (Nicholas Smith); Slyther (Nick Evans); Ashton (Patrick O'Connell); Women in the Woods (Jean Conroy, Meriel Horson)

COMMENTARY: "The Dalek Invasion of Earth" marks the triumphant return of the Daleks to *Doctor Who* after their first appearance in the second serial. Like "The Daleks," this tenth episode is written by Dalek creator Terry Nation, and here he fully indulges in some nihilistic musings about human nature. Rarely has there been a darker or grimmer *Doctor Who* serial. There are two particular incidents that stand out as being especially devastating.

The first occurs midway through the story when resistance survivors Barbara and Jenny encounter "the women in the woods." These two women, filthy and starving, collaborate with the Daleks by sewing clothes for the slave population. Barbara offers them food and the two wretches gladly accept the gift. Then, almost immediately, the women inform on Barbara and Jenny, turning them over to the Daleks. This is perhaps the darkest and most unflinching look at human nature in the entire series. When the camera focuses on the pitiful half-filled sack of fruit the Daleks have proffered as "payment" for the lives of Barbara and Jenny, the writer's point is made abundantly clear: Some humans will sell out their brothers and sisters for even a meager sustenance.

The second scene is no less disturbing. It occurs in the mine at Bedfordshire where Jack Craddock, a human resistance fighter, encounters his robotized brother. Craddock attempts to spark his brother's memories by mentioning his sibling's wife. The roboman's only response is to gun down Craddock in cold blood. There is no moment of hesitation or self-doubt, no moment wherein forgotten humanity is half-recalled. Instead, the roboman kills with a frightening blankness. His human identity is gone totally, subjugated completely by an alien machine. This incident, courtesy of Terry Nation's typewriter, suggest that "quaint" human customs like family and love no longer matter in this futuristic world. In a sense, this scene is echoed in George Romero's *Night of the Living Dead* (1968). In that landmark film, the most foolish of human survivors are unable to deal with the fact that their loved ones have been converted into something horrible, the living dead. They continue to attempt to reason with the zombies, invoking pillars of the "old" society such as religion, family and love. As in *Who*, their reward is inevitably a brutal death.

In "The Dalek Invasion of Earth," like *Night of the Living Dead*, a new social order has been instituted. At the top of the hierarchy is the Daleks, and at the bottom is enslaved humanity. The humans who cannot cope with this, and the conversion of their brothers and sisters to mindless zombies, pay the price for their inability to accept the new social order. Interestingly, the relationship between *Night of the Living Dead* and *Doctor Who* does not end there. The feature film version of this very serial played on a double bill with *Night of the Living Dead* in many cities in 1968! Of course, by then the impact of this *Doctor Who* story had been lost by the change to color photography and the inappropriate addition of slapstick humor.

Beyond the dark look at human nature that permeates "The Dalek Invasion of Earth," this story has other values that make it an exceptional series installment. Not the least of these advantages is the extensive location shooting in and around London. Watching Dalek patrols cross the streets of London may not have the same impact on Americans as on the Brits, but try to recall the image of a flying saucer obliterating the White House, the heavily publicized central image of *Independence Day*, and one will have an idea of how powerful this image was in 1964. Perhaps

John Baxter, the author of *Science Fiction In The Cinema* (1970), assessed the texture and look of this serial best:

> The Doctor and his friends find themselves lost in a future London ruined by atomic war and inhabited by mindless slaves whose electronic helmets dictate their every move. Hunting the small group of uncontrolled humans, three automatons pace to the end of a pier, stand silent for a moment, then at the same moment turn their heads slowly to face the direction of their quarry. The grainy image and natural location, both reminiscent of news footage, convey a special horror.[2]

Baxter has hit the nail on the head with the final sentence. The location, the black-and-white photography, the "cheapness" of the film stock, the isolation of an empty London, and the general eeriness of this serial make it a television horror masterpiece. Again, *Night of the Living Dead* must be mentioned because the appeal of "The Dalek Invasion of Earth" is very similar in some important senses. Both productions gain rather than lose visceral impact with the same budget-saving tactics: hand-held wobbly camera action and grainy prints. They are both examples of a gritty, neo-realistic approach to cinematography: a nightmarish, hallucinatory version of reality. The scene in which Barbara pushes a wheelchair through London and a hand-held camera tracks her progress in closeup and long shot is a strange, surreal and unforgettable image. This is a dramatic occasion when *Doctor Who*'s limited budget actually plays in its favor. "The Dalek Invasion of Earth" is thus a gritty, realistic yet nightmarish peek into a compelling future world.

Interestingly, Nation's teleplay also recounts the birth of this unpleasant reality. His script recalls in detail the progression from human freedom to Dalek subjugation. A freedom fighter informs the captured Doctor and Ian how the Earth was bombarded by meteorites in 2154. After the meteors caused severe damage, a plague began and killed millions of people. Whole continents were wiped out, including Asia and Africa. The plague effectively divided the world into isolated communities. Then the invasion of the Daleks began in earnest and there was almost no resistance. Cities were burned to the ground, and other areas were ruthlessly occupied. This is an inventive but strangely "realistic" sounding scenario — an invasion by cunning enemies that appears first to be not an invasion at all. It is a chilling set-up for the story.

Nation's teleplay also brings the character of Susan Foreman into focus for perhaps the first time. In other episodes she has expressed independence, and refused to submit to a marriage not of her own arranging ("Marco Polo" and "The Aztecs"). Here that characteristic comes to its logical conclusion as Susan finally decides to stay in one place and be married. The scene in which Susan begs David to leave with her in the TARDIS is not so much an example of Susan's cowardice as of her inexperience. Susan wants to do what she has always done: run away with her grandfather to another world, another time. This is how they left things on their home planet, so is it any wonder that when things get difficult in other worlds, her first instinct is return to the womb of the TARDIS? Susan's character arc through the first ten episodes of *Doctor Who* takes her from homelessness and immaturity to self-discovery and, at last, a place that can be her home. This is a most satisfying journey, although one does mourn the loss of Carole Ann Ford, as she offered the series so much enthusiasm.

The only problem involving Susan's departure is the Doctor's line that she has chosen to plant roots because "she is a woman." This is certainly a sexist attitude, firmly in keeping with 1964, but it is nonetheless disappointing to see it played out on *Doctor Who*, a program that in so many respects was really rather forward-thinking. Despite this sexist barb, the final goodbye between the Doctor and Susan certainly tugs at the heart. It is a moment of true feeling and sentimentality, perhaps the most poignant in the series so far.

Less than satisfactory in "The Dalek Invasion of Earth" is the special effects shot of the Dalek spaceship cruising over London. Not to belittle the efforts of the special effects team, but the shot is positively amateurish. A spaceship that looks like a pie plate wobbles in front of a backdrop photograph of London, the wires suspending it painfully obvious. The miniatures inside the mine are also obviously models. And, the climax is rendered confusing by the fact that the explosion of the Dalek mine is stock footage from about five different explosions hacked together in a mismatched montage. As usual, the writing and acting on *Doctor Who* overcomes this weakness in optical effects, but one can always wish that the special effects moments were handled with a bit more panache.

"The Dalek Invasion of Earth" was rewritten and produced as the feature film, *Daleks: Invasion Earth 2150 A.D.* (1966). The original serial, far superior to the color-coated remake, is available in a special two-tape set from BBC/CBS-Fox video.

11. "The Rescue" Written by David Whitaker; Directed by Christopher Barry; Designed by Raymond Cusick; Part I: "The Powerful Enemy" Airdate: January 2, 1965; Part II: "Desperate Measures" Airdate: January 9, 1965

SYNOPSIS: Amidst the rocky mountains of the dead planet Dido, an Earth girl named Vicki tends to her wounded companion, Bennett, aboard their crashed spaceship. They have been trapped on this desolate world for some time, so Vicki is thrilled when her distress call is finally answered. Bennett suggests that the villainous alien Koquillion is behind this rescue signal, but Vicki soon learns that the TARDIS has landed on Dido. The Doctor is horrified that Didonian culture has been destroyed, but Vicki claims the Didonians killed the crew of her ship. The Doctor argues that the Didonians were a peaceful people and realizes that Bennett has been hiding a deadly secret about Koquillion and the true nature of the Didonians.

GUEST CAST: Bennett (Ray Barrett); Space Captain (Tom Sheridan); Koquillion (Sydney Wilson); Didonians (John Stuart, Colin Hughes).

COMMENTARY: Dennis Spooner's "The Rescue" is an intriguing mystery about a "vanished" alien society. In its personal rather than galactic dimensions, the story also makes a nice change of pace from the epic "The Dalek Invasion of Earth." Gratifyingly, this story is not nearly so concerned with action, war, or the fate of mankind. Instead, "The Rescue" focuses admirably on a personal tale of human deceit, as well as the introduction of Vicki, the charming Maureen O'Brien. Although Vicki is a fairly obvious Susan surrogate, O'Brien brings this character to life with a brand of innocence and charm all her own.

Three factors elevate the mystery aspects of "The Rescue" above the average. The first is that very "Whovian" conceit that humans are the *real* danger in space. Like Episode 7, "The Sensorites," "The Rescue" highlights the villainy of a thoroughly despicable human in the form of Ray Barrett's Bennett. Like the Sensorites, the Didonians are described as being friendly and welcoming. Nonetheless, they are destroyed by a human criminal out to line his own pockets. The final revelation of "The Rescue," that there is no Koquillion as such, just Bennett in a frightening alien mask (actually part of a Didonian ritual), highlights the evil of the human Bennett. He is a deceiver, a murderer, an opportunist and a charlatan. Thus it is plain that in *Doctor Who* man is not the evolved *uber mensch* of *Star Trek: The Next Generation.* Instead he is fallible, selfish and replete with twentieth century foibles. Of course, as the later *Doctor Who* adventure "The Ark In Space" clearly states, man is also an incredible creature with an indomitable spirit. It is rewarding that *Doctor Who* allows humanity to be simultaneously *both* of these things.

The second factor that makes "The Rescue" a good serial is the unique and emotional scene in which Barbara shoots down Vicki's harmless pet because it is an "ugly" alien that she thinks is attacking Vicki. This is another occasion in which the main characters of the series are allowed to make mistakes, or commit acts that make them less than heroic. Barbara reacted out of fear and ignorance in killing this creature, but by doing so the viewer learns so much more about her as a person. In the early days of the show, Barbara, Ian and the Doctor sometimes do the wrong things, and they end up hurting people. That reality is the essence, perhaps, of the human condition, and *Doctor Who* captures it in a way that *Star Trek*, by protecting its human heroes from fallibility, never manages. Mistakes happen, human beings learn, and a mistake does not mean that a person cannot be a hero too.

The ending of "The Rescue" is also fabulous. It is one of the best and most mysterious climaxes of the entire series. In the dark cavern of the Didonians, aliens materialize and kill Bennett. Who are they? Are they the spirits of the Didonians? Have they returned from the grave for vengeance? Have the Didonians just been hiding? Has Bennett inadvertently activated some kind of Didonian justice machine in the Hall of Judgment? Or is this strange "afterlife" a natural part of the Didonian life cycle? There is never any answer given for the sudden appearance of the two apparitions at the climax of "The Rescue." Their final act, deactivating the radio which will bring more humans to their world, also hints at something faintly sinister, but again no issue is made of the act. Is this merely a way for the Didonians to prevent further contact with human beings? This mysterious ending perfectly captures the puzzling nature of outer space and other worlds. *Doctor Who* would rarely take this "mysterious" approach to story resolution again, and that is another reason why "The Rescue" is a unique addition to the Whoniverse. In the

'70s, Gerry and Sylvia Anderson's *Space: 1999* would frequently feature enigmatic episode climaxes, but that only served to infuriate American *Star Trek* fans. Still, it is interesting to see *Doctor Who* stray into that enigmatic territory, even if only briefly.

At its essence, "The Rescue" is a simple tale about two people, a murderer and an innocent girl, trapped together on a desolate planet. That simplicity, along with the mysterious ending and hints of Didonian culture, make it a refreshing installment after the grand scale of previous stories. Because it features no real monsters like Daleks or Cybermen, the story is often unremembered or overlooked, but it is nonetheless a terrific addition to the *Doctor Who* roster. "The Rescue" is currently available on videocassette in a two-tape package with "The Romans."

12. "The Romans" Written by Dennis Spooner; Directed by Christopher Barry; Designed by Raymond Cusick; Part I: "The Slave Traders" Airdate: January 16, 1965; Part II: "All Roads Lead to Rome" Airdate: January 23, 1965; Part III: "Conspiracy" Airdate: January 30, 1965; Part IV: "Inferno" Airdate: February 6, 1965

SYNOPSIS: The TARDIS materializes on Earth in 64 A.D. While the Doctor and Vicki travel the Appian Way to Emperor Nero's palace, Ian and Barbara are captured and sold into slavery. Masquerading as a famous musician named Maximus Pettulian, the Doctor is to play his lyre for the notoriously unstable Nero. This causes a problem, as the Doctor has no idea how to play the lyre. Furthermore, the Doctor is mistaken for an assassin! Barbara and Ian also end up in the palace, and find that dangers are everywhere. Nero falls in love with Barbara, Christianity is on the rise, and Nero has concocted a deadly plan to build a new Rome. And then, the fires start....

GUEST CAST: Sevcheria (Derek Sydney); Didius (Nicholas Evans); Centurian (Dennis Edwards); Stall Holder Merchant (Margot Thomas); Slave Buyer (Edward Kelsey); Maximus Pettulian (Bart Allison); Ascaris (Barry Jackson); Woman Slave (Dorothy Rose Gribble); Nero (Derek Francis); Tigilinus (Cup Bearer) (Brian Proudfoot); Tavius (Michael Peake); Delos (Peter Diamond); Locusta (Ann Tirard); Poppea (Kay Patrick); Messenger (Tony Cambden)

COMMENTARY: Dennis Spooner's "The Romans" is perhaps the wittiest and wackiest of all the historical adventures seen on *Doctor Who*. Although it lacks the tension of "The Aztecs," it more than makes up for that deficiency with its exceptional wit and sly prodding of Latin literature. In many senses, the serial is an out-and-out hysterical Roman comedy, not unlike *The Aululuria* by Plautus. There are several typical Roman conventions featured in this story that turn it into an exceptionally literary production.

First there is the outrageous characterization of Nero as a vanity-driven fool and a blunderer (*à la The Aululuria's* Euclio). Also in evidence is the typical Roman preoccupation with sexual subterfuge, here seen in the unique love triangle of Nero's wife, Nero and the unlikely third, Barbara. The Doctor's audacious musical gambit to outwit the Emperor is also aligned perfectly with the precepts of classic drama and comedy. The Doctor plays to Nero's vanity. Since he cannot play the lyre, he claims that only the most talented and insightful of ears will be able to discern his music. When the Doctor then plays *nothing*, the egotistical Nero is unable to admit that he did not hear any music! There are also silly, slapstick chases through the Emperor's palace. Before "The Romans" is over, every schtick is given its shot; a glass of poisoned wine even changes hands several times.

All of these elements make "The Romans" a worthwhile addition to the *Who* canon. They also prove a basic fact about historical adventures on *Doctor Who*. The history stories *only* seem to work well when they have an unusual attitude or stance about the history they visit, when they have a philosophical edge. The edge in "The Aztecs" is the gap between twentieth century morals and Aztec morals. The edge in "The Romans" is the humor, sardonic wit and the allusions to classic literature. Historical adventures which merely plop the time travelers into a situation and force them to fight their way out of a prison offer no edge. No matter how good the period decor or the costumes, a historical adventure must have some substance that sets it apart. That is why "The Romans" resonates, and "The Reign of Terror" does not.

Amidst its humor, "The Romans" also finds time for character development. For perhaps the first time, it is out in the open that Barbara and Ian have fallen in love with another. It has been hinted at before and there has always been a bond between the teachers, but it becomes clear in "The Romans" that the relationship goes well beyond that. The early scene in which Ian and Barbara relax together in the villa and tease one another is a classic moment for these original companions. The Doctor himself runs through a different set of activities in this story as well. He engages in physical combat, a task usually left to the more sturdy Chesterton, and is surrounded by intrigue at the palace. Hartnell plays these humorous and action scenes with an understated grace. It is obvious that comedy comes naturally to this fine actor.

Beyond comedy and character-building, "The Romans" reiterates one of *Doctor Who*'s basic time travel canons. The Doctor unwittingly gives Nero the inspiration to burn Rome. According to the series, such an action is not actually rewriting history, so much as it is nudging it in the right direction. In other words, for history to take its "natural course," the Doctor had to be present in Nero's palace and inspire Nero to take that particular act. Therefore the Doctor is actually *causing* history, *not* rewriting it. This is a subtle distinction, but one worth making.

The Roman Empire has proven a tantalizing era to revisit for nearly all time travel television series. The Emperor Nero encountered time travelers again in Leonard Stadd's *Time Tunnel* entry "The Ghost of Nero." On *Voyagers!*, Rome was visited by Phineas Bogg and his friend Jeffrey in 44 A.D. in the adventure "Cleo and the Babe" by Jill Sherman (aired November 14, 1982), and again in 73 A.D. in the story "Created Equal" by Nick Thiel (aired October 10, 1982). Then there is the "Bread and Circuses" adventure of *Star Trek* which technically is not a time travel story, but nonetheless concerned a "parallel" Roman Empire that has evolved on a faroff planet. Even *Mystery Science Theater 3000* (1989–99) has visited Ancient

Rome. For a span of several episodes, Mike Nelson, the Bots, Pearl Forrestor, Prof. Bobo and Brain Guy find themselves in the court of Nero. In the final moment of the scenario, Prof. Bobo knocked over a lamp and caused the famous fire to begin. None of the aforementioned stories, with the possible exception of *MST3K*, have demonstrated the wit or humor evident in "The Romans," and they exist merely as straight-faced action-adventures.

"The Romans" is currently available on videotape courtesy of BBC/CBS-Fox in a special set with "The Rescue."

13. "The Web Planet" Written by Bill Strutton; Directed by Richard Martin; Designed by John Wood; Part I: "The Web Planet" Airdate: February 13, 1965; Part II: "The Zarbi" Airdate: February 20, 1965; Part III: "Escape to Danger" Airdate: February 27, 1965; Part IV: "Crater of Needles" Airdate: March 6, 1965; Part V: "The Invasion" Airdate: March 13, 1965; Part VI: "The Centre" Airdate: March 20, 1965

SYNOPSIS: Still dressed in Roman garb, the crew of the TARDIS is surprised to feel the craft being dragged down to a bizarre planet. The Doctor deduces that an alien force is holding the ship there, and the TARDIS is soon surrounded by giant ant creatures called the Zarbi. Soon the travelers flee the Zarbi and meet the butterfly-like denizens of the planet Vortis, the Menoptera. The Menoptera once ruled this world, but the peaceful Zarbi, under the influence of an evil life form called "Animus," have grown hostile.

The Menopterans plan an invasion to retake their world while Ian and a Menopteran friend named Vrestin encounter a mutant, wingless strain of Menopterans called the Optera. Vrestin and Ian set about convincing the Optera to join the Menopteran revolution, and the invasion begins. The Menopteran butterfly creatures swoop down from the sky and engage the primitive Zarbi in deadly combat. The battle goes disastrously and the surviving Menoptera soldiers, along with Barbara, hide inside the Menopteran Temple of Light. They formulate a plan to destroy Animus with a "living cell destructor."

The Doctor learns that Animus is located at the center of the planet's magnetic pole. It has harnessed the energy of the planet and has been pulling other energy sources (such the TARDIS) to Vortis so it can survive. The Doctor and Vicki are captured before they can kill Animus, and the Doctor is lead to the "Centre." There he meets his opponent face-to-face and sees that Animus is a giant, tentacled beast, a spider of sorts. Ian and the Menopterans rush to deploy the living cell destructor, but time is running out.

GUEST CAST: Animus Voice (Catherine Fleming); Vrestin (Roslyn DeWinter); Vrootin (Roslyn DeWinter); Hrostar (Arne Gordon); Hrhoonda (Arthur Blake); Prapillus (Joylyon Booth); Hlynea (Jocelyn Birdsall); Hillo (Martin Jarvis); Hetra (Ian Thompson); Nemini (Barbara Ross); Zarbi Operators (Robert Jewell, Hugh Lund, Jack Pitt, John Scott Martin)

COMMENTARY: "The Web Planet" is a tempting target. Many *Doctor Who* fans bash this serial with a vengeance; a 1998 genre magazine listed "The Web

Planet" as the Hartnell serial to "beware of." It is not difficult to see how this serial merited such criticism. It is slow-moving, badly filmed, loosely edited, and incomprehensible, many critics will argue. All of those criticisms may indeed be true, but "The Web Planet" is also a noble experiment, an attempt to do something *completely* different, at least from a visual standpoint. After all, "The Web Planet" showcases a visit to an utterly *alien* domain. The Zarbi, the Menoptera, the Animus and the landscape are totally removed from our reality. The surface of the planet looks like the Moon, the Menoptera are costumed actors who glide about on wires, and the Zarbi are life-size exoskeletons of insectoids. Any such ambitious attempt to dramatize a planet and its inhabitants in such bold non-terrestrial terms deserves at least the benefit of the doubt, even if the serial has too many slow moments.

By this point in *Doctor Who*'s history, the producers were obviously growing more ambitious and confident, and "The Web Planet" reflects their willingness to be brave. They decided to produce a story that was perhaps beyond the means not only of their budget, but also the resources of their the production team. Still, "The Web Planet" is an interesting and unique attempt to create a truly alien world.

One stylistic touch that contributes to this feeling of otherworldliness is the "texture" of the planet's atmosphere. The camera lens was smeared with Vaseline or jelly to give the environs of the Menoptera an unearthly feeling. This is an interesting technique that has been misperceived for 35 years. People just think the whole show is out-of-focus because of the serial's "hazy" appearance. Instead, the clever behind-the-scenes personnel were taking another step to assure that the show would have an alien "air" about it.

Other than this camera technique, "The Web Planet" is experimental in several ways. Non-humanoid aliens are again displayed. Here it is the ant-like Zarbi, not the Daleks, who are the featured villains. It is appropriate to restate that in 1964 the notion of dramatizing non-humanoid creatures was an innovative one, as "The Web Planet" was broadcast well before *Star Trek*, *Lost in Space* and other shows even existed. The Zarbi suits are unquestionably a departure from the ordinary. The ant suit covers an actor from head to toe, with a substantial part of the thorax hanging behind the person's body. The costumed person's legs extend through the underside of the suit to provide the creature's rear legs. The people portraying the Zarbi walk through the serial hunched over, in a kind of "crouching" position so as to hide the length of the human legs and to make the creature seem more insect-like. This is a great design for an alien, and it is very successful overall. The Menopteran suits, unfortunately, are not so good. The hood that makes up the head-piece is obviously sewn cloth, not fur, and the eyes are clearly slits that have been cut through the fabric. Thirty years ago this suit may have looked great, but it is doubtful. Still, the concept is valid, interesting and unique.

The execution of this serial leaves a lot to be desired as well. When the Menoptera fly down to the surface of their homeworld, the wires are clearly visible. And, when the door to the Centre is opened for the Doctor and Vicki, a stagehand can clearly be seen pulling on it for several seconds. The above-ground "walls" on the planet make up the only exterior detailing other than the rocky surface and the black, starry sky. These misshapen walls are weird and surreal all right, but they do not appear to be "sturdy." All these problems conspire to undercut the success of the story, even though something interesting was being attempted.

Also distracting are the alien voices devised for "The Web Planet." The Dalek voices were so successful that it probably seemed natural to duplicate that success. The Menoptera in this story speak in a kind of drawn-out, melodic hum. It is frequently impossible to understand what the Menopteran characters are saying! The Zarbi have no language to speak of, but they make a grating "chirp" sound that quickly drives viewers insane. For long stretches in the story there is nothing happening aurally except this irritating chirp.

"The Web Planet" is a serial that is hard to watch because of the "Vaseline" technique, hard to listen to because of the Zarbi and Menoptera voices, and unintentionally incompetent in execution. That does not leave a lot of territory in which the show can succeed. Unfortunately, the teleplay by William Strutton is the nail in the coffin. Every aspect of this episode is experimental *except* the story, which is a rehash of "The Daleks." Again, two races are fighting over a world. Again, the Doctor and his friends choose the right side and join the revolution. Again there are companion captures and rescues, and again the revolution is successful. There is nothing even mildly original in the text, only in its experimental visual execution. This is a strange reversal for the *Doctor Who* creative team because the situation is usually the opposite. Frequently the story is excellent and the low budget or weak production values undercut the success of the story. In this case, a familiar story coupled with all of the aforementioned problems makes for a notably weak tale. It is visually interesting and innovative, but looks alone cannot sustain a six-part, 148-minute running time.

Noted critic John Baxter, quoted in the "Critical Reception" section of this text, *raves* about this serial. Perhaps that is because an experiment, an attempt to do something bold and different, should never be criticized or demeaned. No one can deny that "The Web Planet" is a sincere effort to stretch the stylistic limits of *Doctor Who*. That it fails more often than it succeeds is not surprising; that it was attempted and produced in the first place is! Fans can judge this controversial episode for themselves since it has been released on videocassette.

In addition to "The Web Planet," author Bill Strutton also contributed two episodes to the Roger Moore series *The Saint* in 1964: "Iris" and "The Rough Diamond."

14. "The Crusades" Written by David Whitaker; Directed by Douglas Camfield; Designed by Barry Newbery; Part I: "The Lion" Airdate: March 27, 1965; Part II: "The Knight of Jaffa" Airdate: April 3, 1965; Part III: "Wheel of Fortune" Airdate: April 10, 1965; Part IV: "The Warlords" Airdate: April 17, 1965

SYNOPSIS: The TARDIS lands on Earth in a beautiful forest at the time of the Third Crusade in Palestine, circa 1191 A.D. King Richard of England (also known as Richard the Lionhearted), Sir William des Tornebu and William des Preaux have fallen prey to a group of attacking Saracens. The Doctor, Ian, Vicki and Barbara arrive in the midst of this surprise attack and save Richard. Unfortunately, William des Preaux and Barbara are carried off by the Saracens and held captive by El Akir, an Emir of Saladin. Akir is a vicious man who has made his name by murdering his own brother! Akir informs them that they will be taken to see Saladin soon.

Eager to save Barbara, the Doctor presents a plan of peace to Richard, who has grown weary of fighting. The Doctor suggests that the King's sister Joanna marry Saphadin, kin to Saladin. This marriage could help end the bloodshed. The Doctor's life is endangered when the Earl of Leicester reveals the plan early. Now it is up to Ian, recently knighted, to save Barbara, Vicki and the Doctor.

GUEST CAST: Richard the Lionhearted (Julian Glover); Joanna (Jean Marsh); Saladin (Bernard Kay); Saphadin (Roger Avon); El Akir (Walter Randall); William des Preaux (John Flint) William des Tornebu (Bruce Wightman); Earl of Leicester (John Bay); Ben Daheer (Reg Pritchard); Luigi Ferrigo (Gabor Baraker); El Akir's Harem (Sandra Hampton, Diane McKenzie, Vivianne Sorre); Saracen Soldiers (Anthony Colby, Valentino Musetti, Derek Ware); Thatcher (Tony Caunter); Chamberlain (Robert Lankesheer); Soldier (Billy Cornelius)

COMMENTARY: "The Crusades" is another straightforward historical adventure, one not very dissimilar from "The Reign of Terror." Its story of captures, rescues and intrigues lacks the suspense of "The Aztecs," the humor of "The Romans" and even the complexity of "The Reign of Terror." As an episode of *Doctor Who*, it is distinguished mainly by the fact that it features two very notable guest stars.

Making his first *Doctor Who* appearance as Richard the Lionhearted is Julian Glover. He would return to *Who* as a Jagaroth villain in the Season 17 episode "City of Death." He is more well-known for his many genre film appearances. He has menaced James Bond in *For Your Eyes Only* (1981), Indiana Jones in *Indiana Jones and the Last Crusade* (1989) and even Luke Skywalker in *The Empire Strikes Back* (1981). He also guest-starred in the tenth episode of *Space: 1999*, "Alpha Child" (1795), and the ninth episode of *Blake's 7*, "Breakdown" (1978). It is interesting that Glover's role in the last *Indiana Jones* film should closely relate to his first *Who* appearance since both involve the "crusades."

Also making the first of three *Who* appearances in "The Crusades" is Jean Marsh. She would return as companion Sara Kingdom in the Terry Nation Season 4 epic "The Dalek Masterplan." In 1989, she would make her final appearance, opposite Sylvester McCoy in the opener of the twenty-sixth season, "Battlefield." Outside *Doctor Who*, Marsh's genre appearances are as numerous and notable as Glover's. She menaced Dorothy and Toto as Princess Mombi in the underrated *Return to Oz* (1985), fought Val Kilmer for possession of a very special baby as Queen Bavmorda in Ron Howard's fantasy pastiche *Willow* (1987) and appeared on the Sylvia and Gerry Anderson series *U.F.O.* (1969), in the episode "Exposed." Outside of the genre, Marsh is probably best remembered for her Emmy-winning turn in *Upstairs, Downstairs* (1975).

It is probably fair to write that "The Crusades" represents the beginning of *Doctor Who*'s loss of interest in the "purely" historical adventures. More would follow ("The Myth Makers," "The Massacre," "The Gunfighters," "The Smugglers" and "The Highlanders") but few would have the impact of the early shows. By Season 4, the bloom was definitely off the rose, and all historical shows were eliminated from the format. In Season 19, 14 years after the broadcast of "The Highlanders," another historical show was produced by John Nathan-Turner. "Black Orchid," however, was more a pastiche of *Jane Eyre* and Alfred Hitchcock films such as *Rebecca* (1940) than an adventure in history. Still, since it did not feature any "sci-fi" elements, it has been categorized as a historical adventure.

Today only Episode 3 of "The Crusades" exists. This 25-minute segment can be seen on the videotape "The William Hartnell Years," available through BBC/CBS-Fox Home video.

15. "The Space Museum" Written by Glyn Jones; Directed by Mervyn Pinfield; Designed by Spencer Chapman; Part I: "The Space Museum" Airdate: April 24, 1965; Part II: "The Dimension of Time" Airdate: May 1, 1965; Part III: "The Search" Airdate: May 8, 1965; Part IV: "The Final Phase" Airdate: May 15, 1965

SYNOPSIS: As a result of a malfunction, the TARDIS and her crew become unstuck in time. The Doctor theorizes that the TARDIS has jumped a time track as a result of something called "Time Friction." No matter what the explanation for their condition, the Doctor and his friends find themselves in terrible jeopardy! They have arrived in a space museum on the planet Xeros as formless "ghosts," only to see their *real* bodies and the TARDIS on display in one of the museum's wings! The Doctor must somehow make things right before time catches up with the travelers and they all end up as lifeless exhibits! To add insult to injury, the travelers are becoming solid, and a war is going on in the museum between the harsh Morok Empire, led by the museum curator Lobos, and the indigenous Xerosian population!

GUEST CAST: Governor Lobos (Richard Shaw); Tor (Jeremy Bulloch); Dako (Peter Craze); Sita (Peter Sanders); Moroks (Billy Curtis, Peter Diamond, Ivor Salter, Salvin Stewart); Dalek (Murphy Grumbar); Dalek Voice (Peter Hawkins)

COMMENTARY: The "Space Museum" starts out powerfully with an eerie, otherworldly atmosphere and central situation, but the teleplay ends rather predictably being yet another planetary revolution story in the vein of "The Daleks" or "The Web Planet." The element of this story that succeeds best is not the retread conflict between Xeros and Morok, but the "time anomaly" hook which opens the tale. The Doctor and his friends find themselves staring down their own fate. If they do not discover a way to change the future and alter their destiny, they will spend eternity as frozen museum displays! This is a frightening scenario, worthy of the macabre *The Twilight Zone*.

The initial premise of "The Space Museum" is also an exploration of one of the most frequently pondered questions in sci-fi film and television. Can the future be changed? Among the films that have asked this question are *Battle for the Planet of the Apes* (1974), *Terminator 2: Judgment Day* (1991) and *Twelve Monkeys* (1995). The Doctor asks himself the same question here, since it is crucial to his continued existence. Can disaster be averted?

The second common sci-fi theme in "The Space Museum" is that of discovering your own death and attempting to alter it. Although this involves changing the future, it is more specific than that. It is a subgenre about the prevention of an unpleasant destiny. This is territory frequently explored by various generations of *Star Trek*, the most notable example being "Time's Arrow," the fifth season cliff-hanger on *The Next Generation*, which found Data discovering his own severed head under San Francisco. The same notion was used in "Visionary" in the third season of *Deep Space Nine*. In this case, Chief O'Brien had to prevent the destruction of the space station which he had witnessed when he "jumped" forward in time. This concept is more specifically reminiscent of "The Space Museum" since in both cases the main characters have jumped off the "railway" of time, and ended up witnessing their final disposition. It is to *Doctor Who*'s credit that it would deal with a concept as complex and adult as a "timeslip" before the first episode of *Star Trek* was written.

Diminishing the effectiveness of this *Doctor Who* tale is the fact that once more there are oppressors holding down the native population of a planet. This idea had already been expressed fully on *Who*, but would sadly be repeated many, many more times. This plot ingredient would recur in the stories "The Macra Terror," "The Dominators," "The Krotons," "Colony in Space," "The Sunmakers," "Underworld," "The Pirate Planet," "The Horns of Nimon," "State of Decay," "The Caves of Androzani," "The Twin Dilemma" "Timelash," "Vengeance on Varos" and "Time and the Rani." Although it is natural that some ideas will be repeated in a series that lasts 26 years, this premise is overused by Serial 15, let alone Serial 100!

Jeremy Bulloch, who plays the youth "Tor" in "The Space Museum," would grow up and reappear on *Doctor Who*. He returns in the eleventh season premiere, "The Time Warrior," as Hal the Archer. Of perhaps more importance, Bulloch played bounty hunter Boba Fett in *The Empire Strikes Back* (1980) and *Return of the Jedi* (1983).

Besides its nifty "hook" of the timeslip, this *Doctor Who* serial is also distinguished by the guest appearance of a frozen Dalek in the space museum! The Daleks would return in force in Episode 16, "The Chase."

All four episodes of "The Space Museum" exist, yet it has not yet appeared on the home video market. It would make an excellent addition to any collection, if only to see how early *Doctor Who* handles similar themes to more recent shows such as "Visionary" on *Deep Space Nine*.

16. "The Chase" Written by Terry Nation; Directed by Richard Martin; Designed by Raymond Cusick & John Wood; Part I: "The Executioners" Airdate: May 22, 1965; Part II: "The Death of Time" Airdate: May 29, 1965; Part III: "Flight Through Eternity" Airdate: June 5, 1965; Part IV: "Journey into Terror" Airdate: June 12, 1965; Part V: "The

Death of Doctor Who" Airdate: June 19, 1965; Part VI: "Planet of Decision" Airdate: June 26, 1965

SYNOPSIS: Having discovered the secrets of time travel, the Daleks track the TARDIS as it leaves the planet Xeros. The Daleks plan to destroy their greatest enemy, the Doctor, and they commit themselves to hunting him down through all of time and space if necessary. The Doctor and his companions learn of this fact from a kind of "time television," a time-space visualizer of the Doctor's invention.

The Daleks pursue the TARDIS to a barren desert world called Aridius, where the Doctor and his friends grapple with an octopus-like creature called a Mire Beast and ferocious sand storms. From there, the chase continues: The TARDIS is pursued to the Empire State Building in the year 1966, to the *Marie Celeste* at sea, and to Frankenstein's House of Terrors, an amusement park ride! The battle royale finally occurs on the planet Mechanus. A Dalek duplicate of the Doctor sets out to kill him, while the travelers face a slew of carnivorous planets. The Doctor, Vicki, Ian and Barbara head for the giant city of the Mechanoids.

The Mechanoids, spherical robots creatures, imprison the Doctor and his group in a prison cell with a human named Steven Taylor, who has been trapped on Mechanus for two years. He tells the new arrivals that 50 years earlier humans intended to colonize this world. They sent robot scouts ahead, but never made it here themselves. In the absence of humans, the robots repaired themselves and became "conscious." Now the humans are but specimens in a zoo.

The Daleks arrive in the city of the Mechanoids and the two robot races engage in all-out warfare and destroy one another. With the danger of the Daleks finally gone, Barbara and Ian realize that they have a functioning time machine to take them home. With the Doctor's help, the Dalek time machine takes Ian and Barbara home to London in 1965.

GUEST CAST: Abraham Lincoln (Robert Marsden); Sir Francis Bacon (Roger Hammond); Queen Elizabeth I (Vivienne Bennett); William Shakespeare (Hugh Walters); Television Announcer (Richard Coe); Mire Beast (Jack Pitt); Dalek Voices (Peter Hawkins, David Graham); Daleks (Robert Jewell, Kevin Manser, John Scott Martin, Gerald Taylor); Malsan (Ian Thompson); Rynian (Hywel Bennett); Prondyn (Al Raymond); Guide (Arne Gordon); Morton Dill (Peter Purves); Albert C. Richardson (Dennis Chinnery); Capt. Benjamin Briggs (David Blake Kelly); Bosun (Patrick Carter); Willoughby (Douglas Ditta); Cabin Steward (Jack Pitt); Frankenstein (John Maxim); Count Dracula (Malcolm Rogers); Grey Lady (Roslyn DeWinter); Mechanoid Voice (David Graham); Mechanoid (Murphy Grumbar); Steven Taylor (Peter Purves); Robot Doctor (Edmund Warwick); London Bus Driver (Derek Ware)

COMMENTARY: Terry Nation's third installment in the ongoing Dalek saga is substantially less interesting than the first two chapters. "The Chase" is just that, an extended chase through time and space with little rhyme, reason or plot substance. While moments of the show are quite droll, particularly the "House of

Terrors" and *Marie Celeste* sequences, other portions seem like pointless dead ends (the Empire State Building encounter, for instance). Still, the serial is finally redeemed by a striking final battle, and the touching farewell wherein Ian and Barbara leave the Doctor and return to their time.

It is easy to see that with this teleplay, Nation and the producers were attempting to perform a "one-up" on the previous Dalek encounter by offering new high points and Dalek set pieces. The first Dalek saga, "The Daleks," had been an unqualified hit. "The Dalek Invasion of Earth," with its London locations and the clever, unexpected shot of a Dalek surfacing from the Thames River, was even more successful. "The Chase" tries to supersede these earlier highs by showing a Dalek rise menacingly out of a sand dune. This moment does not generate exactly the same startling effect, since the Dalek presence on Aridius is already known to the characters, as is the miracle of their increased mobility. Indeed, the whole scene smacks more of a publicity shot than a moment which arises genuinely from the text.

Also, one cannot discount the fact that the more familiar one becomes with a monster, the less frightening that monster appears. Call it the law of diminishing returns. In "The Chase," there is nothing particularly scary about the Daleks. Their mystery and terror was preserved better in "The Dalek Invasion of Earth," which was a positively grim story. This story vacillates uneasily between action and comedy, and once you have an Alabama bumpkin mocking the Dalek trademark style of speech, it is hard to go back and make them a genuine threat. The American redneck is not the only one who ridicules the Daleks in this story. Ian gets to do a wicked Dalek impersonation by holding his nose and squawking out a few choppy sentences. It is rather difficult to maintain the mystique of the Daleks when so many characters are obsessed with mocking them.

There are other strange moments in "The Chase" that do not quite work. Since *Doctor Who* was essentially filmed "as live" back in these early days, there was no time for complex split-screen work. Accordingly, Hartnell's "evil" duplicate is portrayed by a double, *not* through special effects such as the split screen. That is understandable, but this double looks nothing like Hartnell! He is about three inches taller and substantially thinner than the Doctor!

Also, "The Chase" teleplay states that the Daleks have invented time travel, but their capsule is smaller on the outside than on the inside, just like the TARDIS. Does this mean that the Daleks have also discovered dimensional transcendentalism? Do the two discoveries necessarily go hand in hand? This is a point that the script should have addressed.

Where "The Chase" finally gains some momentum is in the final battle in the Mechanoid city. The robotic Mechanoids, impressive spherical creations, fight the Daleks in a tightly edited sequence featuring off-kilter closeups, live action movement, impressive tracking shots, fast zooms backwards and forwards, intense closeups of fire-spitting weaponry and even animated explosions. Also in the mix is model action in the miniature city of the Mechanoids, overhead shots pointed downwards into the battlefield that reveal Dalek and Mechanoid positions, wipes, fades and even superimposition. This war of the robots is an elegant dance of death, and a good enough reason to watch "The Chase." It is a little hard to believe, however, that human-built robots would pose any kind of serious threat to the highly evolved, generations-old Daleks. Still, the battle scenes pack a stylish visual punch.

Even better than the war of the robots is the closing five minutes of the show in which Ian and Barbara say goodbye to the Doctor. It is ironic that Terry Nation has now been responsible for sending off all of the Doctor's companions! He wrote "The Dalek Invasion of Earth," which was the end of Susan's tenure. He also wrote this eloquent farewell, and it could scarcely have been done better. The Doctor is angry and upset that his companions have decided to leave, and at first he refuses to help them. When Vicki convinces him that he must help, Ian and Barbara say their goodbyes and they head on their way in the Dalek time machine in a moment that can be best described as intensely emotional.

This farewell sequence in "The Chase" is ever so much more moving than the departure of a "Melanie" or a "Turlough" because these two London teachers have been established by the series as real people since the first moments of "An Unearthly Child." A wise person once said that you cannot truly love a person until you know their faults. That is certainly true in *Doctor Who*. Barbara's arrogance in "The Aztecs" and Ian's stubbornness in "An Unearthly Child" are just two examples of characters faults. Nonetheless, Ian and Barbara are beloved because they are real. They made mistakes ("The Rescue"), often showed fear ("The Daleks"), but on the whole were brave, intelligent and resourceful.

Saying goodbye to these "real" people in "The Chase" is a painful moment, especially when the Doctor declares that he shall miss them. The sadness of this moment is mitigated somewhat by a short, but surprisingly stylish and well-edited montage of Ian and Barbara gallivanting about 1965 London. Utilizing freeze frames and crazy angles to give the feeling of a world in snapshots, this scene is loads of fun, and even artistically challenging. It suggests that Ian and Barbara, now "frozen" in still-shot, have returned to the regular cycle of linear time — a life where linear moments are followed by linear moments. Of course, this lifestyle is a direct contract to the hustle and bustle, back-and-forth nature of the time traveling they shared with the Doctor. The montage is accompanied by cheery music and a final shot of the two teachers embracing on a bus ... but at the end of the show, the sense of loss is still an overwhelming one. Ian and Barbara were the first, and perhaps the best, of the Doctor's companions. Other companions came and went with regularity, but few demonstrated the same depth of personality as Barbara and Ian.

In the early '80s, there were plans for the Doctor to revisit his friend Ian in the serial "Mawdryn Undead." For undisclosed reasons, Russell did not opt to return to the program, and the Brigadier Lethbridge-Stewart (actor Nicholas Courtney) filled in. Though the Brigadier is always a delightful personality, there would have been something especially touching about the Doctor returning to visit his first companion. After all, the Brigadier never actually traveled through time and space with the Doctor, did he?

"The Chase" makes it clear that Peter Purves (astronaut Steven Taylor), introduced in the final segment of "The Chase," is intended to replace William Russell's Ian Chesterton as the secondary leading man of the series. This was necessary in the early days of *Doctor Who* since the primary lead, Hartnell, was not the physically capable man of action that later Doctors were.

Jacqueline Hill returned to *Doctor Who* in Season 18 in the episode "Meglos" (1980). Sadly, this talented, beautiful actress passed away on February 18, 1993, after fighting cancer. She was 62 when she died.[3] Her memorable portrayal of Barbara Wright certainly puts truth to the lie that the earliest *Doctor Who* females were nothing but screaming ninnies. With the possible exception of William Hartnell, Hill was arguably the strongest presence on the show. She brought to her portrayal of the Coal Hill Teacher such fine qualities as curiosity, kindness, strength and dignity. She was irreplaceable.

Also of passing interest in "The Chase" is the image of American President Abraham Lincoln delivering the Gettysburg Address on the Doctor's time-space visualizer. Although the time travelers do not realize it, also in the audience were the temporal adventurers of *Voyagers!* The episode "The Day the Rebs Took Lincoln" also featured this historic address. This era was also visited by *The Time Tunnel* in the two episodes "The Death Trap" and "The Death Merchant." It makes one wonder if there is some law of television time travelers that forces them all to visit the same eras.

An interesting discontinuity crops up from one event in this story. The TARDIS lands on the *Marie Celeste*. The Daleks pursue Ian and Barbara, and scare the ship's crew right into the water, thus originating the legend of the ghost ship. It is a great, funny moment in *Doctor Who* history. However, the *Marie Celeste* would recur as a reference to a "ghost ship" in no less than three other later *Doctor Who* stories! Jon Pertwee and Katy Manning mention it in "Carnival of Monsters." Tom Baker mentions it to Elizabeth Sladen in "The Android Invasion" (also written by Terry Nation) and Peter Davison and Janet Fielding refer to it in "Mawdryn Undead." Clearly, it is a bit of a *non sequitur* for the Doctor to refer to it in these follow-up circumstances and serials since he knows full well that *he* is, in fact, the cause of the ship's disposition! One would think he might share that little bit of knowledge with Jo Grant, Sarah Jane Smith and Tegan.

The Daleks would return to menace the Doctor in Season 3's "The Dalek Masterplan," the biggest, most spectacular story yet. "The Chase" is available on videocassette in a double-tape set called "The Daleks," along with the twenty-fifth season premiere "Remembrance of the Daleks," starring Sylvester McCoy.

17. "The Time Meddler" Written by Dennis Spooner; Directed by Douglas Camfield; Designed by Barry Newbery; Part I: "The Watcher" Airdate: July 3, 1965; Part II: "The Meddling Monk" Airdate: July 10, 1965; Part III: "A Battle of Wits" Airdate: July 17, 1965; Part IV: "Checkmate" Airdate: July 24, 1965

SYNOPSIS: Steven Taylor, the astronaut found on Mechanus and thought dead, has stowed away on the TARDIS and become the latest of the Doctor's traveling companions. The TARDIS sets down on a rocky English beach and the Doctor, Vicki and Steven venture outside the craft to investigate. They immediately find conflicting evidence about their "time" in the space-time continuum. Steven discovers a twentieth century wristwatch in the sand. This discovery clashes with the Doctor's assertion that they are in the year 1066 A.D., a fact confirmed by the presence of Viking helmets!

At a nearby monastery, the Doctor discovers exactly why this problem has occurred: A member of his own mysterious race, and a fellow time traveler, has arrived in England as well. This entity, known as "The Monk," has none of the Doctor's scruples about interfering in time. In fact, he is plotting to win the Battle of Hastings for King Harold with a supply of atomic weapons! Now the Doctor must battle the Monk to maintain the integrity of Earth's time line.

GUEST CAST: The Meddling Monk (Peter Butterworth); Edith (Alethea Charlton); Eldred (Peter Russell); Wulnoth (Michael Miller); Hunter (Michael Guest); Ulf (Norman Hartley); Viking Leader (Geoffrey Cheshire); Sven (David Anderson); Gunnar (Ronald Rich)

COMMENTARY: Dennis Spooner's "The Time Meddler" is notable in *Doctor Who* history because it is the first episode which pits the Doctor against a member of his own unidentified race. Of course, the name of that race is never whispered, never even mentioned in this story, either by the Doctor or by the Meddling Monk. In fact, the race's name and characteristics would not be highlighted until the final segments of the epic-length Season 6 finale "The War Games" starring Patrick Troughton as the Doctor. This is interesting because it means that Hartnell, through three years of *Doctor Who*, is never actually identified as a "Time Lord." Since that name was not ostensibly created until the end of Troughton's reign, it is possible that Hartnell never even knew the origin of his own character! Of course, when Hartnell returned in the tenth season of *Doctor Who* in "The Three Doctors," his character's identity was well known.

The seeds are planted in "The Time Meddler" that members of the Doctor's race should not interfere in the history of sovereign worlds. It is a rule that is obeyed by the Doctor about as frequently as James T. Kirk obeys the Prime Directive on *Star Trek*, but when the Doctor interferes it is inevitably to help those poor folks who are suffering the domination of evil aliens. What *Doctor Who* as a series never really addresses is the fact that the Doctor is hesitant to interfere in events *before* the twentieth century but he interferes unfailingly in situations after the twentieth century — in other words, "our" future. Does not he realize that someone's future is also someone else's past? That is one moral dilemma and time paradox that the series never really addresses.

Peter Butterworth would return to play the Meddling Monk in "The Dalek Masterplan" in Season 3. And, though all four episodes of "The Time Meddler" exist, the program has not yet been released on videocassette.

SEASON 3

18. "Galaxy Four" Written by William Emms; Directed by Derek Martinus; Designed by Richard Hunt; Part I: "Four Hundred Dawns" Airdate: September 11, 1965; Part II: "Trap of Steel" Airdate: September 18, 1965; Part III: "Airlock" Airdate: September 25, 1965; Part IV: "The Exploding Planet" Airdate: October 2, 1965

SYNOPSIS: The TARDIS arrives on a dying planet in "Galaxy Four." Before the travelers can investigate, a robot examines the TARDIS and then mysteriously heads into the brush. The Doctor, Vicki and Steven nickname the robot a "Chumblie," and soon find out that it is the enemy of two beautiful women in high-necked military uniforms, Drahvins 1 and 2. The time travelers meet the leader of the Drahvins, the icy Maaga, at her crashed spaceship. She warns that more robots, tools of a race called "The Rill," will soon arrive to capture them if they do not help her destroy the crashed Rill spaceship nearby.

Vicki is captured by the Rill, reptilian creatures who communicate telepathically. The Rill tell the Doctor that they offered to escort the Drahvins off the planet peacefully, but that the humanoids are more interested in killing than in cooperating. The Doctor also becomes aware that the Rill live in an ammonia environment and cannot breathe oxygen. There are only four of them left alive and their ship is damaged. With the Chumblies, the Doctor and Vicki help the Rill re-power their vessel. The Rill manage to escape, leaving the Doctor and his companions to face the Drahvin Maaga's wrath.

GUEST CAST: Maaga (Stephanie Bidmead); Drahvin Warriors (Lynn Ashley, Susanne Carroll, Marina Martin); Robot Chumblies (Jimmy Kay, Angelo Muscat, Pepi Poupee, Tommy Reynolds); Voice of Rill (Robert Cartland)

COMMENTARY: "Galaxy Four," the *Doctor Who* third season opener, is an interesting reversal on the Greek idiom that what is good must also be beautiful. Here the ugly (by human standards) Rill are generous, friendly creatures and the beautiful Drahvins are monstrous in their cruelty. As in the earlier "The Sensorites," *Doctor Who* seems to take a particular delight in making humanoids the villains in many of its stories. This is a rare philosophy on science fiction television. Most programs subscribe to the common '50s cliché that beings from other worlds are hideous monsters (*The War of the Worlds* [1953], *The Thing from Another World* [1951]) or invading Oriental hordes (*Buck Rogers* [1939]), *Star Trek*). The clever reversal on viewer expectations appearing in "Galaxy Four" also appeared on *Lost in Space* in its 1966-67 season in Barney Slater's "The Golden Man." In that story, the castaway Robinsons meet two aliens, a beautiful Golden Man and a hideous reptilian beast. In the end, it was the ugly creature who had the beautiful soul. In the '90s, the moral lesson that one should not judge a book by its cover is perhaps a basic one in sci-fi television, with such popular aliens as Odo on *Deep Space Nine* and Worf on *Star Trek: The Next Generation*, but it is again appropriate to establish that *Doctor Who* explored the notion very early in its long history (1965).

William Emms' Target Books novelization and a scant 4 minutes of footage are all that remains of "Galaxy Four," *Doctor Who* episode #18.

The Chumblies, the first "nice" robots to be found in the universe of *Doctor Who*, also make their only appearance in "Galaxy Four." Inside one of the suits is Angelo Muscat, the diminutive actor famous for his portrayal of the mysterious "Butler" to Number 2 in Patrick McGoohan's series *The Prisoner*.

"Galaxy Four" is the late William Emms' only writing credit on *Doctor Who*, but the schoolteacher wrote for other British genre shows, including Trevor Preston's *Ace of Wands* (1970-72). He wrote the four-part episode "The Mind Robbers" which aired in serial format on August 19, August 26, September 2, and September 9, 1970. Unfortunately, a more thorough analysis of Emms' work for *Doctor Who* is impossible, as all four episodes of "Galaxy Four" have been destroyed by the BBC. All that remains of the third season premiere is a-four minute clip. This is a tragic situation as "Galaxy Four," with its alien Rill, robotic Chumblies and evil Drahvins, would surely be of interest to *Doctor Who* fans and genre historians.

This episode was intelligent enough not only to suggest that "ugly" need not equal "bad," it also theorized that other life forms in the universe may not breathe oxygen. Here, the Rill live in an ammonia-based environment. In the '60s, this idea was nothing less than an inspiration. On *Star Trek*, *Lost in Space* and other programs, aliens always breathed the very same air that we do on Earth. *Doctor Who* went against that convention. In the '70s, *Space: 1999* also presented a race of non-oxygen breathers in the second season story "The AB Chrysalis." The aliens in that program breathed chlorine gas.

19. "Mission to the Unknown" Written by Terry Nation; Directed by Derek Martinus; Designed by Raymond Cusick & Richard Hunt; Airdate: October 9, 1965

SYNOPSIS: Space Security has sent special agent Marc Cory and his partner Gordon Lowery to investigate a mystery on the jungle planet Kembel. Cory discovers that the power-mad Daleks are behind the surge of military activity there. He learns that Dalek forces are planning to invade Earth, and the rest of the galaxy as well. Cory makes his report of Dalek activity and prepares to send it into space as a warning to his people. He and Lowery are killed, and Cory's recorded message, which warns the forces of Earth about the Dalek invasion, falls to the ground undiscovered...

GUEST CAST: Agent Marc Cory (Edward de Souza); Malpha (Robert Cartland); Gordon Lowery (Jeremy Young); Dalek Operators (Robert Jewell, Kevin Manser, John Scott Martin, Gerald Taylor); Dalek Voices (David Graham, Peter Hawkins)

COMMENTARY: This unique serial heralds the fourth appearance of the Daleks on *Doctor Who*. Perhaps realizing that "The Chase" had diminished these villains somewhat, Terry Nation plotted a massive return to pure evil and heavy drama with the massive "The Dalek Masterplan." "Mission to the Unknown" is the prologue to that upcoming tale. It is famous in *Doctor Who* history because it features neither the Doctor, his companions nor the TARDIS. This is the only such serial in the series history not to include the Doctor at all.

Sadly, this 25-minute episode has gone the way of "Galaxy Four" and many other early serials. It has been lost forever thanks to the penny-pinching practices of the BBC, and their policy of taping over old *Doctor Who* videos with new programming. "Mission to the Unknown" was novelized in 1993 by *Doctor Who* fan and historian John Peel as part of his two-book adaptation of "The Dalek Masterplan."

20. "The Myth Makers" Written by Donald Cotton; Directed by Michael Leeson-Smith; Designed by John Wood; Part I: "Temple of Secrets" Airdate: October 16, 1965; Part II: "Small Prophet, Quick Return" Airdate: October 23, 1965; Part III: "Death of a Spy" Airdate: October 30, 1965; Part IV: "Horse of Destruction" Airdate: November 6, 1965

SYNOPSIS: The TARDIS lands on the battlefield during the Trojan War just as Achilles and Hector prepare for their final combat. Stunned by the sight of the TARDIS materializing out of thin air, the Trojan Hector is caught by surprise and killed. The Doctor steps out of the TARDIS and is taken for Zeus, the King of the Gods, by the great warrior Achilles. He prevents the Doctor from returning to the TARDIS, which the Doctor identifies as his temple. Achilles claims that he needs the Doctor to boost the fortunes of Agamemnon and his men. They have been fighting here on the plains of Troy for ten long years and yet victory still eludes them. The Doctor goes along with the charade that he is Zeus, but the wily Odysseus of Ithaca has his doubts. He tells the Doctor he has two days to end the war or he will be killed.

Meanwhile, Vicki is captured by the Trojans and renamed "Cressida." The Doctor comes up with a ploy to end the war: an unlikely ruse called a Trojan Horse! After hostilities cease, Vicki remains behind with a Trojan called Troilus. Returning to the TARDIS instead with the Doctor and Steven is Katarina, the young handmaiden of Cassandra.

GUEST CAST: Achilles (Cavan Kendall); Agamemnon (Francis DeWolff); Cassandra (Frances White); Cyclops (Tutte Lemkow); Hector (Alan Haywood);

Menelaus (Jack Melford); Odysseus (Ivor Salter); Paris (Barrie Ingham); Priam (Max Adrian); Troilus (James Lynn)

COMMENTARY: "The Myth Makers," like "Galaxy Four" and most of *Doctor Who*'s third season, has been completely lost due to BBC's practice of destroying old films and videotapes to make room for more modern productions. It is painful to consider how much more money the BBC might make today could it syndicate or release on video Hartnell–era stories such as "The Myth Makers" or "Galaxy Four." Unfortunately, this short-sighted network procedure has not only hurt the coffers of the BBC, it has hurt *Doctor Who* fans around the world.

All that said, "The Myth Makers" appears to have featured some of the same style and wit as the earlier classic entry "The Romans." With the Doctor imitating Zeus, Vicki clashing with Cassandra, and the TARDIS functioning as a "temple," one can imagine that the story had its fair share of humor. Sadly, no new viewers will ever know this for sure. And no one will ever be able to watch Maureen O'Brien's departure from the series either. This is more than just a bit frustrating. The novelization of "The Myth Makers," by original serial author Donald Cotton, is certainly enchanting, as it is written from the perspective of Homer!

If nothing else can be said of "The Myth Makers" as an entry in the Whouniverse, it is at least fun to note that 20th Century–Fox's *The Time Tunnel* once more boldly went back in time to an era *Doctor Who* had already visited in its 1966 story "War of the Gods." In that story, Tony and Doug also met the legendary Odysseus.

21. "The Dalek Master Plan" Written by Terry Nation & Dennis Spooner; Directed by Douglas Camfield; Designed by Raymond Cusick, Spencer Chapman and Barry Newbery; Part I: "The Nightmare Begins" Airdate: November 13, 1965; Part II: "Day of Armageddon" Airdate: November 20, 1965; Part III: "Devil's Planet" Airdate: November 27, 1965; Part IV: "The Traitors" Airdate: December 4, 1965; Part V: "Counterplot" Airdate: December 11, 1965; Part VI: "Coronas of the Sun" Airdate: December 18, 1965; Part VII: "The Feast of Steven" Airdate: December 25, 1965; Part VIII: "Volcano" Airdate: January 1, 1966; Part IX: "Golden Death" Airdate: January 8, 1966; Part X: "Escape Switch" Airdate: January 15, 1966; Part XI: "The Abandoned Planet" Airdate: January 16, 1966; Part XII: "Destruction of Time" Airdate: January 29, 1966

SYNOPSIS: On the jungle world of Kembel, the Doctor, Steven and Katarina uncover the top secret recording made by special agent Marc Cory some months earlier. Another Space Security agent, a dashing young man named Bret Vyon, joins forces with the TARDIS crew to fend off the Dalek invasion plans. They learn the galaxy has been betrayed by Mavic Chen, the Guardian of the Solar System. He has turned over the precious metal "Tiranium" to the Daleks so they can complete work on their ultimate weapon: "The Time Destructor."

The Doctor steals the Tiranium Core of the Time Destructor after witnessing a clandestine meeting between the allied Dalek forces and Chen. With Steven, Vyon and Katarina, the Doctor escapes from the Dalek stronghold in a Dalek spaceship. They hope to alert the Earth authorities about Chen's traitorous deeds before it is too late. Katarina sacrifices her life en route to Earth after a deadly stowaway from the penal asteroid, Desperus, kidnaps her.

The Doctor and his friends arrive on Earth too late. Chen has fingered Vyon as a traitor to humanity. His agent, the fetching Sara Kingdom, shoots Vyon. The Doctor and Steven and Sara then stumble into a "molecular dissemination" device and are transported across space to the swamp world called Myra. There, Sara softens and reveals that Bret Vyon was her brother! When she learns of Mavic Chen's deception, she swears to kill him.

The Daleks arrive on Myra and the Doctor and his friends must contend not only with them, but with the eight-foot-tall, invisible "Vizzians," natives of Myra. Steven, Sara and the Doctor are then apprehended by Daleks. They turn over a false Tiranium core that the Doctor has rigged, and escape to the volcanic world Tigus, where they again encounter "The Monk," a meddling being from the Doctor's race, whom the Doctor thought was trapped permanently on Earth in 1066 A.D. The Monk has vowed revenge against the Doctor and chases him through time and space to Ancient Egypt. The Monk has secretly made a deal with Chen and the Daleks to capture the Tiranium Core and turn over the Doctor. Chen and a Dalek spaceship soon arrive in Ancient Egypt as well. Chen is eventually murdered, and the Doctor is forced to hand over the tiranium core to the Daleks.

After much intrigue in Egypt, the Doctor returns to Kembel and gains possession of the Time Destructor. He activates it, causing time to speed up. The planet Kembel begins to age and die under the ravaging effects of the time machine. The device is too powerful, however, and heroes and villains alike are caught in a temporal web of death...

GUEST CAST: Bret Vyon (Nicholas Courtney); Mavic Chen (Kevin Stoney); Sara Kingdom (Jean Marsh); The Monk (Peter Butterworth); Kert Gantry (Brian Cant); Interviewer (Michael Guest); Bors (Dallas Cavell); Lizan (Pamela Greer); Rould (Philip Anthony); Zephon (Julian Sherrier); Garge (Geoffrey Cheshire); Kirksen (Douglas Sheldon); Trantis (Roy Evans); Karlton (Maurice Browning); Rhynmal (John Herrington); Daxtar (Roger Avon); Borkar (James Hall); Celation (Terence Woodfield); Froyn (Bill Meilen); Scott (Bruce Wightman); Khephren (Jeffrey Isaac); Malpha (Brian Mosely); Hyksos (Walter Randall); Tuthmos (Derek Ware); Trevor (Roger Brierly); Dalek Operators (Robert Jewell, John Scott Martin, Kevin Manser, Gerald Taylor); Dalek Voices (Peter Hawkins, David Graham)

GUEST CAST FROM EPISODE 7 "The Feast of Steven": Sergeant (Clifford Earl); Policemen (Norman Mitchell, Malcom Rogers); Inspector (Kenneth Thornett); Blossom Lefavre (Sheila Dunn); Darcy Tranton (Leonard Grahame); Green (Royston Tickner); Knopf (Mark Ross); Assistant Director (Conrad Monk); Arab Sheik (David James); Vamp (Paula Topham); Clown (Robert Jewell); Cameraman (Steven Machin); Prop Man (Buddy Windrush); Prof. Webster (Albert Barrington)

COMMENTARY: In its original form, "The Dalek Masterplan" ran for a whopping 12 weeks and clocked in at six hours. This exorbitant length made it the longest serial in *Doctor Who* history up to that time. (The record would later be broken by the season-long Colin Baker epic "The Trial of the Time Lord.") Unfortunately, only bits and pieces of "The Dalek Masterplan" exist today. For many years, the entire story was thought lost until two episodes were recovered in 1984 by the Mormon Unification Church of Great Britain during a clean up of a London church.[4] Episodes 5 ("Counterplot") and 10 ("Escape Switch") have thus been saved in their entirety and released on the 1993 BBC/CBS-Fox videocassette "The Daleks: The Early Years." Other than those segments, there are but bits and pieces remaining. The events leading up to Katarina's death as well as various miniature effects shots equaling no more than six minutes are also known to reside in BBC vaults. This means that the bulk of "The Dalek Masterplan," like the two earlier episodes of Season 3, are gone, presumably forever.

"The Dalek Masterplan" is notable for its vicious, cutthroat qualities. Indeed, the effort to return the Daleks to their former level of evil is quite evident here. Although the Daleks lose in the finale, no less than three heroic figures are killed in the process. Katarina, Sara Kingdom and Bret Vyon all pay for this victory with their lives. These deaths are quite shocking, but they certainly prove the point that the Daleks are still a dangerous foe. Sara and Katarina are the first companions ever killed on *Doctor Who*. The only other companion to meet such a horrible fate is the Alzarian youth Adric. He would die in an explosion precipitated by the Cybermen in Season 19's "Earthshock." The deaths, particularly Katarina's, are stunning at this period in television history because it was a rarity for continuing characters to be murdered. In genre television, things like that almost never happened until Terry Nation's other sci-fi epic *Blake's 7* killed off a major character, Gan, in the second season story "Pressure Point." After that, Blake himself, Jenna, Cally and others were all "offed" by the show's producers! The show then made history again by killing off *all* the heroes in the final episode of the series, "Blake."

In America, such a massacre of leads did not occur until 1984 when NBC's *V*, sinking in the ratings, killed off the smart-talking secondary character Elias (actor Michael Wright).

Since Adrienne Hill appeared as Katarina only in "The Myth Makers" and "The Dalek Masterplan," it impossible to judge either the actress' or the character's importance to the *Doctor Who* series. In fact, all that remains of Hill's contribution to the show is a 30-second clip of her struggle with the Desperus criminal Kirksen! This is another *Doctor Who* tragedy since Katarina, as the first companion to lay down her life for the Doctor, is historically quite important.

The dark tone of the "The Dalek Masterplan" mirrored that of "The Dalek Invasion of Earth" in Season 2, but it had one element that the earlier serial had lacked. Episode 7, "The Feast of Steven," was a Christmas story that featured an entirely different cast than the rest of the serial and had nothing to do with the central plot. This was added to the already epic-length program when it was realized that the Christmas holiday fell right in the middle of the show's run. Feeling perhaps that Daleks gliding around murdering people might not be appropriate for the Yuletide mood, this half-hour comedy was inserted into the proceedings.

There are three important guest appearances in "The Dalek Masterplan." Jean Marsh, late of "The Crusades," returns to make her second *Doctor Who* appearance as the doomed Sara Kingdom. She plays a different kind of companion, one more outwardly aggressive and cool than many of the others seen thus far. She would have made a great addition to the *Doctor Who* cast since she seemed to have real chemistry with Peter Purves. However, as the "bad girl" she could not be allowed to live. The morality of the time insisted Kingdom had to be punished for the murder of her brother, Bret Vyon. Marsh, in addition to her troika of appearances on *Doctor Who*, has another interesting connection to the universe of the Time Lord. For a time she was married to Jon Pertwee, the third actor to portray the Doctor.

The second important guest in "The Dalek Masterplan" is Nicholas Courtney. Here seen as space agent Bret Vyon, he would soon return to the world of *Doctor Who* as the stalwart Alistair Lethbridge-Stewart. He would help Patrick Troughton's Doctor clean up the London subway of Yeti vermin in "The Web of Fear," get a promotion and return with UNIT in the Season 6 Cyberman epic "The Invasion." After all this hard work, Courtney became a series regular starring opposite Pertwee's Doctor in Seasons 7–11.

Lastly, Kevin Stoney appears for the first time in *Doctor Who* in "The Dalek Masterplan." He is seen here with pointed fingernails, pointed eyebrows and a shaggy white goatee. He would play another delusional megalomaniac, Tobias Vaughn, without these makeup touches in "The Invasion." Stoney may also be familiar to fans for his appearance as "Talos" of Delta on the *Space: 1999* Year One story "The Last Enemy." He also guest-starred in *Blake's 7* at least twice, in "Hostage" and "Animals."

Also in "The Dalek Masterplan," Peter Butterworth makes his final appearance as "The Meddling Monk." This character, played as a mostly harmless con artist by Butterworth, is clearly an earlier version of the Master. Both characters are renegade Time Lords bent on changing Earth history, and both characters are constantly plotting revenge against the Doctor. The Master is played by both Roger Delgado and Anthony Ainley in a much more traditionally "evil" fashion than Butterworth's rather more buffoonish Monk.

Episode 5 of "The Dalek Masterplan" introduces *Doctor Who* to its first race of "invisible" aliens, the hostile "Vizzians." A more friendly invisible alien would appear, so to speak, later in Season 3 on the planet Refusis in "The Ark." The Daleks would have a second encounter with invisibles in Season 10's *Planet of the Daleks*.

John Peel novelized "The Dalek Masterplan" in 1993 in a two-book series: *The Dalek Masterplan — Mission to the Unknown* and *The Dalek Masterplan — The Mutation of Time*.

22. "The Massacre" Written by John Lucarotti; Directed by Paddy Russell; Designed by Michael Young; Part I: "War of God" Airdate: February 5, 1966; Part II: "The Sea Beggar" Airdate: February 12, 1966; Part III: "Priest of Death" Airdate: February 19, 1966; Part IV: "Bell of Doom" Airdate: February 26, 1966

SYNOPSIS: The TARDIS lands on Earth in Paris of the mid-1500s. By the local architecture, the Doctor determines they have arrived between 1567-1577. He pins the date down further once they reach a pub and overhear that Protestant King Henri of Navarre and Catholic Princess Marguerite of Valois have just been married. The Doctor is now convinced that they have arrived just days short of the St. Bartholomew's Day Massacre of August 19, 1572! While Steven protects a young French runaway named Anne Chaplet from the Catholics who murdered her father in 1562, the Doctor masquerades as his own villainous double, the Abbot of Amboise ... a fire and brimstone clergyman sent to replace Cardinal Lorraine!

When the TARDIS is carted off to the Bastille and set aflame, the Doctor must risk revealing himself. Furthermore, he must prevent the assassination of the Huguenot leader Admiral de Colignay, steer clear of the villainous Abbot whose face he shares, rescue an apothecary named Charles Preslin, and escape from the St. Bartholomew's Day Massacre!

GUEST CAST: The Abbot of Amboise (William Hartnell); Admiral De Coligny (Leonard Sachs); Charles Preslin, the Apothecary (Erik Chitty); Anne Chaplet (Annette Robertson); Tavannes (Andre Morell); Gaston (Eric Thompson); Nicholas (David Weston); Simon (John Tillinger); Roger (Christopher Tranchell) Charles IX (Barry Justice); Catherine DeMedici (Joan Young); Toligny (Michael Bilton); Priest (Norman Claridge); Old Lady (Cynthia Etherington); Captain (Clive Cazen); Guards (Leslie Bates, John Slavid, Jack Tarran); Men (Roy Denton, Ernest Smith); Servant (Reginald Jessup)

COMMENTARY: Significant mainly for introducing the fast-talking Dodo Chaplet at its conclusion, as well as spirited actress Jackie Lane as the newest in a line of replacements for Susan and actress Carole Ann Ford, "The Massacre" is another John Lucarotti–penned historical *Doctor Who* adventure. Like all four predecessors in the third season, "The Massacre" has not been recovered by the BBC; all copies are presumed destroyed. This is yet another considerable loss to *Doctor Who* aficionados since this episode featured a double role for series star Hartnell. It certainly would have been fascinating to see Hartnell play not only the kindly time traveler, but the evil Abbot of Amboise.

It is fair to gamble that the quality of a genre television series may be judged by how well it handles the standards, common themes such as the old "doppelganger" cliché so prevalent in the its history. This perennial theme is visited in *Lost in Space* ("West of Mars"), *Star Trek* ("Mirror, Mirror," "The Enemy Within," "What Are Little Girls Made Of," "Whom Gods Destroy"), *Star Trek: The Next Generation* ("Datalore," "Allegiance," "Second Chances"), *Star Trek: Deep Space Nine* ("Whispers"), *Buck Rogers in the 25th Century* ("Ardala's Return") *Space: 1999* ("Seed of Destruction") and *Blake's 7* ("Weapon"). The doppelganger premise would return to the Whoniverse with more "alien" overtones, rather than the coincidental appearance of a lookalike seen in "The Massacre," in the Tom Baker–era stories "The Android Invasion" by Terry Nation and "Meglos" by Terence Dudley.

23. "The Ark" Written by Paul Erickson & Lesley Scott; Directed by Michael Imison; Designed by Barry Newbery; Part I: "The Steel Sky" Airdate: March 5, 1966; Part II: "The Plague" Airdate: March 12, 1966; Part III: "The Return" Airdate: March 19, 1966; Part IV: "The Bomb" Airdate: March 26, 1966

SYNOPSIS: As the TARDIS lands inside a massive space ark, new companion Dodo has caught a cold. Before long, the time travelers are captured by mute reptilian aliens called Monoids and are taken to the masters of the ship, the human Guardians. The Commander of the vessel tells them that the Monoids are a friendly race of aliens who came to Earth from a dying world many years earlier. The Doctor asks why humans left Earth in the first place, and the answer is startling: Earth is dying. It will soon be burned up by the sun. This ship is headed for the distant world Refusis, a planet 700 years away. This generational ship, this "ark" (as Dodo calls it) is carrying the entire population of Earth (animal, human and Monoid) in miniaturized form to a new life there. The populace will be restored to normal size and awakened when the Guardians, the custodians of the ship, reach Refusis.

Dodo's cold causes a strange disease to spread among the Monoids. The Doctor realizes that this future generation are experiencing the common cold for the first time, so he works quickly to develop a vaccine. His efforts succeed and the Guardians and Monoids are cured. Before leaving in the TARDIS, the Doctor, Dodo and Steven watch on the viewscreen as Earth tumbles from its orbit and is destroyed.

Some time later, the TARDIS lands again on the ark. Seven hundred years have passed and the ark is now nearing the planet Refusis. Monoids have taken over the ship, and the human guardians have become slaves. The Doctor and Dodo are captured by the Monoids and forced to join the first landing party on Refusis. There the Doctor and Dodo discover that the Refusis people are actually non-corporeal, invisible entities who cherish peace. The people of Refusis offer an ultimatum to the inhabitants of the Ark: They may live on Refusis only if Monoids and humans work together in peace. Meanwhile, a secret Monoid bomb waits silently to explode...

GUEST CAST: Commander of the Ark (Eric Elliott); Guardian Zentos (Inigo Jackson); Mellium (Kate Newman); Guardians (Paul Greenhalgh, Stephanie Heesom); Rhos (Michael Sheard); Manyak (Roy Spencer); Baccu (Ian Frost); Monoids (John Caesar, Ralph Corrigan, Edmund Coulter, Frank George); Maharis (Terence Woodfield); Yendon (Terence Baylor); Dassuk (Brian Wright); Venussa (Eileen Helsby); Refusian Voice (Richard Beale); Monoid Voice (Roy Skelton)

COMMENTARY: The concept of a generational space "ark" carrying the remnants of a race to another world has been one of science fiction's most enduring premises. This situation formed the premise of the Harlan Ellison space series *The Starlost* (1973) starring Keir Dullea and has appeared in innumerable other films and television productions as well. Perhaps the earliest film appearance of "the space ark" is in the Oscar–winning George Pal film *When Worlds Collide* (1951), which saw Earthlings fleeing the destruction of their world for the planet Zyra. Since then, the concept has also been evident in the 1979 *Star Trek* novel *The Galactic Whirlpool* by David Gerrold and the 1975 *Space: 1999* episode "Mission of the Darians." *Doctor Who* revisited the "ark" theme in the Season 12 tale "The Ark in Space." Interestingly, that episode also showed the ostensible end of the human race's existence on Earth. A space station, *Nerva*, carried all surviving humans, including the appropriately named Commander Noah, through space until the time when Earth could be inhabited again.

"The Ark" tells the story of man's final exodus from Earth to the distant planet Refusis. Mankind's final destiny would be revised yet again in the Season 21, Davison–era story "Frontios." That story confirmed that man did indeed travel to space after the death of Terra, but that he landed on a world inhabited by the evil Tractators. These alternate (and conflicting) final flights of humanity represent a major discontinuity in the *Doctor Who* series.

What makes "The Ark" a successful story is the fact that, like "The Space Museum," a new twist is put on the "revolution" story so oft-repeated by the series. Here, instead of a "timeslip," the conceit is simply a time-jump. The first half of the story occurs in one era, and the second part brings the Doctor and his companions back to judge the results of their earlier actions. This adds a different context to the adventure, and also shows the inevitable result of interfering in an alien culture. "The Ark" can easily be seen as yet another variation on "The Daleks" or "The Web Planet" since two forces are vying for superiority, and the Doctor has to make things right by choosing a side.

There are two other points of interest in this story, both involving the cast. Roy Skelton, who has been the voice of the Daleks from almost the first day of *Doctor Who*, gives voice to the Monoids. Actor Michael Sheard also makes his first appearance in *Doctor Who* in this serial as "Rhos." He has been a fixture in *Who* history ever since. He has had roles in "The Highlanders" (Season 4), "Pyramids of Mars" (Season 13), "The Invisible Enemy" (Season 15), "Castrovalva" (Season 19) and "Remembrance of the Daleks" (Season 25). This makes him one of the few thespians to have worked with five of the actors playing the Doctor: Hartnell, Troughton, Tom Baker, Davison and McCoy. Outside of *Doctor Who*, Sheard also played a doomed scientist killed by a tentacled space beast in the penultimate episode of *Space: 1999*'s first season, "Dragon's Domain." He also played a Federaton death squad commander in the *Blake's 7* third season adventure "Powerplay."

Paul Erickson, co-author of "The Ark," wrote two 1964 episodes of *The Saint*: "The Scorpion" and "The Damsel in Distress." He also contributed a story to the anthology *Out of the Unknown* in 1965, "Time in Advance." "The Ark" is his only teleplay for *Doctor Who*.

All four parts of "The Ark" still exist today, the first serial of Season 3 to have that distinction. It was released on video in 1999.

24. "The Celestial Toymaker" Written by Brian Hayles; Directed by Bill Sellars; Designed by John Wood; Part I: "The Celestial Toyroom" Airdate: April 2, 1966; Part II: "The Hall of Dolls" Airdate: April 9, 1966; Part III: "The Dancing Floor" Airdate: April 16, 1966; Part IV: "The Final Test" Airdate: April 23, 1966

SYNOPSIS: The TARDIS lands in the dangerous fantasy world of the Celestial Toymaker, a jovial figure who invites the travelers to "play some games" with him. As it turns out, the games are all vicious, malevolent ones. The Doctor is challenged to an enormously complex "Trilogic" game while Dodo and Steven endure Blind Man's Bluff, Musical Chairs, Toy Soldiers and Hopscotch, all against fiendishly clever opponents who take every opportunity to cheat. If they should be vanquished by any one of their competitors, Steven and Dodo are to become the eternal subjects of the smiling but thoroughly evil Toymaker.

GUEST CAST: The Celestial Toymaker (Michael Gough); Joe the Clown (Campbell Singer); Clara the Clown (Carmen Silvera); The Hearts Family (Peter Stephens, Reg Levers); The Dancing Dolls (Beryl Brabham, Ann Harrison, Delia Linden); Cyril (Peter Stephens)

COMMENTARY: "The Celestial Toymaker" is *Doctor Who*'s first excursion into a surreal world or domain "outside" the parameters of time and space. During Season 6, the Doctor would find himself in a not-dissimilar alternate dimension at the whim of yet another villain. That universe, "The Land of Fiction" is seen in "The Mind Robber" and, like the universe of the Toymaker, it features all kinds of traps to avoid and puzzles to solve.

Author Brian Hayles would soon become a regular contributor to *Doctor Who*. He would pen several other stories for the series including "The Smugglers," "The Ice Warriors," "Seeds of Death," "Curse of Peladon" and "Monster of Peladon." He is credited with creating one of *Doctor Who*'s most popular villains/sometime allies: the Martian Ice Warriors. He also has the distinction of writing stories for each of the first three incarnations of the Doctor. Outside of the Whoniverse, Hayles wrote "1 + 1 = 1.5" (1969), a drama concerning overpopulation in a future age Great Britain, for the anthology *Out of the Unknown* (1965–71).

Renowned actor Michael Gough essays the role of the Toymaker in this *Doctor Who* episode, testifying to the program's increased visibility and popularity. Actors of his calibre tend not to appear on "children's shows," especially in the '60s, but Gough made an exception to this rule and found himself going head-to-head with William Hartnell in a dynamic, different style of *Who* adventure. Gough returned to the world of *Doctor Who* in 1981 to play Counsellor Hedin, a treacherous Time Lord. In "Arc of Infinity" he had the distinction of not only sharing scenes with fifth Doctor Peter Davison, but also with the guest-starring future sixth Doctor, Colin Baker. Gough is perhaps most famous to modern American audiences for his portrayals of Alfred the butler in Tim Burton's *Batman* (1989), *Batman Returns* (1992), *Batman Forever* (1995) and *Batman and Robin* (1997). Before his genre appearance on *Doctor Who*, Gough also appeared in producer Herman Cohen's less-than memorable science fiction "monster movie" *Konga* (1961). His other genre appearances include roles in Wes Craven's *The Serpent and the Rainbow* (1987) and the television series *Blake's 7* ("Volcano"). Unfortunately, Gough's first *Doctor Who* performance cannot be adequately reviewed today as only the fourth segment of "The Celestial Toymaker" has been saved from destruction. This installment, "The Final Test," appears on the BBC/CBS Fox tape "The William Hartnell Years."

25. "The Gunfighters" Written by Donald Cotton; Directed by Rex Tucker; Designed by Barry Newbery; Part I: "A Holiday for the Doctor" Airdate: April 30, 1966; Part II: "Don't Shoot the Pianist" Airdate: May 7, 1966; Part III: "Johnny Ringo" Airdate: May 14, 1966; Part IV: "The OK Corral" Airdate: May 21, 1966

SYNOPSIS: The Doctor has come down with a terrible toothache and he needs the services of a dentist, so the TARDIS makes a landing in the blazing Arizona heat. The voyagers in time and space have arrived in the city of Tombstone in the year 1881! The Doctor passes himself and his compatriots off as traveling entertainers to the local marshal, one Wyatt Earp! While Dodo and Steven head to the Last Chance Saloon, the Doctor makes for the nearest dentist office, where he encounters the notorious Doc Holliday.

After a tooth extraction *sans* anesthesia, which has not been invented yet, the Doctor finds more trouble. He is mistaken for Holliday by Seth Harper, a thug who rides with the Clantons. Soon events spiral out of control. Johnny Ringo, a local thug, has also arrived in Tombstone to take his shot at Holliday. The Doctor, now facing Ringo and the Clantons, has no choice but to participate with Wyatt Earp in the famous gunfight at the O.K. Corral on October 26, 1881.

GUEST CAST: Wyatt Earp (John Alderson); Doc Holliday (Anthony Jacobs); Kate Elder (Sheena Marsh): Ike Clanton (William Hurndell); Phineas Clanton (Maurice Good); Billy Clanton (David Cole); Seth Harper (Shane Rimmer); Charlie (David Graham); Bat Masterson (Richard Beale); Johnny Ringo (Laurence Payne); Warren Earp (Martyn Huntley); Virgil Earp (Victor Carin)

COMMENTARY: "The Gunfighters" is famous in *Doctor Who* annals as the worst episode of the entire series. Some attribute the general low quality of the episode to the fact that the historical portions of the story are mostly inaccurate, particularly in regards to Johnny Ringo and Doc Holliday. Others revile the show as inherently silly, since British actors, famous for their "stiff upper lip," are hardly appropriate in the roles of loose-talking, fast-drawing American cowboys. A third problem might best be described as "tired blood." This is, after all, the eighth historical adventure in the series. By now, the formula for these forays into the past is well set: the Doctor is either mistaken for or intentionally doubles as someone indigenous to the time period ("The Reign of Terror": a provincial officer; "The Massacre": the Abbot of Amboise; "The Gunfighters": Doc Holliday), the companions are captured and rescued, and the time travelers escape after making an unusual mark on history (the burning of Rome in "The Romans," the building of the Trojan horse in "The Myth Makers").

In some cases, these historical stories are indeed quite entertaining, particularly "The Aztecs," but the fallacy of time travel stories is that nothing can ever really change and thus any interference on the part of the Doctor and his friends is bound to be minimal. No one can actually go back and stop the Kennedy assassination or, in this case, the gunfight at the OK Corral, so the purely "historical" stories have an element of the predictable to them. The stories that tend to be even less successful are those that involve one major historical event. These are doomed to failure not only because of their predictability and because viewers are more familiar with the "famous" events in history, but also because many viewers are more aware of historical inaccuracies. All this considered, it is easy to see why "The Gunfighters" is not *Doctor Who*'s most high-quality adventure.

The Old West in general, and the gunfight at the OK Corral in particular, has proven another irresistible destination for television time travelers. The cast of *Star Trek* was cast in the role of the Clantons in the third season episode "Spectre of the Gun." Although it was not a strictly time travel story, as the events were taken out of Kirk's mind, the setting was still a familiar one. Other time travels back to the West frequently cover the same territory. *Voyagers!* took its heroes to 1880 to meet Billy the Kid in the 1982 episode "Bully and Billy," and the adventurers of *The Time Tunnel* witnessed the fall of the Alamo in "The Alamo." A more innovative stance on the wild west scenario was seen in "Showdown With Rance McGrew," a 1963 *Twilight Zone* story by series creator Rod Serling. In that episode, a Hollywood cowboy (Larry Blyden) went back in time to the real "Old West" and discovered that quite a bit about his performance and his show's historical details were way off. Unfortunately, "The Gunfighters" did not learn from the example set by Serling's satire, and it is a Western reportedly full of overblown, hambone acting.

Shane Rimmer guest-stars in "The Gunfighters" as Seth Harper, and would soon become a familiar face, if not name, to sci-fi fans. He appeared in three James Bond films, *You Only Live Twice* (1967), *Diamonds Are Forever* (1970) and *The Spy Who Loved Me* (1977), in significant supporting roles. He also guest-starred in the premiere episode of *U.F.O.*, "Identified." He then returned to work with the Andersons again in the *Space: 1999* "alien foam" episode "Space Brain." Rimmer even wrote several scripts for the Andersons' Supermarionation series *Captain Scarlet and the Mysterons* (1967), including "Inferno" and "Expo 2068."

All four episodes of "The Gunfighters" exist, but the episode has not yet been released on videotape, perhaps because of its rather notorious reputation. The novelization by original serial writer Donald Cotton is a lot of fun, not only because one is free to imagine better sets and more appropriate actors, but because it is written from a unique perspective. The story of Dr. Caligari's (the Doctor's) interference at the OK Corral is remembered to a journalist by Doc Holliday on his deathbed! This perspective makes for some amusing and witty writing.

The gunfight at the OK Corral scenario dramatized here by *Who* was recently given the big-screen, big-budget treatment in two Hollywood films: *Tombstone* (1993), starring Kurt Russell as Wyatt Earp, and *Wyatt Earp,* (1993) starring Kevin Costner. True to Hollywood tradition, both of versions played fast and loose with historical accuracy, making "The Gunfighters" in hindsight seem a little less embarrassing.

26. "The Savages" Written by Ian Stuart Black; Directed by Christopher Barry; Designed by Stuart Walker; Parts I–IV; Airdates: May 28, June 4, 11, 18, 1966

SYNOPSIS: The Doctor, Dodo and Steven learn that the civilization on a new planet is split into two diverse factions: the healthy, athletic Elders and the frightened, weak Savages. The City of the Elders is led by a man named Jano. He is obviously part of an "upper class" which possesses all the wealth, technology and knowledge of the world. The Savages, on the other hand, are treated as subhumans with no rights whatsoever. Jano insists the Savages are primitive creatures who should not even be considered life forms by advanced standards. Dodo finds her way into a laboratory and discovers that there is a form of exploitation occurring. The scientist Senta has been transferring the life energy of the Savages into the Elders. This life force drain enables the Elders to live longer and remain vigorous at the expense of the Savages!

When the Doctor protests about the exploitation of the Savages, he is strapped to the soul draining machine himself...

GUEST CAST: Jano (Frederick Jaeger); Avon (Robert Sidaway); Chal (Ewen Solon); Tor (Patrick Godfrey); Exorse (Geoffrey Frederick) Edal (Peter Thomas); Flower (Kay Patrick); Nanina (Clare Jenkins); Wylda (Edward Caddic); Senta (Norman Henry); Savage (John Dillon); Assistants (Christopher Debham, Tony Holland, Andrew Lodge); Guard (Tim Goodman)

COMMENTARY: Ian Stuart Black's first writing assignment on *Doctor Who* introduces the concept of the splintered culture to the series. Although warring cultures had been seen in other stories ("The Daleks," "The Web Planet," "The Space Museum," "The Ark"), the planet of the savages is one that has splintered into two social orders. The story of one people split into dual, duelling societies by technology, values or race is one that would return to *Doctor Who* frequently. The same set-up introduced the popular companion Leela to the series in 1977 in "The Face of Evil." There, the warriors of the "Sevateem" (Survey Team) and the "Tesh" (Technicians) were once part of a homogenous spaceship crew until after many generations their cultures split into strange sects. This same scenario surfaced in the John Boorman–directed 2293 adventure *Zardoz* (1973), which starred Sean Connery as a "savage" Exterminator who learned the truth of both "The Vortex" and the intellectual society that dwelled within it while his own people suffered in barbaric conditions on the world's surface. This type of story seems particularly appealing to the British, and it has also appeared on several *Blake's 7* episodes including the third season episode "Powerplay" and the fourth season adventure "Power." In both those stories, however, the splintered society was separated along lines of sex.

Most often, the splintered society story has been used to expose the dangers of racism or a class society. In "The Savages," it is the treatment of the Savages as subhumans that sparks the righteous indignation and the lesson in morality. *Star Trek* would cover the same territory in "The Cloud Minders," in which the world of Stratos was split between the haves and the have-nots (called Troglytes). On *Who*, the Elders were literally exploiting the physiology of the Savages, draining them of their vitality, while in the *Star Trek* story the Troglytes were being exploited as slave labor.

Ian Stuart Black returned to the Whoniverse to formulate two other episodes: "The Macra Terror," another dark tale of exploitation, and "The War Machines," about the dangers of artificial intelligence. Before working on *Doctor Who*, he penned several episodes of the television series *The Invisible Man* (1959-60) including "Odds Against Death" with co-author Stanley Mann, "Jailbreak," "Bank Raid," "Point of Destruction," "The Vanishing Evidence," "The Prize," "Flight In Darkness," "The Gun Runners," "The White Rabbit," "Man in Power" and "Shadow Bomb." After his work on *Doctor Who*, Black continued to toil in the genre, contributing a teleplay entitled "Another Little Drink" to the Verity Lambert series *Adam Adamant Lives!* (1966-67), a program that in more than one sense is the spiritual ancestor of the hit comedy *Austin Powers* films. In the mid-1970s, Black was also the scribe for nearly half the episodes of the short-lived outer space series *Star Maidens*. His talents were employed in "The Trial," "Test for Love," "The Perfect Couple," "What Have They Done to the Rain?" and "Creatures of the Mind."

"The Savages" serves as the farewell episode to Peter Purves as Steven Taylor. Like Katarina's exit, "The Dalek Masterplan," this departure from the series is today mostly unheralded, since none of the serial "The Savages" survives. Even more depressingly, much of Taylor's era with the Doctor is missing because of the same situation. "Galaxy Four," "The Myth Makers," all but two segments of "The Dalek Masterplan," "The Massacre" and all but one episode of "The Celestial Toymaker" are lost forever. That leaves viewers the chance to see Purves play his part only in the last episode of "The Chase," "The Time Meddler," "The Ark" and "The Gunfighters." Of those stories, only "The Chase" and "The Ark" have been released on videotape thus far.

27. "The War Machines" Written by Ian Stuart Black; Directed by Michael Ferguson; Designed by Raymond London; Parts I–IV; Airdates: June 25, July 2, 9, 16, 1966

SYNOPSIS: The TARDIS arrives on Earth in 1966, and Dodo is thrilled to return home. However, when the duo hits the streets of London, the Doctor immediately senses something evil emanating from the giant new Post Office Tower. He soon meets Prof. Brett, who has designed the world's first supercomputer: W.O.T.A.N. (Will Operating Thought Analogue). Brett boasts it is the most sophisticated computer in history, and he also informs the Doctor that W.O.T.A.N. is about to be linked with a worldwide network of smaller, less-advanced machines. There is more to it even than that, however: The super machine has a central intelligence with a colossal memory data storage facility, and it is able to "think."

Prof. Brett's secretary Polly Lopez and a sailor named Ben Jackson join up with the Doctor when he suspects that W.O.T.A.N. is telepathically controlling humans and draining information from them, including Dodo. Meanwhile,

W.O.T.A.N. is preparing to wage war, and it sets about constructing smaller, mobile, *armed* versions of itself to take over London, Washington D.C., and eventually the world! W.O.T.A.N. has decided that it is better suited to run the world than man is, and it will obliterate mankind if necessary to satisfy its thirst for domination.

GUEST CAST: Prof. Brett (John Karvey); Major Krimpton (John Cater); Tramp (Desmond Cullum-Jones); Major Greene (Alan Curtis); Kitty (Sandra Bryant); Flash (Ewan Proctor); Sir Charles (William Mervyn); Captain (John Rolfe); Corporal (Frank Jarvis); Sergeant (Robin Dawson); Journalists (John Doye, Ric Felgate, Dwight Whylie, Carl Conway); Mechanic (Edward Colliver); Man in Phone Box (John Slavid); War Machine Operator (Gerald Taylor); Kenneth Kendall (Himself)

COMMENTARY: "The War Machines" is even more timely a *Doctor Who* serial now than it was in June and July of 1966 when it originally aired in Great Britain. In those days, a computer with the ability to think was merely a construct of science fiction writers, underline the word *fiction*. In the '90s, machines like W.O.T.A.N. indeed seem much closer to fact than to fantasy. After all, the IBM supercomputer named "Deep Blue" defeated world chess champion Garry Kasparov on Sunday, May 11, 1997, after only 19 moves. The thinking computer, once exclusively the territory of horror or space fantasies, has now crossed over to become part of the tapestry of our "real" lives! Like the imaginary W.O.T.A.N., this advanced IBM machine is incredibly fast (it can execute 200 million possible moves a second) and possesses what some people would think of as situational logic — or, less specifically, the capacity to think. Perhaps there is no need to fret about this victory of machine over man, however. In addition to predicting machines of the nasty, man-hating variety, *Doctor Who* also predicted that more kindly computers would one day beat humans at chess. That friendly robot pup K-9 continually bested the Doctor, a Time Lord, in matches too! If a "thinking" computer is ever produced by man, let all humanity hope it proves to be as loyal and obedient as the cybernetic canine on *Doctor Who*!

Besides auguring the advent of artificial intelligence, "The War Machines" also beat several notable science fiction films to the punch in this story about a machine that believes itself superior to man. Another supercomputer attempted to, and ultimately succeeded in, taking over the world in Joseph Sargent's seminal science fiction film *Colossus — The Forbin Project* (1968) starring Eric Braeden. The same year, a better-remembered machine-gone-mad and no less malevolent creation named HAL debuted in Stanley Kubrick's *2001: A Space Odyssey*. Both of these "thinking computers," like W.O.T.A.N. before them, committed murder and were deceitful in their communications with humans. Unlike W.O.T.A.N., however, neither of these machines was able to read minds. *Doctor Who* would return to the concept of a megalomaniacal computer in Season 10's "The Green Death." In that story, the supercomputer was called B.O.S.S. and it also boasted the ability to interface with human minds.

In addition to its ponderances on artificial intelligence, "The War Machines" also prophesied the creation of interlinked computers, or "networks." That prediction was right on the money too. Perhaps even more interesting was the method used by W.O.T.A.N. to connect not only to other computers, but to people too: the telephone. In a sense then, "The War Machines" forecasted the role of modems in a computer-driven society!

Ian Stuart Black's second script for *Doctor Who* sends off yet another companion, this time the smart-talking Dodo Chaplet. It also introduces Ben and Polly, two characters who would stay with the series through the transformation of Doctors from William Hartnell to Patrick Troughton. Some sources of have also said that "The War Machines" is historically notable because it is the first "modern" adventure featured in the long-running program. That assertion is not true. Season 2's premiere "Planet of Giants" can actually claim that honor.

Disturbing in "The War Machines" is the fact that W.O.T.A.N. refers to Hartnell as "Doctor Who" at one point, a blooper that has been pontificated upon by fans of the series for years. This mistake would never be repeated, except in serial titles and in episode credits.

A full version of "The War Machines" was re-assembled by the BBC and released on videotape in mid-1998.

SEASON 4

28. "The Smugglers" Written by Brian Hayles; Directed by Julia Smith; Designed by Richard Hunt; Parts I–IV; Airdates: September 10, 17, 24, October 1, 1966

SYNOPSIS: Near seventeenth century Cornwall, a group of smugglers are in league with local authorities, including the Town Squire, to transport valuable contraband. More importantly, there is also a secret treasure being stalked by the infamous pirate Capt. Pike and his crew of cutthroats. The only person who knows the whereabouts of the legendary treasure is a local churchwarden. In this time of intrigue and deception lands the TARDIS. After setting the broken wrist of a churchwarden, the Doctor speaks briefly with the gentleman about the secret topic. Unfortunately, the churchwarden is then murdered by pirates. His previous conversation, however, makes the Doctor the number one man on Capt. Pike's list of new targets. Pike is desperate to locate the legendary treasure of Capt. Avery, and he suspects the Doctor now knows where it is hidden!

GUEST CAST: Squire (Paul Whitsun Jones); Churchwarden (Terence de Marney); Capt. Pike (Michael Godfrey); Blake (John Ringham); Cherub (George Cooper); Kewper (David Kelly Blake); Tom (Mike Lucas); Spaniard (Derek Ware); Jamaica (Elroy Josephs); Gaptooth (Jack Bligh)

COMMENTARY: "The Smugglers," which opens *Doctor Who*'s fourth season, is one of the last of the purely historical adventures of the series. This melodrama with pirates, buried treasures and double-crosses is noteworthy, however, for the return of actor John Ringham, last seen as Tlotoxl in "The Aztecs," and also the performance of Paul Whitsun Jones as the immoral Town Squire. He would reappear in the Pertwee Season 9 adventure "The Mutants" as the even more despicable character "The Marshal."

"The Smugglers" has gone the way of "Galaxy Four" and other early *Doctor Who* adventures: Not even a scrap of the serial remains intact. A 1996 videotape special released by Master Vision, *The Doctors — 30 Years of Time Travel and Beyond*, purportedly reveals home movie footage shot during the making of this serial. That may be all that's left of William Hartnell's second-to-last adventure.

29. "The Tenth Planet" Written by Kit Pedler; Directed by Derek Martinus; Designed by Peter Kindred; Parts I–IV; Airdates: October 8, 15, 22, 29, 1966

SYNOPSIS: The TARDIS materializes at an Antaractic military base called Polar Base Snow Cap, just as American space flight Zeus 4 discovers something strange in the cosmic void. Another planet, an exact twin of Earth called Mondas, has somehow slipped into orbit between Mars and Venus. The Doctor warns that Earth should soon prepare for "visitors," and sure enough, a black, torpedo-like object lands at the South Pole just beyond the TARDIS. A military team sent to recover the TARDIS is the first to discover the hostile nature of the Cybermen visitors. Three silver figures, more like robots than human beings, attack the base. The Cyberleader then reveals to the captured command crew and the Doctor that his people were once human beings themselves. When their lifespans on Mondas began to shorten, scientists devised replacement parts of metal and plastic to extend their lives. The Cybermen possess organic brains, but human "weaknesses" such as emotions have been surgically removed! The Cybermen have arrived to take over the Earth and convert the human race into Cybermen!

As 230 Cybermen spaceships speed towards Earth, the Doctor must give up his very life to protect all humankind from a soulless destiny.

GUEST CAST: Gen. Cutler (Robert Beatty); Dyson (Dudley Jones); Barclay (David Dodmead); Astronaut Schultz (Alan White); Astronaut Williams (Earl Cameron); Astronaut Cutler (Callen Angelo); Tito (Shane Shelton); Sergeant (John Brandon); Wigner (Steve Plytas); Radar Operator (Christopher Matthews); Krail (Reg Whitehead); Jalon (Harry Brooks); Technician (Ellen Cullen); Shav (Greg Palmer); Cyberleader Jarl (Reg Whitehead); Cyberleader Krang (Harry Brooks); Cyberman (Greg Palmer); Voice of Cybermen (Roy Skelton, Peter Hawkins)

COMMENTARY: "The Tenth Planet" introduces the popular Cybermen to the *Doctor Who* format. These tall, silver, inhuman monsters have since developed into the most popular of series villains, aside from the Daleks. It is easy to understand why, since the Cybermen are imposing in size, have frightening electronic voices, mimic humanity in a kind of soulless fashion, and are possessed of a single, brutal objective. Unlike the Daleks and their toilet plunger arms, external eyestalks and general immobility, the Cybermen have few flaws that make them less than threatening. They have powerful, crushing arms, not thin metallic limbs with "suckers" on the end. In addition, Cybermen are not so easily blinded or prevented from navigating stairs and ladders. Since their goal is always to turn humans into emotionless automatons like themselves, the Cybermen have a "real" motive rather than just the two-dimensional evil the Daleks represent. Furthermore, they threaten a fate worse than death. The Daleks just kill you. The Cybermen tear you limb from limb and leave the core of your intelligence, your brain, entombed in an emotionless, heartless package.

The Cybermen were invented by physician Kit Pedler and writer Gerry Davis in the '60s when Pedler theorized that medical science would soon reach the point where humans could transplant and substitute not only human limbs, but internal organs as well. The Cybermen are the ultimate speculation about these progressions in advanced medical technology: creatures impervious to damage, composed of metal and plastic parts, so advanced that they have engineered out their own perceived weaknesses ... some might even say their own souls. Like Terry Nation's Daleks, the Cybermen are a brilliant idea well-executed, and far ahead of their time.

It is fair to state that the Cybermen are the inspiration for the Borg, the popular cyborg villains of *Star Trek: The Next Generation* and its spin-off feature film *First Contact* (1996). Like the Borg of *Star Trek, Doctor Who*'s Cybermen are born in human form. Like Cybermen, the Borg graft mechanical parts and limbs onto their organic bodies to "improve themselves." Like the Cybermen, the Borg assimilate other cultures and transform individuals into members of their own race. Like the Cybermen, the Borg eschew personal identity and concentrate on the goals of the "collective." Like the Cybermen before them, the Borg are more advanced each time the *Enterprise* encounters them. The Cybermen even once stated a variation on the line "Resistance is futile" in the Season 5 episode "Tomb of the Cybermen." Also, like the Cybermen before them, the Borg often are seen retreating into hibernation in their own personal cells or wall units. Lastly, both the Borg and the Cybermen can survive in the vacuum of space without dying, as witnessed by the invasion attempt in *Doctor Who*'s "The Wheel in Space" and the *Enterprise* hull-sensor dish sequence in *Star Trek: First Contact.*

When one begins to ponder the parallels between these two alien races, it is not only amazing but rather infuriating! To this author's knowledge, no one associated with *Star Trek*, or the Borg, has ever acknowledged the Cybermen or *Doctor Who* as the inspiration for this *very* popular race. It would certainly be appropriate to do so. As more Cybermen episodes of *Doctor Who* are released on videotape, more fans will see just how derivative a concept the *Next Generation* race really is. Once again, *Doctor Who* was at the vanguard of genre television. In 1966, when *Star Trek* was contemplating pointy-eared Romulans and planets based on 1930s Earth, *Doctor Who* was portraying truly alien races such as the Cybermen. It took *Star Trek* 23 years to come up with the same concept!

Kit Pedler, author of "The Tenth Planet," and his partner Gerry Davis also created a popular British television series entitled *Doomwatch* (1970-72). This program recounted the adventures of the Department for the Observation of Measurement of Science headed by Dr. Quist (actor John Paul). Like *Doctor Who*'s Cybermen stories, *Doomwatch* often dealt with contemporary speculative medical, scientific and environmental dilemmas such as pollution, disease and deforestation. Pedler and Davis wrote many episodes of this television series including the premiere "The Plastic Eaters," "The Red Sky" and "Survival Code." Many other *Doctor Who* writers also wrote for the show, including Brian Hayles ("The Iron Doctor"), Dennis Spooner ("The Logicians"), Terence Dudley ("Waiting for Knighthood") and Robert Holmes ("The Inquest"). *Doctor Who* directors Darrol Blake and Pennant Roberts also showcased their talents on *Doomwatch.*

"The Tenth Planet" is significant in *Doctor Who* lore for beginning the reign of the Cybermen. These villains would return many times, but are most closely associated with the era of Patrick Troughton because the second Doctor grappled with them more frequently than any other incarnation. He encountered them four times: in "The Moonbase," "Tomb of the Cyberman," "The Wheel in Space" and "The Invasion." The central situation of "The Tenth Planet," the destruction of Earth's long-lost twin planet Mondas, would also play a crucial role in the Colin Baker Season 22 story "Attack of the Cybermen."

"The Tenth Planet" represents the end of an important era: This was William Hartnell's *last Doctor Who* serial after three years. His decision to leave the series has been the subject of much controversy ever since his departure. Some insist the actor chose to bow out because he did not like the tenor of the later stories ... that they were too violent and filled with death. Proponents of this theory believe that he was unhappy with the increasingly adult content of the show following "The War Machines." Others insist that Hartnell was dedicated to *Doctor Who* until the very end, but that his health was so bad that he was unable to continue. This theory would seem to be supported by many co-workers and guest stars, including Mark Eden, who confirmed that Hartnell was experiencing physical pain as early as "Marco Polo," the fourth *Doctor Who* serial! Regardless of the reasons for his departure, Hartnell's decision to leave left the producers of *Doctor Who* in turmoil. If the show were to continue, a new actor would be required — but how could the change be explained? Thus, "regeneration" was born. In the closing minutes of "The Tenth Planet," the Doctor grows old and weak, and regenerates for the first time. It is an elegant, inspired solution to a casting problem, and one of *Doctor Who*'s most famous constituents.

Sadly, this historic last adventure of Hartnell's Doctor has been all but destroyed by the BBC's policy of taping over old programs. Although a few seconds depicting the first view ever of the Cybermen, on the frozen plains of the South Pole, still exist, and have been released on the tape "The Cybermen — The Early Years," the bulk of "The Tenth Planet" has been lost by the BBC.

30. "The Power of the Daleks" Written by David Whitaker; Directed by Christopher Barry; Designed by Derek Dodd; Parts I–VI; Airdates: November 5, 12, 19, 26, December 3, 10, 1966

SYNOPSIS: The Doctor has regenerated into a much younger, and rather more eccentric man, and Ben and Polly are not certain that this man with the mop of dark black hair and the penetrating eyes is the same man that they have been travelling with. Making matters more difficult for his companions, the renewed Doctor refers to "the Doctor" in both the past tense and the third person! The new Doctor settles on his new wardrobe: baggy pants held up with suspenders, a bow tie and a rumpled black blazer. He also plays a musical instrument called the recorder.

The TARDIS lands on the planet Vulcan, an Earth colony, in the year 2020. The Doctor discovers a murdered man, a government official from Earth known as an Examiner, and assumes the corpse's identity so as to "legally" investigate a large spaceship that has crashed in a nearby mercury swamp. The Doctor, Polly, Ben and Prof. Lesterson, the colony's scientific authority, board the craft and discover two dormant Daleks there. A third Dalek is missing.

Prof. Lesterson soon revives the Daleks. He believes that they can be used to serve the colony, which has had some difficulties surviving so far out in space. When the Daleks awaken, they claim to be the peaceful servants of mankind, but in secret they assembly a production factory, a conveyer belt producing dozens of additional Daleks! Now it is up to the "new" incarnation of the Doctor to save the planet Vulcan from the rapidly growing Dalek army.

GUEST CAST: Examiner (Martin King); Prof. Lesterson (Robert James); Bragen (Bernard Archard); Quinn (Nicholas Hawtrey); Hensell (Pamela Ann Davy); Valmar (Richard Kane); Resur (Edward Kelsey); Kebble (Steven Scott); Guards (Robert Cuckham, Robert Russell); Daleks (Robert Jewell, Kevin Manser, John Scott Martin, Gerald Taylor); Dalek Voice (Peter Hawkins)

COMMENTARY: The producers of *Doctor Who* took no chances with the first Patrick Troughton serial "The Power of Daleks." Even though the Doctor had changed significantly in wardrobe, character and physical appearance, his old enemies, Terry Nation's Daleks, had not. Of course, in hindsight it is easy to declare that the producers need not have worried. Troughton quickly proved to be one of the best Doctors of all with his unique combination of humor, innocence and eccentric genius.

Unfortunately, Troughton's first time out as the Doctor has been destroyed. In fact, just about all of Troughton's first season was destroyed by the BBC, which may help explain why he is significantly less popular with fans than some of the other Time Lord actors. In three years, Troughton did 21 serials on *Doctor Who*. Of those 21, only six still exist *in toto*, and they have been released on videotape: "The Tomb of the Cybermen," "The Dominators," "The Mind Robber," "The Krotons," "The Seeds of Death" and "The War Games." The eight-part Cyberman story "The Invasion" has also been released on VHS, but it is missing two full episodes. Still, Troughton had the distinction of returning to *Doctor Who* as a "guest star" more than any other actor to play the Time Lord hero, so his excellent work can also be seen in 1973's "The Three Doctors," 1983's "The Five Doctors" and the Colin Baker–era adventure "The Two Doctors" as well. Those appearances help to soften the blow a little, but not much. Troughton is this author's favorite incarnation of the Doctor, and, like many Troughton aficionados, I believe that Season 5, which started with the classic "The Tomb of the Cybermen" and went on to introduce the Yeti and the Ice Warriors, was probably one of the best seasons of *Doctor Who*. This cannot be objectively confirmed, of course, since no episodes of Season 5 exist but for "Tomb of the Cybermen." However, based on the teleplays, novelizations, Troughton's presence as the Doctor and Frazer Hines' presence as Jamie McCrimmon, this seems a fair bet.

The central notion of "The Power of the Daleks," that a terrible evil grows in secret while humanity argues amongst itself, is classic *Doctor Who* material. It puts the Doctor in the role of the Trojan seer, Cassandra. He can warn others all he likes about impending danger and evil, but he is never heeded. As usual, it is only when the Doctor stops depending on the intelligence of others, and acts on his own initiative that the evil is thwarted.

For many years, "The Power of the Daleks" was not available even in novel form because Nation retained all rights to the early Dalek stories. In 1993, that situation changed, and John Peel wrote a novelization of this adventure, #154 in the *Doctor Who* novelization series.

31. "The Highlanders" Written by Gerry Davis & Elwyn Jones; Directed by Hugh David; Designed by Geoffrey Kirkland; Parts I–IV; Airdates: December 17, 24, 31, 1966, January 7, 1967

SYNOPSIS: The TARDIS arrives on Earth in the year 1746, just as Prince Charles Edward ("Bonnie Prince Charlie") is fighting the English King George and the Hanoverian Germans for possession of the English throne. As the Doctor and his friends arrive in this time zone, the historic battle of Culloden Moor has just been fought, and the Duke of Cumberland with his force of English and German soldiers has defeated Prince Edward's highlanders. Devastated by the superior numbers and firepower of the redcoats, a band of highlanders which includes Laird McLairen and young piper Jamie McCrimmon has fled to a rural cottage in the Scottish Glens. There they encounter the Doctor, Polly and Ben, and further danger from the redcoats.

GUEST CAST: Alexander (William Dysart); Laird Colin McLairen (Donald Bissett); Kirsty (Hannah Gordon); Algernon Finch (Michael Elwyn); Solicitor Gray (David Garth); Capt. Trask (Dallas Cavell); Perkins (Sydney Arnold); Sentry (Tom Bowman); Molly (Barbara Bruce); McKay (Andrew Downier); Attwood (Guy Middleton); Highlander (Eric Mills); Woman at Inn (Nancy Gabriel); Sailor (Peter Diamond); English Horseman (Reg Dent)

COMMENTARY: "The Highlanders" was the last historical adventure on

Doctor Who for a dozen years, until Peter Davison's era and the serial "Black Orchid." The end of the historical stories comes not a moment too soon, as the time travel into Earth's history had become a worn-out plot device by the beginning of Troughton's era. In four years this plot idea was used in "An Unearthly Child," "Marco Polo," "The Aztecs," "The Reign of Terror," "The Crusades," "The Romans," "The Myth Makers," "The Massacre," "The Gunfighters" and "The Smugglers" ... ten stories out of 30! By "The Highlanders," all the permutations of this time travel category had been thoroughly explored, yet "The Highlanders," trots out many of the same conventions: the Doctor pretending to be somebody of importance (a German officer), the capture and release of companions, the capture of the villains by the forces of good, and even the attempt to alter history in an oblique but meaningful way. The final idea of bringing someone (Jamie) from the past forward in time to be a companion had already been used with Katarina in "The Myth Makers."

Penned by Gerry Davis, who would later co-write many a Cyberman adventure with Kit Pedler, this story introduces the stubborn, loyal Jamie McCrimmon to the goings-on aboard the TARDIS. Despite his birth in what appears to be a wholly uninspired historical adventure, Jamie, as played by Frazer Hines, ranks as one of the very best companions ever seen on *Doctor Who*. He is a loyal friend to the Doctor, but he also fulfills the "action" role adopted by earlier companions William Russell and Peter Purves (albeit in a less macho manner). In addition, because McCrimmon is from the past, and is not familiar with modern technology, the writers during the Troughton era are able to explain more advanced technical concepts without it sounding like dull exposition. Beyond these matters, Hines has an immediate chemistry with Troughton. Their rapport cannot be considered too highly as a factor in Jamie's success. A very real friendship seems to develop between these excellent actors, and their scenes together are always alive with a *joie de vivre*, a playful kidding that is most enjoyable. Jamie would remain with the Doctor through the rest of Troughton's three-year stint, until forced to part ways with him in "The War Games."

"The Highlanders" shares the same unpleasant fate as "The Power of the Daleks" and the majority of Troughton stories: It has been destroyed by the BBC, and thus no fans can enjoy the historic first meeting of Jamie McCrimmon and the second incarnation of the Doctor.

32. "The Underwater Menace" Written by Geoffrey Orme; Directed by Julia Smith; Designed by Jack Robinson; Parts I–IV; Airdates: January 14, 21, 28, February 4, 1967

SYNOPSIS: The TARDIS materializes on a small island and the Doctor, Jamie, Polly and Ben are immediately apprehended by denizens of the lost city of Atlantis! They are taken underground to a massive metropolis, where they are to be sacrificed to man-eating sharks in honor of the Goddess Amdo. They are saved from this unpleasant destiny by a fellow human from the surface, Prof. Zaroff. Unfortunately, the visitors learn that Zaroff, who has tricked King Thous into believing him a philanthropist eager to restore Atlantis to the planet surface, is experimenting with the Earth's molten core. In truth, Zaroff is planning global destruction with his advanced drilling machinery, and the Doctor must stop him before he drains the oceans into the Earth's core!

GUEST CAST: Prof. Zaroff (Joseph Furst); Damon (Colin Jeavons); Ara (Catherine Howe); King Thous (Noel Johnson); Jacko (Paul Anil); Nola (Roma Woodnutt); Lolem (Peter Stephens); Damon's Assistant (Gerald Taylor); Overseer (Graham Ashley); Guards (Tony Handy, Alex Donald, Tony Douglas)

COMMENTARY: Fantasy writers have for decades been in love with the myth of Atlantis. Was there really ever such a kingdom? What sort of people lived there? What happened to it? How was it destroyed? Were there any survivors? To many imaginative speculators, these mysteries are every bit as compelling as those which surround the extinction of the dinosaurs, or the existence of the Abominable Snowmen (another topic *Doctor Who* would soon tackle). Accordingly, the destiny of the lost city of Atlantis has been the subject of no less than a half-a-dozen genre films over the years. The 12-chapter Republic serial *Undersea Kingdom* (1936), *Siren of Atlantis* (1948) (adapted from the novel by Pierre Benoit), George Pal's 1961 special effects opus *Atlantis, the Lost Continent*, Kevin Connor's *Warlords of Atlantis* (1978) starring Doug McClure and *Doctor Who* guest star Shane Rimmer, and the British television movie *Neptune's Children* (1985) are just a few of the productions that have explored the world of Atlantis, usually in less than successful fashion. One particularly bad film, *Fire Maidens of Outer Space* (1956) even posited the notion that the people of Atlantis evacuated their dying city for one of the moons of Jupiter! The 1970s NBC fantasy-adventure series *The Fantastic Journey* (1977) also suggested a way-out theory in the second episode, "Atlantium": that Atlantis, which looked suspiciously like the Bonaventure Hotel in Los Angeles, and its inhabitants had all been spirited to the Bermuda Triangle! Currently, there is talk in Hollywood that the fourth *Indiana Jones* film will concern, surprise!, the discovery of the lost city of Atlantis!

"The Underwater Menace" was not *Doctor Who*'s solitary exploration of Atlantis. In Season 9, "The Time Monster" rehashed much of the same material. In fact, that Jon Pertwee adventure offered a completely contradictory account of Atlantis' last days. In that story it was another Time Lord, the Master, who destroyed the city by unleashing a time-eating creature called a Chronovore on it. Prof. Zaroff, Amdo and King Thous were nowhere in evidence in "The Time Monster." Despite this flaw, it is a testament to *Doctor Who*'s incredible elasticity that the series effectively features stories in outer space, in the past, outside space in "the Land of Fiction," stories about miniaturized people, and even stories in Atlantis. Despite the disparate nature of these tales, it never seems like the format is being stretched inappropriately.

Interestingly, two elements of "The Underwater Menace" would recur in the film *The Island of the Fish Men* (1978) from director Sergio Martino. This movie, which starred Joseph Cotten, Barbara Bach and Richard Johnson (*The Haunting*

[1963], *Space: 1999*: "Matter of Life and Death"), featured a subplot about a fish-man experiment (they were again used as slave labor, just as in "The Underwater Menace"), and a main story about the ruins of Atlantis!

Despite the fact that the locale is unusual, there are nonetheless several typical *Doctor Who* ingredients at work in "The Underwater Menace." There is the capture of the companions, the power mad human megalomaniac, and again the Doctor's quick thinking which saves the day. In other words, this is essentially a combination of elements that had already worked before on the television series. Whether or not "The Underwater Menace" was an interesting episode remains a mystery today since only Episode 3 has been recovered from the BBC trash heap, leaving yet another Troughton serial completely gutted.

33. "The Moonbase" Written by Kit Pedler; Directed by Morris Barry; Designed by Colin Shaw; Parts I–IV; Airdates: February 11, 18, 25, March 4, 1967

SYNOPSIS: The TARDIS arrives on the moon in the year 2070, where the Doctor, Jamie, Polly and Ben learn that Earth's weather patterns are being regulated from a moonbase on the lunar surface equipped with a fantastic device called a "gravitron." Hobson, the administrator of the Moonbase, also reveals that a deadly disease has infiltrated the installation. Cybermen have somehow contaminated the moonbase's sugar supply with a neurotropic virus that attacks the human nervous system! The Doctor learns that Cybermen must have infiltrated the lunar establishment, and that they are stealing human bodies from the infirmary to make more cyber creatures! Before long, a force of Cyberman marches across the lunar attack and lays siege to the moon installation, just as Hurricane Lucy threatens to destroy Miami, and the gravitron device is sabotaged...

GUEST CAST: Hobson (Patrick Barr); Bendit (Andre Maranne); Nils (Michael Wolf); Voice of Space Control (Alan Rowe); Voice of Controller Rinberg (Denis McCarthy); Sam (John Rolfe); Scientists (Barry Ashton, Derek Calder, Arnold Chazen, Leon Maybank, Victor Pemberton, Edward Phillips, Robin Scott, Alan Wells); Cybermen (John Wills, Peter Greene); Dr. Evans (Alan Rowe); Voice of Cybermen (Peter Hawkins)

COMMENTARY: The much-anticipated return of the evil Cybermen does not disappoint. "The Moonbase" is a frightening serial with plenty of blood-curdling moments, great set design and a satisfying conclusion.

Kit Pedler's script for "The Moonbase" gives first-time *Doctor Who* director Morris Barry the opportunity to indulge in some ghoulish imagery. The sight of an inhuman Cyberman stealing bodies from the lunar base infirmary is enough to cause goosebumps in even the most callous viewer. No wonder Jamie panics and calls the Cyberman a "silver phantom!"

The most frightening scene, however, is that in which all the infected humans of the base rise zombie-like from their beds in the infirmary, their sheets slipping off to reveal the black tendrils of the Cyberman disease infecting their faces. This horrific moment, that of a sickbay full of the "undead" rising to life, has actually reappeared with similarly terrifying results in other sci-fi television series, including the "Space Vampire" episode of *Buck Rogers in the 25th Century* and the "Night Terrors" episode of *Star Trek: The Next Generation.*

Another moment in "The Moonbase" is also frightening. It is not accomplished with special effects or scary monsters, but with acting. There is one instant when the Doctor realizes that the Cybermen must already be inside the moonbase. Troughton's face fills the screen as he logically deduces that the enemy is in the very same room where he stands, the infirmary. It is a chilling realization, well-performed by this talented actor. Also shiver-inducing is the Doctor's remark that there are some dark corners of the universe where the most evil of creatures dwell. It is an icy moment that adds immensely to the mood of the piece.

Also contributing to the verisimilitude of the Cybermen's second appearance is the fact that the moonbase sets, especially the main control room and the gravitron control room, are rather convincing. There are ornate control centers adorned not only with believable work station terminals but also with interesting construction supports, a wall-sized window that looks out on the moon surface, and a platform containing the gravitron mechanism. This is a believable "futuristic" base, probably made more so by the black-and-white photography, which masks the seams.

The climax of "The Moonbase" is one of the best in the series. The Doctor remodulates the gravitron to send the Cybermen and their saucers flying from the surface of the moon into deep space. This is a great alternative to merely "blowing up" the bad guy, and it is perversely thrilling to see the Cybermen blasted into deep space. Serves 'em right! Besides the final use of the gravitron, the concept of a mechanical device controlling weather formations has been the fodder of television science fiction for a long time. Besides its use on *The Bionic Woman* (the 1976 "fembot" episode), the same idea appeared in two further Troughton-era *Doctor Who* serials, "The Enemy of the World" and "The Ice Warriors." Recently, Alex DeWinter (Sean Connery) tried to control the world's weather in the big-screen adaptation of *The Avengers* (1998).

Despite the outright horror of a second Cyberman invasion, "The Moonbase" finds time for a little comedy relief. Troughton fully indulges his penchant for comedy in a very funny "schtick" routine. The Doctor attempts to gather cloth samples from the moonbase crew to analyze the rapidly spreading disease. He gets in the way of the crew, is nearly stepped on, and generally makes a nuisance of himself in an amusing sequence. It is quite a different approach from Hartnell's more serious portrayal of the time traveler; the scene is evidence that Troughton's Doctor is an erratic and kind bumbler, a well-meaning genius, but a genius who is also terribly clumsy! This element of humor makes the Doctor less a two-dimensional hero, and Troughton deserves credit for being the first actor to really incorporate humor into the part. Pertwee's Doctor would retreat significantly from the amount of physical humor displayed by Troughton's, perhaps because he was already well-known throughout England as a comedian. Tom Baker, who usually played grim villains in his movies, would flip expectations again by heightening the outrageous, comical elements of the Time Lord. Sometimes he went overboard playing the comical elements, something which Troughton never did, even in the company of the more "broad" Colin Baker Doctor in "The Two Doctors."

Morris Barry's next Cyberman epic, "Tomb of the Cybermen" is an improvement even over the tense "The Moonbase." Viewers can examine his work on this episode on the tape "Cybermen — The Early Years." Only Episodes 2 and 4 still exist. In this case, at least, that is enough to assess the high quality of this frightening Cyberserial.

34. "The Macra Terror" Written by Ian Stuart Black; Directed by John Davies; Designed by Kenneth Sharp; Parts I–IV; Airdates: March 11, 18, 25, April 1, 1967

SYNOPSIS: On the TARDIS viewscreen is the image of a giant, inhuman claw. What does it mean, and why has it appeared there? The time travelers uncover these answers when they land on a beautiful colony planet in Earth's distant future. One inhabitant, a man named Medok, claims that a race of alien beings called the Macra have infiltrated the colony. When the Doctor sees the hideous, crab-like Macra for himself, he knows the truth. The Doctor learns that the Macra have taken over the colony and are breeding in underground tunnels. They are also producing a gas in the mines that is vital to their continued existence. The Doctor seizes on this weakness and sets about to destroy the gas production unit.

GUEST CAST: Medok (Terence Lodge); Pilot (Peter Jeffrey); Sunnaa (Jane Enshawe); Questa (Ian Fairbairn); Barney (Graham Armitrage); Ola (Gerton Kaluber); Controller (Graham Leaman); Alvis (Anthony Gardner); Chicki (Sandra Bryant); Control Voice (Denis Goacher); Broadcast Voice (Richard Beale); Official (John Harvey); Guards (John Caesar, Steve Emerson, Danny Rae); The Macra (Robert Jewell)

COMMENTARY: "The Macra Terror" revisits one of *Doctor Who's* favorite recurring themes: the exploitation of one race by another. This adventure is different than most ponderings on this theme since in this case humans are actually the good guys. For once, we are not the exploiters! On the contrary, it is the crustacean Macra who are the villains of the tale, brainwashing their human opponents and breeding in the dark tunnels of the colony. This episode also features an element common to many episodes of *The Twilight Zone*. There is one man, in this case Terence Lodge's Medok, who knows what is going on. Of course, just like William Shatner's character in "Nightmare at 20,000 Feet," no one believes his crazy story of a monster.

Graham Leaman, the actor who later played a Time Lord in "The Three Doctors," appears in "The Macra Terror" as Controller. Other than the above information, the overall quality of "The Macra Terror" is unknown since none of the four episodes have been recovered by the short-sighted BBC.

35. "The Faceless Ones" Written by David Ellis and Malcolm Hulke; Directed by Gerry Mill; Designed by Geoffrey Kirkland; Parts I–VI; Airdates: April 8, 15, 22, 29, May 6, 13, 1967

SYNOPSIS: The TARDIS materializes on a runway amidst the hustle and bustle of Gatwick Airport. The airport police load the TARDIS on a truck, and its crew is forced to separate. Polly then witnesses the murder of Insp. Gascoigne and is chased by the killer through a hangar. Later, the Doctor and Jamie run across an exact duplicate of Polly, who claims that she does not know them and that she is merely a tourist from Zurich named Michelle.

Concerned, the Doctor and Jamie investigate Chameleon Tours. The Doctor feels that the Polly doppelganger and the name "Chameleon" spell trouble of an extraterrestrial nature. Hoping to solve the mystery of Chameleon Airlines, Jamie boards one of their planes. It heads unexpectedly into outer space and docks with a spherical space station. There, Jamie discovers compartments of miniaturized young humans! The aliens, called Chameleons, suffered an atomic explosion on their planet and, as a result of the radiation, their bodies lost both individuality and molecular cohesion. Now their race is dying out. The humans on Earth are compatible with the Chameleons, and are being used as a blueprint to help the aliens attain molecular stability. They have captured 50,000 young people already! These missing people will be restored to normal size on the distant homeworld and made use of there.

The Doctor impersonates a chameleon and takes the last flight into space, but is he too late to save Jamie, Polly and the others from exploitation by the faceless aliens?

GUEST CAST: Blade (Donald Pickering); Insp. Gascoigne (Peter Whitaker); Charles Gordon, Airport Commandant (Colin Gordon); Jean Rock (Wanda Ventham); Samantha Briggs (Pauline Collins); Insp. Crossland/Director of the Chameleons (Bernard Kay); Policeman (James Appleby); Spencer (Victor Winding); Jenkins (Christopher Tranchell); Pinto (Madalena Nicol); Ann Davidson (Gilly Fraser); Announcer (Brijit Paul); Pilot (Michael Ladkin); Reynolds (Leonard Trolley); Heslington (Barry Wilsher)

COMMENTARY: "The Faceless Ones" is *Doctor Who*'s interpretation of the material so successfully explored in Don Siegel's paean to the terrors of identity and individuality lost, *Invasion of the Body Snatchers* (1956). In this circumstance, aliens are once more to blame for the resulting chaos, because they are appropriating the identities of friends, companions and family members. Akin to *Invasion of the Body Snatchers*, the terror in this scenario comes when the protagonists encounter people who *should* be familiar, yet are not. The face is the same, but what exists behind it is horribly evil, horribly wrong.

This same brand of horror, that of identity warped and confused, was also effectively showcased in the 1959 *Twilight Zone* story "Mirror Image" starring Vera Miles. In that macabre vignette by Rod Serling, a woman was haunted by the appearance of her own sinister doppelganger in another station of mass transportation, a bus depot. She eventually learns that duplicates are crossing over from a dying parallel dimension to take up permanent residence in this one. "Mirror Image" ends less hopefully than "The Faceless Ones" because the visitors from "the other side" are not vanquished. Still, *Doctor Who*'s "The Faceless Ones" resembles both *Invasion and the Body Snatchers* and "Mirror Image" because it seizes on the selfsame kind of fear and paranoia. One can interpret this as fear of the unknown, or of the inexplicably hostile inside the familiar. It might also represent personal alienation, a kind of mass psychosis, supreme egotism or even a fear of Communism.

Whatever the social subtext (a factor that changes from generation to generation, as equally effective remakes of *Invasion of the Body Snatchers* in 1978 and 1993 demonstrate), "The Faceless One" reminds viewers of the importance of identity and individuality. Indeed, this is one of the hallmark themes of the entire *Doctor Who* series. It is safe to say that the Doctor, with his out-of-fashion clothes and unique genius, represents individuality whilst his enemies, the personality-deficient Cybermen, the swarm organism of the Wirrn and even the corporate mentality of IMC, represent personal identity either sublimated or destroyed. The series can thus be viewed as an examination not only of political revolution and a response to the forces of establishment, but the ultimate triumph of the individual over the more impressive resources and power of "Big Brother."

And what better place to comment on the dehumanization of the individual than a center for mass transport, where hundreds of people are herded into lines, treated as numbers, and met with disdain and dull indifference by overburdened officials? Who has not felt like just "a face in the crowd" while standing in line on an escalator or behind a metal detector? *Doctor Who* suggests there is something wrong beneath the surface of this bustling environment. And sure enough, the activity of the airport is the cloak that shields the activity of the Chameleons, aliens who have already removed 50,000 humans without a trace!

Actress Wanda Ventham guest stars in "The Faceless Ones" as Jean Rock. Like Jean Marsh, Ventham would appear on the series three times. She would first return in Season 15's revisionist version of "The Daemons," called "Image of the Fendahl." Her last appearance was in Sylvester McCoy's Season 24 premiere, "Time and the Rani." Aside from her three *Doctor Who* appearances, Ventham is probably best-remembered for her portrayal of the cool and sexy Col. Lake, assistant to Commander Straker in the Anderson space series *U.F.O.* (1970).

"The Faceless Ones" is Malcolm Hulke's *Doctor Who* writing debut. By the time he joined the series in 1967, he was already a well-established television writer in the genre. He co-wrote with *Star Maidens* creator Eric Paice all six episodes of the 1960 series *Target Luna*, a science fiction program produced by *Doctor Who* creator Sydney Newman. The series, which has been lost due to the BBC's practice of taping over old shows, was geared towards children and featured the adventures the Wedgewood family in space. After "The Faceless Ones," Hulke was a constant presence on *Doctor Who*. He was particularly active during the Pertwee era, in which he wrote "Colony in Space," "The Sea Devils," "Frontier in Space" and "Invasion of the Dinosaurs."

This episode of *Doctor Who* marks the final appearance of Anneke Willis and Michael Craze, the actors portraying companions Polly and Ben. These characters had seen the Doctor through his first regeneration into Patrick Troughton, and been with the show since "The War Machines." Sadly, their exit from the series can no longer be assessed since all four parts of "The Faceless Ones" have been lost by the BBC. It is a shame, because this appears to have been one of the most unique and interesting adventures of the Troughton era.

36. "The Evil of the Daleks" Written by David Whitaker; Directed by Derek Martinus; Designed by Chris Thompson; Parts I–VII; Airdates: May 20, 27, June 3, 10, 17, 24, July 1, 1967

SYNOPSIS: In search of the missing TARDIS, the Doctor and Jamie investigate an antique shop owned by the mysterious Prof. Waterfield. Late at night, they enter the store and the Doctor notices something odd about the collectibles: They are not reproductions, yet they are seemingly brand new. The Doctor theorizes that Waterfield has somehow built a time machine like the TARDIS, and that he is traveling back in time to bring new goods from the Victorian era to the twentieth century!

Waterfield transports the Doctor and Jamie back in time, and they awaken in the Victorian house of Theodore Maxtible in 1866. Maxtible insists he and Waterfield are both victims of a greater power which has kidnapped Waterfield's lovely young daughter, Victoria. Hoping to help, the Doctor is taken to Maxtible's lab where he learns that by using electromagnetism, 144 separate mirrors and a technique called "reflection imagery," the Victorian scientists have invented a time machine. But when they first activated the equipment, inhuman creatures from the future burst into the lab, captured Victoria and ordered Waterfield to go to the future, steal the TARDIS and capture the Doctor and Jamie.

The Doctor suspects he knows who the true villains are, and his suspicions are confirmed when a Dalek rolls into view. In possession of his TARDIS, the Daleks want the Doctor to test humans for them, because the machines have always been beaten by human ingenuity. They call this the "human factor." They feel that if they can isolate this factor and inject it into themselves, they will be invincible. The Doctor has no choice but to obey, and after testing Jamie, the so-called human factor is synthesized in chemical form and injected into three Daleks. The Daleks instantly lose their threatening demeanor and become friendly.

The Doctor and his friends are taken back to Skaro. There the Doctor is granted an audience with the Emperor Dalek, a giant, immobile creature who informs the Doctor that it is now possible to isolate "the Dalek factor." It is this, *not* the human factor, that the Daleks are interested in. They wish to inject it into all the people of the universe, in essence making all creatures Daleks! The Doctor reverses the polarity of the conversion machine and injects several Daleks with the "human factor." Before long, a civil war has erupted on Skaro among the divergent Dalek factions, and the Doctor, Victoria and Jamie are in the middle of it.

GUEST CAST: Prof. Edward Waterfield (John Bailey); Prof. Theodore Maxtible (Marius Goring); Ruth Maxtible (Brijit Forsyth); Kennedy (Griffith Davies);

Mollie Dawson (Jo Rowbottom); Perry (Geoffrey Colville); Toby (Windsor Davies); Bob Hall (Alec Ross); Kemel (Sonny Caldinez); Terrall (Gary Watson); Daleks (Murphy Grumbar, Robert Jewell, John Scott Martin, Gerald Taylor); Dalek Voices (Peter Hawkins, Roy Skelton)

COMMENTARY: David Whitaker's "The Evil of the Daleks" is the second occasion in just one season in which Troughton's Doctor clashes with Nation's evil mutants. Like Troughton's premiere story "The Power of the Daleks," this adventure in its totality has disappeared forever from the BBC film and video vault. The story is nonetheless important to the series because it represents the first time that there is a schism within the Dalek race. In "The Evil of the Daleks," the humanized Daleks fight the "regular" Daleks. In later years, Nation would involve the creator of the Daleks, a madman called "Davros," in another power struggle within the Dalek Empire. Daleks fight it out amongst themselves in the Season 22 story "Revelation of the Daleks," in which Davros is building a new race of Daleks using human parts at a suspended animation mortuary called "Tranquil Repose." The machines also take their infighting to the streets of London in the last Dalek story of the series, the Season 25 premiere "Remembrance of the Daleks." In that tale, Davros is again at the heart of the schism between the standard Daleks and the Imperial Daleks.

"The Evil of the Daleks" also introduces the immobile Emperor Dalek to the series. This creature lives in a different style of casing and has long tubes which connect it to the wall and ceiling. It has an eyestalk but no limbs. The title "Emperor Dalek" would change to "The Supreme Dalek" in Season 17's premiere "Destiny of the Daleks," by Terry Nation. Another version of the Emperor/Supreme Dalek ruler would also be glimpsed in the closing moments of "Remembrance of the Daleks."

Deborah Watling makes her debut as Victoria Waterfield in "The Evil of the Daleks." Like so many of the companions, her contribution to the series as a whole cannot be fairly critiqued. Only one story featuring Victoria survives in whole: "The Tomb of the Cybermen," perhaps the best serial of the entire series. Watling left *Doctor Who* after just a season, but what a season it must have been! As mentioned earlier, Season 5 may have been the most inventive and exciting time the series ever saw with Yeti, Ice Warriors and other fabulous monsters popping up almost constantly. Watling returned to *Doctor Who* in the 1996 semi-professional production *Downtime* starring fellow *Who* alumni Elizabeth Sladen and Nicholas Courtney. The story concerned the Yeti, a creature whom Watling's character Victoria faced in both "The Abominable Snowmen" and "The Web of Fear."

Two portions of "The Evil of the Daleks" have been released on the tape "Daleks — The Early Years."

SEASON 5

X **37. "The Tomb of the Cybermen"** Written by Kit Pedler & Gerry Davis; Directed by Morris Barry; Designed by Martin Johnson; Parts I–IV; Airdates: September 2, 9, 16, 23, 1967

SYNOPSIS: The TARDIS materializes on the barren planet Telos, and the Doctor and his companions quickly run afoul of an archeological expedition led by Prof. Parry. The obsessed archeologist is trying to find the fabled lost tombs of the Cybermen! Also with this excursion are the financiers of the expedition, the mysterious logician Eric Klieg, the domineering woman Kaftan and her huge bodyguard Toberman. Explosive charges are detonated on a craggy outcropping of rock, and the massive entrance to an ancient tomb is unearthed.

Inside the tomb, the Doctor, Klieg and Prof. Parry open a hatch that leads down to a frozen chamber where a giant mechanical hive, the fabled Cyberman tomb, is carved in the ice. Over the protests of the Doctor, Klieg activates a heating unit that will bring the metallic soldiers back to life. Soon the Cybermen awaken, capture the humans and determine that Klieg will be assimilated as a Cyberleader because of his brilliant mind. Toberman is also captured and surgically altered: His arm is removed and replaced by one of Cyberman manufacture.

The Doctor, Jamie, Klieg and Parrt escape to the safety of the control room, but the Cybermen, trapped in the ice cavern below, send up a swarm of cybermats that home in on human brain signals. Meanwhile, the duplicitous Kaftan and Klieg hope to gain control of the Cyberman army, even as the Doctor warns that they are interfering with a force far more powerful than they suspect.

GUEST CAST: Jim Callum (Clive Merrison); Eric Klieg (George Pastell); Prof. Parry (Aubrey Richards); Kaftan (Shirley Cooklin); Toberman (Roy Stewart); Capt. Hopper (George Roubiceck); Cyberman Controller (Michael Kilgarriff), Cybermen (Hans DeVries, Ronald Lee, Tony Harwood, Charles Pemberton, John Hogan, Kenneth Seegar, Richard Kerley, Reg Whitehead)

COMMENTARY: "The Tomb of the Cybermen" is this writer's candidate for the finest *Doctor Who* serial in the entire 159-episode run. It expertly combines a number of disparate elements into a cohesive whole with astonishing success. Foremost there is the "Mummy movie" template from which the central premise of the program is drawn. Beyond its twist on that formula, the serial also features three of the most interesting human villains ever dramatized on *Doctor Who* as well as fantastic sets, rock solid direction from Morris Barry that builds tension throughout the story, a literate script replete with many impressive character moments, and (best of all) the return of the Cybermen at their menacing best. All these factors combine to make "Tomb of the Cybermen" an unforgettable serial.

In assembling their teleplay, authors Kit Pedler and Gerry Davis obviously drew on such films as Universal's *The Mummy* (1932) and the studio's '40s Mummy movies for inspiration. Many elements of these classic films are displayed again, yet made fresh and exciting by their unexpected transplant to a far-off world in the distant future. There is the search and unearthing of a buried tomb, a prerequisite in all Mummy films. Also, "The Tomb of the Cybermen" highlights a character archetype familiar to all aficionados of the adventures of Imhotep and Kharis: the enthusiastic archaeologist who blindly opens the tomb over the protests of someone who knows better, in this case the Doctor. The required peril or "curse" when the explorers open the tomb is also in evidence, but the curse on Telos is, cleverly, not a supernatural one. Instead it is *technological*: a deadly bolt of electricity utilized by the Cybermen as a defense mechanism. This technological menace also substitutes for such common tomb booby traps as pits, falling rocks and collapsing walls.

Eric Klieg, the logician who stubbornly refuses to respect the power he has come to rob, also mirrors a character common to most "archaeological" and Mummy–style films. Indeed, Belloq in Steven Spielberg's *Raiders of the Lost Ark* (1981) and Tim Curry's mischievous character in the recent Michael Crichton hit *Congo* (1995) fulfill the same function in their respective productions. Like Klieg, they are not in the tomb for knowledge or philanthropic reasons, but rather to plunder its riches and gain power. Even the cybermats seen here scurrying around the central control room of the tomb can be seen as a futuristic adaptation of common tomb "vermin" such as snakes, rats or spiders.

Then, finally, there is the revival and rampage of the awakened monster. In *Doctor Who*, this moment is accomplished with special skill by director Barry and the special effects team. It is an awesome sight to watch the Cyberman push their way out of a giant honeycomb and straighten up to full size, almost seven feet tall! Amazingly, the resemblance to mummy movies does not end with the revival of the Cybermen. The Cybermen are remarkably Mummy–like in their unsteady but powerful gait. They shamble and stagger about in herky-jerky style. This dance of the slumbering monster has long been the accepted carriage of the Frankenstein Monster and mummified humans in B-movies.

In another reflection of Mummy movie mores, this technological monster (the Cyberman) has a human brain at its core, as does the revived Kharis. Both are "wrapped," so to speak, in a uniform of a type (either bandages or metal), but both were once human, until altered.

All of these updates and modifications of Mummy tradition elevate "Tomb of the Cybermen" above the level of the average serial. *Doctor Who* would often transplant traditional stories and subgenres to otherworldly venues, but "The Tomb of the Cybermen" is undoubtedly the most successful of such transplant operations.

Other than the setting, "Tomb of the Cybermen" is extraordinary in several other departments, notably in casting and characterization. Kleig, Kaftan and Toberman are among the most compelling villains ever seen in the series, right up there with John Ringham's Tlotoxl in the first season adventure "The Aztecs." They make an effective triangle of evil. Klieg is the deluded and power-hungry villain who is possessed of a supreme ego. Kaftan is the manipulator, the cunning strategist who controls Klieg with her promises and lies. Toberman, of course, is the brawn, the physical threat to the protagonists. In the end, the towering giant is also the soul of this evil group, for it is he who sacrifices his life and defeats the Cybermen by slamming shut the tomb for all eternity. It is appropriate to note that all three of these memorable characters are played with a special verve and passion. George Pastell's Klieg, is particularly effective. He develops his character from minor irritation to full-scale, vicious opponent with a special skill, and his scenes with Troughton crackle with tension and wit. Pastell's most interesting moment comes when Kleig realizes that he has bitten off more than he can chew by attempting to control the Cybermen. Pastell, who plays Klieg as a swaggering, arrogant bully, changes course abruptly in this scene. Without Toberman's brute force, a gun in his hand, or Kaftan's web of promises to buttress him, Klieg is revealed to be little more than a coward. Pastell makes the transition effortlessly. (The actor played Kharis' mentor in Hammer's 1959 *The Mummy*.)

Shirley Cooklin is also effective as Kaftan, one of *Doctor Who*'s best female villains. She is a master manipulator, and a far more resolute villain than the power-mad Klieg. She is more courageous as well. Kaftan is finally killed for her open defiance of the Cyberman.

Roy Stewart plays Toberman, the last of this triumvirate of evil. He is a huge man with a towering physical appearance, not unlike Harold Sakata's Odd Job in *Goldfinger*. He is such a powerful force that Toberman's very appearance is enough to strike fear in the heart(s) of the Doctor. He is seven feet tall, and the episode shows off his amazing physique to good effect. One of the best moments of the serial occurs when this massive man and the mechanical Cybermen are locked in hand-to-hand combat.

"The Tomb of the Cybermen" was filmed on just five sets: the main control room, the doorway and mountain ridge, the target room, the energizer room and the underground tomb. Despite this seemingly limited world, the serial never slows down, and it never is less than interesting to watch. The limited settings heighten the sense of claustrophobia and tension. The Cyberman hive is especially impressive with its twin ladders stretching up the side of the honeycombs, and its "plastic" protective film covering each cell of the tomb. The moment when the plastic film is ripped and the Cybermen descend the staircase is a classic image of horror: the awakening of the juggernaut. It was a moment repeated in the *Star Trek: Voyager* episode "Unity," which saw hibernating Borg (in a similar technological hive) coming back to life.

Barry directs the excellent script by Pedler and Davis in classic horror movie fashion, leaving no horror gimmick unturned. There are scenes of cybermats jumping on unsuspecting victims, surprise moments when a Cyberman target leaps out from behind a wall, and the inevitable scene where Cybermen chase the Doctor up the ladder. As he is almost to safety, they grab his leg and start pulling him down. And, besides the dramatic and horrifying awakening of the Cybermen, there is also the scene in which the villains come, one after the other, up through the tomb entrance, like unstoppable zombies. All of these moments are orchestrated competently and to the end of retaining the menace of the Cybermen. Thanks to Barry, this is probably their scariest appearance on *Doctor Who.*

When "Tomb of the Cybermen" was rediscovered and released on video in 1992, Barry had this to say about his direction of the classic serial:

> "Tomb" had an enormous cast, because there were three lots of people. When you've got so much action and so much running...you've really got to work bloody hard to get your shots right... You've got to pull out all the stops with *Doctor Who*... Try and vary your shots a bit. Make them interesting...[5]

On this, and on all fronts, Barry certainly succeeded. Amidst the Mummy movie setting, the schemes of three villains and Barry's horror movie directing tricks, the Kit Pedler-Gerry Davis teleplay finds time, amazingly, to develop the main series characters too. There is one particularly lovely scene in which Victoria asks the Doctor about his own family, and whether memory is a curse or a blessing. Patrick Troughton replies with a sincerity and frankness that is quite touching, proving again that in many senses his was the most "human" and caring of the Doctor's incarnations. He tells Victoria that he can remember his family when he wants to, but that they "sleep" inside his mind. It is a human moment amidst the horror of the story.

Delightfully, the Doctor even takes the time to ask Victoria if she is going to enjoy traveling with him. That is far different than the approach of Hartnell, Pertwee, Baker, Davison, Colin Baker or McCoy. Of all of the Time Lord's incarnations, Troughton's perhaps had the most dimensions.

"Tomb of the Cybermen" is also significant in *Who* lore because it supports this author's assertion that *Star Trek: The Next Generation*'s Borg are surely the descendants of Kit Pedler's metallic men. Witness these words from the Cyberman in this serial:

> You belong to us. You shall be like us... You will become the first of a new race of Cybermen. You will return to the Earth and control it... You will be the leader of the new race. You will be altered... You have fear, we will eliminate fear from your brain. You will be like us. To die is unnecessary.

Compare that dialogue with two similar passages from the Borg saga in "The Best of Both Worlds Part I," the 1990 third season cliffhanger of *Star Trek: The Next Generation* by Michael Piller:

> Strength is irrelevant. Resistance is futile... Freedom is irrelevant, self-determination is irrelevant. You must comply... Death is irrelevant. Your archaic cultures are authority-driven. To facilitate our introduction into your societies it has been decided that a human voice will speak for us in all our communications. You have been chosen to be that voice.
>
> Resistance is futile. Your life as it has been is over. From this time forward, you will service us.

Both "Tomb of the Cybermen" and "Best of Both Worlds" stress that men will be *altered* to serve the new power. In addition, both the Cybermen and the Borg assert that death is *unnecessary*, or *irrelevant*. And, in both episodes, the process of going from man to Cyborg is referred to as "altering." In "Best of Both Worlds," Data tells Commander Riker that Capt. Picard has been "altered" by the Borg, just as the Cyber Controller in "Tomb of the Cybermen" informs Klieg that he will be "altered." Additionally, both the Borg and the Cybermen rip human beings apart and replace human limbs with robotic ones. Just as Picard gains a mechanical arm as Locutus of Borg, so does Toberman gain a silver robot arm in "The Tomb of the Cyberman."

In terms of drama, both adventures are similar as well because each story is resolved only when the "altered" human is able to break his new programming and fight back. Toberman beats his programming when the Doctor reminds him of his humanity. Picard beats his programming and utters the word "sleep" to Data, indicating to the intrepid android how to destroy the Borg. While the resemblance between these races may indeed be a coincidence, it is nonetheless remarkable. Historically, the Cybermen appeared on *Doctor Who* seven times prior to 1989, the first year the Borg guest-starred on *Star Trek: The Next Generation*, in the episode "Q-Who."

"Tomb of the Cybermen" is also historically important within *Doctor Who* continuity because the Cyber Controller would reappear in the Season 22 Colin Baker story "Attack of the Cybermen." Much of that serial's action takes place in the tombs on Telos. However, the set design does not at all resemble that seen in "Tomb of the Cybermen." Michael Kilgarriff, the actor who portrays the Cyber Controller in this early story, returned to that role in the Colin Baker story.

For many years, "Tomb of the Cybermen" was considered lost. As a result, it gained almost legendary status in *Doctor Who* circles. Those who had seen it on its original broadcast remembered just how good it was. Fortunately, when the serial was recovered in 1992, it not only lived up to expectations, it actually exceeded them. "Tomb of the Cybermen" is available on home video courtesy of BBC/CBS-Fox.

38. "The Abominable Snowmen" Written by Mervyn Haisman & Henry Lincoln; Directed by Gerald Blake; Designed by Malcolm Middleton; Parts I–VI; Airdates: September 30, October 7, 14, 21, 28, November 4, 1967

SYNOPSIS: When the TARDIS lands in the Himalayas, the Doctor and his cohorts meet Prof. Travers, a man hoping to confirm the existence of a species called the "Yeti." As the Doctor prepares to deliver a "ghanta," a Tibetan holy relic, to a local monastery, Victoria and Jamie run across a terrifying Yeti in its mountain lair. Also in the lair are several glowing silver spheres. The Doctor pieces together the puzzle and realizes that the silver spheres are the power units of a nefarious, non-corporeal life form called the Great Intelligence. The Great Intelligence has been deploying robotic Yeti, and psychically controlling a Tibetan monk called Padmasambvha, to transfer himself to another dimension ... Earth's dimension!

Soon, the Great Intelligence begins to manifest itself in the Himalayas, and a deadly substance begins to roll down the mountains...

GUEST CAST: Prof. Travers (Jack Watling); Khrison (Norman Jones); Thonmi (David Spenser); Rinchen (David Grey); Abbot Songsten (Charles Morgan); Padmasambvha (Wolfe Morris); Ralpachan (David Baron); Yeti (Tony Harwood, John Hogan, Richard Kerley, Reg Whitehead)

COMMENTARY: "The Abominable Snowmen" is *Doctor Who*'s attempt to delve into another marginal sci-fi mystery akin to the discovery of Atlantis in "The Underwater Menace." In this case, the subject of interest is the Abominable Snowman, or the Yeti. Nigel Kneale, creator of *Quatermass*, had already explored this idea rather successfully in the BBC-TV production *The Creature* (1954) and the film remake of that story, *The Abominable Snowman* (1957). Featuring future *Doctor Who and the Daleks* star Peter Cushing, this well-done film was directed by Val Guest (*Space: 1999*: "The Rules of Luton," "The A.B. Chyrsalis") and it explored the myth of the Yeti in the land of Tibet. Other than this film, two other Abominable Snowman pictures were made in the '50s: W. Lee Wilder's *The Snow Creature* (1954) and *Man Beast* (1956). As always, *Doctor Who* was not content merely to recycle a popular science fiction idea seen in recent or well-regarded films. Instead, it turned Kneale's concept of the Yeti on its head. In "The Abominable Snowmen," the Yeti were not natural creatures, but robots controlled by an otherworldly, non-corporeal alien menace!

The idea that a hairy beast could actually be a robot was so successful on *Doctor Who* that the concept reappeared several years later on the 1970s American ABC action-adventure program *The Six Million Dollar Man* (1974-1978). In that series, actor Ted Cassidy portrayed Bigfoot. Of course, this incarnation of Sasquatch was no ordinary missing link, he was a bionic robot under the control of aliens Stefanie Powers and Severn Darden (*Conquest of the Planet of the Apes* [1972]). Furthermore, Sasquatch could be activated and deactivated by the aliens, just like the Yeti of "The Abominable Snowmen."

The Yeti also recurred on *Doctor Who* in "The Web of Fear" and even had a guest appearance on the twentieth anniversary special "The Five Doctors." Likewise, the robotic Sasquatch made several return appearances on both *The Six Million Dollar Man* and Lindsay Wagner's sister series *The Bionic Woman*. The Yeti and their silver spheres returned more recently in the video *Downtime* (1996) starring Jack Watling, Deborah Watling, Elizabeth Sladen and Nicholas Courtney. Since the purpose of this book is to officially document antecedents to *Doctor Who*, then it is only fair to note that the dreadful film *Robot Monster* (1953) also posited the notion of hairy robots. In the case of this movie, a robot was portrayed by a man in a gorilla suit and a diving helmet!

"The Abominable Snowman" introduces the Doctor's long association with Prof. Travers. He would encounter Travers and his daughter Anne in "The Web of Fear" later in Season 5. The Doctor would also return for another visit to Travers in the Cyberman adventure "The Invasion." Throughout the entire *Doctor*

Who series, in fact, the Doctor is seen to have a somewhat friendly relationship with people named "Travers." In "Terror of the Vervoids," the commander of the *Hyperion III* is a Travers who knows the Doctor somehow. Their relationship is never clarified, but one wonders if this starship commander is actually a descendent of Anne Travers. A recent book, *Millennial Rites*, also reintroduced the Travers family to the *Who*niverse.

Like the Travers family and the Yeti, the Great Intelligence would also return to menace Patrick Troughton's incarnation of the Doctor in "The Web of Fear."

Today, Episode 2 of "The Abominable Snowmen" exists alone. It has been released on the tape "The Patrick Troughton Years." This is another great loss to *Doctor Who* fandom because the Yeti are such a beloved adversary.

39. "The Ice Warriors" Written by Brian Hayles; Directed by Derek Martinus; Designed by Jeremy Davies; Parts I–VI; Airdates: November 11, 18, 25, December 2, 9, 16, 1967

SYNOPSIS: The TARDIS arrives in the middle of Earth's second Ice Age, when the world's continents are being threatened by encroaching glaciers. The scientists at a nearby installation ask the Doctor how to stop the ice surge, and he realizes ionization is causing the freezing of the planet. The carbon dioxide content of Earth's atmosphere has been unbalanced by the artificial recycling of waste gases. Prof. Clent, the commander of the installation, has been using a device called an Ionizer to heat certain parts of the world and fend off the encroachment of the glaciers, but even that is not helping any more.

While the Doctor works to solve this problem, another scientist, Arden, discovers the body of a strange being frozen in the ice. The scientists thaw the figure and discover that it is an alien — an Ice Warrior from the planet Mars! The Ice Warrior, Varga, strikes Jamie unconscious and carries Victoria away as a hostage.

Soon a squad of vicious Ice Warriors awakens and reactivates its buried spaceship. The Doctor determines that the Ice Warriors must be destroyed before they realize that all life is extinguished on Mars. If they learn that fact, they will have no choice but to conquer Earth. The key to saving the Earth from the ice age and the Ice Warriors rests with mercury isotopes, a sonic cannon, and ammonium sulphide.

GUEST CAST: Clent (Peter Barkworth); Arden (George Waring); Varga (Bernard Bresslaw); Zondal (Roger Jones); Turoc (Sonny Caldinez); Storr (Angus Lennie); Ms. Garrett (Wendy Gifford); Davis (Peter Diamond); Penley (Peter Sallis); Rintan (Tony Harwood); Isbur (Michael Attwell); Computer Voice (Roy Skelton)

COMMENTARY: Proving that in matters of predicting the future, every science fiction television show is hit or miss, "The Ice Warriors" is rife with scientific speculations that viewed 30 years later are interesting, if not entirely accurate. Firstly, the program theorizes that life once existed on Mars. For many years, this was thought to be a fantasy until a Martian fossil was discovered in 1997. Of course, it is doubtful that Ice Warriors ever marched across the surface of the Red Planet, but the discovery that any form of life once existed on Mars adds a bit of relevance to this story today. It makes the possibility of an ancient Martian civilization seem a tad more believable.

On the other hand, this episode also predicts that the Earth will one day be plunged into a Second Ice Age. In 1967, when "The Ice Warriors" was written, there was no such thing as the Greenhouse Effect, but today the polar ice caps are melting, not expanding and encroaching on other continents. And in 1998, much of America's East Coast experienced one of the hottest, most arid summers in recent memory. So, in this situation, *Doctor Who* has been proven wrong.

Otherwise, "The Ice Warriors" is a none-too-subtle *Doctor Who* redress of a popular science fiction film, in this case Howard Hawks' classic fright flick *The Thing from Another World* (1951) starring James Arness as an "intellectual carrot." Here much of the same formula from *The Thing* is duplicated. There is a frozen location and isolated installation (England of the future instead of the Arctic of the 1950s), an alien who is awakened from slumber in the ice, and even a flying saucer. It is difficult to tell whether *Doctor Who*'s rendering of the classic scenario is inventive or merely derivative since the serial has not been released on videotape. Episodes 1, 4, 5, and 6 are known to exist at the BBC, so it is entirely possible that this serial might grace video shelves one day, and be granted a fuller assessment.

This author urges the BBC to assemble the remaining footage and release "The Ice Warriors" so fans will have the opportunity to see more of Troughton's excellent interpretation of the Doctor. This serial is a logical candidate because two-thirds of it are extant. That is more than could be said for "The Abominable Snowmen," "Enemy of the World" or "The Web of Fear"... *Who* classics that now exist only as scraps.

Doctor Who would repeat the scenario of *The Thing* yet again in the Season 13 story "The Seeds of Doom." Like the Thing of Howard Hawks' film, the creature in that serial, the Krynoid, is made of vegetable matter.

Brian Hayles' Ice Warriors make their first historic appearance in this lost story. They would return to menace the Doctor and all of the Earth in Season 6's "Seeds of Death." They would show up yet again, in less menacing form, in Season 9's "The Curse of Peladon." Their last appearance on *Doctor Who* was a return to villainy in the Season 11 sequel to "The Curse of Peladon" entitled "The Monster of Peladon."

40. "The Enemy of the World" Written by David Whitaker; Directed by Barry Letts; Designed by Christopher Pemsel; Parts I–VI; Airdates: December 23, 30, 1967, January 6, 13, 20, 27, 1968

SYNOPSIS: The TARDIS lands at a seaside location in Australia in the year 2030. No sooner have they landed, however, than they are hounded by a hovercraft. The pilot of this ship is convinced that the Doctor is someone called "Salamander." The Doctor and his companions are rescued in a helicopter by a woman named Astrid, who informs them that the Doctor is an exact double of a man determined to achieve total mastery over Earth. This dictator, Salamander, was once a world benefactor who invented and used a device called "The Suncatcher" to manipulate world climate and grow crops for the starving masses of the planet. Now he has killed or discredited most of his political opponents, and he plans to take over the World Zones Organization.

Astrid's superior, Giles Kent, wants the Doctor to double as Salamander and expose the truth of his evil regime. Meanwhile, Jamie and Victoria infiltrate Salamander's organization and gain the dictator's trust. The Doctor discovers that Salamander has kept a secret corps of a hundred people in the bomb shelter below his Sanctum. He has lied to all of them, and told them that the surface of the planet has been devastated by war. They have been responsible for producing the natural disasters plaguing the world ... at Salamander's behest.

Soon, Salamander and the Doctor, exact duplicates, have their final showdown, but Jamie and Victoria are left wondering how exactly to determine which one has survived!

GUEST CAST: Salamander (Patrick Troughton); Astrid (Mary Peach); Fedorin (David Nettheim); Swann (Christopher Burgess); Anton (Henry Stamper); Rod (Rhys McConnachie); Curly (Simon Caine); Giles Kent (Bill Kerr), Donald Bruce (Colin Douglas); Benik (Milton Johns); Denes (George Pravda); Fariah (Carmen Monroe); Griffin (Reg Lyes); Sergeant (Andrew Staines); Guards (Bob Anderson, Elliot Cairnes, Dibbs Mather, William McGuirk)

COMMENTARY: "The Enemy of the World" is yet another unusual *Doctor Who* serial. This tale of a dictator who cons not only a group of gullible underground dwellers but the world itself seems at first blush more appropriate to an American espionage series such as *Mission: Impossible* (1966–72) than to the time traveling, galaxy-hopping *Doctor Who*. In fact, the *Prisoner of Zenda*–like concept of a hero going undercover and mimicking a third-world dictator was the mainstay of that particular Paramount television series. Episodes such as the fourth season premiere "The Code" (1969), which featured *Star Trek* star Leonard Nimoy impersonating a Fidel Castro–type despot, cover much of the same territory as this *Who* serial. As usual, however, the writers of *Doctor Who* were not content to do only one type of story. They again mixed several genres to make this particular story more interesting. As a result, "Enemy of the World" is no ordinary espionage story. It is also a James Bondian super-adventure with a megalomaniacal dictator utilizing a powerful weather control machine (The Suncatcher) to dominate the world, as well as a "future" story (the episode takes place in 2070). These elements would doubtless make "Enemy of the World" a remarkable *Doctor Who* to watch today, especially since it also features a double performance by Troughton as the good Doctor and as the power-hungry Salamander. Unfortunately, like Hartnell's double starring turn in "The Massacre," this serial has been destroyed. Only one of the four episodes, Number 3, has been found. It has been released on the tape "The Patrick Troughton Years" so Troughton fans can at least catch a glimpse of this fine actor portraying a despicable villain.

41. "The Web of Fear" Written by Mervyn Haisman & Henry Lincoln; Directed by Douglas Camfield; Designed by David Myerscough-Jones; Parts I–VI; Airdates: February 3, 10, 17, 24, March 2, 9, 1968

SYNOPSIS: The TARDIS is trapped in a time-space vortex by the powerful grip of the Great Intelligence, the alien force which the Doctor believed was vanquished near Tibet in the 1930s following his adventure at the Det-Sen Monastery. The TARDIS is finally able to break free from the grasp of the evil alien force, and the Doctor brings the TARDIS to Earth in the 1960s in a seemingly abandoned London subway station. There the travelers discover the same cobweb material that attacked the TARDIS, and the Doctor realizes he is witnessing the beginning of another invasion. Once more, the Great Intelligence is planning to break through into reality!

Col. Lethbridge-Stewart, a British officer with a dry wit and a no-nonsense attitude, arrives in the station with a detachment of troops. Unfortunately, the clues surrounding the invasion lead the Doctor, Jamie, Victoria and Lethbridge-Stewart back to their friend from the Himalayas, Prof. Travers. Along with his daughter Anne, Travers has reanimated one of the Yeti robots, and this act has given the Great Intelligence a window back into this world!

A new Yeti army takes control of the subway station, and the Doctor is captured by the Great Intelligence when one of Lethbridge-Stewart's top aides, Sgt. Arnold, turns out to be operating in much the same capacity as Padmasambvha was in the 1930s — as a host for the Great Intelligence.

In response to this alien invasion, Lethbridge-Stewart envisions a multinational task force that will defend the Earth against just such attack. This idea will germinate in a few years and result in UNIT (United Nations Intelligence Task Force).

GUEST CAST: Col. Alistair Lethbridge-Stewart (Nicholas Courtney); Prof. Travers (Jack Watling); Anne Travers (Tina Packer); Lane (Rod Beachman); Silverstein (Frederick Schrecker); Knight (Ralph Watson); Chorley (John Rollason); Wems (Stephen Whittaker); Arnold (Jack Woolgar); Evans (Derek Pollitt); Yeti (Roger Jacombs, Jeremy King, John Levene, John Lord, Gordon Stothard, Colin Warman); Soldiers (Bernard High, Joseph O'Connell)

COMMENTARY: The second Mervyn Haisman-Henry Lincoln story of Season 5 brings back Prof. Travers, the Yeti and the deadly Great Intelligence, all from the lost "The Abominable Snowmen." It also introduces a character who was destined to become one *Doctor Who*'s most beloved recurring personalities: Alistair Lethbridge-Stewart. This fascinating character was brought back in "Invasion" at the behest of frequent *Who* director Douglas Camfield, who first met Courtney while directing "The Dalek Masterplan."[6]

When the Doctor began his exile on Earth and regenerated into his third incarnation, Jon Pertwee, the Brigadier and Courtney both became an integral part of the series. It was during this time that the show took on its most philosophical form, with stories such as "Inferno" and "The Green Death" exploring environmental issues such as pollution, and "Doctor Who and the Silurians" raising questions of genocide. Courtney's role as the Brigadier in those years would frequently be to cast all that social "rubbish" aside, and lead the action scenes. Courtney was thus able to bring a valuable counterpoint to the humanitarianism of the Doctor. In October 1986, Courtney told *Starlog* interviewer Patrick Daniel O'Neill how he developed this important character:

Nicholas Courtney, here seen at an American *Doctor Who* convention, premiered as Alistair Lethbridge-Stewart in episode #41, "The Web of Fear."

> When he was first introduced, the Brig was just an army officer barking out orders. That was very boring... I was eventually allowed to rewrite some of my lines to flesh the man out. Even if the lines weren't there, I tried to think the Brig's character out on my own, and let that show through gestures and reaction shots... The essence of their relationship [the Doctor's and the Brigadier's] was the clash between ... military and ... scientific minds.[7]

It is in "The Web of Fear" that the stern Lethbridge-Stewart, here a colonel, first encounters the strange Doctor from another planet. Although Courtney only worked twice with Patrick Troughton, it was their chemistry that established the ongoing relationship between these two men. This was such a good pairing, ironically, that in the twentieth anniversary celebration "The Five Doctors," Troughton and Courtney are teamed for much of the story, not Pertwee and Courtney.

"The Web of Fear" also sets up the formation of UNIT, another important series concept that would come to full maturity during Pertwee's reign as the Doctor. In addition, it presents the notion of a terror roaming beneath the streets of London; very shortly, Cybermen would use the sewers, not the subway, to plan their invasion in "The Invasion." And Anne Travers would return in the *Doctor Who* Missing Adventure title *Millennial Rites*. That story, which features Colin Baker's Doctor, concerns the emergence of the Great Intelligence on the eve of the twenty-first century.

Despite the historic importance of this story, it too has been destroyed by BBC standard operating procedure. Today only Episode 1 remains intact. The title "The Web of Fear" was repeated in 1971 in the Kit Pedler-Gerry Davis series

Doomwatch. That story had nothing to do with Yeti or subways, but rather with an outbreak of a deadly plague on a remote island.

42. "Fury from the Deep" Written by Victor Pemberton; Directed by Hugh David; Designed by Peter Kindred; Parts I–VI; Airdates: March 16, 23, 30, April 6, 13, 20, 1968

SYNOPSIS: The TARDIS lands once more in modern England, and the Doctor discovers a species of malevolent, extra-terrestrial seaweed attempting to infiltrate a North Shore oil rig. The seaweed is apparently feeding off the natural gas beneath the North Sea, and expelling it in a toxic mix. The situation grows worse as the weed monsters begin to take over human beings telepathically. Meanwhile, Victoria decides she cannot handle any more dangerous situations. In the short time she has been with the Doctor, she has faced Cybermen, Daleks and the Yeti, and she wants to remain on Earth.

GUEST CAST: Harris (Roy Spencer); Maggie Harris (Jane Murphy); Robson (Victor Maddern); Van Lutyens (John Abineri); Megan Jones (Margaret John); Perkins (Brian Cullingford); Price (Graham Leaman); Quill (Bill Burridge); Oak (John Gill); Curney (John Garvin); Chief Engineer (Hubert Rees); Guard (Peter Ducrow)

COMMENTARY: Victor Pemberton's "Fury from the Deep" is *Doctor Who*'s first "invasion of the plants"-type story. Although here it is dangerous, telepathic seaweed causing the trouble, in later stories it would be the spore-born Krynoid ("Seeds of Doom"), the cactus-like, prickly Meglos ("Meglos") and the leafy but malevolent Vervoids ("Terror of the Vervoids"). The notion that vegetable matter can make for a distressing villain is a common one in genre history, given perhaps its greatest treatment in John Wyndham's novel *Day of the Triffids*, and adapted as a less than satisfactory film of the same name in 1963. *Doctor Who*'s "Fury from the Deep" is a reversal of the events seen in that film. In *Day of the Triffids*, the plants are killed by salt water, but in *Doctor Who*, the seaweed *thrives* in sea water.

Evil alien plants also make appearances in all the standard science fiction television series of our age, including *Space: 1999* ("The Troubled Spirit," "The Rules of Luton"), *Star Trek: The Next Generation* ("Shades of Grey"), *Lost in Space* ("The Great Vegetable Rebellion"), *Voyage to the Bottom of the Sea* ("The Plant Man") and *Blake's 7* ("Shadow").

In a sense, "Fury from the Deep" is also another trip to the *Invasion of the Body Snatchers* well already visited in "The Faceless Ones." In this story, people succumb to alien mind control and become the automatons of the villainous seaweed. This theme was a prevalent one in '50s science fiction films, turning up in *It Came from Outer Space* (1953), and *Invaders from Mars* (1953), just to name two.

"Fury from the Deep" also sends off Deborah Watling's Victoria. Her reason for leaving the Doctor, that things have just been too rough for her, certainly has the ring of truth to it. Victoria has the honor of being the Doctor's companion through probably the most dangerous season in *Doctor Who* history. She met the Daleks ("Evil of the Daleks"), the Cybermen ("Tomb of the Cybermen") and the

Ice Warriors ("The Ice Warriors"). She also twice encountered the Yeti and the Great Intelligence ("The Abominable Snowmen" and "Web of Fear"). To top it off, she was accosted by killer seaweed in her final story! That is certainly more than enough peril for any companion to withstand. No wonder the poor girl chose to stay on Earth!

Victor Pemberton, script editor on "The Tomb of the Cyberman" and writer of "Fury from the Deep," went on to write several other episodes of British genre programming. He wrote "The Power of Atep" and "Sisters Deadly," two four-part serials for *Ace of Wands* in 1972.

No episodes of "Fury from the Deep" still exist today, but Pemberton did write the serial's novelization for the Target Book series.

43. "The Wheel in Space" Written by David Whitaker; Directed by Tristan de Vere Cole; Designed by Derek Dodd; Parts I–VI; Airdates: April 27, May 4, 11, 18, 25, June 1, 1968

SYNOPSIS: Space Station W3, the Wheel in Space, is a giant research station on the border of the solar system, and the latest target of the power-hungry Cybermen. They have sent their servants, the villainous cybermats, to sabotage the station. The Doctor and Jamie arrive and discover that the Cybermen have also smuggled themselves aboard. Their plan is to eliminate the Wheel crew and use the station as a jumping-off point to a second invasion of Earth. When the Doctor and Jamie warn the crew of the danger, they are treated as strangers and saboteurs. Only Zoe Herriott, a teenage mathematical genius and astrophysicist, believes their story.

While the Cybermen methodically awaken from bubble-like storage containers, Zoe discovers that Hercules, a nearby star, is about to go nova. The radiation flux will send asteroid shards smashing into the station. Now the Doctor must protect the station from Cybermen *and* the cosmic disaster. Unfortunately, the station's laser beams are inoperative, and the Cybermen are attacking in force! When Zoe expresses her desire to join up with the Doctor, he demands that she be prepared for what awaits. He then transmits portions of previous adventures...

GUEST CAST: Servo Robot (Freddie Foote); Tanya Lernov (Clare Jenkins); Communications Officer Leo Ryan (Eric Flynn); Space Station Controller Jarvis Bennett (Michael Turner); Bill Duggan (Kenneth Watson); Dr. Gimma Corwyn (Anne Ridler); Elton Latham (Michael Goldie); Armand Vallance (Derrick Gilbert); Enrico Casli (Donald Sumpter); Kemel Rudkin (Jevork Malikyan); Sean Flannigan (James Mellor); Chano (Peter Laird); Cybermen (Gordon Stothard, Jerry Holmes); Cybermen Voices (Peter Hawkins, Roy Skelton)

COMMENTARY: "The Wheel In Space," the fourth Cyberman adventure seen in *Doctor Who* and the second Cyberman adventure of the fifth season, is less innovative and exciting than the seminal "The Tomb of the Cybermen." In fact, it is a rather obvious rehash of Season 4's "The Moonbase." In both circumstances, the Cybermen are planning an invasion. In both circumstances, an Earth installation (a moonbase or a space station) is to be the first target. In both instances, the Doctor and his companions are suspected of causing the trouble. The Cybermen also control Earthmen via an unusual methods (a disease in "The Moonbase," hypnosis in "The Wheel in Space") in both programs. And, of course, the Doctor saves the installation not only from the Cybermen, but another danger as well (the graviton in "The Moonbase," the asteroid collision in "The Wheel in Space"). With so many common elements, "The Wheel in Space" is a formula episode all the way.

The introduction of Wendy Padbury as Zoe to the series is perhaps the most innovative element of this serial. Zoe is the first woman aboard the TARDIS in some time who can handle herself in a mature, intelligent fashion. Although she is perhaps the youngest of the female companions, she is far more responsible and adult than Dodo, Polly or Victoria. She is a scientist every bit the Doctor's equal, and a brilliant intellect as well. She is not a screaming, helpless thing like Victoria, nor an adolescent like Dodo. Her character, combining scientific genius, intense curiosity and logic, meshes perfectly with Jamie McCrimmon, who represents action, vitality and energy. The Doctor, especially as portrayed by Troughton, is an unpredictable synthesis of these two characters, sometimes remote and intellectual, sometimes fiercely physical in his solutions to problems. This triumvirate in the TARDIS shares some of *Doctor Who*'s best chemistry since the days of Susan, Barbara, Ian and Hartnell's Doctor. Many great moments would arise from this exciting trio in Season 6, and most of them are available on videocassette.

Episodes 3 and 6 are all that remain of "The Wheel in Space" today. They can be seen alongside episodes of the similar "The Moonbase" on the tape "Cybermen — The Early Years" from BBC/CBS-Fox video.

SEASON 6

44. "The Dominators" Written by Norman Ashby [Mervyn Haisman & Henry Lincoln]; Directed by Morris Barry; Designed by Barry Newbery; Parts I–V; Airdates: August 10, 17, 24, 31, September 7, 1968

SYNOPSIS: A phalanx of Dominator warships cruise above the peaceful planet Dulkis, and one ship in the armada breaks formation and dives into the atmosphere. Soon after landing, two uniformed soldiers, Rago and Toba, exit the craft and scan their surroundings. They have landed to acquire fuel, but to do so they require slave labor. The Dominators order their robot servants, "Quarks," out of their saucer to begin capturing slaves.

The TARDIS arrives as the situation unfolds. Soon after the Doctor and Jamie inspect the Dominator saucer, they are captured by the Quarks. Rago interrogates the two aliens, whom he takes for Dulkians, and wants to know if they will be suitable for slave labor. Aware that he is being tested, the Doctor purposely acts less than intelligent in hopes that the Dominators will see there is no threat on this planet and leave it unharmed.

The Dominators, self-proclaimed masters of ten galaxies, then begin to drill into the earth of Dulkis, exploiting the peaceful Dulkians as slave labor. While Dulkian forces are rallied by Zoe and Jamie, the Doctor learns that the vicious Dominators plan to drill holes in the planet and flood the molten mass of the planet with radioactivity. Then, when the planet explodes, the warfleet will utilize the released radiation as fuel!

GUEST CAST: Rago (Ronald Allen); Toba (Kenneth Ives); Cully (Arthur Cox); Etnin (Malcolm Terris); Tolata (Nicolette Pendrell); Kando (Felicity Gibson); Benex (Walter Fitzgerald); Tena (Brian Kent); Bovem (Alan Gerrard); Teel (Giles Block); Balons (Johnson Bayly); Council Members (John Cross, Ronald Mansell); Quarks (John Hicks, Gary Smith, Freddie Wilson); Quark Voices (Sheila Grant)

COMMENTARY: Morris Barry, the auteur of "The Tomb of the Cybermen," directs "The Dominators" with a strong hand, lending some new life to that old *Doctor Who* standby: the planetary revolution against evil oppressors. In this case, the direction and some fine achievements in makeup and costuming make the story a diverting, if not terribly original, effort.

The *Doctor Who* episodes of the Troughton era tend to highlight experimental camerawork and visual effects, and "The Dominators" is no exception. Here, Barry uses several tricks to define the advanced nature of Dominator technology. Several times during the serial, Dulkians and the Doctor's companions are captured and held for evil "testing." The Dominators press a button on a console and the test subjects are "sucked" back against a smooth wall, as if they are under enormous gravitational strain. This unique effect was actually accomplished by filming the sequence in reverse. The actors began a take by clinging to a wall, and then springing forward suddenly. In reverse, the effect is a startling one, as people are seemingly lifted upwards and backwards right onto the wall.

Then, even more impressively, that wall rotates and turns into an examination table. This special effect is accomplished by a quick 90-degree camera arc, and then a quick cut to the test subjects on a horizontal table. It may sound strange to praise these visual tricks, but they are inventive visual depictions of an alien technology. The effects also have the benefit of being cheap and accomplished without opticals. They are *physical* effects, not computer animation or stop-motion, and thus they have the advantage of appearing natural, even real.

Beyond these tricks, Barry also successfully orchestrates a fair amount of destruction in "The Dominators." The deadly Quark robots are constantly opening fire on something and causing explosions of the most magnificent variety. The effect of a Quark weapon on humans (or Dulkians, in this case) is also an inventive visual gimmick. As the Dulkians are struck by the weapon, the film freezes and then the portion of the film showing the Dulkian's facial features is burned off rapidly. It is as if the weapon causes an implosion of flesh. This is another triumph for a low-budget show. The budget could not handle the expense of flashing animated laser beams, so a cheap but visually dynamic alternative (burning film stock) was used instead. This ingenuity is a common factor throughout *Doctor Who*'s early history.

The presentation of the Dominators is also handled with a high degree of skill. Rago and Toba have thick, jet-black hair, yet ghostly white complexions. Their faces thus appear gaunt and skeletal and their chalky skin seems pinched. In essence, they look like the living dead. Their costumes are also dramatic. The Dominator uniform features a huge "hump" that extends from the upper arm all the way up the length of the neck. This back "hump" suggests that the Dominators have a non-human physique, even that they are encased inside uniforms like turtles are encased in shells. This unusual uniform gives the impression not only of rigidity, a typical Dominator trait, but also of massive shoulders and arms.

The interior of the Dominator spaceship is also stylish and believable. Not only does it come complete with the aforementioned swinging wall/table, but also with a well-designed, lighted "Quark" condition indicator. Whenever one of the Quarks is destroyed, a small icon on the console, shaped like the robots, starts flashing in the background. The multi-level command center, surrounded by convincing "computer" hardware, is among the best sets in the early years of *Doctor Who*. Even the Quarks, with their spiked heads and retractable arms, are convincing in appearance. These machines, perhaps because they were seen primarily as "servants" rather than as villains, have never shared the popularity experienced by the Daleks, the Cybermen or the Sontarans. Despite this, they did make a cameo appearance in the final Troughton adventure "The War Games."

"The Dominators" shares another common trait with all great episodes of *Doctor Who*: humor. Troughton and Frazer Hines get to indulge in their penchant for silliness in the scene wherein they are apprehended and tested by the Dominators. Realizing that they will be killed as threats if they reveal too much, these two distinguished actors put on a most convincing "stupid" show, with the Doctor pretending ignorance of even the most basic machinery (such as a ray gun). Though this scene is terribly silly, it grows naturally out of the drama of "The Dominators." There *is* a reason for the silliness. Such would not always be the case in *Doctor Who*. In some of the later Tom Baker years, the Doctor treated many of his opponents as silly ... something that totally deflated the reality of the program.

With moments of humor, plenty of fireworks, some novel visual conceits and solid production values, "The Dominators" is a strong, if not inspired episode of *Doctor Who*. It can be enjoyed on the BBC/CBS-Fox videotape.

45. "The Mind Robber" Written by Peter Ling; Directed by David Maloney; Designed by Evan Hercules; Parts I–V; Airdates: September 14, 21, 28, October 5, 12, 1968

SYNOPSIS: To escape an erupting volcano on Dulkis, the Doctor takes the TARDIS outside the space-time continuum. Essentially, the capsule now exists "nowhere." Zoe and Jamie are lured out of the TARDIS by visions of their homes, and the Doctor is challenged telepathically by a powerful, unseen foe. The Doctor rescues Zoe and Jamie briefly, but then the TARDIS is ripped apart and the crew ends up in a bizarre dimension: the Land of Fiction!

Zoe, Jamie and the Doctor materialize separately and are confronted by various enigmas. A stranger warns the Doctor that a being called the Master is working against him from a citadel atop the highest mountain in the land. After encounters with the Minotaur, Gulliver, Medusa, Rapunzel and a comic strip character of the year 2000 named "Karkus," the Doctor is taken to the control room of the Master, where he learns that his nemesis is an old man, a writer from 1926 England. He was a prolific writer on his world, but here he is the puppet of the Master Computer. He has sent for the Doctor to replace him as the caretaker of the Land of Fiction.

The alien machine that controls the Land of Fiction needs a man of boundless imagination, a man who will live forever, to take the Master's place. The Doctor refuses to spend eternity as a prisoner of fiction, but the computer retaliates and threatens to reduce Zoe and Jamie to creatures of "fiction."

GUEST CAST: The Master (Emrys Jones); Robots (John Atterbury, Ralph Carrigan, Bill Wiesener, Terry Wright); Redcoat (Philip Ryan); Jamie (Hamish Wilson); A Stranger (Gulliver) (Bernard Horsfall); Children (Barbara Loft, Sylvestra Le Tozel, Timothy Horton, Christopher Reynolds, David Reynolds, Martin Langley); Soldiers (Paul Alexander, Ian Hines, Richard Ireson); Karkus (Christopher Robbie); Rapunzel (Christine Pine); Medusa (Sue Pulford); D'Artagnan/ Lancelot (John Greenwood) Blackbeard (Gerry Wain); Cyrano De Bergerac (David Cannon)

COMMENTARY: "The Mind Robber" stands proudly, even after 30 years, as one of the top ten episodes of *Doctor Who*. It is a stylish, nightmarish excursion into another reality. Peter Ling's script is filled with terror, wonder and even humor. Even better, it is also shocking and unpredictable. In all, it is a stunning and memorable victory for the *Who* creative team, one that comes out of nowhere and sideswipes viewers with its unique vision and soaring imagination.

David Maloney directs "The Mind Robber" with an imaginative eye. Since this story visualizes a heretofore unseen universe, Maloney is free to define it with broad stylistic strokes and interesting visual effects. The story opens with a lava flow and Maloney builds the tension of this scene with techniques such as quick cutting, on-set smoke effects and rapid-fire dialogue from the nearly hysterical Troughton. Once the TARDIS escapes, the tension is diffused, and replaced with an overwhelming sense of fear and dread. Where has the ship landed? Maloney wisely films Troughton in intense closeup as he informs Zoe that they have entered a dimension he knows absolutely *nothing* about. He insists they must be careful because they are at the mercy of the forces of this reality. The sudden shift from the action pace to this frozen closeup of Troughton's worried features sets the stage for what exists outside the TARDIS...a dimension of nothingness.

The "unreality," as the Doctor calls it, is visualized by Maloney as a stark white arena. The sound stage is completely devoid of detail and props, it is just a vast white expanse which seems to stretch to the horizon and beyond. Filmed in long shot, to express the vast isolation of this realm, Zoe and Jamie look like two lost souls in this sea of emptiness. At this point, the sound effect of the Master's white robots is heard. It is a creepy, clicking sound that puts viewers immediately ill at ease. The notion of an unseen, approaching terror is a visceral one. This whole sequence is superbly designed and directed, a show-stopper.

Better yet is what follows. After the TARDIS escapes, it is yanked apart in the cosmic gulf. It is a shocking, unexpected moment when the Police Box splinters into six segments. Then, the control console is seen spinning through blackness, with Zoe and Jamie holding on for dear life. This is one of the most frightening moments in the entire series. The TARDIS has always represented "home" and "safety" on *Doctor Who*, and to see it so easily shattered, its power as "womb" negated, is disconcerting, to say the least. Episode 1 ends as the time travelers, exposed to the forces of evil by the loss of their ship, spiral endlessly through a black void. Who or what they will find in the blackness is a complete mystery. This is perhaps the most effective cliffhanger in the series because the audience has *no idea* what will happen next. Anything is possible.

Once the story settles into the world of fiction, Maloney directs with keen attention to the surreal surroundings. Things drop out of the sky at random, character's faces disappear and re-form into unfamiliar patterns, and people are crushed by the pages of a huge book. In all, it is a terrifying fantasy world that reminds one of some of the great children's literature and films of the twentieth century, including C.S. Lewis' *The Lion, the Witch and the Wardrobe*, L. Frank Baum's *The Wizard of Oz* and Roald Dahl's *Willy Wonka and the Chocolate Factory*. Like those other fantasy landscapes, the Land of Fiction is every bit as much a place of horror as wonder. There is a spine-chilling element of danger to this world, something that children surely associate with the evil Witch of *Oz* or the gruesome fates of the children in *Willy Wonka*. Here, *Doctor Who*'s beloved characters Jamie and Zoe are converted into fiction, faced with terrifying and absurd obstacles like giant glass jars, and hunted by the evil ruler of this realm. "The Mind Robber" may not be believable science fiction to any degree whatsoever, but it is a visual fantasy of the first order, a flight of imagination that would be impossible on more reality-"grounded" technological shows such as *Star Trek* or *Babylon 5*.

"The Mind Robber" also plays close attention to the character details of *Doctor Who*. Peter Ling recalls that Zoe is from the future by having her visualize a character of fiction from the early twenty-first century ... Karkus. It would have been both illogical and unbelievable to suggest that someone from a century ahead would only have affection for creatures and beings from classical and twentieth century literature. Also, Ling provides an appropriate "siren" call for Jamie and Zoe. They are lured out of the TARDIS with visions of their homes. These are insightful details on the author's part, and they add immeasurably to the success of the story.

The final twist of "The Mind Robber," that a human has been abducted and attached to a computer to run this realm, is a classic science fiction concept. It has been seen on *Star Trek* in "Spock's Brain," among others. For its entire run, *Doctor Who* is fascinated by the combination of the human mind and computers. It was a central notion of "The War Machines" and it is an idea that re-occurred in "The Green Death" and "The Face of Evil," among others. As usual, *Doctor Who* expresses the idea that man is superior to machine, and here the Master of the Land is a human being. He needs the computer to "create" all that he dreams, but man is seen as the inspiration, the true creator of this bizarre realm. In a season of invasions and revolutions, "The Mind Robber" is an unexpected, joyful sojourn into memorable fantasy. This smart, terrifying, memorable adventure can be enjoyed today since the episode has been released on VHS.

46. "The Invasion" Written by Derrick Sherwin; Directed by Douglas Camfield; Designed by Richard Hunt; Parts I–VIII; Airdates: November 2, 9, 16, 23 30, December 7, 14, 21, 1968

SYNOPSIS: The Doctor, Jamie and Zoe have returned to Earth to visit with their old friend, Prof. Travers. They discover that he has opened his home to a scientist friend, Prof. Watkins, and his niece Isobel. Isobel informs the travelers that her uncle has disappeared. He was last seen on his way to International Electromatics, a huge conglomerate run by tycoon Tobias Vaughn. Vaughn is the designer and manufacturer of the micro-monolithic computer chip, a revolutionary advance in computers.

Brigadier Lethbridge-Stewart and his new task force, UNIT, assist the Doctor in the investigation of Vaughn, and it is soon obvious that Vaughn has betrayed his people and paved the way for a Cyberman invasion of London! Encased in canisters in the London sewers, thousands of Cybermen awaken and proceed to critical strategic sites all over the city. A cybership in space then transmits a signal through all the micro-monolithic chips created by International Electromatics. These chips are in transistors, televisions, computers and other household devices. The signal makes all of humanity slaves to the Cybermen. The Doctor has rigged a signal jammer for his friends at UNIT, but the majority of the world is now powerless before the invaders!

GUEST CAST: Tobias Vaughn (Kevin Stoney); Tracy (Geoffrey Cheshire); Sgt. Benton (John Levene); Isobel (Sally Faulkner); Gregory (Ian Fairnbairn); Packer (Peter Halliday); Brigadier Lethbridge-Stewart (Nicholas Courtney); Sgt. Walters (James Thornhill); Capt. Turner (Robert Sidaway); Prof. Watkins (Edward Burnham); Major General Rutledge (Edward Dentith); Phone Operator (Sheila Dunn); Workman (Peter Thompson); Policeman (Dominic Allan); Major Branwell (Clifford Earl); Sgt. Peters (Norman Hartley); Patrolman (Walter Randall); Driver (Murray Evans); Cybermen (Ralph Carrigan, Charles Finch, Pat Gorman, Richard King, John Spradbury, Peter Thornton)

COMMENTARY: "The Invasion" is a bit of a letdown after the unique adventure "The Mind Robber." At eight parts it is an overlong story that attempts to recapture some of the early *Doctor Who* glory by rehashing several key ingredients that had gained the series notoriety in the past. Firstly, there is the use of locations in London. In "The Dalek Invasion of Earth," the Daleks ascended from the Thames and chased Barbara Wright across the bridge. In "The Invasion," the Cybermen march on St. Paul's Cathedral. The image is authentic, but when something like this has been done once, the second such attempt is inevitably less successful.

Beyond location, "The Invasion" is yet another space invasion story, something seen not only in "The Dalek Invasion of Earth" but also in "The Tenth Planet" and "The Moonbase." Hence there is nothing really unique about the threat at the heart of this story. Beyond the general style of the story, many details of "The Invasion" are uncomfortably familiar to earlier episodes of *Doctor Who*.

In "The Evil of the Daleks," the Daleks were infused with the human factor, something which mitigates their evil nature. In "The Invasion," a machine is invented to make the Cybermen feel "fear," a human emotion. This is not the only similarity. In "The Dalek Masterplan," Mavic Chen betrays the Earth and the solar system, only to be betrayed himself, and killed by his Dalek conspirators. Tobias Vaughn fulfills the exact same function in "The Invasion." He too is killed by his Cybermen allies when they have no further use for him. The roles are nearly identical, a fact made even more obvious by the casting of Kevin Stoney as Vaughn. He also played Chen in "The Dalek Masterplan!" Also returning is another popular character, Lethbridge-Stewart, from another London invasion story, "The Web of Fear." Indeed, "The Invasion" is so familiar in its details that it almost seems like a remake of many early *Doctor Who* serials. It looks as if the producers had decided to update all the great "invasion" moments for the Troughton era, using the villains of his era, the Cybermen, instead of the Daleks. It is no wonder that after the derivative "The Invasion," the Cybermen were retired from the series for six years, until the Tom Baker Season 12 story "Revenge of the Cybermen." It is clear both with "The Wheel in Space" and "The Invasion" that the writers had nothing new to add to Cyberman lore. These stories diminished their effectiveness considerably. To this day, "The Tomb of the Cybermen" remains the definitive Cyberman adventure.

It is interesting that in "Tomb of the Cybermen," the Cyber Controller recognizes the Doctor from the events in the episode "The Moonbase." Since "The Invasion" also takes place during the second Doctor's incarnation *but* chronologically before the events seen in "The Moonbase," the Cyber Controller should also have recognized him from the events depicted in "The Invasion." Of course, "Tomb of the Cybermen" writers Kit Pedler and Gerry Davis could not have known this at the time they wrote "Tomb," since "The Invasion" was not even written. This is the danger that occasionally crops up in *Doctor Who*. The Doctor encounters his enemies so many times, in the future and in the past, that one needs a score card to remember which Doctors have encountered which opponents in which time periods.

To wit: "The Invasion" takes place in the 1960s with Patrick Troughton, after the Doctor's first regeneration. Yet "The Tenth Planet" (the last Hartnell adventure) occurs in 1986, 20 years after the "The Invasion." In that story, however, the

Doctor is still in his first incarnation! It is enough to drive anybody crazy! And why don't the people of 1986 (in "The Tenth Planet") remember the Cyberman invasion of the '60s? And where is Mondas in this story, since it would not reach Earth for another 20 years?

John Levene, who previously portrayed a Yeti in "The Web of Fear," returns to *Doctor Who* as UNIT's Sgt. Benton. This role would become a regular one for the talented young actor during the Jon Pertwee era. He also guest-starred in "The Android Invasion" with Tom Baker. A video production about the erstwhile Sgt. Benton, created in the late '80s, was entitled *Wartime*.

"The Invasion" has been released on videotape despite the fact that three episodes have been destroyed. On the BBC/CBS-Fox release, Nicholas Courtney narrates the missing portions of the story. Even with nearly an hour of the story missing, "The Invasion" still seems long and drawn out, filled as it is with umpteen captures and rescues.

47. "The Krotons" Written by Robert Holmes; Directed by David Maloney; Designed by Raymond London; Parts I–IV; Airdates: December 28, 1968, January 4, 11, 18, 1969

SYNOPSIS: On the desert homeworld of the Gonds, two exceptional students, Abu and Vana, have been selected to receive the highest honor of Gond culture: They are to be made the companions of the all-powerful Krotons. This is the law of the Krotons, but there is a dissenter among the students at the departure ceremony. He believes it is murder to send the students into the lair of the Krotons.

The Doctor, Jamie and Zoe arrive on the planet and learn that the alien Krotons crashed many years ago on Gond. Since then, they have masqueraded as gods, without ever even being seen by Gonds. Since the crash, the Krotons, malevolent robots, have been draining the brains of Gond's greatest minds to power their damaged dynatrope spaceship. The Krotons were once part of a battlefleet, but two of their crew were killed when they crashed on Gond. The Dynatrope requires four minds to effect transfer to a different point in time and space, so the Doctor and Zoe, with their enormous intelligence, become the Kroton's latest targets.

As Gonds' people revolt against the Krotons, the Doctor must find a way to destroy the villainous mechanical aliens.

GUEST CAST: Selris (James Copeland); Abu (Terence Brown); Vana (Madeleine Mills); Thara (Gilbert Wynne); Eelek (Philip Madoc); Axus (Richard Ireson); Beta (James Cairncross); Student (Bronson Shaw); Custodian (Maurice Selwyn); Krotons (Robert La'Bassiere, Miles Northover); Kroton Voices (Roy Skelton, Patrick Tull)

COMMENTARY: "The Krotons," like "The Invasion" immediately before it, is a familiar story for *Doctor Who*: the planetary revolution against evil oppressors. Unlike "The Invasion," however, there are enough fresh elements in "The Krotons" to make it a successful, exciting drama. The teleplay by first time *Doctor*

Who contributor Robert Holmes is a very good one, filled with interesting moments of humor and danger. Cleverly, it begins not with the revolution, or even with the arrival of the threat (as in "The Dominators"). Instead, the point of attack is a decidedly late one and the teleplay begins *in media res*, with students being sacrificed to the enigmatic Krotons. This is an effective method to start the tale of Gond, and the script unfolds like a mystery.

Piece by piece, the Doctor learns about his mechanical nemesis, but first he must solve the puzzle of the sacrifices and even receive a history lesson about Gond. This approach not only makes the story more compelling and accessible to viewers, it also lessens the sense that one has seen it all before.

Holmes also saw fit to include a large dollop of humor in the story. Here, as in "The Dominators," Troughton gets much mileage out of the comedic aspects of the story. The Doctor is in such a rush to take the Kroton test and join Zoe as a Kroton "companion" that he starts answering the intelligence questions incorrectly. Of course, this failure flusters him further, and he makes even more mistakes. He is not comforted by Zoe, who stands over his shoulder telling him precisely what he has done wrong on each test question. This is a charming moment in *Doctor Who* history, proving the point again that Troughton's interpretation of the Doctor is perhaps the most three-dimensional of all the actors to assume the role. In later serials, the Doctor almost never makes mistakes, and if he does it is usually a ruse to trick an opponent. This version of the Doctor gets flustered, makes mistakes and shows annoyance. It is a wonderful, human portrayal.

After "The Krotons," Holmes became a continuing writing presence on *Doctor Who*. He wrote "The Space Pirates" for Troughton; "Spearhead from Space," "Terror of the Autons," "Carnival of Monsters" and "The Time Warrior" for Pertwee; "The Ark In Space," "The Deadly Assassin," "The Talons of Weng-Chiang," "The Sunmakers," "The Ribos Operation" and "The Power of Kroll" for Tom Baker; "The Caves of Androzani" for Davison; and "The Two Doctors," "The Mysterious Planet" and the first draft of "The Ultimate Foe" for Colin Baker. As this list reveals, Holmes was a prodigious writer, a mainstay on the series. His other credits include "The Inquest" on the Gerry Davis-Kit Pedler series *Doomwatch*, "Shadrach" and "Dr. Jekyll and Mrs. Hyde" for the 1981 fantasy series *Into the Labyrinth*, and the *Blake's 7* episodes "Orbit" and "Killer." Holmes died before he was able to complete work on "The Ultimate Foe" episode of the epic "The Trial of the Time Lord." His work is revered by *Doctor Who* fans around the world, and he is remembered for introducing both the formless Nestene and the evil Sontarans to the series. He is also well regarded for his exciting send-off for Peter Davison's fifth incarnation, the pulse-pounding "Caves of Androzani."

Also making the first of many appearances on *Doctor Who* is Philip Madoc. He portrays the power-hungry Eelek in "The Krotons," but would return at the end of the season to play the villainous War Lord in "The War Games." His *Doctor Who* appearances did not end there. He also portrayed Dr. Solon in "The Brain of Morbius" and Fenner in "The Power of Kroll." Madoc is a common face in British science fiction not only for his work with the BBC Time Lord, but for ITV rival Gerry Anderson. Madoc played the original commander of Moonbase Alpha in "Breakaway," the premiere of *Space: 1999*. He also appeared twice on *U.F.O.* in the episodes "A Question of Priorities" and "Destruction."

"The Krotons" shows what a talented writer and cast can do with a story that recycles elements from previous adventures. It is a memorable serial. The Krotons themselves fail to match the evil of the Daleks. Their costume is less successful as well since their lower half, presumably the legs of the actors, is hidden only by flimsy metal sheets. But the top of the costume, with the crystal-shaped head, is unique and interesting to look at.

Like all but one of the adventures from Season 6, "The Krotons" is available on videocassette.

48. "Seeds of Death" Written by Brian Hayles; Directed by Michael Ferguson; Designed by Paul Allen; Parts I–VI; Airdates: January 25, February 1, 8, 15, 22, March 1, 1969

SYNOPSIS: The T-Mat is the public transportation system of the future, and a supposedly foolproof molecular dispersion device. This day is special, however, because the lunar T-Mat facility has been invaded by the cold-blooded Ice Warriors of Mars! When the T-Mat controls malfunction, the world is thrown into chaos, and it is up to the Doctor, Zoe and Jamie to pilot an old-fashioned rocket, the ZA-683, to the moon and repair it.

The Ice Warriors have a plan to conquer Earth. With the help of a moonbase survivor named Fewsham, they beam alien seeds down to the surface of Earth. These pods, which expand and then explode, carry a killer fungus which causes oxygen starvation and an agricultural famine. It will lower the planet's temperature, making it more like Mars, and hence suitable to the Ice Warriors. When the pods arrive they germinate instantly, and explode a white foamy fungus everywhere. The Doctor deduces that heavy rainfall will exterminate the pods, so he uses the T-Mat to escape from the moon facility with Jamie and Zoe. Time is running out, however, because an Ice Warrior invasion fleet is already en route to Earth.

GUEST CAST: Fewsham (Terry Scully); Chief T-Mat Technician Gia Kelly (Louise Pajo); Radnor (Ronald Leigh-Hunt); Prof. Eldred (Philip Ray); Sir James Gregsor (Hugh Morton); Slarr (Alan Benmon); Computer Voice (John Witty); Brent (Ric Felgate); Osgood (Harry Towb); Locke (Martin Cort); Phipps (Christopher Coll); Ice Warriors (Sonny Caldinez, Tony Harwood, Steve Peters); Grand Marshall (Graham Leaman)

COMMENTARY: Brian Hayle's "The Seeds of Death" opens with the brilliant premise that the T-Mat, a device similar to *Star Trek*'s famous transporter, will one day supplant the rocketship as the most popular means of travel through space. This preference for a new technology over old technology recalls not only the replacement of propeller planes by jets, but also the replacement of records by CDs, and even the replacement of laserdiscs by DVDs. In other words, "The Seeds of Death" perfectly captures the fast-paced twentieth century world of fast-changing technologies.

The personal impacts of such a change are examined in detail in Hayles' teleplay when Prof. Eldred's livelihood, the construction of rockets, is trashed by the advent of this remarkable new device. Strangely, no one seems to care. Everyone has embraced the technology with such enthusiasm that they do not realize either how shaky it is, or how much it has cost certain members of the society. It takes alien sabotage to prove that the T-Mat is not the foolproof luxury its creators claim.

That Hayles was able to write such a profound tale about the impact of technology on man in 1969 is perhaps amazing. Like "The War Machines," this is one *Doctor Who* serial that is more timely now than it was when it first aired.

There can be little doubt, however, that the T-mat (or transmat as it would later become known) is an idea gleaned from Gene Roddenberry's *Star Trek*. In fairness, *Star Trek* did not originate the idea. In all likelihood, *Trek* appropriated the notion of a matter-energy transporter device from *The Fly* (1958), a horror film starring David Hedison and Vincent Price which dramatically demonstrated how such a tool could go disastrously wrong. The idea was not a new one in *Doctor Who* either. In "The Dalek Masterplan," a device called a "molecular disseminator" was tested on William Hartnell's Doctor. It successfully transported Steven, the Doctor and Sara Kingdom to the planet Myra. That *Who* serial aired in late 1965 and early 1966, ten months before *Star Trek* bowed on American television.

Michael Ferguson directs "The Seeds of Death" well, but the story drags in spots despite its interesting premise. This slowdown is due to two factors. The first is that the Ice Warriors are slow, lumbering creatures. Watching them attack is like watching someone wade through molasses. Secondly, Troughton is nowhere in evidence for much of the serial. The Doctor is incapacitated by the Martian fungus early on, and he disappears from the action for a full episode (25 minutes). Without Troughton's impish, powerful central presence, the serial does not fare well in today's climate of fast-paced action-adventure. Ferguson seems to be aware of some of the serial's faults himself, and so he takes steps to make it less routine. The Ice Warrior invasion of the Moonbase is thus filmed, unconventionally for television, from an Ice Warrior subjective point of view. The camera acts as the Ice Warrior's "vision" as the men and women of the base are overtaken. As they are threatened, the officers of the base speak directly to the camera. This technique opens the story with an undeniable visual flair. The effect of the Martian weapon is also interesting from a visual standpoint. It causes first a flash and then a total distortion of the space around the target. It appears as if the film has literally been dragged and shaken to create this illusion. It makes for a frightening weapon when accompanied with a reverberating sound effect.

The special effects conclusion is also noteworthy. The Doctor and Jamie wade through the expanding Martian fungus to activate the "rainfall" at the Weather Control Station. The Ice Warrior fungus is visualized as a very large amount of foam; Troughton is nearly buried in it at one point! The idea of using foam as a menace to sci-fi heroes was later reused in the twentieth *Space: 1999* episode, "Space Brain." In that story, Moonbase Alpha was overrun by alien "antibodies." These antibodies looked like soap foam, just like the fungus in "The Seeds of Death." After *Space: 1999*, the foam trick was used again in the 1978 *Blake's 7* episode "Space Fall."

Lastly, there is one rather nice aspect of "The Seeds of Death" that bears mentioning. The expert in T-Mat systems is a woman, Gia Kelly. She is portrayed in wholly non-sexist terms by both the actress and the script. It is obvious that Kelly is an extremely competent individual. Accordingly, Kelly effectively handles several problems in this story, including the destruction of the Ice Warrior fleet. In all, this was a good span for *Doctor Who* regarding issues of sexism. Not only is Kelly portrayed as competent, but Zoe is always compared favorably to the Doctor in terms of intelligence.

"The Seeds of Death" is a complete serial and is available on videocassette thanks to BBC/CBS-Fox home video.

49. "The Space Pirates" Written by Robert Holmes; Directed by Michael Hart; Designed by Ian Watson; Parts I–VI; Airdates: March 8, 15, 22, 29, April 5, 12, 1969

SYNOPSIS: Interstellar space pirates are the culprits responsible for the theft of several critical space beacons. The TARDIS arrives on one such space beacon just as it is being stripped and disassembled, and the Doctor, Jamie and Zoe find themselves in mortal danger from pirates until Milo Clancey, a friendly space miner, rescues them. Unfortunately, Clancey is unable to save the TARDIS from the villains. The Doctor's fantastic machine has now fallen into the hands of the space pirates, who are led by an unscrupulous character named Caven.

With their future and safe transport in serious jeopardy, the Doctor and his friends must discover the truth about the space pirates and their plot to steal navigational beacons. First, however, they must convince Gen. Hermack of the Intergalactic Space Corps that Clancey is not behind the crimes. Hermack suspects otherwise because the beacons are composed of argonite, a mineral space miner Clancey knows is valuable. Clancey confides that the Issigri Mining Company (IMC), a company he once had a share in, may be responsible for the acts of piracy. On planet Ta, Milo's former business partner, Dom Issigri, may be in league with Caven and the space pirates.

GUEST CAST: Milo Clancey (Gordon Gostelow); Caven (Dudley Foster); Gen. Hermack (Jack May); Dervise (Brian Peck); Warne (Donald Gee); Penn (George Layton); Sorba (Nick Zaran); Madeleine Issigri (Lisa Daniely); Dom Issigri (Edmond Knight); Guards (Anthony Donovan, Steven Peters)

COMMENTARY: From all the available evidence, "The Space Pirates" appears to have been an excellent addition to Season 6. As different from the invasion stories of "Seeds of Death" and "Invasion" as "The Mind Robber" was, this second tale by frequent *Who* scribe Robert Holmes obviously put the second Doctor and his young friends through a different set of obstacles. In "The Space Pirates," the Doctor was working not only to clear the name of an innocent man, but also to recover his beloved TARDIS. That the enemies were space pirates harkens back to Season 4's historical premiere "The Smugglers," while at the same time giving the series a break from cosmic conquerors such as the Cybermen or the Ice Warriors.

Unfortunately, "The Space Pirates" is today impossible to judge as it too has been destroyed by the BBC. Only Episode 2 still exists. It has been included on the videotape "The Patrick Troughton Years" but 25 minutes is hardly enough time to establish whether this story is a lost classic or merely lost.

50. "The War Games" Written by Malcolm Hulke & Terrance Dicks; Directed by David Maloney; Designed by Roger Cheveley; Parts I–X; Airdates: April 29, 26, May 3, 10, 17, 24, 31, June 7, 14, 21, 1969

SYNOPSIS: The TARDIS materializes in a swamp near a man-made trench and the Doctor, Jamie and Zoe deduce they have arrived on Earth during World War I. They soon learn differently however; they have actually landed on an alien world filled with various "war zones." Each zone represents a famous war in Earth history, and thousands of human soldiers have been kidnapped and forced to fight in each locale. Their individual memories have been erased, and they toil forever in the American Civil War, World War I, the Crimean War, the Mexican Civil War and so forth.

All the battlefields are being controlled by a central time zone, an area that can be reached only by a black time machine...a device which the Doctor recognizes as a TARDIS. When the Doctor visits the control center, he learns that one of his own people, a Time Lord, is cooperating with a deadly alien War Lord to build the ultimate army. To this effect, he is studying war and all the battles in human history. Unfortunately, the other Time Lord's own TARDIS ships have a limited life span, and he wants the Doctor's ship! The War Lord and his Time Lord cohort are eventually defeated by a growing human resistance, but the Doctor realizes he has a larger problem: There are over 50,000 human beings trapped on this world! He must return them to their own times, but it is too complicated a task for his TARDIS. Since the War Chief's time machines will not work dependably, the Doctor realizes he has no choice but to contact his own people and ask for help. He is reluctant to do this because he knows that to his people, he is a criminal. By rescuing the humans, he is dooming himself!

The Doctor, Jamie and Zoe flee for the TARDIS, hoping they can escape this world before the Doctor's people arrive. The Doctor explains to his friends how he ran away from his home world. His people can live forever, mold their environment and travel anywhere in time and space, but they choose simply to observe. The Doctor wanted to explore, to get involved. To his people, such action is a violation of their most sacred law.

The Time Lords track down the TARDIS and force the Doctor to stand trial. The War Lord is tried too, and for his vicious acts he is erased from the galactic record, from time itself, and his world is imprisoned behind a force field so it can never again cause harm to other peoples of the galaxy.

When the Time Lords turn their attention to the Doctor, he shows the court images of Quarks, Yetis, Ice Warriors, Cybermen and Daleks. He has fought them all, while the Time Lords sat back and "observed." The Doctor claims that it is not he who has failed in his moral duty, but the Time Lords themselves. Nevertheless, the Time Lords pass judgment.

The Doctor's first punishment is the loss of his dear companions. The Doctor says farewell to Zoe and Jamie as they are dispatched to their individual times and worlds. The Time Lords have wiped their memories clean, so they no longer recall their many voyages with the Doctor. The Time Lords then exile the Doctor to twentieth century Earth and remove the secrets of the TARDIS from his mind during his banishment! Aware that his appearance is known on Earth, the Time Lords trigger his next regeneration and send him hurtling into a dark void...

GUEST CAST: Lady Jennifer (Jane Sherwin); German Soldier (John Liresy); Carstairs (David Savile); Major Barrington (Terence Bayler); Sgt. Willis (Brian Forster); Gen. Smythe (Noel Coleman); Capt. Ransome (Hubert Rees); Sgt. Major Burns (Edmond Webb); Redcoat (Tony McEwan); Commander Gorton (Richard Steele); Military Chauffeur (Peter Stanton); Military Police (Pat Gorman); German (Bernard Davies); Lt. Crane (David Valla); Lt. Locke (Greg Palmer); Von Weich (David Garfield); War Chief (Edward Brayshaw); Sgt. Thompson (Bill Hutchison); Cpl. Riley (Terry Adams); Leroy (Leslie Schofield); Scientist (Vernon Dobtcheff); Harper (Rudolph Walker); Alien Guard (John Atterbury); Arturo Villar (Michael Napier Brown); Petrov (Stephen Hubay); War Lord (Philip Madoc); First Time Lord (Bernard Horsfall); Second Time Lord (Trevor Martin); Third Time Lord (Clyde Pollit); Tanya (Clare Jenkins)

COMMENTARY: The epic-length, 243-minute, ten-episode serial "The War Games" by Terrance Dicks and Malcolm Hulke closes the Patrick Troughton era with a literal and figurative blast. The story begins in deceptively simple fashion in the 1917 time zone, as if this were to be yet another purely historical story in the tradition of "The Highlanders" or "The Crusades." Then, as the mystery builds and the science fiction elements come to the forefront, "The War Games" is revealed to be nothing less than a *Doctor Who* masterpiece about thousands of human soldiers abducted by aliens and forced to fight a never-ending war. The story finally closes not with the solution to this incredibly imaginative scenario, but with the shocking introduction of the Doctor's own people: the mysterious Time Lords. And, finally, the question "Doctor Who?" is addressed after six long years.

David Maloney directs "The War Games" with finesse. It is by turns frenetic, crazy, outlandish and horrifying. The first episode opens with a wonderfully evocative long shot across a barren World War I landscape. The camera tilts down slowly to capture a pool of filthy water and detritus. As the camera zooms in on this polluted water, the reflection of the TARDIS wavers and then materializes in the puddle. Taken by itself, this is an ingenious alternative to the typical beginning of an episode in which there is a simple landscape shot, and the TARDIS just appears in front of the camera. More than that, the pan across this landscape and appearance of the TARDIS in the "swamp" successfully expresses the desolation and isolation of this war zone. The TARDIS stands like a beacon of light amidst all this death and destruction.

There are many further directorial flourishes worth writing about in "The War Games." Almost instantly the Doctor, Zoe and Jamie are caught in a barrage of German machine gun fire. This encounter is delineated in a rapidly edited montage of closeups and explosions. The cuts in this sequence accompany the staccato tempo of the weapons fire in a jarring tempo. This kind of sudden jolt exemplifies the whole tone for the show. Nothing can be taken for granted, not even the emptiness of the landscape. From the first moment of "The War Games," the Doctor is on the run for his life. He evades gunfire, a stampede of Romans and even his own malevolent people. The editing is exceptionally good at conveying that frenetic pace and the frightening chase elements.

Best of all, there is an abrupt stylistic turnaround at the close of the show and suddenly, for the first time, slow-motion photography is employed to denote the inescapable fact that the Doctor can run no longer away. The ultimate enemy, his own people, have finally caught up with him. No matter how fast he runs, it is not fast enough. The dramatic utilization of slow-motion photography in the closing portion of Episode 9 is made doubly effective by all the rapid-fire editing that preceded it throughout the serial. By that point, the audience has been through one fast-paced scrape after another with the Doctor, and the last thing anyone expects is a dramatic slowdown. It is a brilliantly executed visual conceit in that it conveys the whole point of the episode, and heightens the terror of the Time Lord intervention. The slow-motion interlude heightens the importance, and draws out each instant of time as the Doctor tries desperately to escape his own people, who control time.

"The War Games" is significant not only in its stylistic direction, but in its introduction of the Time Lords. Here the Doctor is at last "outed" as a Time Lord. He has to deal not only with another renegade, like the Meddling Monk, but with his whole society. He reveals to Jamie and Zoe that he ran away from his people because he was "bored." He was tired of just sitting back and watching the events of the universe unfold. He wanted to participate, but that decision has made him a pariah. This explanation does not jibe with Hartnell's assertion in "An Unearthly Child" that the Doctor and Susan are exiles, but it is not a direct contradiction either. The Doctor is obviously on a *self-imposed* exile. He cannot go back to his home as long as he disagrees with the policies of his people. Only when the Time Lords become enlightened and join the battle against evil will he be able to end his exile, and go home again.

The Doctor's people are a frightening bunch in "The War Games." In fact, they are probably the nastiest villains seen on *Doctor Who* up to this point. The Doctor is obviously frightened out of his wits by them. And for the first time the audience sees the Doctor give up. When he is unable to outrun or outwit his people, he resigns the game. He knows his travels are over. It is a frightening realization to the audience that the Doctor, the victor over Daleks, Cybermen, Ice Warriors and Yeti, is truly defeated this time. When the Doctor does return to his home world, the image of the Time Lords as frightening specters of death continues. They torture the War Lord with their mental powers, and then wipe him from the face of existence. This is the most horrendous, heartless fate any creature on *Doctor Who* has ever endured. Then, in act of obvious revenge, the Time Lords entrap the War Lord's planet for all of time. A whole planet! The justice of the Time Lords is obviously savage. This is incredibly effective, however, because when the Doctor is on trial, the audience is afraid of what may await him. Running true to form, the Time Lords inform the Doctor that they considered obliterating him and having the whole affair done with!

Of course, Time Lord justice is again savage when it confronts the Doctor and his friends. Jamie and Zoe are ripped from the Doctor, and forced to forget their time with him, an invasion of their very minds, their very identities. Then, essentially, the Time Lords kill the Doctor. Yes, he regenerates into another incarnation, but this second incarnation is sentenced to exile and then killed. As each incarnation boasts a different personality and physical appearance, this Time Lord act is truly comparable to murder.

The interpretation of the Time Lords as an invincible, unstoppable force would not last long. As the series developed further, the urge to explore the issues of the Time Lords became too much to resist. Like the Daleks, the Time Lords eventually became familiar. Over the years, the viewer would become acquainted with their politics ("The Deadly Assassin" and "The Invasion of Time"), their data storage system (the Matrix), their secret incursions into time ("The Mysterious Planet") and their legal system ("The Ultimate Foe"). All of this background reduced the Time Lords from a race of great mystery, grandeur and awesome, almost elemental power, to just another advanced race operating in the galaxy. It is a shame because in "The War Games" the Time Lords are positively frightening and enigmatic.

"The War Games" also finally voices the issue that has been a peripheral ingredient of the *Doctor Who* series since Day One: the need to interfere in the affairs of the galaxy. Patrick Troughton's Doctor eloquently argues in "The War Games" that it is the morality of the Time Lords, not the Doctor, that should be questioned.

It is interesting that *Doctor Who* and *Star Trek* both have a "prime directive," the law that less-developed peoples should be left alone to solve their problems. It is even more interesting to note that *Doctor Who*, as a series, *despises* the non-interference rule and argues cogently that in every battle a person must choose a side. Evil must be vanquished wherever it is found, and a law preventing intervention is just cowardice institutionalized. *Star Trek* says that man must not choose sides, lest he choose wrongly and do more damage than good by interfering. Both series argue the same point and come up with completely opposite answers. Perhaps that is why *Doctor Who* alone is compared to the immortal *Star Trek* in terms of quality.

The last half-hour of "The War Games" is the most heart-wrenching show since Barbara and Ian left the Doctor in Season 2's "The Chase." This farewell between the Doctor and his friends Jamie and Zoe is painful to watch. It is even more sad than the conclusion of "The Chase," because these friends are being forced apart. They do not choose their fates. And, unlike Ian and Barbara, who will always remember their time with the strange man in the TARDIS, Jamie and Zoe are forced to forget everything but their first adventure with the Doctor. It is a terrible justice that the Time Lords enforce, and it is an unforgettable climax. Zoe asks the Doctor if they will ever meet again. The Doctor's response, that time is relative, can hardly shield the sadness in the traveler's eyes. His friends are ripped from him. This is an especially cruel fate considering that Troughton's incarnation of the Doctor is also the most affectionate with companions. For this particular Doctor to be forced to lose his friends is all the more powerful.

This is also the saddest end of any incarnation of the Doctor. Hartnell's Doctor simply grew old and regenerated. Pertwee regenerated after conquering his fear. Baker regenerated only after defeating the Master. Davison died saving Peri's life. Troughton has no such honor. His Doctor, for all intents and purposes, is executed for his crimes. This is an especially controversial ending to "The War Games" when one remembers that it was first considered the conclusion of the whole series! At the time the BBC produced this serial, there was no certainty that the show would reappear the following season. The writers ended *Doctor Who* by killing an incarnation of the Doctor and sending a second regeneration, an amnesiac no less, to twentieth century Earth. Talk about downbeat season finales! "The War Games" takes the cake!

This is story editor's Terrance Dicks' first work on *Doctor Who*. He and Malcolm Hulke deserve great credit for giving the Patrick Troughton era an unforgettable send-off. Dicks continued to write many further episodes of *Doctor Who* including "Robot," "The Horror of Fang Rock," "State of Decay" and "The Five Doctors." He also contributed the story "The Lambda Factor" to the Fred Freiberger–produced second season of *Space: 1999*.

Special effects watchers will note the presence of two pieces of stock footage in "The War Games." The shot of the TARDIS plummeting toward the ocean is from Season 5's "Fury from the Deep." The later shot of the TARDIS parked in space is from "The Web of Fear." This was an unusual choice for "The War Games" since the TARDIS is clearly seen to have cobwebs on it! In "The Web of Fear," this condition was caused by the presence of The Great Intelligence. In "The War Games," the cobwebs make no sense.

"The War Games" is certainly one of the best and most important episodes of the series. In addition to introducing the Time Lords, it also depicts for the first time their home planet. The set design for both the Time Lord planet (only later in the series referred to as Gallifrey) and the World War I zone are very impressive. The Time Lord planet with its rows of TARDIS craft, its smoking and maze-like floors, and its vast, blackness-rimmed courtroom, looks like something out of an early German Expressionist film. It appropriately maintains the mystery of the Time Lord habitat. The World War I zone, complete with barbed wire, trenches and authentic uniforms, is also very well-established. It is a triumph for the production team, the writing staff and the cast. "The War Games" is certainly in the top 20 of all *Doctor Who* episodes despite moments of padding and ineffective plotting. This epic story, the longest during Troughton's tenure, can be examined today on videotape courtesy of BBC/CBS-Fox home video.

A final note: In 1998, *Star Trek: Voyager* opted to retell "The War Games" in quite literal fashion. In a story entitled "The Killing Ground," the crew of *Voyager* has its memory erased. Then each crew member is thrust into a different time zone (including World War II France and Rome) and forced to participate in historic battles. The reason? The presence of an alien race called the Hirogen, who are interested in learning all about the human concept of war. Like "The War Games" soldiers, the amnesiac crew of *Voyager* offers resistance, fights back and eventually wins the day.

SEASON 7

X **51. "Spearhead from Space"** Written by Robert Holmes; Directed by Derek Martinus; Designed by Paul Allen; Parts I–IV; Airdates: January 3, 10, 17, 24, 1970

SYNOPSIS: Exiled to Earth, the new incarnation of the Doctor, a tall man with a hawklike nose and a mop of white hair, is able to convince Brigadier Lethbridge-Stewart that he is the same "Doctor" who has aided him in the past. The Brigadier takes the keys to the TARDIS for safekeeping and agrees to give this strange gentleman a chance to prove himself. Fortunately, the Doctor is soon busy assisting the Brigadier and physicist Liz Shaw of UNIT as they solve a mystery of their own: A cluster of meteors recently crashed in the English countryside. When the Doctor examines the remnants of the meteors he realizes they are not natural, but plastic shells of alien origin!

At a nearby doll and mannequin factory, the villainous Nestene, a collective-consciousness and hive-mind, has arrived from space to conquer the world. This is a familiar operation to this merciless race, which has conquered hundreds of other races throughout the universe. To accomplish their mission on Earth, the Nestene have built an army of indestructible killer mannequins called Autons. These automatons, which are resistant to gunfire, have plastic hands that flip open to reveal deadly weaponry. The Autons are soon shipped to department stores across England, where they wait for the signal to attack.

GUEST CAST: Channing (Hugh Burden); Major General Scobie (Hamilton Dyce); Capt. Munro (Johnny Breslin); Hibbert (John Woodnutt); Ransome (Derek Smee); Seeley (Neil Wilson); Meg (Betty Bowden); Sergeant (Clifford Cox); Reporter (Prentis Hancock)

COMMENTARY: "Spearhead from Space" opens an exciting new era of action for *Doctor Who*. The most noticeable change in the program involves the production's presentation. It is no longer filmed in stark black-and-white. Instead it is shot on 16mm film, and in full color. This new sheen gives the revised series the appearance of being a modern feature film rather than an inexpensive television show. Interestingly, later serials in the Pertwee era would be shot on a combination of film and videotape, causing a jarring transition between the two media. This was not the case with "Spearhead from Space," because studio and location work alike was shot on film.

Beyond the change to color photography, Jon Pertwee assumes the mantle of series star in this story by Robert Holmes. In his first performance as the Doctor, Pertwee stays remarkably true to the character as delineated by Patrick Troughton. He mugs, wallows in the humorous elements of the tale and seems possessed of an entirely childlike innocence. Accordingly, much of the first portion of "Spearhead from Space" focuses on the Doctor's amusing attempts to find a suitable wardrobe for himself, as well as his comedic escape from the hospital. That level of whimsy would not survive beyond Pertwee's initial adventure. Quite soon the comedic actor would find his way to a very different persona. His Doctor quickly develops into the least humorous of all incarnations, and might accurately be described as "grim" in many serials. Instead of reveling in humorous situations, Pertwee's Doctor soon avoids it at all costs. He is positively disdainful of everything even remotely related to it. His Doctor is a brooder, a man obsessed with escaping the prison that the Time Lords have made for him. This is certainly a valid interpretation for the role, especially considering the Doctor's situation. It is different from the Troughton approach, just as Troughton's was different from Hartnell's. Pertwee saw himself as a gadget-loving dandy, a futuristic James Bond, and although he admired Patrick Troughton, he felt that the Doctor, as an admired cult hero and larger-than-life figure, should not be a prevaricator. Whereas Troughton sought to wring suspense out of each story by making the audience wonder if the Doctor could survive, Pertwee altered that dynamic. He saw the Doctor as a figure of certainty, a mother hen protecting the young. He was rock-solid, larger-than-life, implacable in his values.

It seems fair to state that any actor taking over a popular role from another performer must bring his own sensibilities to it. That is why Roger Moore succeeded Sean Connery so ably in the role of James Bond. Had he tried to do the same things in the same ways as Connery, the Bond series would not have survived the '70s. Likewise, Pertwee updated the image of *Doctor Who* to make the Time Lord fit with the new decade. His Doctor is suave, debonair, dashing and a man of action.

Pertwee's incarnation is clearly obsessed with hard-driving physical action, something that terrified earlier incarnations. This penchant for fisticuffs and chases can be seen already in "Spearhead from Space." In Pertwee's first serial he not only indulges in an old-fashioned car race, but also a more dangerous wheelchair chase. Later stories would find him using Venusian karate to disable foes, a skill akin to Mr. Spock's famous Vulcan nerve pinch. Clearly the previous half-decade, which saw the advent of *Star Trek* (1966–69), *The Man from U.N.C.L.E.* (1964-68), *The*

Prisoner (1966–67) and other action-oriented sci-fi programming, had made a huge impact on this new, revised *Doctor Who.*

The new setting also had incalculable impact. In many senses, the world of *Doctor Who* is severely narrowed by the exile on Earth concept. Suddenly the Doctor cannot time-hop, or visit other planets. Instead he is limited to Earth in just one time period. This leads to several stories that are rehashes of the invasion theme already so fully explored by series in its first six years, or even variations on traditional espionage and "mad scientist" tropes. However, if the writers of *Doctor Who* had proven anything over the years, it is that they thrive when placed under restriction. Rewardingly, inventive writers "escaped" the limited setting of twentieth century England by sending the Doctor to alternate worlds ("Inferno," "The Time Monster") and on Time Lord–authorized secret missions to outer space ("Colony in Space," "The Mutants"). Still, this work on Earth in the service of the Brigadier creates an impression that few writers could have foreseen. The Doctor, science advisor to UNIT and secret agent of the Time Lords, is now firmly part of the establishment instead of a rebel railing against it!

"Spearhead from Space" introduces Caroline John as Liz Shaw, the Doctor's assistant. She is a character in the mold of earlier companions Barbara Wright and Zoe. In other words, she is bright, independent and tough. Female roles had also changed in the late '60s, and *The Avengers*' Emma Peel (Diana Rigg) was all the rage in 1970. Thus Liz Shaw was designed as a character who could take care of herself. She did not need the Doctor to rescue her all the time. Unfortunately, the writers seemingly did not know how to develop a believable relationship between the Doctor and a female companion who did not require rescue. As a result, John left her post after only four serials.

Far more successful was the integration of Brigadier Lethbridge-Stewart, actor Nicholas Courtney, into the series. With his rigid military viewpoint, this character was an excellent foil for the humanitarian new Doctor. Their frequently saucy banter, reminiscent of the McCoy-Spock relationship on *Star Trek*, brought some delightful moments to the new and improved *Doctor Who.*

Aside from a new appearance, a new Doctor, a new location and a new supporting cast, "Spearhead from Space" is otherwise a surprisingly traditional story. Once again the threat of extra-terrestrial "invasion" has been trotted out. This time the formless Nestene, with their blank-faced Autons, are the villains of the week. Since this is such a tired premise, the invasion elements of the story are a lot less interesting than the subplot concerning the Doctor's arrival and integration into UNIT. There is one unforgettable scene in "Spearhead from Space," however. The Auton mannequins burst out of a London shop window and begin killing people on the streets! The location work, the color photography and the unearthly villains all combine to make this a memorable moment. The Nestene are not the most interesting nor charismatic villain seen on *Doctor Who*, yet they were also selected to open Season 8 ("Terror of the Autons").

Observant *Who* watchers will note Prentis Hancock in this episode as a journalist. He would return as Salamar in "Planet of Evil" and as the Captain of the

Guard in "The Ribos Operation." He was also the regular character Paul Morrow on *Space: 1999* Year 1.

"Spearhead from Space" is available on home video. Generally Jon Pertwee is considered in America to be among the most popular of the Doctors. Though he falls behind Tom Baker, he invariably finishes ahead of the other actors. Accordingly, a good number of the Pertwee–era episodes have been released on videotape. Unlike those of Troughton's era, very few Pertwee–era episodes have been destroyed by the BBC.

52. "Doctor Who and the Silurians" Written by Malcolm Hulke; Directed by Timothy Combe; Designed by Barry Newbery; Parts I–VII; Airdates: January 31, February 7, 14, 21, 28, March 7, 14, 1970

SYNOPSIS: At a nuclear power plant in Derbyshire, something beneath the Earth is causing critical power losses. The Doctor travels deep into the caves to investigate and discovers that beneath the surface of England dwell the Silurians ... ancient lizard people. Millions of years ago the Silurians ruled the Earth with advanced science and technology that foretold them of an approaching calamity. They believed a rogue planet was going to collide with the Earth, and they consequently retreated underground. They set their computer systems to awaken them when the danger had passed, but the rogue planet turned out to be a wandering satellite — the moon! It never collided with the Earth, but went into orbit instead. As a result, the "alarm clock" system of the Silurians was never activated, and for centuries they have slept in hibernation beneath the surface of the planet. Now the activity of the nuclear power plant has awakened them. Understandably, the Silurians are horrified to discover that their planet is in the hands of evolved rodents.

Realizing that both humanity and the Silurians can rightfully claim the Earth as their own, the Doctor attempts to negotiate a peace between the two disparate life forms. Unfortunately, extremists on both sides are unwilling to share the planet, and a group of Silurians attempt to destroy the Van Allen belt around the Earth.

GUEST CAST: Dr. Charles Lawrence (Peter Miles); Dr. Quinn (Fulton Mackay); Dr. Meredith (Ian Cunningham); Major Baker (Norman Jones); Ms. Dawson (Thomasine Heiner); Edward Masters (Geoffrey Palmer); Davis (Bill Matthews); Spencer (John Newman); Roberts (Roy Branigan); Capt. Hawkins (Paul Darrow); Squire (Gordon Richardson); Travis (Harry Swift); Doris Squire (Nancie Jackson); Doctor (Brendan Barry); Cpl. Nutting (Alan Mason); Private Wright (Derek Pollitt); Nurse (Gillian Toll); Receptionist (Sheila Knight); Silurians (Paul Barton, Simon Cain, John Churchill, Dave Carter, Pat Gorman, Nigel Johns); Silurian Voice (Peter Halliday)

COMMENTARY: Every so often, a story comes along in *Doctor Who* that is so good, so well-done, so full of possibilities, that it reminds one how vibrant and experimental a television series it can be. "Doctor Who and the Silurians" is one such serial. It is an extremely inventive story because it plots an invasion not from outer space, but from inner space. More impressive than this variation on a theme is the serious moral dilemma that is raised by the ascendence of the dinosaur-like Silurians.

The problem is this: Who has the right to rule the Earth? In this case, the answer is difficult to determine. Both the Silurians and the humans are indigenous to the planet. Who should be superior? Is it only "natural" that these enemies should fight to extinction to see who has the right to rule? In his wisdom, the Doctor realizes both species have a valid claim. He accordingly acts as negotiator, diplomat and peacemaker, a role the Doctor would play repeatedly during the Pertwee years, and this story is made ever so much more interesting by the fact that *all* of the Doctor's peace attempts fail. In the end, "Doctor Who and the Silurians" tells us there can be no peace between disparate races. This is a startling conclusion, and one wonders if it was meant to be an allegory for civil and racial strife among humans.

"Doctor Who and the Silurians" is spellbinding also for its non-traditional handling of its protagonists. At the climax, the Brigadier merrily bombs the Silurians back underground, literally into the stone age. This is an act that surely makes him the ultimate villain of this particular piece. He has made peace impossible and, with a typical military mentality, outmaneuvered the opponent. The Doctor is not at all happy about this solution of "might over right," and his relationship with Lethbridge-Stewart obviously degenerates after this incident. How often in American television dramas do main characters do such unappealing things, things that might be considered wrong? It is a credit to writer Hulke that he should deepen the Brigadier's character in this fashion. It is not unexpected, perhaps, for Hulke to do so since he is among the most socially conscious of the *Doctor Who* writers. His stories always have a moral point, either about pollution, exploitation, racism or the military mentality. "Doctor Who and the Silurians" is perhaps his finest teleplay for the series.

It is an interesting change in the Doctor's *modus operandi* that in this serial he is seen as a facilitator and negotiator. Previously he always took sides in situations. He jumped in and vigorously fought for one side or the other. This change is perhaps a result of Mr. Spock's fame. Like Spock, the Doctor is an alien amidst humans. The writers apparently realized that the Time Lord had to somehow be very much above his human comrades in UNIT. He had to be set apart in a way. One way to accomplish this was to have him act on an agenda different than the Brigadier's. Suddenly he is no longer a participant in the insurrection or revolution, but a negotiator trying to bring peace without violence. Pertwee's Doctor would thus frequently make comments about humanity's barbarism. Like Spock, he became the mirror through which mankind could judge itself. This is an interesting modification of the *Doctor Who* tradition.

Star Trek: Voyager revisited many of the same themes as "Doctor Who and the Silurians" with its story of evolved dinosaurs, "Distant Origin" (1997). Like the Silurians, the alien race called the Voth developed on Earth and consider humans to be nothing more than lower life forms. And, like the Silurians, the Voth were prepared to do anything to reclaim their heritage as the most evolved race in the galaxy, even destroy the humans aboard *Voyager*.

"Doctor Who and the Silurians" is famous in *Who* lore because it is the only serial to feature the words "Doctor Who" in the title. Fans can view this landmark episode in the two-tape set released by BBC/CBS-Fox video.

53. "Ambassadors of Death" Written by David Whitaker; Directed by Michael Ferguson; Designed by David Myerscough-Jones; Parts I–VII; Airdates: March 21, 28, April 4, 11, 18, 25, May 2, 1970

SYNOPSIS: A bizarre message from space heralds the return of Recovery craft 7, a spaceship that has been to Mars. Three spacesuited astronauts return from the mission, but they have been transformed into radioactive monsters capable of killing merely by touch. When the Doctor learns that Gen. Carrington and Prof. Taltallian are somehow involved in this strange incident, and that the astronauts are not humans at all, but alien diplomats, he knows the only to solve the mystery is to fly the next mission to Mars himself.

GUEST CAST: Dr. Taltallian (Robert Crawdon); Van Leydon (Rick Felgate); Cornish (Ronald Allen); Wakefield (Michael Wisher); Grey (Ray Armstrong); Gen. Carrington (John Abineri); Dobson (Ivan Moreno); Lefee (Steve Peters); Lennox (Cyral Shaps); Assistants (Joanna Ross, Carl Conway); Michaels (Neville Simons); Quinlan (Dallas Cavell); Masters (John Lord); Champion (James Haswell); Control Room Assistant (Bernard Martin); Parker (James Clayton); Alien (Peter Noel Cook); Alien Voice (Peter Halliday); Soldier (Max Faulkner)

COMMENTARY: "Ambassadors of Death" is the return of a popular *Doctor Who* theme first explored in the first season serial "The Sensorites." Like that story about human exploitation of an alien planet, this story suggests that aliens are frequently friendly, and that humans are often "the bad guys." In this case, there is another deluded madman running amok, much like Bennett in "The Rescue." In "Ambassadors of Death," Gen. Carrington is willing to propagate a worldwide conspiracy to keep the peaceful aliens (who thrive on radiation) from making successful and peaceful first contact with Earthmen.

"Ambassadors of Death" also treads into the territory of another science fiction television standby: the alien who kills by accident, without malevolence. Like the Horta who kills to protect her young in *Star Trek*'s classic first-year episode "Devil in the Dark" or the evolving young creatures in the *Buck Rogers in the 25th Century* second season episode "The Crystals," the trio of alien ambassadors in *Doctor Who* cannot be held responsible for the murder and mayhem that ensues. After all, emitting radiation is a characteristic of their race! They require radiation as humans need air. Although they kill by touching humans, this is an inadvertent act. It also relates back to the moral of the destroyed but not forgotten "Galaxy Four": that creatures who are ugly or different need not necessarily be evil.

After two invasion stories in Pertwee's freshman season, "Ambassadors of Death" is certainly a change of pace. It proves itself to be the template for the second type of story featured in Pertwee's era: the Madman in Control story. Sometimes the madman is a scientist ("Inferno"), sometimes a businessman ("The Green

Death") and sometimes a man of the military like Gen. Carrington. All the trouble in this *Doctor Who* subgenre can be traced back directly to the fact that the villainous madman is either (a) paranoid, (b) dangerous and out of control, ignoring all warnings about safety and logic, or (c) convinced that he should rule the world. Again, this formula belies the heavy influence that the enormously popular James Bond film series had on *Doctor Who* in the early 1970s. The Doctor was now encountering villains who would have been right at home facing down Sean Connery or Roger Moore on the big screen. The "madman"-style story replaced the planetary revolution story during this time period of *Doctor Who* because that earlier prototype (introduced in "The Daleks") could not be utilized while the Doctor was exiled on Earth.

Max Faulkner, yet another "unsung" guest star in *Doctor Who*, appears in this serial as a soldier. He would later be a very strange member of UNIT in the Tom Baker story "The Android Invasion." He also appears in "The Monster of Peladon," "Planet of the Spiders," "Genesis of the Daleks" and "The Invasion of Time." Faulkner also guest-starred in "Ring Around the Moon," the fourth episode of *Space: 1999*, as technician Ted Clifford. And, speaking of *Space: 1999*, that series also featured aliens who thrived on radiation in the two-part Year 2 adventure "The Bringers of Wonder."

"Ambassadors of Death" has not yet appeared on the home video market, despite the fact that the serial is known to be intact in black-and-white.

54. "Inferno" Written by Don Houghton; Directed by Douglas Camfield & Barry Letts; Designed by Jeremy Davies; Parts I–VII; Airdates: May 9, 16, 23, 30, June 6, 13, 20, 1970

SYNOPSIS: Prof. Stahlman, an irritating, self-righteous genius, has been working on a top-secret project of enormous importance. The Stahlman Project, or "The Inferno" as it is commonly known, is a complicated scheme to drill through the Earth's crust to the untapped energy sources at the planet's core. Since the Stahlman project involves the use of top secret drilling equipment, several nuclear reactors and many scientific geniuses, UNIT is assigned to maintain a security presence at the Stahlman project site.

While the Brigadier complains about the assignment, the Doctor seizes this opportunity to tie the TARDIS console to an "Inferno" nuclear reactor without telling anyone but Liz Shaw. With her assistance, he attempts to override the Time Lord blocks on his dematerialization equipment. After one failure, the TARDIS console sweeps the Doctor into a parallel universe. He quickly discovers that England is ruled by a fascist organization called "The Republic." Despite the fact that Elizabeth Shaw is a security officer and the Brigadier a one-eyed martinet, the Doctor recognizes with worry that there are some strange similarities. Stahlman's "Inferno" project exists in this universe as well, and it turns out to be very dangerous. The Doctor realizes the impact that Inferno could have on his Earth, and must find a way back to his dimension as soon as possible.

GUEST CAST: Prof. Stahlman (Olaf Pooley); Sir Keith Gold (Christopher Benjamin); Harry Slocum (Walter Randall); Petra Williams (Sheila Dunn); Private Wyatt (Derek Ware); Greg Sutton (Derek Newark); Patterson (Keith James); Latimer (David Simeon); The Mutants ("Primords") (Dave Carter, Pat Gorman, Walter Henry, Philip Ryan, Peter Thompson)

COMMENTARY: Ever since Jerome Bixby's immensely popular "Mirror, Mirror" premiered on *Star Trek* on October 6, 1967, every sci-fi television program worth its salt has highlighted at least one alternate or "parallel" dimension story. If one were to judge a genre show solely by how well it tackles the standards (androids experiencing emotions, the generational space ark, the sentient machine, time travel, etc.), then the alternate universe category would certainly be one of the most important benchmarks. The alternate universe has become one of the most popular and enduring of all clichés within the realm of sci-fi television — so much so that a recent series, Fox's *Sliders* (1995-1999), is actually built around the premise of overlapping dimensions, each one slightly different from the other. Otherwise, the "alternate" universe tale is most often concerned with evil, other-universe interpretations of *dramatis personae* ("Crossover," "Through the Looking Glass" and "Shattered Mirror" on *Star Trek: Deep Space Nine*) or slightly off-kilter futures in which traumatic events have caused significant changes in the behavior of the main characters ("Another Time, Another Place" on *Space: 1999*; "The Hand of the Goral" on *Buck Rogers in the 25th Century*; "Parallels" and "All Good Things" on *Star Trek: The Next Generation*). Interestingly, the point of all of these parallel-dimension stories tends to be the escape back home, to the canon universe. The trick is not to learn about the new universe, or adapt to residence in this twisted, parallel version of series reality, but rather brief survival in a cutthroat environment until the opportunity to return arises. *Doctor Who*'s interpretation of the alternate dimension story, "Inferno" is quite different in some senses.

"Inferno" follows the pattern of the typical alternate dimension story in some basic respects, particularly in that the supporting cast is permitted to indulge in playing "evil" and even adorn themselves with unusual character affectations. The Brigadier goes without his moustache, but he mysteriously has a sinister eye patch, much as Mr. Spock in the classic "Mirror, Mirror" wears a beard. However, the ultimate point of Don Houghton's teleplay is not merely the delineation of a sinister sister existence, but the avoidance of a problem that threatens both universes. In this case the deadly Stahlman project, not the alternate universe, is the real focal point of the story. The Doctor is able to view Inferno's effect in the fascist world of the Republic and then return to his own world in time to stop it. Thus the story is not merely one of action-packed escapes and thrills, but one of didacticism as well. The example of the evil otherworld and its destruction allows viewers and the Doctor alike to see the deadly result of overmining and the ruthless penetration of the Earth's precious resources. Thus when the Doctor returns home, the action really begins and the tension mounts. The Time Lord must convince the Brigadier and Liz to believe his story and save this version of the Earth before it is too late. The viewers, like the Doctor, have already seen what will happen if he fails in his mission.

"Inferno" is a wonderful episode of *Doctor Who* for this reason. Not only does it feature excellent performances by the talented supporting cast and Pertwee, but it has an eloquently stated message about man's tendency to exploit and destroy the resources of his world. The parallel dimension is the tool by which author Houghton shows viewers the final result of Stahlman's project. This is something that could not be shown without the device of the alternate dimension.

Doctor Who does not often explore alternate dimensions, perhaps because the series could visit so many other interesting places (E-Space, history, the future, the Land of Fiction, inner space). That alone makes "Inferno" one of the most unusual and compelling of *Doctor Who* stories. Because of its unique style, and didactic structure, it must surely rank as one of the 25 best serials in the long-running series.

Pertwee found his niche as the Doctor by this story. His Doctor is the man who knows best, who is wise, and who can foresee the danger lurking around the corner. Yet he is also the Doctor who is almost never heeded. Thus it is up to him to force his way (using vehicles, stinging words and even fisticuffs) to a solution. His Doctor is the man railing alone against an irrational, self-destructive society. His is a very different kind of Doctor from the time and space traveler to other worlds, the aimless wanderer who would ally himself with any rebel faction and (in a team effort) defeat the powerful oppressors.

Like many episodes of Pertwee's era, "Inferno" wears its environmentalist heart on its sleeve. The writers from this period became obsessed with the plundering of Earth's resources, and the Stahlman Project obliquely forecasts such scientific disasters as Three Mile Island as well as short-sighted actions like the destruction of the Brazilian Rain Forest. In "Inferno," science races forward, hand in hand with government, without ever assessing the risks to Mother Earth or the human race. It has long been the purview of science fiction film and television to inform or even "warn" viewers about societal dangers under the mask of escapism. "Inferno" follows proudly in this decision. Just as *Star Trek* commented on the Vietnam War ("A Private Little War"), overpopulation ("Mark of Gideon") and race hatred ("Let That Be Your Last Battlefield"), *Doctor Who*'s writers sought to preserve the environment from science and government ("Inferno") and big-business ("Colony in Space" and "The Green Death").

"Inferno" leaves an indelible mark on the Doctor. He is an eyewitness to the destruction of an entire planet. This is a vision that scars him for some time. Liz also comes off very well in this, her last story. The viewers learn that even in an alternate dimension she is a person of great moral courage. She sacrifices herself to save the Doctor and his world. What could be more heroic? Perhaps most interesting of all is the interpretation of the Brigadier on the parallel Earth. His military mentality has taken over his personality and he is a callous martinet, a puppet of a fascist regime. All in all, "Inferno" offers some of the deepest and most impressive character development in the entire series. It is an incredible success for the show, especially considering fan worries that "invasions from space" would take the lion's share of the action in the new exile situation.

Don Houghton returned to write "Mind of Evil" in Season 8, a story about corporal punishment. He also contributed two four-part stories to *Ace of Wands*, "Now You See It, Now You Don't" (1970) and "Nightmare Gas" (1971). Houghton also wrote for the strange genre series *Sapphire and Steel* (1979-1982) starring *Absolutely Fabulous* star Joanna Lumley and *Man from U.N.C.L.E.* hearthrob David McCallum. Houghton's *Doctor Who* debut, a seven-part epic, is now available on videocassette.

SEASON 8

55. "Terror of the Autons" Written by Robert Holmes; Directed by Barry Letts; Designed by Ian Watson; Parts I–IV; Airdates: January 2, 9, 16, 23, 1971

SYNOPSIS: Using a weapon called a tissue compressor gun, which shrinks victims down to doll size, an exiled Time Lord called the Master hooks a Nestene container up to the control panel of a massive satellite dish in England. A concerned Time Lord contacts the Doctor just as he is introduced to his new assistant, the beautiful Jo Grant, and warns the Doctor of the Master's arrival.

Soon the Master's nefarious invasion plan unfolds. He takes over a plant which produces thousands of plastic daffodils, and an Auton army travels by bus all across England to distribute these flowers to passersby. The Doctor discovers that the daffodils are deadly weapons that shoot a plastic film around unsuspecting humans and cause immediate asphyxiation! Worse, 450,000 of the devices have already been distributed! The Doctor must now stop the Master's plan before a Nestene invasion force arrives.

GUEST CAST: The Master (Roger Delgado); Rex Farrel (Michael Wisher); McDermott (Harry Towb); Time Lord (David Garth); Radio Telescope Director (Frank Mills); Prof. Philips (Christopher Burgess); Goodge (Andrew Staines); Rossini (John Baskcomb); Museum Attendant (Dave Carter); Brownrose (Dermot Twohy); Mrs. Farrel (Barbara Leake); Telephone Mechanic (Norman Stanley); Policeman (Bill McGuirk); Auton Policeman (Terry Walsh); Auton Leader (Pat Gorman); Auton Voice (Haydon Jones)

COMMENTARY: "Terror of the Autons" is yet another "invasion from space" story. It is a repeat of the threat seen only four serials earlier, in "Spearhead from Space." This serial is distinguished only by the fact that it successfully plays on some old horror movie notions and introduces two important characters to the series: the Master and Jo Grant.

Perhaps the *raison d'être* of "Terror of the Autons" is to dramatize plastic dolls coming to life and attacking people. These are certainly effective images, ones that have been seen in horror films and genre television since time immemorial. Among the most notable examples are the evil "Talky Tina" who threatened Telly Savalas in *The Twilight Zone*'s 1964 entry "Living Doll" and the Brad Dourif–voiced "Chucky" from the 1988 frightfest *Child's Play* and its sequels *Child's Play II* (1990), *Child's Play III* (1991), and *Bride of Chucky* (1998). Still, *Doctor Who*'s writers have always proven that they can work any notion into a series script, and here a devil doll makes an intriguing villain. The plastic spouting daffodils are inventive, if somewhat surreal and cartoonish. They seem more appropriate to the camp series *Batman* (1966–1969) than to *Doctor Who* and the grim, black-garbed "Master."

Katy Manning's Jo Grant first appears in "Terror of the Autons." Manning is a delightful presence on the series, and a favorite companion of many fans. There is no doubt, however, that the character also represents huge step backwards from the tough-minded recent companions like Liz Shaw and Zoe. Jo is a screamer and a buffoon. She is constantly being captured, and in need of rescue. Nonetheless, her innocent, youthful naiveté blends well with Pertwee's harsh-tongued interpretation of the Doctor. The Doctor never really needed to show his soft side with Liz Shaw, as she was perfectly capable of blasting a retort right at him. With her mousy demeanor, Jo brought out the tenderness of this particular incarnation of England's favorite Time Lord.

Roger Delgado also makes his first appearance as the villainous Time Lord known as "The Master" in this Season 8 opener. He is a menacing presence, but he would be better used in later stories which do not require him to use such gimmicks as a lethal telephone and poisonous daffodils. Delgado shortly became a regular presence on *Doctor Who*, and appeared in all five serials of this season. Delgado was very much a gentleman and a beloved presence on the set of *Doctor Who*. His reign as the Master was cut tragically short when he was killed during a stunt on the set of a film in 1973. He was so popular in the role of the Master that the character was dropped from the series for three years following his untimely death. His shoes were just too big to fill.

The character of the Master is a modification of other characters seen earlier on *Doctor Who*. The Doctor had already met the jovial Time Lord renegade the Meddling Monk in "The Time Meddler" and "The Dalek Masterplan." Troughton encountered a far more sinister renegade in "The War Games." The Master is clearly based on these characters in that he is sinister and devious but also shares a sort of witty relationship with the Doctor.

More obviously, the Master is based on Arthur Conan Doyle's nemesis for Sherlock Holmes: Professor Moriarty. Just as Moriarty is obsessed with killing Holmes, so is The Master obsessed with murdering the Doctor. And, as in the Holmesian equation, on *Doctor Who* both men are geniuses of roughly equal intelligence. The producers of *Doctor Who* undoubtedly realized that the series would quickly grow stale if the brilliant Doctor were constantly facing Earthmen of lesser mental agility. Accordingly, they gave him an enemy equal in skill. This solution had its own problems, however. It became rather unbelievable that the Master and the Doctor locked horns in every serial and neither one succeeded in eliminating the other. Anyone could write the climax of these serials: The Master's plan is foiled by the Doctor, but the Master lives to fight another day. This repetitive scenario introduced a feeling of predictability to the series that was hard to overcome, even with well-written adventures.

Even more than that, the Master reacts illogically and unbelievably in "Terror of the Autons." He has gone to a great deal of trouble to plan the invasion with the Nestene. Suddenly, as his plan is reaching its climax, the Doctor is able to convince the Master that the Nestene do not need his help any more and will undoubtedly kill him. What does the Master do? He turns around and helps the Doctor! It is hard to believe that the Master would not have thought of this possibility on his own, and that he needed the Doctor to explain it to him. This abrupt about-face undermines the intelligence of the Master significantly. It is a poorly written moment and one that lacks believability.

"Terror of the Autons" introduces the new and improved Time Lords. This is the first such being, other than the Master, seen since "The War Games," and the producers altered the concept of this race considerably between the end of Season 6 and the beginning of Season 8. Here the Time Lord is not menacing at all but downright comical. He floats in the air, looks ridiculous in a suit, and seems more like a petty government bureaucrat than an elemental force of nature that watches over the Time Streams. This was the first "demystification" of the Time Lords. Alas, it would not be the last.

With all these problems, "Terror of the Autons" is a mixed bag. The story is downright dull since another Auton invasion had been recently repelled, and the Robert Holmes teleplay offers no new information about the hive-mind race. Jo Grant, while being lovely, charming and impeccably portrayed by Katy Manning, is undeniably a step backwards into the '60s for female companions, and the Master's plan with devil dolls and poison daffodils seems silly. Couple these problems with the use of a Time Lord as a comedic element rather than an imposing villain as seen in "The War Games," and one begins to sense the unsatisfactory nature of the story. Even with chase scenes, a daring escape from a racing bus and horror movie imagery concerning living dolls, the episode seems hackneyed and slow-moving today.

To date, "Terror of the Autons" has been the last appearance of the Nestene and the Autons in *Doctor Who*. The episode is available on videocassette.

56. "Mind of Evil" Written by Don Houghton; Directed by Timothy Combe; Designed by Raymond London; Parts I–VI; Airdates: January 30, February 5, 13, 20, 27, March 6, 1971

SYNOPSIS: At Stangmoor Prison, Jo and the Doctor witness the demonstration of a revolutionary new process which extracts evil brain impulses from criminals. The Doctor is skeptical about any device that alters the human mind, but he listens as Prof. Kettering lectures. The machine has been invented by the mysterious Dr. Emil Keller, and it eliminates antisocial brain impulses, in theory leaving a rational individual behind. Once extracted, the evil impulses are stored in a reservoir box. The machine has already been used successfully in over 100 cases, but the Doctor learns that Dr. Keller is not who he appears to be, and that the mind-altering machine is rapidly gaining a living, malevolent consciousness.

GUEST CAST: Barnham (Neil McCarthy); Prof. Kettering (Simon Lack); Dr. Summers (Michael Sheard); Green (Eric Mason); Chin Lee (Pik Sen Lim); Fu Peng (Kristopher Kum); Vosper (Hadyn Jones); Mailer (William Marlowe); Senator Alcott (Tommy Duggan); Officers (Dave Carter, Martin Gordon, Bill Matthews, Barry Wade); Linwood (Olive Scott); Bell (Fernanda Marlowe); Charlie (David Calderisi); Costworth (Patrick Godfrey); Fuller (Johnny Barrs); Prisoner (Matthew Walters)

COMMENTARY: Don Houghton's "Mind of Evil" is a meditation on corporal punishment. A scientist has built a device that can extract evil from the brain, but what is left after this process? In Houghton's script, it is suggested by the Doctor that a man missing part of his mind, even the evil part, is less than human. Therefore the story discusses not only the morality of punishing and experimenting on prisoners, but the basic nature of human life. "Mind of Evil" says that evil is an essential part of man. This philosophy mirrors the *Star Trek* story "The Enemy Within" in which Capt. Kirk was split into two beings, one good, one evil. The good captain quickly learned that he was not an effective leader without his negative half. Similarly, the inmate (Barnham) who goes through the Keller Machine Process in "Mind of Evil" is left zombie-like by the extraction of his evil impulses.

With its unique ability to dramatize the fears of those minds it attacks, the monstrous Keller Machine foreshadows some of influential American horror films of the '80s. As in *A Nightmare on Elm Street* (1984), the results of attacks in dream or trance states are dramatized by physical evidence on the corpse. Just as Freddy Krueger's victims frequently die with five razor slices across their teenage bellies, so do the Keller Machine's victims die with evidence of "unreal" rat attacks, drownings and so forth. In this case, however, the scars result when victims *themselves* create these conditions from within their terrified psychology. The evidence is not caused by the presence of a supernatural specter of death.

"Mind of Evil" heralds the second appearance of Roger Delgado's renegade Time Lord. Once more the Master has a plan to cause massive death and destruction, and as usual he has no real motive to do so except that he is "evil." In some senses the Master is the most two-dimensional and juvenile of all the villains created on *Doctor Who*. He is not engineered to be evil like the Daleks. He is not brutal by lack of emotions like the Cybermen. He does not want to commit genocide to save his people like the Silurians or the Sea Devils do. He is just evil. He wants to cause world wars, destroy the Earth and kill the Doctor just because he is mean and "bad." Why does he hate the Doctor so much? This question is never explained in the series, although past incidents on Gallifrey are often enigmatically referred to. It has been suggested that the Master and the Doctor were once close friends and that they had a falling-out over something. (Fans have even speculated that the Doctor and the Master are brothers.) Still, the Master is a less than satisfactory character because he is always committing evil acts just for the pure unadulterated evil of it, not because he has an agenda or a valid motive. Sometimes he wants to take over the Earth ("Terror of the Autons"), sometimes he wants to cause chaos and destruction ("Mind of Evil") and sometimes he just wants to kill the Doctor ("Castrovalva"). In other words, he is easy to fit into any story that requires a threat. Dressed all in black, the Master is a simplistic bad guy who can fill in for writers when they do not have a reason for characters in the drama to legitimately threaten the Doctor. He is a crutch: Hey, just throw in the Master, he hates the Doctor! That is all that one need say, and the Master has often been used in exactly that capacity.

In later years, the Master would grow a little, particularly in instances where he is forced to save the Doctor rather than destroy him ("The Five Doctors," "The Ultimate Foe"). Writers of later stories would also finally find legitimate motivation for his actions: He has reached his final incarnation and must steal, kill, threaten and plot to gain a new body. In these early days, however, the relationship between the Master and the Doctor is a two-dimensional one. Only Delgado's exceptional performance, not the character conception, makes the Master effective.

"Mind of Evil" exists only in a black-and-white print and has recently been released on videotape.

57. "The Claws of Axos" Written by Bob Baker & Dave Martin; Directed by Michael Ferguson; Designed by Kenneth Sharp; Parts I–IV; Airdates: March 13, 20, 2, April 3, 1971

SYNOPSIS: A strange organic spacecraft crashes near the Nuton Power Complex and a national emergency is declared. UNIT forces including the Doctor, Brigadier Lethbridge-Stewart and Jo Grant arrive on the scene. They soon receive a transmission from the aliens called "Axos," who request assistance. The Axos are gold skinned, curly-haired, bulb-eyed creatures who claim that their culture is dying, and that their science has taken an organic rather than mechanical path. They want to remain on Earth until their damaged ship can be replenished. In exchange, they offer to share Axonite, a valuable power source, a chameleon of elements, a "thinking" molecule.

After examining the element, the Doctor learns that the Axonite, the Axos themselves, and even their ship are all part of a single living, vampiric entity which can destroy the whole world. The Doctor is backed into a corner and forced to divulge the complicated equations of space-time travel to the Axos when they threaten to extract Jo's life force.

GUEST CAST: Chinn (Peter Bathurst); Bill Filer (Paul Crist); Hardiman (Donald Hewlett); Winser (David Saville); Axon Man (Bernard Holley); Capt. Harker (Tim Piggot-Smith); First Radar Operator (Michael Walker); Second Radio Operator (David March); Axon Woman (Patricia Gordino)

COMMENTARY: "The Claws of Axos" is yet another "invasion from space" story featuring an appearance by the Master. It is notably more successful than

"Terror of the Autons," however, because the Axos organism is an interesting and unique villain. The notion of the Axos space creature as a kind of living spaceship with a vicious snout and thumping organic walls is well-designed by Kenneth Sharp. A living spaceship with organic qualities would repeat as the central theme of the *Star Trek: The Next Generation* third season story "Tin Man" and in *Star Trek: Voyager*'s "Scorpion." In fact, "The Claws of Axos" introduces perhaps for the first time on British or American television the concept of alien technology based on an organic rather than "computer-based" technology. This bio-mechanical look reappeared on the *Doctor Who* series several times, notably in "Terror of the Zygons" and "The Android Invasion." This look is all the rage right now in American sci-fi cinema, as evidenced by its appearance in the *Alien* foursome, the *Predator* film series and more recent hits such as *Independence Day* (1996). All of these epics display alien technology that is as much organic as mechanical, so "The Claws of Axos" deserves some recognition for first visualizing this unique concept.

"The Claws of Axos" successfully translates a longstanding human myth into a new venue. Here the Axon organism is revealed to be the outer space wandering equivalent of a vampire. Space vampires have since proven irresistible, showing up in diverse films such as Tobe Hooper's *Lifeforce* (1985), the *Buck Rogers* 1980 episode "Space Vampire" and the derivative *Babylon 5* (1994) story "Soul Hunter." A second space vampire appeared in the *Doctor Who* Season 18 adventure "State of Decay."

"The Claws of Axos" continues the *Doctor Who* trend begun in the Pertwee era of exposing human bureaucracy and greed. In the Dave Martin-Bob Baker teleplay, the British government wants to control distribution of the Axonite so it can make a killing selling the material to other countries. This is a particularly selfish attitude. Minister Chinn, with his shoot-first-and-ask-questions-later attitude, is also a less than positive example of the human species. The Doctor, of course, rails against this selfishness. Again, this is sort of the "Mr. Spock" phase of the Doctor's character, wherein he is shown to be more advanced than those who surround him.

Not so effective in "The Claws of Axos" is the costume for the Axos beasts. These creatures are certainly grotesque and misshapen, but with their floppy "spaghetti arms" they look only mildly threatening.

There is also a significant special effects blunder in this story. There is a shot of Sgt. Benton and another UNIT officer fighting the Axonites in their moving Jeep. This scene was filmed in front of a blue screen, apparently so an image of the landscape could be rear-projected behind the fight. Through some goof-up, no scene was added to the background. The men are thus fighting in front of a totally blue screen! This shot lasts for several seconds and the error is obvious to even a casual observer.

Despite this production error, "The Claws of Axos" is a visually interesting if not terribly innovative *Doctor Who* serial. The Master's role is once again ill-defined, and the character switches sides at the drop of a hat. The Axon organism is nonetheless an exciting threat, and the Doctor's final "time loop" solution would become a recurring element in the series. In fact, casting a villain into a time loop (as the Doctor does to the Axos) is the standard operating procedure of the Time Lords. They commit this act in the Season 15 story "Image of the Fendahl." The Doctor is himself is caught in a time loop in "The Armageddon Factor" in Season 16 and "Meglos" in Season 18.

"The Claws of Axos" is available on videotape.

58. "Colony in Space" Written by Malcolm Hulke; Directed by Michael Briant; Designed by Tim Gleeson; Parts I–VI; Airdates: April 10, 1, 24, May 1, 8, 15, 1971

SYNOPSIS: The Master has stolen a file from the Time Lord memory circuit and the Time Lords are worried about the theft. The file concerned the Doomsday Machine and its location in time and space. Realizing that they have inadvertently allowed the universe to be endangered, the Time Lords send the Doctor and Jo to a barren world in the distant future. The Doctor and Jo are quickly captured by settlers who fear the new visitors are prospectors and that a mining company is going to sweep in and turn the world upside down with industry and machinery.

The Doctor takes the side of the colonists and confronts Capt. Dent of the IMC (Intergalactic Mining Company). Dent intends to mine this planet because it is rich in duralinium and can supply Earth with the valuable building substance for years to come. While this conflict plays out, the Doctor and Jo begin to realize that the Primitives, the indigenous inhabitants of the planet, may be hiding a deadly secret from the galaxy. The Master and the Doctor, working to opposite ends, must then confront the Guardian, a leftover from the distant past when the Primitives were a technologically advanced race.

GUEST CAST: The Master (Roger Delgado); Time Lords (John Baker, Graham Leamon); Servo Robot (John Scott Martin); Leeson (David Webb); Jane (Sheila Grant); Martin (John Line); John Ashe (John Ringham); Mrs. Martin (Mitzi Webster); Winton (Nicholas Pennell); Mary Ashe (Helen Worth); Norton (Roy Skelton); Primitive (Pat Gorman); Caldwell (Bernard Kay); Capt. Dent (Morris Perry); Morgan (Tony Caunter); Holden (John Herrington); Allen (Stanley McGeach); Alien Priest (Roy Heyman); Leeson (John Tardaff); Guardian (Norman Atkyns)

COMMENTARY: "The Colony in Space" is a Western–style frontier story transplanted to the far reaches of outer space. The villains of the piece are the same as one might find in any story of the American frontier: wealthy companies bent on taking the land away from poor settlers. Even the threat from wild Indians is transcribed successfully to this venue in the form of native "Primitives." This serial is a very successful "Western in space" because it finds interesting analogies for all of these cowboy conventions. Other science fiction productions that have attempted to bring the Western to outer space, notably the film *Moon Zero Two* (1969) starring James Olsen and Catherine Schell and the American television series *Battlestar Galactica* (1978), have been much less artful and less interesting because they have focused on mimicking classic Western films like *The Magnificent Seven* or *High Noon* rather than creating a believable situation on another planet. Whereas *Doctor Who*'s "The Colony in Space" echoes elements seen in Westerns, *Battlestar Galactica* attempted a much more literal translation of the genre. Several episodes of that series such as "The Lost Warrior," and "The Magnificent Warriors" actually featured swinging saloon doors, cowboy hats and shootouts in the streets. The Glen Larson series mimicked the physical conventions of the Western, but not the essence of the frontier situation. Obviously, this conceit was hard to accept. Cowboy hats on a planet thousands of light years away from Earth? Identical architecture too? This belied a lack of imagination rather than an inventive transposition of genres.

Doctor Who's "Colony in Space" is a much more intellectual blending of Western and space opera since it relies not on genre retreads of *High Noon* or *The Magnificent Seven* and recycled sets and costumes. Instead it creates a frontier situation, a social structure similar to that of the Old West. The mining companies controlled from back on Earth (read: "East") represent greed and civilization while settlers try to eke out a living in the rough environment of the frontier planet ("West"). They must contend not only with bad soil that won't grow their crops, but with savage, incomprehensible aliens called Primitives (read: Native American Indians), whom they fear.

In addition to its translation of Wild West trappings, "Colony in Space" is another anti-business polemic. The big bad IMC represents the greed and the selfish aspects of man's nature. The mining company is willing to kill to possess the land, echoing films such as *McCabe and Mrs. Miller* (1973). The story is also pro-environment, since the colonists are portrayed as salt-of-the earth farmers and decent, hard-working folk, while the Company men are seen as cutthroat strip-miners. The fallen culture of the Primitives also represents a diatribe against civilization and technology. The Primitives killed themselves off with nuclear weapons! Only in returning to their "natural" roots has this race finally achieved happiness and peace. "Colony in Space" is filled with subtext such as this, and it is one of the most intellectually interesting shows of Pertwee's era. In a sense this is a "revolution" story, but its Western–style overtones and heavy didactic quality elevate it beyond the average.

"Colony in Space" is also a unique story because it is the first non–Earth adventure since the end of Season 6. It is good for the Doctor and Jo to get away for a time from the repetition of alien invasions, mad scientists and uncooperative modern bureaucracies. The only element that ties this episode to the rest of the season is the presence of the Master. More interesting, however, is the chance to see Pertwee explore another world, something which he had heretofore been denied, as his incarnation was limited to Earth. This adventure expands the Pertwee mystique because finally the viewers see the third Doctor indulge in the kind of traveling that earlier incarnations took for granted.

"Colony in Space" has been novelized by serial writer Malcolm Hulke under the title *Doctor Who and the Doomsday Weapon*.

59. "The Daemons" Written by Guy Leopold [Robert Sloman & Barry Letts]; Directed by Christopher Barry; Designed by Roger Ford; Parts I–V; Airdates: May 22, 29, June 5, 12, 19, 1971

SYNOPSIS: In the quiet English village of Devil's End, a world-renowned archaeologist named Prof. Horner is planning to open an ancient barrow at the ominously named Devil's Hump. Superstitious townfolks, including Miss Gilbert Hawthorne, are certain that if he succeeds in unearthing the barrow beneath their town church, doom and disaster will result.

At UNIT headquarters, the Doctor works to unravel the lost secrets of the TARDIS, but is interrupted in this task by Jo's seemingly endless ponderings on the subject of science versus superstition. The Doctor insists there is no such thing as witchcraft, magic or superstition, but Jo is not convinced. The Doctor's tone changes suddenly when he realizes that the Devil's Hump barrow will be opened during Beltane, the greatest occult festival of the year! He races to the scene, but is too late.

A devil creature called Azal is released from the barrow, and the Doctor realizes that it is actually an alien life form from a planet 60,000 light years away. This alien, from a world called Damos, is capable of diminishing and enlarging not only himself, but any objects he chooses. The Doctor explains to Jo that the Daemon race exists on the far side of the Milky Way, and that they came to Earth 100,000 years ago. They are responsible for the many legends of horned monsters such as the Minotaur of Crete, the Hindu demons and even Satan himself. While man was evolving, the Daemons had already developed sophisticated science and technology. All the "black magic" on Earth is actually a remnant of this advanced science! The Doctor confides that the Daemons are not evil creatures, but simply amoral. They assist Earthlings only on their own terms, and everything is a lab experiment to them. The Doctor is afraid that the awakened Daemon will now end this particular experiment and destroy the Earth! Making matters worse, the Master has orchestrated Azal's revival!

GUEST CAST: Azal (Stephen Thorne); The Master (Robert Delgado); Prof. Gilbert Horner (Robin Wentworth); Miss Hawthorne (Damaris Hayman); Harry (James Snell); Osgood (Alec Linstead); Thorne (John Owens); Bok (Stanley Mason); Tom Girton (John Croft); Winstanley (Rollo Gamble); Garvin (John Joyce)

COMMENTARY: *Doctor Who* has always been a series that pinpoints successful stories and then exploits those stories as a template for future adventures. The *Time Machine* scenario of "The Daleks" has been repeated innumerable times. The quest scenario originated in "The Keys of Marinus" returns in the "Key to Time" saga of the Tom Baker era. The "trial" motif of "The War Games" inspires a similar adventure in "The Trial of the Time Lord." Similarly, the *Quatermass* television productions clearly led to the central thematic concept of the Jon Pertwee era: that of a brilliant scientist struggling in England to stave off alien invasions.

***Quartermass and the Pit*, a 1958 science fiction epic by Nigel Kneale, was the spiritual ancestor of *Doctor Who* episode #59, "The Daemons."**

"The Daemons" is a new *Doctor Who* prototype that is repeated in "Pyramids of Mars," "Image of the Fendahl," "State of Decay" and others. In the "Daemons"–style subgenre, the plot is always identical: An ancient evil, based on legend and mythology, has been unearthed. It begins to awaken. The only way to destroy this burgeoning evil is by using the traditional "occult" devices and symbols that were believed to stop the evil in ages past. In "The Daemons," the rites of black magic, including human sacrifice, are intrinsic to Azal's power. In "Image of the Fendahl," the use of salt and the pentagram symbol are invoked. In "State of Decay," a stake destroys the Great Vampire. The "Daemons" prototype is certainly a dramatic one because it plays on the seemingly insatiable human need to believe that ancient sagas of spooks, demons and monsters have a basis in fact. Usually, *Doctor Who* suggests that the historical monster is actually an alien creature come to rule or conquer Earth.

Despite its popularity, the roots of the "Daemons" prototype are obvious, making "The Daemons" perhaps the most derivative of all *Doctor Who* serials. Consider the film *Quatermass and the Pit* (1967), or its television counterpart of the same name, produced in 1958. An excavation in London at Hobb's Lane (i.e. "Devil's Lane") unearths an ancient human skull. Also beneath the ground is a buried alien spaceship from which a terrible psychic force emerges. The dead owners of the spaceships, horned alien beings, are revealed to be the source of human legends about demons. The force of psychic energy affects people around the excavation, and is thus equated with the demonic possession of the living. The alien terror is finally ended when a crane made of iron is driven through the alien nemesis. In essence, *Quatermass and the Pit* originated the "Daemons" prototype!

With the *Quatermass* plot specifics established, it is only too easy to see the similarities to "The Daemons." Once again, an excavation is causing trouble. Once again, the excavation has a frightening name relating to Satan. Once more it is revealed that human legends of demons are actually based on encounters with an extraterrestrial force. If one substitutes the eccentric scientific genius of the Doctor for the eccentric scientific genius of Dr. Quatermass, the parallels are complete. Clearly, "The Daemons" owes a huge debt to *Quatermass and the Pit*. The number and sequence of similar events cannot be coincidental.

That said, "The Daemons" is nonetheless a competent and well-executed serial. Pertwee considered it to be among the best of his reign as the Time Lord. Still, it is hard to laud a production, no matter how slick or well-produced, that borrows all of its creativity from another source. Despite this borrowing of *Quatermass* concepts, "The Daemons" did spawn many follow-ups in *Doctor Who* including the aforementioned serials. "Image of the Fendahl" even begins with the unearthing of a human skull millions of years old, the same act which precipitates the excavation in *Quatermass and the Pit*! To some *Doctor Who* fans, this kind of repetition may not be bothersome, but it automatically disqualifies "The Daemons" and "Image of the Fendahl" from positions of honor in the *Doctor Who* canon. It would be one thing if "The Daemons" explored a similar concept, but it is quite another thing to repeat every element of *Quatermass and the Pit*. What makes *Doctor Who* so frequently a great series is the way it appropriates a popular film or work of literature like *The Incredible Shrinking Man*, *Fantastic Voyage* or *The Mummy* and then takes the story a step beyond the earlier production by overturning convention or adding something unexpected. Had "The Daemons" used *Quatermass and the Pit* as a starting point, and then added a dose of original thinking, this author might instead be complimenting the ingenuity of the author. Sadly, "The Daemons" proves that *Doctor Who* has derivative moments as well as inspired ones. Some *Doctor Who* fans may euphemistically refer to this serial as an affectionate "homage" to the works of Nigel Kneale and the *Quatermass* series, but that is not an apt description. A homage is defined as a story which somehow harkens back to and celebrates another work in spirit and intent. A story which repeats every element of an earlier work and yet does not acknowledge that work is not an "homage." It is imitation.

Doctor Who fans can judge the adventure for themselves, as "The Daemons," a very popular and well-liked serial, has been released on videotape.

SEASON 9

60. "Day of the Daleks" Written by Louis Marks; Directed by Paul Bernard; Designed by David Myerscough-Jones; Parts I–IV; Airdates: January 1, 8, 15, 22, 1972

SYNOPSIS: A troop of resistance fighters from a Dalek-controlled future have traveled back through time to assassinate Sir Richard Styles, a man they deem responsible for the Dalek takeover of Earth. Using a time vortex magnetron device found on the corpses of one of the guerrillas, the Doctor and Jo travel to the twenty-second century and are captured by the Daleks. They escape and return to the present to prevent the assassination of Styles, but the Daleks and their minions (ape-soldiers called Ogrons) return to the twentieth century as well. A show-down occurs at Styles' lavish country estate just as a critical peace conference is about to commence.

GUEST CAST: Twenty-Second Century Human Controller (Aubrey Woods); Capt. Yates (Richard Franklin); Ariat (Anna Barry); Roaz (Scott Fredericks); Shura (Jimmy Winston); Sir Reginald Styles (Wilfrid Carter); Miss Paget (Jean McFarlane); Girl Technician (Deborah Brayshaw); Monica (Valentine Parker); Manager (Peter Hill); Senior Guard (Andrew Carrane); Guard at Work Center (George Raistrick); UNIT Radio Operator (Gypsie Kemp); TV Reporter (Alex MacIntosh); Guerrilla (Tim Condren); Ogrons (Rick Lester, Maurice Bush, David Joyce, Frank Menzies, Bruce Wells, Geoffrey Todd); Daleks (John Scott Martin, Rick Newby, Murphy Grumbar); Dalek Voices (Oliver Gilbert, Peter Messaline)

COMMENTARY: Sci-fi film and television is frequently obsessed with the notion that by traveling to the past, mankind destroys his own future. Accordingly, films such as *The Terminator* (1984) echo "Day of the Daleks" in surprising detail. In both productions, guerrilla soldiers send warriors back in history to prevent a war that kills most of the human race and leads to a planet Earth dominated by killing, inhuman machines (whether they be Daleks or terminators). Consider also that it is the actions of these selfsame warriors that actually lead to the eventual takeover by the nemesis they have sought to defeat!

In "Day of the Daleks," a resistance fighter named Shura destroys the peace conference and thereby triggers the war which makes Earth vulnerable to Dalek domination. In *The Terminator*, the machines send a robot after Reese, a robot whose control microchip is actually responsible for causing the war and creating terminators in the first place! Both stories emphasize that time is a deadly cycle, and that those unfortunates who try to tamper with their own existence inevitably end up causing the misery of the future.

This story has also been in seen in *Planet of the Apes* (1968), in which astronauts travel to a future ruled by apes. The apes would never have been able to gain control, however, if the astronauts had not come to the future in the first place and provided a spaceship in which the apes go back in time! This was also the central theme in David Gerrold's (i.e., Noah Ward) contribution to the *Logan's Run* (1977) television series. In "Man Out of Time," scientist David Eakins learns that his invention of time travel is responsible for causing the nuclear holocaust which created Logan's world! Clearly this scenario is a popular one but it is surprising how closely James Cameron's *The Terminator* follows the scenario presented in "Day of the Daleks."

"Day of the Daleks" introduces the fierce Ogrons, ape-like servants to the Daleks. Interestingly, the design of the Ogron uniform is quite derivative of the gorilla uniform in *Planet of the Apes*. In both productions, the evolved ape creatures wear dark leather vests with a sash draped across the front of the uniform. The outfits are too similar to be coincidental, so one has to wonder if the repetition was intentional.

"Day of the Daleks" introduces a brilliant concept to *Doctor Who*: the Blinovitch Limitation Factor. This is the theory that a person can not repeatedly go back and try to change the same event in history over and over again. The Blinovitch Limitation Factor apparently limits this possibility. This "law" explains why the Daleks cannot go back and re-fight the battle of 2164 seen in "The Dalek Invasion of Earth," and why the time-traveling Master cannot go back to the incidents in "Mind of Evil" and try to beat the Doctor one more time, this time with knowledge of how the Doctor defeated him in the first place. The Blinovitch Limitation Factor is really a "throwaway" line in "Day of the Daleks," but it would be incorporated as a crucial element of the Peter Davison story "Mawdryn Undead."

Even with a troop of Ogron soldiers, there is an inherent cheap quality to "Day of the Daleks." The production only had two Daleks to work with and thus had to constantly reshoot and reposition the camera to make it appear as if more Daleks were around. This made "Day of the Daleks" Pertwee's least favorite *Doctor Who* adventure. He told *Starlog* interviewers Karen Flunk Blocher and Teresa Murray in 1991 that he not only disapproved of this story, which he called dreadful, but he despised the Daleks themselves.

> I thought the Daleks ridiculous with their sink pumps and egg whisks, and tennis balls stuck all over them. ... ["Day of the Daleks"] was dreadful, dreadful. And yet, funnily enough, it's quite a popular one. The videocassette sells well.[8]

Many fans would probably disagree with this assessment of the Daleks' menace, and the serial in question. The story is a sound one that was repeated almost lock, stock and barrel in *The Terminator*. It is merely the low budget that keeps this *Doctor Who* story from being completely successful.

61. "The Curse of Peladon" Written by Brian Hayles; Directed by Lennie Mayne; Designed by Gloria Clayton; Parts I–IV; Airdates: January 29, February 5, 12, 19, 1972

SYNOPSIS: In the great castle of Peladon, the young Prince's most trusted aides, Chancellor Torbis and High Priest Hepesh, are fiercely divided on the issue of admission into the Galactic Federation. Torbis supports the Prince's petition to enter the peaceful organization of worlds, and believes that the Federation can put an end to superstition on Peladon. Hepesh feels that the Federation will attempt to control Peladon and extinguish its rich historical traditions. He also fears the curse of Peladon will kill any who dare support this bid for Federation membership. Almost immediately after leaving the throne room, Torbis is killed by the beast Aggedor, the legendary protector of Peladon. Hepesh attempts to convince the young prince that this death is a signal and that the Curse of Peladon is no myth. The prince, however, has already invited the delegates of the Federation.

Along with the Doctor and Jo, who are mistaken for Earth delegates, the Federation representatives arrive. From Alpha Centauri comes a cyclopean Hermaphrodite Hexapod. From Arcturus comes a mechanically sustained creature with a devilish face and small, wiry appendages. And from Mars arrive the Ice Warriors Izlyr and Ssorg. The Ice Warriors are nearly killed by a falling statue of Aggedor and Arcturus is almost murdered when someone sabotages his life support system. The Doctor must determine who is manipulating the "curse" of Peladon...

GUEST CAST: Prince Peladon (David Troughton); Hepesh (Geoffrey Toone); Torbis (Henry Gilbert); Izlyr (Alan Bennion); Ssorg (Sonny Caldinez); Alpha Centauri (Stuart Fell); Voice of Alpha Centauri (Ysanne Churchman); Arcturus (Murphy Grumbar); Voice of Arcturus (Terry Dale); Grun (Gordon St. Clair); Aggedor (Nick Hobbs); Guard Captain (George Giles); Amazonia (Wendy Darvens)

COMMENTARY: "The Curse of Peladon" is another exciting winner for the *Doctor Who* creative team. It features a believable alien culture trying to escape a sort of superstitious "Dark Ages," suspense and intrigue, some great fight scenes, interesting aliens and a thoughtful message about the dawn of enlightenment.

Hayles' story opens with a shot of the menacing Castle of Peladon. This is an evocative matte painting that immediately sets the mood for the dangerous adventure that follows. Even better, the Peladonian culture is crisply established as "divided" from the first scene when men of opposing positions, one representing reason and one representing religion, fight over the course of the future. This sets up the dynamic that will dominate the majority of the serial. It is ironic that the group which espouses a return to traditional values and religion is actually the sect that has betrayed Peladon and entered into secret negotiations with the alien Arcturians!

"The Curse of Peladon" is presented as a compelling mystery. Who is committing the murders, and why? Naturally there are many suspects, including the Prince, Hepesh, Grun, the Ice Warriors, the Alpha Centauri diplomat and the Arcturian. There is even a short time when it seems that the mythical beast of Aggedor may indeed by a supernatural force of vengeance. It is especially rewarding that the Ice Warriors, the Doctor's merciless opponents in "The Ice Warriors" and "The Seeds of Death," are not the culprits. Interestingly, the Doctor displays a bit of racism in his dealings with these Martians. He suspects them immediately of being villains solely because of past experience. He even makes a derogatory remark about them to Jo along the lines that "you can't trust Ice Warriors." The error of his prejudice is fully revealed to the Doctor when the Ice Warriors save him from the Arcturan diplomat, the real villain of the piece. This is rewarding because already the trend in the Pertwee era is to make the Doctor a character who is never wrong. In "The Curse of Peladon," the Doctor has a chink in his armor: discrimination.

The Ice Warriors would return one more time in the Season 11 sequel to this popular story, "The Monster of Peladon." In that adventure, a renegade band of violent Ice Warriors star as the villains along with a miner from Earth. Here, however, the Ice Warriors are depicted as a logical and peaceful race which has overcome violent instincts. This is one of the few times in *Doctor Who* history that a race is permitted to evolve over time from villainy to peace. The Daleks have certainly never made such a jump.

With the Ice Warriors, the green Alpha Centauri, the Arcturan diplomat (who resembles the Martian leader in 1953's *Invaders from Mars*), and the hairy beast Aggedor in evidence, the BBC costume department certainly had its hands full with "The Curse of Peladon." Aggedor, Alpha and the Ice Warrior costumes reappear in "The Monster of Peladon."

As is typical with the Pertwee–era *Doctor Who* serials, there is an extended fight sequence in this serial. The Doctor is forced into the arena with Grun, champion of the Prince. This fight is well-choreographed, fast-paced and indicative of Pertwee's penchant for physical violence. It would have been inconceivable to place either Hartnell or Troughton into the arena with a warrior the size of Grun, but Pertwee more than holds his own. He is the first Doctor in the series who does not require a "second" male lead to perform the stunts. This fetish for fights made the '70s' *Doctor Who* more like *Star Trek*, a series in which the fate of planets, empires and starships often hinged on a right cross or karate chop from the intrepid Capt. Kirk. It is a little harder to accept, perhaps, in *Doctor Who* because the Doctor is supposed to be a peaceful time traveler who thinks his ways out of dilemmas. When he regenerated into Pertwee, the Doctor must have inherited an excess of testosterone.

"The Curse of Peladon" also features a few romantic scenes for Katy Manning's Jo Grant when she romances the prince of Peladon. The introduction of this human element is far more interesting than any number of fight scenes. Romance of any kind was usually barred from this long-running series, although young Susan did settle down and marry the resistance fighter David in "The Dalek Invasion of Earth." Still, the romantic scenes between Peladon and Jo are unexpected and well-played by both Manning and young David Troughton — the son of actor Patrick Troughton! In fact, the son of the Doctor's second incarnation is very good throughout the story, successfully conveying the King's political inexperience but willingness to do the right thing. Patrick Troughton was surely proud to see his son perform a role on this very special series.

"The Curse of Peladon," for all of its obvious intrigue, romance, fast-paced action, well-designed aliens and message about the dawn of an enlightened age, is somewhat reminiscent of the *Star Trek* story "Journey to Babel." In that story, a group of alien diplomats were aboard the *Enterprise* when murders began. The mystery came about because Capt. Kirk did not know which alien faction was behind the crimes. In the end, it was learned that the mineral wealth of a disputed planet (also attempting to gain admission into the Federation) was the issue that prompted the murders. "The Curse of Peladon" shares every one of those elements. The term "Federation," ostensibly borrowed from the Roddenberry series, is one that would repeat in *Doctor Who* many times.

For those people who like to play "name that tune," the Venusian lullaby which the Doctor sings so ably to the sleepy beast Aggedor in "The Curse of Peladon" is actually a nonsense-dialogue version of the song "God Rest Ye Merry Gentlemen"! Audiences can enjoy Pertwee's vocal styling in "Curse of Peladon" for themselves since the episode has been released on videocassette.

62. "The Sea Devils" Written by Malcolm Hulke; Directed by Michael Briant; Designed by Tony Snoaden; Parts I–VI; Airdates: February 26, March 4, 11, 18, 25, 1972

SYNOPSIS: The S.S. *Pevensey Castle* is destroyed at sea with all hands aboard. Meanwhile, the Master has been tried, convicted and sentenced to life imprisonment in a French Chateau which has been converted into a top security prison. The Master's plan to escape from incarceration coincides with further disappearances at sea. The Doctor soon learns that the Master and a sister-race to the Silurians, the Sea Devils, are in cahoots. In an attempt to make peace and avert the fate of the Silurians, the Doctor is lowered into the Sea Devil shelter in a diving bell. The Navy attacks, angering the Sea Devils, and the Doctor is left in a position to choose. Who should survive: Man or Sea Devil?

GUEST CAST: The Master (Roger Delgado); George Trenchard (Clive Morton); Capt. Hart (Edwin Richfield); Robbins (Royston Tickner); Bowman (Alec Wallis); Barclay (Terry Walsh); Jane Blythe (Jane Murphy); Hickman (Hugh Futcher); Clark (Declan Mulholland); Wilson (Brian Justice); Mitchell (David Griffin); Ridgway (Donald Sumpter); Drew (Stanley McGeagh); Walker (Mattin Boddey); Watts (Brian Vaughn); Girton (Rex Rowland); Myers (John Caesar); Lovell (Christopher Wray); Summers (Colin Bell); Admiral (Norman Atkyns); Radio Operator (Neil Seiler); Sea Devils (Peter Forbes-Robertson, Pat Gorman)

COMMENTARY: "The Sea Devils" is the second piece of the so-called Silurian-Sea Devil trilogy. The first story was Season 7's excellent "Doctor Who and the Silurians." Ironically, the final part of this troika occurs not in Pertwee's era, but in Peter Davison's. Season 21's "Warriors of the Deep" sees the angry Silurians and the Sea Devils combining forces and launching their final attack on the human race.

"The Sea Devils" once again puts the Doctor in the role of third-party mediator. He is neither human nor reptilian, so he is the perfect person to negotiate a peace between the two races. As in "The Silurians," any agreement between the two diverse cultures is not possible, and extremist forces on both sides take steps to win at all costs. Therefore, the Doctor fails for the second time to insure a peaceful future. At the end of "Doctor Who and the Silurians," he had to watch as the

Brigadier bombed the Silurian shelters and cut them off from the surface. In "The Sea Devils," he is forced to take a much more active role in the destruction. As the Master so tactfully tells the Doctor, he is responsible for mass murder by destroying the Sea Devil habitats. The Doctor, of course, is not happy about this act, but he was forced to make a choice. The drama in "The Sea Devils" rises from the fact that the Doctor can no longer remain neutral. This time he is forced to choose a side and bloody his own hands. The Doctor elects to save humanity in the end, but the cost both to the Sea Devils and to the Doctor's soul is enormous.

The effectiveness of Malcolm's Hulke's "The Sea Devils" is doubled by the fact that the *Doctor Who* production team was permitted to shoot at various authentic locations and granted access to Naval equipment, including the *HMS Reclaim*. The island stronghold of the Master, another effective and eerie locale, was Norris Castle in Ryde. The naval scenes were lensed at both Portsmouth and Whitecliffe Bay.[9] Like "Doctor Who and the Silurians" before it, "The Sea Devils" is an exciting, well-photographed battle between two races which have an equal claim to rule the Earth. Fans can see "The Sea Devils" today on videocassette.

63. "The Mutants" Written by Bob Baker and Dave Martin; Directed by Christopher Barry; Designed by Jeremy Bear; Parts I–VI; Airdates: April 8, 15, 22, 29, May 6, 1972

SYNOPSIS: The Time Lords want the Doctor to deliver a message pod to an unknown destination in space and time. Realizing he has little choice, the Doctor and Jo take the sphere into the TARDIS and are transported into another wild adventure.

In the thirtieth century, an orbiting space station called *Skybase* has been established around the planet Solos. It is run by the vindictive Marshal, a human officer who enjoys hunting Solonian mutants for sport. The Marshal is upset because a Terran Administrator has just arrived to grant the Solonians their long-sought independence from Earth. Realizing that this will threaten his hobby, the Marshal hires a Solonian named Varan to assassinate the Administrator. The assassination is carried out and then blamed on the Solonian dissident Ky, Varan's chief political rival. The Doctor and Jo encounter Ky as he is escaping captivity, and learn that the Time Lord sphere is intended for him. The message it carries concerns the "mutts" (mutants who dwell on the surface of the planet), thesium radiation and a little-understood act of evolution...

GUEST CAST: Ky (Garrick Magon); Marshal (Paul Whitsun-Jones); Stubbs (Christopher Coll); Administrator (Geoffrey Palmer); Investigator (Peter Howell); Varan (James Mellor); Cotton (Rick James); Sondergaard (John Hollis); Jaeger (George Pravda); Guards (David Arlen, Damon Sanders, Martin Taylor); Solonians (Reg Crenfield, Roy Pearce, Brychan Powell, Damon Sanders, Vic Taylor, Peter Whitaker); Mutants (Laurie Good, Nick Thompson Hill, John Scott Martin, Mike Mungaven, Rick Newby, Eddie Sommer, Mike Torres); *Skybase* Guards (Keith Ashley, Dave Carter, Dennis Plenty, Ron Tingley, Terry Walsh, Donald Waterman)

COMMENTARY: As in "The Curse of Peladon" and "Colony in Space," the wily Time Lords once again free Pertwee's Doctor from exile and send him on a dangerous secret mission in Bob Baker and Dave Martin's unique adventure "The Mutants." It is yet another Third Doctor story which comments on the moral repercussions of race exploitation, pollution of the environment and the tyranny of colonialism. The Marshal, an official from Earth, takes special pleasure in lording it over the peaceful inhabitants of Solos. He treats them as subhumans and plans to remake their world in the image of Earth. He does not care that this will kill the natives. And, as evidenced by his operation with Varan, the Marshal enjoys turning the primitive Solosians against one another. In human history this technique of turning one faction of a less-advanced society against another so the imperialists can remain in control is all too common. *Doctor Who*, a British program, courageously points out the inequity of this situation. All of these stories again prove that Pertwee's age was perhaps the most socially relevant and moralistic of *Doctor Who* periods.

"The Mutants" is also a transformation story. This, like the alternate universe, the doppelganger or the living machine, is also a subgenre of sci-fi television. Other transformation programs include "The Crystals," a 1981 episode of *Buck Rogers* in which beings evolve from featureless mummies to physically perfect humans in a week. The gimmick of the story is that the *Searcher* crew has misinterpreted the transformation: Buck and the others believe the transformation is from human to mindless mutant, and they try to stop it before a beautiful young girl becomes a monster. *Star Trek: The Next Generation* produced a 1990 transformation story entitled "Transfigurations," in which a man persecuted by his people is picked up by the *Enterprise*. Over a period of weeks it is discovered that this ugly humanoid has a gift for healing others. At the close of the show he evolves into a perfect being who radiates a blinding yellow glow. All of these stories follow the theme common in *Doctor Who* that something ugly can develop into something beautiful. Here the ugly Mutts are just a step along the road to perfection. Beyond its transformation elements, this serial explores what happens when a person tries to prevent another from attaining his destiny.

Paul Whitsun-Jones plays the Marshal in this story, returning to *Doctor Who* for the first time since his 1966 appearance in Season 4's premiere "The Smugglers." "The Mutants" is not yet available on videocassette.

64. "The Time Monster" Written by Robert Sloman; Directed by Paul Bernard; Designed by Tim Gleeson, Parts I–VI; Airdates: May 13, 20, 27, June 3, 10, 17, 1972

SYNOPSIS: The Master experiments with T.O.M.T.I.T. (Transmission Of Matter Through Interstitial Time), a device which can reduce matter to light waves and then transport it to different places. The Master is using T.O.M.T.I.T. to summon a creature called "Kronos," who exists outside space-time among a race of beings known as Chronivores, or "time eaters." When Kronos appears, it sucks the life out of a human scientist named Stuart Hyde. Affected by the temporal distortion, Hyde ages from 25 to 80 in just a few seconds.

The Doctor knows that Kronos is the most powerful of all the Chronivores. The Ancient priest of Atlantis once controlled him using a time crystal, and now the Master is using the same 4,000-year-old crystal to capture the chronivore for some dastardly purpose! The Doctor and Jo time travel to Atlantis to stop the Master's plan, but if Kronos is unleashed there, the city will be totally destroyed.

GUEST CAST: The Master (Roger Delgado); Stuart Hyde (Ian Collier); Krasis, High Priest of Atlantis (Donald Eccles); Dr. Ruth Ingram (Wanda Moore); Kronos (Marc Boyle); Face of Kronos (Ingrid Bowers); King Delios (George Cormack); Queen Galleia (Ingrid Pitt); Lakis (Susan Penhaligon); Dr. Percival (John Wyse); Minotaur (David Prowse); Hippias (Aidan Murphay); Neophyte (Keith Dalton); Knight (Gregory Powell); Dr. Cook (Neville Barber); Proctor (Barry Ashton); UNIT Sergeant (Simon Legree); Crito (Derek Murcott); Miseus (Michael Malker); Roundhead (Dave Carter); Knight (Gregory Powll); Window Cleaner (Terry Walsh); Guards (Richard Eden, Laurie Goode, Nick Hobbs, Christopher Holmes, Melville Jones, Jonas Kerr, Geoffrey Morgan); Councillors (Edmund Bailey, Wilfred Boyle, Colin Cunningham, Reg Lloyd, Peter Penny, Bill Whitehead); Serving Girls (Yyvonne Ashley, Alison Daimler, Susan Patrice); Sedan Carriers (Yinka Adebiyi, George Gragney, Peter Johnson, Francis Williams); Trumpeters (Andrew Dempsey, Jamie Griffin, Jeremy Higgins, Marc Landers)

COMMENTARY: "The Time Monster" is *Doctor Who*'s second foray into Atlantean lore. The first was the Season 4 adventure "The Underwater Menace," which showed the destruction of Atlantis. "The Time Monster" also dramatizes the destruction of the city, but it is in completely different circumstances! In "The Underwater Menace," the Doctor destroyed Atlantis to stop the evil Dr. Zaroff from draining Earth's oceans. In "The Time Monster," it is Kronos who eliminates the mythical kingdom. Since "The Underwater Menace" has been destroyed by the BBC, perhaps this discontinuity in *Doctor Who* history no longer matters.

"The Time Monster" introduces a race of beings outside time called Chronivores. This is their only appearance in *Doctor Who*, although several other beings are described throughout the series as "existing outside time," including the bored Eternals in Season 20's "Enlightenment." Another *Doctor Who* element seen in "The Time Monster," the battle of TARDISes (TARDI?), would reappear in Episode 116, "Logopolis."

The legendary Minotaur makes an appearance in "The Time Monster" and is played by David Prowse. Prowse is world-renowned for giving body to Darth Vader in the *Star Wars* trilogy. Between his assignment on *Doctor Who* and his stardom in *Star Wars*, Prowse also appeared in the Year 2 *Space: 1999* episode "The Beta Cloud." The Minotaur's legend would also be rewritten and transposed to an alien planet in the Season 17 *Doctor Who* story "The Horns of Nimon." Troughton's Doctor also encountered the Minotaur in the Land of Fiction in "The Mind Robber."

The other notable guest star in "The Time Monster" is Ingrid Pitt as Galleia. She had already acted with Pertwee in *The House That Dripped Blood* (1971), an

Ingrid Pitt, here being assaulted by a vampirized Jon Pertwee in *The House That Dripped Blood* (1970), guest-starred in *Doctor Who* episode #64, "The Time Monster."

Amicus horror anthology written by *Psycho* author Robert Bloch and also starring Peter Cushing (*Doctor Who and the Daleks*).

"The Time Monster" was writer Robert Sloman's first contribution to the series. He would also write the environmentally minded farewell to Jo Grant, Season 10's "The Green Death," as well as the last story of the Pertwee era, "Planet of the Spiders." "The Time Monster" is not yet available on videocassette.

SEASON 10

65. "The Three Doctors" Written by Bob Baker and Dave Martin; Directed by Lennie Mayne; Designed by Roger Liminton; Parts I–IV; Airdates: December 30, January 6, 13, 20, 1973

SYNOPSIS: A beam of energy traveling faster than the speed of light hits Earth and materializes strange creatures who seem intent on capturing the Doctor.

On Gallifrey, home planet of the Time Lords, the inhabitants are aware of the problem. A black hole is sucking energy from space, and the universe is being consumed. The Time Lords cannot muster the energy to stop the drain, and they have only enough power to give the Doctor some much needed assistance. Although it is a flagrant violation of the First Law of Time, the Gallifreyans pull the earlier incarnations of the Doctor from their individual time streams and attempt to deposit them in the Third Doctor's time frame.

Soon the first three incarnations of the Doctor are teaming up in the anti-matter universe to stop the architect of this destruction: the villainous Omega. Omega was once the solar engineer of Rassilon, the Gallifreyan who was sent to gain mastery of a black hole. Omega succeeded in his mission and trapped the power of a black hole so that the Time Lords could harness that power and successfully travel through time. Unfortunately, the Time Lords' benefactor was himself trapped in the anti-matter universe. He is unable to return, and is causing the cosmic energy drain for revenge. Now he hopes the presence of the Doctor will allow him to escape from the eye of the black hole.

GUEST CAST: Doctor Who (Patrick Troughton); Doctor Who (William Hartnell); Dr. Tyler (Rex Robinson); President of the Time Lord High Council (Roy Purcell); Mr. Ollis (Laurie Webb); Omega (Stephen Thorne); Chancellor (Clyde Pollitt); Time Lord (Graham Leaman); Ms. Ollis (Patricia Prior); Corporal Palmer (Denys Palmer)

COMMENTARY: "The Three Doctors" starts off a wonderful tenth season for *Doctor Who*. It is a funny, involving story that unites all the actors who have portrayed the curmudgeonly Time Lord up to this point. The only disappointment is the small part accorded the original Doctor, William Hartnell. This was a necessary adjustment, however, since Hartnell was sick during the shooting.

Still, the joyous celebratory feeling of "The Three Doctors" creates a special installment of *Doctor Who*. The best parts come about when Troughton and Pertwee share the stage. These vastly different actors have instant chemistry — or rather anti-chemistry. Their Doctors bicker, throw temper tantrums and sass one another with regularity. Pertwee even refers to Troughton as "incorrigibly frivolous." How right he is! What a perfect description of the innocent and childish second incarnation of the Time Lord! This meeting of Doctors is also a joy because it depicts a rendezvous that no person should ever have to face. How would anyone like to be forced to encounter themselves at high school age? At 13? At seven? At an immature 430? It is no wonder that the ever-serious Pertwee shows considerable disdain for his younger, more fun-loving self. The Doctor has matured since those days, after all! Now he is a grown-up, more physically and socially adept than ever before.

This difference between Doctors is beautifully expressed in the decision-making processes exemplified by each Doctor in "The Three Doctors." Pertwee, as always, comes across as an intense physical presence. His method is a proactive one. He is a linear-thinking negotiator and mediator. He attempts to deal with Omega through logic and understanding. Troughton's Doctor comes along and takes a completely different approach. He stumbles around clumsily, laughs at his own jokes and makes a general nuisance of himself. All this activity causes the impatient Omega to reveal a lack of self-control. Thus Troughton's seeming incompetence is actually a ruse to draw out the weakness of the enemy! "The Three Doctors" is a brilliant show because it so clearly delineates these differences in strategies between Doctors.

Hartnell's Doctor also appears periodically, and he is characterized as the "Oracle" of *Doctor Who*. He is the all-knowing, all-wise elder statesman of the series. Though this depiction contrasts somewhat with Hartnell's years on the show when he was shown to be a crotchety, temperamental character, it is appropriate after ten years to lionize the acting giant who originated the role of the Doctor. Accordingly, the later incarnations treat Hartnell as sacred, and they mind his every word. Hartnell, for his part, treats Pertwee and Troughton like squabbling children. His initial shock at seeing his replacements is very funny. "Oh, wonderful," he says, "I've been replaced by a clown and a dandy!" That is just one of the funny moments in the serial. In another one, Troughton alludes to the fact that he and Pertwee are both "copies" of Hartnell.

Other than matters of personality and ego, "The Three Doctors" also adds significantly to Time Lord lore. For the first time since "The War Games," the audiences get a lingering look at the Time Lord home planet. Disappointingly, it is an average-looking "space age" control room. It does not at all seem indicative of the powerful telepaths who once put the Doctor on trial, sent away his companions and exiled him to Earth. The control room could easily be the bridge of a starship on *Star Trek*. The Time Lords have thus officially transitioned from superior, mysterious aliens to just another alien race, like the Vulcans or the Klingons.

Beyond the disappointment of the control room, "The Three Doctors" reveals the history of solar Engineer Omega. It also unveils for the first time the source of Time Lord power: a black hole! This is all fascinating information, but familiarity tends to breed contempt. The more the audience knows about the Time Lords, the less menacing and enigmatic they become. *Doctor Who* was at its best in "The War Games" when the Time Lords were shown to have mist-enshrouded corridors, endless rows of TARDIS capsules and menacing evil alive in their granite, cold eyes. The saga of the Time Lords and Omega would continue in the Season 20 opener, "Arc of Infinity."

"The Three Doctors" is a landmark show not only because Time Lords are at the heart of it, but because of the nostalgia factor. How wonderful it is to see Hartnell and Troughton back in action again. Sadly, this would mark Hartnell's last appearance on the series. In "The Five Doctors" his incarnation would be played by Richard Hurndall. Troughton returned to the Whoniverse two further times: in the twentieth anniversary special "The Five Doctors" and the 1985 episode "The Two Doctors" with Colin Baker. For trivia buffs, the film segment of Troughton displayed on the Time Lord screen in "The Three Doctors" is cut from the destroyed serial "The Macra Terror."

As a reward for his actions in saving the universe from Omega, the Time

Lords give the Doctor full use of the TARDIS once again, ending officially the "exile" years on *Doctor Who*. Accordingly, the series would soon take off for destinations unknown, leaving UNIT and Earth behind.

"The Three Doctors" may not be the most taut, well-written serial ever seen on *Doctor Who*, but it is an enjoyable romp filled with old friends and good humor. It is the perfect anniversary show. Fans can revel in every silly moment of it on BBC/CBS-Fox home video.

66. "Carnival of Monsters" Written by Robert Holmes; Directed by Barry Letts; Designed by Roger Liminton; Parts I–IV; Airdates: January 27, February 3, 10, 17, 1973

SYNOPSIS: His exile ended, the Doctor offers to take Jo to Metebelis III, but the TARDIS sets down somewhere other than the programmed destination. When the traveling duo sees a crate of chickens and a box labeled "Singapore," the Doctor and Jo realize they are on a terrestrial cargo ship. They meet the passengers and crew of the ship and learn that they are bound for Bombay in the year 1926. This strikes a chord with the Doctor: The ship is the S.S. *Bernice*, a vessel that vanished two days from Bombay, never to be heard from again. While the Doctor and Jo investigate this mystery, a plesiosaurus rears its head in the ocean nearby!

On the planet Inter Minor, two traveling entertainers from Lurma, Vorg and Shirna, unload the "Scope," a cylindrical, man-sized machine with a viewing orb on top. They are here to entertain the inhabitants of Inter Minor. The Scope is a giant peepshow which displays many worlds inside. There is something wrong with the Scope, so Vorg looks into the miniature world and locates the malfunction. There is a strange blue box generating an electrical field ... the Doctor, Jo, the TARDIS and the *Bernice* have somehow ended up miniaturized inside the peep show! To make matters worse, they are not alone. Also inside the scope are the omnivorous Drashigs from the moon of Grundle, creatures so fearsome that they once ate a crashed spaceship and its crew!

The Doctor and Jo must escape from the cosmic equivalent of an ant farm before the xenophobic inhabitants of Inter Minor decide it is best to destroy the Scope and its miniature "infestation" altogether.

GUEST CAST: Vorg (Leslie Dwyer); Shirna (Cheryl Hall); Kalik (Michael Wisher); Pletrac (Peter Halliday); Orum (Terence Lodge); Andrews (Ian Marter); Claire (Jenny McCracken); Captain (Andrew Staines); Functionary (Stuart Fell)

COMMENTARY: "Carnival of Monsters" is a brilliant *Doctor Who* story that effectively turns the tables on civilized mankind. It is not helpless animals who are caged in a zoo this time, but sentient humanity! When Jo points out how awful and inconsiderate this captivity is, the Doctor pointedly asks her if she has ever owned a bowl of goldfish. The point, that mankind is just as bad as the owners of the Scope, is established superbly and with a minimum of preachiness. The situation of humans trapped in a zoo has been a sci-fi trope for decades. The idea was splendidly realized in a classic 1959 *Twilight Zone* episode starring Roddy

McDowall and Susan Oliver, "People Are Alike All Over." The animated *Star Trek* series explored the same concept in David P. Harmon's story "Eye of the Beholder" (1974).

Robert Holmes' "Carnival of Monsters" is a nicely visualized adventure packed with classic *Doctor Who* moments and images. Not only is the Doctor miniaturized again, as in Season 2's premiere "Planet of the Giants," but there are cameo appearances from favorite villains such as the Cybermen and Ogrons. The fact that the *Bernice* crew is unaware of its fate and locked inside a "time loop" is a concept already utilized in both "The Claws of Axos" and "The Time Monster," but it makes an effective addition to this adventure. Jo's frustration with the *Bernice* crew as they endlessly repeat the same few moments of insipid dialogue is quite funny.

The main menace of the piece, the Drashigs, are probably the best designed and scariest of the *Doctor Who* monsters in the '70s. The scene wherein the Drashig first blasts out of the swamp is a show-stopping cliffhanger. This horrible, dinosaur-like creature is all pointed teeth and gaping maw. Frequently, when monsters jump up in *Doctor Who,* they are ridiculous rather than scary ("Time and the Rani," "The Invisible Enemy," "The Web Planet"). In "Carnival of Monsters," no silly costume mitigates the horror of the Drashig ascent.

The sequence in the Drashig marsh is also convincing from a special effects standpoint. The Doctor employs his sonic screwdriver to keep the omnivores back, and in the process generates a series of impressive live-action detonations. Three Drashigs, in a separate but nonetheless impressive miniature shot, then retreat. It is only when the Drashigs attack the *Bernice* and Kalik on Inter Minor that the visual effects falter. In these sequences, the Drashigs are clumsily matted with live footage of the actors. As a result of this process, the Drashigs seem to vary wildly in scale from one shot to the next. It is unfortunate that a low budget caused sloppy effects work because the Drashigs ultimately lose the considerable menace they generated in the swamp sequence.

"Carnival of Monsters" is also humorous in its depiction of the obsessive-compulsive Inter Minor culture. The Minorans might best be described as a race of intergalactic customs officials. They cling to bureaucratic red tape, quote transportation regulations and express horror that living life forms have been imported to their world without a license. They are also unnaturally obsessed with cleanliness and germs. This officious, anal-retentive alien race is author Holmes' parody of government bureaucrats, and his observations are hence both funny and wicked. Holmes would later write a stinging indictment of the British tax system, *Doctor Who*'s "The Sunmakers," which is similarly brutal in its representation of tax collectors and government officials.

Actor Ian Marter appears in "Carnival of Monsters" as *Bernice* officer Andrews. He would make an exciting return to the world of *Doctor Who* as Harry Sullivan, companion for Tom Baker's Fourth Doctor, in Season 12. Marter is also one of the many contributors to the *Doctor Who* Target Book novelizations. He has written adaptations of "The Ark in Space," "The Sontaran Experiment," "The Reign of Terror" and "Enemy of the World." At one point during the '70s, Marter co-wrote with Tom Baker the screenplay for a *Doctor Who* motion picture to be called *Doctor Who Meets Scratchman*. The project never came to fruition and Marter's final appearance on *Doctor Who* was in the Season 13 story "The Android Invasion."

There are a couple of interesting trivia notes in "Carnival of Monsters." Firstly, Vorg and Shirna constantly refer to the captured humans as "Tellurians." This is a name not frequently associated with Earth. Did author Robert Holmes mean for the actors to say "Terrans"? Or, perhaps, is Earth in the future renamed Tellura? This strange nomenclature goes unnoticed by the Doctor and Jo throughout the story. It is repeated by the Androgum Shockeye in Holmes' later serial "The Two Doctors."

In another strange moment, Vorg talks to the Doctor in the dialect of a "carnie," a showman. The Doctor is confused and says he does not understand the language. This directly contrasts information the Doctor shares with Sarah in Season 14's "The Masque of Mandragora." In that adventure, he reveals that it is a Time Lord gift to understand all languages of all times and worlds encountered. If that is the case, why is the Doctor unable to understand Vorg in "Carnival of Monsters"?

More importantly than issues of language, the time stream is irrevocably altered at the conclusion of this story because the S.S. *Bernice* continues on its voyage to Bombay uninterrupted. Earlier in the story, however, the Doctor informed Jo that the disappearance of the *Bernice* was as significant a naval mystery as the loss of the *Marie Celeste*. If this is the case, the return of the *Bernice* to 1926 will wreck the time line and forever alter history! What if an ambitious journalist decided to write a book about the disappearance of the *Bernice*? Well, suddenly, that book can no longer exist because the *Bernice* never disappeared in the first place! Maybe that journalist then never wrote a second book and consequently did not win the Pulitzer Prize. Or maybe the journalist wrote something else, perhaps an article that exposed a political regime and caused the downfall of a government, a government that did not fall in the original time line because the author wrote about the disappearance of the *Bernice* instead! Granted, this is a far-fetched scenario, but *Doctor Who* has always made a special point of noting that any change in time can have disastrous repercussions. Obviously, at the end of "Carnival of Monsters," the *Bernice* should not be allowed to return to 1926.

For sheer audacity of story concept, "Carnival of Monsters" is a *Doctor Who* victory. In what other television series would a seagoing vessel from 1926 be trapped in an intergalactic ant farm on a planet of anal-retentive customs officials? All the elements of this serial jell so nicely that one is tempted to consider it one of the most entertaining of all *Doctor Who*s.

67. "Frontier in Space" Written by Malcolm Hulke; Directed by Paul Bernard; Designed by Cynthia Kljuco; Parts I–VI; Airdates: February 24, March 3, 10, 1, 24, 31, 1973

SYNOPSIS: In the far future, Earthmen and Draconians are the dominant life forms in the Milky Way galaxy ... and they do not cohabitate well. Both possess vast empires and both are fiercely protective of their borders. In recent months, many Earth ships have been hijacked by what authorities suspect are Draconian marauders. When the TARDIS lands in the middle of this delicate diplomatic situation, the Doctor begins to believe that Earth and Draconia are being played against each other by a puppet master behind the scenes. When the Master makes an appearance, the Doctor's suspicions are confirmed. But it turns out that the Master is also being manipulated by a dark force...

GUEST CAST: The Master (Roger Delgado); Stewart (James Culliford); Hardy (John Rees); President of Earth (Vera Fusek); Gen. Williams (Michael Hawkins); Draconian Prince (Peter Birrel); Draconian Emperor (John Woodnutt); Earth Soldiers (Laurence Harrington, Stanley Price); Newscaster (Bill Mitchell); Draconians (Bill Wilde, Roy Pattison, Ian Frost); Ogrons (Michael Kilgarriff, Rick Lester, Stephen Thorne); Dalek Voice (Michael Wisher)

COMMENTARY: This epic-length, galaxy-spanning adventure features a complex plot to precipitate war and control the galaxy. It also accurately foreshadows the style and substance of both *Babylon 5* and *Star Trek: Deep Space Nine* in its layered depiction of intergalactic politics, intrigue and deception. In "Frontier in Space," the behind-the-scenes Daleks bounce the Draconians and the Earth forces against each other in much the same fashion that the villainous Dominion of the Gamma Quadrant would manipulate the Klingon Empire against the United Federation of Planets in the fourth season of *DS9*. In both cases it is the secret third party (The Daleks/The Dominion) who stand to gain the most by a war among other Empires/Federations. In both cases it is barely controlled race hatred and distrust between man and alien (Draconian/Klingon) that precipitates the war.

In both the *Star Trek* and *Doctor Who* universes, this prejudice against aliens is a common trait to the military person. In "Frontier in Space," Gen. Williams is personified as a man who has known mostly hate for 20 years and who cannot see the "enemy" as a sentient being. Like Admiral Cartwright in *Star Trek VI: The Undiscovered Country*, Lt. Styles in "Balance of Terror" or any of the frequently seen hate-filled military men in *Doctor Who* ("Doctor Who and the Silurians," "The Sea Devils," "Warriors of the Deep," etc.), distrust and racism is the order of the day when dealing with other cultures. *Doctor Who* is unique among genre programming in that it is one of the few such productions not to glamorize a military hierarchy. *Babylon 5*, *Star Trek*, *SeaQuest DSV*, *Battlestar Galactica*, *Buck Rogers in the 25th Century* and even to an extent *Space: 1999* all feature central situations in which the military is considered heroic. In *Battlestar Galactica* it goes beyond that. Soldiers are not just heroes, they are saviors! Not so in *Doctor Who*. Though the Brigadier is certainly a positive role model, he and the Doctor frequently argue ("Inferno," "The Three Doctors," "The Green Death") about how to handle a situation. After all, it is the Brigadier, the most positive characterization of the military mentality in the series, who destroys the Silurians in "Doctor Who and the Silurians." *Doctor Who*, in addition to being anti-business ("Colony in Space"), anti-bureaucracy ("Carnival of Monsters") and anti-pollution ("Inferno"), is also anti-military ("Ambassadors of Death")! Nowhere is that more evident than in the central situation of "Frontier in Space" with jingoistic generals maneuvering to start a war.

Doctor Who is not the only series to foresee a war between the planet Earth and a race of aliens called Draconians. The Draconians were the recurring villains in the first year of *Buck Rogers in the 25th Century* in 1979. Those Draconians were not six-foot-tall lizards but fanatical soldiers in quasi-samurai armor led by the forces of the beautiful Princess Ardala (Pamela Hensley) and Killer Kane (Michael Ansara).

"Frontier in Space" is the last *Doctor Who* appearance of Roger Delgado's "Master." It was shortly after production on this serial that his car went over a mountainside during a dangerous film shoot. The Master finally returned in the 1976 episode "The Deadly Assassin." He was seen there as a desiccated, skeletal figure, rather than in his familiar guise from "Terror of the Autons," "Frontier in Space" and others. Ironically, the Master's role in Delgado's last *Who* story is among his best. For once the Master is not "just being evil." His actions are clearly motivated since he is in the employ of the Daleks. This is the kind of believable circumstance that needed to be exploited more frequently in the series to explain the Master's aberrant, antisocial behavior and make him more than a one-note villain. It should come as no surprise to anyone that this despicable villain would sell himself as a mercenary to the most lethal force in the galaxy, the Daleks.

Making a guest appearance in "Frontier in Space" is the Drashig from the previous episode, "Carnival of Monsters." Also returning is Michael Kilgarriff, the actor who portrayed the Cyber Controller in "The Tomb of the Cyberman." He plays an Ogron, one of the ape-soldiers of the Daleks who first appeared in "Day of the Daleks" and had a cameo appearance in "Carnival of Monsters."

The epic story of "Frontier in Space" would be concluded in the much-awaited full-scale return of the Daleks in the next episode. Ironically, much of the backstory about Draconian and human relationships that had been so carefully constructed in "Frontier in Space" was ignored in favor of a standard Dalek-style adventure on the planet Spiridon. Instead of working on a galactic scale, "Planet of the Daleks" represented a return to the revolution story seen so frequently on *Doctor Who*. The Thals would be back, as would yet another race of "invisibles."

"The Frontier in Space" is available in a two-tape VHS pack from BBC/CBS-Fox home video.

68. "Planet of the Daleks" Written by Terry Nation; Directed by David Maloney; Designed by John Hurst; Parts I–VI; Airdates: April 7, 14, 21, 28, May 5, 12, 1973

SYNOPSIS: On the jungle world of Spiridon, Jo and the Doctor join up with two Thal warriors who have come to the planet to destroy the Dalek threat. The Daleks have mastered invisibility thanks to Spiridon collaborators. Soon a Dalek transmission, reporting that there are 10,000 of the killing machines on Spiridon, is intercepted. The Doctor realizes that an invasion force of that size is enough to sweep through this part of the galaxy unchallenged. Manipulating the unusual Spiridon icecanoes, volcanoes that form the solid core of Spiridon, the Doctor plans to keep the Dalek army on ice.

GUEST CAST: Vabor (Prentis Hancock); Taron (Bernard Horsfall); Wester (Roy Skelton); Codal (Tim Preece); Rebec (James How); Marat (Hilary Minster); Latep (Alan Tucker); Dalek Operators (Murphy Grumbar, John Scott Martin, Cy Town); Dalek Voices (Roy Skelton, Michael Wisher); Dalek Supreme (Tony Starr)

COMMENTARY: Terry Nation's return to the *Doctor Who* universe after a seven-year absence is something less than the momentous occasion it could have been. "Planet of Daleks" is the same old "revolution against the oppressors" formula that has graced *Doctor Who* since Nation first contributed the landmark serial "The Daleks" in December 1963. Once more the Daleks are plotting evil against the Thals and the universe ("The Daleks"). Once more the Daleks have developed a kind of invincible weapon (in "The Dalek Masterplan" it was the Time Destructor, in "Evil of the Daleks" it was the Dalek Factor). Once more the Daleks have made slaves of a planetary population (just like the Aridians in "The Chase"). Once more the secret of invisibility is involved (as it was on the planet Myra in "The Dalek Masterplan"). Once more there is a Dalek "revival" scene as the deadly machines come to life (David Whitaker's "The Power of the Daleks"). And, of course, the Doctor defeats the Daleks in the end with a clever strategy. What is even more tiresome is that the Daleks are not actually annihilated completely ... only slowed down (like "The Dalek Masterplan" in which they are reverted to embryos at the conclusion). In other words, "Planet of the Daleks" is a disappointing and derivative return to pure *Doctor Who* cliché. It is all the more unsatisfactory considering the complex political strands involving galactic empires that were introduced in "Frontier in Space." This is one story where the buildup and opening acts are more satisfying than the conclusion. Where are the Draconians in "Planet of the Daleks"? The Earth President? It does not seem right to start a story on a galactic scale and then end it on an out-of-the way planet without involvement from any of the major players.

Perhaps there is a different way to look at "Planet of the Daleks." Just as every actor who plays James Bond must flirt with Miss Moneypenny, master Q's gadgets and defeat terrible megalomaniacs, so must each incarnation of *Doctor Who* go through the same paces as his predecessors. Each Doctor must defeat the Daleks. Each Doctor must defeat the Cybermen. Each Doctor must affect historical time periods, etc. Seen in this light, "Planet of the Daleks" is obviously a second attempt to generate some kind of successful chemistry between this version of the Doctor and his most famous opponents. "Day of the Daleks," despite its clever plot, has a low-budget look and feel to it, and this story rightfully takes place on a much grander canvas than the earlier serial. Still, it is easy to understand why the Daleks are markedly less effective with Pertwee than they were with Troughton or Hartnell. Pertwee's era is the beginning of what might be termed "modern *Who*." It is in color, and it has a higher budget. And, thanks to the social consciousness of Malcolm Hulke and Roger Sloman, it is a more adult in its interpretation of the universe. Pertwee himself is a no-nonsense, imposing physical presence. It is obvious that this tall, physically fit gentleman has little to fear from the Daleks. Next to him they look shrunken.

There is also the issue of familiarity. By now the Daleks are over ten years old, still trying to control the universe, and still screeching "Ex-ter-min-ate." "Frontier in Space" had interesting political overtones, but once the camera again focuses directly on the Dalek menace with their "sink pump" arms and grating mechanical voices, the series is essentially back to square one or, perhaps more appropriately, Serial 2.

The era of the Daleks ("The Daleks," "The Dalek Invasion of Earth" and maybe even the first half of "The Chase") was long gone by 1973. Like the later *Nightmare on Elm Street* films prove, there is a danger in showing a monster too often. He loses his ability to scare the audience. Perhaps the best "late" appearance of these popular monsters in *Doctor Who* occurs in the 1975 story "Genesis of the Daleks." In that story, Nation has something new to say about the Daleks. He examines their roots and the reasons for their malevolence. By 1975 it was also necessary to introduce a human threat in the form of Dalek originator Davros to make the Daleks more interesting and more menacing.

Despite the flaws, it is still nice to see the Thals again in "Planet of the Daleks." This is the first appearance of the pacifist race since Episode 2, "The Daleks." These particular Thals are even more interesting because they are portrayed by two very familiar *Who* faces. Vabor is essayed by Prentis Hancock, veteran of "Spearhead from Space" and soon to appear in "Planet of Evil," "The Ribos Operation" and *Space: 1999*. Bernard Horsfall, who tackles the role of Tabor, is equally recognizable. He played Gulliver in the excellent "The Mind Robber" and one of the Time Lord judges in "The War Games." In later years, he would play a Time Lord again in "The Deadly Assassin."

A familiar voice is heard in "Planet of the Daleks" too. Roy Skelton, voice of Cyberman, Kraals, Monoids and the Daleks from day one, again enunciates the threats of the treacherous creatures from Skaro.

69. "The Green Death" Written by Robert Sloman; Directed by Michael Briant; Designed by John Burrowes; Parts I–VI; Airdates: May 10, 26, June 2, 9, 16, 23, 1973

SYNOPSIS: In the village of Llanfairfach, Wales, Panorama Chemicals is polluting the environment with its new industrial complex. The Doctor, Jo and the Brigadier investigate Panorama Chemicals, all for different reasons and with different agendas. What they uncover is a subterranean river of green slime, a nursery for giant mutated maggots and, most deadly of all, a super-intelligent computer called B.O.S.S. (Bimorphic Organizational System Supervisor) calling the shots! In the course of the adventure, Jo falls in love and decides to leave UNIT.

GUEST CAST: Prof. Clifford Jones (Stewart Bevan); Dr. Thomas Stevens (Jerome Willis); Ted Hughes (John Scott Martin); Elgin (Tony Adams); Dai Evans (Mostyn Evans); Milkman (Ray Handy); Hinks (Ben Howard); Dave (Talfryn

Thomas); Fell (John Rolfe); Minister of Ecology (Richard Bale); Nancy (Mitzi McKenzie); Cleaner (Jean Burgess); James (Roy Skelton); B.O.S.S. (John Dearth); Bert (Roy Evans); Guards (Alan Chuntz, Billie Horrigan, Brian Justice, Terry Walsh)

COMMENTARY: "The Green Death" combines several familiar *Doctor Who* elements. Firstly, there is the sentient, megalomaniacal computer called B.O.S.S. This device harkens back to W.O.T.A.N. in the Hartnell story "The War Machines." In conjunction with this examination of another living machine, "The Green Death" also presents an environmental theme and green slime, two components observed in Pertwee's Season 7 story "Inferno."

Other than these familiar *Doctor Who* constituents, "The Green Death" presages the arrival of a major sci-fi subgenre of the mid-'70s: the Revenge of Nature! In "revenge of nature" films, giant animals and insects are born from pollution, chemicals or radiation spills. Once free, these enlarged vermin wreak havoc on the world. The giant maggots and fruit flies of "The Green Death" would eventually give way to even more disgusting and far-fetched threats. There were giants rats created by chemical growth hormones in *Food of the Gods* (1976) and gigantic, telepathic ants mutated by a radiation spill in *Empire of the Ants* (1977). Another "revenge of nature" film which predicted nature would rebel against insecticides was *Kingdom of the Spiders* (1976) starring William Shatner and Tiffany Bolling. All these films harken back to '50s monster movies such as *Them!* (1954), *Beginning of the End* (1957) and *Tarantula* (1955)—movies which showed the horrible results of atomic bomb testing or human meddling in "God's Domain." The "revenge of nature" cycle was a reiteration of this theme, but with the more chic, '70s threats of industrial pollution and manmade chemicals substituting for atomic horror.

"The Green Death" was the last story to feature Katy Manning as Jo Grant. Since she was conceived in a sexist light as a screaming, helpless woman, it is only natural that the character would be sent off on equally degrading terms. She falls in love and leaves UNIT without a second glance. In other words, *Doctor Who* suggests that a woman cannot be married and have a career. That Jo must accompany her new husband, a scientist at the commune-like "Nuthatch," to the Amazon is no excuse. She could simply take a leave of absence from UNIT and return after the trip. Of course, a "married" companion for the Doctor would be a lot less provocative, wouldn't she?

Nonetheless, Manning was a delightful presence despite the sexist concept of her character. She and Pertwee shared some terrific chemistry, and Pertwee once stated that his Doctor was a protector, which is why he wore a cloak so frequently ... to pull companions into his fold. In this regard, Jo was a more successful match with the Doctor than the independent-minded Liz Shaw. Manning herself is a rather notorious figure in *Doctor Who* circles because in the early '90s she posed nude with a Dalek.

SEASON 11

x **70. "The Time Warrior"** Written by Robert Holmes; Directed by Alan Bromly; Designed by Keith Cheetham; Parts I–IV; Airdates: December 15, 22, 29, January 5, 1974

SYNOPSIS: A Sontaran soldier crashes his spherical spacecraft on Earth after a disastrous engagement in the ongoing Rutan-Sontaran intergalactic war. Linx has arrived in Britain during the Middle Ages and he quickly makes a partner of the villainous English knight Irongron, who has been waging a war against his neighbor, Edward of Wessex, while the King is off fighting a foreign war.

When Linx uses his technology to kidnap twentieth century scientists and bring them back in time to repair his spaceship, the Doctor and his new companion, the nosy journalist Sarah Jane Smith, travel back in time to prevent the Sontaran's escape.

GUEST CAST: Linx (Kevin Lindsey); Prof. Rubeish (Donald Pelmear); Irongron (David Daker); Bloodaxe (John J. Carney); Eleanor (June Brown); Edward of Wessex (Alan Rowe); Hal (Jeremy Bulloch); Meg (Sheila Fay); Eric (Gordon Pitt); Sentry (Steve Brunswick)

COMMENTARY: A lively adaptation of Mark Twain's *A Connecticut Yankee in King Arthur's Court*, "The Time Warrior" revealed that even after ten years on the air, *Doctor Who* was still full of lively surprises. The ecology themes that had so dominated the previous season are nowhere in evidence in this premiere. Instead, the story abounds with humorous antics as a Time Lord and a Sontaran, rather than a nineteenth century American, equip knights in shining armor with new technologies. Instead of Twain's most interesting conceit, knights on bikes, *Doctor Who* illuminates the age with robots and rifles. The Doctor counters the Sontaran devices with homemade fireworks. The battles generated are thus unique and well-choreographed at the same time that they are amusing.

"The Time Warrior" also introduces the Sontarans. These thick-necked, pasty-faced, leather-clad cloned warriors would prove so popular that they would soon find themselves in the top tier of *Doctor Who* villainy, surpassing even Brian Hayle's Ice Warriors. In recent polls the favorite villains were (in order) Daleks, Cybermen, Sontarans. This is amazing since the Sontarans actually appear in far fewer episodes than either the Cybermen or the Daleks do. The Sontarans returned to menace Tom Baker in "The Sontaran Experiment" and "The Invasion of Time" and then appeared opposite Patrick Troughton and Colin Baker in the 1985 story "The Two Doctors." In the Season 15 story "The Horror of Fang Rock," *Doctor Who* fans finally met the long-talked-about but never-seen Sontaran nemesis, the Rutans.

The premiere serial of Season 11 is another opportunity for the able Jon Pertwee to strut his stuff. Here he becomes involved in an extended duel and proves himself to be a capable swordsman. He also engineers a daring escape from a firing squad. All this running and jumping makes the Doctor resemble Robin Hood more than a renegade Time Lord of Gallifrey, but it also makes for an exciting serial. Of the first three incarnations of the character, only the athletic Pertwee could pull this off.

Amidst the humor, the action and the introduction of the Sontarans, "The Time Warrior" also unveils actress Elizabeth Sladen as the fire-tongued journalist Sarah Jane Smith. Sladen is a talented actress who brings enthusiasm and a tart wit to *Doctor Who.* After her first season with Pertwee she would stay with the series for another two-and-a-half seasons. She would meet the Sontarans again, the Daleks (twice), the Cybermen and many other menaces in her adventures through time and space with Pertwee and Tom Baker. So popular was Smith that she was recalled to duty in the twentieth anniversary special "The Five Doctors." She is also the only "human" companion of the Doctor's to be honored with a spin-off: In 1981, a pilot called *K-9 and Company: A Girl's Best Friend* starred Sladen and the popular robotic canine. Though the program did not go to series, it has the distinction of being the only network "spin-off" of *Doctor Who.* The producers could not have picked a better companion to star in her own series, as Sladen is a charismatic screen presence who exudes competence and bravery. Many fans insist that the Doctor has never had a better companion than Sarah Jane, and they may be right. Recently, Sladen recreated the role in the 1996 production *Downtime*, which concerned a Yeti incursion in the 1990s.

The beautiful Elisabeth Sladen joined Jon Pertwee in *Doctor Who*'s season 11 premiere, episode #70, "The Time Warrior."

"The Time Warrior" also features a substantial performance by Jeremy Bulloch (*Star Wars*' Boba Fett) as Hal the Archer. Bulloch had previously been seen back in Season 2's "The Space Museum." Kevin Lindsey, who here portrays Linx, would be back as a different Sontaran (Styre) in Season 12's "The Sontaran Experiment." He also appears in "Planet of the Spiders," as Cho-je.

This action-packed first contact with the Sontarans is available on videotape.

71. "Invasion of the Dinosaurs" Written by Malcolm Hulke; Directed by Paddy Russell; Designed by Richard Morris; Part I: "Invasion" Airdate: January 12, 1974; Parts II–IV, Airdates: January 19, 26, February 2, 9, 16, 1974

SYNOPSIS: After the Doctor and Sarah defeat Linx in the Middle Ages, the TARDIS returns to twentieth century London. To the surprise of the time travelers, the city appears to be evacuated. Telephones are disconnected, and there are looters running madly through the city. Sarah and the Doctor are confused by this strange situation, but confusion transforms to shock when a flying dinosaur swoops down from overhead and nearly kills them!

The Doctor suspects that the dinosaurs have been brought forward in time by a technology similar to the Gallifreyan device known as a "time scoop." But why would someone bring dinosaurs to the twentieth century? The answers comes in the form of betrayal. Some of the most prominent men in UNIT and the British government believe that Earth should return to a "Golden Age" before overpopulation and pollution can take their toll. They intend to destroy all human life on Earth with the dinosaurs, and then repopulate it with their own "chosen" colonists, who are already sequestered aboard a phony spaceship.

GUEST CAST: Charles Grover (Noel Johnson); Gen. Finch (John Bennett); Butler (Martin Jarvis); Prof. Whitaker (Peter Miles); Cpl. Norton (Martin Taylor); Mark (Terence Wilton); Adam (Brian Badcoe); Ruth (Carmen Silvera); Private Bryson (Colin Bell); Robinson (Timothy Craven) Sgt. Duffy (Dave Carter); Phillips (Gordon Reid); Lt. Shears (Ben Aris); Private Ogden (George Bryson); Looters (Alan Bull, Leslie Noyes, Terry Walsh); UNIT Soldiers (Leslie Bates, David Bills, John Caesar, Ian Elliott, Pat Gorman, Richard King, James Muir, Brian Nolan, Louise Souchez, Geoffrey Witherick); Golden Age People (Geoffrey Brighty, Lyn Howard, Rory O'Connor, Annette Peters, Judy Rodger, Barry Summerford, Ken Tracey)

COMMENTARY: The temptation to feature dinosaurs on *Doctor Who* was apparently too great for the producers of the decade-old series to resist. By 1974, there had been a sort of visual renaissance with improved special effects making dinosaur films more believable than ever. Irwin Allen had produced a remake of *The Lost World* (1960) with "real" lizards doubling as dinosaurs, but it was probably Ray Harryhausen's landmark dinosaur-Western picture *The Valley of Gwangi* (1969) that convinced producers that dinosaurs could be "done right" on television. (In Season 10, the dinosaur-like Drashigs in "Carnival of Monsters" seemed quite believable at points.) This notion was one consequently shared by other genre producers, because shortly after "Invasion of the Dinosaurs" debuted, stop-motion dinosaurs would make a splash on American television in the popular Saturday morning NBC series *Land of the Lost* (1974-76). Of course, dinosaur motion pictures can be traced back further even than these relatively late examples. There are dinosaur films evident in virtually every decade of the twentieth century: *The Lost World* (1925), *King Kong* (1933), *Lost Continent* (1951), *One Million Years B.C.* (1967), *The Land That Time Forgot* (1975), *My Science Project* (1985) and *Jurassic Park* (1993). The summer smash of 1997 was *The Lost World: Jurassic Park*, yet another dinosaur-on-the-rampage movie. Obviously, Dinomania is one fad that translates well from one generation to the next. This said, "Invasion of the Dinosaurs" is not considered a good *Doctor Who* serial. Since it is unavailable for review in 1998, a brief analysis of this serial by *Doctor Who* fan and writer Paul Mount is included below:

> Not for one moment do these dinosaurs convince; some brief appearances are better than others, but none is ever really acceptable... It's virtually unheard of for an entire *Doctor Who* story to be totally ruined because of ineptly executed special effects, but when the effects are as central to the proceedings as in this case, how can any other facet even hope to hold water?[10]

Obviously, "Invasion of the Dinosaurs" is no *Jurassic Park*. Nonetheless, it has to go down in history as a unique serial because it turns the recurring UNIT character Mike Yates into a misguided villain! He is shown to be a part of the conspiracy in "Invasion of the Dinosaurs" and a betrayer to UNIT, although he does save the Doctor's life. Still, this was a bold step for the series to take in the early '70s, and it can be interpreted as evidence that the era of "black-and-white" *Doctor Who* stories was truly over in more than the literal sense. Moral complexity entered the series permanently, even consuming friends of the righteous Time Lord. This unexpected character arc is truly a delightful development. *Star Trek*, even as late as 1991, has never had the courage to make a beloved central character do something wrong. When the notion that Saavik, a member of the *Enterprise* crew, might be a traitor was suggested in early drafts of *Star Trek VI: The Undiscovered Country*, it was rapidly vetoed by Gene Roddenberry. *Doctor Who* acted rather more boldly and opted to do something different and innovative. Still, the character of Mike Yates was not through yet. He would appear one more time in a heroic capacity in Jon Pertwee's last serial, "Planet of the Spiders."

Besides bad special effects and a stunning role for Richard Franklin's Mike Yates, "Invasion of the Dinosaurs" is a *Doctor Who* milestone because it is the last serial written by scribe Malcolm Hulke. Once more there is a social agenda at the core of his writing. This time the central theme concerns, in Hulke's words, "these people who have this very lovely idea of 'The Golden Age,' but sometimes people with very good, altruistic ideas can overlook the main issue."[11] This is a reversal of many of the ecological stories. The point here is that sometimes people with the passion to make a better world also lack the capacity to make good decisions. Obviously, the team behind "The Golden Age" is not evil, they want to make the world a better place, like the people in the "Nuthatch" in "The Green Death." Their plan to make the world better, however, is an atrocious one that will bring about millions of deaths. This is an undoing of many 1970s *Doctor Who* philosophies. "Invasion of the Dinosaurs" tells viewers that times change, philosophies differ, and there can be evil even in the most unexpected and innocuous places.

This serial also has the honor of introducing "The Whomobile," a combination of hovercraft, rocketship and car. This silver, winged craft was built at the expense of Jon Pertwee, who thought that the Doctor should sport a more advanced vehicle than old Bessie. The Whomobile, replete with a license plate that reads "WHO," reappears in the final story of the Pertwee era, "Planet of the Spiders." Ever the great showman, Pertwee also frequently drove to charity and fan events in this amazing, fully operational mock-up.

"Invasion of the Dinosaurs" has not been released on video because of a mistake made by the BBC. While BBC personnel were sifting through their film and video vaults and destroying episodes of *Doctor Who* right and left, they erred. They destroyed the first episode of "Invasion of the Dinosaurs" (which was titled "Invasion" to preserve the secret of the dinosaur presence) instead of the Troughton Cyberman epic "The Invasion." Thus "Invasion of the Dinosaurs" is an unseen but oft-remembered addition to Pertwee's era of action.

72. "Death to the Daleks" Written by Terry Nation; Directed by Michael Briant; Designed by Colin Green; Parts I–IV; Airdates: February 23, March 2, 9, 16, 1974

SYNOPSIS: The Doctor and Sarah joyfully head to the planet Florana for a swim in the effervescent waters there, but the TARDIS is unexpectedly sidelined by a total power drain. Sarah and the Doctor soon learn that they have arrived on Exillon, a planet where Earth's Marine Space Corps and the Daleks have been competing for the valuable mineral Perennium, which is needed to stop a virulent plague ravaging the Outer Colonies. Like the TARDIS, the Dalek and Earth ships are confined to Exillon by a strange power source.

A friendly Exillon native, Bellal, informs the Doctor and Sarah that the power-draining mechanism is powered by the abandoned city of his ancestors. Pursued by the Daleks, the Doctor survives the deadly booby traps of the metropolis and causes the city's main computer to have a "nervous breakdown."

GUEST CAST: Lt. D.N. Galloway (Duncan Lamont); Jill Tarrant (Joy Harrison); Lt. Peter Hamilton (Julian Fox); Commander Stewart (Neil Seiler); Capt. Richard Railton (John Abineri); High Priest of the Exillons (Mostyn Evans); Spaceman (Terry Walsh); Bellal (Arnold Yarrow); Golal (Roy Heymann); Dalek Voices (Michael Wisher); Dalek Operators (John Scott Martin, Cy Town)

COMMENTARY: Terry Nation's "Death to the Daleks" seems an improvement over Season 10's "Planet of the Daleks." Unlike the earlier adventure, Dalek involvement in this story is peripheral rather than central. They too are trapped on this world and, interestingly, an alliance is made with them! Of course, the Daleks prove to be as treacherous as ever, but the Doctor has anticipated that fact and defeats them with the help of a noble human. Perhaps the reason that the Daleks are more interesting in this story than in the previous one is because they serve the plot of "Death to the Daleks" rather than being the *raison d'etre* for the story. Here the Daleks are just one obstacle among many. The Doctor must free the TARDIS, stop a deadly plague on the Outer Colonies, fathom the lost city, escape the Exillons and avoid the Daleks. That is more than enough adventure for just one serial! "Death to the Daleks" also serves as the introduction of another key *Doctor Who* story prototype.

Having introduced the Daleks and Thals in "The Daleks" and the quest template in "Keys of Marinus," Nation creates another *Doctor Who* subgenre in "Death to the Daleks." Call it the "brain teaser." The alien city in this serial is filled with intellectual puzzles and mazes which the Doctor must decipher if he is to find his way to the control room. Although this notion had been seen way back in "The Tomb of the Cybermen," it is given full focus here. The Doctor solves each riddle, avoids death and reaches his goal. The idea of intellectual booby traps and intelligence tests for the Doctor reappear in "Pyramids of Mars" and "The Five Doctors," among others. In all these stories, the Doctor encounters ancient conundrums and has to stretch his thinking to solve them. Interestingly, this is also one of the central conceits of the *Indiana Jones* film series, especially the last part of the trilogy, *Indiana Jones and the Last Crusade* (1989). The "brain teaser" is a perfect scenario for Pertwee's Doctor because he is always portrayed as a logical genius. He excels in those scenes in which he must reason out a scenario by using logic and science. Accordingly, the ancient city in "Death to the Daleks" makes a more interesting nemesis for him than the Daleks do. Tom Baker approaches "the brain teaser" in a totally different fashion in "Pyramids of Mars." He acts scatterbrained, makes gestures, talks to himself and then seemingly picks a course of action at random. After the threat is gone, his Doctor then explains his solution in a humorous or witty fashion. Which approach is better depends, perhaps, on which incarnation one favors.

The moral ambiguity raised in "Invasion of the Dinosaurs" also figures prominently in "Death to the Daleks." Lt. Galloway is portrayed throughout the tale as a selfish collaborator. Yet at the end of the story, he sacrifices his life to destroy the Dalek ship. This is not the typical *Doctor Who* characterization of a collaborator. Usually a character is either good or bad. Shades of gray have at last been introduced, and Galloway's death is a good example of that. His sacrifice has much more impact because the character is not a saint. He has been seen as cowardly and selfish, but in the end he proves his courage. This dual nature is what humanity is all about.

After "Death to the Daleks," the Daleks would return in Season 12's excellent "Genesis of the Daleks." "Death to the Daleks" is available on videocassette.

73. "The Monster of Peladon" Written by Brian Hayles; Directed by Lennie Mayne; Designed by Gloria Clayton; Parts I–VI; Airdates: March 23, 30, April 6, April 13, 20 27, 1974

SYNOPSIS: On the planet Peladon, King Peladon has been succeeded by his daughter, Queen Thalira. As a member of the Galactic Federation, Peladon has a duty to serve that organization during its war with Galaxy 5. The trisilicate mineral that makes up much of Peladon's rocky core is crucial in the war effort. The Federation depends on trisilicate as the basis of much of its technology, including heat shields and electronic circuitry. Unfortunately, this situation has caused several old conflicts to boil again. The traditionalists and the progressives of Peladon are once again at odds. The traditionalists wonder why they should break their backs mining for offworlders. The progressives remember King Peladon's wish to join the Galactic Federation and want to make that dream a reality. Consequently Aggedor, the Beast of Peladon and the legendary protector of the people, once again rears his head to kill those who threaten the planet.

GUEST CAST: Queen Thalira (Nina Thomas); Chancellor Ortron (Frank Gatliff); The Queen's Champion, Blor (Michael Crane); Ettis (Ralph Watson); Commander Azaxyr (Alan Bennion); Alpha Centauri (Stuart Fell); Voice of Alpha Centauri (Ysanne Churchman); Vega Nexos (Gerald Taylor); Eckersley (Donald Gee); Sskel (Sonny Caldinez); Rima (Roy Evans); Miner (Max Faulkner); Preba (Graeme Eton); Gebek (Rex Robinson); Captain (Terry Walsh)

COMMENTARY: This sequel to "The Curse of Peladon" is less exciting and interesting than the dynamic political serial that inspired it. The audience has seen all the elements of "Monster of Peladon" before, and the political dynamic of the planet, superstition versus technology, is much the same too. Hayles reveals nothing new about this interesting battle. Furthermore, Queen Thalira is just as inexperienced and naive as her father was in "The Curse of Peladon." It is a little too convenient that she should fulfill a role identical to the one her father played 50 years earlier.

There are other annoying repetitions as well. Aggedor, or the image of Aggedor, is once again being manipulated to scare traditionalists and cause strife; the alien diplomats are again assembled; the true villains of the piece are a mystery. "The Monster of Peladon" is much the same story as "The Curse of Peladon"! Perhaps this serial was a money-saver for *Doctor Who*: the Alpha Centauri costume, the Aggedor costume, the Peladonian costumes, the castle painting and the Ice Warrior costumes are all reused here.

The Ice Warriors return to their ways of evil in "The Monster of Peladon," perhaps because audiences prefer to see the Martians as villains rather than as allies. The explanation for the shift back to evil is a renegade faction of the Ice Warrior populace. This is a believable explanation, certainly, but how did the renegade militia get its hands on an Ice Warrior battleship? Wouldn't the legitimate government of the Ice Warriors report this theft so it could not be blamed for any actions taken by violent renegades in an official vessel of the Martian government?

"Monster of Peladon" is available on video in a two-tape set.

74. "Planet of the Spiders" Written by Robert Sloman; Directed by Barry Letts; Designed by Rochelle Selwyn; Parts I–VI; Airdates: May 4, 11, 18, 25 June 1, 8, 1974

SYNOPSIS: A blue crystal from Metebelis III in the Doctor's possession becomes the object of an extended chase. Metebelis III is now ruled by giant, malevolent spiders who require the crystal to carry out the "Great One's" plan to conquer the Earth. When Sarah is apprehended and taken to Metebelis III, the Doctor must risk everything to save his friend. In addition to the spiders, the Doctor is confronted by the Great One. Although the Doctor rarely feels fear, he is terrified by this horrible creature. In fighting it, the Doctor lays down his life and triggers another regeneration...

GUEST CAST: Mike Yates (Richard Franklin); Sgt. Benton (John Levene); Prof. Clegg (Cyril Shaps); Luton (John Dearth); Barnes (Christopher Burgess); Mos (Terence Lodge); Keaver (Andrew Staines); Cho-je (Kevin Lindsey); Tommy (John Kane); Policeman (Chubby Oates); Soldier (Pat Gorman); Man With Boat (Terry Walsh); Hopkins (Michael Pinder); Tramp (Stuart Fell); Arak (Gareth

Hunt); Sabor (Geoffrey Morris); Neska (Jenny Laird); Regg (Joanna Monro); Tuar (Ralph Arliss); Guard Captains (Walter Randall, Max Faulkner); Ken-Po (George Cormack); Spider Voices (Ysanne Churchman, Kismet Delgado, Maureen Martis)

COMMENTARY: The Pertwee era of *Doctor Who* comes to an end after four years with a rousing, action-packed adventure. "Planet of the Spiders" leaps from one chase to another, one special effect to another, one planet to another, until finally, in the end, there is the shocking death of the third Doctor.

At times during "Planet of the Spiders," Pertwee and the *Who* production team seem to be announcing their intention to beat the excitement of all the *James Bond* films combined. The central set piece of this story is an action scene that begins as a gunfight at UNIT headquarters. This fight then develops into a car chase between Bessie and the Whomobile. This is great fun because these two vehicles, in addition to being unusual, characterize the two sides of the Doctor's personality. One is antique and traditional, the other a technological wonder. Unexpectedly, the car chase becomes an aircraft chase incorporating an autogyro like the ones seen in *You Only Live Twice* (1967) and *The Road Warrior* (1981). Even more unexpectedly, the aircraft pursuit transforms into a waterbound hunt utilizing a hovercraft and a motorboat. This portion of the chase is reminiscent of the speedboat chase through the Everglades in *Live and Let Die* (1971); it also foreshadows the use of a hovercraft in the final moments of Jackie Chan's hit *Rumble in the Bronx* (1996). The action finally culminates with one great stunt: The Doctor leaps from his speeding hovercraft onto the motorboat. This is undoubtedly the most expensive and elaborate action sequence seen throughout the entire 26-year run of *Doctor Who*, and it is the perfect capper for Pertwee's era. It seems as if the writers and the producers finally threw up their hands in resignation and indulged Pertwee in his fondest dream: a chase using multiple vehicles and encompassing all kinds of terrain.

An ironic touch in "Planet of the Spiders" is that much of the action occurs on Metebelis III, a planet which Pertwee's Doctor repeatedly attempted to visit in episodes such as "Carnival of Monsters" and "The Green Death." Well, the Doctor finally gets to stay on Metebelis III for awhile, and he is killed! It is a dark touch, but a humorous and ironic one.

All in all, Pertwee is granted a far more uplifting death than either of his predecessors. Hartnell's Doctor just faded away after being absent from large portions of the serial "The Tenth Planet." Even more disturbing, Troughton's Doctor was executed by the Time Lords after being forcibly separated from his companions. Pertwee's death is the classic death of a hero, and firmly in keeping with his stature as a macho figure of action. He faces his utmost fear (though it is hard to imagine Pertwee's Doctor really being afraid of anything!) and defeats the Great One before ultimately losing his life.

What did the loss of Pertwee mean for the series? Well, Pertwee's era had less varied stories because of the "exile" premise, but he always brought a stylish dash to the show. He made the Doctor a noble, respectable figure. He carried several repetitive formula stories (the invasion and mad scientist plots mainly) with his charismatic presence. Furthermore, he never mocked the material. Pertwee always played the part of the Doctor seriously. He honored it and made it his own. Tom Baker, another excellent Doctor, would not always maintain the respect for the part that Pertwee had so clearly demonstrated.

Besides the fast pace and the action scenes, "Planet of the Spiders" is a return to two of the oldest *Doctor Who* stories. It is both a "revolution against oppressors" story, (the *Time Machine* template) and an "invasion from space" story (*Quatermass* template). Strangely, this combination of old formulas is not at all bothersome in this story, perhaps because of the breakneck pace. The giant black spiders are effective villains, exploiting arachnophobia for all its worth. There is also a running *Invasion of the Body Snatchers* motif, with the spiders "possessing" human beings. All these elements work together to generate a splendid finale for Pertwee.

Actor Gareth Hunt guest stars as rebel leader Arak. He later went on to fame by playing Mike Gambit on *The New Avengers* (1976-1977) opposite Joanna Lumley and Patrick Macnee.

Pertwee's *Doctor Who* swan song is available on videocassette.

SEASON 12

75. "Robot" Written by Terrance Dicks; Directed by Christopher Barry; Designed by Ian Rawnsley; Parts I–IV; Airdates: December 28, 1974, January 4, 13, 18, 1975

SYNOPSIS: The Doctor has regenerated, but his new persona is erratic and mischievous. While the Doctor begins to discover who he is this time, a villainous robot created by Prof. Kettlewell, and exploited by Miss Winters of the Think Tank Organization, initiates a campaign of terror in London. It steals a deadly UNIT disintegrator, commits murder and commences a countdown to nuclear destruction. The Doctor and Sarah attempt to stop the machine, only to learn that it is not only growing into an emotional being, but growing up ... to gargantuan proportions!

GUEST CAST: Miss Winters (Patricia Maynard); Robot (Michael Kilgarriff); Prof. Kettlewell (Edward Burnham); Jellicoe (Alec Linstead); Short (Timothy Craven); Guard (John Scott Martin); Chambers (Walter Goodmans)

COMMENTARY: Tom Baker's first story as the Doctor begins like a retread of many familiar "mad scientist" stories from Jon Pertwee's earthbound era. The Think Tank organization and Scientific Reform Members featured here clearly echo the lunatic conspirators of Operation Golden Age in "Invasion of the Dinosaurs." The robot itself is a tool for world domination, not too dissimilar from the Keller Machine in "Mind of Evil" or the meglomaniacal B.O.S.S. computer in "The Green Death." With the Brigadier and UNIT also very much in evidence, "Robot" is eerily reminiscent of the classic Pertwee exile stories from Seasons 7 and 8. The TARDIS, space travel and life on other worlds are only tangentially referred to in this twelfth season premiere. Surprisingly then, "Robot" is quite a conservative debut for the new, wildly eccentric fourth Doctor. Despite this lack of experimentation, there are also a few elements of interest in the Terrance Dicks–written serial.

The Kettlewell robot's inability to harm human beings perhaps stems from the famous "Three Laws of Robotics" established by legendary SF writer Isaac Asimov in the mid-'50s. These rules had earlier been applied to Dr. Morbius' wonderful Robby the Robot in the 1956 space epic *Forbidden Planet.* The Laws were also the primary feature of the 1964 *Outer Limits* episode "I, Robot," starring a young Leonard Nimoy. *Aliens* (1986) and *Star Trek: The Next Generation* have also made use of these important rules of civilized robotic conduct. Perhaps more importantly than this acceptance of Asimov's ideas, "Robot" highlights a reappearance of several themes from *King Kong* (1933) and Madame De Beaumont's fairy tale *Beauty and the Beast.* Accordingly, the Kettlewell robot becomes obsessed with Sarah Jane Smith and sets about to protect her from all the chaos and destruction of the story. It is plain that the robot has fallen in love with this woman ... and on several occasions he refuses to harm her. At the close of the tale he even removes her from danger. Because the robot expands to King Kong size at the serial's climax, the similarity to *King Kong* is further cemented. The scene in which the giant robot scoops up the tiny Sarah in his giant hand and carries her around is the final connection. Sarah's plight is the same as that of Fay Wray and many other monster movie damsels-in-distress since the 1930s. Furthering the analogy to *King Kong*, the UNIT forces fill in for the policeman of New York City, or the biplanes circling the Empire State Building, by attacking this menace without mercy. Ironically, when the Doctor finally succeeds in destroying the robot, it is a less-than-joyous moment because the teleplay has sentimentalized the machine to a high degree. The robot's connection to King Kong is almost too apparent. It seems wrong that the Doctor has no problem wiping out this machine — it is so clearly sentient and emotional. The Doctor always defends the weak and the manipulated, and the K-1 robot of "Robot" is surely not responsible for his destructive actions. This is a strange *Doctor Who* because the Doctor shows no regret whatsoever for ending the robot's existence. Maybe it is the effect of the recent regeneration.

The special effects waver in effectiveness. The robot costume is a victory, an imposing, silver creation with heavy arms, a massive torso and a regal, crown-like head packed with red lights. The scene in which the robot grows to 100 feet tall is initially both dramatic and convincing as well. However, a UNIT tank pulls into the foreground of one battle shot ... and it is obviously a tiny model, something one expects to see in a *Godzilla* film perhaps. When the giant robot grabs Sarah, the young reporter is represented by a limp rag doll. Never for a moment is Sarah rendered believably by the special effects team. Like "Claws of Axos" and

"Carnival of Monsters," there are also some horrendous matte jobs in evidence throughout the final scenes.

"Robot" may be a less-than-innovative tale but Tom Baker grabs the role of the Doctor with unexpected vigor. He announces immediately his intention to return humor to the world of *Doctor Who* by mugging and carrying on shamelessly. The "wardrobe" sequence in which the Doctor tries on the garb of a Viking warrior and a clown goes way over the top ... but Baker's charming screen persona, bulging eyes and infectious smile make it all endurable. Of course, this shift to silliness is totally at odds with Pertwee's serious interpretation of the character, but if history has shown *Doctor Who* anything it is that each new Doctor must be completely different from the one who preceded him. Baker's interpretation is squarely within that tradition.

"Robot" is solid science fiction entertainment. It is certainly not a bad story, although many fans do refer to it as a stinker. Like most "first" stories of new Doctors ("Spearhead from Space," "Castrovalva," "The Twin Dilemma," "Time and the Rani"), the script's thematic and philosophical elements are nil. The threat in "Robot" is perhaps a simple one, like the Auton invasion in "Spearhead from Space," but the robot is certainly an unusual and sympathetic character with some depth.

Perhaps most refreshingly, the two central figures in "Robot" are women. Winters is the piece's villain, and she is portrayed as a cold-hearted, emotionless monster. Sarah, the protagonist, is played by Sladen as a woman who is comfortable with her emotions and stereotypical "female" qualities. The scene in which Winters and Sarah clash over the robot's emotional ability is an interesting confrontation between two interpretations of contemporary female behavior. Winters is a scientist and a professional who has cut off the nurturing, more stereotypical elements of her character. She torments the robot, and confuses it with her vicious directives ... showing all the maternal warmth of a Lady Macbeth. Sarah, on the other hand, is immediately intuitive about the robot's inherent humanity. She builds a relationship with the machine, and brings out its tender side with love and friendship. Although this battle between women may be viewed by some as a sexist dynamic, it is nonetheless an interesting subtext to an otherwise straightforward tale.

"Planet of the Spiders" said goodbye to Jon Pertwee, and it is appropriate also to view "Robot" as the end of an era. This is the last "mad scientist" story to appear on *Doctor Who* for some time. It is also the departure of Nicholas Courtney and the Brigadier from the series' regular format. As a motivating factor in stories, UNIT would no longer be significant in the years to come. The fourth Doctor would furthermore break with tradition by visiting Earth far less frequently than any of his predecessors. Accordingly, the *Doctor Who* universe opened up considerably and the seasons to come were among the most exciting and unusual yet seen.

Ian Marter, Andrews in "Carnival of Monsters," makes his first appearance as Harry Sullivan in "Robot." Unfortunately, Harry would prove to be a rather redundant character and would be written out of the show after just one season.

Baker's Doctor, like Pertwee's, simply did not require a "second male lead" to fill the physical action requirements. Since Baker could handle fight scenes with expertise, there was little for Harry Sullivan and Ian Marter to do but provide comedy relief and cause problems. Marter explained it best in a *Starlog* interview shortly before his death in 1986:

> They didn't make the character as well-written as it could have been ... it seems a great mistake to believe you make a character bigger by surrounding him with idiots. You actually do the opposite. Harry may have been a bit of a bumbler, but he was also a trained doctor ... and they never let him be one.[12]

Marter very well expresses the problem with many companions over the years. Obviously the producers felt that another vigorous male lead would diminish the importance of the Doctor. Accordingly, Baker's Doctor never again had a mature male companion accompany him. Marter, who had very much the same appeal as William Russell's Ian Chesterton, could have added some charming moments to the series, but he was never allowed to. In his last two stories, "Terror of the Zygons" and "The Android Invasion," Marter's Sullivan is lobotomized even further and plays an inexpressive automaton for long stretches! Companions are always problematic on *Doctor Who* because, as Jon Pertwee once established, they are essentially helpless translators to the public. They are helpless, so the Doctor can rescue them, and they are stupid, so the Doctor can *translate* the science fiction concepts to them (surrogates for the audience). Some companions, of course, are more successful than others.

Tom Baker's premiere story is available on videocassette.

76. "The Ark in Space" Written by Robert Holmes; Directed by Rodney Bennett; Designed by Roger Murray-Leach; Parts I–IV; Airdates: January 25, February 1, 8, 15, 1975

SYNOPSIS: The Doctor, Sarah and Harry disembark from the TARDIS to find themselves aboard a highly advanced but apparently abandoned space station. In a vast hall sleep remnants of the human race; the Doctor marvels at the giant cryogenic chamber which cradles the future of mankind. But something destructive is feeding on the sleeping humans: a race of sentient insects called the Wirrn.

The first human medtech, a woman named Vira, revives from suspended animation and informs the visitors that they are on space station Nerva. The hundreds of people in cryogenic freeze represented the best brains of Earth when disaster loomed. Dangerous solar flares eradicated all human life on the planet long ago, and those suspended on Nerva are to represent the future. Vira awakens Commander Noah, who is convinced that Sarah, Harry and the Doctor are dangerous "regressives" out to sabotage Nerva's mission. If Earth is ever to be recolonized and the human race is ever to live again, the Doctor and his companions must convince Noah of their innocence and prevent the Wirrn from feasting on the remnants of the once-proud human race.

GUEST CAST: Vira (Wendy Williams); Commander Noah/Lazzar (Kenton Moore); Rogin (Richardson Morgan); Lycett (John Griegg); Libri (Christopher Masters); Voice of the High Executive (Gladys Spencer); Wirrn Operators (Stuart Fell, Nick Hobbs)

COMMENTARY: "The Ark in Space" is an exciting episode that foreshadows many of the key story elements that would later make *Alien* (1979) such a hit. Like *Alien,* "The Ark in Space" features frozen humans in cryogenic sleep who are menaced by a monster on the loose. The creature sabotages the ship, travels through the vents, breeds inside humans and is finally ejected into space. Of course, these elements are hardly new to film or television. *It! The Terror from Beyond Space* (1958) probably deserves the honor as the first movie version of this story. *Space: 1999* also featured a terrific and terrifying monster-in-space story entitled "Dragon's Domain" (1975), and the *Alien* films seem just as derivative of that adventure as they do of this particular *Who* ... especially since Brian Johnson designed the special effects for both productions. *Alien* director Ridley Scott also worked at the BBC early in *Doctor Who*'s history. In fact, Scott was originally tapped to design the Daleks for Serial 2, "The Daleks." He was too busy, however, and the assignment was given to Scott's office mate, Raymond Cusick!

"The Ark in Space" has other descendants. The third film of the *Alien* series, 1991's *Alien*^{3}, opens with creatures breaking into sealed suspended animation chambers, the same image that opens "The Ark in Space." The *Star Trek* Borg, in addition to their Cybermen–like characteristics, also make a habit of absorbing all the knowledge and memories from the humans they assimilate. This is a technique also utilized by the Wirrn, another a hive-mind race.

"The Ark in Space" introduces a new philosophy to the series. In the early '70s and even in the '60s, mankind was derided as a selfish, deluded creature who would destroy his fellow man and the natural resources of his planet to gain the most knowledge, the most prestige, the most wealth or the most land. In the mid-'70s, this paradigm shifts. Instead, the Doctor marvels about the indomitable human spirit in "Ark in Space" and other serials. Perhaps this shift in tone is a result of *Star Trek*'s unreserved optimism about humanity. Most sci-fi television in the mid-'70s repeated *Star Trek*'s optimistic philosophy, and eschewed the early '70s pessimism that made the Pertwee *Doctor Who* serials and the Andersons' *U.F.O.* such thoughtful visions. In 1976, even the lugubrious *Space: 1999* was revised to incorporate the utopianism of *Star Trek.* For *Doctor Who,* this shift comes at a good time. When a new actor takes on the role of the Doctor it is expected that the philosophies and moods of the show will change too. This type of shift keeps the series remarkably fresh, and "The Ark in Space" is indeed a lively installment. The British viewing audience apparently agreed, because "The Ark in Space" was watched by 14 million people! This was the highest number ever for *Doctor Who,* and a benchmark which new producers and directors were always measured against afterwards.

Reflecting this new optimism about humanity, "The Ark in Space" offers a fascinating conceit. In the future, the people of Earth have become intensely specialized. Vira is a medtech and thus untrained in leadership. Noah is bred for leadership, but when he is transformed into a Wirrn, it is up to Vira to overcome her "specialization" and rediscover her humanity and latent leadership ability. "The Ark in Space" states succinctly that every human can be more than he or she was designed to be. A crisis can reveal hidden skills and talents that lie beyond the limitations of one's assigned role. This comment on specialization reflects a business trend that was began in the '70s and lasted well into the '80s. Workers were more efficient, many experts believed, if they only did one thing. The pendulum has now swung the other way. With '90s downsizing and re-engineering, the valuable worker is not the one who can only do just one task. On the contrary, modern companies seek multi-task workers. Amazingly, *Doctor Who* was pondering the shortcomings of worker specialization as early as 1975. In 1997, the Ethan Hawke–Uma Thurman film *Gattaca* conveyed much the same message.

"The Ark in Space" predicts yet another sad end for the planet Earth. "The Ark," a Hartnell–era story, predicted that the Earth would fall out of orbit and man would spend generations traveling to the distant world Refusis. This particular *Who* story seems to contradict the events in "The Ark," but *Doctor Who* revisionists have attempted to fit it all together. In *The Terrestrial Index*, Jean-Marc Lofficier suggests the events seen on Nerva during this serial occur many millennia before the end of the planet. This story is just one of the Earth's many peaks and valleys before the final end dramatized in "The Ark." After all, "The Ark" took place in the fifty-seventh Segment of Time, some million years after the twentieth century! This rationalization is certainly believable, but it is just a rationalization. At this stage in its history, *Doctor Who* is not strong on continuity. Just witness the Atlantis debacle of "The Underwater Menace" and "The Time Monster." In this regard, *Doctor Who* is less advanced than *Star Trek*, *Space: 1999* or other series of the time period which did attempt to maintain continuity. Of course, *Doctor Who* had more problems to handle. It had a history of 12 years to consult. *Star Trek* and *1999* each lasted less than five years, so fewer incongruities cropped up. Of note to continuity buffs: A dead Wirrn shows up briefly in the Season 16 story "The Stones of Blood."

"The Ark in Space" is the first *Doctor Who* serial to be lensed completely on videotape, and the studio-bound serial thus has a cheap look about it. The well-written story overcomes this shortcoming, but it is clear that the days of the stylish *Doctor Who* episodes like "The Dalek Invasion of Earth," "The War Games" and "The Mind Robber" are long gone. Color may have been added to the mix, but style is missing.

"The Ark in Space" is a classic serial, and it ranks as one of the best episodes of the series. It is a compelling, tense story about the future of mankind, and it gives Baker's new Doctor plenty of trouble to handle. It can be enjoyed on home video.

○ **77. "The Sontaran Experiment"** Written by Bob Baker & Dave Martin; Directed by Rodney Bennett; Designed by Roger Murray-Leach; Parts I & II; Airdates: February 22, March 1, 1975

SYNOPSIS: The Doctor, Sarah and Harry use the Nerva transmat system to reach Earth. There they commence repairs on terrestrial transmat equipment so Vira can beam down members of the recently revived human race. While the Doctor toils with the orb-shaped transmat units, Sarah and Harry head off to explore this uninhabited Earth. In no time, the Doctor and his companions have run afoul of the survivors of a Galsec rescue mission ... survivors who claim that a deadly alien is conducting evil experiments on the them! The Doctor learns that the truth is even worse than he imagined. The Sontarans have resurfaced, with deadly plans for Earth. Now the only way to stop an invasion of the planet is for the Doctor to engage Field Major Styre in deadly hand-to-hand combat!

GUEST CAST: Sontaran Field Major Styre (Kevin Lindsey); Krans (Glyn Jones); Efrak (Peter Walsh); Roth (Peter Rutherford); Vural (Donald Douglas); Galsec Colony Prisoner (Brian Ellis)

COMMENTARY: There is not a lot of story substance to this brief (two-part) *Doctor Who* adventure. The fault for this paucity of drama lies not with the writers, or the production team, but with an accident! During the location shooting of "The Sontaran Experiment," Tom Baker tripped over the Doctor's long scarf and broke his collarbone! Since the series lead was incapacitated, the producers had no choice but to reduce the scope of the story. As a result, "The Sontaran Experiment" is a short, action-packed adventure that is very *Star Trek*–like in its flavor. Here, the common *Trek* conceit that major problems can be resolved by physical combat (a solution seen in "Arena," "Amok Time," "The Gamesters of Triskelion," "Bread and Circuses" and "The Savage Curtain") is translated to *Doctor Who*. The duel between the Sontaran and the Doctor is still entertaining because the Doctor usually attempts to solve problems through his wit and intelligence, not his skill with fisticuffs.

"The Sontaran Experiment" is the first reappearance of the Sontarans since Season 11's premiere "The Time Warrior." Actor Kevin Lindsey, last seen in "Planet of the Spiders," again essays the role of a Sontaran. Delightfully, these clone aliens have not been humanized even a bit. Here, the nasty Styre tests Sarah's resistance to fear, and watches as snakes and crawling rocks attack her. He later continues his research, testing human resistance to fluid deprivation and immersion! A very nasty character indeed. In an especially rewarding moment of continuity, Sarah recognizes the Sontaran as Linx (the character in "The Time Warrior"), but in fact he is merely a clone of Linx.

Even though "The Sontaran Experiment" is short, it is not without some visual aplomb. The serial opens with a long, slow pan across a desolate landscape. A gray, ashen sky cloaks the earth, winds blow audibly on the soundtrack and a circle of rusted orbs (transmat receptacles) become visible. With just one shot of this desolate landscape, the locale of this serial (a world where no human has set foot for a thousand years) is masterfully established. Later information by the Doctor that this area of wilderness is actually Trafalgar Square of the future adds to the eeriness of the terrain.

The idea of a temporally misplaced human setting foot on future Earth would recur in the multi-part adventure "The Mysterious Planet," part of the "Trial of the Time Lord" season. In that story, companion Peri echoed Sarah Jane's comment in "The Sontaran Experiment" that the place was "creepy."

Also exquisitely creepy is the roving robot servant of the Sontarans, on display throughout much of the serial. It has an elongated, squat head and two mechanical "whiskers" near its mouth that move back and forth to time with a bizarre electronic pulse. Though the robot is never seen again in *Doctor Who*, it is an interesting tool for the Sontarans to utilize, especially as it is able to shoot out restraining ropes which capture unsuspecting humans.

Other visual and dramatic details make "The Sontaran Experiment" a less-empty-headed experience. The gaunt, bearded spacemen in their grungy, dirty spacesuits nicely evoke the feeling of a marooned expedition. The hand held, subjective camera which "creeps" up on Sarah at various points in the serial adds suspense, and the mention that space station Nerva (from "The Ark in Space") is "The Lost Colony" suggests that society has gone on, with Earth and inhabitants becoming little more than a legend, as we recall Roanoke or Atlantis.

Other than the action scenes and the special effects sequences with the robot scavenger, there is little of philosophical interest in "The Sontaran Experiment." It is an entertaining, short serial. It could have been a bit more effective, perhaps, with a different title. The title "The Sontaran Experiment" undercuts the tension since the viewer knows from square one that the clone villains are responsible for the torture and disappearance of the Galsec rescue crew. In a series wherein villains recur so frequently, perhaps it would have been better *not* to tip viewers off about the identity of the alien here.

Because of its short length, "The Sontaran Experiment" has been released on video in a two-tape pack with "Genesis of the Daleks."

78. "Genesis of the Daleks" Written by Terry Nation; Directed by David Maloney; Designed by David Spode; Parts I–VI; Airdates: March 8, 15, 22, 29, April 5, 12, 1975

SYNOPSIS: The Doctor is hijacked in mid-transmat beam by a fellow Time Lord. The Gallifreyans have another mission they wish the Doctor to undertake, this one concerning his long-time nemesis, the Daleks. The latest temporal projections by the pensive Time Lords suggest that the Daleks will eventually destroy all other sentient life forms and become the dominant creatures in the universe. The Time Lords want the Doctor to go back to the planet Skaro, the homeworld of the Daleks, and either prevent their creation or somehow re-engineer them to be less hostile.

With Sarah and Harry accompanying him, the Doctor arrives on war-torn Skaro. The mass destruction they witness suggests that the 1,000-year war between the humanoid Kaleds and Thals is nearly at an end because of a scarcity of equipment and manpower. Together, the companions encounter Davros, the horribly scarred creator of the Daleks. Davros has engineered love, compassion and humanity out of his prized creations, and the Doctor has an agonizing choice to make. If he destroys the Daleks in their infancy, is he any better than the Daleks?

GUEST CAST: Davros (Michael Wisher); Nyder (Peter Miles); Gen. Ravon (Guy Siner); Sevrin the Thal (Stephen Yardley); Time Lord (John Franklyn-Robbins); Kavell (Tom Georgeson); Morgren (Ivor Roberts); Tane (Drew Wood); Gerrill (Jeremy Chandler); Ronson (James Garbutt); Dalek Voice (Roy Skelton); Daleks (Keith Ashley, Max Faulkner, John Scott Martin, Cy Town); Thals (Max Faulkner, Michael Lynch)

COMMENTARY: "Genesis of the Daleks" is nothing less than a *Doctor Who* classic. Although it is yet *another* Dalek story, it is, for once, a Dalek story about something other than conquering other planets and flashy exterminations. It eloquently debates the infamous "Adolf Hitler" time travel question.

For many years, sci-fi writers have asked this endlessly fascinating interrogative regarding the notorious Nazi butcher: "If I could travel back in time and kill Adolf Hitler as a baby, should I do so?" This question is so compelling because of humanity's dual nature. As a helpless infant, Hitler is but an innocent. As an adult, however, he is a monster responsible for war crimes and attempted genocide. Is it right to punish Hitler retroactively by killing a baby and therefore stopping the evil he will unleash as an adult? Of even more personal relevance to the time traveler is this related question: "Shall I become a monster as bad, if not worse, than Hitler himself by going back in time and executing a baby?" Does such an evil create a greater good? Or is murder an act of evil, even when practiced on as hideous a creature as Hitler?

Furthermore, if a traveler should change history and kill Hitler, what will happen to the timeline? In the absence of Nazi Germany, will a greater evil spring up in Communist Russia? In a United States obsessed by the Red Scare? In Mussolini's Italy? What if by killing Hitler, something worse is accidentally unleashed? The ramifications of this scenario are endless, which is why the issue is so very compelling.

In exploiting these profound questions of morality, writer and Dalek creator Terry Nation has found the perfect format in which to spin a superb *Doctor Who* serial. What greater moral dilemma is there in time travel? Is it right to destroy even the monstrous Daleks in their infancy? The Doctor's final realization is that the evil of the Daleks will also cause great *good.* People across the universe will be united, learn to trust one another and revel in the joys of liberty and freedom because of the evil of the Daleks! Without the Daleks, all of those wonderful things are lost forever. This is the yin and yang of the universe. Without evil, good loses its value and its meaning. This artful finale of "Genesis of the Dalek," in which Tom Baker's Doctor voices this truism, is a satisfying, thought-provoking solution to the "Adolf Hitler" question ... and one of *Doctor Who*'s greatest moments as sci-fi television.

The same provocative moral question would be explored more pedantically in a talky fifth season *Star Trek: The Next Generation* story entitled "A Matter of

Time." In that adventure, Capt. Jean-Luc Picard mentions a temporal ethics class and the Adolf Hitler dilemma by name. In this episode, he has two actions to take, each one having various ramifications. With the help of a time traveling scholar, he makes his decision.

"Genesis of the Daleks" is memorable not only for its philosophical strands, but also for the introduction of another fascinating villain. The Daleks have always lacked an individual face, and Nation rectifies that situation by unveiling the hideous Davros. Evil as the Daleks are, Davros is worse. The Daleks at least have an excuse for their unpleasant disposition: They were engineered that way. Davros, a man of ambitions and emotions, has no such excuse. Like Hitler himself, Davros is the epitome of human(oid) evil. He has no compassion, no love, no genuine goodness within him. Interestingly, "Genesis of the Daleks" suggests in rather subtle fashion that Davros may be this way because of the extent of his physical injuries. With his glowing mechanical eye, his mobile chair, his life support system and his back brace, Davros is more machine than man. In essence, he is an earlier version of Darth Vader. Like Vader, Davros is a man whose life is sustained completely through machinery and prosthetics. Like Vader, Davros is a pasty-white being trapped within the mechanisms that maintain his existence. Like Vader, Davros has succumbed completely to evil and sells out his own people, much as Vader seeks to murder his own son in *The Empire Strikes Back* (1980). Even beyond matters of physical and psychological similarities, Darth Vader and Davros perform similar dramatic functions within their respective productions. They both lead armies of relentless, faceless killers with amazingly bad targeting skills (the storm troopers of *Star Wars* and the Daleks of *Doctor Who*). In fact, the design of R2D2 is awfully similar to that of the Daleks as well...

Any television show that can take a well-established villain and revitalize it, update it and give it added depth has achieved a victory. "Genesis of the Daleks" not only reveals the origins of the Daleks and explains their antisocial behavior, it also develops the character of the Doctor. His dilemma in this story is perhaps the toughest one any incarnation faces. Moral uncertainty is now firmly ingrained in the series. In the early days, the Doctor did not bat an eye when destroying the Dominators, the Krotons, the Daleks or the Cybermen. For the first time, the Daleks are seen in shades of gray. Like the Silurians or the Sea Devils in "Doctor Who and the Silurians" and "The Sea Devils," even the most evil villains are no longer treated in black-and-white fashion. Perhaps "Genesis of the Daleks" truly represents the beginning of *Doctor Who*'s adulthood, its emergence into realistic drama. Accordingly, Tom Baker's performance in this program is an astonishing one. Any doubts about his ability to successfully handle the serious aspects of the series are completely erased. He is captivating throughout.

Also indicating a more balanced, realistic view of life, the Thals in "Genesis of the Daleks" are treated as bitter creatures just as unattractive as the Kaleds. They are as destructive as Davros, and even use their own doomsday weapon, a powerful new missile. This is a change from "The Daleks," a serial in which the Thals are depicted as innocent pacifists in the vein of the Eloi in *The Time Machine*

(1960). No longer is the destruction of Skaro by these races a simply a matter of good versus evil. Both races are now treated as short-sighted and self-destructive.

"Genesis of the Daleks" is one of the ten best *Doctor Who* serials. The Daleks are good villains, but they work better when there is less of them on-screen. In "Genesis of the Daleks," the Daleks do not blossom into full destructive beauty into the final installment, and that fact makes their presence all the more powerful at the climax. "Genesis of the Daleks" has been released on videotape with "The Sontaran Experiment."

79. "Revenge of the Cybermen" Written by Gerry Davis; Directed by Michael Briant; Designed by Roger Murray-Leach; Parts I–IV; Airdates: April 19, 26, May 3, 10, 1975

SYNOPSIS: After completing the mission to Skaro, the Doctor, Harry and Sarah are returned to Nerva. However, they have been returned (via a Time Lord power bracelet) 1000 years too early! In this time, the station is fulfilling its original function as a beacon to space freighters. Fortunately, the TARDIS is programmed to find the Doctor in any time period, and it will eventually drift through time to their current position. In the meantime, the Doctor, Sarah and Harry discover that the crew of the station has fallen prey to a deadly plague. The Doctor believes that the Cybermen are to blame when he learns that the remnants of the planet Voga have entered Earth's solar system. The Cybermen want Voga, "The Planet of Gold," obliterated since it was the mines of Voga that provided the gold necessary to defeat the Cybermen during the great Cyberwar hundreds of years earlier. Before long, the Cybermen show their metallic faces, and the Doctor and his friends are caught in a deadly conflict between the Cybermen and Voga ... which is preparing to launch a devastating Sky-striker missile at Nerva!

GUEST CAST: Commander Stevenson (Ronald Leigh-Hunt); Kellman (Jeremy Wilkins); Leter (William Marlowe); Warner (Alec Wallis); Vorus (David Collins); Magrik (Michael Wisher); Tyrum (Kevin Stoney); Sheprah (Brian Grellis); Cyberleader (Christopher Robbie); Cybermen (Melville Jones, Pat Gorman)

COMMENTARY: "Revenge of the Cybermen" brings back Kit Pedler's and Gerry Davis' deadly Cyborg soldiers for the first time since "The Invasion" (1969) and their brief cameo appearance in "Carnival of Monsters" (1973). Unfortunately, this story has but little of the impact of the early, frightening, Troughton–era Cybermen stories such as "The Tomb of the Cybermen" or "The Moonbase." Nor is "Revenge of the Cybermen" a particularly skillfully updated rendering of these popular villains, like the previous Dalek installment "Genesis of the Daleks." Instead, the same elements seen in Troughton's landmark shows "The Moonbase" and "The Wheel in Space" are dutifully recycled in adequate if uninspired fashion.

The plague seen infesting Nerva in "Revenge of the Cybermen" is the same ploy that was used by the Cybermen in "The Moonbase." The setting of "Revenge of the Cybermen" (an isolated space station) is also the setting of "The Wheel in

Space." The attack of the vicious cybermats also recurs from "Wheel in Space." Little originality has been added to the mix since Troughton essayed the role of the Doctor six years earlier.

Still, there are a few fresh pieces of Cyberman lore on display. The most important is Voga, the Planet of Gold. Before this story, gold was never identified as a substance dangerous to Cybermen. That in itself is a continuity error, since "The Tomb of the Cybermen" takes place generations after the Cyberman defeat depicted in this story. Since Voga played such a crucial role, gold's importance as a weapon should have been considered by Klieg, Kaftan and the others in the "The Tomb of the Cybermen." Of course, that serial was written long before it was decided that gold would be the Cyberman Achilles' heel. Still, this is an historical incongruity. Gold would play an important role in all future Cybermen stories including "Earthshock" in the Davison era, "Attack of the Cybermen" in the Colin Baker era and finally "Silver Nemesis" in the McCoy era.

Also for the first time, "Revenge of the Cybermen" mentions the First Cyber War. Exactly when and where this war takes place is a mystery, but Voga's crucial part in the defeat is noted. It is left uncertain if the Cyber War refers to either of the twentieth century invasion attempts, seen in "The Tenth Planet" and "Invasion." This is unlikely since Voga did not feature in those tales.

To discuss "Revenge of the Cybermen" further is unnecessary. It is a solid action story with good performances and a high entertainment quotient. It as enjoyable and competent as any average episode of *Star Trek*. Baker is again outstanding as the Doctor, and it is good to see the evil Cybermen again after their long absence. One only wishes they could have been updated in a clever fashion and inserted into a story that was more philosophical or intellectually stimulating. Still, the Cybermen remain one of *Doctor Who*'s most enjoyable villains. The Vogans are also interesting, if less villainous. They are depicted as humanoid creatures with receding hairlines, big foreheads and strange eyebrow ridges. In a sense, virtually every alien race on *Star Trek: The Next Generation* also fits this description!

"Revenge of the Cybermen" is available on videocassette.

SEASON 13

80. "Terror of the Zygons" Written by Robert Banks Stewart; Directed by Douglas Camfield; Designed by Nigel Curzon; Parts I–IV; Airdates August 30, September 5, 13, 20, 1975

SYNOPSIS: The TARDIS materializes in Scotland near Loch Ness. Several North Sea oil rigs have been attacked by a monster and Brigadier Lethbridge-Stewart has requested the Doctor's help in solving the puzzle. The alien Zygons, led by the Warlord Broton, are behind the massacres. Their homeworld was destroyed in a solar catastrophe millennia ago, and many of their ships have been roaming the galaxy looking for a planet that can be modified to accommodate their life form. Broton's ship has been on Earth for many generations, but only recently reactivated. The Zygons have also awakened a native beast from their planet: the Skarasen. Broton can control the Skarasen monster with a special control device. His master plan is to destroy the polar ice caps and breed herds of the Skarasen on the Earth's surface. To do this, however, the Zygons will have to destroy mankind.

GUEST CAST: Broton/Duke of Forgill (John Woodnutt); Munro (Hugh Martin); Huckle (Tony Sibbald); Angus McRannald (Angus Lennie); Cabler (Robert Russell); Radio Operator (Bruce Wightman); Sister Lamont (Lillian Walker); Corporal (Bernard G. High); Soldier (Peter Symonds); Zygons (Keith Ashley, Ronald Gough)

COMMENTARY: "Terror of the Zygons" is an amalgam of familiar *Doctor Who* conventions. First and foremost it is an "invasion from space" story like the 1969 serial "The Invasion" or 1964's "The Dalek Invasion of Earth." Secondly, it is a "body snatchers" story like the Troughton–era "The Faceless Ones," but with duplicates of Harry and the Duke of Forgill instead of Polly Lopez. Thirdly, it returns to the world of North Shore oil rigs, a locale already explored in the Troughton killer-seaweed story "Fury from the Deep" and tangentially in the Pertwee–era story "The Sea Devils." "Terror of the Zygons" is also a serial squarely in the tradition of "The Daemons," because once again an Earth legend, this time the Loch Ness Monster, is revealed to be an alien being. Finally, if one is nit picking, "Terror of the Zygons" even follows the visual example of "The Claws of Axos" because Zygon technology is delineated in organic rather than mechanical terms. The monster special effects are also familiar, recalling the Drashigs in "Carnival of Monsters" and the inadequately depicted prehistoric beasts in "Invasion of the Dinosaurs."

Despite the re-use of these *Doctor Who* ingredients, "Terror of the Zygons" is nonetheless a riveting and horrifying adventure. The Zygon costumes are incredible to behold. These brown, fleshy creatures have barnacles up and down their bodies and small, piggish faces set back in their giant arrowhead skulls. When *Doctor Who* premiered in America during the '70s, the Zygons were featured prominently in magazine articles and television commercials about the series, probably because they are so interesting and effective as an extraterrestrial design. The Zygon spaceship, although reminiscent of the biomechanical Axos, is nonetheless masterfully designed with misshapen organic knobs and strange tables and cabinets in evidence everywhere. It is not a ship in which humans would feel comfortable, and the unconventional interior makes that plain. The Skarasen is not handled nearly so effectively. It frequently appears to be an inexpressive puppet. Apparently not much has been learned since the "Invasion of the Dinosaurs" debacle.

In addition to set design, "Terror of the Zygon" repeats other elements of "The Claws of Axos." In the first story, a duplicate of British agent Filer was created by the organic vampire creature to stop the Doctor. Here, a duplicate of the Doctor's friend Harry is utilized for the same purpose.

"Terror of the Zygons" has few original notes in its teleplay, but even considering the weak special effects there is a feeling of underlying tension evident in this story. The early Tom Baker stories all have the same *joie de vivre*, and an air of "legitimate" horror-grounded science fiction that the original *Star Trek* featured in spades too. Perhaps it is because Sladen and Baker share an obvious chemistry. They handle each story with a remarkable grace and intensity, and just the right note of fun...even when the story is deadly serious, and even scary. There is nothing tongue-in-cheek about their performances, just something miraculously energetic in the face of a well-written teleplay. "Terror of the Zygons" is the same old invasion stuff, but it is fast-paced, suspenseful and slicker than many older stories. In this sense, *Doctor Who*'s repetition of old stories might be seen as a sincere attempt to improve on past victories, rather than merely as a lack of creativity. Adding to the rollicking spirit of fun is the welcome presence of Courtney's Brigadier Lethbridge-Stewart. This marks his last appearance in the series until 1982 and the episode "Mawdryn Undead."

This adventure is referenced by Sylvester McCoy's seventh incarnation of the Doctor in the twenty-fifth season opener "Remembrance of the Daleks." "Terror of the Zygons" has been released on videocassette courtesy of BBC/CBS-Fox home video.

81. "Planet of Evil" Written by Louis Marks; Directed by David Maloney; Designed by Roger Murray-Leach; Parts I–IV; Airdates: September 27, October 4, 11, 18, 1975

SYNOPSIS: In the year 37,166, an eight-man survey team from the Morestran Empire is attacked on Zeta Minor, the most distant planet in the known universe. Dr. Sorenson, the only survivor of this expedition, has been spending his time collecting rock samples near a mysterious Black Pool that is completely alien in composition and does not even reflect light.

While en route to London, the TARDIS detects a space emergency signal and lands on Zeta Minor. The Doctor and Sarah soon encounter Sorenson and a Morestran Space Service rescue ship. When they all attempt to leave Zeta Minor, however, they are confronted with a horrible anti-matter monster. When the ship attempts to lift off, it is pulled inexorably back to the planet. The Doctor makes for the Black Pool and attempts to communicate with the anti-matter alien that dwells within. Stunned by the telepathic link, he falls into the pool of the unknown and disappears...

GUEST CAST: Salamar (Prentis Hancock); Vishinsky (Ewen Solon); Dr. Sorenson (Frederick Jaeger); Braun (Terence Brook); Baldwin (Tony McEwan); Morelli (Michael Wisher); De Haan (Louis Mahoney); Anti-Matter Monster (Michael Lee); Sorenson Monster (Douglas Stark, Ray Knight)

COMMENTARY: Louis Marks' "Planet of Evil" is another stylish *Doctor Who* adventure which (like "The Ark in Space") could easily be named a precursor to

Ridley Scott's *Alien* (1979) Much of the initial situation is identical to that of the first film in this profitable outer space horror film series. In both adventures, a spaceship is drawn to a geologically strange world by a distress call. The crew of the spaceship encounters the remnants of a previous expedition (an alien one in *Alien*) and brings an extraterrestrial horror aboard their ship. As the ship leaves the planet, the alien force runs free and starts killing crew members left and right. The planet in *Alien* is at the edge of known space somewhere near Zeta Reticuli. The planet in *Doctor Who* is also at the frontier of the universe, on a planet called Zeta Minor. Of course, the "monster on the loose" subgenre is a common one, so it is both difficult and unjust to state that one production has "appropriated" the notion from another. Yet it is significant that *Doctor Who* visited themes that were popular later in the decade, and indeed, even today (*Alien Resurrection* [1997]). Although the dramatic concept of characters dying in an isolated situation probably originated all the way back in the Agatha Christie story *Ten Little Indians*, *Doctor Who* is among the first television shows to transpose the setting to space.

Despite the fact that the "monster on the loose" is a common plot, one particular scene in *Alien* and "Planet of Evil" does bear mentioning for its similarity. In "Planet of Evil," several dead bodies are ejected into space. This same idea is dramatized in almost identical fashion in *Alien* (1979) and Disney's *The Black Hole* (1979), with silver coffins launched out of tubes into space. Both films premiered four years after "Planet of Evil" debuted on the BBC. Later, this idea of "burial at space" was repeated not only in *Star Trek II: The Wrath of Khan* (1982) but in *Starship Troopers* (1997).

Beyond the alien monster concept at the heart of the story, "Planet of Evil" involves the concept of anti-matter. Like the doppelganger, the alternate universe and the living machine, the anti-matter story is yet *another* classic sci-fi television idea that every program worth its salt seems honor-bound to explore. In its first season, *Star Trek* presented the confusing "The Alternative Factor," about an evil anti-matter duplicate of an alien man named Lazarus. *Space: 1999* went twice to the same anti-matter well in both the Year One story "Matter of Life and Death" and the Year Two adventure "A Matter of Balance." *Doctor Who*'s take on the material is less cerebral and far more horrific than either of the aforementioned productions. The entire story seems to exist solely for the horrifying moment when the Sorenson anti-matter beast reproduces and roams the halls of the fleeing spaceship. Appropriately, this is the most tense moment in the show. Vishinsky and Sarah flee for the bridge, attempting to stop the horrible alien creatures from destroying them. The creatures finally do break in, and only the Doctor's quick thinking and use of the TARDIS saves his friends from death.

"Planet of Evil" also features that old *Doctor Who* chestnut, the misguided scientist. Following in the tradition of Prof. Stahlman in "Inferno" or Dr. Maxtible in "The Evil of the Daleks," Sorenson attempts to tamper "in God's domain" in this adventure. Ironically, Sorenson is treated with uncommon sympathy despite his meddling with the balance of nature. He is saved from his fate by the anti-matter people, and even given knowledge of a new power source by the Doctor...a source that can save his dying people! This is a far kinder fate than Stahlman's or Maxtible's. "Planet of Evil" seems to suggest that good intentions make all the difference. Sorenson's goal is honorable, even if his discovery of living anti-matter will cause disaster throughout the universe. Sorenson's return to normality also points out that the anti-matter beings in "Planet of Evil" are not really evil at all. They are merely protecting the fabric of space from those who are ignorant enough to weaken it.

One of the factors that makes "Planet of Evil" such a joy to behold is the impressive alien jungle built indoors on the sound stage. This is a lush, beautiful set with bubbling swamps and fleshy plant pods. Quick cuts of the jungle interior reveal slime-coated trees, bizarre alien cacti, strange egg-like protrusions and even organic spaghetti-like growth from the trees. Taken as a whole, this set is remarkably evocative of an alien habitat. The portal between dimensions, a black pool of nothingness, is also effectively depicted as a reflectionless, circular pond. With steam machines running in the background, gloomy lighting, strange animal sound effects and densely packed jungle vegetation, the illusion of otherworldliness is vividly presented. It is a triumph for the production team, and particularly for designer Roger Murray-Leach (who also designed The Liberator for *Blake's 7*). Also worthy of praise are the bevy of tools and devices designed by the production team to depict the Morestran culture. From futuristic grave markings (of men with names like Egard Lumb) to hand-held mining equipment and even a one-eyed "oculoid tracker," "Planet of Evil"'s visual touches never disappoint. The effectiveness of the sets and props is undercut only slightly by the fact that some of the serial is lensed on film, some on videotape, and the transitions are jarring.

Not only is the planet surface a wonder of design, but so is the interior of the Morestran spaceship in "Planet of Evil." It is elegant in its simplicity: a stark space battleship that contrasts well with the dense, random nature of the jungle on Zeta Minor.

Prentis Hancock, last seen as a Thal in "Planet of the Daleks," has his juiciest *Doctor Who* role as Controller Salamar in "Planet of Evil." Ironically, "Planet of Evil" aired during the same year as *Space: 1999* Year One. In that series, Hancock also played a character with the rank of "Controller," but Paul Morrow was a much more sympathetic man than the power-hungry Salamar in this story.

"Planet of Evil" is available on videocassette, and is well-worth checking out for its connections to the popular *Alien* saga.

82. "The Pyramids of Mars" Written by Stephen Harris [Lewis Greifer, Robert Holmes]; Directed by Paddy Russell; Designed by Christine Ruscoe; Parts I–IV; Airdates: October 25, November 1, 8, 15, 1975

SYNOPSIS: The TARDIS returns to UNIT Headquarters a half-century too early, and the Doctor and Sarah become involved in a deadly adventure. Prof. Scarman, an archaeologist, has been transformed into a servant of Sutekh, a malevolent god of destruction who, 7000 years earlier, was trapped on Mars by Horus, the Osirian God of Light. Now Scarman and a troop of mummy-like automatons are building a rocket that will free Sutekh from his pyramid-like jail. The Doctor attempts to destroy the rocket, but Sutekh captures the explosion in a time-loop stasis field. The Doctor steps through a time corridor to face the evil Sutekh himself, but Sutekh has learned of another craft that can free him from his imprisonment: the TARDIS!

GUEST CAST: Marcus Scarman (Bernard Archard); Lawrence Scarman (Michael Sheard); Ernie Clements (George Tovey); Dr. Warlock (Peter Copley); Namin (Peter Maycock); Collins (Michael Bilton); Ahmed (Vik Tablian); Sutekh (Gabriel Woolf); Mummies (Nick Burnell, Melvyn Bedford, Kevin Selway)

COMMENTARY: "Pyramids of Mars," widely considered a classic *Who* serial, has been the subject of many essays, including Ian Towey's thoughtful exploration in *Dreamwatch* ("A Journey to the Dark Side, *Doctor' Who's* Pyramids of Mars," 1995). There is some justification for praise as "Pyramids of Mars" is an exciting, well-acted story. However, the serial owes a heavy debt to earlier *Doctor Who* episodes such as "The Tomb of the Cybermen" and "The Daemons." "Pyramids of Mars" exploits many of the same *Mummy* film conventions as the classic fifth season Troughton serial, particularly the newly-discovered tomb, the awakening of a monster from hibernation and the appearance of shambling robotic men. Unlike "The Tomb of the Cybermen," however, these ingredients are not so successfully integrated in "Pyramids of Mars."

To wit: why are the robots of Sutekh wrapped in bandages, other than to make them resemble mummies? It is certainly a striking image, but it is nonsensical. Why is the rocket shaped like a pyramid? Is this a believable design for a craft that must reach escape velocity, or merely an attempt to suggest that ancient Egyptian technology is based on the vessels of extraterrestrials?

In "The Tomb of the Cybermen," all of the action arose *logically* out of the story, and believable analogies were found to accommodate *Mummy* film elements. The cybermats were tomb vermin like rats or snakes. The electrified doors, the targeting room and the Cyberman energizer were old-fashioned booby traps. Every element of the drama thus fit the *Mummy* mold *believably*, from the curious archaeology team to the slow, grinding stomp of the mummy-like Cybermen. "Pyramids of Mars" also makes use of the props of Egyptian mythology. The sarcophagus, the Mummy and even the pyramid are all reinterpreted as tokens of an alien influence. Yet these symbols are not integrated in the teleplay as either logical or convincing analogies for said alien technology. Why does a sarcophagus house a time portal? Where is the logic in this construction? How does form express purpose? Why are the robots of Sutekh garbed in bandages? What is the intrinsic value of bandages to humanoid robots? Would bandages not impede function rather than aid it? Most importantly, where did these robots come from in the first place? Horus would certainly not leave evil robot servants on Earth for Sutekh to command — and Sutekh himself is trapped on Mars, unable to interact with other beings except on a purely mental plane! The presence of the robots in this story is illogical and unmotivated dramatically. "Pyramids of Mars" loses some essential credibility because it takes advantage of Egyptian lore without *translating* Egyptian lore as a believable alien technology.

Like "The Daemons," "Pyramids of Mars" again suggests that ancient mythology, this time that of the Sun Gods, the Osirians and Horus, is actually true. Supposedly, all of these legendary characters were extraterrestrials who came to Earth millennia ago and formed the basis of myth. This story element established, "Pyramids of Mars" is thus obviously another rehash of *Who* convention. Remember the "Daemons" prototype? In it, beings from another world arrived on Earth generations ago and formed the basis of human mythology. Already this idea has been used in Season 13 in "Terror of the Zygons" in regards to the Loch Ness Monster. These mythological elements are also fairly illogical in "Pyramids of Mars." Why did the Osirans use sarcophagi, pyramids and mummy-like robots? Why are these elements important to their culture? Why did the ancient Egyptians adopt these symbols? Why did Horus construct the tomb in Egypt to grant access to the dominion of Sutekh? With the technology to trap an indestructible being such as Sutekh on Mars, why couldn't the Osirans erect a force field on Earth so the path to Sutekh would be blocked to primitive man? How peaceful and benevolent were these aliens if they left such a destructive force within our reach? These questions are also unanswered, and "Pyramids of Mars," for all its Egyptian motifs, finds no logical purpose for ancient Egyptian paraphernalia. It is the same story as "The Daemons," but Egyptian lore stands in for demonology.

StarGate (1994) also used Egyptian motifs to power its high-powered action story, but in that film these elements were used with considerably more logic. The alien soldiers of Ra wore fierce Jackal helmets and carried laser staffs to scare the native population of a distant world. It was a fearsome, believable uniform, unlike the ill-defined robot mummies. *StarGate* also explored the myth of Ra, but in a fashion that made sense. An alien set himself up as dictator on a primitive planet of slaves, and his powerful ship brought light and power. Thus Ra could make day out of night, and the legend of the "Sun" God was born. "Pyramids of Mars" is not so lucid in its explanations.

"Pyramids of Mars" also relies on an unlikely coincidence. Is it not convenient that Dr. Scarman's brother, a Victorian man born of the nineteenth century, has invented a communications device that can pick up signals from Mars at exactly the same time that Sutekh is breaking free of his tomb? According to the serial, the message "Beware Sutekh" had been transmitting for eons, but the Doctor discovers it at a most serendipitous time ... at the same moment in time that Sutekh's forces are gathering for escape, in fact! Although all drama must rely on coincidence to some extent, this particular convergence of events strains believability, as does Scarman's invention of such a powerful machine in pre-technological 1911. Coincidence has given way to contrivance.

Writer Ian Towley praises "Pyramids of Mars" on the basis that it features elements of Gothic style:

> From the shots of rattling door handles and winding secret, dusty hidden passageways, to images of the good Doctor's assistant fleeing up a flight of moss-covered

> steps dressed in a flowing white gown, "Pyramids of Mars" episodes are suffused with intentional Gothic images and references.[13]

Of course, *Doctor Who* has constantly mixed literary genres in sly fashion. That the series should explore Gothic themes over its long run is a natural development. However, how successfully are Gothic elements *really* established in "Pyramids of Mars"? The Towley essay stresses that "Pyramids of Mars" is Gothic primarily because there is such a clear differentiation between the light-hearted good guys and the frowning, obsessed bad guys. That is a distinction that could also be observed in virtually any other *Doctor Who* serial (or any modern genre drama from *Goldeneye* to *Star Trek: First Contact*). It is hardly a trait found here and here alone. After all, the evil-obsessed Daleks are visibly different from the light-hearted Doctor in "The Evil of the Daleks," a serial set in Victorian England. Is that story also "Gothic" since good and bad are differentiated visually?

Gothic qualities should include not only the *differentiation* between good and evil, but also violent incidents that occur in remote surroundings. By that definition as well, virtually any episode of *Doctor Who* could be defined as Gothic. Although "Pyramids of Mars" does occur at the isolated Stargrove house and is rife with violence, the same isolated setting and predilection for death could be pinpointed easily in "The Daemons," "The Curse of Peladon," "The Wheel in Space," "The Horror of Fang Rock" or "Ghost Light." Praising "Pyramids of Mars" on the basis of its mild Gothic style is perhaps less than illuminating.

Gothic literature has also been seen as the Romantic response to the rationalism of the Enlightenment period of literature. Accordingly, a prime characteristic of Gothic storytelling is the tug-of-war for possession of the hero or heroine's soul. Bram Stoker's *Dracula* was perhaps the ultimate Gothic protagonist — simultaneously frightening and alluring. He was a devil, yet he was also a powerful devil with qualities attractive to women. In this sense, neither Sutekh nor Scarman in "Pyramids of Mars" is delineated in traditional Gothic terms. They cast no spell, and are *markedly* unattractive. Additionally, the Doctor never intentionally wavers in his dedication to Sutekh's destruction, nor does he find Sutekh's brand of megalomania to be attractive or alluring. Sarah, if she is indeed the Gothic maiden down to her "flowing white gown," should harbor some kind of attraction to the grisly Sutekh. This does not occur, and Sarah remains like the Doctor, dedicated to killing Sutekh throughout. In this sense, "Pyramids of Mars" is notably anti–Gothic in its depiction of protagonists and villains. Sarah wears a gown in "Pyramids of Mars," all right, but it is Victoria's gown from the Troughton era. Are all of Victoria's episodes thus "Gothic" as well? Questions of wardrobe alone cannot qualify this serial as particularly Gothic.

Despite several ill-defined elements of Egyptian literature, there is no doubt that "Pyramids of Mars" remains an entertaining serial. It is filled with menace and has one scene of astonishing power. The Doctor takes Sarah to a future in which he has not intervened to stop Sutekh and Scarman. Sutekh has destroyed the Earth and it is a lifeless, windswept desert. It is a frightening vision that makes

Sutekh's destruction all the more imperative. Rather than praising *Doctor Who* as a Gothic vision, it should be praised for this kind of startling imagery. The series often relates, in the most striking visual terms possible on its budget, the incredible ramifications of interference and non-interference. *Doctor Who* is valuable as sci-fi drama because finds striking visual conceits which highlight the decision-making process. It visualizes *possibilities* like no other television series. The dead Earth in "Pyramids of Mars," the Dalek-controlled future in "Day of the Daleks" and even the alternate reality of "Inferno" all reflect how one person's action or inaction can change the path of a person, a country, a world or even the universe.

The influence of its literary and filmic forebears can be judged today on the "Pyramids of Mars" video release.

83. "The Android Invasion" Written by Terry Nation; Directed by Barry Letts; Designed by Philip Lindley; Parts I–IV; Airdates: November 22, 29, December 6, 13, 1975

SYNOPSIS: The Doctor and Sarah arrive in a quaint English village not far from Britain's Space Defense Center. To their surprise, they find that the village is not "real," but rather a full-scale mock-up of the original. They have not arrived on Earth at all, but in the midst of a devious Kraal test. The village, its inhabitants and even the Space Defense Center itself are all part of a Kraal invasion strategy, and a human astronaut, presumed lost, is a collaborator!

GUEST CAST: Astronaut Guy Crayford (Milton Johns); Morgan (Peter Welch); Cpl. Adams (Max Faulkner); Styggron (Martin Friend); Grierson (Dave Carter); Harry Sullivan (Ian Marter); Chedaki (Roy Skelton); RSM Benton (John Levene); Kraal (Stuart Fell); Col. Farady (Patrick Newell); Matthews (Hugh Lund); Tessa (Heather Emmanuel)

COMMENTARY: Terry Nation's first non-Dalek teleplay since "The Keys of Marinus" in *Doctor Who*'s first season is an atmosphere-laden suspense chiller. Both the *Invasion of the Body Snatchers* (1956) motif of familiar people acting unemotionally and *The Stepford Wives* (1975) conceit of android duplicates are in evidence to enhance the disturbing mood of the story. In particular, the first half hour of this serial is masterfully executed. The viewers share the mystery with the Doctor and Sarah as they observe the strange behavior of the Evesham village denizens. Something is obviously wrong with these "doppelganger" people, and it is very unnerving to see human beings act in such bizarre, mechanical fashion. Letts' camerawork captures this strangeness effectively with intense close-ups of blank, emotionless faces and static long shots that reveal the emptiness (mental and physical) of the false terrain. The ultimate terror occurs when the Doctor finally faces his own android duplicate. The android Doctor is portrayed as a joyless, imposing thing of ruthless purpose. Baker, who is quite good in villainous roles such as Prince Khoura in *The Golden Voyage of Sinbad* (1974), exudes menace as the lifeless duplicate of the Time Lord, and the difference between the buoyant, lively real thing and the walking automaton is quite pronounced.

"The Android Invasion" also introduces one of the great sci-fi television fallacies to *Doctor Who*. Ever since "The Mark of Gideon" aired on *Star Trek* in 1969, genre productions have been obsessed with artificial "duplicate" settings. In "The Mark of Gideon," Capt. Kirk found himself aboard an exact duplicate of the *Enterprise*. It was so authentic that all the controls worked. This idea was repeated frequently in other shows. *U.F.O.* produced a tale entitled "Reflections in the Water" which featured a precise duplicate of the SHADO headquarters deep under the surface of the ocean. Not to be outdone, a fully functioning replica of Moonbase Alpha was explored in the *Space: 1999* story "One Moment of Humanity." *Doctor Who*'s "The Android Invasion" similarly presents an entire town and Space Defense Center duplicated in incredible (and accurate) detail. Of course, the fallacy of this particular situation is that any alien race intelligent and resourceful enough to build perfect replicas of starships, moonbases, control rooms and entire towns is also resourceful enough to solve their problems without resorting to primitive methods such as invasion.

All of Evesham and the Space Center is constructed by the Kraals just so they can *test* their androids. Would it not have been more logical to take the androids to the real Evesham and introduce them one at a time, rather than to recreate miles of forest vegetation, the town pub, the general store and everything else from that area on Earth? The central premise of "The Android Invasion," though eerie, is revealed to be flawed. All the valuable resources that went into the Kraal scenario could have been better spent ensuring the success of the actual invasion. No wonder the Kraals are outmaneuvered in the climax! For a race of brilliant scientists, they are surprisingly inept and unimaginative.

"The Android Invasion" features androids who are similar in appearance to the Fembots in several episodes of the American television series *The Bionic Woman*. In both series, androids are revealed to sport faces filled with circuitry and round, lifeless orbs for eyes. The idea of android duplicates replacing important citizens was seen not only in *The Stepford Wives*, which premiered just months before "The Android Invasion." It was also the premise for the short-lived series *Beyond Westworld* (1980). In that series (based on the Michael Crichton film), protagonist Connie Selleca tracked down androids who had escaped from the Delos Amusement Park. These machines were bent on the destruction of man, and they attempted to take over nuclear submarines and other important human installations to achieve their aim. They managed these tricks by duplicating exactly the appearance of important personnel. In other words, *Beyond Westworld* is a total duplication of ideas on view in "The Android Invasion"!

This *Doctor Who* adventure also suffers from the absence of the Brigadier. How is it that the Kraals realize Lethbridge-Stewart will be away in Geneva at the exact time of their invasion? Would it not behoove the Kraals to have an android duplicate of this important person, just in case his schedule changed and he returned to London? As small a thing as a schedule change could thus completely disrupt their invasion plan! Again, the ridiculous nature of the Kraal invasion is exposed by this little detail. Roger Ebert often calls this kind of contrivance "the idiot plot."

"The Android Invasion" highlights the final appearance of Ian Marter as Harry Sullivan. Marter has little to do here as Sullivan but play a sinister duplicate. This was also his task, ironically, in the Season 13 opener "Terror of the Zygons."

Despite all these problems, "The Android Invasion," like "Terror of the Zygons" or "Pyramid of Mars," overcomes the goofy plot. There is again the satisfying feeling of series growth in this serial. It is yet another take on a television cliché, but these clichés have become immensely enjoyable and even nostalgia-provoking over the years. It is rewarding to see *Doctor Who* tackling the same subjects that motivated *Star Trek* or *Space: 1999*, or any other classic '70s outer space show. As always, *Doctor Who* manages to come through it all with a high entertainment quotient. Perhaps it is the presence of Tom Baker that somehow makes all these rehashes seem fresh and enjoyable. Perhaps it is the touches of humor injected into each Season 13 script. For whatever reason, "The Android Invasion" is thoroughly enjoyable.

"The Android Invasion" is available on VHS.

84. "The Brain of Morbius" Written by Robin Bland [Terrance Dicks]; Directed by Christopher Barry; Designed by Barry Newbery; Parts I–IV; Airdates: January 3, 10, 17, 24, 1976

SYNOPSIS: When the TARDIS unexpectedly veers 1000 parsecs off course and lands on a storm-ridden planet, the Doctor learns the Time Lords are responsible for the detour. This is the planet Karn, where the renegade Time Lord Morbius was vanquished and consequently destroyed. Led by the ancient priestess Maren, the Sisterhood of Karn also protects the sacred Elixir of Life on Karn. The Doctor and Sarah soon become aware of a plot by the obsessed Dr. Solon — a plot which will involve the theft of the valuable elixir and the resurrection of the villainous Morbius. Unfortunately, for Solon to complete his plan, he requires the Doctor's head ... literally!

GUEST CAST: Dr. Meheni Solon (Philip Madoc); Condo (Colin Fay); Maren (Cynthia Grenville); Ohica (Gilly Brown); Sisters (Sue Bishop, Janie Kells, Gabrielle Mowbray, Veronica Ridge); Voice of Morbius (Michael Spice); Monster (Stuart Fell)

COMMENTARY: When *Doctor Who* is at its best, it combines literary and filmic sources in inventive, unpredictable fashion. "The Brain of Morbius" proves that *Doctor Who* fails when it adapts its inspirations too literally, and does not attempt a new twist on the material. For all of its otherworldly settings, "The Brain of Morbius" is in essence a rather slavish and uninspired takeoff on events from the Universal *Frankenstein* films. Images and characters are mercilessly recycled. The Sisterhood of Karn fills in for the torch-bearing villagers, Solon's assistant Condo is Ygor, and Dr. Solon himself is a surrogate for the mad Frankenstein. Even Sarah's brief bout with blindness harkens back to the Frankenstein Monster's encounter with a sightless hermit in *Bride of Frankenstein*. Terrance Dicks is one of the best writers for *Doctor Who*, but it is obvious that he also was unhappy with this serial. When he saw the route it was taking, he removed his name and substituted the pseudonym "Robin Bland." That name perfectly captures the feel of the story. It *is* bland, and lacking in originality. Even the production values are subpar. The show has a garish look to it, and the monster costume is ludicrous. The Morbius beast, with twin eyestalks poking out of a transparent fishbowl helmet containing a rubbery human brain, must represent a nadir in *Doctor Who* monster design. It is a ridiculous creation that lacks menace.

"The Brain of Morbius" also rehashes a genre that really needed no homage: the disembodied brain-transplant story. This type of story, inevitably featuring a human brain (or head) in a jar, was the mainstay of science fiction films like *Donovan's Brain* (1953), starring a young Nancy Reagan, and the incomparably wretched *They Saved Hitler's Brain* (1964). That *Doctor Who* would stoop to emulate these rather forgettable films demonstrates two facts. The first is that *Doctor Who* writers and producers looked for inspiration in even the most ludicrous places. This is, perhaps, an admirable trait. The second fact is that there are some ideas which are just inherently ludicrous, and need no homage. That is the case with the "brain in the jar" genre. Steve Martin finally put it all to rest in 1983 with the hysterical send-up *The Man With Two Brains.*

The name of the Time Lord Morbius certainly must harken back not only to mythology, but also to the 1956 film *Forbidden Planet,* which emphasized the alien-induced brain boost of one Dr. Morbius (Walter Pidgeon).

Talented thespian Philip Madoc returns to *Doctor Who* for the first time since 1969. He is appropriately loony and sinister as Dr. Solon, but the role is not nearly as interesting as that of the War Lord in "The War Games."

"The Brain of Morbius" is available on video in a "special edition" so fans can view this Frankenstein pastiche first-hand.

85. "The Seeds of Doom" Written by Robert Banks Stewart; Directed by Douglas Camfield; Designed by Jeremy Bear; Parts I–VI; Airdates: January 31, February 7, 14, 21, 28, March 6, 1976

SYNOPSIS: At Antarctica Camp 3, scientists Moberly, Winlett and Stevenson unearth a vegetable pod the size of a basketball. This strange pod was buried nine layers deep in the ice, which means it is over 20,000 years old, and from the late Pleistocene Period. Pictures of this amazing discovery are transmitted back to England, and Sir Colin Thackeray and Deputy Dunbar of the World Ecology Bureau decide they need the help of a scientific advisor in uncovering the mysteries of the pod's origin. They contact UNIT, and the Doctor and Sarah are soon involved.

Almost instantly, the Doctor suspects that the pod originated not on Earth, but on a distant planet. He asks that an urgent message be sent to Antarctica instructing the scientists to keep the pod under constant guard. The Doctor and Sarah then head immediately for Antarctica themselves. When they arrive, they learn that the Doctor's instructions have not been obeyed, and that the "Krynoid" pod has attacked one of the scientists.

The Krynoids are "galactic weeds" that travel through the universe. Seeds are dispersed by mother plants across space and they land on planets. Once safely on a world, the pods release parasitic shoots which attack animal life. Those infected organisms are then transformed into adult Krynoids. The Doctor warns that another adult Krynoid could consume all life on Earth in a matter of days. The Doctor's troubles escalate as a crazy millionaire and plant lover named Chase becomes obsessed with the acquisition of the Krynoid pod, a second Krynoid pod is discovered to be at large, and an adult Krynoid approaches primary germination...

GUEST CAST: Moberly (Michael McStay); Stevenson (Hubert Rees); Winlett (John Gleeson); Sir Colin Thackery (Michael Barrington); Deputy Dunbar (Kenneth Gilbert); Harrison Chase (Tony Beckley); Scorby (John Challis); Hargreaves the Butler (Seymour Green); Keeler (Mark Jones); Major Beresford (UNIT) (John Acheson); Sgt. Henderson (Ray Barron); Chauffeur (Alan Chuntz); Amelia Ducat (Sylvia Coleridge); Guards (Harry Fielder, David Masterman); Voice of the Krynoid (Mark Jones)

COMMENTARY: Season 13 ends with a non-stop blast of excitement entitled "The Seeds of Doom." Once again, *Doctor Who* returns to the territory of *The Thing from Another World* (1951) for a story about an extra-terrestrial entity found buried in the ice. Like "The Ice Warriors" in Season 5 or "Gethsemane" on *The X Files* in 1997, this discovery leads to much terrestrial and extraterrestrial trouble. The primary cause of the difficulty in "Seeds of Doom" is not just the frightening Krynoid, a creature whose rapid growth and voracious appetite is truly frightening, but the human turncoat Harrison Chase. As a *Doctor Who* nemesis, Chase is very much in the tradition of Mavic Chen in "The Dalek Masterplan" or Tobias Vaughn in "The Invasion." He is a man who sides with the enemy and encourages an invasion. This familiar type is given a strange twist in "The Seeds of Doom" in that he is depicted as a plant lover. He loves plants so much that he wants them to rule the Earth! Just ponder it: Love is the basis for the destruction of the human race!

"The Seeds of Doom" follows the entire life cycle of the Krynoid monster and has an epic scope only imagined on shows such as *Star Trek*. As usual, however, the imagination of the writer far exceeds the limited production budget. Although Banks-Stewart has written of a giant monster destroying a mansion, the miniature effects are not at all satisfactory in depicting this event. In the tradition of the Godzilla films, the Krynoid is obviously a man in a suit, or rather a "tent." Also rather hokey are the UNIT laser weapons which fire light pulses. The laser blasts resemble giant "flashes" from modern cameras, not deadly beams of light. Even with these problems, "The Seeds of Doom" is a serial filled with action and adventure. The suspense mounts as the Krynoid grows stronger and stronger. Perhaps that is why it all works so well. Whenever faced with a villain that changes, grows and increases in strength, the mood of *Doctor Who* gets frenetic. "The Seeds of Doom" is no exception. By the time Sarah and the Doctor are fleeing the Chase mansion and facing assault by angry plants, the show has taken a frantic turn.

Alien plant life also formed the basis of "The Rules of Luton," a *Space: 1999* episode by Fred Freiberger, and later re-appeared as a threat in *Doctor Who* in "Terror of the Vervoids." The Krynoids never made a reappearance in the series despite their effectiveness in this story.

Perhaps the only disappointment in "The Seeds of Doom" is the absence of Nicholas Courtney as the Brigadier. Just as in "The Android Invasion," UNIT is seen to be under the charge of a less-than-satisfactory replacement. The Brigadier would also not appear in the Season 14 Earth–based story "The Hand of Fear."

"Seeds of Doom" author Robert Banks-Stewart also penned a 1966 episode of *Adam Adamant Lives!* entitled "The Sweet Smell of Disaster." The producer of that series was none other than Verity Lambert, the first producer of *Doctor Who* back in 1963.

"The Seeds of Doom" is available on videocassette.

SEASON 14

86. "The Masque of Mandragora" Written by Louis Marks; Directed by Rodney Bennett; Designed by Barry Newbery; Parts I–IV; Airdates: September 4, 11, 18, 25, 1976

SYNOPSIS: While the Doctor and Sarah transfer the TARDIS' control to an auxiliary command center, the craft is pulled into a cosmic vortex — a spiral of strange space crystals. This is the Mandragora Helix, an energy force that exists in space near Earth. A red meteor of helix energy heads right for them and infiltrates the TARDIS. Unknowingly, the Doctor and Sarah bring this evil energy to Earth when they arrive in the village of San Martino in fifteenth century Italy. The Mandragora life form joins forces with the destructive Demnos cult and plans to destroy a banquet where several philosophers, scholars and rulers (including the Duke of Padua, the King of Geneva, Senora of Florence and Leonardo Da Vinci) are in attendance. In other words, it is a perfect time to interfere in the Renaissance and plunge mankind back into the darkness of fear and hatred! The Demnos cult, which has existed since the third century B.C. in ancient Rome, is the perfect power base for the Mandragora energy. Somehow, the Doctor must stop this unholy alliance of alien energy and human evil.

GUEST CAST: Count Federico (Jon Laurimore); Capt. Rossini (Antony Corrick); Giuliuano (Gareth Armstrong); Marco (Tim Pigott-Smith); Hieronymous (Norman Jones); High Priest (Robert James); Soldiers (James Appleby, John Clamp, Pat Gorman); Pikemen (Peter Walshe, Jay Neill); Titan Voice (Peter Tuddenham); Dancers (Peggy Dixon, Jack Edwards, Alistair Fullarton, Michael Reid, Kathy Wolff); Entertainer (Stuart Fell)

COMMENTARY: Louis Marks' "The Masque of Mandragora" has the honor of having been filmed on location at Portmeiron, the charming town designed by

Sir William-Ellis which doubled as the inescapable "The Village" in Patrick McGoohan's classic series *The Prisoner*. Beyond visual appeal, this serial also has the distinction of being the first *Doctor Who* to occur before the twentieth century since the Jon Pertwee story "The Time Warrior" in Season 11. The subjects of this historical tale are superstition, astrology and the dawn of the Renaissance. If the Doctor is unable to save mankind from the dark forces of the Mandragora Energy Helix, man will be forever doomed to live in the shadow of the Dark Ages. Of course, the Doctor does win out and the Renaissance occurs.

The Mandragora Helix is not a particularly frightening or effective villain, as it is just a ball of red energy. It needs a human being to take on a "face," and so the thrust of this story is mostly escape and capture, a common time-waster in far too many *Who* serials. Still, Tom Baker handles the action elements nicely. He indulges in swordplay, escapes on a horse and is constantly involved in fisticuffs. All of this physical action proves that Pertwee's era had left an indelible mark on the series. It would not be until McCoy's era that the Doctor was again less than a physically fit action hero. In McCoy's era, it was the Doctor's companion Ace who was involved in the fight scenes!

Of all Marks' teleplays, including "Planet of Evil," "Planet of Giants," "Day of the Daleks" and "The Masque of Mandragora," this serial is the one that is perhaps most sumptuously realized. Everything from costume to set design is quite impressive. The story, if not as innovative as "Planet of Evil," is at least diverting. It is also the first story to introduce the TARDIS' second control room. This set is beautifully Victorian in style with wood panels and an ornate central control panel. An effort is made to suggest that the second Doctor, Patrick Troughton, preferred this control room. His recorder is even found in it. However, this control room was never seen in the Troughton era. It is interesting that references to Troughton's era are made with both the recorder in "The Masque of Mandragora" and Victoria's dress in "Pyramids of Mars." Was this because the producers recognized that Baker had more in common with the eccentric, lovable Troughton than either Hartnell or Pertwee? Or was it an acknowledgment that many people felt the series was at its best and most innovative during Troughton's reign?

"The Masque of Mandragora" is available on videocassette.

87. "The Hand of Fear" Written by Bob Baker & Dave Martin; Directed by Lennie Mayne; Designed by Christine Ruscoe; Parts I–IV; Airdates: October 2, 9, 16, 23, 1976

SYNOPSIS: The TARDIS materializes in a giant quarry in England. The Doctor and Sarah are unaware that explosives have been set there, and are caught in a massive detonation. The Doctor is wounded but safe, but Sarah is found injured in the rubble, grasping a most strange fossil: a severed humanoid hand! This strange artifact is the hand of Eldrad, a silicon-based life form from the planet Kastria. In short order, Eldrad has possessed Sarah, attacked a nuclear power station and become obsessed with resurrecting its entire body. When Eldrad grows incredibly powerful, the Doctor is forced to take Eldrad back to Kastria, where he/she/it plans to avenge itself upon the populace that shattered its body millions of generations ago.

GUEST CAST: Dr. Carter (Rex Robinson); Intern (Renu Setna); Abbott (David Purcell); King Rokon (Roy Skelton); Guard (Robin Hargrave); Prof. Watson (Glyn Houston); Driscoll (Roy Boyd); Miss Jackson (Frances Pidgeon); Elgin (John Cannon); Eldrad (Judith Paris); Kastrian Eldrad (Stephen Thorne)

COMMENTARY: "The Hand of Fear" is a splendid *Doctor Who* serial. Like "The Three Doctors," "The Daemons" and "Pyramids of Mars," it concerns a villain who longs for vengeance after many generations in captivity or exile. Like Omega, Azal and Sutekh, Eldrad is the embodiment of awakening evil. Undoubtedly this gallery of villains represents *Doctor Who*'s philosophy about the nature of evil: it may rest ... but it never dies! Just as Sutekh was once dealt with by Horus, so was Eldrad once thought vanquished by King Rokon of Kastria. One must remain ever vigilant, or the villains long ago thought destroyed will return to take over once more. Perhaps this is *Doctor Who*'s view of contemporary politics: preparedness is all, or old enemies will crawl out of the woodwork.

"The Hand of Fear" also utilizes the imagery of another horror film subgenre: the living hand! The severed hand which walks on its own digits has been seen in *The Beast With Five Fingers* (1947) starring Peter Lorre and *The Hand* (1981) starring Michael Caine, to name just two. The concept has become so familiar that it has been ridiculed in the genre spoofs *Evil Dead II: Dead by Dawn* (1987) and of course *The Addams Family* (1991), which features the playful "Thing." The crawling hand effects of "The Hand of Fear" are handled quite competently.

Proving again the diversity of *Doctor Who*'s video and filmic sources, "The Hand of Fear" is also a silicon life form story, another standby of all sci-fi television. Considerably more malevolent than the Horta in *Star Trek*'s "Devil in the Dark," the rock monsters in *Space: 1999*'s "All That Glisters" and the MicroBrain of *The Next Generation*'s "Home Soil," Eldrad is the only silicon-based life form in television history who assumes humanoid form. And what a form it is! When Eldrad first appears in her female guise, she is a shapely, purple-skinned creature with glowing reflective stones and lavender crystals accentuating her beauty. This costume is an elegant one. The later suit, worn by Stephen Thorne, is not as powerful as the shapely female version of Eldrad. Interestingly, Eldrad modeled herself on Sarah's DNA and that is why she becomes female for a time. This is the same conceit used in *Species* (1995); the adult creature Sil in that film resembles Eldrad to a large degree, having an elongated head and flesh that is non-human in appearance.

"The Hand of Fear" is the final serial to feature Elisabeth Sladen (Sarah Jane Smith), who had been with the show since the last Pertwee season. After leaving, Sladen declared she would never again act in the *Doctor Who* universe. To her credit, she reversed that decision and appeared in the *Doctor Who* spin-off *K-9 and Company* as well as the twentieth anniversary special episode "The Five Doctors." Since Tom Baker backed out of the celebratory story, Sladen was again matched with Pertwee for most of her scenes. "The Hand of Fear" culminates in an emotional conclusion when the Doctor and Sarah finally part ways. The scene is a tender one that is well-played by both Baker and Sladen. It is sad to see Sarah go, because she was always such a good companion. Clever, resourceful, witty and sharp, she became the standard-bearer for all future *Doctor Who* females. Sladen left an indelible mark on the series; her farewell is available on videocassette through BBC/CBS-Fox.

88. "The Deadly Assassin" Written by Robert Holmes; Directed by David Maloney; Designed by Roger Murray-Leach; Parts I–IV; Airdates: October 30, November 6, 13, 20, 1976

SYNOPSIS: Inside the TARDIS, the Doctor has a vision of himself in the Panopticon of Gallifrey. He sees himself assassinating the Time Lord President! When the TARDIS materializes on Gallifrey, the Doctor learns it is Presidential Resignation Day, the day the President will resign his office and name his successor. The Doctor knows he must warn the president of the impending danger, but only ends up at the scene of the crime, holding the very rifle that has murdered the President. The Doctor is accused of murder, but already he suspects that he has been framed by an old enemy: the Master! Now the Doctor must follow the Master into the Time Lord matrix, a computer system containing all of Time Lord History and knowledge. Inside the machine, however, the Master is waiting....

GUEST CAST: Chancellor Goth (Bernard Horsfall); Castellan Spandrell (George Pravda); Coordinator Engin (Erik Chitty); Commander Hildred (Derek Seaton); Commentator Runcible (Hugh Walters); Cardinal Borusa (Angus McKay); The President (Lewellyn Rees); Gold Usher (Maurice Quick); Time Lords (John Dawson, Michael Bilton); The Master (Peter Pratt); Solis (Peter Maycock); Transgram Voice (Helen Batch)

COMMENTARY: The Master's first appearance since 1973's "Frontier in Space" is another action-packed *Doctor Who* adventure full of intrigue and excitement. The political assassination aspects of the story recall John Frankenheimer's *The Manchurian Candidate* (1962), but *Doctor Who* proves again that it ahead of its time by introducing a marvelous new device to the series at the same time that it exploits the old assassination subplot. In this case, the device of importance is the data storage system called the Matrix. The Matrix, in which a person's mind actually "enters" another reality, predicts the advent of virtual reality in the late '80s and early '90s. In truth, "The Deadly Assassin" is a virtual reality story before virtual reality existed! Later sci-fi productions such as William Shatner's *Tek War* (1995) have also included a virtual reality world identically termed "The Matrix." Films such as *The Lawnmower Man* (1992), *Disclosure* (1994) and *Virtuosity* (1995) also featured virtual reality confrontations not unlike the ones seen first in *Doctor Who* in 1976! The Disney film *Tron* (1982) also followed in "The Deadly Assassin"'s footsteps by depicting the otherworldly interior of an advanced computer. It is truly amazing that *Doctor Who* predicted virtual reality technology and visited the interior mind of a computer long before the premiere of *Star Wars* and the Atari–video game revolution of the late '70s. Author Robert Holmes deserves much credit for his forward-thinking teleplay. "The Deadly Assassin" is 20 years ahead of its time.

The "virtual reality" combat between Goth (the Master's pawn) and the Doctor is rehashed in the final confrontation between the Valeyard and the sixth incarnation of the Doctor in "The Ultimate Foe" episode of "The Trial of the Time Lord." Interestingly, several elements inside the Matrix in "The Deadly Assassin" also mimic the imaginary apparitions of the pleasure planet in the classic *Star Trek* story "Shore Leave." In both adventures, a Samurai and a biplane are featured as "mental" menaces for the heroes. What is even stranger than this repetition is that in "The Trial of the Time Lord" the Time Lords insist that the Matrix cannot be corrupted. Have they completely forgotten the events of "The Deadly Assassin"? Not only has the Matrix system been corrupted, it has been completely subverted. The Master is the final authority in this virtual reality world!

"The Deadly Assassin" also has historic value because it is the first story since 1973 to feature action on Gallifrey. Once more, exposure to the Time Lord planet results in demystification of the advanced race. Obviously the creative team which had developed the Time Lords as menacing, telepathic giants with the power of life and death was long gone. Now the Time Lords are no more mysterious or advanced than the Vulcans on *Star Trek*. The Time Lords are supposed to be the most advanced race in the cosmos. Somehow in realistic color and with the typically low *Who* budget, their civilization seems less than impressive. Also, the fact that Time Lord politics are seen to be much as the same as Earth politics is a disappointment. The more the audience sees the Time Lords, the more Gallifrey seems just like planet Earth.

The second historical point of interest in "The Deadly Assassin" is that this is the only *Who* serial in history in which the Doctor is not accompanied by any companion whatsoever. As a result, Baker spends much time talking to himself, obviously for the benefit of any confused viewers. Sherlock Holmes should never be without Watson, as this story proves.

The Master returned in his desiccated, dying form in "The Keeper of Traken" before metamorphosing into actor Anthony Ainley. The Matrix and Time Lord politics would again play critical roles in "The Invasion of Time," "Arc of Infinity" and "The Trial of the Time Lord." Like most stories in Season 12–14, "The Deadly Assassin" also features a high level of physical action. For these reasons, Baker's early years are extremely popular in America. The notion that battles can be won through a well-placed right cross, a staple of the original *Star Trek*, is a traditional, comforting one that makes *Doctor Who* seem less British and more accessible to American audiences. Though it is a violation of the Doctor's essentially non-violent nature, it nonetheless makes for exciting television.

"The Deadly Assassin" is available on videocassette through BBC/CBS-Fox home video.

89. "The Face of Evil" Written by Chris Boucher; Directed by Pennant Roberts; Designed by Austin Ruddy; Parts I–IV; Airdates: January 1, 8, 15, 22, 1977

SYNOPSIS: The Doctor arrives in a splintered society. Out in the jungle live the savages of the Sevateem. Hidden up in a mountain with their advanced technology is the tribe called the Tesh. When the Doctor befriends Leela, a savage warrior of the Sevateem, he learns that both tribes are descended from a spaceship crash many generations ago. Even worse, the Sevateem (Survey Team) and Tesh (Technicians) are both being menaced by a megalomaniacal computer called Xoanon. When the Doctor sees that Xoanan's face matches his own, he realizes he has been on this planet before...

GUEST CAST: Xoanan (Tom Baker, Rob Edwards, Anthony Frieze, Roy Herrick, Pamela Salem); Andor (Victor Lucas); Calib (Leslie Schofield); Tomas (Brendan Price); Sole (Colin Thomas); Neeva (David Garfield); Lugo (Lloyd McGuire); Guards (Tom Kelly, Brett Forest); Jabel (Leon Eagles); Gentek (Mike Elles); Acolyte (Peter Baldock)

COMMENTARY: "The Face of Evil" is another full scale, action packed *Doctor Who* triumph. It features the splintered, savage societies seen in genre films like *Zardoz* (1973) as well as in earlier *Doctor Who* episodes such as "The Savages." Also in evidence is the monster from the id concept, a highlight of *Forbidden Planet* (1956). Despite these familiar sources, the central conflict of the serial is a fresh one because the Doctor is drawn into the conflict between Xoanan, the Tesh and the Sevateem by a mistake he made in his past. Rarely does the Doctor face the consequences of his past actions; this is a notable and dramatic exception to that rule. Here, viewers learn for the first time that the Doctor sneaked out on UNIT during the events of "Robot." Because the Doctor was erratic at that time, having just regenerated, he ended up on this distant world and repaired the computer Xoanan ... sharing his mental imprint with it. Since he was unstable at the time, the computer became unstable as well!

In "The Face of Evil," the Doctor must undo the damage he has done to the computer Xoanan, a descendent of such crazed computers as HAL in *2001: A Space Odyssey* (1968) and Colossus in *Colossus: The Forbin Project* (1968). In some senses the evil Xoanan, with its penchant for self-preservation and deceitful relationship with human beings, might also be seen as a precursor to later mad computers such as Proteus in *Demon Seed* (1977) and the Nostromo computer, affectionately called "Mother," in Ridley Scott's *Alien* (1979).

Chris Boucher, the author of "The Face of Evil," contributed a dynamic teleplay. He peppers the story with action, and the monsters of Xoanan's subconscious are well-dramatized by the special effects crew in much the same manner as the anti-matter aliens in "Planet of Evil." Boucher soon became a regular fixture of the season; he went on to write the excellent "The Robots of Death," one of the ten best *Doctor Who* serials, and "Image of the Fendahl." His credentials as a sci-fi television writer extraordinaire are also cemented by his many writing efforts on Terry Nation's stellar television series *Blake's 7*. For that space adventure he penned "Shadow," "Weapon," "Trial," "Star One" (1979), "The City at the Edge of the World," "Rumors of Death" and "Deathwatch" (1980). In 1981 he wrote

Louise Jameson accompanied the fourth incarnation of the Doctor as the savage huntress Leela in episode #89, "The Face of Evil."

"Rescue" and the final episode of the series, "Blake." In the '80s, Boucher formulated his own vision, the short-lived *Star Cops* (1987).

Boucher's lively "The Face of Evil" teleplay is given form by inspired direction from Pennant Roberts, director of "Time Squad," "Mission to Destiny" and "Bounty" on *Blake's 7*. Before "The Face of Evil" he had directed episodes of the Gerry Davis–Kit Pedler science fact-fiction series *Doomwatch*, including "Waiting for a Knighthood" and "Enquiry" in 1972.

Most delightful of all in "The Face of Evil" is the arrival of Louise Jameson as the huntress Leela. This fine actress brings danger, humor and pure sex appeal to her portrayal of this "primitive" warrior. Like Sladen before her, Jameson immediately establishes a rapport with Baker's Fourth Doctor. These two performers would go on to share many delightful "companion" moments. The only sad thing about Louise Jameson's Leela is the fact that the role would not last. The character appeared on *Doctor Who* for only a fleeting season and a half. Still, Jameson is the first woman allowed to fulfill the role of "action hero" which actors William Russell, Peter Purves, Michael Craze and Frazer Hines filled in the early days of the series. Also, Leela is surely the direct predecessor of the physically active Dalek–basher Ace, the last companion during the 26-year run of *Doctor Who*. Leela is an enormously appealing character not only because she is spirited and physically competent. Since she is from a primitive culture, the Doctor often has to explain technical and historical details to her. This causes some very funny exchanges between the super-advanced Time Lord and the super-primitive huntress. *Doctor Who* had not been able to exploit this kind of dynamic since Jamie, another so-called "primitive," travelled with Troughton's second incarnation of the Doctor.

90. "The Robots of Death" Written by Chris Boucher; Directed by Michael Briant; Designed by Kenneth Sharp ; Parts I–IV; Airdates: January 29, February 5, 12, 19, 1977

SYNOPSIS: The Doctor and Leela step out of the TARDIS to find they are aboard a huge, tank-like vehicle traversing a windswept desert planet. They have also landed in trouble: Crew members on the colossal rig are being murdered by an unseen assailant who leaves "corpse markers" on each victim. The corpse markers are typically used to signify when a humanoid-robot has been destroyed, so someone who has a familiarity with robots is behind the deaths. The Doctor and Leela find that this crew and its society are completely dependent on robots. There are three models on this rig: the Dumbs (mute robots), the Vox and the SuperVox. The Doctor quickly deduces that the robots have overcome their peaceful programming and are killing humans.

Things get even more complicated when the Doctor discovers that crewman Poole and a robot named D84 are actually agents sent by "the Company" to discover what is amiss on the rig. Surprisingly, the robots are not to blame after all! They have been reprogrammed by a brilliant human scientist named Taryn Kapel. Raised by robots, Kapel believes that the machines must rise up and kill their human masters. He has overridden the prime directive of the robots so they will do just that. Now the Doctor and Leela are caught amidst Kapel's robot revolution....

GUEST CAST: Commander Uvanov (Russell Hunter); Toos (Pamela Salem); Dask (David Ballie); Pow (David Collings); Borg (Brian Croucher); Zilda (Tania Rogers); Cass (Tariq Yunus); Chub (Rob Edwards); D84 (Gregory De Polnay); SV7 (Miles Fothergill); Robots (John Bleasdale, Mark Cooper, Peter Langtry, Jeremy Ranchev, Richard Seager, Mark Blackwell Baker)

COMMENTARY: "The Robots of Death" is one of the ten best *Doctor Who* serials for a variety of reasons. From a visual standpoint alone, the episode is unique and beautifully done. The costumes and sets are uniformly lavish. The robots are streamlined creatures garbed in Oriental serving clothes to suggest their status as "underlings." Their faces are "polite" masks consisting of thick plastic lips, wide inhuman eyes and a molded mop of curly hair. Thus they are pleasing to look at as they perform their duties. In other words, the robots are the smiling faces of the underclass ... pleasant to look at as they toil for their masters.

By contrast, the men and women aboard the mining craft wear elegant, impractical costumes that sparkle in a gaudy, decadent fashion. Each human character is also garbed in an ornate headdress, to indicate his or her individuality (in contrast to the robots' conformity). Their human eyes are also heavily made-up to give them a regal, far Eastern appearance. The makeup also lends to the feeling that these humans are concerned only with physical appearance and "outward" surface values such as wealth and physical beauty. Too often on *Doctor Who* the costumes are of a clichéd, "Buck Rogers" future vision with aliens garbed in capes, silver epaulets and tights. Not so here. The costumes and makeup are masterfully evocative of an alien culture indulgent in its own luxury. This echoes the main theme of the serial, that robots have become the new underclass of the galaxy while humanoids dedicate themselves totally to leisure.

The luxurious interior of the mining vessel, more like a massive ocean liner than a utilitarian working mining vessel, is also nicely contrasted with the planet exterior. Outside there is no luxury at all: only wind and endless dunes of sand. Despite the reality of this situation, the crew members carry on *inside* as if they do not have a care in the world. They gossip, indulge in feasts and insult one another with self-assuredness. They do not realize how unsafe their cocooned environment has become.

Beyond the many visual flourishes, "The Robots of Death" is a grand mystery in the tradition of Agatha Christie's *Murder on the Orient Express*. Each character aboard the craft has a mysterious past, a secret identity and a reason to kill. This duplicity makes the mystery an engrossing one, and the guest characters are well-played. Commander Uvanov is particularly three-dimensional. He begins the story as a cruel, cold commander, but once he has been fingered as the murderer he develops a more "humane" demeanor. In the end, he has forsaken the symbols of his culture and rank (i.e., arrogance and cruelty) and helped solve the mystery. It is rare when there is a believable character arc on *Doctor Who* among the guest cast, but Uvanov bucks the odds and comes across as a realistic human being. The remainder of the cast, all possessing secrets and spewing venom with expertise, are also strong performers.

One of the most innovative aspects of "The Robots of Death" is Chris Boucher's conceit that there is secretly an agent of "the Company" monitoring events on the craft. This conceit has become *de rigeuer* for Hollywood science fiction movies in the '80s and '90s. Ash is a company representative in *Alien* (1979), Burke is one in the sequel *Aliens* (1986) and Benny secretly represents Martian government interests in *Total Recall* (1990). The "false" team member who harbors a secret has also appeared in *Species* (1995) (Ben Kingsley), *Predator* (1987) (Carl Weathers) and *Leviathan* (1989) (Richard Crenna). *Doctor Who* anticipates the importance of this convention in "The Robots of Death" by making David Collings a secret agent. Even more unconventionally, Collings' Agent Pow is a useless secret agent! He becomes paralyzed by his fear of robots, and is unable to accomplish his mission. Collings returned to *Doctor Who* in the Davison–era story "Mawdryn Undead." He also played the elemental force "Silver" in the cult British series *Sapphire and Steele*.

The robot rebellion in "The Robots of Death" is presented with great style. Michael Briant shoots the murders of the crew from point-of-view, subjective perspective, keeping the identity of the culprit a secret. The final sequence, in which the killer robots roam the ship and attempt to penetrate the bridge, is an effective climax and one that recalls the action-packed conclusion of the earlier "Planet of Evil."

Best of all, there is an engaging subtext concerning the nature of a class society. The robots are essentially slaves in this alien culture. Yet they are unfailingly polite and servile ... or are they? The humans treat the robots only as things, never granting the robots such basic "human" rights as courtesy or even civility. The leisure-minded humans have become so comfortable treating the robots in this fashion that they are unable to conceive of "killer" robots. In fact, humans have grown so lazy and complacent that their race would die out without the robots who serve them and maintain their culture. *Doctor Who* is thus taking an opportunity to comment on the acceptance of poverty and solitude by the upper class. The humans have become so conditioned to the bad treatment of the robots that their eyes are closed to the danger the lower class truly represents to them. The status quo between the rich and the poor will not remain unchanged, "The Robots of Death" warns, even when the lower class is robotic! This is certainly a cautionary tale that touches on issues of race relations, a class society and even the eventuality of race warfare. All it takes to inspire the lower class to rebel is one man with a taste for power. In this case, that man is Taryn Kapel, a man who grew up with robots and saw how unfairly they were exploited by society.

"The Robots of Death" is a brilliant serial filled with danger, humor and intrigue. It is available on videocassette.

91. "The Talons of Weng-Chiang" Written by Robert Holmes; Directed by David Maloney; Designed by Roger Murray-Leach; Parts I–VI; Airdates: February 26, March 5, 12, 19, 26, April 2, 1977

SYNOPSIS: In Victorian London, the Doctor and Leela run afoul of a Chinese magician named Chang and his evil homunculus, Mr. Sin. These two villains serve a criminal from Earth's fifty-first century, Magnus Greel, who is known in his own time as "The Butcher of Brisbane." In the far future, Greel was the Minister of Justice of the Supreme Alliance, a man who conducted top secret experiments in time travel; one such experiment, "The Zygma Experiment," brought him back to this time. Unfortunately, he was separated from his Time Cabinet and he now seeks it in Victorian London. Unlike the TARDIS, his method of time travel is unsafe. It has left him drained and dying. To combat the effects of such dangerous time travel, the villainous Greel has been employing a process called organic distillation. He has been draining the life forces of beautiful young females....

GUEST CAST: Li H'Sen Chang (John Bennett); Magnus Greel (Michael Spice); Prof. Litefoot (Trevor Baxter); Jago (Christopher Benjamin); Mr. Sin (Deep Roy); Teresa (Judith Lloyd); Cleaning Woman (Vaune Raymond); Singer (Penny Lister); Ho (Vincent Wong); Lee (Tony Then); Coolie (John Wu); Kyle (David McKail); Ghoul (Patsy Smart)

COMMENTARY: "The Talons of Weng-Chiang" is another great *Doctor Who* serial that follows in the footsteps of "The Daemons" and "Pyramids of Mars." As per the "Daemons" prototype, an unnatural force, this time a man from the future, has inspired legend—this time, ancient Oriental legend. Magnus Greel, Mr. Sin and his dragonhead laser weapon are responsible for the stories of "Weng Chiang," a much-feared god who blows fire from his mouth and whose eyes grow white with otherworldly light. As is usual for *Doctor Who*, the force from the future is exploiting humans for a devious purpose. Here Greel uses the Weng-Chiang myth to gain followers (the Tong) and find a way back to health. Despite the familiar template, "The Talons of Weng-Chiang" is filled with authentic Victorian detail and many frightening moments. It is Grand Guignol at its best, as giant rats gnaw on Londoners and a grotesquely deformed Greel steals the youth and vigor from beautiful young women.

The story is worthwhile not only for its macabre elements and Victorian overlay, however. It is also an entertaining "fish out of water" story with Leela consistently misunderstanding and misinterpreting the behavior of the people around her. By allowing Leela to act as a commentator on Victorian society, author Robert Holmes manages to expose the vicissitudes of that generation. For instance, Prof. Litefoot makes an issue out of talking about death in front of a lady, but of course Leela has seen more death than this man ever will! And isn't it ridiculous that a woman should pretend to be dainty and take only one lump of sugar when she would prefer two? The sexism and traditions of the Victorian era are ridiculed.

It is a pleasure also to finally see the Doctor garbed in the traditional uniform of Sherlock Holmes. The Doctor has always been reminiscent of Arthur Conan Doyle's great detective: he is an expert in deductive reasoning, a brilliant scientist and an eccentric personality. His various companions are equivalent in spirit to John Watson. And, of course, the Doctor even has his own "Moriarty" in the person of the Master. Tom Baker would later play Sherlock Holmes in a BBC production of *The Hound of the Baskervilles*. He is a natural for the part, and he looks good in the accoutrements. Louise Jameson also gets to put her hair up and shed her animal skins in exchange for the regal dress of a Victorian lady. To her credit, she appears appropriately uncomfortable in this garb, just as Leela should.

A touch that is less effective in "Talons of Weng-Chiang" is the casting of Caucasian John Bennett in the role of Chang. Although Bennett is adequate in the part, it is inappropriate that a non–Asian was chosen to play this part. Although Bennett is equipped with prosthetics over his eyes to heighten his resemblance to Asians, it is nonetheless a long-standing entertainment cliché to have Caucasians play Orientals. Chang, with his pidgin English, could easily be interpreted as a racist portrayal of Chinamen.

"The Talons of Weng-Chiang" is a strong serial that adequately ends a very good season. Though it is not as brilliant as "Robots of Death," it is nonetheless further evidence of *Doctor Who*'s maturing production values. Like all stories that season, the production values and historical details of "The Talons of Weng-Chiang" are sterling. Perhaps this is why so many people consider the early Baker era to be the halcyon years of the series. The production values are high, there is searing drama, good science fiction concepts and hard-driving action. There is also witty banter between the Doctor and companions Sarah and Leela. Although the stories may not be as thoroughly inventive as "The War Games," "Tombs of the Cybermen" or "The Aztecs," they are nonetheless sturdy outlines on which to build entertaining serials. So successful were these early Baker seasons that a book about Philip Hinchcliffe's years as producer (Seasons 12 to 14) was published by Boxtree in 1995. Featuring an introduction by Baker, Adrian Rigelsford's *Classic Who: The Hinchcliffe Years, Seasons 12–14* features behind-the-scenes information about the series from "Robot" to "Talons of Weng-Chiang." The thrust of the work is that *Doctor Who* was never better than during these landmark seasons. With excellent stories such as "The Ark in Space," "Genesis of the Daleks," "The Seeds of Doom," "The Face of Evil" and "The Robots of Death" produced during this span, it is easy to understand why such an assertion has been made. It would also be fair to state, however, that *Doctor Who*'s first season, which includes "An Unearthly

Child," "The Daleks," "The Keys of Marinus," "The Aztecs" and the lost "Marco Polo" is every bit as good if not better than any Baker season. Seasons 5 and 6, with "Tomb of the Cybermen," "The Krotons," "The Mind Robber" and "War Games" and Patrick Troughton's delightful portrayal of the Doctor, could also be referred to as a "golden age" in *Who* history.

Of course, Tom Baker's era is more popular today; it is also more accessible than Hartnell or Troughton stories since it was filmed in color and features more advanced special effects. On the other hand, Baker's early days, with their fistfights and sci-fi tropes such as duplicate androids, killer plants and doppelgangers, is undeniably influenced by the success of the American *Star Trek*.

"The Talons of Weng Chiang" is available on videocassette.

SEASON 15

92. "The Horror of Fang Rock" Written by Terrance Dicks; Directed by Paddy Russell; Designed by Paul Allen; Parts I–IV; Airdates: September 3, 10, 17, 24, 1977

SYNOPSIS: Fang Rock Lighthouse is a beacon in the night for all errant travelers, and on one night it catches the attention of more than one extraterrestrial force. The Doctor and Leela arrive amidst the thick bands of fog, and so does a misplaced Rutan scout! This gelatinous mass of protoplasm, a shape shifter, hails from Ruta 3, an icy planet. The Rutans, who developed in the sea and then adapted to land, are still fighting their endless war with the Sontarans, and this Rutan wants to use Earth as a launch point for a final assault on the Sontarans. With Leela's help, the Doctor uses a blast of gunpowder to force the Rutan scout down the stairs of the lighthouse. Although this gambit stops it momentarily, there is an even larger problem: The Rutan scout has sent a message to a nearby mothership. The Doctor must now contend with the Rutans in orbit as well!

GUEST CAST: Reuben (Colin Douglas); Vince (John Abbott); Ben (Ralph Watson); Col. Skinsale (Alan Rowe); Palmerdale (Sean Caffrey); Adelaide (Annette Woolett); Harker (Rio Fanning)

COMMENTARY: In science fiction and horror films, the lighthouse has long been a location of mystery and terror. John Carpenter used the location to great effect in his 1979 homage to the tradition of ghost stories, *The Fog*. Before that, it appeared in other films, and always seemed to harbor horrible secrets. Humanity's last stand in *The Day of the Triffids* (1963) was at an isolated lighthouse. Bert I. Gordon's *Tormented* (1960) also wove a tale of vengeful ghosts around its lighthouse location. "The Horror of Fang Rock" is a solid sci-fi story, not a supernatural one, but there is the same feeling of gloom evident throughout the story. The legend of the Fang Rock Beast, a creature who rose from the sea 80 years ago to destroy men and women, gives the story an horrific aura that relates it to the supernatural tradition of lighthouse films.

Otherwise, "The Horror of Fang Rock" is another foray into the *Ten Little Indians* prototype. A group of diverse characters gather at an isolated location only to be killed off one by one by a mysterious assailant. This template has been used in hundreds of horror movies, and it recurs many times in *Doctor Who*. "The Ice Warriors," "The Abominable Snowmen," "Robots of Death" and many others fit within this formula. The concept of an alien arriving from space and stalking isolated human beings would recur in the 1987 film *Predator*.

Terrance Dicks' teleplay at last introduces the enemies of the Sontarans. The Rutans had been mentioned as far back as 1974's "The Time Warrior," but never seen. This story reveals them to be a creepy, non-humanoid life form capable of shape-shifting. It is thus an early version of Odo and the Founders, as dramatized on *Star Trek: Deep Space Nine*.

At the climax of "The Horror of Fang Rock," Leela's eyes change colors after the explosion of the Rutan mothership. According to Peter Haining, a *Doctor Who* authority and historian, this event occurred because Louise Jameson's eyes could no longer accommodate the brown contact lenses she had worn since "The Face of Evil." From this story forward, Jameson's beautiful *blue* eyes would be seen on the series.

93. "The Invisible Enemy" Written by Bob Baker & Dave Martin; Directed by Derrick Goodwin; Designed by Barry Newbery; Parts I–IV; Airdates: October 1, 8, 15, 22, 1977

SYNOPSIS: In the year 5000 A.D., Capt. Safran's shuttle is bound for Titan, a moon of Saturn, when it encounters a deadly cloud in space. Shortly before docking at a Titan space station, the crew is infected with an alien virus called "The Nucleus." The compromised shuttle crew takes over the base, and Nucleus determines that it is an ideal place to breed and multiply.

Aboard the TARDIS, Leela and the Doctor pick up a distress call from Titan and set a course for the space station. In mid-flight, the Nucleus intercepts the TARDIS and sends a bolt of energy through the main control unit. The Doctor makes contact with the controls and is zapped by the alien material. Before the Doctor becomes host to the Nuclues, miniaturized clones of Leela and the Time Lord are sent into his body to combat the infection. The plan fails, and Nucleus's power grows. With the help of a cybernetic dog called K-9, Leela and the Doctor must stop the spread of Nucleus.

GUEST CAST: Station Administrator Lowe (Michael Sheard); Prof. Marius (Frederick Jaeger); Capt. Safran (Brian Gellis); Silvey (Jay Neill); Meeker (Edmund Pegge); Crewman (Anthony Rowlands); Voice of Nucleus (John Leeson); Nucleus Operator (John Scott Martin); Nurses (Nell Curran, Elizabeth Norman); Opthamalogist (Jim McManus); Dr. Cruickshank (Roderick Smith); Hedges (Kenneth Waller); Dr. Parsons (Roy Herrick); Medic (Pat Gorman)

COMMENTARY: "The Invisible Enemy" is an inspired twist on *Fantastic Voyage* (1966). In this case, it is the Doctor and Leela who are miniaturized and sent inside a body (the Doctor's!) to stop the growth of a deadly disease organism. The story is inventive not because it sends miniature clones on the trip, but because it turns the *Fantastic Voyage* scenario on its head. Instead of accomplishing their mission, the miniaturized clones *die* and the disease, a sentient being, escapes through the Doctor's tear ducts and is enlarged to normal size. A heretofore microscopic organism arrives in the real world to divide and conquer! This is a brilliant conceit, and one that improves on the concept motivating the 1966 film. If one believes the oft-heard remark that there are no new stories, only new ways of telling stories, then "The Invisible Enemy" is as original and exciting as any good television drama. The story may have its origin in another production, but there is a high degree of creativity in taking that production to the next step.

On the down side, "The Invisible Enemy" is also one of those infrequent *Doctor Who* serials where there is some bad speculation about science. "The Ice Warriors" predicted the worldwide encroachment of the polar ice caps, an idea made ridiculous in the face of anticipated global warming. Similarly, "The Invisible Enemy" dates the first successful cloning experiment in the year 3922, almost 2000 years after the "factual" year of cloning, 1997! Still, in 1977, who could have known that the miracle of cloning was but 20 years away?

"The Invisible Enemy" is significant for the introduction of the marvelous cybernetic organism K-9. The robot was added to *Doctor Who* to capitalize on the popularity of recent *Star Wars* celebrities R2-D2 and C-3PO. *Battlestar Galactica* would premiere a year after K-9's first appearance; the "cute" robot on that ABC show was another cybernetic dog called Muffitt. Unlike K-9, however, Muffitt was basically a "dumb" robot. It could yap and run around, but it could not fire laser blasts, speak or compute complex mathematical figures. In many senses, K-9 is the perfect companion for the Doctor. He is loyal and tolerant. He is resourceful, and even imaginative. He can also deliver exposition believably, thanks to his powerful memory banks. K-9 perfectly combines the intelligence of a computer and the cuddliness of a dog. He is a wonderful addition to *Doctor Who* and would become the Doctor's all-time most popular traveling companion.

This episode is a winner not only because it introduces K-9 and a twist on *Fantastic Voyage*, but because it widens the believability of the *Doctor Who* universe. The Bi Al Facility, a galactic "General Hospital," is one example of this expansion. Previously, space stations and moonbases had been seen, as well as alien colonies. No medical facilities, however, had been shown in the program. The Bi Al facility introduced here is a believable futuristic installation packed with doctors, nurses and other specialists. This setting would also be the central one of UPN's *Mercy Point* (1998).

The Swarm of the Nucleus also makes for a terrifying new type of villain for this series. This kind of disease entity would become "in fashion" in the mid-'90s in the UPN series *The Burning Zone* (1996). *Star Trek: Voyager* featured a 1997 story entitled "Macrovirus" which also concerned a disease organism's unprecedented "growth" into the human world.

A Time Lord's best friend, K-9, was introduced in episode #93, "The Invisible Enemy." Artwork by Mindy Easler.

Fans watching for repeat guest stars should recognize not only Michael Sheard of "Pyramids of Mars," but also Frederick Jeager, who portrayed Prof. Sorenson in "Planet of Evil."

94. "Image of the Fendahl" Written by Chris Boucher; Directed by George Spenton-Foster; Designed by Anna Ridley; Parts I–IV; Airdates: October 29, November 5, 12, 19, 1977

SYNOPSIS: On twentieth century Earth, a human skull has been found beneath a dormant volcano. It is over eight million years old, which means it existed long before human life evolved on Earth. Working within an English priory, Dr. Fendelman activates a dark force inside the skull. Using an X-ray machine, he has found a pentagram lining the back of the find. He believes this symbol is a neural relay wherein an enormous supply of energy is stored.

Shortly after his arrival, the Doctor fears that the Fendahlin, a creature from Time Lord mythology, is involved. He returns to the TARDIS with Leela and heads for the home planet of the Fendahl (designated by Time Lords as "The Fifth Planet"). According to myth, it was destroyed 12 million years ago, but the Doctor finds that the planet is actually caught up in a repeating time loop. The Time Lords have intervened to keep that world from affecting the rest of the universe.

Returning to Earth, the Doctor learns that Dr. Stael, the leader of a local coven, has captured scientist Thea Ransome to use in his worship of the alien Fendahl. The ancient skull transforms Thea into a Fendahl. Thea becomes the center of a gestalt hive-mind, defended by 12 Fendahlin worm organisms. Dr. Fendelman also learns that his name means "Man of the Fendahl" and that it has always been his programmed destiny to bring the Fendahl back. The Fendahl programmed man's evolution so one day man would recover the skull and reactivate the species. Using the tools of black magic, including salt, the Doctor fends off the alien worms....

GUEST CAST: Thea Ransome (Wanda Ventham); Martha Tyler (Daphne Heard); Dr. Fendelman (Denis Lill); Ted Moss (Edward Evans); Maximillian Stael (Scott Fredericks); Adam Colby (Edward Arthur); David Mitchell (Derek Martin); Hiker (Graham Simpson); Jack Tyler (Geoffrey Hinsliff)

COMMENTARY: Chris Boucher's third contribution to *Doctor Who* is probably his weakest. Although the teleplay is interesting, it once more owes a clear debt to the "Daemons" prototype. Last seen in "The Talons of Weng-Chiang," this overused plot template is again called in to service a *Doctor Who* serial. Ancient legends and superstitions, again relating to demonology, actually reflect an alien life form which visited Earth in antiquity. Symbols such as the pentagram are *actually* related to that alien. And, of course, traditional occult tools such as salt are used to vanquish the alien. Once more *Doctor Who* owes a great deal to *Quatermass and the Pit* (1967), a film which began in an identical fashion to "Image of the Fendahl." In that film, it was a five-million-year-old skull that was discovered. In "Image of the Fendahl," it is an eight-million-year-old skull that triggers events. Since "Image of the Fendahl" does not even bother to modify the "Daemons" prototype to incorporate a mythology other than ancient black magic and demonology, it can be seen as a pretty straight remake of "The Daemons." At least "Pyramids of Mars," "The Talons of Weng-Chiang" and "The Terror of the Zygons" drew on different ethnic legends.

Doctor Who's return to the "Daemons" prototype can be seen in two different lights. The first is perhaps a more flattering explanation. One can say that *Doctor*

Who, by reusing this story in at least five serials, features a consistent thematic thread throughout its run. The series postulates repeatedly that the basis of human legend is not human imagination, but alien intervention. The repetition of the prototype is thus intentional.

The less flattering view of the repetition is merely that *Doctor Who* recycles the same story out of lack of creativity, or laziness. Of course, even if one were to take the view that *Doctor Who* set out to purposefully "explain" the origins of ancient mythology, the series cannot necessarily be praised for this effort. After all, *Quatermass and the Pit* popularized the concept at an earlier time. *Doctor Who* is thus a subscriber to formula, not an inventor. Also, *Star Trek* played with this idea in the 1960s. The *Enterprise* encountered the god Apollo in "Who Mourns for Adonais." They found that this "god" was merely an extraterrestrial who once lived on Mount Olympus. "Who Mourns for Adonais" played into the "Daemons" prototype before "The Daemons" aired.

Nevertheless, "Image of the Fendahl" is an engrossing serial. The story opens at night. A lone camper is pursued through a misty forest by the unseen forces of evil. This scene is evocative of many horror films, including *An American Werewolf in London* (1981) in which hikers stray onto the fog-covered moors and are attacked by werewolves. As usual, *Doctor Who* uses standard horror film imagery to elevate its story of an ancient evil once more awakening. The gestalt organism is another version of Sutekh, Azal or Eldrad, a vanquished evil waiting to be activated through man's tampering. "Image of the Fendahl" also represents the age of the horror *Who*. In seasons 12–15 there is an abundance of horror imagery. This element would soon be abandoned in favor of a satirical view of the universe. By Davison's era, horror was nearly gone from the format, replaced with sci-fi potboilers.

"Image of the Fendahl" marks the second appearance of three-time *Doctor Who* guest star Wanda Ventham. She would return in the premiere of the seventh Doctor, "Time and the Rani."

Director George Spenton-Foster made his debut on the Time Lord's series with "Image of the Fendahl." He conducts this story effectively yet it is hard to overcome the repetitive plot elements. Spenton-Foster cut his teeth in the genre by producing the anthology series *Out of the Unknown* (1965–1971). In 1965 and 1966 respectively he directed "The Counterfeit Man" and "Lambda I." After he helmed "The Ribos Operation" in Season 16 of *Doctor Who*, he moved on to helm several episodes of its BBC sister series *Blake's 7*, including "Weapon," "Pressure Point" and "Voice from the Past" (1979).

Curious fans could make an interesting day of television viewing by screening "Image of the Fendahl," now on videocassette, after watching the Pertwee–era serial "The Daemons." Such a comparison would reveal just how little originality is evident in this serial. The main point of interest is not the central plot, or the frightening theme that an ancient evil has been guiding human evolution, but that the Time Lords dealt with the Fendahl by erecting a time loop around their world. This echoes their punishment of the War Lord and his people in Serial 50, "The

War Games," and puts truth to the lie that Time Lords never "interfere" in galactic events. It is also interesting to learn that the Fendahl affected not only Earth mythology, but Time Lord mythology as well. A young Doctor once heard the fairy tale of the Fendahl, and was obviously frightened by it. After the ease with which the Doctor dispatches the Fendahl in this story, it is difficult to understand why the Fendahl are considered so fearsome. Disappointing in "Image of Fendahl" is K-9's absence from the action. After his promising debut in "The Invisible Enemy," his cameo appearance here does not satisfy. Fortunately, the charming robot would see action in the next serial, "The Sunmakers."

Wanda Ventham, seen here as SHADO's resourceful Colonel Lake in the series *U.F.O.*, appeared on three episodes of *Doctor Who* including "The Faceless Ones" (episode #35), "Image of the Fendahl" (episode #94), and "Time and the Rani" (episode #148).

95. "The Sunmakers" Written by Robert Holmes; Directed by Pennant Roberts; Designed by Tony Snoaden; Parts I–IV; Airdates: November 26, December 3, 10, 17, 1977

SYNOPSIS: The TARDIS lands on Pluto where there is a breathable atmosphere and a huge technological city. The governing body of this planet is the Company. Officials in the Company become aware that the TARDIS has landed illegally on the roof. There is a huge fine for such a thing — 500 talmars. The Gatherers are dispatched to collect the money and discover more about the TARDIS. The Doctor and Leela flee the Tax Gatherers and end up in the Undercity where tax evaders and outlaws called "The Others" exist. The Doctor and Leela learn that Pluto has six artificial suns circling it, one for each Megropolis, and all are provided by the Company at cost. The people are taxed heavily for the suns by an alien creature called a Usurian. The all-important Collector, Chief Representative of the Company, becomes aware of the Doctor's history of economic disruption and orders him liquidated.

GUEST CAST: Citizen Cordo (Roy Macready); Gatherer Marn (Jonina Scott); Goudry (Michael Keating); Gatherer Hade (Richard Leach); Synge (Derek Crewe); Mandrel (William Simon); Veet (Adrienne Burgess); Collector/Usurian (Henry Woolf); Nurse (Carole Hopkin); Guard (Tom Kelly)

COMMENTARY: "The Sunmakers" is a delightful *Doctor Who* serial full of wit and parody. The Robert Holmes teleplay is rife with satirical jabs at the bureaucracy and tax practices of the British government. In being so pointedly absurd and overtly humorous, "The Sunmakers" forecasts the path that future *Whos* would take. The predilection for horror tropes ("Planet of Evil," "Pyramids of Mars," "Seeds of Doom," "The Invisible Enemy," "Image of the Fendahl") would soon end, and humor would replace it as the order of the day. "The Sunmakers," however, is quite different from later stories (such as Douglas Adams' farce "The Pirate Planet") in that the satirical elements do not overwhelm the story and compromise the validity of *Doctor Who*'s "reality." In "The Sunmakers," a humorous and satirical situation is at the center of the plot, but the characters and actors do not mock the situation. They do not treat the situation, or the *Doctor Who* universe, with overt humor or disdain. Instead, the actors move seriously about their silly tasks, making the serial all the funnier because it is played straight. Once the tongue-in-cheek aspects of Baker's performance overwhelm the series ("The Pirate Planet," "The Ribos Operation"), *Doctor Who* takes a dive in credibility. The result is that the series overall, rather than an individual situation or culture, is mocked.

"The Sunmakers" incorporates humor seamlessly into the *Who* format. Leela has never had the benefit of being "taxed," so it is with great difficulty that she comes to comprehend the situation on Pluto. She likens the paying of taxes to a sacrifice one makes to a god! There are other funny situations in "The Sunmakers," including the final destruction of the Usurian. What better weapon to use against a businessman than the threat of inflation? The absurdity of income, sales and insurance taxing is also uncovered in this story when it is established that the people of Pluto are taxed for the use of the sun! Although this is a ridiculous tax, it makes sense in the situation. Those Usurians spent all that money providing the people with six suns, and they have to have some recompense, right? That absurd logic is what makes "The Sunmakers" so enjoyable. Like the best of science fiction, "The Sunmakers" examines a current problem and then projects it logically and ruthlessly into a futuristic scenario. The creation of an alien race obsessed with profit foreshadows not only the money-grubbing Sil in "Vengeance on Varos," but the alien Ferengi on *Star Trek: The Next Generation*. The Ferengi, like the Usurians in "The Sunmakers," have built their society around money. Everything is a matter of fines, bribes, payoffs and profit. This is important because before "The Sunmakers" most alien races on television were bent on conquering other planets, not accumulating wealth. In the '80s, the Ferengi and Sil were created primarily as a response to Reagonomics and the era of the "yuppie." The context spurring "The Sunmakers" was not the Reagan Revolution, however, but the era of the "tax and spend" Labour Party in Great Britain.

The Usurians are also cleverly named by Holmes. "Usury" is defined as an excessive or illegal rate charged to a borrower. The tax-crazy Usurians, then, truly exemplify their name.

Michael Keating appears in "The Sunmakers" as Goudry. This diminutive performer has become a cult figure in sci-fi circles for his portrayal of the cowardly Vila throughout the four-year run of *Blake's 7*. He was once on the short list to play the Doctor in *Doctor Who*, but Sylvester McCoy was eventually cast instead.

96. "Underworld" Written by Bob Baker & Dave Martin; Directed by Norman Stewart; Designed by Dick Coles; Parts I–IV; Airdates: January 7, 14, 21, 28, 1978

SYNOPSIS: At the boundary of the known universe, the Doctor and Leela board a Minyan patrol vessel. The craft's presence is surprising to the Time Lord because Minyos was destroyed 100,000 years ago on the other side of the galaxy. The Doctor explains Minyos history to Leela: Well before the creation of the non-intervention policy, the Time Lords visited Minyos and introduced new technologies and even the secret of regeneration to the culture. In a matter of time, the war-like Minyans rebelled, and the Time Lords evacuated Minyan outposts. With the Time Lords gone, the Minyans fought amongst themselves and they destroyed their civilization and planet. The Time Lords questioned their role in this holocaust and settled on the non-interference directive.

Now the Doctor and Leela have found that a Minyan ship survived the ancient disaster. Its crew is in search of the P7E, a long-lost spaceship containing the genetic heritage of their race! With the Doctor's help, the P7E is found to be at the core of a recently formed planet. Unfortunately, it is ruled by the malevolent ship's computer, the Oracle.

GUEST CAST: Jackson (James Maxwell); Orfe (Jonathan Newth); Herrick (Alan Lake); Tala (Imogene Bickford-Smith); Idas (Norman Tipton); Idmon (Jimmy Gardner); Rask (James Marcus); Tarn (Godfrey James); Ankh (Frank Jarvis); Klimt (Jay Neill); Lakh (Richard Shaw); Naia (Stacey Tendeter); Oracle (Christine Pollon)

COMMENTARY: Mythology is once again at the heart of *Doctor Who* in "Underworld." Unlike the "Daemons" prototype, however, "Underworld" uses elements of mythology translated into a futuristic setting. The creatures in the story are not responsible for generating mythology (as in "The Daemons" or "Image of The Fendahl"), they are merely echoing it. In particular, "Underworld" is a futuristic translation of several Greek "Tartarus" stories. The P7E is actually phonetically "Persephone." P7E also fulfills the same role as the heroine Persephone. Like the beautiful young maiden, the P7E has become trapped in an underworld. And, again like its namesake, the P7E is the object of a heroic quest. This mythological overlay on an outer space story is a conceit that was used again in "The Horns of Nimon," a story that transplanted the Ariadne and Minos myths of Crete to a distant planet. Nimos is an anagram of Minos.

Other than its mythological context, "Underworld" is a story packed with familiar *Doctor Who* images. The class differences between the Trogs and the Overseers echo the relationship between the Savages and the Elders in "The Savages," among others. That established, "Underworld" is obviously another "revolution" story in the mold of "The Daleks," "The Web Planet" and "Colony in Space."

Another classic *Who* element at work here is the domination of man by computer. In this case, the great Oracle runs the underworld domain. The Oracle is a retread of Xoanan in "The Face of Evil," as well as the identically named "Oracle" in the *Star Trek* third season story "For the World Is Hollow and I Have Touched the Sky." "Underworld" also stresses the importance of a genetic "race" bank, a critical device in the *Space: 1999* Year One story "Mission of the Darians" (1975). With all of these common elements, "Underworld" is hardly a superlative or creative *Doctor Who* story. Like most episodes of the Leela–Doctor–K-9 era, however, it is action-packed and fast paced.

Most significantly, "Underworld" reveals some critical Time Lord history. It was the disaster of contact with Minyans in the distant past that led these advanced beings to adopt an official policy of non-intervention. In *Star Trek: The Next Generation*, the Federation also adopted its Prime Directive of non-interference after a disastrous first contact with another alien species, the Klingons. It is interesting that *Doctor Who* should reveal this particular story because it is presented in the light that the Time Lords were right to stop interfering. Their meddling, after all, caused a race to destroy itself. Despite this example, the official line of *Doctor Who* has frequently been that it is necessary to interfere in the affairs of others when tyranny threatens freedom. Certainly Troughton's Doctor argued cogently for interference in "The War Games." "Underworld" seems to suggest that the Time Lords are right for sitting back and observing instead of joining in to help the forces of good.

x **97. "The Invasion of Time"** Written by Graham Williams & Anthony Read; Directed by Gerald Blake; Designed by Barbara Gosnold; Parts I–VI; Airdates: February 4, 11, 18, 25, March 4, March 11, 1978

SYNOPSIS: The Doctor collaborates with the Vardan military in an invasion of Gallifrey, the home planet of the Time Lords. As reward for his treachery, the Doctor is made the new puppet president of the Time Lords. Soon, however, it becomes clear that the Doctor has not betrayed his people after all. In fact, he has been trying to learn the truth about the Vardans. There is another force, far more ruthless, awaiting a shot at Gallifrey: the militaristic Sontarans!

GUEST CAST: Borusa (John Arnatt); Andred (Chris Tranchell); Kelner (Milton Johns); Vardan Leader (Stan McGowan); Savar (Reginald Jessup); Gold Usher (Charles Morgan); Rodan (Hilary Ryan); Nesbin (Max Faulkner); Chancery Guard (Christopher Chistou); Gomer (Dennis Edward); Ablif (Ray Callaghan); Presta (Gai Smith); Jasko (Michael Mundell); Guard (Eric Danot); Commander Stor (Derek Deadman); Sontaran (Stuart Fell)

COMMENTARY: "The Invasion of Time" represents the end of an era. Not only do Leela and the original K-9 leave the series in this serial, but the very tone of the entire *Doctor Who* series soon changed. Ever since Tom Baker took over the role in Season 12, *Doctor Who* had been involved in terrifying horror stories, often set in outer space. There was the Grand Guignol of "The Talons of Weng-Chiang," the *Alien*–like scenario of "Planet of Evil," the *Thing*–like situation of "Seeds of Doom," the horror of inhuman duplicates in "The Android Invasion" and giant insects preying on humanity in "The Ark in Space." After "The Invasion of Time," all that would change. The series would become more comical and less horrific. As for "The Invasion of Time" itself, it is a pure action formula. Like "Underworld" before it, the story is essentially of the "revolution" (*Time Machine* template) mode. Here it is the once-fearsome Time Lords themselves who must revolt against first the Vardans and then the Sontarans.

By adapting the common revolution story (a concept seen in *Doctor Who* from Serial 2, "The Daleks") to the Time Lord world, the *Doctor Who* creators did a great disservice to the series. This episode is the ultimate demystification of the Time Lords. Now they are reduced to being just another civilization trying to regain control of their world. No longer are they the superior, telepathic giants of "The War Games." Instead they are but another "oppressed" faction, like the Thals, forced to revolt against alien exploiters. Like "The Deadly Assassin" before it, "The Invasion of Time" demystifies other aspects of Time Lord culture, including politics and the virtual reality matrix system. The saddest element of this story is the demystification of the TARDIS itself. The last portion of the serial is an extended chase through the interior of the Doctor's mysterious craft. Amazingly, the interior of the ship is depicted as being constructed of *brick and iron.* There is a latticed iron lift, and many corridors where bricks are obvious. The series was apparently too cheap to come up with an exciting new idea for the interior of the TARDIS, and so represented it in completely inappropriate twentieth century Earth terms. This is an unforgivable blunder. The TARDIS, with its faulty controls, malfunctioning chameleon control and telepathic abilities, has always been part of the Doctor's mystery. After this serial, the TARDIS could be part of any brick house or apartment building on Earth. This is one incident in which the *Doctor Who* design team fails totally.

Just as underwhelming as the chase through the TARDIS is the send-off for Louise Jameson's wonderful companion, Leela. She is married off to a Time Lord, an astonishing insult to this resourceful, assertive companion. This act is so completely out-of-character for the warrior of the Sevateem that it makes one gasp in disbelief. Surely a more realistic send-off could have been conceived. It would have been entirely preferable for Leela to be killed while defending the Doctor from the Sontarans. That would have been a noble end, wholly in keeping with Leela's character. To simply marry her off and force her to settle down on Gallifrey is not only out-of-character, it is sexist!

Beyond these problems, character motivations in "The Invasion of Time" are murky. The Doctor has engineered an alien invasion by the Vardans so as to make the Time Lords confront their complacency? Now that's a good idea! Is he so confident in his abilities and so supremely opinionated that he has the right to subject an entire world to the attack of an aggressive alien species? The Doctor's life had been threatened many times before "The Invasion of Time," and yet he had never done anything so cowardly or idiotic as betray an entire world to an invasion force. Even if he wanted to know the secret source of the invasion (the Sontarans), there were surely easier ways than endangering millions of innocent people! This has to rank as one of the dumbest plots ever seen on *Doctor Who.*

Also rather unbelievable is the notion that a Time Lord who has once been exiled and tried for murder could assume the Presidency. There is no rule in the Gallifreyan constitution prohibiting such an ascension? The Time Lords have certainly grown very forgiving since "The War Games." In that story, they wanted to obliterate the Doctor for his actions, and yet now he is made President! This not only demystifies the Time Lords, it makes their laws quite unbelievable.

About the only positive aspect of the "The Invasion of Time" is the welcome return of the Sontarans. These alien villains had last been seen in Season 12's "The Sontaran Experiment." "The Invasion of Time" is an unsatisfactory end to a very good era of *Doctor Who*.

SEASON 16

98. "The Ribos Operation" Written by Robert Holmes; Directed by George Spenton-Foster; Designed by Ken Ledsham; Parts I–IV; Airdates: September 2, 9, 16, 23, 1978

SYNOPSIS: With K-9 Mark II in tow, the Doctor is summoned to the domain of the White Guardian. The Guardian, a bearded man in white jacket and hat, tells the Doctor about the legend of the Key to Time. The Key is a perfect cube that maintains the equilibrium and balance of time. There are six segments of the Key to Time, all of them hidden throughout the cosmos. When assembled, the key is a very powerful and dangerous tool. The White Guardian insists that the segments must be retrieved and assembled before the universe is plunged into eternal chaos. The segments can be disguised in any shape, form or size, so the Doctor is given a key segment locator, a sort of electronic divining rod.

The White Guardian also warns the Doctor that the Black Guardian desires to own the Key to Time for an evil purpose. The Doctor must not let the Black Guardian win in this quest or the universe will forever suffer the consequences. Teaming up with a saucy and arrogant Time Lady named Romana, the Doctor and K-9 set out on the quest. The first segment is known to be on the planet Ribos, a world of devastating winters. There, the Doctor and his friends encounter some scam artists, a deposed dictator and a mysterious substance known as "jethrick."

GUEST CAST: Guardian (Cyril Luckham); Garron (Iain Cuthbertson); Unstoffe (Nigel Plaskitt); Graff Vynda-K (Paul Seed); Sholakh (Robert Keegan); Captain (Prentis Hancock); Shrieves (Oliver Maguire, John Hamill); Binro (Timothy Bateson); Seeker (Ann Tirard)

COMMENTARY: The "quest" concept, introduced to *Doctor Who* in Terry Nation's first season serial "The Keys of Marinus," returns to motivate Season 16 of *Doctor Who*. All six serials produced in this season ("The Ribos Operation," "The Pirate Planet," "The Stones of Blood," "The Androids of Tara," "The Power of Kroll" and "The Armageddon Factor") are elements in the Doctor's ongoing search for the powerful "Key to Time." The first story of this quest series, "The Ribos Operation" begins powerfully with the White Guardian luring the TARDIS to his domain. Following the Doctor's introduction to this supreme being, there is a well-written briefing about the Time Lord's new mission. Equally enjoyable and stimulating is the presentation of Mary Tamm's Time Lady, Romana. She is immediately established as a brilliant thinker and a quick wit. In other words, she is Sarah Jane Smith but one step improved.

"The Ribos Operation" introduces the concept of two Universal Guardians to *Doctor Who*. The White Guardian represents good and the Black Guardian represents evil. Before Season 16, there had never been any reference in the series to any such "supreme beings." In fact, it was always assumed that the Time Lords were the most powerful beings in creation. It was only in the Tom Baker era, when the Time Lords became thoroughly demystified in stories such as "The Deadly Assassin" and "The Invasion of Time," that it became necessary to create another race above them, a race of "elemental" force and supernatural power. Had the concept of the Time Lords seen in "The War Games" survived, the creation of the Guardians in this season would never have been necessary. Accordingly, the White Guardian that the audience becomes acquainted with in "The Ribos Operation" is an overly familiar (and unchallenging) god entity who can bend time, space and reality to his will.

In science fiction television, such god-beings have become a cliché. *Buck Rogers in the 25th Century* introduced a race of similarly named Guardians in 1981. In the story "The Guardians," Buck and the Searcher had to deliver an all-important green box belonging to the Guardians to a distant planet. While the box was out of Guardian control, time was distorted. Essentially then, the series postulated the same idea as "The Ribos Operation." *Buck Rogers* repeated *Doctor Who*'s notion that the ultimate control of time was in a tool (box/key) possessed by a race of universal Guardians. A much less benevolent god being also turned up on the first episode of *Star Trek: The Next Generation* in 1987. In "Encounter at Farpoint," the entity called "Q" was also able to bend time and space to his will. In stories such as "All Good Things," "Q" returned to wreak havoc with the space-time continuum. The problem with "Q" and the Guardians in *Doctor Who* is that as soon as a program attempts to personalize a god-being, that being no longer resembles a god, but a human being. *Space: 1999* overcame this problem by never showing the mysterious cosmic intelligence that guided Moonbase Alpha through adventures such as "Black Sun" and "The Testament of Arkadia"; the character, appearance and mechanisms of the cosmic force was able to remain a mystery, and hence somewhat believable. As soon as *Doctor Who* introduced the god-like Guardians with their lawn chairs and Earth-style wardrobe, the series automatically limited itself in how these powerful creatures could be portrayed. Despite this problem, Cyril Luckham is charming as "The White Guardian," and he successfully sets up the premise that will spur this season of *Doctor Who*.

Entirely more successful is the integration of the Time Lady Romana into the

Mary Tamm joined the quest for the Key to Time in *Doctor Who* season 16 as the first incarnation of the Time Lady Romana.

TARDIS control room. She is physically competent like Leela, and perhaps the first female since Zoe to be an intellectual match for the Doctor. Importantly, Romana is also the Doctor's equal in acerbic wit. As a result, "The Ribos Operation" and all episodes of Season 16 are alive with banter and character chemistry. Mary Tamm and Tom Baker shoot sparks at each other in their performances, and both characters come out of the adventures seeming all the stronger. This supports Ian Marter's theory about companions. The more intelligent and challenging a companion is, the better that companion will make the Doctor look. As a result of this chemistry between Tamm and Baker, the best moments in the season are those in which they clash over protocol.

Unfortunately, many *Doctor Who* viewers found Mary Tamm too aggressive as Romana. They were not yet ready for a female companion of her stature. The general attitude towards her was one of irritation. Who does she think she is telling the Doctor what to do? In this case, the show introduced a character that the audience was not yet ready to accept. Tamm's replacement in Season 17, Lalla Ward, turned Romana into a helpless little innocent. No longer would she challenge the Doctor, or face down enemies with courage. This softer interpretation of the Time Lady made the second incarnation of Romana one of the dullest companions in the run of the series.

Although the premise of the Key to Time saga and the introduction of the feisty Romana are laid out expertly in Robert Holmes' teleplay, the substance of the actual Ribos adventure is considerably less than enthralling. It is a mediocre story about small time con men trying to steal money from a deposed dictator. It is intentionally a "small" story featuring neither galactic wars, the "Daemons" prototype, nor the awakening of any evil villains. These factors should make for a diverting serial and indeed "The Ribos Operation" is very different from all the *Who* serials that precede it. However, the pacing of the story is slow, and the exposition about jethrick, Vynda-K's conflict and the powers of the Ribos mystical seer is fairly tedious and uninteresting. The fun of this story was presumably to come in seeing the Doctor and Romana stoop to the level of the con men to attain the jethrik that is actually the first segment to the Key to Time. Unfortunately, this is not really a worthy effort and the Time Lord, Romana and K-9 seem to play only a peripheral importance in the plot.

The guest performances in "The Ribos Operation" are uniformly two-dimensional, with Garron, Unstoffe and Vynda-K coming across fairly badly. They are broad comic caricatures rather than believable characters. Since the supporting cast overplays their antics, Tom Baker ups the ante and also indulges in some over-the-top behavior. Everyone tries so hard to make "The Ribos Operation" seem funny that its profound lack of humor becomes only more obvious. This is one story where the so-called sense of humor goes over like a lead balloon. The boring, seemingly endless finale in the catacombs does little to enlighten the show either. And since there is no social subtext in "The Ribos Operation," *à la* "The Sunmakers," the serial is a very empty one aside from the premise and companion it unveils early on.

Although it is thematically interesting to send the Doctor to a variety of third-world planets in the Key to Time saga, one cannot help but measure these stories against 15 years of antecedents. If the Key to Time were not involved, the Doctor would *never* end up on such a dull collection of worlds as he encounters this season! That said, "The Ribos Operation" looks like a masterpiece compared to the second installment in the saga, "The Pirate Planet."

"The Ribos Operation" is available on videocassette.

99. "The Pirate Planet" Written by Douglas Adams; Directed by Pennant Roberts; Designed by John Pusey; Parts I–IV; Airdates: September 30, October 7, 14, 21, 1978

SYNOPSIS: In search of the second segment of the Key to Time, the Doctor, Romana and K-9 end up on a planet-sized spaceship, Zanak, piloted by a malevolent creature called the Captain. So far the Captain has "jumped" his pirate planet onto other worlds including Granados, Bandraginus V and Calufrax. Each time he has made a jump, he has sucked all the life forces and minerals right out of these victimized worlds. His next target is Earth.

While the telekinetic Mentiads launch an attack on the Captain, the Doctor discovers that the Captain's purpose in reducing worlds to rubble is even more devious than it seems. Locked behind the bridge, safe in protective "Time Dams," is the ancient body of Queen Xanxia, Zanak's former ruler. She is using a holo projector and the life forces of the vanquished planets to restore herself to a youthful, holographic body. A hostage of the Captain, the Doctor is forced to walk the plank after making this discovery....

GUEST CAST: The Captain (Bruce Purchase); Mr. Fibuli (Andrew Robertson); Balaton (Ralph Michael); Pralix (David Sibly); Kimus (David Warwick); Mula (Primi Townsend); Citizen (Clive Bennett); Nurse (Rosalind Lloyd); Mentiad (Bernard Finch); Guard (Adam Kurakin)

COMMENTARY: "The Pirate Planet" is among the weaker serials in *Doctor Who*'s 26-year run. This is a surprise since author Douglas Adams is a well-respected name in sci-fi circles for his popular novel *The Hitchhiker's Guide to the Galaxy*. By so stylishly penning Arthur Dent's odyssey across the universe, Adams brought satire and absurdist, existential humor to new levels. Adams' characters asked questions about the meaning of life and were invariably met with a resounding "huh?" from a universe filled with bureaucracies, depressed androids, Infinite Improbability Drives and restaurants in time bubbles. His humorous vision of an utterly pointless universe captured the imaginations of many Americans and Brits alike in the early '80s. So successful was *The Hitchhiker's Guide to the Galaxy* that Adams continued the cycle with three other novels: *The Restaurant at the End of the Universe*; *Life, the Universe and Everything;* and *So Long, and Thanks for All the Fish*. With stellar credentials and a unique vision, Adams could have been a powerful force for creativity on *Doctor Who*.

Such was not the case, at least not immediately. His sarcastic, absurdist style did not mesh at all with the values and moralities long established on *Doctor Who*. His seemingly intractable belief in the meaninglessness of life could never be reconciled with the Doctor's penchant for helping others. Indeed, why help the Thals, the Menoptera, the Minyans or even the people of Earth if the universe is just a purposeless arena, and man is but a monkey with language? No, the Doctor has always been a creature of purpose and morality, and those facts are at odds with the muse that guides Adams' irreverent genius.

Adams would soon become story editor of *Doctor Who* and his tenure would drag the series further into the dangerous realm of tongue-in-cheek, over-the-top humor. Adams' silly plotting, coupled with Tom Baker's penchant to jump head-first into comedy, makes "The Pirate Planet" a farce. Later stories of the Adams reign are not nearly so objectionable. In fact "City of Death" is a great episode of *Doctor Who*. Still, "The Pirate Planet" has a plethora of problems. The most disturbing issue is that the plot is not treated with respect. Instead, the tone is a smarmy, self-satisfied one. The moral universe of *Doctor Who* is not taken seriously, but cruel-heartedly mocked instead. The story is built on a silly jumble of random incidents rather than a believable and linear teleplay. It hops disjointedly from one location to another so rapidly and with so little rhyme or reason that "The Pirate Planet" appears to have been improvised on the set. The disparate elements include the Mentiad cult, the struggle of a blooming telepath, a space-hopping planet, the search for the second piece of the Key to Time, an ancient Queen trying to restore herself to life using holographic technology, the exploitation of other worlds and even a threat to Earth. Since all the events in the story are treated as just a "cosmic" joke, there is no sense of menace or jeopardy throughout the serial and no real sense of importance either. This kind of attitude passed in *Hitchhiker's Guide to the Galaxy* because that "universe" had no *history*. Readers came to it with no expectations or preconceived notions. When they found something brilliant, irreverent and utterly unique, they rightfully rejoiced. What a world view this writer espoused! It was fantastic and fun and *funny*. But *Doctor Who* had 15 years of proud history to live up to by the time of "The Pirate Planet." The sudden shift to sarcasm and a devil-may-care attitude was jarring and untrue to *Who* tradition.

The teleplay of "The Pirate Planet" is a melange of *Who* clichés. The revolution of the Mentiads is yet another insurrection against oppressors ("The Daleks," "The Web Planet," "The Space Museum," "The Ark"). The attempt of the villain to restore him/herself to youth and power recalls "The Hand of Fear," "Pyramids of Mars" and "The Abominable Snowmen," among others. The space pirate angle had already been seen as well in "The Space Pirates." The subtext about strip-mining and ecological exploitation is also a repeat offender in the *Doctor Who* hall of shame, familiar to viewers from "Colony in Space" and "The Green Death," to name two. A secret cult with a great power, the Mentiads in "The Pirate Planet," was also the starting point of the stories "The Masque of Mandragora" (the Demnos Cult) and "The Brain of Morbius" (the Sisterhood of Karn). *Doctor Who* has always been a strong science fiction vision because it updates itself periodically and revisits earlier stories with a new "adult" veneer, but such is not the case in "The Pirate Planet." These many ingredients are simply tossed together incoherently. Each element of the story is introduced and then rapidly forgotten in favor of the next jokey set-piece.

Even when *Doctor Who* finds itself telling a bad or derivative story, other elements frequently make the show bearable. Baker is an actor who can carry a story simply with his powerful eyes. He is that good an actor. Unfortunately, the performances in "The Pirate Planet" are embarrassing from start to finish, and another cause of the serial's failure. Actor Bruce Purchase portrays the villain of the piece, the Captain. He shouts every one of his lines in a booming theatrical voice, almost as if trying to be heard at the back of a theater auditorium. He melodramatically rolls the letter "r" each time he uses it. Is this a believable or realistic depiction of a space pirate, hardened by years in space stealing, robbing and escaping the authorities? Or is this a camp performance that mocks the character of the Captain and the *Doctor Who* universe? The weaker the Captain's material gets in "The Pirate Planet," the louder Purchase shouts. As a consequence, his performance is grating, and his scenes are about as funny as root canal. He is an unfunny character given life in a distinctly unfunny, distasteful fashion. His camp "Captain" would be right at home on the American television series *Batman*.

Alas, Baker does not fare much better. He reaches inappropriately for humor in every possible scenario in "The Pirate Planet." When playing against Purchase, he too resorts to screaming his lines. This increase in volume is supposed to be funny? Fortunately, Mary Tamm retains her dignity as Romana and wears a pained expression throughout the proceedings. K-9 fares the best of all the main characters because at least he is given something purposeful to do. He engages an evil robotic nemesis, the Captain's parrot, in a fierce laser battle. His victory over the robot bird, which resembles Boba Fett in a strange way, is the best scene in the serial.

"The Pirate Planet" fails from a production standpoint as well. The story calls for the creation of "air cars." Inadequately re-dressed *motorboats* are used to double as these futuristic vehicles, and atrocious matte work makes the air car flying sequences embarrassing to watch. Also less than adequate is the "linear induction tunnel," a *Jetsons*–esque conveyer belt that speeds characters from one end of a long hallway to another. The matte work is, again, terrible. The actors stand in front of a blue screen and throw their hands up helter skelter, as if surfing. On the blue screen behind them, the corridor whizzes by rapidly.

It is hard to find good in "The Pirate Planet." As a critic of science fiction television, one is always inclined to give a production the benefit of a doubt if a story is written, acted and produced with sincerity. Otherwise, there will *always* be something to find fault with. It should not be forgotten that these are episodes that are often written and filmed in a matter of days or weeks yet are held up to intense scrutiny after 20 years. *Star Trek*, *Space: 1999* and *Doctor Who* are not perfect visions by any means, but each television series so frequently reaches a level of greatness for its medium that there is something praiseworthy in each adventure. A tongue-in-cheek story which is not only disrespectful to *Doctor Who* tradition, but which brashly mocks it, is hard to defend or compliment. It is a sad day when a story is inappropriate even within *Doctor Who*'s elastic format. One thing no self-respecting series should ever have to endure is a campy farce filled with self-loathing. This opinion, however, is not shared by many *Dr. Who* scholars and viewers.

"The Pirate Planet" is available on videocassette.

100. "The Stones of Blood" Written by David Fisher; Directed by Darrol Blake; Designed by John Stout; Parts I–IV; Airdates: October 28, November 4, 11, 18, 1978

SYNOPSIS: The Doctor and Romana assemble the first two pieces of the Key to Time aboard the TARDIS and soon learn that the third piece is on Earth in England. The TARDIS materializes near a circle of ancient rocks not unlike Stonehenge. These rocks are called "The Nine Travelers" and there are two scientists, Prof. Emilia Rumford and her local friend Vivien Fay, examining them. Rumford is confused because her topological survey of the rock circle indicates that the rocks have moved positions! The Doctor adds to the mystery when he discovers blood stains in the grass nearby. There are also large footprints — from a creature that would weigh at least three and a half tons!

The Doctor soon recognizes that alien, blood-sucking rocks are responsible for a series of local attacks. These rocks are actually the Ogri, silicon life forms from Tau Ceti. The Doctor realizes the aliens exist in two domains and he crosses over to a spaceship trapped in hyperspace. The Doctor is convinced that this was once a convict ship and that Vivien Fay and her Ogri cohorts are escaped criminals! The Doctor then inadvertently releases from the prison ship two life forms who call themselves "The Megara." They are noncorporeal computerized entities who serve as the law of the Galactic Federation. They are judge, jury and executioner. And they have determined that the Doctor must be executed for breaking the seal on their compartment....

GUEST CAST: Prof. Rumford (Beatrix Lehmann); Vivien Fay a.k.a. Cessair Diplos (Susan Engel); DeVries (Nicholas McArdle); Martha (Elaine Ives-Cameron); Megara Voices (Gerald Cross, David McAlister); Campers (James Murray, Shiren Taylor)

COMMENTARY: "The Stones of Blood" finds *Doctor Who* solidly back on track after two missteps, "The Ribos Operation" and "The Pirate Planet." It spotlights an inventive plot that includes several horror movie elements missing from the series since "Image of the Fendahl" in Season 15. At first the story looks to be another "Daemons" prototype featuring an extraterrestrial masquerading as a mythical god, this time Calleich. However, the story takes a fascinating and thoroughly unexpected turn when the Doctor unleashes the Megara aboard the hyperspace vessel. Suddenly the story becomes delightfully preoccupied with verbal fencing and legal trickery instead of blood-sucking rock monsters. The last half of the serial functions as an insightful indictment of Britain's legal system. The legal machines, "The Megara," have gotten so carried away obeying the technicalities of the law that they have forgotten what it means to actually dispatch justice. They destroyed their creators in accordance with the letter of the law, but never once considered that such a mass execution was not justified. This is a brilliant conceit and it makes for one of the funniest and most enjoyable serials of *Doctor Who* in many a season. Legal trickery and the inhumane nature of a machine's justice had been visited in Terry Nation's Season 1 serial "The Keys of Marinus," but satire was not the method of that exposé. "The Stones of Blood" is exuberantly funny in its portrayal of a legal system that has not really served the people it was intended to protect.

Also delightful in "The Stones of Blood" is the presence of Beatrix Lehmann as Prof. Rumford. She is a chatty old woman who bores the Doctor with her incessant conversation about the driest of subjects. Nonetheless she makes a wonderful companion in this story, and Baker plays off her in witty fashion. Baker had this to say in *Starlog* #115 about a Rumford–type traveling partner:

> I wanted this old lady to be the companion. She would have a stick, because she would have a very bad hip. You could have had great fun with the Doctor saying, "Come on...we've got to go fast," and she obviously can't go fast. Now it strikes me as being in a wonderful surreal area — how fast are the monsters who are following us? ...Just because they're moving slowly doesn't mean they can't catch us, because *we're* only moving slowly. Because I'm not going to leave my beloved companion who has an arthritic hip, am I? And so there would be tension and great humor there.[14]

Based on Baker's chemistry with guest star Lehmann, his concept of a decrepit companion may have been a good one to explore. After all, Rumford proves an able assistant in "The Stones of Blood." She fixes the Doctor's portable hyperspace portal with K-9's help, and even stands face-to-face with the slow-moving Ogri. There is no denying that she is an intelligent and resourceful woman. The only reason to disqualify this character from companionhood is audience demographics. It is unlikely that "the fathers would be kept interested" by looking at a woman in her late sixties! Still, Lehmann is a delightful guest star, and portions of "The Stones of Blood" unfold very much in the humorous/tense style Baker outlined in the above passage. Again, it is essential to stress that this is the kind of humor that *Doctor Who* does well. It does not mock the series; Lehmann's character is not ridiculed or treated like a cosmic joke. Nor is the nearly immobile threat of the Ogri considered a cause of derisive laughter. Instead, the laughter comes naturally out of the elements of this scenario: an elderly, talkative woman, a slow-moving villain and a dangerous situation. Because of Prof. Rumford's interaction with the Doctor, as well as the surprising courtroom ending of "The Stones of Blood," this serial is a witty and totally enjoyable addition to the *Doctor Who* roster of episodes. For inventive characters and situations, it is unmatched.

"The Stones of Blood" is available on videocassette.

101. "The Androids of Tara" Written by David Fisher; Directed by Michael Hayes; Designed by Valerie Wallender; Parts I–IV; Airdates: November 25, December 2, 9, 16, 1978

SYNOPSIS: The TARDIS sets down on the world of Tara, the location of the fourth segment of the Key to Time. After changing into authentic Taran gear, Romana sets off with the key locator to find the object of the quest. She quickly finds the key segment at the foot of a statue. She is met there by Count Grendel, a local chieftain who realizes that this strange woman is the exact likeness of a woman he has taken prisoner in his dungeon: Princess Strilla! Grendel wants this dead ringer for Romana to marry him and validate his claim to Tara's throne. He feels that this marriage, coupled with Prince Reynart's assassination, will assure his domination of the planet. Meanwhile, the Doctor is captured and forced to repair an android duplicate of Reynart, who is to be coronated as King of Tara in just a few hours.

GUEST CAST: Grendel (Peter Jeffrey); Zadek (Simon Lack); Prince Reynart (Neville Jason); Farrah (Paul Lavers); Lamia (Lois Baxter); Till (Declan Mulholland); Archimandrite (Cyril Shaps); Kurster (Martin Matthews)

COMMENTARY: "The Androids of Tara" is a remarkably self-assured romp that blends swashbuckling heroics with a wicked sense of humor. Only on *Doctor Who* could a quasi-medieval world incorporate futuristic humanoid androids! Despite this strange, temporally confusing setting, the story has superb pacing. Even better than the breakneck pace, the humor once again arises believably and realistically out of the situation rather than from some kind of tongue-in-cheek poke at the universe of the series. Romana's protests that she is not an android as the surgeon Lamia prepares to cut her up, the android George's obvious lack of equilibrium on the throne of Tara, K-9's final predicament in the moat and the Doctor's deluxe, castle-spanning swordfight with the villainous Grendel are all charming, beautifully executed moments. Although science fiction played no part in the Rob Reiner film *The Princess Bride* (1987), "Androids of Tara" nonetheless tackles some of the same fairy tale elements. There is a beautiful princess trapped by an evil lord, a ridiculous sword duel between men who each claim to be the greatest swordsman of the land, and many moments of verbal banter and witty asides. It may not be classic *Doctor Who*, but it sure is *fun*.

Mary Tamm plays not only Romana but the Princess Strilla as well. She thus follows in the great tradition of series leads William Hartnell and Patrick Troughton. Respectively, they played the Abbot of Amboise in "The Massacre" and Salamander in "The Enemy of the World." It is interesting to note, however, that there are so many doubles of Time Lords in outer space. Already "The Androids of Tara" coupled with the aforementioned serials establish random doublings of physical identities in the galaxy. Is there some secret to Time Lord physiology that the audience does not yet know about? Why are duplicates of their bodies constantly showing up on other, more primitive planets?

At first glance, "The Androids of Tara" is yet another unimportant story in the *Doctor Who* saga. The fate of galaxies are not in the balance, and warring empires are not fighting for control of Earth — but the story is still an enjoyable and valuable one. The method to the producer's madness in the "Key to Time" saga is to highlight backwater, previously unvisited worlds so that popular *Doctor Who* villains like the Daleks or the Cybermen would not interfere with the quest aspects of the stories. After all, who would care about the Key to Time if a group of Daleks showed up? In this respect, Season 16 is certainly a bold experiment. There is not one famous *Doctor Who* villain featured in the season except the cameo shot of the Wirrn corpse (from "Ark in Space") in "The Stones of Blood." This is shocking, since the previous two Tom Baker years had seen the return of at least one "popular villain" per season (the Sontarans in Season 15's "Invasion of Time," and the Master in Season 14's "The Deadly Assassin"). An attempt to be inventive and lead a program in interesting new directions should always be applauded, and there is little doubt that even with the hit-or-miss nature of the Season 16 stories, the producers were leading *Doctor Who* to new destinations. "The Androids of Tara" evens the score for Season 16: So far there had been two failures ("The Ribos Operation" and "The Pirate Planet") and two successes ("The Stones of Blood" and "The Androids of Tara").

"The Androids of Tara" is available on videocassette.

102. "The Power of Kroll" Written by Robert Holmes; Directed by Norman Stewart; Designed by Don Giles; Parts I–IV; Airdates: December 23, 30, 1978, January 6, 13, 1979

SYNOPSIS: The Key to Time locator has sent the TARDIS to the swamps on the moon of Delta Magna. In no time, Romana is captured by gunrunner Rom Datt, who immediately takes her to a tribe of green-skinned humanoids called Swampies. She is to be sacrificed there to a god called "Kroll." The Doctor is also captured, but by uniformed human beings who operate the local Methane Catalyzing Refinery. The humans consider the Swampies to be ignorant savages and of no importance. The humans have been producing so much protein from this installation that they want to build ten Methane Catalyzing Installations on the moon. Unfortunately, this mass construction would squeeze the Swampies right off their own planet.

The Swampies, who call the humans "dryfoots," are planning a revolution to stop the human developers, and soon the giant god Kroll, a gargantuan squid, rears its ugly head amidst the swamps. The Doctor suspects that the mystery of Kroll is not yet solved and decides to confront the colossal beast. As he is grabbed by one of Kroll's tentacles and almost eaten, the Doctor realizes where the fourth segment of the Key to Time is hidden.

GUEST CAST: Thawn (Neil McCarthy); Ranquin (John Abineri); Fenner (Philip Madoc); Varlik (Carl Rigg); Skart (Frank Jarvis); Dugeen (John Leeson)

COMMENTARY: *Doctor Who* returns to serious business with "The Power of Kroll," an exciting serial laced with social commentary. Also obvious is the serial's resemblance to the film *King Kong* (1933). Here members of a primitive native tribe worship another gigantic creature, a squid instead of an ape. They sacrifice women to this beast, and even dance around in squid (ape?) suits during their ceremonies. Kroll, clearly King Kong's double, goes on a rampage in the latter half of the serial and attacks the white men who have attempted to injure it. Beyond that obvious filmic template, however, "Power of Kroll" has a great deal on its mind ... especially considering its placement in a season of lightweight but entertaining tales. "The Power of Kroll" raises questions about genocide, race hatred and the exploitation of land, to name just a few social issues. Delightfully, *Doctor Who* is back to exploring the same themes that it found so provocative in the Pertwee era. Although all this has been seen before in *Doctor Who*, it is refreshing after socially irrelevant stories such as "The Ribos Operation," "The Pirate Planet" and "The Androids of Tara."

Holmes' script also draws strong parallels between the situation of the Swampies and the predicament of the Native American peoples in the United States. Consider: The Swampies and the American Indians have been removed from their ancestral home and transplanted to less than ideal land. The Swampies, relocated to the moon of Delta Magna, are scorned by the officers of the Earth company (white men) and even referred to as savages. Thawn, the leader of the Caucasians, calls these creatures subhumans and he rejects attempts to educate or "enlighten" them with Earth knowledge and morality. Swampie skin is green instead of red, but the analogy is plain despite the switcheroo. The Swampies are an exploited race, just like the Indians in America. Especially damning is the Company's decision to move the Swampie reservation again now that there is actually something of value on the moon of Delta Magna. They do not care that the Swampies' religion ("Kroll Worship") is tied to their current location. The Swampies are treated as cattle that can be moved about without trouble.

Also insightful is the inclusion of a liberal group of humans called "The Sons of Earth." This radical group is characterized as a toothless political entity, more concerned with dogma than the actual disposition of the Swampie people on the distant moon of Delta Magna. Modern-day liberal bleeding hearts?

Neil McCarthy's portrayal of Thawn is a good one. He is a man who believes unquestioningly in his own racial superiority. He would rather exterminate the Swampies as a race then be forced to live in harmony with them. McCarthy successfully paints a picture of total race hatred. Philip Madoc, last seen in "The Brain of Morbius," also shows up in "The Power of Kroll" in the thankless role of Fenner. Of interest to trivia buffs is John Leeson's appearance in this story as the morally wavering Dugeen. Leeson gave a voice to K-9 in Seasons 15 and 16.

In addition to strong social commentary and a moral stand on genocide and racism, "The Power of Kroll" culminates in a shocking conclusion: Kroll *is* the Key to Time segment! This comes as quite a surprise, and it foreshadows the conclusion of the Key to Time saga in "The Armageddon Factor." This conclusion does raise some very important issues, however. Since the Doctor has taken the Key/Kroll, what of Swampie religion? It is crushed! How will these people live once their "god" has been destroyed? This problem is never addressed.

Secondly, the Doctor makes an issue of saving Astra's life in "The Armageddon Factor." He refuses to force her to exist as a segment of the Key to Time. He shatters the key to its component parts so Astra can remain human. But what of Kroll? Why didn't the Doctor comment on the fact that Kroll too had to give up its life to form the Key? Was Kroll's life worth less because it was non-human? Another question is this: Has the Key to Time actually melded with Kroll, or was Kroll designed by the White Guardian to hide the Key? If so, why? What was the logic in creating the entity? This is another story where solutions are not clear. Still, "The Power of Kroll" is a powerful tale, and another positive show in the Key to Time epic.

"The Power of Kroll" is available on videocassette.

103. "The Armageddon Factor" Written by Bob Baker & David Martin; Directed by Michael Hayes; Designed by Richard McManan-Smith; Parts I–VI; Airdates: January 20, 27, February 3, 10, 17, 24, 1979

SYNOPSIS: The planets Atrios and Zios have been at war for many years when the Doctor, Leela and K-9 arrive in search of the last piece to the Key to Time. They encounter a war-hungry marshal and learn that an invisible planet hides between the two nearly destroyed worlds. When the Doctor's opposite number, "the Shadow," takes possession of the Doctor's TARDIS and kidnaps the Princess Astra, the Doctor realizes fate may favor the Black Guardian in this quest. The Doctor, K-9 and Leela also encounter Mentallis, a deadly Ziosian computer bent on annihilation! Saving the day, the Doctor assembles the Key to Time and then, realizing its power, smashes it. This earns him the everlasting enmity of the Black Guardian

GUEST CAST: Marshal (John Woodvine); Princess Astra (Lalla Ward); Shapp (Daryl Harries); Merak (Ian Saynor); Hero (Ian Liston); Heroine (Susan Skipper); Guard (John Cannon); The Shadow (William Squire); Drax (Barry Johnson); The Black Guardian (Valentine Dyall)

COMMENTARY: "The Armageddon Factor" is an unsatisfactory serial, and a disappointing ending to the Key to Time saga. With negatives outweighing the positives, the mediocre qualities of this episode cause the Key to Time experiment to end in a draw. There are three weak stories, the convoluted "The Ribos Operation," the weak "The Pirate Planet" and the mediocre "The Armageddon Factor." There are also three good stories, the superlative "The Stones of Blood," the fun "The Androids of Tara" and the thought-provoking "The Power of Kroll." Although this is perhaps not a bad average for sci-fi television, it is not very good for *Doctor Who*. One would be hard-pressed to name even one overtly "bad" or uninteresting story in Seasons 12–15. In Season 16, there are three such stories.

The problems in "The Armageddon Factor" are similar to those that plagued "The Ribos Operation." The story is needlessly padded out at six parts. For long stretches, the Doctor, Romana and K-9 are kidnapped and rescued, *ad nauseam*, and the plot moves forward at a snail's pace. The story also has some incoherent sequences that have nothing whatsoever to do with the central plot. Why are the Doctor and fellow Time Lord Drax shrunken down to ant-size for a brief interlude? How does this fit into the story? Why does the story open with a glimpse of the "propaganda" television programming on Atrios, if that conflict is only to be a peripheral part of the overall adventure?

Coincidence also plays a large part in teleplay. Is it not suspicious how Time Lord countryman Drax conveniently appears and assists the Doctor in a difficult situation? Or how the all-powerful Key to Time can be tricked into operating with only five parts?

The Shadow, the Black Guardian's champion, is not well characterized either. He is a cartoony presence rather than a serious menace. He mouths threats, balls his fists in a rage, and generally acts in the exaggerated style of a silent film villain. What is his motivation for being such a despicable creature? Why did the Black Guardian pick this character for his champion instead of someone *really* clever like the Master? With his skull-face mask and "comic book" appearance, the Shadow is a precursor to Skeletor in the film *The Masters of the Universe* (1987), which starred future icons such as Courtney Cox (*Scream*) and Robert Duncan McNeill (*Voyager*). Amazingly, the similar-looking Skeletor in that film sends his minions after the powerful "Cosmic Key," a device that, oddly enough, controls time. In other words, Skeletor's quest is identical to that of the Shadow's in the Key to Time saga! Someone in Hollywood must have been watching *Doctor Who*'s 1978 quest.

Thematically, "The Armageddon Factor" concerns the horror of an eternal war. This particular theme has been seen in *Star Trek*'s similarly named "A Taste of Armageddon," *Deep Space Nine*'s "The Armageddon Game," *Space: 1999*'s "The Last Enemy," *Battlestar Galactica*'s "Saga of a Star World" and *Deep Space Nine*'s "Battle Lines," to name but a few. The notion had also been visited several times on *Doctor Who* in serials such as "The Daleks." "The Time Warrior" also introduced the neverending war scenario in regards to the conflict between the Sontarans and the Rutans. "The Armageddon Factor" thus has precious little to add to any of these stories, so the bulk of the serial is uninteresting. The story finally redeems itself in the closing moments when the Doctor chooses to save a human life and negate the entire Key to Time quest rather than doom Astra to eternal entrapment as a puzzle component.

It is typical *Doctor Who* genius to send a character in search of an important object only to have it all be a wild goose chase. With "The Armageddon Factor," *Doctor Who* suggests it is the journey, not the destination, that is important. Of course, the Doctor will pay for his final act in this story. The Black Guardian will return to torment him in Season 20 stories such as "Mawdryn Undead," "Terminus" and "Enlightenment."

"The Armageddon Factor" is available on videocassette.

SEASON 17

104. "Destiny of the Daleks" Written by Terry Nation; Directed by Ken Grieve; Designed by Ken Ledsham; Parts I–IV; Airdates: September 1, 18, 15, 22, 1979

SYNOPSIS: The Doctor, a regenerated Romana and a K-9 with laryngitis return to war-torn Skaro to find the Daleks desperate! The villainous exterminators have returned to their homeworld to unearth their long-dead creator Davros because only a humanoid mind is capable of ending the Dalek's long stalemate with another robot race, the humanoid Movellans. When the Movellans catch wind of the Dalek plot, they apprehend the Doctor and force him to give *them* a humanoid advantage over the Daleks and Davros.

GUEST CAST: Tyssan (Tim Barlow); Commander Sharrel (Peter Straker); Agella (Suzanne Danielle); Lan (Tony Osaba); Davros (David Gooderson); Jall (Jenny Casdagli); Veldan (David Yip); Daleks (Mike Mungarvan, Cy Town); Voice of the Daleks (Roy Skelton)

COMMENTARY: The Daleks are back in an adventure penned by their creator Terry Nation. The rub this time is that the Daleks have found themselves in an endless war with the humanoid Movellans that neither side can win. The only possible way to end the standoff is the so-called "human" factor, last featured in the Troughton-era adventure "The Evil of the Daleks" (Season 4). In "Destiny of the Daleks," the Daleks and the Movellans require the inspiration, illogic and mistakes of a plain old, simple human being to win the conflict once and for all. Nation's teleplay insightfully visualizes this theory about man versus machine with the simple game of "Rock, Paper, Scissors." The Doctor demonstrates this playground game several times with Romana, and he effectively shows how humans (or humanoids) make random choices with variable results. Then the Movellans play together and constantly stalemate one another. Through a simple game, the robot mind has been exposed as uncreative.

One has to wonder how IBM's Deep Blue would "feel" about this revelation, since the so-called human factor did not help Kasparov defeat the machine. A computer familiar with every option and every move possible in a game is more than a match for the random thinking patterns of humans. Or is it? Everything about computers is designed by man, after all. Its chips, its circuits, its memory, its programming all come from the minds of human beings. A computer victory in chess is merely the victory of a good programmer, not of "machinery." These issues are at the heart of "Destiny of the Daleks" and it is nice to see that *Doctor Who* still has faith in the indomitable spirit of man.

For years, a significant portion of *Doctor Who* fans have considered Season 17 to be the worst in the series. Many of them feel that Douglas Adams, though undeniably brilliant, did not mesh well with the series as story editor. "Destiny of the Daleks" has therefore not been a popular story. So unhappy was John Nathan-Turner with the presentation of the Daleks in this serial that he retired them until Season 21. This is perhaps an unfair assessment, as the Daleks are presented in this story just as they have always been presented in the past. They are shown to be ruthless, evil creatures. The essential difference is not in how the Daleks are portrayed, it is in how others *react* to them. The Doctor in particular dispatches Daleks handily. He throws his hat on a Dalek's eyestalk ... and it is completely immobilized. No wonder the Daleks cannot win a war — they cannot even pull a hat off their heads. Instead of removing the hat, the Dalek spins in circles and fires its lasers in all directions. It is so trigger-happy that it nearly fries Davros! The Daleks are not the only ones mocked by this story: Davros does not come off well either. The Doctor pats his bald cranium affectionately, shakes his ancient hand and generally treats the creator of the Daleks as an object of derision. Davros is portrayed just as menacingly as he was in "Genesis of the Daleks," but others relate to him as a fool instead of as a fearsome opponent. In the end, the Doctor traps Davros and defeats the Daleks with ridiculous ease.

That said, there is one person in "Destiny of the Daleks" who does treat the Daleks like a menace: Lalla Ward's new Romana. When the Daleks break through a wall and surround her, the actress screams at the top of her lungs. It is an appropriate response to the terror of ten galaxies, and one is gratified that Romana did not attempt to make light of her opponents. However, this also shows a shift away from the strong-minded, sharp-tongued Romana of Mary Tamm; it would be impossible to imagine Tamm's first incarnation of the Time Lady screaming about *anything*. She was much more composed. However, it is important to remember that when a Time Lord or Lady regenerates, the personality changes as well. It was absolutely correct of Ward to play Romana in an entirely different fashion than Tamm. Still, it is sad to see a strong female character changed to a more traditional damsel in distress.

"Destiny of the Daleks" is a solid production. Although the spaceship effects are weak, the set design inside the Movellan ship is very impressive. The Movellans themselves are fantastic-looking aliens. They wear skin-tight white uniforms and have long, Cleopatra–style hair. Their eye makeup also reflects an ancient Egyptian design. The casting assists the reality of the Movellans as well. Each of the aliens is portrayed by men and women with splendid physiques. Their physical attractiveness is made doubly powerful by the skin-tight uniforms. The Daleks

Lalla Ward played a more girlish, less assertive incarnation of Romana in seasons 17 and 18 of *Doctor Who*.

also seem to be more numerous than they were in early serials such as "Day of the Daleks," requiring fewer breaks in the action to go back and reshoot sequences with doubles. The world of Skaro, seen in "Genesis of the Daleks," is also recreated with flair.

With good production values and a solid sci-fi concept at its core, "Destiny of the Daleks" is far from a failure. It is an entertaining serial and far better than at least three of the stories from the previous season. Although the Daleks have lost their teeth, *Doctor Who* retains in its first Season 17 adventure a sense of suspense and fun. Some degree of its success must lay squarely with story editor Douglas Adams.

"Destiny of the Daleks" is available on videocassette.

105. "City of Death" Written by Douglas Adams & Graham Williams; Directed by Michael Hayes; Designed by Richard McManan-Smith; Parts I–IV; Airdates: September 29, October 6, 13, 20, 1979

SYNOPSIS: On the barren, rocky surface of Earth at the dawn of time, a spherical spaceship with three spidery landing struts prepares for takeoff. There is a malfunction, and the vessel explodes in midair. At the moment of the catastrophe, the Jagaroth pilot, Scaroth, is splintered into a dozen pieces. Over the span of several million years, the pieces of Scaroth attempt to perfect time travel so the pilot can avoid the accident that sent his soul scattered across time and space.

One incarnation of Scaroth, known as Count Scallioni, is operating in twentieth century Paris. He has been selling famous art pieces to pay for time travel research. His game in the twentieth century is to steal the *Mona Lisa* from the Louvre and sell many *originals* made by Da Vinci at his behest centuries earlier to various art collectors...all of whom believe they are buying the only original! The Doctor realizes that Scaroth cannot succeed because the fallout of his ship's explosion was the impetus necessary to create the human race. If Scaroth succeeds, mankind will never be born!

GUEST CAST: Count/Scaroth (Julian Glover); Countess (Catherine Schell); Duggan (Tom Chadbon); Kerensky (David Graham); Hermann (Kevin Flood); Louvre Guide (Pamela Sterling); Soldier (Peter Halliday)

COMMENTARY: "City of Death" is a brilliant story from script editor Douglas Adams and co-author Graham Williams. It is innovative, humorous and thoroughly enjoyable. There is not one sarcastic or snide element in the story that makes one feel bad for enjoying *Doctor Who*. It is a terrific serial filled with great guest appearances, impressive location shooting, witty lines and an unexpected conclusion. Unlike "The Pirate Planet," this adventure handles the *Doctor Who* universe respectfully while still finding ample opportunity for appropriate comedy.

Julian Glover returns to *Doctor Who* after his 1964 turn in "The Crusades." Glover also appeared on the *Space: 1999* episode "Alpha Child." In the '80s he was in three blockbusters: *The Empire Strikes Back* (1980), *For Your Eyes Only* (1981) and *Indiana Jones and the Last Crusade* (1989). His co-star in "City of Death," Catherine Schell, is also a *Space: 1999* alumnus. She guest-starred in the Year One adventure "Guardian of Piri" and returned as the shape-shifting Maya in Year Two. Schell has also appeared in the James Bond film *On Her Majesty's Secret Service* (1969), *Return of the Pink Panther* (1975) and the Hammer space Western *Moon Zero Two* (1969). Another guest star, David Graham, appears as the Russian scientist Kerensky; Graham was one of the first men to ever voice the villainous Daleks way back in 1963. He also contributed his vocal skills to episodes of Sylvia and Gerry Anderson's Supermarionation series *Thunderbirds* (1965). The last guest star of note is John Cleese of Monty Python fame. He appears in one short, hilarious scene at the Louvre. With an incredibly pretentious woman at his side, Cleese dissects the TARDIS as a work of art. While these two self-satisfied art critics comment on the police box, the Doctor, Romana and Duggan run inside it and cause it to vanish. This dematerialization does not keep Cleese and his partner from continuing their conversation. This is Cleese's sole shot in *Doctor Who*, and it is a memorable one. Significantly, all of the guest stars seem to have a ball in "City of Death" playing rotten, scheming people. Glover and Schell seem especially comfortable in scenes with Tom Baker. They each remark at least once that no one could possibly be as stupid as the Doctor pretends to be. Of course, Baker's clumsiness in this story contributes to that obvious assumption. However, Baker is clearly using the Troughton method of portraying the Doctor: He fiddles about, stumbles over things and makes a fool of himself to draw out the enemy. In the end, of course, the Doctor is victorious.

"City of Death" has marvelous visual appeal. The production company lensed a great deal of footage in Paris, and the French city is captured in glorious detail. The only downside is the fact that, as usual, the location work is all shot on film and the studio work is done on video. Therefore, there are jarring transitions between the two. The sequence at the dawn of time is also visually appealing. The Earth is shown to be a barren world with mustard mountains and endless tracts of sand and rock. When the TARDIS arrives in this distant past with its beacon flashing, the image recalls on old one in *Doctor Who* history: the ship's arrival in prehistory in "An Unearthly Child." The Jagoroth spaceship is also a marvel of design. It resembles a giant one-eyed spider as it lifts off from the surface of the planet.

Very few genre television series could accommodate a story that begins as an art heist and then transmutes into a time travel story at the dawn of man. *Doctor Who* does it smoothly, and Douglas Adams deserves much of the credit for its funny, inventive aspects. There is a wonderful, witty exchange wherein the Doctor attempts to tell Scaroth that meddling in time is wrong. To the delight of *Doctor Who* fans everywhere, Scaroth responds that meddling is *exactly* what the Doctor does. Baker replies that he is "a professional" in such matters.

"City of Death" guest star Catherine Schell had previously starred in the 1969 space Western *Moon Zero Two* as well as *Space: 1999.*

"City of Death" also deserves credit for unveiling a scene that would be repeated blow-for-blow in the final *Star Trek: The Next Generation* episode "All Good Things": The Doctor takes a human being, Duggan, back to prehistory to stop Jagoroth. He says the barren landscape will one day be the Atlantic Ocean. He then runs his hands through the primordial soup and comments on the creation of man. If the Jagaroth are not stopped, life will never commence here. Almost line-for-line, the god-being "Q" repeats this sequence in "All Good Things."

Q brings Captain Picard back to prehistory. He states the barren landscape will one day be Picard's hometown, Lavarre. He then runs his hand through the primordial soup and says that if an eruption of "anti-time" is not stopped, human life will never evolve. The first passage below is from *Doctor Who*, the second from *Star Trek: The Next Generation*:

> The amniotic fluid from which all life on Earth will spring. The amino acids fuse to form minute cells, cells which eventually evolve into vegetable and animal life. You, Duggan.... It's inert, there's no life in it yet.
>
> —*Doctor Who*, "City of Death" by Douglas Adams

> This is you [Picard]. I'm serious. Right here. Life is about to form on this planet for the very first time. A group of amino acids are about to combine to form the first protein, the building blocks of what you call life. Strange, isn't it? Everything you know, your entire civilization, it all begins right here in this little pond of goo.
>
> —*Star Trek: The Next Generation*, "All Good Things" by Brannon Braga and Ronald Moore

Not only is dialogue, setting and plot scenario similar, so is the character dynamic. In both cases, a superior, time traveling entity introduces a mystified man to his earliest stages of development. This author does not assert that *The Next Generation* "stole" this scene from *Doctor Who*, merely that the situations are identical. But "City of Death" *was* aired 15 years before "All Good Things" was conceived. Interestingly, there is another small *Star Trek* connection in "City of Death." Captain Janeway of *Voyager* also met with Leonardo Da Vinci in the final episode of Season 3, "Scorpion."

"City of Death" is a great Adams–era story and among the best *Who* serials produced. It is available on videocassette.

106. "The Creature from the Pit" Written by David Fisher; Directed by Christopher Barry; Designed by Valerie Wallender; Parts I–IV; Airdates: October 27, November 3, 10, 17, 1979

SYNOPSIS: When Romana installs a Mark III Emergency Transceiver, the TARDIS lurches out of control and materializes in a jungle on planet Chloris. The Doctor and Romana look around and find a giant metallic eggshell that measures 400 meters! The creature who once inhabited this organic spaceship has been cast into a mineshaft by the tyrant of the planet, Lady Adrasta. The Doctor communicates with the alien blob, who reveals that it is Ambassador Erato, a Tythonian. It was tricked into the pit by Adrasta 15 years ago. It was sent on a peaceful trading mission to Chloris and wanted to trade metal ore from Tythonis for chlorophyll from Chloris. Erato's race will wither and die without the life-sustaining chlorophyll. The Doctor exposes Adrasta's crimes, but Erato is not quite as peaceful as he claims. His people intend to destroy the Chloris solar system by a bouncing a neutron star against the Chloris sun! The plan is already in motion and only 24 hours remain until the catastrophe occurs.

GUEST CAST: Lady Adrasta (Myra Frances); Madame Karela (Eileen Way); Engineer Doran (Terry Walsh); Torvin (John Bryans); Edu (Edward Kelsey); Organon (Geoffrey Bayldon); Huntsmen (Philip Denyer, Dave Redgrave); Guard Master (Tommy Wright); Ainu (Tim Munro); Tollund (Morris Barry)

COMMENTARY: "The Creature from the Pit" is another inventive serial. So forward-thinking is this 1979 production that it too would have an impact on the 1987 series *Star Trek: The Next Generation*. Witness the premiere story of that series "Encounter At Farpoint." The new *Enterprise* arrives at a world and discovers that a life form is being exploited by the rulers of the Bandi city. It is tortured and forced to perform tricks for the Bandi. The crew learns that the life form is actually an amorphous jellyfish-type creature that is attempting to communicate with them. Yet no one has been able or willing to understand it! In "Creature from the Pit," the blob creature recurs, the exploitation occurs (the creature is used by Adrasta to terminate her opponents), the failed attempts at communication recur, and the alien's effort to destroy the oppressor also recurs. Although the creatures in "Encounter at Farpoint" are mates, that distinction is a small differences in a similar story. Again, this author is not attempting to suggest that any *Star Trek* authors plagiarized *Doctor Who*, only that *Doctor Who* managed to tackle several concepts that have long been lauded on *The Next Generation*. Indeed, the sequel to *Star Trek* has often been praised as the greatest science fiction television show in history, but a close examination of it reveals many sources of inspiration including not only *Doctor Who* but especially *Space: 1999*, *U.F.O.*, the film *Aliens* and even the often-derided *Battlestar Galactica*. Though *The Next Generation*'s lineage may be a subject for an entirely different book, the purpose of this text is not only to note *Doctor Who*'s antecedents, but also its descendants. In this case, as in "City of Death," *The Next Generation* was clearly not the originator of the concepts it has often been praised for. It is fair to say that in regard to "Encounter At Farpoint," *Doctor Who* explored the premise earlier ... and better.

Humor again plays a central role in "The Creature in the Pit." The story is taken seriously, but the Doctor and Romana encounter some seriously strange characters, including Bayldon's Organon and the incompetent Torvin. It is probably for this reason that many fans do not like "The Creature from the Pit." Nonetheless, this episode is on solid ground from a dramatic perspective. The quest to communicate, and the impediments that stand in the way of such communication, have been explored not only in *Doctor Who* but also in *Star Trek* episodes such as "Metamorphosis" and "The Devil in the Dark." *Doctor Who* takes the concept a bit further by making the hard-to-understand alien a less-than-perfect creature himself. The Tythonian Ambassador Erato at times comes across as vengeful and uncaring. Who can blame him, however, after his treatment by Adrasta? Still, this is quite a step, because the Horta in "Devil in the Dark" and the Companion in "Metamorphosis" were shown to be creatures of pure good, creatures who could not possibly harbor an evil thought. *Doctor Who* took the same concept and made the alien a more well-rounded (no pun intended) character.

107. "Nightmare of Eden" Written by Bob Baker; Directed by Graham Williams & Alan Bromly; Designed by Roger Cann; Parts I–IV; Airdates: November 24, December 1, 8, 15, 1979

SYNOPSIS: The starliner *Empress* comes out of hyperspace on top of the survey vessel *Hecate*. The TARDIS materializes on the *Empress* too, and the Doctor assesses the situation: All the matter where the ships are joined is in a state of flux, and highly unstable.

In the cargo area of the *Empress*, the Doctor and K-9 discover a shipment of a highly addictive narcotic substance called Vraxoin. The Doctor has seen entire planets reduced to what he calls "idiotic complacency" by this drug, which causes agonizing withdrawal symptoms. The Doctor learns that Secker, the *Empress* pilot, was addicted to the Vraxoin when the hyperspace accident occurred. While the Doctor examines a Vraxoin tube, he is assaulted by an unseen assailant, and the Vraxoin is stolen. In the meantime, Romana has met Dr. Tryst, a zoologist of some repute. It is his greatest wish to catalogue every species in the galaxy, and he now has a machine to help him do just that: the C.E.T. (Continuous Event Transmitter), which is currently projecting an image of life on the distant planet Eden.

Romana learns that the C.E.T. creates more than a simple hologram: It actually *converts* life forms and their natural surroundings into magnetic signals. When Secker is attacked by an alien beast at the intersection of jumbled matter, the Doctor suspects that a life form has escaped from this unique machine! Somehow, the accident, the Vraxoin and the C.E.T. machine are joined together in a conspiracy of disastrous proportions....

GUEST CAST: Capt. Rigg (David Daker); Prof. Tryst (Lewis Fiander); Major Stott (Barry Andrews); Officer Fisk (Geoffrey Hinsliff); Capt. Dymond (Geoffrey Bateman); Della (Jennifer Lonsdale); Secker (Stephen Jenn); Costa (Peter Craze); Mandrels (Robert Goodman, David Korff, James Muir, Jan Murzynowski, Derek Southern); *Empress* Passengers (Annette Peters, Maggie Peterson, Peter Roberts, Lionel Sansby); Crew People (Richard Barns, Eden Philips, Sebastian Stride); Computer Voice (Pamela Ruddock)

COMMENTARY: "The Nightmare of Eden" is a variation on that old 1970s Reese's Peanut Butter Cups television commercial which goes: "You got your chocolate in my peanut butter," to which another person replies, "No, you got your peanut butter in my chocolate!" In *Doctor Who*, however, it is two spaceships that get "into" each other courtesy of an ill-timed hyperspace miscalculation. This wild premise leads unexpectedly to a story about virtual reality, as well as a pastiche of police "drug" adventures like *The French Connection* (1973). That said, this immensely clever story is also intensely silly. Fortunately there is enough invention to keep "The Nightmare of Eden" lively throughout. The surprise ending, that the alien Mandrels from Eden are themselves the source element of the drug Vraxoin, recalls Frank Herbert's *Dune* and the secret that the spice comes from the giant worms of Arrakis.

Much of the action involves the C.E.T. machine. In some senses, the C.E.T. is a more advanced version of the Mini-Scope device seen in the Pertwee story "Carnival of Monsters." Like the Scope, the C.E.T. can collect both live specimens and a natural habitat. And, like the Drashigs in "Carnival of Monsters," the Mandrels are some very unfriendly creatures to encounter in *any* arena. In another sense, however, the C.E.T. is a deeper exploration into the world of virtual reality. Like the Time Lord Matrix seen in "The Deadly Assassin" and "The Invasion of Time," this device can project a different world which humans can physically enter. It is amazing that *Doctor Who* predicted virtual reality devices in stories as early 1976, 1977 and 1979.

Perhaps the C.E.T. can also fairly be described as an early version of the popular holodeck seen in *Star Trek: The Next Generation* because it "traps" people inside of it, just like the malfunctioning holodecks in stories such as "The Big Goodbye" and "11001001." The C.E.T. is an effective storytelling instrument in "The Nightmare of Eden," however, because it is integrated into the mystery, not used merely for its own sake. In the *Star Trek* holodeck stories, the audience is always acutely aware that the device and the story it services are ridiculous. Why would anyone willingly use a holodeck after it broke down in "110010001," "Angel

One," "The Big Goodbye," "A Fistful of Datas" and "Emergence," to name but a few of these tales? The very concept of setting an adventure inside a holodeck, an arena where nothing is real and nothing matters, is a dramatic cheat anyway. It is an excuse to widen *Star Trek*'s appeal by featuring different settings that don't legitimately fall within its format parameters. Delightfully, "The Nightmare of Eden" is not an excuse to set a story in the '40s like "The Big Goodbye," or in the Old West like "A Fistful of Datas" or even in the world of James Bond, like the *Deep Space Nine* story "Our Man Bashir." Instead, the C.E.T. serves the dramatic purpose of the teleplay: It is a drug-smuggling venue. Just imagine it: virtual reality drug smuggling! Now that is something that Crockett and Tubbs on *Miami Vice* (1984–1988) never had to contend with!

As *Doctor Who* is prone to do, "The Nightmare of Eden" mixes genres to form a new and unique whole. Major Stott and the drug smuggling angle of the program recall cop shows and films such as *The French Connection.* The accident and the passengers of the space liner recalls the intrigue of *Murder on the Orient Express.* These components jell nicely with the "pure" SF elements of hyperspace, rampaging monsters and the amazing C.E.T. machine. The "ocean liner in space" angle of this serial would be repeated not only in the *Doctor Who* serial "Terror of the Vervoids" (in which dangerous cargo, Vervoids instead of Mandrels, break out and wreak havoc) but also in Luc Besson's imagery-laden space opera *The Fifth Element* (1997).

"The Nightmare of Eden" is one of *Doctor Who*'s few forays into the subject of drug abuse. The narcotic Vraxoin is referred to as something that has destroyed entire worlds with its addictive effects. There is one frightening moment in this serial when Romana is almost forced to take the drug, for which there is no known antidote. In later years, *The Next Generation* also did a "just say no" to drugs story entitled "Symbiosis."

108. "The Horns of Nimon" Written by Anthony Read; Directed by Kenneth McBain; Designed by Graeme Story; Parts I–IV; Airdates: December 22, 29, 1979, January 5, 12, 1980

SYNOPSIS: Soldeed is the gullible but ambitious ruler of Skonnos. His world has been promised great military strength by an unseen creature called "The Nimon." All Soldeed must do to attain it is send young men and women and valuable hymetusite crystals into a labyrinth in tribute to "The Nimon." Since this is not a pleasant fate, Skonnos has been importing the crystals and the sacrifices from a neighboring world, the peaceful Aneth.

The Nimon is actually an alien with humanoid body and a head shaped like a bull's. This alien has been hoarding hymetusite crystals in an effort to bring his race to Skonnos through a black hole. This is a typical ploy of the Nimons. They have drained one planet after another of both precious people and resources. To accomplish this task, they always send forward a scout who promises greedy rulers power. Now the Doctor, Romana and K-9 must not only stop the Nimon and shut down the black hole portal to Crinoth, but find their way out of the labyrinth to boot!

GUEST CAST: Soldeed (Graham Crowden); Seth (Simon Gipps-Kent); Sorak (Michael Osborne); Teka (Janet Ellis); Skonnos co-pilot (Malcolm Terris); Pilot (Bob Horney); Sezom (John Bailey); Nimons (Bob Appleby, John Hacker, Robin Sherringham); Voice of the Nimon (Clifford Norgate)

COMMENTARY: Like Season 15's "Underworld," which revised the mythology of Persephone (P7E), "The Horns of Nimon" is an attempt to remake the legend of Minos, Ariadne, Theseus and the Minotaur in an outer space setting. The analogies work quite well on a surface level. "Skonnos" is a jumble of the name "Knossos." Soldeed's name comes from maze creator "Daedalus," but his role is that of Minos of Crete. He transports innocent Anethians (Athenians) to die in the labyrinth. The maze serves as a housing facility for the alien Nimons, who physically resemble the mythological man-beast called the Minotaur. Finally, the Anethian Seth is Theseus. Although the mythological aspects fit together well, this story nonetheless begs the question: why? What was to gain by translating the Minotaur legend to *Doctor Who*? What is *Doctor Who*'s feelings about the ancient Greek myth? What does the audience learn about the Doctor in "The Horns of Nimon"? Just because mythological elements are cleverly grafted into a serial does not necessarily mean it is particularly good or insightful. All it really means is that someone knows their myths. There is, however, the British holiday season of the "panto" or pantomime, and "The Horns of Nimon," which aired around Christmas, seems obliged to offer typical "panto"-style in-jokes and references.

The mythological or panto elements barely mask that "The Horns of Nimon" is another "revolution" story like "The Daleks," "The Web Planet" and "The Sunmakers." Once again the Doctor stops the exploiters, here the Nimon, and helps the Anethians regain freedom. The Season 17 serials are so inventive in their structure and imaginings compared to the "The Horns of Nimon," which is memorable only in its superficial, mythologically based trappings, not in its content.

Writer Anthony Read would tackle the same material again in 1981. He directed an episode of the British fantasy series *Into the Labyrinth* that was entitled, appropriately enough, "Minotaur." Like "The Horns of Nimon," "Minotaur" revised the myth of Minos and Crete, this time to accommodate the series cast members as new versions of Daedalus, Ariadne and Theseus. Who better to direct that story than someone who had already handled the translation of the same antique material adequately on *Doctor Who*?

The Nimons, with their pull-over masks and short white stubs as horns, are not the most convincing aliens ever seen in *Doctor Who*. For trivia's sake, it is interesting to note that the Minotaur had already been seen before in *Who*. David Prowse played the beast in the Pertwee serial "The Time Monster."

109. "Shada" Written by Douglas Adams; Directed by Pennant Roberts; Designed by Victor Meredith [Unfinished serial; no airdate/intended to be six parts]

SYNOPSIS: In Gallifreyan lore, Shada is the Time Lord penal planet. The galaxy's worst criminals (Zygons, Daleks, Rasputin, etc.) are incarcerated there.

Shada's location is a secret, its existence unconfirmed, but Skagra, an alien scientist bent on galactic conquest, has begun the search for it. He believes that Salyavin, a criminal Time Lord, is held there. Skagra intends to free Salyavin and take over the galaxy, but first he must find Shada with the help of a book called *The Ancient Law of Gallifrey*, which reveals the location of the prison.

Kindly old Prof. Chronotis has been teaching peacefully at Cambridge for many years — 300, in fact! He is a Time Lord and he has had *The Ancient Law of Gallifrey* in his care for some time. He contacts the Doctor and Romana and asks them to take the book off his hands. He wants it returned to Gallifrey so it cannot be stolen or used by an evil force. The Doctor and Romana agree to visit Cambridge and take care of this important errand, but when they meet with Chronotis the elderly Time Lord discovers the book has disappeared! A human graduate student, Chris Parsons, has borrowed it! Now the Doctor and his friends must save the galaxy before Skagra gets his hands on that book.

GUEST CAST: Prof. Chronotis (Denis Carey); Skagra (Christopher Neame); Chris Parsons (Daniel Hill); Porter (Gerald Campion); Victoria Burgoyne (Clare Keightley); Caldera (Derek Pollitt); Constable (John Hallett); Passenger (David Strong); Krargs (James Coombs)

COMMENTARY: It has often been stated that "having" is not so great a thing as "wanting." Such is probably the case with the legendary *Doctor Who* serial "Shada." This unfinished adventure has been talked about at length in fan circles since 1980. All through the decade, saddened fans mourned its incomplete status and speculated intently about it. Many *Who* fans believed it would have been the greatest episode of *Doctor Who* ever, one that would miraculously reveal Season 17 in a whole new, presumably more positive, light. Others felt that given its placement in the Adams years of *Doctor Who*, it probably would not have been very good if it *had* been finished. This debate raged, and it was fueled by contradictory comments from producer Graham Williams, who insisted the serial would have been a masterpiece, and Adams himself, who thought the serial had its share of problems.

Years after "Shada" has been released on videotape in its incomplete form, the fan furor has died down. Everyone who wanted to see it has now seen it for themselves, and can judge objectively its merits. Although critical pieces of the story are missing, it is possible to speculate from the recent video release how the serial was coming together. It does not rank as a great episode of *Doctor Who*. It is an interesting story, but even within the context of Season 17, "Shada" does not seem as inventive as "City of Death" or "The Nightmare of Eden." (It is perhaps more epic in scope than "Horns of Nimon" and "The Creature from the Pit.") Arguably, it also has more zip than does "Destiny of the Daleks." Quality-wise, "Shada" falls somewhere in the middle of the Season 17 roster. This in not a left-handed compliment since Season 17 is a more inventive and successful year than Season 16. If only "The Pirate Planet" had been left unfinished instead...

"Shada" was never completed because of a two-month BBC technical crew strike during the 1979 holiday season. When the episode was cancelled by the BBC in January 1980, all of the location shooting in and around Cambridge and the Thames had been completed. All but three or four days of studio filming were complete as well.[15] By the time John Nathan-Turner, the new *Doctor Who* producer, stepped up to assemble Season 18, it was impossible to put the pieces of "Shada" back together again. Cast and crew members had all moved on to other commitments. The serial was officially dead, and the fan mythology about it began to grow. Pieces of "Shada" were first shown as part of "The Five Doctors" in 1983, when Tom Baker refused to appear in the anniversary special. More than ten years later, the existing footage of "Shada" was edited together with some verbal narration and released "as is" by the BBC. The debate was then over, and the fans finally got what they wanted. Today "Shada" is rarely discussed.

Thematically, "Shada" has interesting flourishes. The central concept is one of a Time Lord penal planet. It is hard to imagine why the Time Lords would ever need a penal planet. History shows that they either obliterate their enemies from the face of time ("The War Games"), trap them in time loops ("Image of the Fendahl," "The Invasion of Time") or erect force fields around their planets ("The War Games"). With that kind of strong-arm justice, a Time Lord prison seems unlikely and unnecessary. Still, it would have been great to see cameo appearances by a Dalek, a Cyberman and a Zygon. One has to wonder however, why a Dalek or a Cyberman would be so dangerous that they would be housed in this top secret prison. Cybermen and Daleks are just drones, not individual geniuses who need to be kept from the universe at large. More innovative is Skagra's idea to take over the universe. He wants to imprint all sentient minds in the universe with his own mental pathways. Talk about megalomania carried to an extreme! It also would have been interesting to meet Prof. Chronotis, yet another Time Lord who has elected to live on Earth, following in the footsteps of Ken Po in "Planet of Spiders" and the Meddling Monk in "The Time Meddler."

The character name Prof. Chronotis recurs in the Douglas Adams novel *Dirk Gently's Holistic Detective Agency*. "Shada" is available in its unfinished form on videocassette.

SEASON 18

110. "The Leisure Hive" Written by David Fisher; Directed by Lovett Bickford; Designed by Tom Yardley-Jones; Parts I–IV; Airdates: August 30, September 6, 13, 20, 1980

SYNOPSIS: In need of a vacation after a bad day at Brighton Beach, the Doctor and Romana high-tail it to Argolis, home of the galaxy-famous Leisure Hive. Because of a recent war with a reptilian race called the Foamosi, all Argolin life now exists within the pleasure domes. Unfortunately, the Leisure Hive, once the tourist highlight of the ten galaxies, is going bankrupt. It is out-of-date, the radiation shields are failing, and there has been an offer to buy the sinking enterprise. All the Argolins have in their favor is that they have been conducting experiments with tachyon technology. The Doctor is impressed to see a tachyon device that utilizes "unreal transfer," but soon learns the hard way that the technology is unsafe. Soon, Romana and the Doctor are caught in a deadly plot to destroy Argolis.

GUEST CAST: Mena (Adrienne Corri); Pangol (David Haig); Morix (Laurence Payne); Hardin (Nigel Lambert); Vargos (Martin Fisk); Brock (John Collin); Stimson (David Allison); Klout (Ian Talbot); Chief Foamasi (Andrew Lane); Argolin Tour Guide (Roy Montague); Generator Voice (Clifford Norgate)

COMMENTARY: Virtual reality gets a third tweak in David Fisher's "The Leisure Hive" as yet another V.R. system similar to the C.E.T. in "The Nightmare of Eden" malfunctions. This tachyon generator actually tears an Argolis tourist limb from limb! This is one of the serial's grislier moments, but perhaps not as grisly overall as the picture Adrienne Corri's Mena paints of life after a deadly war. She and her people have become sterile, and unless something is done immediately, the Argolin race will become extinct. *Doctor Who* has always been anti-war, in serials as diverse as "Doctor Who and the Silurians," "The Daleks" and "Destiny of the Daleks," and "The Leisure Hive" falls squarely in this tradition.

Issues of old age are also addressed in this story. Amazingly, it is the Doctor who is affected by this malady. It is rare in the series for the Doctor to become sick himself, although it did happen in Season 15's "The Invisible Enemy." It is even more rare for the Doctor to be seen as vulnerable, but that is exactly what happens when the Argolin time flow machine ages the Doctor several hundred years. It is sad to watch as this powerful, virile man loses his faculties to creeping senility. *Star Trek* featured a similar "aging" story entitled "The Deadly Years" in its second Season. *Star Trek: The Next Generation* would also do an aging story in its second season, "Unnatural Selection."

"The Leisure Hive" also introduces the concept of recreation planets to sci-fi television. Though *Star Trek* episodes made references to "Wrigley's Pleasure Planet," that world was never actually visited by the *Enterprise* and "Shore Leave" is more a mystery than an intentional excursion. "The Leisure Hive"'s world of recreation and pleasure is echoed in later series such as *Deep Space Nine* and *The Next Generation,* both of which highlight a pleasure world called Risa in episodes "Captain's Holiday" and "The Game."

In terms of *Doctor Who* continuity, "The Leisure Hive" is significant because it sees the removal of the "Randomizer" from the TARDIS control panel. For those who do not recall this instrument, the Randomizer was installed at the end of the Key to Time saga. It caused the TARDIS to traverse the universe without any specific destination. This was done so that the angry Black Guardian could not track the Doctor after his destruction of the Key to Time. The Randomizer was in place all through Season 17. In John Nathan-Turner's first serial, he instructed that the Randomizer be removed so the Doctor could again be in control of his TARDIS and his destiny. This was probably a good idea. It is quite one thing to go somewhere only to find that you have not arrived where you intended (a common plot device in the early years of *Doctor Who*). It is quite another to simply travel about aimlessly, never knowing where you going to land next. The Randomizer was difficult from a logical standpoint as well. It is a huge coincidence that it would land the Doctor on Skaro, the homeworld of his nemesis, the Daleks in "The Destiny of the Daleks." The Randomizer also inhibited drama because the Doctor could not now go to Earth even if he wanted to. It was a wise decision to remove it. This act, however, would have repercussions for the Doctor in Season 20, because the Black Guardian would indeed catch up with him.

Adrienne Corri, who plays the gold-skinned Mena with such dignity, is a familiar face to genre buffs. She appeared in the films *Devil Girl from Mars* (1954), *Corridors of Blood* (1958) with Boris Karloff and Christopher Lee, *Moon Zero Two* (1969) and *A Clockwork Orange* (1971).

"The Leisure Hive" is available on videocassette.

111. "Meglos" Written by John Flanagan & Andrew McCulloch; Directed by Terence Dudley; Designed by Philip Lindley; Parts I–IV; Airdates: September 27, October 4, 11, 18, 1980

SYNOPSIS: On Tigella, the glowing Dodecahedron is the source of all the planet's energy. Although it is supposedly inexhaustible, the power cells of the massive device have recently begun to fluctuate. Zastor, the ruler of Tigella, is worried. Unless the Dodecahedron's fluctuations can be controlled, the Tigellans will lose power to their underground city and be forced to live on the harsh surface of their world where vicious, carnivorous plants rule the jungles. To make things more difficult, Zastor leads a divided people. There are two factions, the Savants and the Deons, and each is equal in size and influence. They ruthlessly oppose each other on the critical issue of the Dodecahedron. To the Savants it is but a scientific instrument, a device that powers the city. To the Deons, however, it is a god.

On the planet Zolfa-Thura, a xerophyte creature (a plant resembling a cactus) called Meglos hires mercenaries to steal the Dodecahedron. Meglos is also aware of the Doctor's impending arrival and he traps the Time Lord in a chronic hysteresis, a time loop! This will keep him from assisting Tigella. Meglos then changes his face into a duplicate of the Doctor's! Disguised as the Doctor, Meglos travels to Tigella to meet with Zastor. His plan is to steal the Dodecahedron from the Tigellans.

GUEST CAST: Lexa (Jacqueline Hill); Zastor (Edward Underdown); Deedrix (Crawford Logan); Caris (Colette Gleeson); Capt. Grugger (Bill Fraser); Brotocac (Frederick Treves); George Morris (Christopher Owen); Tigellan (Simon Shaw)

COMMENTARY: If fans watching "Meglos" are suddenly struck with the notion that they recognize the actress portraying Lexa, there is a good explanation. The actress essaying this role is Jacqueline Hill, the beautiful and talented performer who played classic companion Barbara Wright from "An Unearthly Child" to "The Chase," the first 16 serials in *Doctor Who* history. It is a pleasure to see Hill again, especially in a role that has some significant differences from the Barbara Wright all *Doctor Who* fans love. Lexa is unlike Barbara in her religious fanaticism, but there is surely a touch of Yitaxa in Hill's haughty interpretation of the role. (Yitaxa is the Aztec god Barbara impersonated in the memorable "The Aztecs.")

Other than the reappearance of an old friend, "Meglos" is a straightforward *Doctor Who* adventure with less of an accent on humor than virtually any recent entry. Instead, it is a return to the moral lesson first established in the Season 1 entry "The Keys of Marinus": man must work together and build his own future. He cannot depend on devices that alter his behavior (as in "The Keys of Marinus") or those that promise paradise (the Dodecahedron in "Meglos"). Both serials end with the Doctor destroying the object of value. Man, *Doctor Who* preaches, is better off living on his own ingenuity than depending on a device for artificial utopia.

"Meglos" is also the return of the "doppelganger" motif, which by Season 18 had been seen in the series almost too many times to document. Hartnell met his double at least twice, in the serials "The Chase" and "The Massacre." Troughton met his doppelganger in "The Enemy of the World." Ian Marter saw Harry Sullivan doubled in both "The Terror of the Zygons" and "The Android Invasion." "The Android Invasion" also featured doppelgangers of Sarah Jane Smith and the fourth Doctor. The first Romana encountered a lookalike on Tara in "The Androids of Tara." "Meglos" follows in the tradition of these other stories by making an evil version of Tom Baker's cheery Doctor. In this case, the doppelganger's perfect appearance is at points marred by the protrusion of cactus spears.

The doppelganger is not the only genre cliché in "Meglos." The evil plant is also back. By this point, the Doctor had already been menaced by evil seaweed in "Fury from the Deep" and the Krynoids in "The Seeds of Doom." After defeating the cactus man in "Meglos," the Doctor would again face evil plants in "Terror of the Vervoids."

"Meglos" is Terence Dudley's first directorial contribution to *Doctor Who*. He would later helm "Four to Doomsday" and "The King's Demons" for Davison's fifth incarnation. Before working for the Time Lord, Dudley directed episodes of *Doomwatch* in 1970 including "Tomorrow, the Rat" and "You Killed Toby Wren." For the 1972 season of *Doomwatch*, he wrote and directed the season premiere "Fire and Brimstone." He also wrote "Waiting for a Knighthood," which was helmed by frequent *Who* director Pennant Roberts.

With another *Who* veteran, Don Houghton, "Meglos" scribe Anthony Read wrote the fifth adventure of *Sapphire and Steele* in 1981.

112. "Full Circle" Written by Andrew Smith; Directed by Peter Grimwade; Designed by Janet Budden; Parts I–IV; Airdates: October 25, November 1, 8, 15, 1980

SYNOPSIS: The Doctor and Romana have been summoned to Gallifrey, and a Time Lord summons cannot be ignored. Romana is afraid she is being recalled since her apprenticeship with the Doctor is finished. She does not wish to return to the static environment of Gallifrey, and fate intervenes: The TARDIS becomes trapped in E-Space (Exo-Space) as opposed to N-Space (normal space). The Doctor theorizes that the TARDIS has traveled through a rare phenomenon known as a CVE (Charged Vacuum Emboitement). They are now entrapped forever in Exo-Space unless they find another CVE through which they can return!

On Alzarius, the Doctor and Romana encounter a teenager named Adric, a refugee from a downed starliner from the planet Terredon. This young mathematical genius warns the duo about something called Mistfall. The Doctor is curious about this legend and heads out with K-9 to investigate it. He approaches a marsh and watches in horror as scaly, hideous monsters ascend from it...

GUEST CAST: Varsh (Richard Willis); Keara (June Page); Tylos (Bernard Padden); Nefred (James Bree); Omril (Andrew Forbes); Dexeter (Tony Calvin); Garif (Alan Rowe); Draith (Leonard Maguire); Rysik (Adrian Gibbs); Login (George Baker); Marshman (Barney Lawrence); Marshchild (Norman Bacon)

COMMENTARY: The story arc that will result in the loss of Romana and K-9 from the *Doctor Who* format begins in "Full Circle." This story by Andrew Smith is also the first of what fans refer to as "The E-Space Trilogy." While trying to get Romana back safely to Gallifrey, the Doctor ends up trapped with the TARDIS in a sort of pocket universe where space has a green hue. The TARDIS will remain trapped in Exo-Space for the next two serials, "State of Decay" and "Warrior's Gate." Exo-space will ultimately be the final home of Romana as well.

Other than this new galactic venue, "Full Circle" is very much in the tradition of earlier *Doctor Who* stories. It once again highlights a society which has lost sight of its heritage. Unlike the people of the Sevateem in "The Face of Evil," however, the Alzarians have actually assumed the heritage of another society, that of the Terradonians. This is a minor twist on the cliché of the splintered world descended into barbarism, but it is enough of a shift to make the story's antecedents less obvious. The scenario also provides for a startling revelation at the climax. Adric and all his friends are descendants of the hideous Marshmen!

Beyond this concept, "Full Circle" revisits common *Who* clichés. The first concerns K-9. The poor dog seems to spend half his tenure on *Doctor Who* being destroyed ("The Stones of Blood," "Warrior's Gate") or repaired ("Destiny of the Daleks," "The Leisure Hive, "Image of the Fendahl"). Was the cybernetic canine that difficult to integrate into the formula? At least K-9 did not suffer the indignity of the companion called Kamelion, a shape-shifting robot introduced in "The King's Demon." Kamelion came aboard the TARDIS only to remain hidden until his final appearance half-a-season later in "Planet of Fire." Clearly, however, K-9 caused some problems for the production team from a purely mechanical standpoint (hence his absence from "The Power of Kroll"). The robot was controlled by remote control and was obviously limited in what kind of terrain he could traverse. Still, it is a shame that this charming, loyal character spends so much time sidelined. In "The Full Circle" his decapitated head is used as a club by the Marshmen. Oh, the indignity of being a dog!

"The Full Circle" is also familiar because it revisits arachnids as agents of evil, recalling "Planet of the Spiders." The episode "Full Circle" also coincides with a *Space: 1999* title from 1975. On *1999*, "The Full Circle" was also an evolutionary story. The men and women of Alpha passed through a mist (mistfall?) and ended up as devolved cavemen. "The Full Circle" on *1999* preceded the *Doctor Who* story by five years.

Since the groundwork is laid in "Full Circle" to eliminate Lalla Ward's Romana from the series, it is only natural that a new companion should be introduced. Accordingly, Matthew Waterhouse makes his first appearance as Adric. Waterhouse is a charming young actor and a welcome addition to the cast. He works especially well with Tom Baker and Lalla Ward. For the first time since Ian, Susan and Barbara, there is a legitimate "family"-style relationship in the TARDIS. The Doctor is the father; Romana is the matriarch; Adric is the precocious teen; K-9 the beloved pet. This dynamic would only continue until the conclusion of "Warrior's Gate," however. Adric would lose his mother, his pet and his father (to regeneration) in just a few short weeks. Waterhouse also has the distinction of playing the first companion since Katarina and Sara Kingdom in "The Dalek Masterplan" (1965) who meets an unpleasant end: He is killed in the Season 19 story "Earthshock." His death actually pleased many series fans. Today there are "I Hate Adric" message boards and websites all over the Internet! Like another genre teenager, Wesley Crusher, young men are not usually well-received in sci-fi television. Perhaps they remind some fans too much of themselves?

113. "State of Decay" Written by Terrance Dicks; Directed by Peter Moffatt; Designed by Christine Ruscoe; Parts I–IV; Airdates: November 22, 29, December 6, 13, 1980

SYNOPSIS: The TARDIS is still trapped in E-space and has materialized on an unfamiliar world. The Doctor and Romana are unaware that Adric has stowed away and they set out to explore. They are quickly captured by a group of angry rebels. Kalmar, the leader of the resistance, informs the travelers that his people are fighting for their lives against the repressive King Zargo and Queen Camilla, despotic rulers who reside in luxury in a massive tower that dominates the landscape. The Doctor and Romana join the fight against the tyrants but make a powerful discovery: The King and the Queen are not natives of this planet. They are also travelers from N-Space!

Adric is captured by Lord Aukon, the sinister minion of Zargo and Camilla, and taken to the tower-spaceship. The Doctor realizes that a rescue attempt is now imperative if Adric is to survive. Zargo, Aukon and Camilla are the original crew of the ancient spacecraft from N-Space. They have survived here for 1000 years by draining and then feasting on the blood of the peasants. They are vampires! Even worse, they are supplying blood to a terrible entity hidden beneath the tower. The Doctor is familiar with this gigantic entity because the Time Lords battled it generations ago. The Great Vampire, as it is known in Gallifreyan lore, must now be destroyed at all costs.

GUEST CAST: King Zargo (William Lindsay); Queen Camilla (Rachel Davies); Lord Aukon (Emrys James); Tarak (Thane Bettany); Ivo (Clinton Greyn); Habris (Iain Rattrary); Kalmar (Arthur Hewlett); Marta (Rhoda Lewis); Karl (Dean Allen); Roga (Stuart Fell); Veros (Stacy Davies); Zoldaz (Stuart Black); Guard (Alan Chuntz)

COMMENTARY: Although "State of Decay" takes place in Exo-Space instead of on Earth, it is yet another example of the "Daemons" prototype. Once again the source of a legend is found to have an extraterrestrial source and the method of execution (a stake) is an ancient, legendary one. The mythology plundered this time is from the genre of vampirism. Even within the confines of *Who* lore, "State of Decay" recalls another vampire story, the Pertwee–era "Claws of Axos." Space vampires have also been seen in *Lifeforce* (1985), which was based on a Colin Wilson novel entitled *Space Vampires*, a 1981 *Buck Rogers in the 25th Century* episode (also called "Space Vampires") and the low-budget 1966 Curtis Harrington production *Queen of Blood*. In that story, astronauts John Saxon and Dennis Hopper discovered a space vampire who was the last of her alien race.

Terrance Dicks' first story since "Robot" in Season 12 is a disappointment because it is also reminiscent of the Season 15 entry "Image of the Fendahl." In both stories, the villain (either the Fendahl gestalt or the Great Vampire) is revealed to be an ancient enemy of the Time Lords, one which was thought vanquished eons ago. Though Dicks is one of *Who*'s best writers, "State of Decay" does not represent his best work. The third element in the story is also derivative: a revolution against oppressive rulers. Of course, the *Time Machine* template had been at work on the series since episode 2, "The Daleks," and was seen in *Doctor Who* as recently as "The Horns of Nimon" and "The Pirate Planet."

The re-use of early *Who* elements begins to become really oppressive at this point in the series' history. Already "Meglos" took a new stab at the doppelganger clichés. "The Full Circle" was to some extent a "forgotten heritage" story like "The Ark" or "The Face of Evil." "State of Decay"'s problems are along the same lines. Though *Doctor Who* has proven to be a good show by reusing clichés and common situations in new ways, nothing new is added to any of these tropes in Season 18. In many ways, John Nathan-Turner's first season represents more of a slump than the much maligned Season 17. At least in that season there were inventive if rather oddball stories such as "The Creature from the Pit" and "The Nightmare of Eden." They may not be perfect *Doctor Who*, but at least they stretched the series in new directions. Unfortunately the same cannot be said for "State of Decay."

"State of Decay" is available on videocassette in a three-pack with "Full Circle" and "Warrior's Gate."

114. "Warrior's Gate" Written by Steven Gallagher; Directed by Paul Joyce; Designed by Graeme Story; Parts I–IV; Airdates: January 3, 10, 17, 24, 1981

SYNOPSIS: Trapped in the substratum universe of E-Space, the Doctor suggests that the solution to their entrapment may lie in a random coin toss. Adric takes this theory rather too seriously and programs coordinates into the TARDIS based on a random sampling using one coin toss as a reference. When engaged, the TARDIS is sent spinning through a time vortex. The door to the TARDIS blasts open and the Doctor and his companions encounter the legendary Time Winds. This elemental force of nature sweeps through the TARDIS and K-9 is caught in it. As the Time Winds waft through the type 40 capsule, another strange occurrence is witnessed: An alien humanoid named Biroc breaks into the TARDIS and operates the central control column.

The TARDIS arrives at the intersection of E-Space and N-Space, the point where positive and negative universes merge. This pocket of matter, called "The Zero Point," is rapidly shrinking. The Doctor investigates and comes across an ancient gateway replete with a set of mirror-like entrances to other worlds and other times.

The gateway is protected by giant robots called Gundans, but the Doctor encounters Biroc again and together they pass through the gateway where the Doctor learns of Biroc's people, the Tharil. The Tharil were once the controllers of a galaxy-spanning empire. Now they are slaves to the heartless Rorvik and his Slavers. The Doctor helps to liberate the Tharil, but he is forced to leave two of his most beloved companions behind in E-Space...

GUEST CAST: Biroc (David Weston); Rorvik (Clifford Rose); Packard (Kenneth Cope); Laslo (Jeremy Gittins); Aldo (Freddie Earlie); Sagan (Vincent Pickering); Royce (Harry Waters); Lane (David Kincaid); Gundan (Robert Vowles)

COMMENTARY: "Warrior's Gate" is a good story by Stephen Gallagher as well as a major downer for *Who* fans. This is another sad goodbye to two more companions, along the lines of "The Chase" or "The War Games." But one is glad that Romana and K-9 will have a life together somewhere...even if it is not with their Time Lord friend. John Leeson, the actor who voiced K-9 in Seasons 15, 16, and 18, would have preferred a rather different death for the beloved robot:

> K-9 should have gone out on a heroic mission and been blown to smithereens within full sight of the Doctor. Tears would be shed — but that would be THE END. That would be clean and final and heroic and good and wonderful. ...But then, as everyone knows, it didn't happen that way.[16]

Indeed, K-9 is merely injured in "Warrior's Gate." Perhaps a better term for it is hobbled, or made lame. This is a rather terrible situation, obviously akin to having one's beloved pet fall ill with a terminal disease. No one wants to see a pet suffer, and certainly no *Doctor Who* fan or K-9 lover wants to see the robot dog injured as badly as he is in "Warrior's Gate." This fate is effective on one hand, and not so effective on the other. It works well, perhaps because it is realistic. It adds a verisimilitude to the Doctor's universe that K-9 should be wounded in such a horrible fashion and be forced to remain behind. *Doctor Who* companions are frequently sent off to be married and the stories take on an unbelievable, "fairy tale" feeling. Not so here. There is real pain and genuine emotion in the pet's departure. However, the manner of K-9's injury is not entirely believable. This is a creature who has been shattered, blasted and gutted. Yet he is always reassembled as good as new with what seems like a minimum of effort. Thus K-9's wound in "Warrior's Gate" is just one in a long line of "on the job" injuries for this cybernetic organism rather than a surprise that leaves audience members gasping in shock. Of course, had the situation been different, had the Doctor been anywhere in N-Space, he might have saved his pet. Maybe that fact makes K-9's fate more tragic.

What is it that makes K-9's permanent departure from *Doctor Who* so sad? Ironically, it is the very thing that made him such a popular companion in the first place. Like any good cat or dog, K-9 loves the Doctor unconditionally. The Doctor can badger him, neglect him or snap at him, but K-9 will always wag his tail and be a loyal friend. Although K-9 is a robot, he is also a creature of unconditional love. Fans responded to this characteristic and an emotional bond was forged. K-9 is as beloved as Lassie, Benji or any other cinematic or television dog. Because he is cute as well as smart, he hits a tender spot in all pet-loving fans. One thing is for certain: K-9 was missed after "Warrior's Gate." There was never another companion like him.

Of course, Romana also leaves in "Warrior's Gate." It is sad to see the Time Lady go, of course, but not nearly so sad as saying goodbye to K-9. Why? There are two reasons. The first is that Romana had been personified by two actresses. Many fans no doubt already felt as if Romana had left the series when Tamm was replaced by Ward. The audience had already lost Romana once. Secondly, it is an accepted fact in *Doctor Who* that humanoid companions *leave*. It is expected. All fans know it is just a matter of time before the current companion leaves, and is replaced by a new one. K-9's departure was much more serious, because he was not human and thus not affected by contracts, better job offers or salary disputes. No one expected the pet to leave for a better part in another BBC drama. He could have stayed in the *Doctor Who* family forever.

Romana's journey had been a part of *Doctor Who* since the beginning of Season 16. She started out in "The Ribos Operation" as an arrogant young spitfire. She wanted to do things her own way. She learned many things from her time with the Doctor, including patience, compassion and humor. In "Warrior's Gate," this journey is complete, and the Romana who stays behind to help the Tharils is a very different person than the one who first stepped aboard the TARDIS during the Key to Time saga. Obviously, this journey would have seemed all the more powerful had only one actress played the part (either Tamm or Ward). As it stands now, Ward's softer interpretation of Romana negates some of the character's self-sacrifice in "Warrior's Gate." Romana's choice seems appropriate because Ward's Romana has always been "nice." Imagine the impact of Tamm's haughty Romana choosing to join the struggle of the Tharils.

Obviously, the departure of beloved friends is what pops to mind first when discussing "Warrior's Gate." Perhaps this is not really fair because the story itself is quite effective. It introduces the "Time Winds," a frightening elemental force that had never been featured on the series before. It also has a nice kind of "karma" to it. The oppressors (the Tharils) have now become the oppressed. They have tasted their own poison, and have been changed forever by this fact. The teleplay is a fresh, exciting one that makes good use of science fiction concepts such as time gates, space slavers and the fall of galactic empires. What else could anybody want? The Tharils, with their lion-like countenances, foreshadow the appearance of Vincent on the American television series *Beauty and the Beast* in 1988.

With "Warrior's Gate," an era of *Doctor Who* ended. K-9 and Romana were left behind, and the next few stories took on a gloomy atmosphere. By the end of the season, Tom Baker would also leave *Doctor Who*, the third emotional departure in one year!

115. "The Keeper of Traken" Written by Johnny Byrne; Directed by John Black; Designed by Tony Burroughs; Parts I–IV; Airdates: January 31, February 7, 14, 21, 1981

SYNOPSIS: On its return to N-Space, the TARDIS enters the region of space known as the Mettula Orionsis, controlled by the Traken Union. Almost immediately upon crossing into this territory, an old man appears inside the TARDIS control room. He is the Keeper of Traken and he has assumed control of the vessel. The Doctor and Adric are told that an all-pervading evil is coming to Traken. When they arrive on Traken, they think they have found it in the strange, evil statue called the Melkur. In fact, the Melkur is more than a statue…it is the TARDIS of an old nemesis named the Master! The Master is on Traken to steal the life force of Consul Tremas, young Nyssa's father!

GUEST CAST: Consul Tremas/The Master (Anthony Ainley); The "Dying" Master (Peter Pratt); The Keeper of Traken (Denis Carey); Melkur (Geoffrey Beevers); Consul Seron (John Woodnutt); Kassia (Sheila Ruskin); Katura (Margot Van Der Burgh); Neman (Roland Olivers); Fosters (Philip Bloomfield, Liam Prendergrast

COMMENTARY: Johnny Byrne's first credit on *Doctor Who* is a story that falls squarely in the genre of "evil awakening" that has been so prevalent *Who* history. Just like Sutekh in "Pyramids of Mars," Eldrad in "The Hand of Fear," the Mandragora power in "Masque of Mandragora" and the Fendahline Gestalt in "Image of the Fendahl," the Master in "The Keeper of Traken" manipulates people and events around him so he can be restored to health and vitality.

Anthony Ainley plays Consul Tremas, but only in the final seconds of the story does he step into the role left vacant by the death of Roger Delgado in 1973. Ainley would reappear as the Master in "Logopolis," "Castrovalva," "Time Flight," "The King's Demons," "The Five Doctors," "Planet of Fire," "Mark of the Rani," "The Ultimate Foe" and "Survival." His reign as the evil Time Lord would pit him once more against Tom Baker, five times against Davison, once against Colin Baker and once against McCoy. Ironically, by appearing in "The Five Doctors,"

After meeting Tom Baker in episode #115, "The Keeper of Traken," Sarah Sutton's Nyssa went on to become the most trusted companion of the fifth Doctor.

Ainley was able also to encounter Pertwee and Troughton. This means that he has worked with all incarnations of the Doctor but Hartnell's.

Ainley's version of the Master differs from Delgado's in some ways. Ainley is perhaps a more elegant, more handsome figure than his predecessor. He is chic in his black velvet uniform and black gloves. His incarnation also lacks a certain humility about himself that made Delgado's Master both wily and witty. Instead, Ainley's personification is one of very little humor. His Master is a creature that you would dare not lock eyes with. He has a cold, cruel demeanor. Ainley is also fortunate that the Master is marginally better written during his reign than the role was back in the '70s. In episodes such as "The Five Doctors" and "The Ultimate Foe," the Master *almost* becomes a three-dimensional villain at last.

"The Keeper of Traken" also introduces the lovely Sarah Sutton. She plays Nyssa, a new companion to replace Romana. While Nyssa is strong on science and mathematics, she is not nearly so strong in personality. Once Peter Davison takes over the role of the Doctor, it is very much an issue of the bland acting with the bland. Nyssa is just not a very charismatic character. She is dependable, friendly and helpful, but not particularly spirited. The new, more fiery companion would arrive in the next story, "Logopolis," in the form of Janet Fielding's abrasive Tegan.

Episode writer Byrne was one of the script editors for Year One of *Space: 1999*. He wrote many outstanding adventures for that series, including (in the first season) "Matter of Life and Death," "Another Time, Another Place," "Force of Life," "End of Eternity," "The Troubled Spirit," "Mission of the Darians" and "The Testament of Arkadia." For Year Two of the ITC series he penned "The Metamorph," "The Immunity Syndrome" and "The Dorcons." He would return to *Doctor Who* to write "Warriors of the Deep," the final adventure in the Silurian and Sea Devil saga.

There is nothing new or particularly exciting in "The Keeper of Traken" to elevate it to the level of classic *Who*. It only enforces the notion that Season 18 was merely marking time rather than going forward. Perhaps with the impending departure of Baker, the producers felt it better to offer conservative, familiar stories about "evil awakening" than to send the series in a new direction, only to have a new actor and a new Doctor cause yet another shift or upheaval. For whatever the reason, Season 18 is one of the least ambitious and least interesting. Adric, Nyssa and Tegan are all introduced in separate stories...which should give them all adequate time to develop into three-dimensional characters. Such is not the case, however. During Season 18, one is acutely aware that these characters have none of the realism of Barbara and Ian, the vigor of Jamie and Zoe, or the zip of Sarah and Leela.

"The Keeper of Traken" is available on videocassette.

As air flight attendant Tegan Jovanka, Janet Fielding accompanied the fifth incarnation of the Doctor through many dangers in seasons 19–21.

116. "Logopolis" Written by Christopher H. Bidmead; Directed by Peter Grimwade; Designed by Malcolm Thornton; Parts I–IV; Airdates: February 28, March 1, 14, 21, 1981

SYNOPSIS: The TARDIS's chameleon circuit, as always, is in need of repair, and so the Doctor sets course for the planet of mathematical geniuses: Logopolis. Unfortunately, the Master has brought Logopolis to a standstill by destroying its main computer. The Doctor reveals to his friends Nyssa, Adric and the newly arrived Australian stewardess Tegan that Logopolis is the keystone of the universe, part of something called the "causal nexus." Its continued existence is crucial to the fabric of creation. The Logopolitan equations hold everything together, and without them existence will unravel! The Doctor and the Master join forces to save all of creation, but there is a heavy price to pay: The final battle claims the life of the fourth incarnation of the Doctor.

GUEST CAST: Aunt Vanessa (Dolore Whiteman); Detective Inspector (Tom Georgeson); The Master (Anthony Ainley); The Monitor (John Fraser); Security Guard (Christopher Hurst)

COMMENTARY: Like all previous regeneration shows, "Logopolis" closes an era. This is Tom Baker's farewell to *Doctor Who*, and it is certainly an emotional one. By the time "Logopolis" was produced, Baker had portrayed the Doctor for seven years, twice as long as any other actor. In that span, Baker virtually re-made both the role and the series. He *was* the Doctor. During his reign, *Doctor Who* developed from a sometimes juvenile series to an always adult sci-fi program filled with humor, horror and satire. Baker's era also saw some of the best companions, including K-9, Sarah and Leela. It highlighted some of the best, most involving stories ever, including "City of Death," "Genesis of the Daleks" and "The

Ark in Space." More importantly, Baker brought the series new visibility and recognizability all over the world. His serials were the ones that became a hit in America in the late '70s. To Americans, Baker was *Doctor Who* as much as Sean Connery was James Bond. It did not matter to Americans that three actors had played the part before him. He was the first Doctor most Americans saw, and as a result, Baker's image was inexorably tied to the series. Stubborn Americans never got over his departure; no later Doctor ever met with the same level of popularity.

Why is Baker so popular? The best answer is probably that Baker had fun with the part, and it showed. He winked at the audience and let them know he was enjoying the adventure as much as they were. Sometimes he crossed the line and winked a bit too much. This was limited mostly to isolated incidences in his later years, "The Pirate Planet" being the most blatant example. Besides the fact that he reinterpreted the role of the Doctor to make it considerably more fun, Baker oversaw an era in which the show became "Americanized." In "The Deadly Assassin" and others, he was drawn into physical brawls much like Captain Kirk had been. Even more so than Pertwee's time, Baker's days embraced hard action as well as solid genre concepts. The production values also improved significantly and thus the show was more believable in look and feel, enough so as to be enjoyed even by image-conscious Americans. Baker also participated in a long era of compelling horror. "Planet of Evil," "Pyramids of Mars," "The Seeds of Doom," "The Android Invasion," "Image of the Fendahl" and "The Ark In Space" were all suspenseful and horrific excursions. Baker thus became a kind of invincible figure. He could relieve tension with his quick wit, and he always beat the horrible bad guys. The audience was safe with this powerful figure.

As the Doctor, Baker had charisma. He carried weak serials purely by the strength of his personality, and the obvious love he had for both the character and his show. How can one adequately describe his energy, his *joie de vivre*? His facial expressions and mannerisms were funny, and his rapport with his companions was genuine. With the first Romana there was actually an element of sexual tension, a *Moonlighting*-type relationship. With Sarah, he was a protector. He teased her and goaded her, but loved her like an uncle. He was quick with witty comebacks, he was lighthearted, yet also serious. He often lost his temper in the same scene that he flashed that toothy smile. He was such a well-rounded Doctor it is hard to say enough about him. Perhaps his own words can describe the complexity of the fourth Doctor best:

> The kind of character who always fascinates me is the fiendish type, having lots of thoughts at the same time, combining patience with kindness, fun with anger. I like that complexity of character.[16]

When Baker left *Doctor Who* after "Logopolis," he left some big shoes to fill. This big, funny man with the mop of curly hair, the buggy eyes and the huge grin would be missed.

Accordingly, "Logopolis" has the mood of a funeral. Baker delivers his most morbid, humorless performance in seven years. It is his death, after all, that the story concerns. Baker seems preoccupied with his exit, and when his death finally occurs it is a stark, show-stopping moment. He smiles one last time and then suddenly seven years of laughs, adventure and fun are gone forever. No matter how good the later actors, *Doctor Who* would never be the same.

The story of "Logopolis" is rather convoluted. The specifics of "block transfer" and mathematics are not particularly interesting as drama. How do the equations keep the universe together? Why does the Master destroy Logopolis and then seek to save it? Why is the control center of Logopolis a duplicate of Earth twentieth century technology? The answers to these questions are addressed in only the muddiest of ways. One needs a good rewinder to follow the trail of logic in "Logopolis." Even more confusing is this creature who shows up every now and again: the Watcher. He warns the Doctor of his death early in the tale — but who is he? Is he the fifth incarnation come back in time to insure that he will exist? Is he the "ghost" of the fourth Incarnation? Is he a figure outside the Doctor who sacrifices his life to give the Doctor a further incarnation? The Doctor has regenerated three times before and nothing like this has ever happened! What is the audience to make of it all? Although it is by no means necessary to explain "everything" in a story, some clarity would have helped to focus "Logopolis."

Despite the flaws, the infinite regression scene early in the serial, with a TARDIS inside a TARDIS inside a TARDIS, is rather amusing, as is the TARDIS's shrinking sequence on Logopolis. However, it is virtually impossible to enjoy or appreciate the specifics of this adventure on its own terms. The sense of gloom in "Logopolis" *overwhelms* the audience. It is one of those shows that viewers do not want to watch, yet cannot turn away from. The story introduces Tegan and actress Jane Fielding, a character and actress who would provide many good moments on the series. It is a tremendous disservice to present Tegan in "Logopolis." No newcomer, now matter how good, can compete with the final exit of a master. Consequently, there is something quite sad about seeing Tom Baker surrounded in his last moments by three companions whom he hardly knows. K-9, Leela, Romana or Sarah should be there with him. Instead, he makes his final voyage with three people the audience really has no interest in yet.

"Logopolis" is available on videocassette.

SEASON 19

117. "Castrovalva" Written by Christopher Bidmead; Directed by Fiona Cumming; Designed by Janet Budden; Parts I–IV; Airdates: January 4, 5, 11, 12, 1982

SYNOPSIS: The regenerated Doctor, a young blond man, is deeply confused and badly shaken after his recent traumatic experience. When Adric is captured by the Master, Tegan and Nyssa take the Doctor to the planet Castrovalva, a world that is supposed to have restorative effects on injured Time Lords. As the Doctor recovers, he realizes that Castrovalva is too good to be true. The city is a trap that cannot be escaped, an example of "recursive occlusion." If the Doctor, Tegan and Nyssa cannot find a way out of Castrovalva soon, they will be killed when the city folds in on itself!

GUEST CAST: The Master (Anthony Ainley); Head of Security, Pharos Project (Dallas Cavell); Ruther (Frank Wylie); Shardovan (Derek Waring); Mergrave (Michael Sheard); Pertreeve (Neil Toynay); Child (Souska John)

COMMENTARY: The Peter Davison era begins with a conservative, almost tame story about the Master's trap for the regenerated Doctor on the invented world of Castrovalva (named after the M.C. Escher print). The serial exists primarily to introduce Davison as Tom Baker's successor, and as a result is devoid of any substantial meaning or interest. It is a puzzle story that ends, appropriately, when the puzzle is finally solved. This sort of "empty" story is expected in a post-regeneration adventure, and Davison's is not the first to lack thematic density. "Spearhead from Space" and "Robot" were not the most innovative *Doctor Who* stories either. Nor are Colin Baker's and McCoy's introductions ("The Twin Dilemma" and "Time and the Rani").

Davison is a very capable actor, and he brings stolid heroism and youthful sincerity to his portrayal of the Doctor. Physically, Davison is a young, slim, attractive man. With his blond hair and puppy-dog eyes, he is the most traditionally handsome actor to play the Time Lord. This is a bit strange and disconcerting, however, because the Doctor has never been what one would consider traditionally handsome. How far the series has come from its beginning! In 1963, the Doctor was a cranky old man with white hair. In 1983, he is a beautiful young specimen of virile manhood. Already Davison seemed to have one strike against him. Judging solely by appearance, he seemed neither alien nor different. He was as traditional a leading man as Bruce Boxleitner in *Babylon 5* or William Shatner in *Star Trek*; quite frankly, such an "average" television look does not do justice to the character of the Doctor. First and foremost, the Doctor is alien. The subversive, unusual casting of the Doctor has always highlighted this fact, from Hartnell to Tom Baker. Davison breaks with tradition because not only is he beautiful, he is also very young. There is simply no way that a man his age, even the best actor in the universe, could convey the breadth of the Doctor's experience. Hence Davison cannot carry off the wisdom of Hartnell and Pertwee nor the sense of world-weariness and know-it-all authority that Troughton and Baker expressed with such ease. He would have to work hard to cut out his own niche, and find a different aspect of the Time Lord.

Although many will certainly say it is unfair to criticize Davison's performance purely on his looks and age, who can deny that appearance plays a critical role in how people are perceived? Davison is a great actor, and he grew adequately into the role of Doctor, but he did not make the instant connection that the others did. He had to build that connection solely through trial and error, through the process of performing in the role. His task was tough because he was not aided at all by his physicality. Baker's performance was great, but there was also something that *felt* right, even from the first moment of "Robot," about his wild eyes, his crazy hair and his prominent teeth. There are many *Doctor Who* fans and writers who feel that Davison was the best actor ever to play the Doctor because he once more grounded the series in believability. The jokes of the Baker era were gone, and Davison brought a serious, respectful tone to his portrayal. Good or bad, Davison was a conventional choice to play the Doctor. The positive aspect of this choice was that the stories would not be overshadowed by a larger-than-life central performance. Of course, many stories in the Davison span are bland and repetitive of early *Doctor Whos*, so at least a larger-than-life performance would have given them something distinctive.

Davison is quite good at expressing confusion, weakness and irritability in "Castrovalva." He also proves he is a talented mimic, at times taking on characteristics of Hartnell and Troughton. These scenes are delightful, and they remind the viewer that Hartnell, Troughton, Pertwee, Baker and now Davison are supposed to be the same person. This is something that was not always obvious with the other actors. Perhaps it is Davison's very youth and lack of experience that allows him to acknowledge that others have played this part before him. It is hard to imagine the proud Tom Baker intentionally mimicking Pertwee, and thereby recognizing a portrayal other than his own. So perhaps Davison deserves credit for respecting *Doctor Who* tradition and acknowledging past triumphs. This alone makes him likable.

The specifics of "Castrovalva" are not terribly interesting. "The Zero Room," essentially an isolation ward aboard the TARDIS, is mentioned for the first time...but it is destroyed in the course of the story, so it does not reappear. The Escher–like qualities of the city of Castrovalva are also well-designed and interesting. But beyond the visual conceit that the Doctor and his friends are trapped in an Escher painting, the story has precious little of interest. It is just one more plan (by the Master) to destroy the Doctor.

"Castrovalva" is the third "Master" story in a row; frankly, a little of the Master goes a long way. He is not an interesting enough villain to clash with continually, one story after another. Since Davison's fifth incarnation of the Doctor is in no condition to face him down in "Castrovalva," much of the story seems out of balance. The end result is that one shakes one's head in disbelief that the Master cannot defeat an incapacitated Doctor. He goes up against the minds of Tegan and Nyssa...and loses. Additionally, it strains credulity that the Master never just kills the Doctor flat-out. He reprograms the TARDIS, and invents a planet, all to entrap and kill the Doctor. Why does he not whip out the Tissue Compressor blaster and shoot the Doctor in any one of their numerous encounters? For this reason, almost all stories involving the Master are a failure. Everyone knows the Master *cannot* kill the Doctor because the series would then end. Everyone also knows that the Doctor *cannot* kill the Master because then he could not return to menace him again. It is the law of predictable television. It would be like having

Khan (Ricardo Montalban) as the guest villain on *Star Trek* every week. After awhile, he would begin to look like a boob because he can never kill Captain Kirk. Kirk would look equally incompetent for never killing Khan! It is a sad fact that the Master stories represent *Doctor Who* grinding over the same material again and again. Innovation is missing.

"Castrovalva" does show the beginnings of an ensemble that would provide some good moments in serials to come. Janet Fielding and Stacy Sutton have sizable parts in this story and they perform very well, both becoming more three-dimensional than in their earlier appearances with Tom Baker. They get to fly the TARDIS and save the Doctor's life, a lot more than many other companions get to do. Matthew Waterhouse's Adric spends most of the serial pinned to the ceiling of the Master's TARDIS, so he has little chance to interact with Davison's new Doctor.

Fiona Cumming, like *Who* directors George-Spenton Foster, Michael Briant, David Maloney, Pennant Roberts and Derek Martinus, helmed several episodes of *Blake's 7*, including "Rumors of Death" and "Sarcophagus" in 1980. Cumming returned to the Davison era for "Snakedance," "Enlightenment" and "Planet of Fire."

"Castrovalva" is available on videocassette.

118. "Four to Doomsday" Written by Terence Dudley; Directed by John Black; Designed by Tony Burrough; Parts I–IV; Airdates: January 18, 19, 25, 26, 1982

SYNOPSIS: The TARDIS lands inside an enormous spaceship where Monarch introduces himself as the supreme ruler of the planet Urbanka in the Inokshi solar system of the galaxy RE 1489. His ship is headed to Earth, which he last visited 2,500 years ago.

The Doctor learns that the Urbankans have perfected a method of attaining immortality. They have transferred human souls into microchips in android bodies, eliminating emotion and humanity from what Monarch calls the "Flesh Time." The Doctor discovers that the Monarch is planning to depopulate the Earth with a deadly poison so he can mine the planet for silicon and create more "soul" microchips. Monarch used up the resources and polluted the atmosphere of his own world with his technology. All of this has been done so that the megalomaniac can learn the secret of faster-than-light travel and travel back in time to the Big Bang. He earnestly believes he will find himself there — that he is God...!

GUEST CAST: Monarch (Statford Johns); Persuasion (Paul Shelley); Enlightenment (Annie Lamber); Bigon (Philip Locke); Princess Villagra (Nadia Hamman); Kurkutji (Illario Bisi Pedro); Lin Futu (Ben Kwouk)

COMMENTARY: Davison's era finds its voice in "Four to Doomsday," an innovative story that explores what it means to be flesh and blood. In this adventure, the Doctor and his friends encounter a being who can capture all of a human's memories and personality and transfer them into an android body. These androids are immortal and have the semblance of "humanity," but do they still possess souls?

Can a soul survive a memory transfer to a control chip and insertion into an artificial form? This question is the heart of "Four to Doomsday," and it is explored in fascinating, thought-provoking fashion. It is an effective storytelling technique to have a captured Athenian philosopher, Bigon, be an android himself...since Greek civilization is in many senses the cornerstone of modern Western culture. Who better to ask such questions about the nature of man and his spirit than a Greek philosopher? Since his people founded the values the modern audience thrives on, it is only right that Bigon should confront the dilemma himself. The final and most important revelation in "Four to Doomsday" is that Monarch has not submitted himself to the dehumanizing procedure. He denounces "Flesh Time" as primitive, yet he is unwilling to risk his *own* soul on his "miraculous" process.

The high price of immortality has been investigated in many genre television series. *Space: 1999* expressed the idea that immortality led to boredom ("Guardian of Piri") and deviant behavior ("End of Eternity"), sterility ("Death's Other Dominion") and even self-indulgence at the expense of others ("Mission of the Darians"). *Star Trek* treads similar ground, expressing the notion that it is mortality which defines mankind as a species (*Star Trek: Generations*). *Doctor Who* suggests that there is a very high price to pay for immortality: one's soul! Of course, examinations of immortality are less prominent in *Doctor Who* than in other genre series because the Doctor is virtually immortal. It is hard to preach against immortality as boring, perverse or against nature when the Doctor seems to lead such a joyous life. Similar to the conceit that frames "Four to Doomsday," *Star Trek* unveiled a second season story entitled "I, Mudd" in which Uhura was tempted to shed her human body for an immortal, android replacement.

"Four to Doomsday" is also an early example in sci-fi television of a currently in-vogue subgenre: "the alien abduction" story. This story is the bread and butter of Chris Carter's *The X Files* and has been prominent in *Star Trek*s of later generations, particularly *Voyager* ("The '37s") and *The Next Generation* ("Schisms"). Like those stories, "Four to Doomsday" suggests that aliens have been stealing humans for generations for nefarious purposes.

"Four to Doomsday" also touches on another tent pole of *Doctor Who* stories: the invasion. The Urbankans plan to loot the Earth for its silicon and destroy the population, harkening back to "The Android Invasion," "The Invasion" and "The Dalek Invasion of Earth." Fortunately, that oft-reused aspect is downplayed and the serial does not seem overly repetitive. There are even a few new wrinkles, such as the Doctor's climactic space walk, in which he uses a cricket ball to provide himself with some much needed momentum, and Tegan's theft of the TARDIS.

All in all, "Four to Doomsday" is a well-told adventure that focuses on the issue of what it means to be human. There is a notable lack of humor, but this is post–Tom Baker *Doctor Who* with its reliance on story-telling, not laughs. For the most part, that template works in Davison's sophomore outing.

119. "Kinda" Written by Christopher Bailey; Directed by Peter Grimwade; Designed by Malcolm Thornton; Parts I–IV; Airdates: February 1, 2, 8, 9, 1982

SYNOPSIS: When Nyssa falls ill, the TARDIS lands on Deva Loka, a jungle paradise. While Nyssa recuperates, the Doctor, Tegan and Adric discover an Expeditionary Force from Earth looking to resettle the planet. Members of this expedition have been disappearing mysteriously, and the leaders blame the Kinda, the planet's natives. The Kinda women are telepathic, having a gift called "the Voice." Two Kinda have been taken hostage by the Expeditionary Force in hopes that this will stop the disappearance of their team members. Meanwhile, Tegan finds herself possessed by an evil, snake-like life form called the Mara.

GUEST CAST: Hindle (Simon Rouse); Aris (Adrian Mills); Panna (Mary Morris); Karuna (Sarah Prince); Sanders (Richard Todd); Anicca (Roger Milner); Todd (Nerys Hughes); Dukkha (Jeffrey Stewart); Anatta (Anna Wing); Trickster (Lee Cornes)

COMMENTARY: "Kinda" is another return to a philosophy often re-visited in *Doctor Who*: A love of "nature" is once again equated with wisdom. Like the Swampies in "The Power of Kroll" and the Primitives in "Colony in Space," the Kinda natives are depicted as wise, kind creatures who have embraced nature and are all the better for it. Conversely, Earth people are seen as scheming, land-consuming racists who have lost their bonds with the natural world. In "Kinda," technology is made useless, and the defeat of the evil Mara results not from technology's function but from its *physical appearance*. The solar panels that reflect the evil of the Mara at the climax represent a mythological, anti-technological solution to the problem, recalling the death of Medusa (who could not see her reflection) in the Perseus legend. Thus *Doctor Who* again states that evil will be conquered not through machines or science, but through man's deepest racial memories, and a return to the truths of nature. That "evil cannot look upon itself" is not a rational conclusion to the serial...it is a blatantly superstitious one instead. The Kinda, who are so at one with their environment and each other that they can communicate telepathically, can understand this solution because they are in touch with "nature" and "natural beliefs." The humans, with their robotic survival suits, artificial domes and synthetic uniforms, are unable to connect with their base human-ness to defeat the Mara.

"Kinda" also suggests that evil can enter the unconscious minds of good people through the world of dreams. This idea would be popularized in America in 1984 after the premiere of Wes Craven's *A Nightmare on Elm Street*. Like the Mara in "Kinda," murderer Freddy Krueger enters the dreamscapes of the innocent and reshapes them to his own evil blueprint. "Kinda" is the first Mara story in *Doctor Who*, but these villains would soon return in a sequel entitled "Snakedance." The Mara are not particularly memorable or dangerous opponents after the events of "Kinda" because the Doctor knows how to defeat them, so it seems strange then that "Kinda" would be singled out for a sequel story. Accordingly, much of "Snakedance" is not about conquering evil, but about escaping from jail and trying to find the repossessed Tegan before the same old evil awakens.

The new *Doctor Who* TARDIS ensemble encounters some difficulties in "Kinda." Sutton's Nyssa is sidelined in the first few moments of the adventure, and does not reappear until the wrap-up. Ostensibly, this was done to better establish Fielding's Tegan, but it is an obvious ploy. The producers perhaps realized that "Logopolis" was not a fair debut for the excellent Fielding, since virtually every element in that story was overshadowed by Tom Baker's departure. Still, it is hardly fair to enhance a character at the expense of another. The sidelining of Nyssa in "Kinda" reveals that the *Who* writers of the '80s were not nearly so facile with an ensemble cast as the writers in the '60s were. In the days of Hartnell, there were often four plots running simultaneously to accommodate the Doctor, Susan, Ian and Barbara. "The Aztecs" is an example of just such a well-done ensemble piece. All the character subplots fit together well, and each character has an important role to fulfill. Nyssa's illness in "Kinda" has the unpleasant smell of a writer's ploy rather than that of legitimate dramatic motivation.

"Kinda" is available on videocassette.

120. "The Visitation" Written by Eric Saward; Directed by Peter Moffatt; Designed by Ken Starkey; Parts I–IV; Airdates: February 15, 16, 22, 23, 1982

SYNOPSIS: On Earth in 1699, a spacecraft crashes in the English countryside. The aliens aboard the craft attack the inhabitants of a nearby mansion, killing them with green laser beams! Behind this attack is a Terileptil, a hideous turtle-like alien. The Doctor, Mace and Nyssa find the Terileptil spacecraft and realize who they are up against. This Terileptil is working with comrades in London to engineer the complete annihilation of the human race. They are using contaminated rats to spread a horrible infection! The Doctor offers to return the aliens to their homeworld, but they are exiles. They want the Earth to be their home, and it must be rid of human vermin to be an adequate one.

GUEST CAST: Richard Mace (Michael Robbins); Android (Peter Van Dissel); The Squire (John Savident); Charles (Anthony Calf); Ralph (John Baker); Elizabeth (Valerie Fyfer); Villager (Richard Hampton); Miller (James Charlton); Poacher (Neil West); Terileptil (Michael Melia); Head Man (Eric Dodson)

COMMENTARY: Eric Saward's first teleplay for *Doctor Who* is weak stuff. It is a hodgepodge of old *Doctor Who* stories with nothing new thrown into the mix. The alien interfering in the past and threatening the future of Earth is recycled from "The Time Meddler," "The Time Warrior," "The Masque of Mandragora," "The Abominable Snowmen," "The Time Monster" and "The Horror of Fang Rock." The climax of the story, that alien interference and the Doctor's response to it precipitates a major historical event, is also familiar. The fire at Pudding Lane in "The Visitation" is analogous to the start of the Renaissance in "The Masque of Mandragora," the burning of Rome in "The Romans" and the Battle of Hastings in "The Time Meddler." The killer virus of the Terileptels is also a rehashed plot element, similar to the Kraal plot in "The Android Invasion."

Even beyond these similarities, "The Visitation" recalls the entire "invasion" prototype seen throughout *Doctor Who*. Earth has been invaded or almost invaded in "The Dalek Invasion of Earth," "The Tenth Planet," "The Faceless Ones," "The Abominable Snowmen," "The Ice Warriors," "The Web of Fear," "The Invasion," "The Seeds of Death," "Spearhead from Space," "Terror of the Autons," "The Claws of Axos," "Invasion of the Dinosaurs," "Planet of the Spiders," "Terror of the Zygons," "The Pyramids of Mars," "The Android Invasion," "The Seeds of Doom," "The Masque of Mandragora," "Image of the Fendahl" and "Four to Doomsday." By "Visitation" there had been 120 serials of *Doctor Who* and 21 of those featured an invasion of some sort. That is more than 16 percent of the television series as a whole! Clearly this premise had been worn threadbare by this time. Is there really anyone who believes that this invasion of Earth will not be thwarted, after the Doctor has thwarted all previous attempts?

Of course, there is the theory that each new Doctor must go through the same paces as his predecessors. Times may change, but the situations our heroes face do not. Thus "The Visitation" is Davison's invasion story. Those who watch for such things will be relieved to know that Davison handles the situation just as competently, if not as stylishly, as Hartnell, Troughton, Pertwee and Baker.

With such a hackneyed premise, there is very little room for "The Visitation" to succeed. Even the Tereliptil android who resembles the Grim Reaper recalls other *Doctor Who* villains based on folklore, specifically the alien Loch Ness monster in "The Terror of the Zygons," the robot Yeti in "The Web of Fear" and "The Abominable Snowmen." While it is refreshing that companions Nyssa and Adric are allowed to save the day in "The Visitation," that distinction is not enough to push the serial into the category of entertaining. "The Visitation" is a failure in imagination, and a bad omen for the program's nineteenth season. There were already two relatively weak stories ("Castrovalva" and "The Visitation") just four serials into Davison's reign as the Doctor. And "Kinda" and "Four to Doomsday," though solid sci-fi stories with interesting themes, are in no way great *Doctor Who* serials. In fact, these stories are not even in the second rung of "very good" stories.

Ironically, Nathan-Turner's decision to eliminate humor from the series format only weakens the fabric of "The Visitation" and other Davison stories. With a trite, oft-repeated premise, humor might have been the only thing that could have redeemed this serial. It is overlong and dull.

"The Visitation" sees the destruction of the Doctor's trusted sonic screwdriver. When Nathan-Turner took over as producer, he expressed the belief that with K-9 and his sonic screwdriver, the Doctor was dispatching his villains too easily. Hence, K-9 and the sonic screwdriver were removed from the series. In the case of the sonic screwdriver, this belief was ridiculous. The sonic screwdriver was always just an instrument, like a phaser or a tricorder on *Star Trek*. It was a legitimate tool of the "profession," not a gimmick or problem solver. The sonic screwdriver was important in "Carnival of Monsters," "The Ark in Space," "The Sontaran Experiment" and others, but it never saved the day. That privilege was always reserved for the Doctor. There is a lingering shot of the destroyed sonic screwdriver in "The Visitation," suggesting this is a momentous occasion in the Doctor's travels. It is a silly assumption that the destruction of a sonic screwdriver would be so traumatic an experience. With everything else he stored in the TARDIS, the Doctor does not own a spare? Even if he did not, he would only have to purchase another one at a Time Lord hardware store.

"The Visitation" is available on videocassette with the two-part serial "Black Orchid."

121. "Black Orchid" Written by Terence Dudley; Directed by Ron Jones; Designed by Tony Burrough; Parts I–II; Airdates: March 1, 2, 1982

SYNOPSIS: On June 11, 1925, the TARDIS arrives at a rail station in rural England. A car is waiting at the station to pick the Doctor up for a game of cricket. The Doctor is surprised, but his affection for cricket prompts him to go with his companions to the home of Lord Cranleigh. The Doctor and his companions are soon involved in a costume ball, a complicated murder mystery and a tale of secret identities involving a lost explorer and his onetime fiancée.

GUEST CAST: Lady Cranleigh (Barbara Murray); Sir Robert Muir (Moray Watson); Lord Cranleigh (Michael Cochrane); Brester (Brian Hawksley); Tanner (Timothy Block); Latoni (Ahmed Khalil); Constable Cummings (Andrew Tourell); The Unknown (Gareth Milne); Sgt. Markham (Ivor Salter)

COMMENTARY: "Black Orchid" is a delightful serial from start to finish. It is appropriate that this sci-fi television series should dramatize a story out of Romantic literature and the Victorian Age because *Doctor Who*, like novels of the period, expresses the importance of individuality over reason, and highlights a generally optimistic feeling about the world. Although this optimism was not always evident in Pertwee's era of ecologically friendly episodes, it has since become an important ingredient in *Doctor Who*. Like Charlotte Brontë's *Jane Eyre* or Daphne Du Maurier's *Rebecca*, "Black Orchid" is a romantic mystery of the highest order. In this case, the terrifying secret in the attic is not someone's insane wife, but someone's insane child. And, as in all good Romantic literature, the fantasy of "mistaken identity" plays a crucial role in the story.

It may seem strange that *Doctor Who* should eschew science fiction for this two-part episode and opt instead for a Victorian-style mystery, but the premise of "Black Orchid" fits so well within *Who* parameters that it seems inevitable. Mistaken identity has been an element in *Who* serials as diverse as "The Massacre," "The Enemy of the World," "The Androids of Tara" and "Meglos." The dark secret which a host zealously hides from the main characters is also reminiscent of the futuristic riff on *Frankenstein* called "The Brain of Morbius." Dark secrets and hidden passageways also play a part in "The Curse of Peladon" and "Pyramids of Mars." Thus the earmarks of the Victorian genre are well-established in *Who* history. It is not a format stretch to produce "Black Orchid," just an unexpected and delightful variation. Many who write about *Doctor Who* refer to "Black Orchid" as the first "historical" adventure since "The Highlanders" (1966). This is a valid claim, but the interest of "Black Orchid" is not specifically historical reenactment, as in "The Romans," "The Gunfighters" or other "historical" adventures. On the contrary, "Black Orchid"'s purpose is to pay homage to *Jamaica Inn*, *Jane Eyre* or *Wuthering Heights*. Its style might better be described as *literary* instead of historical. Perhaps it is most accurate to state that "Black Orchid" is the first serial since "The Highlanders" which does not feature genre elements other than the TARDIS and the Doctor himself. In whatever way one chooses to describe "Black Orchid," it is a success.

The production values are superb. The early 1900s are recreated in a loving, authentic fashion. The costumes are elegant and colorful, and the set design of the ominous Cranleigh mansion recalls the mysterious dwellings fans remember from epics like *Jane Eyre* or *Rebecca*. Even more delightful than the lush sets is the fact that *Doctor Who* personalities are finally delineated in some realistic, insightful ways. Adric, for one, seems more three-dimensional than before. In "Black Orchid" he is not just a smart mathematician who is impulsive and loyal to the Doctor, he is also a typical teenage boy who stuffs his face with food at a party and is too embarrassed to dance. Tegan, ever the extrovert, dances the Charleston and is the life of the party. Refreshingly, Fielding is permitted to do something other than whine about returning home (an earmark of Tegan). Her natural effervescence is unbottled as never before, and it is beautiful to witness. Davison gets to show off his athletic prowess by playing cricket, a delightful pastime which the Doctor rarely finds time to enjoy. Nyssa also plays an important role. She shows her fiendish, mischievous side when she agrees to wear Ann's costume and thereby create the mistaken identity scenario. Sutton plays a double role in the serial, and she has never looked lovelier or been more charismatic. For once, the ensemble really meshes well and seems true-to-life. There is a sense of a family just as there was in the days of Ian, Barbara, and Susan.

Thematically the teleplay is intensely interesting as well. Everyone wears a mask, both figuratively and literally. Though all the guests at the party wear costume masks, the central characters in the drama also mask their true identities in other ways. The Doctor is obviously not who or what he claims to be. He is a Time Lord "masking" himself as a human being (and specifically as a human doctor). Ms. Cranleigh wears the mask of propriety and friendliness, but she harbors an evil secret. Nyssa and Ann delight in masking and switching their identities by adorning the same outfit and mask. George Cranleigh, of course, wears the mask of the Harlequin clown to hide his deformity and his insane nature. Because no one is really what he or she pretends to be, the story is a charming mystery and one of *Doctor Who*'s liveliest serials. It is the best Season 19 story, hands down.

There is another element of "Black Orchid" that bears some close examination. When the Doctor is in trouble with the law, he invites Mr. Muir into the TARDIS to prove his story is authentic. This is a strange moment because the Doctor usually takes pains to keep people away from the TARDIS, lest time be altered. In "An Unearthly Child," the Doctor was horrified when Barbara and Ian forced their way into the time machine. Why the sudden change of heart after centuries of time travel? Perhaps it is because Davison exudes a natural innocence and naiveté as the Doctor. Clearly, that is becoming his niche. He is the sensitive, trusting Time Lord, the one who even allows strangers aboard the TARDIS (a story element that would be repeated in "Earthshock").

Interestingly, *Star Trek: Voyager* also attempted to exploit the *Jane Eyre* milieu in the early episodes "Cathexis" and "Persistence of Vision." In both stories, Capt. Kathryn Janeway interacted in a holonovel along the lines of *Jane Eyre*. She became governess to two children whose father hid a strange secret in the attic. It is interesting to contrast *Doctor Who*'s and *Voyager*'s efforts with the same material. In *Voyager*, the Victorian milieu is essentially a time-waster. It is promptly abandoned once the "real story" begins and Janeway is forced to leave the holodeck. Thus it serves no dramatic or character purpose except to enlighten the viewer that Janeway likes Victorian novels. There is always the knowledge in these holodeck stories that the adventure is not real and thus does not really matter. In *Doctor Who*, the characters actually find themselves enmeshed in a real Victorian mystery. The danger is real, the characters are real, and that milieu is revisited in loving fashion. The premise is not just an excuse for some great set design and an unrelated sci-fi premise.

"Black Orchid" is available on videocassette in a two-box set with "The Visitation."

122. "Earthshock" Written by Eric Saward; Directed by Peter Grimwade; Designed by Bernard Lloyd-Jones; Parts I–IV; Airdates: March 8, 9, 15, 16, 1982

SYNOPSIS: A Cyberman plot to destroy the Earth has grave repercussions for the Doctor and Terran history. Once the Cybermen have taken over a space freighter, they set it on a collision course with Earth. If the freighter collides with the planet, its anti-matter engines will ignite and the resulting explosion will kill all life. Even more significantly to the Cybermen, the explosion will totally destroy the Unity Conference being held on Earth — a conference at which many dignitaries from alien worlds are in attendance. Adric gives his life to save mankind, and the resulting collision occurs not in the future, but in the past. The Cyberman plot has caused the extinction of the dinosaurs!

GUEST CAST: Lt. Scott (James Warwick); Prof. Kyle (Clare Clifford); Capt. Briggs (Beryl Reid); Executive Officer Berger (June Bland); Ringway (Alec Sabin); Cyberleader (David Banks); Cyberlieutenant (Mark Hardy); Sgt. Mitchell (Ann Holloway); Walters (Steve Morley); Snyder (Suzi Arden); First Trooper (Anne Clements); Second Trooper (Mark Straker); First Crew Member (Mark Fletcher); Second Crew Member (Chris Whittingham)

COMMENTARY: From the first exciting android battle under the Earth's surface to Adric's shocking death, "Earthshock" is an exciting, fast-paced *Doctor*

Who adventure. Peter Davison's era, jump-started with the stylish "Black Orchid," now rockets into full swing with a classic story that bears comparison with many of the best serials in the program's long history.

"Earthshock" works well for a number of reasons. Firstly, the Cybermen return after a seven-year absence. They are just as merciless, as evil and as frightening as ever. What a pleasure it is to see these great villains on the march once again, especially in a story that supports their frightening dynamic. In true Cyberman form, the evil cyborgs leave a deadly logic puzzle aboard the star freighter for Adric to unravel. The logic puzzle is nicely reminiscent of the Cyberman tomb traps in "Tomb of Cybermen."

Secondly, the casting in "Earthshock" is wonderfully idiosyncratic. Beryl Reid portrays Captain Briggs. Reid is an older woman with flaming red hair and a sharp tongue. She is a totally inspired choice to play this part. She looks as if she has been flying this same dull space run for a dozen years, and her dry humor and cranky demeanor is wonderfully unconventional and reminiscent of "real" life. When was the last time there was a character this unusual in command of a spaceship in *Star Trek*? Many *Doctor Who* fans disliked the casting of Reid in this critical part because they feel that her forte is humor, not drama. "Earthshock" proves that fear to be misplaced. Reid is funny as Briggs, but *appropriately* funny. She handles the part with respect, and this strange, surly old woman makes for a very memorable freighter captain.

Beyond a good guest appearance and the return of the Cybermen, "Earthshock" socks it to the audience with surprise after surprise at the climax of the story. Most dramatically, Adric is killed! He is the only companion to suffer this fate since Katarina and Kingdom died in "The Dalek Masterplan." This destiny is especially shocking coming from *Doctor Who*, a family-oriented show if ever there was one. No one would have expected the producers to so mercilessly kill off a teenage boy! Harry Sullivan, Steven Taylor or Ian Chesterton perhaps, because they were grown men and capable of taking care of themselves — but Adric? Poor young Adric who saw his brother die in E-Space? Adric the orphan? Adric, the boy who loves the Doctor like a father? Yes. This death is one of the most dramatic and effective surprises in any *Doctor Who* serial because it seems so cruel, so horrible and so random. Fortunately, Adric's death is handled in a believable fashion that fits the tenor of the adventure. "Earthshock" spirals out of control, until finally the Doctor can do nothing to help his friend. For once, the Doctor is unable to save the day. It is a powerful climax. It also makes Davison's Doctor more sympathetic and believable. Suddenly, this is not the infallible version of the Doctor, but a fallible one like Hartnell in "The Aztecs" or Troughton in "The War Games." It is rewarding that Davison and "Earthshock" scribe Eric Saward permitted this shocking event to occur, with the Doctor just a helpless bystander.

The second surprise is equally incredible: The destruction of the spaceship precipitates the extinction of the dinosaurs! This revelation rivals some of the greatest *Who* serials in history for shocking finales. The audience had already learned how the Doctor's journey had affected Earth history before. He was responsible for the *Marie Celeste* incident ("The Chase") and the burning of Rome ("The Romans"), among other things. Here the Doctor's travels cause him to play a part in the destruction of the dinosaurs. So much for not interfering in the history of other planets!

"Earthshock" is also dramatic because it allows Peter Davison to fly off the handle and dramatize an enraged Doctor. He attacks the Cyberman leader at the end of the story and kills him outright. This is a brutal act, but one that is wholeheartedly deserved. Throughout the history of the series, the Time Lord rarely expresses all-consuming rage. He does so here, and the moment is beautifully performed by Davison. All reserve, all civilization, all reason are stripped away in a moment and the Doctor reacts to the loss of his friend in a most...human fashion. It too is a powerful and memorable moment.

To fully underline the impact of Adric's death, the *Doctor Who* theme music is not heard over the end credits. Instead, there is just a closeup of Adric's shattered mathematics badge as the credits roll by.

From a genre standpoint, "Earthshock" is something of a turning point as it fully integrates *Star Trek* terminology and technology into *Doctor Who*. The star freighter's faster-than-light drive is referred to as "warp drive." This drive is also powered by an anti-matter–matter mix, just like the *Enterprise*'s. This is a rather shocking and blatant steal from *Star Trek*, and wholly unexpected. From here on in, however, the term "warp drive" would be heard fairly frequently even though it was an invention of Gene Roddenberry, not the *Who* production team.

"Earthshock" is a stunner, and a very good latter-day *Doctor Who* serial. It is available on videocassette.

123. "Time Flight" Written by Peter Grimwade; Directed by Ron Jones; Designed by Richard McManan-Smith; Parts I–IV; Airdates: March 22, 23, 29, 30, 1982

SYNOPSIS: A supersonic jet has disappeared in flight and the Doctor believes that Golf Victor Foxtrot has disappeared through time. A second Concorde is prepared with the TARDIS on board to retrace the flight of the first airliner. This Concorde also goes through a time slip and lands deep in a prehistoric jungle. The Doctor is certain they have travelled back in time at least 140 million years to the Jurassic era! Close by in the wilderness is Victor Foxtrot, and beyond that stands a strange pyramid and the wreckage of an advanced spaceship. Trapped in this distant past is not only the evil Master, but the entire race of the Xeraphin...all in one organism, all with one personality. The Doctor remembers that the Xeraphin were once humanoid. They lived on Xerophas before it was destroyed in the Vardon-Kosnax War. They were a highly developed race, and apparently they were able to combine their mental forces to create a single bioplasmic body for their people. The Master knows that he will possess incredible power if he can tie the brainpower of this group entity into his own damaged TARDIS.

GUEST CAST: The Master (Anthony Ainley); Capt. Urquhart (John Flint); Anithon (Hugh Hayes); Kalid (Leon Ny Taiy); Zarak (Andre Winterton); Adric

(Matthew Waterhouse); Terileptil (Chris Bradshaw); Melkur (Graham Cole); Sheard (Brian McDermott); Angela Clifford (Judith Byfield); Andrews (Peter Cellier); Bilton (Michael Cashman); Capt. Stapley (Richard Easton); Scobie (Keith Drinkel); Prof. Hayter (Nigel Stock); Security Guard (Tommy Winward)

COMMENTARY: The momentum of "Black Orchid" and "Earthshock" collapses in "Time Flight," another dreadful story that rehashes the boring Master-Doctor dynamic that appears so frequently in the Davison era.

The concept of a modern jet lost in a prehistoric time is reminiscent of a 1961 episode of Rod Serling's *The Twilight Zone*. In "The Odyssey of Flight 33," a commercial airliner went through a time-slip and ended up flying over a prehistoric jungle filled with brontosaurs and other dinosaurs. Although it did not concern prehistory, the Stephen King novella and miniseries *The Langoliers* (1995) also concerned an airliner's flight through a crack in time. "Time Flight" is probably not as interesting nor as frightening as these two stories, and it adds little to *Doctor Who* history. It seems hindered mainly by its budget, which could afford neither prehistoric monsters nor a convincing prehistoric jungle set. All of "Time Flight"'s prehistoric scenes are filmed on the sound stage, and it shows. The alien jungle of "Planet of Evil," way back in 1975, was dramatized more believably than the world shown in this story.

Although "Time Flight" is enlivened by an enlarged role for Sarah Sutton's Nyssa, and a surprise cameo by Matthew Waterhouse as the specter of Adric, there is little else of excitement here. The Xeriphans, a gestalt organism like the Fendahl ("Image of the Fendahl"), are not the most memorable of alien races. The Doctor's final solution to sabotage the Master's TARDIS is reminiscent of "The Time Meddler" and "The Dalek Masterplan" wherein Hartnell's version of the Time Lord removed precious components from the Meddling Monk's time machine. The Master himself had already lost components of his TARDIS to the Doctor in the Pertwee–era story "Terror of the Autons." So both premise and solution are rather weak in "Time Flight." Perhaps that is why Davison and Sutton have both said in interviews saying that this is their least favorite story.

"Time Flight" ends Davison's freshman season in ignominious fashion. Of the seven serials produced in this season, two are great ("Black Orchid" and "Earthshock"), two are good ("Four to Doomsday" and "Kinda") and three are weak ("Castrovalva," "The Visitation" and "Time Flight"). That is not a great average for the series, and it is obvious that entropy was starting to seep in. "The Visitation," had it been produced in the first three or four years of the series, might be considered a great story. Within its historical context, however, it is an uninventive rehash of previous invasion stories. That is very much the case in "Time Flight" as well, another regurgitation of the Master-Doctor feud that for some inexplicable reason seems to interest rather than frustrate many *Doctor Who* fans.

Despite the weak nature of several Season 19 stories, by "Time Flight" Davison is firmly in command as the Doctor. He has shown rage, innocence, naiveté, athletic ability and even a kind of low-grade charm. Season 20 would prove to be a better year for Davison's fifth incarnation.

SEASON 20

124. "Arc of Infinity" Written by Johnny Byrne; Directed by Ron Jones; Designed by Marjorie Pratt; Parts I–IV; Airdates: January 3, 4, 10, 11, 1983

SYNOPSIS: Omega, the Time Lord engineer trapped in the dimension of anti-matter, attempts to possess the Doctor. The TARDIS is recalled by the Time Lords to Gallifrey, who are worried because a force from the anti-matter universe is trying to join with the Doctor in this universe. This malevolent force, if it fails to cross over successfully, could cause mutual annihilation on a galactic scale. Unfortunately, the only way to permanently sever a temporal bonding is for one of the participants to be killed. In this case, the Time Lords feel they have no choice but to issue a warrant for the Doctor's execution.

GUEST CAST: Colin (Alistair Cummings); Lord President Borusa (Leonard Sachs); Commander Maxil (Colin Baker); Councillor Hedin (Michael Gough); Omega (Ian Collier); Robin Stuart (Andrew Boxer); Chancellor Thalia (Elspet Gray); Cardinal Zorac (Maximillian Harvey); Castellan (Paul Jericho); Ergon (Malcolm Harvey); Hotel Clerk (Maya Wolfe); Receptionist (Guy Groen)

COMMENTARY: *Doctor Who*'s twentieth anniversary season begins with an entertaining if uninspired tale from the pen of frequent *Space: 1999* writer Johnny Byrne. "Arc of Infinity" picks up the plot strand of "The Three Doctors." It reinvokes the story of Omega, the Time Lord engineer who was trapped in the world of anti-matter while capturing a black hole for Gallifrey to utilize as a power source. If nothing else, this story is well-timed, since it has been exactly ten years since Hartnell, Troughton and Pertwee fought Omega to the death in "The Three Doctors." Also contributing to the feeling that this is a momentous season for *Doctor Who* is the return to Gallifrey for the first time since "The Invasion of Time" in Season 16. As with all Gallifrey stories, the Matrix is also featured in "Arc of Infinity."

In addition to the evil Omega, there are some other familiar faces in "Arc of Infinity." Michael Gough, the Celestial Toymaker himself, returns for the first time since the Season 3 story "The Celestial Toymaker." Also present is Colin Baker as Commander Maxil. Baker was not recognizable, perhaps, when "Arc of Infinity" aired in 1983, but he soon would be: He is the sixth actor to play the Doctor. His first serial as the Time Lord, "The Twin Dilemma," would come at the end of Season 22.

It is not quite honest to say that the recurring character Borusa is also a familiar face. He is not. He is a familiar *name*. The character Borusa had already appeared in "The Deadly Assassin" and "The Invasion of Time." Leonard Sachs portrays Borusa in "Arc of Infinity" but Angus McKay and John Arnatt played him in "The Deadly Assassin" and "The Invasion of Time," respectively. Yet another actor, Philip Latham, would play Borusa in "The Five Doctors" at the end of Season 20. Considering all this casting and recasting, Borusa is apparently a Time Lord who likes to regenerate frequently.

Although "Arc of Infinity" is certainly an adequate story, it has some notable flaws. It's an incredible coincidence that the "arc of infinity," a region of outer space, should lead right to Earth — and that the Doctor should find his way right back to the inadvertently abandoned Tegan. Also, the Matrix is compromised yet again, this time by Omega. The Master has infiltrated the thing, and so has Omega, and yet in the upcoming "The Trial of the Time Lord," the Gallifreyans insist that the Matrix *cannot* be tampered with. "The Deadly Assassin" and "Arc of Infinity" offer cogent historical evidence to the contrary.

"Arc of Infinity" also continues an unfortunate trend developing in the later serials of *Doctor Who*. There is a terrible temptation to bring favorite villains back again and again, at the cost of original stories and more interesting themes. Omega returns in "Arc of Infinity." The Black Guardian returns in "Mawdryn Undead," "Terminus" and "Enlightenment." The Master returns in "The King's Demons" and "The Five Doctors." Every villain in Season 20 is a repeat offender, someone who had been seen on the series before. With such a long history of interesting villainy, it became harder and harder for writers to resist bringing back baddies for one more round. This fact nearly murdered the originality of the series. Consider that in seven years, the fourth incarnation of the Doctor met the Daleks twice, the Cybermen once and the Sontarans twice. Thus in 43 serials, famous bad guys only popped up five times (about ten percent of Tom Baker's run). That is quite different from the later years, when it seemed like every old *Doctor Who* monster was being trotted out to lift the ratings. In Davison's first two seasons, he faced repeat villains (Cybermen, the Master, the Kinda in "Snakedance," Omega) in eight serials...about 50 percent of the time!

"Arc of Infinity" also continues the unfortunate but ongoing demystification of the Time Lords. There is nothing particularly special about them anymore. Their mystery has been permanently lost. "The War Games," in which they were fierce elemental creatures with granite eyes, was a long time ago indeed.

"Arc of Infinity" is available on videocassette.

125. "Snakedance" Written by Christopher Bailey; Directed by Fiona Cumming; Designed by Jan Spoczynski; Parts I–IV; Airdates: January 17, 18, 24, 25, 1983

SYNOPSIS: The TARDIS arrives in the Scrampa Solar System and materializes on Mynosa, the third planet in the Federation and the former homeworld of the cruel Sumeran Empire. The Doctor has not set the TARDIS controls for this planet, so he is puzzled and a little frightened. He is a aware that the Mara, the evil beings of the Sumeran Empire, once existed on this world and may be trying to revive themselves through some devious means. To make matters worse, Tegan is having bad dreams about a cavern and a subterranean passageway shaped like a snake's head.

GUEST CAST: Ambril (John Carson); Tanha (Colette O'Neil); Dojjen (Reston Lockwood); Prince Lon (Martin Clunes); Drydale (Brian Miller); Fortune Teller (Hilary Sesta); Hawker (George Ballantine); Chel (Jonathan Moins)

COMMENTARY: In "Snakedance," the Doctor must once again prevent an ancient evil from awakening. Although it is the Mara in this case, the plot of a slumbering evil bent on returning to consciousness has been the fodder of "Image of the Fendahl," "Kinda," "The Masque of Mandragora," "The Brain of Morbius" and "The Pyramids of Mars." That the evil should choose one of the Doctor's dear friends recalls Sarah's role as servant to Eldrad in the Tom Baker–era "The Hand of Fear." Therefore this sequel to "Kinda," like so many Davison–era adventures, is not very original, nor very exciting. There is also a major flaw. Since the Mara were defeated in "Kinda," the Doctor should be able to defeat the beast again in "Snakedance." Yet circumstances prevent that from happening: The Doctor is captured and locked up for much of the story, and when he does break free, he loses track of Tegan's whereabouts. In other words, the story provides reasons (mostly lame) why the Doctor and the Mara cannot reconnect for a final confrontation before the end of the serial.

Since "Snakedance" is such a thoroughly average tale, only the production values could possibly render it watchable. Unfortunately, the production is sabotaged by a few things. First, the costume that young prince Lon must wear during the final Mara ceremony is atrocious. It consists of a gold lamé skirt with a crown that looks as if it was stolen from the Statue of Liberty. In this costume, Lon looks like a participant in a drag queen revue more than the hero of the Galactic Federation. This look of femininity is exaggerated by the fact that actor Martin Clunes can only be described as, well, beautiful. He has piercing eyes and full, red lips. When put in a dress, the result is unsettling and perverse to say the least. This is in no way meant to put down Clunes or his interpretation of the part. In fact, he gives a terrific performance in "Snakedance" as the bored young prince. He is appropriately arrogant, a behavior he pays for when it leads him to be absorbed by the Mara. Still, that costume does not do much for his masculinity.

The special effects in "Snakedance" are also subpar. For the final rebirth of the Mara, a rubber snake substitutes for a real one. Though no one expected *Anaconda*–style special effects in 1983, a little believability would have helped. At times the snake appears as if it is an inflatable toy rather than the symbol of the menacing aliens.

There is one place where the production values do stand up well. "Snakedance" showcases an alien bazaar, a kind of cosmic flea market of weird peddlers, fortunetellers and merchants. The visualization of this scene and the strange inhabitants is just right. Many extras mill about and the merchants seem appropriately individual and authentic. A cosmic flea market is a world never before visited by

Mark Strickson debuted as the treacherous Turlough in episode #126, "Mawdryn Undead."

Doctor Who, so it is a fresh, exciting image that enlivens the early portion of the show.

Like its predecessor "Kinda," "Snakedance" is available on videocassette.

126. "Mawdryn Undead" Written by Peter Grimwade; Directed by Peter Moffatt; Parts I–IV; Airdates: February 1, 2, 8, 9, 1983

SYNOPSIS: At a Boy's School in the English countryside, a young student named Turlough steals the antique car of his mathematics teacher, Alistair Lethbridge-Stewart. He does not have a license to drive and he totals the vehicle. Thrown from the vehicle, he has an out-of-body experience. While unconscious, he is introduced to the Black Guardian. This sinister being promises to help Turlough escape from Earth. First, however, Turlough must murder someone called "the Doctor."

Meanwhile, the TARDIS encounters a gigantic spaceship that has been trapped in a warp ellipse around Earth for 3,000 years. A metamorphic symbiotic regenerator, a device apparently stolen from the Time Lords on Gallifrey, is also aboard. The Doctor meets Mawdryn, who claims that his people stole the symbiotic regenerator and attempted to become immortal. But the machine merely mutated them: All eight of the crew will live forever, but they are in mortal pain and just want to die. They cannot do so without the help of a Time Lord, so they want the remaining eight of the Doctor's regenerations so they can die in peace. The Doctor is understandably reluctant to do this, since it would mean the end of his existence as a Time Lord. Meanwhile, Turlough plots to kill the Doctor...

GUEST CAST: Alistair Lethbridge-Stewart (Nicholas Courtney); Mawdryn (David Collings); The Black Guardian (Valentine Dyall); Headmaster (Angus MacKay); Ibbotson (Stephen Garlick); Dr. Runciman (Roger Hammond); Matron (Sheila Gill); First Mutant (Peter Walmsley); Second Mutant (Brian Darnley); Young Nyssa (Lucy Baker); Young Tegan (Sian Pattendon)

COMMENTARY: "Mawdryn Undead" is Season 20's first great serial. It makes appealing, innovative use of complex *Doctor Who* time travel conceits such as the "Blinovitch Limiting Factor," a time travel theorem first mentioned in the Pertwee–era story "Day of the Daleks." It also features a strong guest appearance by the beloved Nicholas Courtney as a retired Lethbridge-Stewart.

Even more rewarding than these highpoints, the character Mawdryn is basically treated throughout "Mawdryn Undead" as a sympathetic character. Although his people have stolen Time Lord technology to reap the benefits of immortality, they have paid the ultimate price for that theft. They now exist in a lingering "undead" state. No creature, even a criminal, should have to endure the lingering pain which Mawdryn and his cohorts have been facing for centuries. Thus Mawdryn is a more sympathetic villain than those usually painted in *Doctor Who*. Accordingly, he does not force the Doctor to give up his life; he knows merely that the Doctor must help if he is to save his own friends. There are no ray guns forcing the Doctor to save Mawdryn. Instead, the Doctor chooses to make the sacrifice when it becomes obvious that Tegan and Nyssa will be forever trapped without his aid. This is a great dilemma for the Doctor, and it shows new sides of his personality.

Davison's face conveys the difficulty of this decision in expert fashion. The Doctor knows that if he gives up his future regenerations, he will be as mortal as Tegan or Turlough. That knowledge flashes across Davison's face for a split second before it is replaced by a mask of iron resolve. Then the Doctor simply does what he has to do. It is one of the best moments for Davison's young incarnation.

Nicholas Courtney reveals new shades of Alistiar Lethbridge-Stewart in "Mawdryn Undead." He is no longer the cocksure military man of the Jon Pertwee era. Though he retains his dry wit and sharp tongue, it is clear that the Brigadier has mellowed over the years. It is sad to see him, however, living in a tiny, ratty cottage. It seems unrealistic that his UNIT pension would not provide better for a man of his stature and importance, someone who gave his entire professional life to the armed forces. It is delightful to hear Courtney (the Brigadier) talking of his days in UNIT, recalling old enemies and friends such as Benton (now a used car salesman!). This is a very sentimental *Who* serial because the series remembers and honors its own history, and the importance that Lethbridge-Stewart played in the late '60s and early '70s adventures. David Collings also returns for the first time since Season 14. The "Robots of Death" actor plays Mawdryn in this story and does a terrific job as the less-than-honorable creature who is desperate for the relief of death. Collings has acted in other science fiction productions, notably *Sapphire and Steele.*

"Mawdryn Undead" also brings Valentine Dyall's Black Guardian back to the series. The Black Guardian is still smarting from the Doctor's destruction of the Key to Time at the end of Season 16, and is hellbent on destroying him. To that end, the "Turlough" experiment begins. Turlough is the newest companion to the show, a young man played by Mark Strickson. Turlough is ostensibly a unique and different companion because he is out to kill the Doctor. This is indeed an unusual experiment as far as companions go, but it never really works. Everyone knows that Turlough cannot succeed in his quest, or the series will end. He is very much the same kind of two-dimensional threat as the Master. He keeps trying to kill the Doctor, and he keeps failing. The end result of all this failure is that Turlough merely looks incompetent, rather than threatening. His presence also gives the series a kind of *Lost in Space*, "Dr. Smith" presence. In the next three serials, everybody *knows* that Turlough is up to no good, while the good-hearted Doctor seems oblivious to it at all. Turlough, though bold in concept, does not work as a companion.

Lethbridge-Stewart's return to *Doctor Who* successfully explores the age-old question of time travel. Can the same person exist as two different people in the same time period? *Doctor Who*'s answer is that if such a thing should happen, the Blinovitch Limitation Factor kicks in and causes mutual annihilation. Only the presence of the Time Lord machinery (it absorbs the energy from the explosion) keeps annihilation from occurring in this story. In *Space: 1999*'s "Another Time, Another Place" (1975), destruction occurred to only one version of the "self" when Helena Russell encountered an older doppelganger on a duplicate Earth. In other science fiction television series, people have met themselves without such a disaster occurring. Jadzia Dax met up with a descendent who is carrying an identical symbiont, but no explosion results in "The Children of Time." Similarly, Bill and Ted meet themselves without any problem whatsoever in the less-than-contemplative hit *Bill & Ted's Excellent Adventure* (1988).

In the original draft of "Mawdryn Undead," the Doctor met up with Coal Hill School Teacher Ian Chesterton, his first companion from 1963. William Russell was apparently unavailable or not interested in resuming the role, and the story was adapted to feature the Brigadier. Although it is always great to see Courtney, a revisit from Russell might have been a more special moment. He had been out of the series for 18 years. The Brigadier's last appearance was in "Terror of the Zygons," only eight years earlier. Also, it strains believability that the Brigadier would retreat from life and become a mathematics instructor at an out-of-the way boy's school. He was always a fighter. He also successfully repelled several invasions of Earth in the stories "The Web of Fear," "The Invasion," "Spearhead from Space," "Terror of the Autons" and the aforementioned "Terror of the Zygons." It seems unlikely that UNIT would not retain his services in at least an advisory capacity! Courtney would return in just three episodes for "The Five Doctors." His last appearance on the series was in the 1989 serial "Battlefield."

"Mawdryn Undead," like "Earthshock" and "Black Orchid," is an outstanding serial of the less-than-sterling Davison era. It is filled with both heart and menace, and the story remains involving throughout. It is available on videocassette.

127. "Terminus" Written by Steven Gallagher; Directed by Mary Ridge; Designed by Dick Coles; Parts I–IV; Airdates: February 15, 16, 22, 23, 1983

SYNOPSIS: Turlough continues to plot murder, while the TARDIS hooks up with a space liner of some kind. All over the ship, the booming announcement of Terminus Incorporated is heard. The voice orders all passengers with mobility to disembark immediately, before sterilization procedures follow. The Doctor realizes that they are aboard the futuristic equivalent of a leper ship! This is the "terminus" where the Lazars come to die. Terminus also happens to be the name of the Lazar disease that is decimating their culture. The Doctor accesses the ship charts and learns an interesting fact: The Terminus ship lies at the exact center of the universe!

Nyssa is captured by a robot drone and mistaken for a diseased Lazar. She is to be led to an alien animal called a "Garm" and then taken into the "Forbidden Zone" where a cure can be attempted. First, however, Nyssa is escorted to a ward of sick and dying Lazars. She is appalled by the conditions, as well as the cavalier treatment of the sick. Nyssa soon realizes that she has been infected with the dreaded disease. She has little hope for survival unless this mysterious cure can help her.

GUEST CAST: Olvir (Dominic Guard); Kari (Liza Goddard); Inga (Rachel Weaver); Eirak (Martin Potter); Valgard (Andrew Burt); Bor (Peter Benson); Sigurd (Tim Munro); The Black Guardian (Valentine Dyall)

COMMENTARY: At face value, "Terminus" is a rather grim story. Despite the preoccupation with pain, suffering and disease, and the sterile, metal surroundings of the spaceship, the story nonetheless has an optimistic ending. The concept of an outer space "leper" ship is a good one that is handled well by the teleplay and dramatized effectively by the production team. Unless one considers the installations in "The Moonbase" and "Revenge of the Cybermen," the story of a plague ship had not been previously visited on the series, so some new ground was finally broken. *Star Trek: The Next Generation* would later offer a story entitled "Haven" by Tracy Torme. This 1987 adventure also featured a leper ship and a deadly disease. An important character stays behind with the lepers to cure the illness, just like in "Terminus," in which Nyssa leaves the Doctor's company to help the Lazarians.

Of greatest importance in "Terminus" is Nyssa's expanded role. Sarah Sutton's character is finally given something worthwhile to do in this, her last story on *Doctor Who.* Gratifyingly, Nyssa's decision to become the Florence Nightingale of the Terminus station seems very right, very true to this quiet, understated character. Although Nyssa was never the most charismatic of companions, she was certainly among the most loyal. She nursed the Doctor to health in "Castrovalva," and never once left him, as Tegan had done (albeit accidentally) in "Time Flight." Unlike Tegan, Nyssa really wanted to travel with the Doctor, and she was quite a useful friend in many adventures. She was one of the few companions who could fly the TARDIS ("Mawdryn Undead"). She could also solve problems without the Doctor's assistance ("The Visitation" and "Four To Doomsday"). She may not have had the wit of Sarah Jane Smith, the physical appeal of Leela or the intellect of Romana, but Sutton's Nyssa always managed to exude dignity in a quiet, unassuming kind of way...much like the embodiment of the Time Lord she accompanied. She is less flashy than her TARDIS–mate Tegan, but she has heart. Also, she is not a screamer! That fact alone counts heavily in her favor when one considers companions such as Melanie of the Sylvester McCoy era.

Nyssa's final moment in "Terminus" is an emotionally rewarding one for fans who have traced the character's development. Despite the sadness at her departure, it is good to see that Nyssa will be leaving the Doctor for a purpose and a mission all her own. It is better that she go off and help the sick rather than stop somewhere and conveniently fall in love and marry. Sutton's best moments in *Doctor Who* are in the charming "Black Orchid" and "Terminus."

Otherwise, "Terminus" reflects the style of the Peter Davison era in that there is very little humor in evidence and much of the drama's running time is devoted to the lesser companions' travails in and around vents and corridors. Here Turlough and Tegan perform that rather unhappy, unrewarding task. (Turlough would get to do it yet again in "Resurrection of the Daleks.") Perhaps this is payback for "Kinda" in which Nyssa got a headache and was sidelined for the whole story so Tegan could be highlighted. In "Terminus," Sutton gets to act her heart out and sink her teeth into a meaty, meaningful part while Janet Fielding's Tegan whines and crawls through pipes *ad infinitum*.

"Terminus" also reveals once more that the Turlough experiment is not working at all. The character is presented as incompetent, rather than a menace. It is hard to see why the Black Guardian puts up with him. Then again, remember the ridiculous "Shadow" in "The Armageddon Factor"? The Black Guardian obviously has trouble finding good help! In "Terminus," Turlough tries to sabotage the TARDIS, but only half-succeeds. He tries to escape to the TARDIS and leave the others, but he fails in that effort as well. These mistakes do nothing to make the character either likable or believable. The whole "kill the Doctor" subplot would be dropped in the next story.

"Terminus" is a well-presented story that shows Nyssa at her strongest and most appealing. The story was directed by skilled technician Mary Ridge. Before "Terminus," Ridge had overseen some of the best episodes of *Blake's 7*, including the similarly named "Terminal" (1980). She also directed "Rescue," "Power," "Animals," "Headhunter" and the final show of the series, "Blake."

Nyssa's final adventure is available on videocassette.

128. "Enlightenment" Written by Barbara Clegg; Directed by Fiona Cumming; Designed by Colin Green; Parts I–IV; Airdates: March 1, 2, 8, 9, 1983

SYNOPSIS: The crew of the TARDIS find itself aboard a sailing vessel from Edwardian England, circa 1901. After meeting the vessel's commanding officer, Striker, and detailing several temporal anachronisms, the Doctor realizes that this sailing vessel is involved in a race: a race through outer space! It is competing against several ships from many eras in Earth's history. Striker's main opponent is Critas, a Greek sailor!

Striker informs his new guests that he and his people are racing for two reasons. The first is that the participants need a diversion, and the second is that a prize awaits the victor. That prize is nothing short of "enlightenment," the knowledge of the past and the future! The beings involved in this race are not human beings, but Eternals. The Doctor is shocked by this because the Eternals exist outside of time, in the corridors and shadows of eternity. Their minds are empty and tired because they have lived so long. They require the thoughts and inspiration of

Ephemerals, human beings, to keep them entertained. If the wrong Eternal wins this race, the universe will forever suffer the consequences.

GUEST CAST: Capt. Striker (Keith Barron); Marriner (Christopher Brown); First Officer (James McClure); Jackson (Tony Caunter); Capt. Wrack (Lynda Barron); Mansell (Lee John); Critas the Greek (Byron Sotiris); Colier (Clive Kneller); Helmsman (John Cannon); The White Guardian (Cyril Luckham); The Black Guardian (Valentine Dyall)

COMMENTARY: "Enlightenment" is a beautifully told story punctuated by some startling and surreal outer space imagery. The sight of seagoing sailing ships slicing through space is a memorable visual trick, one that is new to the *Who*niverse. However, the idea of oceangoing vessels traversing the ocean of space had also been seen in the Japanese animated series *Star Blazers*. In that series, the Japanese World War II battleship *Yamato* was upgraded to spaceship! Likewise, a 1978 *Star Wars* ripoff entitled *Message from Space* also featured a giant, Hornblower–era sailing vessel in deep space. This film from Kinji Fukasaku is eclectic in its imagery, recalling everything from *The Seven Samurai* to the dismal *Star Crash*. Still, the special effects in *Message of Space*, like those in "Enlightenment," are decent if not groundbreaking.

Barbara Clegg's teleplay ponders the truth about immortality. In fact, immortality had become the most popular theme in Peter Davison's era, perhaps because the series itself had become somewhat immortal by surviving 20 years! Still, immortality had already played a part in "Four to Doomsday" and "Mawdryn Undead" and it would later return to precipitate Borusa's evil deeds in "The Five Doctors." The immortals in this story are "The Eternals," and they are seen to be creatures who are rather bored with their longevity. Thus to *Doctor Who*, immortality is something of a trap. The Eternals need the enthusiasm and joy for life that Ephemerals (humans) exude. They also need the thoughts of humans because they have lived so long they have already thought of everything. Hence they amuse themselves with games like this space race. That immortality consists largely of boredom has been the subject of *Star Trek* ("Requiem for Methuselah") and *Space: 1999* ("End of Eternity"), among others. The 1986 film *Highlander* also explored the issue, but the focus there was the loneliness of immortality in a mortal-dominated world, not boredom. The term "Eternal" was one used in *Zardoz* (1973) to describe the immortal inhabitants of the year 2293.

"Enlightenment" also brings to an end the Turlough–Black Guardian subplot. It is satisfactorily concluded, and Turlough is revealed to be a good guy at heart after all. After "Enlightenment," Turlough would stay with the Doctor as just a "regular"-style companion. His first two serials had proved without a doubt that the *Doctor Who* format could not sustain a character with an ulterior motive. After all, Turlough was inside the TARDIS for much of his stay. Why did he not kill the Doctor while the Time Lord was sleeping? For those who say that Time Lords do not sleep, remember Hartnell's nap in "The Rescue"! The subplot ends in "Enlightenment" for good, as does the recurring Black Guardian character.

Cyril Luckham, the White Guardian of "The Ribos Operation," also makes a guest appearance in this story to end the Guardian saga.

While it is refreshing that John Nathan-Turner chose to pick up on various elements from Season 16 in Season 20, the Guardian saga has never been this author's favorite. Somehow the Guardians, one in white, one in black, tend to make the universe of *Doctor Who* almost cartoonish. A cosmic intelligence should be more than just an embodiment of evil or good. It should have some mystery and some incredibly, otherworldly form. The universe is too complex a place to be separated only into evil and good (why not a Grey Guardian?). But *Doctor Who* has always very much been a series of absolutes.

Portions of "Enlightenment" also recall the Season 6 Patrick Troughton finale, "The War Games." In both stories, humans are abducted by aliens for a nefarious purpose. In both stories, the humans are plagued with significant memory gaps. And finally there is also the discovery in "Enlightenment" of electronics equipment in an age before electronics were invented; that mirrors the discovery of alien machinery in the World War I era in "The War Games." This repetition of familiar elements is not particularly troubling, and "Enlightenment" is still an enjoyable adventure.

"Enlightenment" is available on videocassette.

129. "The King's Demons" Written by Terence Dudley; Directed by Tony Virgo; Designed by Ken Ledsham; Parts I–II; Airdates: March 15, 16, 1983

SYNOPSIS: The TARDIS is acting finicky again and Turlough suggests rather indelicately that it is time for a refit. Tegan is unhappy too because she wants to go home. Her wish is granted, but not quite in the way she expects. The TARDIS arrives on Earth yet again, but it is not the Earth Tegan grew up in. In fact, it is March 4, 1215. The TARDIS has arrived in England just in time to uncover another of the Master's dastardly plots. This time, he is using a shape-shifting android called Kamelion to prevent the signing of the Magna Carta!

GUEST CAST: The Master (Anthony Ainley); King John (Gerald Flood); Kamelion (Chris Padmore); Ranulf (Frank Windsor); Isabella (Isla Blair); Sir Gilles (James Stoker); Hugh (Christopher Villiers); Sir Geoffrey (Michael J. Jackson); Jester (Peter Burroughs); Lute Player (Jacob Lindberg)

COMMENTARY: "The King's Demons" seems like small potatoes for *Doctor Who*. Essentially the story asserts that Earth's future will collapse if the Magna Carta is not signed at this critical juncture in history. While it is doubtless that this document is historically important, is it really so important that the entire future of civilization will collapse without the signature? If man is ready to develop democracy, he will develop it with or without the signing of Magna Carta, right? Besides, what makes the Master believe he will become the ruler of the Earth, just because the Magna Carta is not signed in 1215? Why is he bothering with Earth again anyway? He is a Time Lord, able to live forever and go anywhere he wishes! What does Earth offer him that he is so desperate to possess it? And is it really necessary to draw the Doctor into this plan, just to discredit King John? Is that not tempting fate just a bit too much? After all, the Master has been defeated in every encounter with the Doctor since 1971! That should probably tip off the Master to the fact that he should keep the Doctor *as far from his plans as possible*! Why does the Master always draw such attention to his schemes, when they might actually succeed if he were more discreet?

The fallacy of time travel stories like "The King's Demons" is that there are always far more appropriate time periods in which to exploit the native populace on Earth than the one that is actually selected by the villain. The Master could have gone back to visit the tribe of Gum seen in "An Unearthly Child" and provided them with fire. Thus he would be seen as nothing less than a god. No one would dare oppose him. With his Tissue Compressor Gun at his side, the Master would be invincible in that time period.

Or better yet, he could go back to the primordial soup seen in "City of Death" and destroy it. The Earth would belong to him and he would never need humans again. Why go back instead to a time period when it is necessary to battle politics, knights, the population and even the Plague to succeed? It makes no sense dramatically.

"The King's Demons" is also reminiscent of a 1966 *Time Tunnel* episode entitled "Revenge of Robin Hood." In that adventure (penned by Leonard Stadd) Robin Hood (Don Harron) forced King John to sign the Magna Carta and therefore assure freedom of his subjects. Thus "The King's Demons" is not even original in its setting and Magna Carta dynamics!

Sci-fi television trivia hounds should recognize Isabella in "The King's Demons." She is portrayed by Isla Blair, a guest star in the *Space: 1999* episodes "Journey to Where" (another time travel story involving the British Isles, this time in 1339) and "War Games." She also appeared in the first season *Blake's 7* adventure "Duel."

"The King's Demons" has been released on video in a two-box set with a re-edited version of "The Five Doctors."

130. "The Five Doctors" Written by Terrance Dicks; Directed by Peter Moffatt; Designed by Malcolm Thornton; Airdate: November 25, 1983

SYNOPSIS: An unseen evil plucks the first five incarnations of the Doctor from their individual time lines and deposits them on Gallifrey. Only the fourth incarnation does not appear, trapped instead in limbo. Together with many companions from adventures past, the various Doctors play a deadly game inside "the Death Zone" of Gallifrey. Eons ago, the Gallifreyans kidnapped aliens from all over the universe and deposited them in this zone. Then they made the aliens fight one another to the death. Now the Doctor has been brought to this game along with his worst enemies, including Daleks, Yeti and Cyberman! All the incarnations of the Doctor realize that somehow, some way, they must get to the Mountain of Rassilon and find the answer. They learn that they are just pawns in an attempt by a secret traitor to possess the Ring of Rassilon, which will provide its owner with life eternal.

GUEST CAST: Doctor Who, First Incarnation (Richard Hurndall); Doctor Who, Second Incarnation (Patrick Troughton); Doctor Who, Third Incarnation (Jon Pertwee); Sarah Jane Smith (Elisabeth Sladen); Susan Foreman (Carole Ann Ford); Brigadier Lethbridge-Stewart (Nicholas Courtney); The Master (Anthony Ainley); Lord President Borusa (Philip Latham); Chancellor Flavia (Dinah Sheridan); Rassilon (Richard Matthews); The Castellan (Paul Jericho); Cyberleader (David Banks); Cyber Lieutenant (Mark Hardy); Jamie McCrimmon (Frazer Hines); Zoe (Wendy Padbury); Liz Shaw (Caroline John); Capt. Yates (Richard Franklin); Crichton (David Savile); Voice of K-9 (John Leeson); Dalek Voice (Roy Skelton); Dalek Operator (John Scott Martin); Commander (Stuart Black); Sergeant (Ray Float); Guard (John Tallents); Cyberscout (William Kenton); Raston Robot (Keith Hodiak); Yeti (Lee Woods); Cybermen (Graham Cole, Richard Naylor, Gilbert Gillan, Emyr Morris Jones, Myrddian Jones, Lloyd Williams, Alan Riches, Ian Marshall-Fisher, Mark Bassenger)

COMMENTARY: Season 20 ends with a sentimental story celebrating two decades of *Doctor Who*. Besides the inspiring appearances of *Doctor Who*s past Patrick Troughton and Jon Pertwee, the story also finds time to highlight historic companions Sarah Jane Smith (Elisabeth Sladen), Susan Foreman (Carole Ann Ford), K-9 (John Leeson) and the Brigadier (Nicholas Courtney). Companions Jamie (Frazer Hines), Zoe (Wendy Padbury), Liz Shaw (Caroline John) and Mike Yates (Richard Franklin) also make cameo appearances. It is great to see *all* of them again. The villains join the party as well in the form of Daleks, Yeti and Cybermen. With all these memorable guests, "The Five Doctors" is a joyous birthday party. As such, it is certainly a triumph.

There are some low points in the production. The saddest fact, of course, is that William Hartnell has been dead for ten years by the time of "The Five Doctors." Amazingly, Richard Hurndall (now also deceased) does a beautiful job of recapturing this essential First Incarnation. It is a high compliment to state that Hurndall is Hartnell–esque in his approach to the role. He recaptures the magic and eccentricity of this beloved First Doctor.

The second disappointment is that Tom Baker opted not to attend the celebration. An historic opportunity is missed. Of course, Baker had only been gone from the show for two years at this point, and that was apparently not long enough a time to separate himself from the role that made him a household name in England and in the United States. The fourth Doctor is missed in "The Five Doctors." Because of Baker's refusal to participate, the fans missed the only opportunity to see Doctors 2, 3, 4 and 5 in the same production. A reunion show today would be a rather sad thing since Pertwee and Troughton are now dead too. A gathering of *Doctor Who*s today would, amazingly, feature Tom Baker as the elder statesmen — the oldest living actor to play the Doctor in the series. Would a show uniting Baker, Davison, Colin Baker, McCoy and McGann engender the same nostalgic feelings so evident in "The Five Doctors"? Perhaps ... perhaps not. The show's landmark early days would be left unrepresented without Hartnell, Troughton or Pertwee along for the fun. And it would be impossible to even contemplate the recasting of Troughton and Pertwee's incarnations. Hurndall pulled off the Hartnell replacement well here, but recasting three of the eight Doctors would spark only confusion and sadness.

Since Baker did not make himself available for "The Five Doctors," he is represented in the serial by footage from the lost adventure "Shada." At the time of broadcast, this stop-gap measure seemed at least moderately acceptable, since the public had never been privy to any of that footage. In 1983 it seemed that they really were seeing "new" Baker film.

As in "The Three Doctors" (1973), the highlight of "The Five Doctors" is the interaction among the various incarnations of the Time Lord. Pertwee and Troughton resume their bickering, testy relationship as if a day has not passed since the 1973 celebration. The first incarnation of the Doctor is again treated by later Doctors as the wise, elder statesmen of the series, and he is the one who solves the central problem of the serial. Davison is for some reason kept occupied in the Time Lord city while his previous incarnations join up in the castle of Rassilon. Only in the final minutes of the last episode is Davison permitted to stand side-by-side with his legendary peers. Delightfully, the young fifth incarnation more than holds his own against these consummate scene stealers. Davison has found his niche as a sincere, naive version of the Time Lord, and he is as much a part of the legend as Pertwee or Troughton. One just wishes all the leading actors had more time together in "The Five Doctors." They spend so much time apart that it is hard to tell how they feel about seeing their fourth regeneration (Davison).

"The Five Doctors" reveals more about Time Lord history, including the Dark Times before the non-intervention directive. The Time Lords were apparently quite the scoundrels in ancient times, scooping up aliens from other planets and forcing them to fight in the rough terrain of Gallifrey. This makes sense historically, however, and seems to fit in with the Time Lord brutality so obvious in "The War Games."

The key to the story in "The Five Doctors," transcribed in Old High Gallifrey of course, is that Time Lord architect Rassilon engineered a method of removing would be tyrants from the planet. The lure of immortality, he assumed, would be too much to resist. He was right, and Lord President Borusa suffers a horrible fate in Rassilon's trap. He will be alive forever inside the coffin of Rassilon. This is a creepy, macabre climax to the celebratory show, and a satisfying resolution to the story.

The final moments of "The Five Doctors" are echoed by the last act of the 1989 film *Indiana Jones and the Last Crusade*. The Nazi villain Donovan (*Doctor Who* guest star Julian Glover) is asked to choose the cup of Christ from among several cups. He chooses the wrong cup, and meets with a horrible fate. Indiana Jones then chooses a cup, and is told that he has "chosen wisely." Similarly, in this 1983 *Who* adventure, Borusa chooses to take the ring of Rassilon and meets with a horrible fate. The spirit of Rassilon then communicates with the various incarnations of the Doctor and asks them if they want the ring. When they refuse, Rassilon also notes that they have "chosen wisely." Even the situation leading up to this scenario is identical. In both stories, the hero must navigate the evils of an ancient tomb/castle before he can claim the prize at the end.

There is an incongruity in "The Five Doctors" that results in some confusion. In the castle of Rasillon, Troughton's incarnation runs across the phantoms of companions Zoe and Jamie. He realizes they are false because the Time Lords erased their memories and sent them back to their homes ... and therefore they should not remember him. However, these events occurred in the last Troughton saga "The War Games." Immediately following the departure of Zoe and Jamie, the Time Lords forced a regeneration on Troughton and exiled him to Earth. Unless Borusa pulled Troughton's incarnation from a brief five-minute span between Zoe and Jamie's departure and his own exile in "The War Games," Troughton's Doctor should not be privy to this information. And the text of the serial makes clear that Troughton is pulled not from the events of "The War Games," but from a visit to the Brigadier on Earth! Therefore this scene represents a major discontinuity in *Doctor Who* history. Of course, there is always the possibility that Patrick Troughton's Doctor somehow managed to outfox his Time Lord captors and remain alive in the Troughton persona at the same time that part of his personality regenerated into third incarnation Jon Pertwee. Perhaps because Troughton's Doctor saved the Time Lords from Omega in "The Three Doctors," the Time Lords rewarded him in some fashion (as they did Pertwee) and allowed him to continue his existence in a different time stream. Or, more realistically, writer Terrance Dicks just made a mistake that resulted in a continuity error.

Troughton would appear once more in *Doctor Who* in the serial "The Two Doctors" (1985). This makes him the only Doctor to have worked not only with his predecessor (Hartnell in "The Three Doctors") but with three of his descendants (Pertwee, Davison and Colin Baker). Unfortunately, Pertwee would not appear again on *Doctor Who*. He died in New York City of a heart attack in 1996.

"The Five Doctors" was originally released on videotape on its own. In 1993, the tape was reissued in a "special edition" form along with the previous serial "The King's Demons." As is typical with these box sets, that means that *Who* fans must buy a less-than-satisfying serial at the same time they purchase a delightful one.

SEASON 21

X **131. "Warriors of the Deep"** Written by Johnny Byrne; Directed by Pennant Roberts; Designed by Tony Burrough; Parts I–IV; Airdates: January 5, 6, 12, 13, 1984

SYNOPSIS: While Earth stands on the brink of annihilation in the year 2084, two subterranean enemies from the past, the Silurians and the Sea Devils, arrive to take advantage of humanity's warlike nature. Inside Sea Base 4, the Doctor, Turlough and Tegan must prevent the reptilian creatures from launching proton missiles that could instigate the final conflict between the Eastern and Western Blocs. The Doctor also contends with the Myrka, a deadly Silurian-Sea Devil dragon capable of massive destruction.

GUEST CAST: Commander Vorshak (Tom Adams); Commander Icthar (Norman Comer); Sauvix (Christopher Farries); Bulic (Nigher Humphreys); Lt. Preston (Tara Ward); Maddox (Martin Neil); Nilson (Ian McCulloch); Karina (Nitza Saul); Scibus (Stuart Black); Tarpok (Vincent Brimble); Dr. Solow (Ingrid Pitt); Paroli (James Coombes); Myrka (John Asquith); Sea Devils (Mike Braben, Steve Kelly, David Ould)

COMMENTARY: With "Warriors of the Deep," *Doctor Who* was once again ahead of a fad. This 1984 story about an underwater installation attacked by non-human forces debuted five years before Hollywood became obsessed with the very same science fiction notion. In 1989, America was flooded with a deluge of underwater "monster" films very similar in tone and content to "Warriors of the Deep." In that one year alone, the country was treated to *Endless Descent* starring Jack Scalia, Roger Corman's *Lords from the Deep*, Sean Cunningham's *Deep Star Six*, George Cosmatos' *Leviathan* and James Cameron's *The Abyss*.

Johnny Byrne's third *Doctor Who* episode is the final adventure in the trilogy begun in Season 7 with "Doctor Who and the Silurians" and continued in Season 9's "The Sea Devils." "Warriors of the Deep" sees the reiteration of the themes evident in both of those previous serials, specifically that even in a battle of two equally "right" species, one side must be chosen. In this case, as in "The Sea Devils," the Doctor chooses to side with humanity. This is perhaps the most important stance on morality taken throughout the series. This is quite different from *Star Trek*'s stance on life; *Star Trek* believes peace can be maintained, disparate cultures can work together, and fighting and warfare can be abolished. Though perhaps *Star Trek*'s philosophy is more optimistic, *Doctor Who*'s is undoubtedly the more realistic, once human nature is considered. *Star Trek* has the luxury of being concerned with other worlds. In "Warriors of the Deep," it is Earth that is the battlefield. How would the United Federation of Planets respond to the presence of an alien race with an equal claim to possession of Earth? Would the citizens of the Federation share their paradise with a lizard species? Or would they want Starfleet to intervene to stop the "invaders"? This is one story that *Star Trek* has never tackled, perhaps because it would put a chink in Roddenberry's belief that all races can ultimately be friends.

"Warriors of the Deep" is the least philosophical of the Silurian-Sea Devil adventures. It is the most action-packed and self-contained and therefore the most tense of the trilogy. In this sense, the Doctor really has very little time to reflect thoughtfully before making his decision and taking sides. The proton missiles are going to launch, the Sea Devils are inside the base, and he has to do something fast or millions of people will die. To Davison's credit, he is able to embody the

Doctor's moral dilemma in the midst of pyrotechnics, the ridiculous-looking Myrka beast and the story's relentlessly fast pace.

Davison's Doctor is particularly adept at making the Doctor's dilemmas in morality identifiable. Davison's era constantly saw the Doctor facing questions of moral uncertainty in stories such as "Earthshock," "Black Orchid" and "Mawdryn Undead." In "Resurrection of the Daleks," he would also have to decide if it was right to murder Davros in cold blood. "Warriors of the Deep" fits in with these stories because the young Doctor has to make a tough decision. In the process, he learns what kind of person he is. This is clearly Davison's niche. He is not the experienced, world-weary traveler like Pertwee. He does not take Hartnell's schoolteacher approach to time travel. He is not the humorous man who champions the cause of the innocent without question like Troughton or Tom Baker. Instead he is the "innocent"! He is the Doctor who learns about himself and his morality as he travels. In some senses, the Doctor seems to be aging in reverse. Not only is he younger in appearance, he seems less experienced in the ways of the universe. As each incarnation must be different from ones that preceded it, Davison's interpretation is successful.

"Warriors of the Deep" is available on videocassette. Many fans dislike this serial intensely because of the design and execution of the Myrka creature. Some fans even insist this is one of the worst three serials in *Doctor Who* history. Considering "Time Flight," "The Awakening," "The King's Demons" and other weak stories of the Peter Davison era, that is a difficult assertion to prove.

132. "The Awakening" Written by Eric Pringle; Directed by Michael Owen Morris; Designed by Barry Newbery; Parts I–II; Airdates: January 19, 20, 1984

SYNOPSIS: At Tegan's insistence, the Doctor sets a course for the village of Little Hodcombe, England, in the year 1984. She wants to visit her grandfather, Andrew Verney. When the TARDIS arrives, the Doctor clashes with Malus, "the God of War." The Doctor realizes that the Malus is focusing the energy of human thoughts. That means the alien is harnessing the thoughts created by the participants in a local war games recreation! The Doctor asks a participant, Sir George Hutchinson, to stop the games because the Malus is fueling himself from the activity. Hutchinson refuses, because he is under the influence of the evil alien. The Doctor speculates that Malus was a living entity somehow re-engineered as an instrument of war and sent to Earth to clear the way for an invasion. Now he must break the alien's hold on Hutchinson's mind.

GUEST CAST: Sir George Hutchinson (Denis Lill); Joseph Willow (Jack Galloway); Will Chandler (Keith Jayne); Andrew Verney (Frederick Hall); Col. Wolsey (Glyn Houston); Jane Hampden (Polly James); Trooper (Christopher Saul)

COMMENTARY: "The Awakening" is a two-part *Doctor Who* serial in the tradition of "The Sontaran Experiment," "Black Orchid" or "The King's Demons" since it clocks in at a running time just under an hour. Thus "The Awakening" is roughly equivalent to a typical American hour-long drama. When put in this context for purpose of qualitative judgment, it becomes obvious how narratively primitive and lackluster "The Awakening" is in compared to *Star Trek*, *Space: 1999* or even *Battlestar Galactica*. The characters are two-dimensional, the action is motivated by coincidences and the sci-fi concepts utilized are fresh from the recycling bin of genre clichés.

Yet another old standby has been pulled from the *Doctor Who* vaults to spur the action in Eric Pringle's sole contribution to the series. The concept of an ancient evil reawakening and causing havoc is nowhere more thinly dramatized than in this serial. As in "Pyramids of Mars," "The Masque of Mandragora, "The Daemons," "Image of the Fendahl" and "The Hand of Fear," the Doctor in "The Awakening" must stop an extraterrestrial horror before it emerges from its slumber and destroys the Earth. Malus is less memorable a villain than Sutekh, Eldrad, Azal or even the Mandragora Helix, so this is truly a by-the-numbers adventure. Even the concept of disparate time zones meeting with one another is reminiscent of earlier *Who* stories such as "The War Games."

"The Awakening" once again leads the series back to Earth. In all, Davison's Doctor had visited Earth in more than half of his stories. Out of 16 adventures thus far, Davison's Time Lord had been to Terra in ten. This was a break with the situation in the later years of the Tom Baker era, when Earth was visited only once per season ("The Stones of Blood" in Season 16, "City of Death" in Season 17 and "Logopolis" in Season 18). This trend in Seasons 19–21 reveals a lack of imagination and creativity. It is much easier to visit Earth than to develop a realistic alien society, and so the Doctor went back to Terra again and again. As a result, *Doctor Who* of this period is almost unrelentingly boring.

The paucity of imagination evident in "The Awakening," "The Visitation" and "Snakedance" is hard to understand, much less tolerate. *Doctor Who* is a series that sports the most elastic format of any series in history and yet old plots, time-worn ingredients and oft-repeated stories carry new adventures. Invasions, evil awakening and the "Daemons" prototype were all old, old stories by this time, and nothing can satisfactorily explain their constant reappearances. For this reason, Seasons 19–21 are among the most dull and uninventive of the entire series from a narrative standpoint.

Although the occasional brilliant story ("Mawdryn Undead," "Black Orchid") crops up, the vast majority are familiar hokum. In a series that can go backwards and forwards in time, to any planet in this or alternate universes, even to domains outside of time and space, stories like "The Awakening" betray a laziness on the part of producers and writers. *Doctor Who* of this era is content to repeat past glories rather break new ground. Some fans might find comfort in this obvious recycling of elements, but others merely find it infuriating. "The Awakening" is another candidate for the worst serial in *Doctor Who* history because it is so unoriginal, so unambitious, so familiar.

133. "Frontios" Written by Christopher Bidmead; Directed by Ron Jones; Designed by David Buckingham; Parts I–II; Airdates: February 2, 3, 1984

SYNOPSIS: The TARDIS drifts into the Veruna System in the far future and hovers over the planet Frontios, where the Doctor says mankind will seek refuge after Earth is destroyed. The TARDIS is unexpectedly buffeted in a meteor storm and forced to land. The Doctor and his friends learn that the planet is being bombarded by unknown attackers. The attackers come not from outer space, but underground. There are deadly creatures there called "Tractators." These hideous beasts command immense gravitational forces. Gravis, the leader of the Tractators, has been abducting humans because the Tractators need living flesh to power their machinery. The Doctor soon learns that the Tractators are building a giant gravity motor in the center of the planet. They intend to steer Frontios through the galaxy and begin nesting on other inhabited worlds.

GUEST CAST: Plantagenet (Jeff Rawle); Range (William Lucas); Norna (Lesley Dunlop); Brazen (Peter Gilmore); Capt. Revere (John Beardmore); Gravis (John Gillett); Warnsman (Jim Dowdall); Orderly (Richard Ashley); Deputy (Allison Skilbeck); Retrograde (Raymond Murtagh); Tractators (William Bowen, George Campbell, Hedi Khursandi, Michael Malcolm, Stephen Speed)

COMMENTARY: *Doctor Who* was obsessed with man's ultimate fate since the first days of the series. William Hartnell, Jackie Lane and Peter Purves voyaged with the last remnants of civilization to a new home on the distant world of Refusis in "The Ark." Tom Baker, Ian Marter and Elisabeth Sladen awoke the last representatives of the race to repopulate a regenerated Earth in "The Ark in Space." In "Frontios," Peter Davison likewise leads Janet Fielding and Mark Strickson through another adventure involving the final destiny of man. Although all three of these stories tell markedly different, and sometimes contradictory, stories about the end of Earth and the final fate of humanity, all three serials express the common opinion that cataclysm will one day engulf the Earth and cause a new dawn for the race, perhaps in space, or perhaps on another world. This speculation is based firmly on science, which tells us that in several billion years our sun *will* die out. Ever a series of optimism, *Doctor Who* believes that man will still be alive to see that event.

Still, "Frontios" is a rather grim tale about a human colony facing gruesome death from the evil, inhuman Tractators. The Tractators are an interesting alien race because they incorporate human body parts and human intelligence into their very technology. This is a concept that has not been explored before on the series. The Cybermen are just the opposite of the Tractators. They have removed human limbs and organs and replaced them with robotic parts. The Tractators actually employ human bodies as we might use a metal pipe, a motor, a computer or a cog. This conceit is incredibly disturbing, and it fits well within *Doctor Who* tradition that the Doctor should stop this exploitation rather than let man die in such an ignoble manner.

"Frontios" is a return to that old chestnut, the *Time Machine* template, which defined so many of the early serials. The Tractators clearly fill in for the Morlocks, and the human colonists are surrogates for the Eloi. In *The Time Machine*, the

Morlocks also used human bodies ... but for food and slave labor, not for machinery parts. The essence of the story is still the same.

The biggest question about "Frontios" is how to reconcile it with events seen in the aforementioned serials "The Ark" and "The Ark in Space," both of which also purport to document the final portion of mankind's odyssey. Attempts to make sense of the *Doctor Who* universe in this fashion are very popular and fans have long speculated about seeming incongruities like this one. Jean-Marc Lofficier calls this effort "retconning"[18] or retroactive continuity. In his book *The Terrestrial Index*, Lofficier explains away the discrepancies in the following way. "The Ark in Space" takes place somewhere around 17,000 A.D. This new society lives on Earth peaceably until millions of years after that date. Then Earthmen flee the planet in "Frontios" and "The Ark" respectively. This is a believable, logical extrapolation of the events seen in these episodes, but it is important to remember that "retconning" is entirely subjective. Unlike series such as *Star Trek: The Next Generation*, which maintained a clarified continuity until the revisionism of *First Contact* in 1996, *Doctor Who* is not so successful in its feeling of unity. The origin of the Daleks had changed from "The Daleks" to "Genesis of the Daleks," and certainly the future of man was another area of discontinuity. Still, "retconning" appears to be a very enjoyable pastime in *Who* circles. In fact, that is often the fun of sci-fi television series: trying to make all the pieces fit together.

134. "Resurrection of the Daleks" Written by Eric Saward; Directed by Matthew Robinson; Designed by John Anderson; Parts I–II; Airdates: February 8, 15 1984

SYNOPSIS: When the TARDIS is unexpectedly pulled into a dangerous time corridor, the Doctor, Turlough and Tegan are forced to confront a temporal incursion by the Daleks! Their seemingly endless war with the Movellans is finally over. The Daleks lost the war and were totally defeated. The Movellans finally attained victory by developing a deadly virus that killed Daleks. The Daleks were forced to run to the corners of the universe to escape this disease, and are no longer a major player in galactic events. A small group of Daleks has risked a return to Earth's galaxy to fetch Davros from a penal vessel. They believe that he can find a cure for the virus. And, true to form, the Daleks also have a new plan for galactic conquest. They have created perfect duplicates of Tegan and Turlough and now they wish to make a genetically perfect duplicate of the Doctor to act as their agent. They want the three agents to go to Gallifrey and assassinate the members of the Time Lord High Council.

GUEST CAST: Stein (Rodney Bewes) Styles (Rula Lenska); Col. Archer (Del Henney); Commander Lytton (Maurice Colbourne); Prof. Laird (Chloe Ashcroft); Sgt. Calder (Philip McGough); Davros (Terry Molley); Mercer (Jim Findley); Osborn (Sneh Gupta); Trooper (Roger Davenport); Crew Members (John Adam Baker, Linsey Turner); Calloway (William Sleigh); Dalek Voices (Brian Miller, Royce Mills); Dalek Operators (Toby Byrne, John Scott Martin, Tony Starr)

COMMENTARY: The first Dalek story in five years (since 1979's "Destiny of the Daleks") is an exciting action-adventure filled with flashy pyrotechnics. The Daleks exterminate and connive in a welcome return to the menacing ways they dramatized in classic stories such as "The Dalek Masterplan" and "The Chase." Although the hand of Dalek creator Terry Nation is missing, this serial still accomplishes its purpose: making the Daleks *effective* villains once again. Many *Who* fans felt that "Destiny of the Daleks" mocked these evil creatures and effectively ended their reign as believable villains. After considering this argument, producer John Nathan-Turner retired the Daleks until he felt they could be done right again. "Resurrection of the Daleks" is well-named because its primary purpose is to resurrect the terrifying nature of the Daleks that audiences had felt so palpably in early serials such as "The Daleks" and "The Dalek Invasion of Earth." Since this serial's aim is simply to be a rollicking adventure with the Daleks once again providing glorious villainy, the serial succeeds. It may not have the philosophical underpinnings of "Genesis of the Daleks" or even "Destiny of the Daleks" (which was about the difference between mechanical and human minds), but it is nonetheless a solid actioner.

"Resurrection of the Daleks" features several fast-moving battle scenes. In an impressive opening sequence, a squad of Daleks storm the prison ship and the scene successfully recalls the opening battle aboard the Blockade Runner in *Star Wars*. Later in the story, another Dalek is pushed out a window and explodes into a million pieces once he hits the street. This stunt is accomplished with panache. The only problem is that, as always, the Daleks love to shout out their own problems in that highly irritating metallic screech. Before the Dalek is pushed out the window, a soldier shoots off its eyestalk. The Dalek thus begins to shout, for all his enemies to hear, "Vision impaired, I cannot see; vision impaired, I cannot see." It is a ridiculous moment. One would think that the military-minded Daleks would have some kind of back-up vision system in case their vulnerable eyestalk was shot off! Even if this was not so, why announce the problem to the enemy?

Unfortunately, "Resurrection of the Daleks" also brings Davros back to life. This character had served his purpose quite well in both "Genesis of the Daleks" and "Destiny of the Daleks," but he brings nothing new to his last several appearances in the series ("Resurrection of the Daleks," "Revelation of the Daleks" and "Remembrance of the Daleks"). By bringing Davros back in every later Dalek adventure, the producers only succeeded in proving that the Daleks couldn't cut it as villains on their own any more. Davros' presence, his individuality, is what sparks the outbursts of villainy in all later Dalek stories. It was Davros who built a new Dalek army in "Revelation of the Daleks" and Davros who pursued the Hand of Omega in "Remembrance of the Daleks." As for the mutated, armored beasts (the Daleks), they are seen more as shock troops than as legitimate villains with their own agenda in these latter sojourns. This is unfortunate because the true terror of the Daleks in the early days was in their total inhumanity. They were not humanoid, did not share human values and they needed no "individual" face to make them terrifying. They were like a swarm of bees, and just as terrifying. As audiences became more familiar with the Daleks and more immune to their particular brand of horror, the producers kept inserting Davros into the action to make the story more personal. What they should have done was staged a full-fledged *Doctor Who* blow-out with the Daleks fighting the Cybermen for possession of a human-populated colony somewhere. Now that would have made a fantastic story that would not require Davros to stimulate the action.

"Resurrection of the Daleks" features one incredibly tense scene in which a Dalek has shed its destroyed armor suit and is scurrying around a warehouse. Once freed, this horrible little ball of slime begins attacking every human it can gets its misshapen claws on. This sequence foreshadows a similar scene in the 1986 film *Aliens* in which a grotesque face-hugger breaks loose in a laboratory. This is the first time that a Dalek mutant (apart from their costumes) was displayed in such a threatening fashion. The revelation in this story that they are pretty violent, disgusting creatures even *without* their protective suits also makes them seem more menacing than in previous adventures.

Amidst all the fireworks and exploding spaceships, the Doctor once again learns a lesson about himself in "Resurrection of the Daleks." He decides that he is responsible for the evil of the Daleks, and so he appropriates a huge laser rifle and levels it point-blank at Davros. Of course, the Doctor hesitates. He finds that even with good reason, he is unable to kill in cold blood. This is another classic Davison moment, and one that effectively dramatizes the Doctor's sense of morality.

Janet Fielding's Tegan also says goodbye to *Doctor Who* in "Resurrection of the Daleks," and her farewell has an abrupt air to it. It is not really integrated into the drama, especially considering the stylish goodbyes to Nyssa in "Terminus" and Adric in "Earthshock." Tegan simply has a temper tantrum and says she has seen too much violence. She then runs off into a warehouse and disappears. It is a shocking and poorly integrated moment, yet it *does* have the uncomfortable feel of reality to it. No trumpets play, no preposterous mate shows up to marry her. Instead Tegan just breaks down and leaves. As a farewell, it is more shocking than sad, and it works rather well. It is a surprise and it is illogical but of course, life is seldom predictable or logical, is it? The abrupt nature of Tegan's departure leaves viewers gasping in shock and dismay. The departure is perhaps made a little less effective because Tegan returns to say goodbye one more time after the Doctor and the TARDIS have already left. This was apparently the producer's way of suggesting that Tegan was not really mad at the Doctor after all, just having a bad moment. It would have been a more effective moment if Tegan just left and did not come back at all.

Was Tegan an effective companion? Janet Fielding certainly imbued Tegan with loads of personality and charm, but how many times did writers force this great actress and this interesting character to whine about going home? Dramatically speaking, it is not very interesting to feature a character who wants to leave all the time. Has Tegan no interest in the Doctor, or the universe he shows her? Why is she so unhappy all the time? These characteristics make Tegan less successful than

Sarah Jane, Romana or Leela. Fielding had the talent to make Tegan the most interesting and well-loved of all companions, but the writers never gave her a really good story to sink her teeth into. Although the character was possessed in stories such as "Kinda" and "Snakedance," what else did Fielding really get to do besides whine and cry? She complained her way through "Time Flight" and "The King's Demons," to name just a few episodes. She showed beautiful charm and *joie de vivre* in "Black Orchid," but that was the exception, not the rule. One is not at all happy to see the lovable Tegan leave, but it certainly makes sense. It is obvious that of all the companions the Doctor ever had, she was probably having the least fun.

"Resurrection of the Daleks" is available on videocassette.

135. "Planet of Fire" Written by Peter Grimwade; Directed by Fiona Cumming; Designed by Malcolm Thornton; Parts I–IV; Airdates: February 23, 24, March 1, 2, 1984

SYNOPSIS: Because Tegan is gone and the Doctor is depressed, Turlough suggests a visit to a tropical island. Before a decision can be made, the Doctor and Turlough hear Kamelion cry out in pain. He has connected himself to the TARDIS and is hurt. Turlough runs to the main console to see if something there is affecting the robot. Instead, he overhears a distress call from his own homeworld, Trion. Convinced that the Custodians are searching for him, he sabotages the console so the Doctor will not hear the call and offer aid. Soon, the Doctor, Kamelian, Turlough and an American biology student, Perpigillium "Peri" Brown, become enmeshed in adventure on Sarn, a planet of intense volcanic activity. As the time travelers encounter the Master, Turlough is also forced to confront the mysteries of his own history...

GUEST CAST: Malkon (Edward Highmore); The Master (Anthony Ainley); Timanov (Peter Wyngarde); Sorasta (Barbara Shelley); Amyand (James Bates); Prof. Howard Foster (Dallas Adams); Roskal (Jonathan Caplan); Lomand (John Alkin); Zuko (Max Arthur); Trion (Ray Knight); Lookout (Simon Sutton)

COMMENTARY: "Planet of Fire" combines two common *Doctor Who* story threads. The first is the oft-seen conceit of a civilization that has lost knowledge of its heritage and returned to barbarism after a spaceship crash. On *Doctor Who* these stories include "The Face of Evil" and "Planet of the Spiders." The second might be called "the Master trap." In this style of *Who* serial, the evil Master plots to destroy the Doctor while at the same time trying to gain power, escape imprisonment or ensure his own longevity. Stories of this type include "The Deadly Assassin," "The Keeper of Traken," "The King's Demons," "Terror of the Autons," "Castrovalva," "Logopolis" and "Time Flight." With all these predecessors, "Planet of Fire"'s roots are derivative. The serial is still noteworthy, however, because it dispatches with Mark Strickson's Turlough and introduces new companion Peri Brown, played by actress Nicola Bryant.

Turlough was never the most successful of the Doctor's companions. He was introduced with a great flourish in "Mawdryn Undead," but he was frequently dramatized as incompetent while under the dominion of the Black Guardian ("Mawdryn Undead," "Terminus," "Enlightenment"). With his treacherous, ineffectual nature, Turlough recalled the worst aspects of Jonathan Harris' Dr. Smith on *Lost in Space.* Turlough was always looking out for himself, and always working within his own dark agenda, but somehow the Doctor tolerated him. After the Black Guardian angle was dropped, Turlough had nothing to do in stories such as "The Awakening," "Frontios" and "Resurrection of the Daleks." He became a standard male companion like Harry Sullivan or Adric. Athletic incarnations of the Doctor such as Tom Baker and Peter Davison can handle the action elements of the series themselves, however, and do not require a second male lead. Mark Strickson was always competent, but the role of Turlough offered nothing of substance for him to do. He could not save the day because that was the Doctor's job. He could not handle all the action because, again, that the was the Doctor's bailiwick. As a result, Turlough is one of the most underdeveloped parts in *Doctor Who* history, especially when one remembers "real" individuals like Ian, Barbara, Susan, Zoe and Jamie. Essentially the duty of all modern companions is to be captured and then rescued by the Doctor. Though Turlough was conceived to break this mold, the experiment failed. He became exactly what the producers had hoped to avoid: another boring companion. In the introduction to the novel *Turlough and the Earthlink Dilemma* (1986) by Tony Attwood, Mark Strickson acknowledged the problem:

> One of the problems of being a companion on *Doctor Who* is that you would really, of course, like to be playing the Doctor… There just isn't time for everyone to play a leading part, or to have their character developed… You may have noticed that Turlough spent a great deal of time kept captive in various states of bondage. It was always a disappointment to me that there seemed to be no getting around this problem.[19]

That Strickson was able to make Turlough a slightly different breed of companion at all is relevant. "Planet of Fire" ends the saga of Turlough in a satisfactory manner, with the young man finally able to return home to Trion after many years of exile.

Nicola Bryant makes her debut as Peri in "Planet of Fire." Peri would accompany Davison's Doctor through one more adventure, and then become the companion of Colin Baker's mercurial sixth incarnation. Peri is a controversial figure in *Who* fandom, the focal point of a rather dramatic schism: Some fans love her for her sassy persona, and others despise her because they do not like Bryant's voice, which many call "whiny" or "nasal." There can be no denying that Bryant's Peri was a perfect foil for the sixth Doctor. Since he was played as a raging egotist by Colin Baker, it was necessary to have someone puncture his balloon of arrogance. Peri accomplished the task quite successfully. And really, she was not whiny in the same way Tegan had been. Instead, she complained about the Doctor's erratic new nature and his attitude problems. Baker's persona would have been positively insufferable without Bryant's Peri to keep him in line.

Nicola Bryant played Peri, first companion to Colin Baker's erratic Time Lord, in serial #135, "Planet of Fire."

"Planet of Fire" also features a guest appearance by Peter Wyngarde as Timanov. Wyngarde is recognizable not only for his portrayal of Jason King in the early '70s ITC action series *Department S*, but also for his rendition of Klytus, evil minion of Ming the Merciless in the 1980 film *Flash Gordon*.

136. "The Caves of Androzani"

Written by Robert Holmes; Directed by Graeme Harper; Designed by John Hurst; Parts I–IV; Airdates: March 8, 9, 15, 16, 1984

SYNOPSIS: The Doctor and Peri land on the barren world Androzani Minor. Inside the caves there, the Doctor reveals why always he wears a celery stalk on his lapel: It is a restorative for Time Lords should they encounter a substance to which they are allergic. While examining the caves, Peri slips and falls into a pile of strange organic material. The Doctor rescues her, but finds the same compound sticking to him. He realizes they have both been stricken with the terminal disease Spectrox Toxemia.

Meanwhile, the Doctor and Peri learn that Sharez Jek and his army of androids have been fighting Gen. Chellak and his army. Jek has not only built an entire android army, but he has hoarded an important substance called Spectrox. Morgas and the President of the Androzani Major Presidium are desperate to take this material from him because it doubles the average human life span. Gen. Chellak's soldiers have been on Androzani Minor for six months trying to get the Spectrox away from Jek. Jek, who was once disfigured horribly by Morgas, wants only one thing: revenge. Dying from Spectrox Toxemia, the Doctor must navigate his way through this deadly situation, but in saving Peri's life, he is forced to regenerate once again.

GUEST CAST: Sharez Jek (Christopher Gable); Morgas (John Normington); Salateen (Robert Gelnister); Stotz (Maurice Roeves); Chellak (Martin Cochrane); Krelper (Roy Holder); Timmin (Barbara Kinghorn); President (David Neal); Soldier (Ian Staples); The Doctor (Colin Baker); The Master (Anthony Ainley); Adric (Matthew Waterhouse); Nyssa (Sarah Sutton); Tegan (Janet Fielding); Turlough (Mark Strickson); Voice of Kamelion (Gerald Flood)

COMMENTARY: "The Caves of Androzani" is an exciting last chapter in the life of the fifth Doctor. Like many great episodes of *Doctor Who*, this serial finds energetic life in the manner by which it adapts a literary or filmic forebear into a futuristic situation. The template of "The Caves of Androzani" is the movie version of Gaston Leroux's novel *The Phantom of the Opera*.

In "The Caves of Androzani," Sharez Jek is the exploited main character who has been tormented by years of suffering. He is a scientist rather than a composer, but he is still a genius whose talents have been denied and exploited. Like the Phantom, Jek has been scarred in a terrible accident, and he can never forgive the man he deems responsible. In *The Phantom of the Opera* that man is a music thief; in "The Caves of Androzani" it is the doublecrossing businessman Morgas. Jek hides behind a mask and refuses to show his disfigured face to any other living soul. Instead of haunting a Parisian opera house and its subterranean tunnels, the masked Jek haunts the dark mines of Androzani Minor. Completing the analogy to *Phantom of the Opera*, the one thing that Jek really longs for in his miserable life is companionship and love from a beautiful woman. He captures Peri (who fills in for previous actresses in the role such as Mary Philbin in 1925 and Jane Seymour in 1983), but she is repulsed by his real face.

"The Caves of Androzani" is audacious in its futuristic stylings, and it is filled with androids, bat-monsters and spaceships. Had all stories of the Davison era been this inventive, *Doctor Who* fans would indeed find much to celebrate.

Beyond the *Phantom of the Opera* framework, "The Caves of Androzani" is an action-packed story with a pace that never lets up. There is an undercurrent of urgency in every scene because the viewer is acutely aware that the Doctor and Peri are dying. This tension builds as the Doctor is kidnapped and taken away from Androzani Minor by gunrunners. He manages to return to the planet, but by then the clock is ticking and he must survive a crash, an encounter with a monster bat and a mudslide to save his friend Peri. Only when the Doctor finally succumbs to Spectrox Toxemia does the viewer finally find time to breathe. And then, of course, comes the surprise of the regeneration. "The Caves of Androzani" is one of the most exciting *Doctor Who* stories in the entire series and a real triumph for producer John Nathan-Turner.

Even with a template culled from classic literature and a structure of action, "The Caves of Androzani" finds time to contemplate the corporate mentality. *Doctor Who* had condemned big business before, in stories such as "Colony in Space" and "The Green Death," and "The Caves of Androzani" also takes a dim view of it. Here it is the conniving, power-hungry Morgas who echoes the great robber barons of the 1890s. He is a ruthless exploiter of people, a man who thrives on accumulating wealth. Appropriately, Morgas is unseated by his immediate underling the moment he leaves his office on Androzani Major. This quick transition of power calls attention to the cutthroat mentality of the businessman. People are not important except as consumers, and one mistake leads to a change in personnel. The final indignity for Morgas is that his sheltered bank accounts and vacation home are also confiscated. He has nothing left, and so he resorts immediately to thievery. Actor John Normington effectively takes Morgas from a position of complete control to one of total loss. His performance is a highlight of the show.

Also good is Christopher Gable as Sharez Jek. Even in a mask, Gable emotes successfully as this tragic figure. Jek is not evil, simply twisted and perverted by his experiences. Accordingly, Jek's pleas for understanding and love cannot help but seem heartbreaking. Gable, perhaps understanding *The Phantom of the Opera* analogy, turns in a very sympathetic, powerful performance. Jek is one of the best performed villains in the series in years.

"The Caves of Androzani" ends with the death of the Doctor's fifth incarnation. Peter Davison has been granted a particularly noble death: He dies to save his friend Peri. This is quite satisfying, and also different. Hartnell's Doctor simply expired of old age. Troughton's Doctor was executed by the Time Lords. Pertwee's Doctor died when he conquered his fear in "Planet of the Spiders." Tom Baker's Doctor died saving the galaxy from the Master. Davison's final moments are equally noble as Baker's and Pertwee's, but perhaps more sentimental. This Doctor has always been a man intent on examining his own morality. In "The Caves of Androzani" he blames himself for getting Peri sick, and he risks everything to save her. It is a powerful moment, one highlighted by the guest appearances of former series regulars Fielding, Waterhouse, Sutton, Strickson and even the robot Kamelion.

With "The Caves of Androzani," the Davison era ends. It is a great send-off to an epoch that is perhaps less successful than any that had preceded it. In "popularity polls," Davison's Doctor usually ranks second or third among Doctors. He is always behind Tom Baker, but sometimes ahead of Jon Pertwee. This author attributes Davison's popularity to his sincerity as the Doctor. He may not have been affectionate like Troughton, but he was a serious, thoughtful man who exuded innocence and genuine kindness. The reason that Season's 19–21 are weak have little to do with Davison's portrayal of the Time Lord. On the contrary, it is uninspired stories like "The Visitation," "The Awakening," "The King's Demons" and "Planet of Fire" which create the impression that the series was resting on its laurels rather than boldly heading into the '80s. The lack of humor in the Davison era also contributes to the lack of enthusiasm this writer feels for the period.

The last few moments of "The Caves of Androzani" forecast the direction the series would take. Colin Baker sits up on the TARDIS floor and tells the camera that his regeneration has occurred not a moment too soon. His expression is one of disdain, and his tenor one of pure arrogance. This is a wonderful and exciting shock after the kind, gentle qualities of the fifth Doctor. Many fans would not appreciate Colin Baker's portrayal. The sixth Doctor even referred to his previous generation at one point as representing "feckless youth." This no doubt upset many purists, but it is important to remember that Pertwee's Doctor showed irritation towards Troughton's in "The Three Doctors" by calling him "frivolous." Thus Baker's new attitude was quite in keeping with previous adventures.

The excellent "The Caves of Androzani" is available on videocassette.

137. "The Twin Dilemma" Written by Anthony Steven; Directed by Peter Moffatt; Designed by Valerie Wallender; Parts I–IV; Airdates: March 22, 23, 29, 30, 1984

SYNOPSIS: Earth twins Romulas and Remus, who possess incredible mathematical skills, are kidnapped by aliens from the planet Jaconda and escorted to the safe house of the great gangster Mestor, on Titan 3. Aboard the TARDIS the Doctor has "renewed." Besides his bad taste in clothing, this incarnation of the Doctor also seems prone to wild mood swings. One moment he is confident and happy and the next he is threatening and violent. The Doctor and Peri soon join up with a police officer, Hugo Lang, in search of the missing twins. This hunt takes them to Jaconda. The forests there have been destroyed, and the part slug–part human giant gastropods have taken over the world. Mestor has captured the twins in order to move two lesser planets into the same orbit as Jaconda. He needs the geniuses to calculate this complex move. The Doctor meets up with the boys and informs them that this plan is dangerous: It might very well cause an explosion that could rip a hole in the universe! Mestor believes this explosion will allow the thick-skinned gastropod eggs to stretch across the universe and take root on many distant worlds.

GUEST CAST: Edgeworth/Asmael (Maurice Denham); Lt. Hugo Lang (Kevin McNally); Mestor (Edwin Richfield); Sylvest (Dennis Chinnery); Noma (Barry Stanton); Drak (Oliver Smith); Fabian (Helen Blatch); Elena (Dione Inman); Romulus (Gavin Conrad); Remus (Andrew Conrad); Chamberlain (Seymour Green); Prisoner (Roger Nott); Jacondan Guard (John Wilson)

COMMENTARY: Colin Baker arrives with full force in "The Twin Dilemma." Although this story is not at all popular with *Doctor Who* fans because of one isolated incident (the Doctor's attempt to strangle Peri), it is nonetheless thematically interesting. "The Caves of Androzani" had pulled from the example of *The Phantom of the Opera* to tell its gripping story, and accordingly "The Twin Dilemma" also finds inspiration in other genres. In this case it is not classic literature or macabre films, but the television "cop" drama or police movie. It all fits rather nicely into this convention. The newly regenerated Doctor assumes the role of the fallen cop, the experienced avenger who has made a mistake (attempting to hurt Peri). He no longer trusts himself or his instincts and he goes into retirement (seeking to become a hermit on Titan). Of course, he is drawn out of this self-imposed retirement to solve an important case. This is a familiar police movie dynamic seen in *Striking Distance* (1993) and others.

The cop drama aspect of "The Twin Dilemma" is clear in other regards too. The evil slug Mestor is the Crime Boss, the evil head of a crime syndicate, like Jabba the Hutt in *Return of the Jedi* (1983). He even comes complete with his own gang of thugs. He resorts to criminal activity to get what he wants by kidnapping the twins. He then orders his abductees incarcerated at his "safe house," a common term of cop dramas or mob movies such as *The Bodyguard* (1991) or *The Godfather* (1972).

In "The Twin Dilemma," there is also the presence of officer Hugo Lang, the cop who wants only revenge for the destruction of his squadron. He fits the genre cliché of the vigilante cop. Asmael is also a piece of the puzzle in the crime movie aspect of the serial. He is the honorable man gone bad, the one who works for a villain, but in the end demonstrates his real colors and saves the hero's life. Throw in a souped-up star freighter with an illegal license plate, a space police station of the future, and two kidnapped children with an ability that the crooks require, and it is obvious that "The Twin Dilemma"'s roots are in *Starsky and Hutch*, *T.J. Hooker* and the like. Taken on these terms, and seen as another wild and woolly *Doctor Who* genre pastiche, it emerges as an interesting story highlighting a unique conceit. This kind of original template may not make for the best adventure ever, but it gives the show a different feeling ... an eccentricity that was missing in so many of the uninventive stories of the Davison reign.

The cleverness of "The Twin Dilemma" has been repeatedly overlooked by those who see only that Colin Baker is not what they expect or like in a lead actor-character during this story. The newly regenerated Doctor is prone to acts of violence. He is irritating and wholly pompous. He is also scornful of his previous incarnation. Sensitive *Doctor Who* fans rebelled at this interpretation of the Time Lord, and shouted angrily that "the Doctor would not do that." Instead, they should have applauded the attempt to do something new on the series, especially after such tiresome stories as "The Awakening" and "Time Flight." A series can never grow or survive without change and reinterpretation. Nathan-Turner and Colin Baker set out to make the Doctor alien again. As a Time Lord, he would not have the same morality, nor the some standards of courtesy and politeness as the humans he traveled with. This was a fact also conveyed quite well in the Hartnell and Tom Baker stories, so it was certainly not without precedent in *Doctor Who*. Baker said this of his interpretation of the Time Lord:

> He has many facets to his personality, and, bearing in mind that he is an alien, some are difficult for humans to understand. When he's a little curt to his assistant. Impatient. Irascible. I think that these are very important aspects.... For him to behave exactly the same way as a human behaves would be a shame.... In casual conversation he won't always be polite. That's a human concept.[20]

The Doctor's sudden bout with physical violence in "The Twin Dilemma" is disturbing, but then, it is supposed to be! When was the last time there was such a surprise in *Doctor Who*? Fortunately, the brief choking of Peri is not gratuitous, it comes directly from the situation at the core of "The Twin Dilemma." The Doctor is suffering from the effects of a bad regeneration. He is not responsible for his actions. Why is it impossible to believe that in a moment of sickness, the Doctor would attack someone he loves? Is this so out of character or so mean-spirited as fans have claimed? The Doctor expresses remorse after the event — so much remorse that he plans to become a hermit!

Other fans dislike Baker because his patchwork outfit is visually abrasive. That kind of criticism does not even merit a considered response. It is obvious that the doctor's new outfit resembles his brash new characteristics. The negative reaction to Baker only shows that some *Doctor Who* fans rival *Star Trek* fans in the groping attempts to control the direction of a series they feel is "theirs." *Star Trek* fans attempted to stop the death of Spock, undo the destruction of the *Enterprise*, and otherwise interfere in the decisions made by the *Star Trek* production teams. It is sad to see the same level of nitpicking interference in the universe of *Doctor Who*. Baker is one of the most charismatic performers in the history of the series. He may not be innocent and kind, like Davison, but it is obvious that as an actor he takes chances.

He also has a love of the English language. His tongue rolls over the words in "The Twin Dilemma" with a delicious sense of delight and fun. Baker's portrayal is an unpredictable one, in a sense more reminiscent of Tom Baker than any other Doctor. Colin Baker's incarnation uses language and vocabulary in a challenging way. He uses words to tease, to mock, to inveigle and to convey the inherent intelligence and arrogance of the Time Lord. Baker's opening performance is astonishing. He makes an excellent Doctor.

How does "The Twin Dilemma" compare to premiere stories of new Doctors? It is more substantive than "Spearhead from Space" (an old-fashioned invasion-from-space story) and "Time and the Rani," and less convoluted than "Castrovalva." Though it is not as good as "An Unearthly Child," it is roughly equal in quality to "Robot," Tom Baker's first story. "The Twin Dilemma" shows much more inventiveness than fully half of the adventures dramatized during the Davison era. The cop drama sheen masks the repetitive elements of the story. All in all, it's a lot better than people have made out to be, *especially* for a post-regeneration story.

"The Twin Dilemma" is available on videocassette.

SEASON 22

138. "Attack of the Cybermen" Written by Paula Moore; Directed by Matthew Robinson; Designed by Marjorie Pratt; Parts I–II; Airdates: January 5, 12, 1985

SYNOPSIS: A Cyberman incursion on Earth sends the Doctor and Peri back to the planet Telos, home of the Cybermen. The Doctor informs Peri that Telos was not always their homeworld: The Cybermen adopted it and in the process destroyed the indigenous life forms there, the highly advanced Cryons. On Telos, the Doctor discovers from a group of renegade Cryons that the Cybermen plan to use the TARDIS and another captured time ship to change the web of time. They intend to go back and prevent the destruction of their original homeworld, Mondas. The Cyberman plan to divert Halley's Comet to crash into Earth, making it defenseless before the arrival of Mondas. This change in history will cause a tear in the fabric of the universe so enormous that all creation could be destroyed!

GUEST CAST: Commander Lytton (Maurice Colbourne); Cyber Controller (Michael Kilgarriff); Griffiths (Brian Glover); Russell (Terry Molloy); Cyber Leader

(David Banks); Cyber Lieutenant (Brian Orrell); Cybermen (John Ainley, Pat Gorman, Thomas Lucy, Roger Pope); Varn (Sarah Green); Rost (Sarah Berger); Flask (Faith Brown); Threst (Esther Freud); Bates (Michael Attwell); Policemen (Mike Braben, Michael Jeffries); Bill (Steven Churchett); Crytons (Trisha Clarke, Maggie Lynton, Irela Williams)

COMMENTARY: In "Attack of the Cybermen," *Doctor Who* again reuses the *Time Machine* template that served it so well over 22 years. For the first time in their long history as villains, the Cybermen are given their own oppressed "Thals" in the form of the appropriately named sub-zero creations called Cryons (Cryonics? Cryogenics?). This plot development is not very interesting, nor is the repeat appearance of the revolution story. The Cyberman have always been interesting enough without this version of "the Thals." The inclusion of the Cryons only shows how uninventive *Doctor Who* can be. Why take a villain more interesting than the Daleks and then saddle them with common factors inherent to the Dalek story?

The biggest problem is not its familiar plot, but that it revisits a world seen in the memorable Season 5 story "Tomb of the Cybermen." This would have been fine had the two serials matched *at all* in visual detail. As it stands, the tomb seen in "Attack of the Cybermen" does not all resemble the memorable tomb discovered by Troughton back in the 1960s. The tombs are not the only things that have changed. The Cyber Controller, though played again by Michael Kilgarriff, also looks different as well. At this point in *Who* history, "The Tomb of the Cybermen" was considered lost, so perhaps the designer of this serial assumed that no one would remember the look of the earlier show. This was a short-sighted decision, however. Now that "Tomb of the Cybermen" has been recovered and released on video, the differences in set design and costume design are unnerving, and hard to explain as well.

If it is a ritual that each Doctor must go through the same paces as his predecessors, than "Attack of the Cybermen" is Colin Baker's big shot with the evil cyborgs. He proves himself more than ready for the encounter with this frightening nemesis. He is tough, resourceful and every bit as clever as his predecessors. He even gets to be the Time Lord equivalent of *Rambo* by blasting the Cyber Controller to pieces. "Attack of the Cybermen" also begins an interesting association between Colin Baker and the Doctor's second incarnation. First, the sixth Doctor returns to the site of Troughton's greatest story. Later, he meets Troughton's incarnation in the flesh in "The Two Doctors"! The association would have been complete had the "Timelash" teleplay also featured a painting of the second Doctor, rather than one of Pertwee's third incarnation.

"Attack of the Cybermen" is strong on trivia touches, if not on originality. Totter's Lane is revisited for the first time since "An Unearthly Child," although it looks markedly different. Foreman's Scrapyard would be visited by the Doctor again in "Remembrance of the Daleks," but the junkyard would once again have a different look to it. Even the long-malfunctioning TARDIS chameleon circuit is repaired for a time upon landing at 76 Totters Lane. This is a nice touch because the equipment first broke down when the TARDIS *left* 76 Totters Lane in "An Unearthly Child." Michael Kilgarriff is back as the Cyber Controller, and the outdoor sequences representing Telos are again lensed at Gerrards Cross Quarry. Another familiar face shows up playing Commander Lytton: actor Maurice Colbourne. This graduate from "Resurrection of the Daleks" is developed into a more three-dimensional character in this serial. The events of "Tomb of the Cybermen" and "The Tenth Planet" are also recalled in the teleplay of "Attack of the Cybermen."

The process of "building" Cybermen out of organic organisms is shown in more detail in "Attack of the Cybermen" than in any previous story. These scenes would be recalled in similar, albeit gorier fashion in the 1996 film *Star Trek: First Contact*, which highlighted a Borg attempt to assimilate the crew of the NCC-1701-E.

139. "Vengeance on Varos" Written by Philip Martin; Directed by Ron Jones; Designed by Tony Snoaden; Parts I–II; Airdates: January 19, 26, 1985

SYNOPSIS: Varos is a poverty-stricken world built on an ancient insane asylum, and the guards and officers who once ruled Varos have become the rich elite. The descendants of the original inmates are the poor underclass. The government on Varos is extremely cynical. They have only two profitable exports: The first is the rare Zytton ore; the second is a selection of videotapes of public executions! The governor of Varos is a decent man trying to build a better planet for his people, but he has opened negotiations with the reptilian creature Sil, a representative of the Galitron Mining Company. The governor is up for re-election, and his position is weak, but he still demands that Sil pay seven credits for each unit of the Zytton. Sil refuses and, with the help of the treacherous Chief Officer, hopes to oust this governor, take control of Varos and buy all the Zytton at ridiculously low prices.

Into this situation arrives the Doctor, who is need of the Zytton ore to repair the TARDIS. He and Peri unexpectedly become the main attraction in a violent Varos television entertainment.

GUEST CAST: Governor (Martin Jarvis); Sil (Nabil Shaban); Jondar (Jason Connery); Chief Officer (Forbes Collins); Arak (Stephen Yardley); Etta (Sheila Reid); Areta (Geraldine Alexander); Maldak (Owen Teale); Bax (Graham Cull); Quillam (Nicolas Chagrin); Priest (Hugh Martin)

COMMENTARY: "Vengeance on Varos" is a return to greatness for the 22-year-old *Doctor Who*. This is an uncommon serial, one which draws its inspiration not from classic literature or popular film, but from a once-relevant public drama concerning what English citizens and elected officials referred to in the mid-'80s as "video nasties." Video nasties were horror movies and videos such as *Faces of Death* which featured gory special effects and graphic violence. At the same time that England's Margaret Thatcher was expressing her hatred for these productions, much the same stance was being taken in America by the Moral Majority. Sadly, watchdog groups like the Moral Majority and the National Viewers' and Listeners' Association in Great Britain proved woefully inept at discerning the difference between artless snuff-style movies like the aforementioned *Faces of Death* and horror masterpieces like Sam Raimi's *The Evil Dead* and Wes Craven's *A Nightmare on Elm Street.* Even the fantasy-oriented family drama *Doctor Who* was accused of being too violent during this time. It was a very unpleasant period, and represented a pendulum swing back to the more restrictive, conservative sensibility of the 1950s.

"Vengeance on Varos" responds to this true-life drama by sending the Doctor to a world that is, an essence, one big "video nasty." Varos is a violent planet where the citizens harbor a deep bloodlust. Their only form of entertainment is violence. They revel in public torture, executions and terror. The reason for this bloodlust, ironically, is revealed to be a sense of hopelessness created by the government itself. The people are ignorant of literature, and television is the only outlet in their repressed society. Education and humanity are also missing from their lives; all the government cares about is getting rich from the sale of the Zytton ore. Appropriately, "Vengeance on Varos" is a violent show in which the Doctor is constantly exposed to perilous and "public" situations. In a sense, "Vengeance on Varos" foreshadows the 1987 film *The Running Man*, which also put its protagonist into a futuristic society where television sates the public demand for violence and for bread and circuses.

Beyond the real-life social problems from which "Vengeance of Varos" is drawn, the serial also confronts issues around a "true" democracy. On Varos, all citizens vote on important issues merely by punching a button on a television console. The duty and responsibility of casting a vote has become as easy and as rote an act as opening a can of beer or walking to the refrigerator. Since voting has become so easy and so common, the people no longer make responsible decisions. Instead they use the vote only as another opportunity to inflict pain and torture. The politicians are punished if they lose a vote, so the people constantly choose to make the politicians lose, whether they agree with their viewpoint or not. Inflicting pain has become more important to them than doing what is right. Regarding politics and bloodlust on Varos, Bob Dole might ask appropriately, "Where's the outrage?" It is an ugly culture and a dark look at humanity, but one that is not so hard to believe. Voter turnout in the 1996 United States presidential election was the lowest in history. With electronic town meetings all the rage, how long is it before voters can simply vote on the Internet? Take that possibility one step forward with the advent of WEB television, and soon Americans will be voting on the television in their living rooms, just like the citizens of Varos. Many Americans have not been happy with the tone of recent elections. How will they feel when the duty to vote does not require even a trip to a voting center? Or when voting is as perfunctory a duty as setting the VCR? Before WEB television and before the Internet, *Doctor Who* was already tackling this controversial issue.

There is more to recommend "Vengeance on Varos" than its take on video nasties and the meditation on the nature of democracy. The serial is also given what might be called a "classic" structure by its framing sequences. At the beginning and end, the camera returns to two Varos citizens as they watch the events of the main story on their television. These citizens operate as a sort of Greek chorus as they comment on the action, cast their votes and personalize the drama on Varos. This is a clever stylistic conceit and one of the few later *Doctor Who*s to attempt so interesting a literary technique. In "Vengeance on Varos," it is just one compelling facet in an excellent story.

Perhaps "Vengeance on Varos" is most important to sci-fi television history because of the important character it introduces. That character is the evil Sil. Played by Nabil Shabin, this creature is one of *Doctor Who*'s most popular "late" villains. He was so appreciated in "Vengeance on Varos" that he would return in Season 23 for the episode "Mindwarp." Still, Sil is a significant creation not simply because he is played with weasly skill by Shaban. On the contrary, Sil is a forerunner of the alien race known as the Ferengi that were introduced in 1987 (two years after "Vengeance on Varos") on *Star Trek: The Next Generation*. Like the Ferengi, Sil's people are short in size and physically repulsive. Like the Ferengi, Sil's people are seen to have disgusting eating habits. Sil does not eat grubworms, but small, living fish creatures. Still, the effect is the same. More crucial than eating habits or physical appearances, the Ferengi and Sil's Thoros-Betans share a society based on capitalism. Profit, not political conquest, is the most important factor to these two alien cultures. All that matters to Sil is striking unfair bargains that amass for him as much wealth as possible. That description also suits the character Quark and the other Ferengi creatures seen in many episodes of *The Next Generation* and *Deep Space Nine*. Sil also makes a very theatrical, larger-than-life villain for Bakers "big" portrayal of the Time Lord.

In the guest star category, "Vengeance of Varos" offers a surprise. The young rebel Jondar is played by Sean Connery's son Jason. After his appearance on *Doctor Who*, Connery would become the star of the popular drama *Robin of Sherwood*.

"Vengeance on Varos" has been released on videotape. It looks especially interesting today to an America that has become obsessed with the daily violence and fistfights of *The Jerry Springer Show*.

140. "The Mark of the Rani" Written by Pip & Jane Baker; Directed by Sarah Hellings; Designed by Paul Trerise; Parts I–II; Airdates: February 2, 9, 1985

SYNOPSIS: At the start of the Industrial Revolution, the Doctor and Peri run afoul of two renegade Time Lords: the Master, and the beautiful Rani. The Rani, like the Doctor, was exiled from Gallifrey. She is less maleficent than the Master, but bent on completing her own mission. To preserve the denizens of the planet she rules, she requires a chemical found only in the human brain. Without this chemical, however, the human brain cannot rest, and insanity and hyperactivity results. The Rani has been coming to Earth for centuries to drain human minds. She was present during the Trojan War, the Dark Ages, the American War of Independence and now the Luddite Rebellion. The Doctor must prevent the

Jason Connery (son of Sean) guest-starred in *Doctor Who* adventure #139, "Vengeance of Varos," before finding fame in *Robin of Sherwood*.

Rani's draining of Earth's greatest minds and thwart the Master's plan to destroy the Industrial Revolution.

GUEST CAST: The Master (Anthony Ainley); The Rani (Kate O'Mara); Lord Ravensworth (Terence Alexander); Jack Ward (Peter Childs); Luke Ward (Gary Cady); Guard (Richard Steele); Tim Bass (William Ilkley); Edwin Green (Hus Levent); Sam Rudge (Kevin White); Drayman (Martin Whitby); Young Woman (Sarah James); Older Woman (Cordelia Ditton); George Stephenson (Gawn Grainger)

COMMENTARY: Female villains are a rarity in *Doctor Who*, so it is with a real sense of pleasure that fans watched the highly competent and threatening renegade Time Lady "the Rani" being introduced in this serial. Beautiful, sexy and so intelligent that the Doctor regards her as superior to himself, the Rani is a memorable villain. She is so memorable, in fact, that she would return in Sylvester McCoy's premiere adventure "Time and the Rani." Kate O'Mara plays the role with considerable charm and wit in "The Mark of the Rani."

"The Mark of the Rani" is buoyed by some fine production values. Much of the story was lensed at the Ironbridge Gorge, a great location that looks like a holdover from the 1800s. Also impressive is the interior of the Rani's TARDIS. It is a nightmarish place. The central control panel has a magnificent, functioning gyroscope on top, and all around the command center are strange jars which contain things that seem to be dinosaur embryos. Interestingly, the script never reveals why the Rani has these creatures in her TARDIS. It is just a weird, macabre touch. It nicely reinforces the notion, however, that the Rani has been present through all of Earth's history.

The central plot of "The Mark of the Rani" concerns the Rani's attempts to drain the minds of human beings for a vitally needed chemical. This is a good premise for a *Doctor Who* plot, and one that would be recalled in the *Star Trek: The Next Generation* fifth season cliffhanger called "Time's Arrow." In that adventure, aliens from a distant world traveled back to the early 1900s to steal the life force of human beings in San Francisco.

Where "The Mark of the Rani" does not work specifically is in the Master's plan for world domination. He believes that by controlling the geniuses of the Industrial Age, he can rule the planet. This is another incredibly idiotic idea. The Master surely possesses more intelligence himself than all the geniuses of the 1800s combined! He has knowledge of physics, time travel, dimensional transcendentalism and other things that Earthmen can have no awareness of. What genius can they possibly provide that he does not already possess? And again, why is he bothering with Earth at all? This is reminiscent of the idiot plot in "The King's Demons," which saw the Master trying to take over the Earth by (gasp!) preventing the signing of the Magna Carta. As always, a little of the Master goes a long way. Even though Ainley is a marvel in the part, the character is badly conceived. With O'Mara carrying the burden of villainy in "The Mark of the Rani," the Master is extraneous.

"The Mark of the Rani" is still a thoroughly enjoyable *Doctor Who* adventure due to Colin Baker's irrepressible presence as the Doctor. He puns his way through the show (making reference to "Peri"-pheral vision at one point) and he genuinely seems to be having fun. This jubilant portrayal of the Doctor compensates for the hazy nature of the Master's plot. In a sense, Colin Baker has very much the same kind of screen presence as Tom Baker. When he is the Doctor, people watch *him* as much as they watch the details of the show. He can carry a weak story just by virtue of his powerful persona. Many fans may deride Baker's portrayal of the Time Lord, but one thing that they can never claim is that he is boring. True to form, Baker is an engaging screen presence throughout "Mark of the Rani." Though it is in no way as inventive a serial as "Vengeance on Varos," it is certainly a solid addition to the *Doctor Who* episode roster.

"The Mark of the Rani" is the first *Doctor Who* script by Pip and Jane Baker. They would later pen "Terror of the Vervoids," "The Ultimate Foe" and "Time and the Rani." Other than their *Doctor Who* credits, this team is probably best known in the U.S. for writing "A Matter of Balance" for Year Two of *Space: 1999*.

"The Mark of the Rani" is available on videocassette.

141. "The Two Doctors" Written by Robert Holmes; Directed by Peter Moffatt; Designed by Tony Burrough; Parts I–III; Airdates: February 16, 23, March 2, 1985

SYNOPSIS: The second and sixth incarnations of the Doctor, Jamie McCrimmon and Peri become involved in a Sontaran plot to learn the secrets of time travel. Involved in the deadly plot is a treacherous scientist, Dastari, and his creation, the highly evolved Androgum, Chessene. The sixth Doctor must come to the rescue when the second Doctor is genetically mutated into an Androgum, a barbaric warrior creature of insatiable appetites.

GUEST CAST: The Doctor (Patrick Troughton); Jamie McCrimmon (Frazer Hines); Shockeye (John Stratton); Chessene (Jacqueline Pearce); Dastari (Laurence Payne); Stike (Clinton Greyne); Dona Arana (Aime Delamain); Oscar (James Saxon); Anita (Carmen Gomez); Varl (Tim Raynham); Technician (Nicholas Fawcett)

COMMENTARY: "The Two Doctors" calls former series stars Patrick Troughton and Frazer Hines out of retirement to share one more exciting adventure with current leads Colin Baker and Nicola Bryant. Accordingly, there is an overwhelming feeling of nostalgia and joy evident in this serial as these old friends are revisited. The episode opens in a rather stylish fashion, too. The first sequence aboard the TARDIS is filmed in black-and-white and begins with the Doctor and Jamie. It looks exactly like a scene from a late 1960s adventure. Then, slowly, the picture transforms to color and the audience realizes this is not an adventure from 1968, but a brand new one. Amazingly, Troughton and Hines look much the same as they did all those years ago, and the illusion works very well. Hines in particular looks like he has not aged a day in 19 years.

Unfortunately, the action that brings these heroes back to duty is marred somewhat by an historical incongruity. "The Two Doctors" establishes that Troughton's Doctor has been sent on a mission for the Time Lords. This directly contradicts the evidence of the early series history. It was quite well-established in "The War Games" that the Doctor had been *on the run* from the Time Lords for some time. He did not want them to find him, lest he be recalled to Gallifrey. He was so determined not to encounter the Time Lords that he was almost willing to leave thousands of humans trapped on an alien world in the adventure "The War Games." The notion that Troughton's Doctor might be called to perform a task for the Time Lords is completely out-of-synch with *Who* history. Notably, Jamie had never even *heard* of the Time Lords before his last adventure in "The War Games." How then could he be on a mission for the Time Lords in "The Two Doctors," which surely occurs before Victoria's last adventure ("Fury from the Deep")? Again, mincemeat is made of early *Doctor Who* continuity. Although many fans have lauded Nathan-Turner for bringing an increased sense of continuity to the series, it seems the opposite is true. Under his leadership, frequent continuity errors regarding the Troughton era occurred ("The Five Doctors" and "The Two Doctors"). It was actually Pertwee's Third Doctor, not Troughton's second incarnation, who occasionally went on a mission for the Time Lords. Troughton, like Hartnell before him, was on the run from the powerful, vengeful race of Gallifrey. Despite this problem, it is indeed a delight to see performers Troughton and Hines back in action. Perhaps one can speculate that after Troughton saved the Time Lords in "The Three Doctors," he was allowed to live out the rest of his incarnation in a separate time stream. Maybe he went back to the 1700s and picked up Jamie again!

"The Two Doctors" is a serious adventure concerning the discovery of time travel, but it is also a delightful black comedy. The Androgums are apparently a race of beings who will eat anything. Shockeye spends the whole serial trying to sink his teeth into Peri and Jamie. Thus he mouths all sorts of suggestive dialogue concerning these two specimens, drooling about how juicy and tender they look. This is about as racy as *Doctor Who* ever gets! The scene in which Troughton becomes an Androgum and eats a 12-course meal is also quite funny. His Doctor was always the funniest of the bunch, and it is only fitting that he be brought back in an exciting adventure with humorous overtones.

Although the moments of humor are many in "The Two Doctors," so are the moments of violence. Shockeye spends half the serial chasing people with a butcher knife, an innocent restauranteur is killed, the Sontarans meet a brutal end, and the Doctor uses violent methods to overcome both Chessene and Shockeye. Many fans objected to this heightened violence, but that was part of the show's new sheen after the departure of Peter Davison. It was more adult, more outrageous, more violent, more edgy and ultimately far more nihilistic (as evidenced by heavy stories such as "Vengeance on Varos," "Mindwarp," "Terror of the Vervoids" and "The Ultimate Foe").

Delightfully, Baker proves in "The Two Doctors" that he has strong chemistry with both Hines and Troughton. In "The Five Doctors," Peter Davison was hardly permitted to interact with his predecessors. Baker and Troughton enjoy several moments together near the climax of "The Two Doctors," and prove they are a formidable team. The banter is not as saucy as that between Pertwee and Troughton, but a new dynamic is found instead. Baker seems to react with bemusement to the escapades of his former self. For his part, Troughton acts the innocent and pretends not to know how he gets into such dire predicaments. It is a shame that Troughton and Baker never shared another episode. They are the most underrated actors in *Doctor Who* circles.

Jacqueline Pearce, the president of the Federation in Terry Nation's series *Blake's 7*, plays Chessene in "The Two Doctors," and Laurence Payne, who appeared in the Hartnell–era story "The Gunfighters" and in the Season 18 opener "The Leisure Hive," co-stars as Dastari. It is John Stratton as Shockeye, however, who steals the show. He really sinks his teeth into the role of the Androgum butcher. It is one of the meatiest guest spots in many a course.

"The Two Doctors" was shot on location in Seville, Spain, and the results are breathtaking. At points, Troughton and John Stratton are seen running through the streets of Spain in their "best" restaurant outfits. Baker, Bryant and Hines pursue them through alleys and side streets in a chase scene, and it has a sense of verisimilitude often missing from *Doctor Who*.

"The Two Doctors" reveals more about Time Lord history. Apparently it is

Although Jacqueline Pearce had already made her mark on science fiction television with her portrayal of *Blake 7's* Servalen, she returned to outer space to menace Colin Baker and Patrick Troughton as the Androgum Chessene in episode #141, "The Two Doctors."

the Rassilon Imprimateur gene which permits the Gallifreyans to journey through the ages. This is interesting because it suggests that the Time Lords are *engineered* creatures. They manipulate time and space by means of a genetically engineered cell.

"The Two Doctors" is available on videocassette courtesy of BBC/CBS-Fox home video.

142. "Timelash" Written by Glen McCoy; Directed by Pennant Roberts; Designed by Bob Cove; Parts I–II; Airdates: March 9, 16, 1985

SYNOPSIS: The Kontron Tunnel, also known as a "timelash," deposits the TARDIS on the planet Karfel. The Doctor has been there once before; many years before, he set up a treaty of cooperation between the people of Karfel and their neighbors, the Bandril. The Treaty has recently been abrogated and the Bandrils have threatened to attack. Karfel is currently ruled by a vicious dictator called the Borad. He disposes of political opponents by hurling them into the timelash. He has recently sent a young woman named Vena — the daughter of the Doctor's old friend Maylin — into it. She has landed in Victorian England at the turn of the century. With the help of Vena, H.G. Wells and Peri, the Doctor must stop the Borad, his appointed governor Tekker and a monster called the Morlox. If he cannot, war will again erupt between the Bandril and Karfel.

GUEST CAST: Tekker (Paul Darrow); Vena (Jean Anne Rowley); H.G. Wells/Herbert (David Chandler); Maylin (Neil Hallet); Katz (Tracey Louise Ward); The Borad (Robert Ashby); Mykros (Eric Deacon); Kendron (David Ashton); Gazak (Steven Macintosh); Aram (Christine Kavanaugh); Tyheer (Martin Gower); Android (Dean Hollingsworth); Old Man (Denis Carey); Sezon (Dicken Ashworth); Guard (James Richardson)

COMMENTARY: It had to happen eventually. *Doctor Who* has always been such a grand and far-reaching assimilator of concepts and themes from previous science fiction films and literature that it was only a matter of time before it returned, quite literally, to its dramatic roots. In "Timelash," *Doctor Who* audaciously suggests that author H.G. Wells found inspiration for his story *The Time Machine* not in his own imagination, but in his alien experience on the planet

Karfel! Of course, this is the most unabashed of ironies because it is *Doctor Who* which found inspiration and dramatic life in the works of H.G. Wells, not vice versa. *Doctor Who* explores this notion in "Timelash" with a kind of wink-and-jab at the viewer. It is a fun premise.

The Doctor obviously represents the Time Traveler in *The Time Machine* and Vena is the inspiration for the Eloi love interest Weena. Even more amusingly, after years of featuring surrogate Morlocks (in the form of Daleks, Monoids, Zarbi and even Cybermen), "Timelash" finally introduces an alien monster called, appropriately, "Morlox." Only *Doctor Who* would have the temerity and pure brass to so thoroughly rib the author who motivated so many of *Doctor Who*'s stories. "Timelash" uses the commonly used *Time Machine* template, last seen in "Attack of the Cybermen." Although this story has been done to death on *Doctor Who*, this clever connection to H.G. Wells and *The Time Machine* makes "Timelash" memorable and ironic, if not original or perfectly executed.

The serial fails because of its limited budget. The Karfel sets seem strangely bland, and the timelash effects are less convincing than those seen on *The Time Tunnel* almost 20 years earlier. For these reasons, "Timelash" is not a favorite of *Doctor Who* fans or the production team. There has also been much talk in *Who* circles about guest star Paul Darrow's over-the-top performance as Tekker. Much beloved for his portrayal of the lead character Avon in *Blake's 7*, Darrow has been criticized for his theatrical performance in "Timelash." This is perhaps an unfair assessment. Darrow attempts to bring a larger-than-life, theatrical air to this character; if at times he overreaches, it is a result of ambition and sincerity. The most unsatisfactory thing about Tekker is not Darrow's performance, but the long, unconvincing wig the actor wears.

Pertwee's incarnation of the Doctor and Katy Manning's Jo Grant make brief appearances in "Timelash" courtesy of a wall-painting and locket photograph, respectively. The Doctor's journey with Jo Grant to Karfel is undocumented, but *Who* continuity expert Jean-Marc Lofficier has speculated the trip occurred between the events of "The Three Doctors" and Grant's final adventure, "The Green Death."

"Timelash" is also noteworthy because it is one of the only "original" serials of Season 23. "Attack of the Cybermen," "Revelation of the Daleks," "The Mark of the Rani" and "The Two Doctors" are sequels which bring back popular guest stars Anthony Ainley, Patrick Troughton, Davros and the Cyber Controller. Only "Vengeance on Varos" and "Timelash" did not revisit characters seen in other serials. Despite this nearly constant re-use of familiar characters and villains, Season 22 nonetheless stands out as one of the strongest since the Tom Baker era. "Timelash" is sabotaged by a low budget, but as far as creativity goes, it is well ahead of "The Awakening" or "The Visitation."

143. "Revelation of the Daleks" Written by Eric Saward; Directed by Graeme Harper; Designed by Alan Spalding; Parts I–II; Airdates: March 23, 30, 1985

SYNOPSIS: The TARDIS lands on the planet Necros. The Doctor wishes to pay his final respects to an old friend, Prof. Stengos. The renowned Stengos has been interred at the cryogenic facility at Tranquil Repose, where people with fatal diseases are stored in suspended animation until a cure for their illnesses can be found. Running the mortuary, however, is the villainous Davros. He is converting the "sleeping" populace of Tranquil Repose into a new brand of Dalek. This is necessary since his own Daleks have betrayed him. Even worse, Davros has been sending other bodies in the Tranquil Repose population to a food processing plant. The bodies of the sick are being sold to the starving masses of the galaxy as "protein"!

GUEST CAST: Davros (Terry Molloy); Arthur Stengos (Alec Lindstead); Natasha (Bridgit Lunchblosse); Kara (Eleanor Bron); Vogel (Hugh Walters); Jobel (Clive Swift); Grigory (Stephen Flynn); D.J. (Alexei Sayle); Orcini (William Gaunt); Bostock (John Ogwen); Takis (Trevor Cooper); Lilt (Solin Spaull); Mutant (Ken Barker); Computer Voice (Penelope Lee); Dalek Voices (Royce Mills, Roy Skelton); Daleks (Toby Byrne, John Scott Martin, Tony Starr, Cy Town)

COMMENTARY: The Daleks are trotted out in yet another *Doctor Who* adventure of little distinction. Although it is rewarding that Colin Baker's short-lived incarnation enjoyed the opportunity to face these historic baddies, there is nothing new or exciting in the story itself. The Daleks are back, and the tiring Davros is back as well ... but a sequel, even a good sequel, is the last thing *Doctor Who* needs at this juncture. In a season of sequels, even the enjoyable "Revelation of the Daleks" feels like territory already fully mined by the series. By now the Dalek stories have become incredibly interchangeable. This one is as competent as "Resurrection of the Daleks," but that is hardly high praise. In fact, fans writing about *Doctor Who* on the Internet constantly confuse the events in "Resurrection of the Daleks," "Revelation of the Daleks" and "Remembrance of the Daleks." The days of stylish black-and-white epics like "The Daleks" or "The Dalek Invasion of Earth" are long gone.

The foundation of the plot in "Revelation of the Daleks," that Davros is creating Daleks out of human parts, recollects the fate of Theodore Maxtible in the early Troughton serial "The Evil of the Daleks." Another inspiration of "Revelation of the Daleks" is obviously *Soylent Green* (1973), a film also featuring human beings unknowingly eating other human beings during a food shortage.

SEASON 23: "THE TRIAL OF THE TIME LORD"

144. "The Mysterious Planet" Written by Robert Holmes; Directed by Nicholas Mallett; Designed by John Anderson; Parts I–IV; Airdates: September 6, 13, 20, 27, 1986

SYNOPSIS: The TARDIS is pulled to an ominous space station and the Doctor is forced to stand trial before his fellow Time Lords. The prosecutor, a grim fellow called the Valeyard, opens the case against him. The Doctor is charged with conduct unbecoming a Time Lord, and the Valeyard proposes to demonstrate his case by showing the court two typical examples of the Doctor's criminal behavior.

On the viewscreen, the Doctor's visit to the planet Ravalox is dramatized. This is evidence taken directly from the Matrix, the Time Lord data storage system. When the Doctor asks how the Matrix was able to gather this data when no Time Lord but he was present, the Valeyard admits that the Doctor's TARDIS was, in Earth lingo, "bugged."

On the viewscreen, the Doctor's travails on Ravalox begin. The Court watches as the Doctor and Peri explore the strange planet in the Stellion galaxy. It is of the same mass as Earth. More than that, the planet reminds Peri of a wet November on Terra. The Doctor is curious because, according to Gallifreyan records, Ravalox was destroyed by solar flares. This world, though wild, seems to thrive. The Doctor and Peri learn that two fortune hunters, Sabalom Glitz and Dibber, are on the planet to steal a secret tape from underground vaults. To get it, they must first defeat Drathro, a robot that runs on black light energy. In the course of the adventure, the Doctor and Peri learn that Ravalox is actually Earth!

GUEST CAST: The Valeyard (Michael Jayston); The Inquisitor (Lynda Bellingham); Katryca (Joan Sims); Glitz (Tony Selby); Dibber (Glen Murphy); Merdeen (Tom Chadbon); Drathro (Roger Brierly) Broken Tooth (David Rodigan); Balazar (Adam Blackwood); Grell (Timothy Walker); Humker (Bill McColl)

COMMENTARY: The first chapter of "The Trial of the Time Lord" is a stunner. It opens with perhaps the greatest special effects moment in any episode of *Doctor Who.* The camera glides smoothly towards an ominous space station with multiple technological protrusions and a giant tower rising from its center. The camera then races across the perimeter of the station while stars flash by in the background. A beam of blue light extends upwards into space and catches the TARDIS. The TARDIS, seen from a high angle to suggest menace and doom, spirals downwards into the space station. It is an accomplished visual trick that perfectly captures the mood of the serial. On the soundtrack, the tolling of a bell is heard, suggesting a kind of day of reckoning. Even before the Doctor or the characters in the trial have been seen, a feeling of doom has been created through this interweaving of fine effects work and incidental music.

"The Mysterious Planet" then leads the Doctor into a trial for his very life. His opponent is the Valeyard, a sinister, humorless figure played to a tee by Jayston. It is clear that this Time Lord wants blood. The story's mood, and the dark nature of the Valeyard, make the Time Lords a frightening race for perhaps the first time since "The War Games." The trial then leads immediately into an adventure on the planet Ravalox and many questions are asked. Where is Peri? Why is the Doctor on trial? Who is the Valeyard? Is the Matrix showing what actually happened, or has it been tampered with again? As with all good mysteries, none of these questions are answered in the first act of the story. Instead, suspense and horror heightens throughout "The Mysterious Planet," leaving one eagerly awaiting the next installment.

The events on Ravalox are interesting, if not terribly original. Once again the *Time Machine* template has been brought out of mothballs. Here it is the robot Drathro (a great design with huge metal horns) who commands the hellish underworld, while on the surface mankind lives in ignorance and poverty. As usual, the Doctor sets the situation right. What is important in "The Mysterious Planet," however, is not the political dynamic, but the questions raised. Why is the mercenary Glitz there? What is so important on Ravalox that he would risk his life to possess it? Even more importantly than that, why has Earth been moved from its position in space and renamed Ravalox? All of these questions reveal "The Trial of the Time Lord" to be an epic mystery in the tradition of the great *Doctor Who* stories.

Although "The Mysterious Planet" and "The Trial of the Time Lord" experiment as a whole are extremely praiseworthy, it is only fair to mention that *Doctor Who* is not the first time travel television series to put its central figure on trial for his life: The derivative series *Voyagers!* did it first, on January 16, 1983. An episode entitled "The Trial of Phineas Bogg" is remarkably like "The Trial of the Time Lord" in more ways than one. First, the Voyager's superiors recall him to headquarters (the space station in "The Mysterious Planet"). Phineas Bogg (the Doctor) is accused of violating Voyager ethics (Time Lord conduct). Evidence from Bogg's time machine is played on the screen (as is testimony from the Doctor's TARDIS in "The Trial of the Time Lord"). The visual evidence condemns Bogg, but it has been tampered with (as the Matrix has been tampered with throughout the Doctor's trial). The prosecutor is actually to blame for this deception in *Voyagers!*, just as the prosecutor, the Valeyard, is responsible in *Doctor Who*. The villainous prosecutor escapes, but Bogg catches up with him (just as the Valeyard escapes only to be stopped by the Doctor in "The Ultimate Foe"). In the end, the Voyagers and the Doctor are exonerated of crimes and allowed to continue on their adventures. The similarities are many and obvious. Fortunately, there are four individual stories incorporating "The Trial of the Time Lord," and the trial scenario is a framework rather than the only element of the story. Thus "The Trial of the Time Lord" is infinitely more complex than "The Trial of Phineas Bogg."

It is interesting for the Doctor to be put on trial again for his acts of intervention, but there is quite a bit of evidence that the Doctor should bring forward but does not. He should first remind the Time Lords that he has twice saved them from the mad Omega (in "The Three Doctors" and "Arc of Infinity"). That would certainly be a mitigating factor! He should then remind them that he saved Gallifrey from the Master and Borusa in "The Deadly Assassin" and "The Five Doctors," respectively. Thirdly, he should point to his community service. He several times completed missions specifically for the Time Lords ("The Two Doctors," "The Mutants," "Colony in Space," "Genesis of the Daleks" and "The Brain of Morbius"). Even more significantly, he has already been tried for this very crime and been found guilty ("The War Games"). He served his sentence and was pardoned by the Time Lords themselves. Do not all these events constitute "mitigating circumstances"?

"The Mysterious Planet" introduces another popular recurring character: Sabalom Glitz. The rogue is portrayed in a serious fashion in both this serial and in "The Ultimate Foe" by *Ace of Wands* star Tony Selby. Glitz would reappear one last time in "Dragonfire," but by the time of that serial he was played mostly for laughs.

Once again, a different and seemingly contradictory fate for the planet Earth is presented. The Earth was destroyed in "The Ark" and "Frontios" and rendered uninhabitable in "The Ark in Space." Now *Doctor Who* seems to suggest that most of the planet's populace was killed when the planet was mysteriously "moved" two light years. Only a few people survived, but they reverted to barbarism (another *Who* cliché like "The Face of Evil"). If this is the case, then was Earth/Ravalox eventually returned to its position in space so the people of Nerva could repopulate it, or did the Ravalox "move" occur after the Nerva resettlement, and before the final migration from Earth to Refusis or Frontios? If it did occur before the events of "Frontios" and "The Ark," then how did it get back to its correct position in space? Once again, series history and continuity has gone right out the window.

"The Mysterious Planet" is available on videocassette with "Mindwarp," "Terror of the Vervoids" and "The Ultimate Foe" in "The Trial of the Time Lord" box set available from BBC/CBS-Fox.

145. "Mindwarp" Written by Philip Martin; Directed by Ron Jones; Designed by Andrew Howe-Davies; Parts I–IV ; Airdates: October 4, 11, 18, 25, 1986

SYNOPSIS: The Doctor's trial on the Time Lord space station continues. The Valeyard ruthlessly continues his case, and his second bit of evidence from the Matrix is the Doctor's most recent adventure. The action took place on the world of Thoros-Beta in the last quarter of the twenty-fourth century.

The TARDIS arrives in the pink-hued surf of Thoros-Beta. The Doctor and Peri are apprehended by the security forces of Dr. Crozier. After meeting Crozier, the Doctor and Peri run into the enemy they encountered on Varos: Sil! The Doctor reveals to Peri that Thoros-Beta is the homeworld of Sil's people, the Mentors. Peri and the Doctor are taken to Crozier's lab and they soon learn why they have been detained. Kiv, a Mentor leader, is dying from ongoing brain swell. He needs a new body, and Crozier hopes to transfer the Mentor's entire persona into a new body before Kiv dies. Unfortunately, Peri is the perfect choice to play host to this monstrous creature. Although the Doctor and the Warlord, King Yrcanos, attempt to stop the transfer, they are too late...

GUEST CAST: The Valeyard (Michael Jayston); The Inquisitor (Lynda Bellingham); King Yrcanos (Brian Blessed); Sil (Nabil Shaban); Kiv (Christopher Ryan); Crozier (Patrick Ryegart); Matrona Kani (Alibe Parsons); Frax (Trevor Laird); The Lukoser (Thomas Branch); Tuza (Gordon Warnecke)

COMMENTARY: "Mindwarp" is the darkest story in "The Trial of the Time Lord" season, and perhaps in *Doctor Who* history. The Doctor apparently switches sides and tortures Peri, the detestable Sil plots evil, Peri's soul is destroyed on an operating table, and King Yrcanos commits brutal murder at the behest of the Time Lords. It is a show filled with evil, madness and violence. This is appropriate, however, since this is the second act of a grand mystery. The evil is most prevalent here so that the hero's situation looks grim before the uplifting climax. Just as *The Empire Strikes Back* is the darkest of the *Star Wars* films, so is "Mindwarp" the darkest of the "Trial" adventure.

"Mindwarp" is probably the least-liked episode of "The Trial of the Time Lord" for a number of reasons. Not only is it gloomy and murky, but the story has no real payoff after the drama that has preceded it. Unlike "The Mysterious Planet," which was a self-contained adventure on Ravalox with a clear beginning, middle and conclusion, "Mindwarp" does not appear to have a conventional climax. Instead, it ends with the Doctor being pulled out of time by the Time Lords, and the violent massacre by King Yrcanos. The central issues of the serial, including Kiv's regeneration, Sil's maneuvering, the Alphan revolution and Dr. Crozier's experiments, are left unresolved. In this case, the surprise of such a wild conclusion is worth a few dangling plot strands. The serial's ending moments are tense as the Doctor jumps one hurdle after another to save Peri from the soul transfer surgery. His ferocity and determination recalls the best moments of the last Peter Davison serial, "The Caves of Androzani." Then, suddenly, when he is at the door of the operating room, the TARDIS pulls the Doctor away. It is a gut-wrenching moment. Fan and viewer expectations are completely turned upside down as the Doctor finds himself unable to help his friend. There is no happy ending this time. Instead, Peri loses her life to Kiv's consciousness. There can be no last-minute reversal of this key plot element because the Time Lords cause Yrcanos to kill Peri and Crozier in the operating theater. Peri's life ends, and the Doctor is unequivocally responsible for putting her in this dangerous situation. It is a shocking ending but an effective one.

"Mindwarp" is a welcome return to the great days of early *Who*, when not all stories were retreads of past glories. This is an original adventure told with style and large dollops of horror. The memory of tired seasons 19–21 are obliterated by new energy and a fatalist attitude.

Despite the commendable in-your-face attitude and rock 'em sock 'em finale, there is something distinctly ugly about "Mindwarp." From the set designs of Sil's retreat to the cold sterility of the operating room, this is not a pretty serial to watch. Kiv and Sil are disgusting, Yrcanos is unsympathetic and Crozier is mad. Even the Doctor seems insane at points. "Mindwarp" seems infused with evil and menace. The world of *Doctor Who* is no longer a safe place at all.

Interesting guest appearances also make "Mindwarp" memorable. Brian Blessed makes his first appearance on *Doctor Who* as Yrcanos. He is famous to sci-fi fans for his guest appearances on *Space: 1999* in "Death's Other Dominion" and "The Metamorph." He also played Vultan, King of the Hawkmen, in the 1980 Dino DeLaurentiis film *Flash Gordon*, and a religious zealot in the *Blake's 7* adventure "Cygnus Alpha." Blessed is not the only *1999* alumnus in "Mindwarp": Alibe

Parson also appears as Matrona Kani. She played Zienia Merton's replacement, named "Alibe," in a few episodes of *Space: 1999* Year Two. Nabil Shabin also returns as the Ferengi–like character Sil. His part is not crucial to the plot of "Mindwarp," and so he comes off as just another unpleasant facet of the story.

Especially confusing in "Mindwarp" is the continued assertion by the Time Lords that the Matrix cannot be tampered with or compromised. Have they forgotten the events of "The Deadly Assassin," "The Invasion of Time" and "Arc of Infinity"? Once again, this production team has lost track of series continuity.

"Mindwarp" also represents a goodbye of sorts to Bryant's companion Peri. The character meets a horrible end in this story, probably the worst end of any companion in the series. But is it real? The truth would be revealed in the final portion of "The Trial of the Time Lord."

146. "Terror of the Vervoids" Written by Pip & Jane Baker; Directed by Christopher Clough; Designed by Dinah Walker; Parts I–IV; Airdates: November 1, 8, 15, 22

SYNOPSIS: The Doctor mourns the tragic death of Peri but is forced to begin his defense nonetheless. As per Gallifreyan law, he has been given access to the Matrix to build his case. He tells the court that he is showing them an adventure that has not yet occurred. His defense is that his behavior will improve in the future!

The Matrix viewscreen shows the Doctor and his new companion Melanie as they attempt to stop the germination of a race of monstrous plant people (Vervoids) aboard a space liner called the *Hyperion III*. When the Doctor destroys the Vervoids, the Valeyard suggests there is a new issue to consider: Article 7. He believes the Doctor is guilty of genocide.

GUEST CAST: The Valeyard (Michael Jayston); The Inquisitor (Lynda Bellingham); Prof. Lasky (Honor Blackman); Commodore (Michael Craig); Rudge (Denys Hawthorne); Janet (Yolande Palfrey); Doland (Malcolm Tierney); Bruchner (David Allister); Grenville (Tony Scoggo); Kimber (Arthur Hewlett); Edwarde (Simon Slater); Duty Officer (Mike Mungarvan); First Guard (Hugh Beverton); Second Guard (Martin Weedon); Atza (Sam Howard); Ortezo (Keon Davis); Mutant/Ruth Baxter (Barbara Ward); First Vervoid (Peppi Borza); Second Vervoid (Bob Appleby)

COMMENTARY: "Terror of the Vervoids" is the best serial in "The Trial of the Time Lord." It expertly references Agatha Christie's *Murder on the Orient Express* in its tale of passengers on an isolated vehicle. Of course, each passenger harbors a secret identity and a sinister agenda. To cement the reference, the producers of "Terror of the Vervoids" put the novel *Murder on the Orient Express* in the hands of guest star Honor Blackman. "Terror of the Vervoids" takes Christie's premise and sends it off in a wild new direction. The *Hyperion* boarders (Mogars) are surrogate foreigners, the Doctor is the stolid detective, and there are murders aboard the *Hyperion III*, but there is no analogy in the novel for the carnivorous Vervoids. Still, it is an excellent story filled with tension and suspense. With its classic battle between the Doctor and a race completely inimical to human life, it recalls classic Tom Baker adventures like "The Seeds of Doom" and "Planet of Evil."

The main plot, however, raises some questions within the context of the larger trial story. The first question concerns the charge of genocide. How dare the Time Lords charge the Doctor with attempted genocide when they once sent him on a mission of genocide themselves. Do they not recall that they interrupted the Doctor's journey and forced him to destroy the Daleks as embryos in the Tom Baker story "Genesis of the Daleks" (1975)? It smacks of Time Lord hypocrisy that they would dare raise this issue to the Doctor. After all, the Doctor acts in "Terror of the Vervoids" not to destroy the aliens, but to preserve humanity. Did the Time Lords feel he committed genocide in "Doctor Who and the Silurians" and "The Sea Devils"?

The second issue involves the Doctor's choice to present a "future" story as evidence. How does he have access to the future? Even though the Time Lords have mastered time travel, this court proceeding must be occurring within a specific context, a specific moment inside or outside of linear time. How can the Time Lords or the Doctor know of an adventure that has never occurred? In "Frontios," the Doctor established that Time Lord knowledge could go so far and *no further*, so how does "Terror of the Vervoids" fit within this explanation? Secondly, why bother with a future adventure anyway? Why does the Doctor not use "Colony in Space," "The Mutants," or "The Two Doctors" as evidence? In those adventures, he was used by the Time Lords to interfere at their behest! With over 900 years of history, one would think that the Doctor could find some events in his life that would exonerate him, instead of digging into the future.

The lovely Honor Blackman guest-starred in "Terror of the Vervoids" (episode #146) almost 21 years after her appearance in the role shown here: James Bond's love interest, Pussy Galore, in *Goldfinger* (1964).

The last issue of believability in "Terror of the Vervoids" involves the new companion Melanie Bush (actress Bonnie Langford). She has already met the Doctor by the time of the events on the *Hyperion* in "Terror of the Vervoids." Their introduction is unseen, but this is a "future" adventure after their initial meeting. Yet, amazingly, Mel first begins her journey with the Doctor in the adventure "The Ultimate Foe," immediately following the testimony of this adventure. In that story, her *first* with the Doctor, she already has knowledge of the "Terror of the Vervoids" but it has *not occurred* for her yet. In other words, the Doctor never actually meets Mel. Her involvement with the Doctor is a time paradox!

Honor Blackman appears in "Terror of the Vervoids" as Dr. Lasky. This beautiful actress has made quite a mark in the superspy and sci-fi genre. She starred opposite Patrick Macnee in *The Avengers*, a series also created by *Doctor Who* progenitor Sydney Newman. She later costarred opposite Sean Connery as Pussy Galore in the 1964 James Bond blockbuster *Goldfinger*.

The captain of the *Hyperion III* in "Terror of the Vervoids" is named Travers. This is a common character name in *Doctor Who*, having appeared in "The Abominable Snowmen," "The Web of Fear" and "The Horror of Fang Rock," to name just a few. Is Capt. Travers a descendent of the Prof. Travers the Doctor befriended in the Himalayas in "The Abominable Snowmen"? The name recurs so frequently in *Who* that one has to wonder about it.

147. "The Ultimate Foe" Written by Robert Holmes, Pip & Jane Baker; Directed by Christopher Clough; Designed by Michael Trevor; Parts I–II; Airdates: November 29, December 6, 1986

SYNOPSIS: The Master, Sabolom Glitz, Melanie and the Doctor prepare the Doctor's defense. In the course of ending the Trial, the Doctor learns that the Time Lords have been dishonest with him. This trial is but a mockery to keep him silent. The Time Lords are responsible for moving Earth and renaming it Ravalox. Furthermore, the Matrix has been tampered with, by the Valeyard. Therefore, Peri is not really dead and the Doctor is not really guilty of genocide. The only mystery remaining involves the identity of the Valeyard: He is not who he appears to be. In fact, he is the Doctor himself: a frightening evil figure in his final regeneration!

GUEST CAST: The Valeyard (Michael Jayston); The Inquisitor (Lynda Bellingham); The Master (Anthony Ainley); Glitz (Tony Selby); Popplewick (Geoffrey Hughes); Keeper of the Matrix (James Bree)

COMMENTARY: "The Ultimate Foe" is one of the most densely packed hours of *Doctor Who*. Answers and explanations fly at the viewer in quick succession, and they do not always appear to make sense. So, for the record, here is the tally on how the epic story finally culminates.

First, Peri did not die on Thoros-Beta because of the Doctor's interference; she survived and married King Yrcanos. Presumably she will live happily ever after. Secondly, the Doctor was tried to mask the unethical activity of the Gallifreyan High Council — activity which the Doctor nearly discovered during the events of "The Mysterious Planet." Specifically, the Time Lords moved the planet Earth from its position in space to another position two light years away, a position once held by the world called Ravalox. The Time Lords moved the Earth because a group of criminals called the Andromedan Sleepers had stolen the Time Lord Matrix duplicate storage tape and hidden it there. The Time Lords made sure that the Andromedan beings could not find Earth and retrieve the all-important data storage tape. Unfortunately, in transporting the Earth across space, the Time Lords damaged its biosphere and killed millions of people. The Time Lords, realizing the Doctor would discover this horrible crime, used the Doctor's last regeneration, a villainous creature called the Valeyard, to prosecute his earlier self. If the Valeyard succeeded in winning the case against the Doctor, the High Council would have rewarded him with the remainder of the Doctor's regenerations. In other words, the Valeyard prosecuted an earlier version of himself in order to prolong his own life. The censored moments between Glitz and Dibber in "The Mysterious Planet" were edited out of the trial Matrix transcript by the Valeyard because they revealed the importance of the Time Lord storage tape. The events which seemed to place the Doctor in a bad light (torturing Peri in "Mindwarp"; destroying the communications equipment in "Terror of the Vervoids") were false images created by the Valeyard. Interestingly, the Time Lords themselves must have contravened the laws of time so that two Doctors could cross the time streams of one another. This was an act strictly forbidden in "The Three Doctors."

Lastly, the Master arrived in "The Ultimate Foe" not to save the Doctor, but to gain control of the real Matrix storage tape and take over the planet of Gallifrey. Either the Time Lords or the Doctor himself were smart enough to booby trap the tape so when the Master opened it, he could not access the secrets of the Time Lords. Instead, he was trapped in time.

If this lengthy explanation sounds complicated, there is a good reason. "The Ultimate Foe" moves at such a breakneck pace that the many answers fans had been left hungering for in "The Mysterious Planet," "Mindwarp" and "Terror of the Vervoids" were not always clear. This author watched "The Ultimate Foe" serial five times before catching all elements of the story. Any solution that is this complex can hardly be called successful, yet "The Ultimate Foe" does in the end resolve the mystery set up so expertly in earlier "Trial" stories. The final episode should have been twice as long, and not so packed with information. Still, it is challenging, intellectual drama, and how often does that play on television?

Although parts of "The Ultimate Foe" are confusing, other parts stand out as great *Doctor Who* moments. The ending, with the Valeyard reasserting himself as a force of authority on Gallifrey, suggests that evil will never die. It is a chilling climax. Also worthy of discussion is the fact that the Valeyard is the last incarnation of the Doctor. This great champion of morality will one day become as hypocritical, as selfish and as consumed with evil as Time Lord renegades like the Master and the Rani. This is the nihilistic vision of the Colin Baker era that so many fans loathe. The Doctor's future is now written, and it is filled with evil. The Doctor, in the person of the Valeyard, will one day resort to the same tricks as the Master did in "The Deadly Assassin" and "The Keeper of Traken" so he can extend his own life span. "The Trial of the Time Lord"'s ultimate message is that morality withers in the face of extinction. The Doctor abandons many incarnations (presumably 12) of goodness and morality, a shocking conceit, not at all in keeping with the clear black-and-white morality of the series' early days. More than that, it is a challenging notion that forces fans and viewers to recalibrate their opinions of the Doctor. No more is he the incorruptible creature of good.

If parts of "The Ultimate Foe" seem familiar, it is with good reason. As the Doctor fights himself (the Valeyard) in the Matrix, the story becomes for ten minutes a strict rehash of the Doctor-Master battle inside the Matrix in "The Deadly Assassin."

In the end, the important question about "The Ultimate Foe" is about meaning. What does the trial mean within the context of *Doctor Who*? For one thing, the Time Lords are exposed as villains. They have interfered and lied to cover their tracks. They have killed millions, and changed the fate of a planet. They are meddlers too, but unlike the Doctor they meddled only to preserve their superiority, not to help others. The Time Lords have become the greatest villains ever seen in the series. They are worse than the Master, the Daleks or the Cybermen, because they are so hypocritical in their conveyance of "justice." "The Ultimate Foe" is the last word on Time Lords; Gallifrey would never be visited again. Where can you go after exposing the super race as a bunch of lying, conspiratorial hypocrites? For too long the Gallifreyans were depicted as just another alien race with the ability to control time travel. Harkening back to "The War Games," the Time Lords of "The Ultimate Foe" dispense a most evil justice. The Time Lords are monsters.

Sadly, "The Ultimate Foe" is also the last adventure of Colin Baker's Doctor. After the show went on hiatus, BBC executive Michael Grade decided the best way to improve the show's ratings was to cast a new actor as the Doctor. They offered Colin Baker one four-part serial to end his reign. He made an alternate suggestion: one more season as the Doctor. They refused his offer and his era ended without a regeneration scene. Still, in the season-and-a-half that Colin Baker reigned as the Doctor, the series improved immensely. The series took on dark overtones in episodes such as "Vengeance on Varos," "Mindwarp" and "The Ultimate Foe." "The Mysterious Planet" and "Timelash" were inventive, if not completely successful. This was a direct contrast to the rehashes seen throughout the Peter Davison era.

More than story content, however, Baker's era saw the advent of a new and different kind of Doctor. He was flamboyant like Tom Baker, but he was the edgiest incarnation of the Time Lord yet. He brandished words like weapons, and he had a vicious streak. Despite this, he also defended the galaxy as vociferously and as loyally as ever before. He faced tragedy and horror in "The Trial of the Time Lord," perhaps the most personal story seen in *Doctor Who*. To this day, Colin Baker is not a favorite incarnation of the Doctor, but there is no doubt that he oversaw a turbulent and exciting era in the *Who* storyline. He proved that he had the charisma and screen presence to stand toe-to-toe with consummate scene stealers like Patrick Troughton and Frazer Hines. In the years following his departure, Baker's tough, challenging interpretation of the Doctor would be missed, especially as the writing declined considerably.

SEASON 24

148. "Time and the Rani" Written by Pip & Jane Baker; Directed by Andrew Morgan; Designed by Geoffrey Powell; Parts I — IV; Airdates: September 7, 14, 21, 28, 1987

SYNOPSIS: The TARDIS is ambushed in space, and the Doctor regenerates into a short, middle-aged, dark-haired man. The TARDIS lands on Laekertia, its doors are pried open and the renegade Time Lady, the Rani, enters the craft. She orders her Tetrap servant Urak to leave Mel unconscious on the floor and bring the Doctor back to her lab. The Rani is hatching a deadly plan to exact revenge upon the galaxy that has wronged her. She has captured Earth geniuses such as Albert Einstein and Louis Pasteur and put them in cryogenic chambers. After a few checks, the Doctor realizes that the Rani is preparing to explode a dark matter asteroid. When she does so, it will cause a supernova and destroy the planet. She requires the minds of Einstein and Pasteur to make the final calculations, but it is only a matter of time...

GUEST CAST: The Rani (Kate O'Mara); Ikona (Mark Greenstreet); Beyus (Donald Pickering); Sarn (Karen Clegg); Urak (Richard Gauntlett); Faroon (Wanda Ventham); Lanisha (John Segal); Special Voices (Peter Tuddenham, Jacki Webb)

COMMENTARY: "Time and the Rani" is a weak debut for Sylvester McCoy's seventh Doctor. It is a low-brow, empty story with an implausible plot, ridiculous monsters and a total lack of any overriding theme or viewpoint. It is startling in its banality, especially after the complexity of Season 23 and the magnum opus "The Trial of the Time Lord."

The first disappointment in "Time and the Rani" is the abrupt regeneration sequence. This is the first time since "The War Games" (1969) that a *Doctor Who* lead actor has not "morphed" into the next. It is thus distinctly troubling to watch "Time and the Rani" open with the injured Doctor already unconscious on the floor. Before his face is visible, he regenerates into McCoy. This is the worst regeneration scene in the series, brought on by Colin Baker's understandable unwillingness to return in a cameo after being forcibly retired from the show. It does not matter what the circumstances were; the opening of "Time and the Rani" is abrupt and unacceptable in terms of direction and believability. The producers should have allowed the "Baker" corpse to shift a little, and recall via flashback the highlights of his all-too-short era (including companions Peri and Mel, and even Glitz). In addition, it is hard to believe that the sturdy TARDIS would be so badly buffeted in the time-space vortex that it would induce a regeneration. How many times has the TARDIS been shaken this badly before without such a drastic happening? The regeneration in "Time of the Rani" smacks of necessity, not of drama.

A second disappointment is Bonnie Langford's transformation as companion "Mel." In "Terror of the Vervoids" and "The Ultimate Foe," she was a go-getter, a solid new companion for the Doctor. She showed initiative and faced dangerous situations with composure. In "Time and the Rani," Mel has been changed into an idiot. She runs and screams her way through the entire serial. Although she still helps free the Doctor, she does so in the most grating manner. When confronted with the Tetraps, Melanie throws her hands up and screams at the top of her lungs in the sexist tradition of '50s horror movie damsels. It is a strange change to an already ill-defined character.

The worst element of "Time and the Rani" is the teleplay itself. It mercilessly rehashes a number of *Doctor Who* stories including the *Time Machine* template (Rani equals Morlocks; Laekertians equal Eloi). It also revisits the ludicrous notion seen in "The Mark of the Rani," that Earth geniuses can help Time Lords solve complex calculations about time and space. Even brilliant Earthmen like Einstein would have difficulty with dimensional transcendentalism and block transfer equations. If the Rani needs geniuses, why not kidnap the mathematicians of "Logopolis" instead of twentieth century Earthlings? Since the Rani needs the Doctor to bring her plan to fruition, "Time and the Rani" also serves as a "Master trap" story, only with O'Mara's baddie stepping in for Anthony Ainley's Time Lord. With all of these problems, "Time and the Rani" is the most uninventive serial since the Davison era. The only original element of the show is the Rani's interesting attempt to convince the Doctor that she is Mel. O'Mara has wicked fun playing Mel as a smiling, perky bitch.

Although it is a pleasure to see beautiful actress Wanda Ventham (late of "The Faceless Ones" and "Image of the Fendahl") again in this story, she is made to look ridiculous in the Laekertian regalia. The Laekertians are a race of mustard yellow aliens who wear flowing, baggy robes. They look like something out of a 1930s *Flash Gordon* serial. Still, the Laekertians are not as ridiculous in appearance as the crazy-eyed Tetrap beasts, one of the worst monster designs in *Doctor Who* history. The Tetraps are no more believable than the Mickey Mouse costumes at Disneyland.

Because of all these problems, McCoy's Doctor is hardly given a masterful debut. He is competent in the role. He is a talented physical comedian, and this skill is in evidence in "Time and the Rani." Like a vaudevillian of the highest stature, McCoy tips his hat to each defeated villain and swaggers around the TARDIS like Charlie Chaplin (with an umbrella doubling for a cane). He is amusing to watch, and his interpretation of the Doctor would improve over time. In the last two seasons in particular, McCoy would be given a more interesting context in which to operate (the notion that the Doctor is perhaps not a Time Lord after all, but an elemental force of nature). Stories such as "Silver Nemesis," "Ghost Light" and "The Curse of Fenric" would also reveal McCoy's Doctor to have a dark side, and a kind of strange master plan. In these early days of the McCoy era, however, it is primarily the actor's humor and slapstick physical tricks which are in evidence.

It is safe to assert that McCoy's Doctor is probably the most popular of all post–Tom Baker portrayals. Fans seem to prefer mature men in the lead role of *Doctor Who*. Colin Baker, Peter Davison and Paul McGann still carry, at least in appearance, the baggage of youth. They are good-looking, physically capable, aggressive and vigorous. McCoy, like Troughton and Tom Baker, is more seasoned in his portrayal. He does not run around and fight to assert his manhood. *Doctor Who* fans do not mind arrogance in their Time Lord, if it is not coupled with youth. Perhaps the feeling is that the arrogance and self-confidence of Hartnell, Troughton, Pertwee, Tom Baker and McCoy has been earned. The older Doctors also make for stronger relationships with companions. With Colin Baker, McGann and Davison, there is the uncomfortable feeling that some of these Doctors are sexually attracted to companions such as Nyssa, Peri and Grace Hollowell. With the more mature Doctors, the attitude towards the companions is avuncular, harmless.

"Time and the Rani" is available on videocassette.

149. "Paradise Towers" Written by Stephen Wyatt; Directed by Nicholas Mallett; Designed by Martin Collins; Parts I—IV; Airdates: October 5, 12, 19, 26, 1987

SYNOPSIS: The Doctor and Mel watch a video brochure of Paradise Towers, a Terran resort community, on the viewscreen. The Doctor finds the twenty-first century community architecturally fascinating but Mel just wants to go swimming. When they arrive at the complex, the travelers discover immediately that it bears no resemblance to the promotional materials they were just scanning. The place is littered with garbage and infested with rats. It is a hell of blight and poverty.

The Doctor and Mel soon cross paths with a gang of redhead girls called the "Red Kangs," a militaristic outfit called the "Caretakers," cannibalistic "Rezzies" (residents) and the infamous architect of Paradise Towers: Kroagnon, builder (and destroyer) of Miracle City. Can the Doctor and Mel build a community out of this splintered society before Kroagnon's forces murder everyone?

GUEST CAST: Chief Caretaker/Kroagnon, the Great Architect (Richard Briers); Deputy Chief (Clive Merrison); Tilda (Brenda Bruce); Tabby (Elizabeth Spriggs); Fire Escape (Julie Brennon); Bin Liner (Annabel Yuresha); Pex (Howard Cooke); Blue Kang Leader (Catherine Cusack); Young Caretaker (Joseph Young); Yellow Kang (Astra Sheridan); Maddy (Judy Cornwell)

COMMENTARY: "Paradise Towers" is a great *Doctor Who* story. On the surface it appears to be yet another example of the future society fragmented and splintered over time (like the Sevateem and the Tesh in "The Face of Evil") but it is actually much more than that. It is *Doctor Who*'s ultimate statement on diversity and integration, and as such it is amazingly cohesive and persuasive. In "Paradise Towers," the denizens of a giant apartment complex include the overfed, cannibalistic "Rezzies," the remnants of a security force called "Caretakers," maintenance droids running wild, and gangs of foraging girls called "Kangs." The history of Paradise Towers is recorded for the Doctor's benefit on the apartment complex walls by unseen graffiti artists. The drawings of these wall-scrawlers are reminiscent of paintings found in prehistoric caves and are equally important, because they record the development of a society that has lost literature and knowledge and reverted to barbarism. All the inhabitants of Paradise Towers live separate, violent lives until the Doctor brings the community together in a "town meeting." Facing a threat greater than all of their splintered groups combined, the inhabitants of the complex band together to defeat Kroagnon. They do so by using their own separate strengths in a common cause. Their diversity is what makes them powerful. The Rezzies stop the robots with knitted tablecloths of their invention, the Kangs use their skill in archery to help turn the tide of battle, and Pex overcomes his cowardice to become a hero. The battle to save the community is a moment of unity, and a strong statement from *Doctor Who* that people of different ideals, races and colors can work together to do great things. "Paradise Towers" also suggests that people will come to this understanding and tolerance of one another only when there is a common threat.

Even beyond the powerfully conveyed central message, "Paradise Towers" has much to offer a keen-eyed viewer. Each element of the apartment society reflects a different aspect of modern culture. The Rezzies, who live in comfort in beautiful apartments, are representative of the modern middle class. The Rezzies are delineated as overweight consumers who care most about a good meal. They have cut themselves off from the events outside their tiny compartments, and they concentrate only on their own comfort. They would rather eat innocent people than address issues of social change in their community. They are short-sighted, complacent consumers. Only when crime enters their pristine part of the world, in the form of the killer robots, do the Rezzies rejoin the community.

The Caretakers represent the ultimate military mentality. These men are fascists who rule over the other denizens of Paradise Towers simply because they wear black uniforms. They accept favors and grant privileges to those who help them. They also obey an archaic set of rules that has nothing to do with morality or current social mores, but only with all-important tradition. They do not even understand why they follow orders, or in what context their rule book was written. The Doctor is able to fool them easily because they have no understanding outside the lock-step conformity of their brotherhood.

The Kangs represent inner city gangs. They have no homes and no education. They have their own laws and their own "colors." Anyone who challenges their colors is immediately branded an enemy. All these various groups are used by scribe Wyatt to expose an element of modern society. It is done in a teasing way, rather than a heavy-handed one, and it affords the serial an admirable density of subtext.

Wyatt's teleplay of "Paradise Towers" also finds humor in the society. The Kangs have adopted names for themselves, but without books to guide them, these names are rather strange. Two very funny Kang names are "Bin Liner" and "Fire Escape"! Also quite funny is the manner in which the Doctor is able to use the Caretakers' love of rules against them. Though many fans object to this slapstick humor, it arises naturally out of the situation in "Paradise Towers." It is hence more than appropriate and McCoy handles these facets with finesse. His second outing is far superior to the lifeless "Time and the Rani."

"Paradise Towers" is also enlivened by the great set design of Michael Collins. The apartment complex is beautifully designed. It is a lush architectural community with stylistic flourishes such as arches and walkways. Appropriately, the beauty is marred by trash and generations of debris. It is a perfect example of urban blight. Every element of apartment living has been skillfully updated not only to reflect updates in technology, but also years of degeneration in the hands of a culture that has forgotten it. In a sense, Collins' job as designer was difficult because he first had to picture the ultimate apartment of the future. Then, he had to imagine that apartment's degradation after years of use. Like the rest of "Paradise Towers," Collins work is convincing and it supports the issues raised by the teleplay.

Perhaps the only disappointment in "Paradise Towers" is the depiction of the villain Kroagnon. Like many other villains in the early McCoy era, Kroagnon is a kind of "cartoony" threat. Actor Richard Briers is made up to resemble Adolf Hitler, but his threats and the nature of his evil are over-the-top. He is a comic book villain from *Batman*, not a believable threat to the Doctor and the community of "Paradise Towers." Had Kroagnon's villainy been established in more realistic terms, "Paradise Towers" would be even more successful.

"Paradise Towers" is available on home video. Like "Vengeance on Varos" and "Mawdryn Undead," it represents latter-day *Doctor Who* at its most stimulating.

150. "Delta and the Bannermen" Written by Malcolm Kohll; Directed by Christopher Clough; Designed by John Asbridge; Parts I — IV; Airdates: November 2, 9, 16, 1987

SYNOPSIS: The Doctor and Mel are the ten billionth customers to pass through a cosmic toll booth. Their prize is a free time travel trip to the opening of Disneyland in 1959. En route, they meet a stowaway on the bus, a girl named Delta. The Doctor learns that Delta is no ordinary woman, but the Chimeron Queen! Delta's people have been attacked by the Bannermen, an evil alien race, and all but destroyed. The sadistic Gavrok, leader of the Bannermen, will not be satisfied until all the Chimerons are dead. This includes the escaped Queen.

GUEST CAST: Delta (Belinda Mayne); Billy (David Kinder); Gavrok (Don Henderson); Burton (Richard Davies); Weismuller (Stubby Kaye); Murray (Johnny Dennis); Hawk (Morgan Deare); Gorony (Hugh Lloyd); Tollmaster (Ken Dodd); Aldon (Leslie Meadows); Vinny (Martyn Geriant); Chimeron Princess (Carley Joseph); Bollit (Anita Graham); Callon (Clive Condon); Arex (Richard Mitchley); Young Chimerons (Jessica McGough, Amy Osborn); Chimerons (Russell Brook, Ian McClaren, Tim Scott); Lorells (Robin Aspland, Jeff McCulloch, Justin Myers, Ralph Salmins)

COMMENTARY: Christopher Clough, the director who handled the complexity of "The Ultimate Foe" so admirably, returns to helm another interesting *Doctor Who* story in McCoy's era. He would prove so adept at juggling action that he would return for "Dragonfire," "The Happiness Patrol" and "Silver Nemesis." His work on "Delta and the Bannermen" is strong, but the story itself reflects a continuation of the comedic direction taken by "Paradise Towers."

Like Wyatt's "Paradise Towers," which was rife with satirical jabs at the middle class and the police, "Delta and the Bannermen" strays heavily into the world of absurd comedy. This *Doctor Who* is reminiscent of Douglas Adams' brand of humor and his view of a silly galaxy bereft of meaning or purpose. In "Delta and the Bannermen," Earth artifacts such as highways, toll booths, vacation trips and tourism are adapted to an outer space setting and to the *Doctor Who* universe. These items are brought to life but make no particular point, and therefore the wild, comedic touches are lapses into silliness. *Doctor Who* is not the universe of *Hitchhiker's Guide to the Galaxy.* Although there is room for humor, it must always be handled in a way that builds logically from the drama. "The Sunmakers" and "Paradise Towers" are two good examples of *Doctor Who* stories filled with humor, but which also make serious points about modern life. What is the point in "Delta and the Bannermen"? Are viewers to believe that in all the planets of all the galaxies, Disneyland is to remain a tourist attraction? Disneyland and toll booths in space only detract from the realism of *Doctor Who*'s universe.

It is also rather significant that there are now time travel tours to Earth's past. When did this begin? Do the Time Lords know about it? They used the Doctor as their agent to prevent the galaxy at large from obtaining time travel in stories such as "Attack of the Cybermen" and "The Two Doctors"! What has changed? When did time travel become a common thing? If it is so common, why did the Hartnell Doctor rarely run into other "tourists" during his forays into history in such stories as "The Crusades," "The Reign of Terror," and "The Aztecs"? Furthermore, how do alien species survive the destructive forces of time travel at all? In "The Two Doctors," viewers learned that the Rassilon Imprimateur gene is what enables the Time Lords to survive the stress of temporal voyages. This is another case in which the Nathan-Turner production team has thrown *Doctor Who* continuity out of the window. If "Delta and the Bannermen" were a great adventure seriously examining a new aspect of the universe, it might be forgiven for so cavalierly throwing out convention. It is not, however, and one is hard-pressed to fit the events of this story into *Doctor Who* history. Even the best "retconning" would have a hard time with this one!

151. "Dragonfire" Written by Ian Briggs; Directed by Christopher Clough; Designed by John Asbridge; Parts I — III; Airdates: November 23, 30, December 7, 1987

SYNOPSIS: On the planet Iceworld, also known as Svartos, the despot Kane has purchased a ship's worth of men to serve as soldiers. These "Chosen Ones" are to be frozen in cryonic tubes until needed. The Doctor and Mel visit Iceworld and run into Sabolom Glitz there. They also meet a young human girl named Ace who is waitressing at the ice cream bar. Ace reveals that a dragon lives under Iceworld. The hunt for the dragon is soon on, but it turns out to be the key to a puzzle. The dragon leads the Doctor to a polydimensional scanning imager. This historical archive machine informs the Doctor that Kane has been exiled from his home planet and banished to Svartos. His lover, Ixanna, killed herself to avoid the humiliation of arrest and trial. The Doctor also learns that Kroanon, Kane's homeworld, has been destroyed in the 3,000 years that Kane has been marooned here. The "dragon" is in reality a computerized jailer, and inside its skull is the "dragonfire," the power component that will allow Kane to escape from Svartos forever.

GUEST CAST: Sabalom Glitz (Tony Selby); Kane (Edward Peel); Belaze (Patricia Quinn); Karcauer (Tony Osoba); Customer (Shirin Taylor); Henderson (Ian Mackenzie); Stellar (Miranda Borman); McLuhan (Stephanie Fayerman); Bazin (Stuart Organ); Zed (Sean Blowers); Pudovkin (Nigel Miles-Thomas); The Creature (Leslie Meadows); Announcer (Lynn Gardner); Archivist (Daphne Oxenford); Arnheim (Chris MacDonnell)

COMMENTARY: "Dragonfire" takes the Time Lord to a fascinating ice world called "Svartos" and once again sends him on a quest, invoking the memory of "The Keys of Marinus" and the Season 16 "Key to Time" saga. It also introduces the '90s-style companion Ace (actress Sophie Aldred). Unfortunately, the serial is made less-than-enthralling in parts by confusing plotting, an obvious ripoff from a popular film and the cartoonish interpretation of the main villains. Despite these failings, it is nonetheless an enjoyable, action-packed serial. It is not great, but nor is it awful, or wholly uninventive.

The confusing plotting in "Dragonfire" concerns a small blond-haired girl who is seen at regular intervals. She has accompanied her mother to Iceworld for a shopping trip. She smiles, wanders into the central action, crawls into Kane's ice bed, and is the last human face seen in the serial. Who or what this child represents is a complete mystery. Why is she there at all, in her strange silver dress? This incomprehensible facet of the story wastes time and distracts from the Kane subplot. Is the girl's presence an attempt to warn mothers not to leave their children unattended in shopping malls? Does the girl represent the plight of the innocent caught up in adult turmoil? Is she an alien creature with a secret agenda? Or is she just the producer's niece? Her name in the credits is "Stellar," suggesting, perhaps, that she is a Star Child *à la 2001: A Space Odyssey*. What are viewers to make of her? Thematically, what does she tell us about this story?

The second embarrassing feature in "Dragonfire" is the design of the dragon. It is a blatant ripoff of the creature seen in the *Alien* saga. The creature sports a long, banana-shaped head, biomechanoid skin and long protrusions emanating from its back. The only way it could appear more derivative of the alien in the Ridley Scott film is if the actual costume from *Alien* were appropriated and used by *Doctor Who*. Apparently the writer of this serial also had *Aliens* on the brain because there is an unfortunate sequence in "Dragonfire" in which two of Kane's soldiers confront the being. One of the soldiers is a macho woman (*à la* Private Vasquez in *Aliens*) who drones on at length about the importance of carrying a big gun. She and her partner then track the alien underground with a hand-held scanning device. It malfunctions and the soldiers start to panic. "Oh, no, it's all around us! I've lost the signal! It's coming straight at us," they shout, turning the horror and tension of the *Aliens* into a monster movie cliché. Then the ultimate ripoff comes: The motion scanner detects not an evil alien, but a little blond girl! Of course, this is Stellar, who seems to serve no purpose in the story! As all *Aliens* fans remember, the space marines in that film also uncovered a young blond girl (Newt) with their motion scanner! This entire *Aliens* interlude has no connection whatsoever with the main plot of "Dragonfire," which concerns Kane's attempt to escape exile on Svartos and wreak revenge on his jailers. Therefore the ripoff is doubly surprising. Rarely does *Doctor Who* pick up a film strand so randomly, and for such little narrative purpose. At the very least, the producers could have waited to ripoff *Aliens* until an entire serial merited it, rather than cramming all these *Aliens* clichés into one five-minute sequence in "Dragonfire."

Beyond these problems, Kane is depicted in "Dragonfire" as another campy villain. He could just as easily be Mr. Freeze on *Batman* as a villain in *Doctor Who*. He wears a white uniform just so viewers do not forget to associate him with "ice," and he is incredibly cartoonish in his attempts to be evil. Not for a moment is he dramatized as a believable or realistic character. Only in his final self-sacrifice does the character achieve any kind of dignity. Tony Selby's Glitz has also taken an unfortunate turn since "The Trial of the Time Lord." In that tale, he was a villainous rogue with a degree of charm. In "Dragonfire," this space pirate has been reduced to a comical blunderer. He is a buffoon and a target of humor, instead of the legitimate, dramatic character introduced in "The Mysterious Planet."

Although "Dragonfire" has its share of problems, there are some highpoints. The moment when the ice spires of Svartos separate from the planet and form a giant, crystalline spaceship is a vision of wonder and awe. It is a great special effect sequence. Secondly, the story introduces Sophie Aldred as Ace. She is the best companion for the Doctor since the first incarnation of Romana in the Tom Baker era. On the surface she seems like a smart-mouthed teenager, but Ace is so much more than that. In her time with the Doctor, Ace develops into a realistic personality. She is the most athletic and capable of all the companions. She fires missile launchers at Daleks and beats them up with a baseball bat ("Remembrance of the Daleks"). She has a fetish for explosives ("Dragonfire") and even destroys a Cyberman spaceship ("Silver Nemesis"). Secondly, she has a "real" friendship with the Doctor; they do not simply smile and get along with one another. Instead, she questions his motives and argues with him repeatedly. Fortunately, it is not in that pat, whiny companion way. Instead, she calls the Doctor on the carpet for keeping secrets from her ("Ghost Light," "Curse of Fenric") and playing games with the fate of the world. Ace is also depicted as a needy person of low self-esteem ("Dragonfire") who despises her mother ("The Curse of Fenric"). The viewer has even seen some of Ace's romantic dalliances ("Remembrance of the Daleks") and faced the dark side of her nature ("Survival"). It has been a long time since so much has been known about a *Doctor Who* companion.

With the advent of Aldred's Ace also comes the departure of Langford's Melanie. She was a problematic companion at best. It was hard to relate to her because she and the Doctor never actually "met" in the context of any adventure. She simply showed up, uncelebrated and unheralded, in "Terror of the Vervoids." The viewer knew nothing of her background, her history, her likes or her dislikes. The audience does not even know why she travels with the Doctor at all. Also,

Mel underwent a dramatic character revision between the end of Season 23 and the beginning of Season 24. When she joined up with McCoy, she suddenly became a screaming ninny. Though Langford and Melanie were always pleasant to have around, there is no connection between the viewer and this character. She is probably the least developed and most unsatisfactory of all the Doctor's companions throughout the series. It is a testament to Langford's acting skills that her moment of departure in "Dragonfire" is filled with as much emotion as it is. McCoy also performs beautifully in that moment. His response to Melanie's departure is a great example of passive-aggressive behavior. The Doctor feels happy for his companion, sorry for himself, mad at the universe, and rather confused. It is a decent farewell to a companion who never worked very well.

"Dragonfire" is available on videocassette.

SEASON 25

152. "Remembrance of the Daleks" Written by Ben Aaronovitch; Directed by Andrew Morgan; Designed by Martin Collins; Parts I — IV; Airdates October 5, 12, 19, 26, 1988

SYNOPSIS: The Doctor and Ace travel to Coal Hill School in 1963. In a sense this is a trip home for the Doctor. He was here once before, with his granddaughter Susan. Together they picked up two teachers (Barbara and Ian) and began a long series of temporal adventures. Now, however, the Doctor has returned for a very important item: the hand of Omega. Unfortunately, two warring factions of Daleks want this device (a remote stellar manipulator that customizes stars), and they are willing to destroy London to get it. Interestingly, the Doctor has an ulterior motive, a plan to wipe the evil Daleks from the face of creation once and for all. But will Davros, the Dalek Emperor, fall for his ruse?

GUEST CAST: Group Captain "Chunky" Gilmore (Simon Williams); Sgt. Mike Smith (Dursley McLinden); Rachel (Pamela Salem); Allison (Karen Gledhill); Ratcliffe (George Sewell); Headmaster (Michael Sheard); Harry (Harry Fowler); The Girl (Jasmine Breaks); Embery (Peter Hamilton Dyer); Vicar (Peter Halliday); Martin (William Thomas); John (Joseph Marcell); Kaufman (Derek Keller); Davros (Terry Molloy); Dalek Operators (John Scott Martin, Hugh Spight, Tony Starr, Cy Town); Dalek Voices (John Leeson, Royce Mills, Brian Miller, Roy Skelton)

COMMENTARY: "Remembrance of the Daleks" is probably the best Dalek story since Terry Nation's "Genesis of the Daleks" in 1975. It is filled with impressive battles, great special effect sequences and fun historical references. And, ending 25 years of speculation, a Dalek soldier hovers successfully up a staircase! The serial also introduces the special-forces Dalek, an imposing, ominous, tank-like creation. Perhaps more significant than the Dalek improvements or the high quality special effects is the fact that "Remembrance of the Daleks" relies heavily on *Doctor Who* trivia and history. Unfortunately, this reliance on matters of continuity raises more questions than it answers. However, any show that can inspire hours of speculation has to be at least moderately worthwhile. In that regard, *Doctor Who*'s "Remembrance of the Daleks" succeeds admirably. This serial could be talked about for days before all topics are exhausted.

On a basic, visual level, the twenty-fifth season premiere features the best pyrotechnics yet seen on *Doctor Who*. In the exciting opening battle in Totter's Lane and the final combat in the streets of the London, the Daleks spit green laser beams at one another and at the British military. The series has indeed come a long way since "The Daleks." Back then, the Daleks spit only a blast of steam. The effect of their blast on human beings was accomplished by causing the film image to become "negative." In "Remembrance of Daleks" *Doctor Who* has finally entered the age of *Star Wars* (1977) and zippy visual effects. The opening outer space shot is a tacit acknowledgment of this fact. "Remembrance of the Daleks" commences with a lingering pan across a massive Dalek spaceship. It is reminiscent of the Star Destroyer's approach to Tatooine in George Lucas's film.

The last Dalek adventure of the series finally does away with the loathsome creatures. Although Davros escapes the destruction of his ship, Skaro and the Daleks are both destroyed by the Hand of Omega in the conclusion of "Remembrance of the Daleks." In essence, the Doctor has finally committed the genocide of the Daleks which he planned way back in "Genesis of the Daleks." But this creates an interesting discontinuity in *Doctor Who* history. It was established in "The Dalek Invasion of Earth" that the adventures seen in "The Daleks" occurred "millions of years in the future." Those are the Doctor's words, as mouthed by William Hartnell. However, in "Remembrance of the Daleks" Skaro is seen to be obliterated by the supernova of its sun *in the year 1963*. In other words, all of history has now been altered. The Doctor cannot travel to Skaro with Ian and Barbara in "millions of years" in the adventure "The Daleks," because Skaro is long gone by that time! Also, what about the Thals? In this time period in Skaro history (equivalent to Earth 1963), the Kaleds and the Thals still co-exist on the planet Skaro! They are fighting their ten millennium war of attrition, as detailed in "Genesis of the Daleks"! The Daleks on the attack in "Remembrance of the Daleks" are delineated as being "from the future," but their home planet is clearly destroyed in the present (again, 1963). This means the Daleks and Davros will *never even be born*. This also means that *all* the events of *all* the Dalek adventures can no longer occur. Essentially, the Doctor has given the Daleks a retroactive abortion in "Remembrance of the Daleks." Indeed, since he has destroyed their planet before he ever encountered them in the first place, they cannot even exist in the future to travel back in time to 1963 in "Remembrance of the Daleks"! Thus the Hand of Omega cannot be used to destroy them, since they were never born in the first place! Whew! Can anyone say time paradox?

Besides the fact that the climax of "Remembrance of the Daleks" changes all of *Doctor Who* history and makes mincemeat of series continuity, it also reveals the Doctor in a distinctly unkind perspective. He is now responsible for genocide (the crime the Time Lords tried him for in "The Trial of the Time Lord"). He has destroyed not only the Daleks, but the kindly Thals. He is a cosmic murderer! Didn't he decide in "Genesis of the Daleks" that great good could come out of the evil of the Daleks? That worlds would unite in peace and friendship to stop the Dalek threat? What changed his mind?

The second continuity problem in "Remembrance of the Daleks" involves the Hand of Omega. The teleplay suggests that the first Doctor was planning to hide the Hand of Omega when he was interrupted by Ian and Barbara in Totter's Lane during the first half-hour of "An Unearthly Child." Only now, six incarnations later, is the Doctor returning to take care of the important Time Lord device. Wow! The Doctor is one hell of a procrastinator! In six incarnations he never went back to complete his mission. Perhaps that is the beauty of time travel. As long as a Time Lord is alive, he or she can go back to any time and complete any task. Although apparently six incarnations of the Doctor have passed since the events of "An Unearthly Child," the seventh Doctor goes back to Totter's Lane just the day after he left with Susan, Ian and Barbara in the first place. Incredible! Still, how is it that William Hartnell's self-confessed "exile" came to be doing a mission for the Time Lords? Or did he flee Gallifrey and steal the Hand of Omega from the Time Lords? Is that why he was afraid of being caught or pursued by the Time Lords in "The War Games," because of this theft? If so, why didn't the "Hand of Omega" come up in the trial? All the details between an "An Unearthly Child" and "Remembrance of the Daleks" do not form a cohesive whole. Rather, the connection of these two stories just raises more questions. Still, it is delightful that the story is awash in *Doctor Who* details. Coal Hill School is seen again, as is Totters Lane, the Daleks and Davros. There is also mention of the twenty-first century invasion dramatized in "The Dalek Invasion of Earth." Perhaps the greatest trivia touch of all is the fact that, while in Ian Chesterton's science lab, Ace flips through a book entitled *The French Revolution.* Of course, this was the book that Barbara lent to Susan in the opening scenes of "An Unearthly Child"! For audience members, that event occurred 25 years ago, but in linear time Ace is holding this book just hours after Susan did. Again, this is an incredible moment that calls attentions to the vicissitudes of time travel.

"Remembrance of the Daleks" also is the first *Doctor Who* story to suggest that the Doctor has a kind of foreknowledge of all the events he plays a part in. He operates by a secret plan in this story, and he has plotted every development from point A to point Z. In other words, he is shown to be a virtually infallible agent of destiny. In stories such as "The Curse of Fenric," "The Greatest Show in the Galaxy" and "Silver Nemesis," he would also be shown to be acting within the guidelines of a secret plan. Everyone he encounters, every time period he ventures to, every feint or thrust on his part is an element of that master plan. This is an exciting new interpretation of the Time Lord. It makes him look devious, conniving and far less jovial than one might think. That is why McCoy does so well

George Sewell, shown here as defender of the Earth Alec Freeman in *U.F.O.*, switched sides and betrayed the planet to the Daleks in *Doctor Who* episode #152, "Remembrance of the Daleks."

with the role. On the surface he is all humor and happiness, but he hides a deep brooding side and an incredible sense of strategy. The only problem with this new approach is that the Doctor's character can at times come across as boring. Since all the universe is but a chess game to him, he is never surprised, never taken off guard and never in any real jeopardy. He has planned out everything to the last detail, and thus the universe of *Doctor Who* loses its essential characteristic of spontaneity. Still, it is an interesting attempt on the part of the producers to show the Doctor in a different context. Realizing perhaps that the Time Lord angle had been completely exhausted in "The Trial of the Time Lord," the series set out in a new direction and the Doctor came to represent much more of a mystery. It was a return to the early days of the series when no one knew who the Doctor was. After "Remembrance of the Daleks" the Doctor is not merely a Time Lord of Gallifrey any more. Instead he is the elemental force of "good." Or is he? Is he actually an agent of another, more frightening type? What is the secret that he hides so zealously in "Silver Nemesis"? This is a great new mystery in *Doctor Who*, and one that is never solved. Finally, after 20 years, viewers are again invited to ask "Doctor Who?"

"Remembrance of the Daleks" also has a number of good guest performances. Michael Sheard ("Pyramids of Mars," "The Invisible Enemy") returns to play the brainwashed Headmaster of Coal Hill School ... a character who would have been very familiar to Barbara and Ian had they not disappeared the day before the events of this story. George Sewell also appears as the white supremacist character Ratcliffe. Sewell is most famous for his portrayal of Col. Alec Freeman in *U.F.O.* He appeared in the film *Journey to the Far Side of the Sun* (1969), which was also produced by Gerry and Sylvia Anderson.

The historic last appearance of the Daleks is available in a two-box set with the classic adventure "The Chase."

153. "The Happiness Patrol" Written by Graeme Curry; Directed by Christopher Clough; Designed by John Asbridge; Parts I—IV; Airdates: November 2, 9, 16, 1988

SYNOPSIS: Terra Alpha is the TARDIS's latest destination. The Doctor and Ace look around this failed Earth colony and discover that events have taken a very surreal and nasty turn. The planet's ruler is Helen A, an infuriating woman who has enacted a special edict: everyone must remain happy, all the time, in every way imaginable. This nonsensical rule is enforced by the Gestapo-like Happiness Patrol. If anyone, such as the Killjoys, should fail to comply with the happiness law, Helen A has provided a number of exquisite penalty options. An unhappy inhabitant can be executed by the Happiness Patrol. Or a criminal can face the inhuman monster known as "Candy Man." This bizarre creature is composed entirely of candy and finds "happiness" in force-feeding syrupy sweets to the convicted!

GUEST CAST: Helen A (Sheila Hancock); The Candy Man (David John Pope); Joseph C (Ronald Fraser); Gilbert M (Harold Innocent); Daisy K (Georgina Hale); Priscilla P (Rachel Bell); Susan Q (Lesley Dunlop); Harold V (Tim Barker); Silas P (Jonathan Burn); Trevor Sigma (John Normington); Earl Sigma (Richard Sharp); Wences (Philip Neve); Wulfric (Ryan Freedman); The Killjoy (Mary Healey); Newscaster (Ann Hulley); Victim (Cy Town); Doorman (Tim Scott); Snipers (Mark Carroll, Steve Swinscoe)

COMMENTARY: "The Happiness Patrol" feels like a leftover from Season 24, and borderline absurd stories such as "Paradise Towers" and "Delta and the Bannermen." It is more political satire, more absurdist comedy, than a serious exploration of sci-fi concepts and themes. Nevertheless, the notion that everyone on Terra Alpha must be happy at all times or face the terrible repercussions invoked by the government is an explosive and controversial notion. In fact, "The Happiness Patrol" looks a lot more interesting and insightful today than it did in 1988 when it first aired, perhaps because our culture was less obsessed with political correctness ten years ago than it is in 1998. Today, after seeing politically correct drivel like *SeaQuest DSV* as well as a P.C. version of *Star Wars* (in which Han Solo shoots Greedo *only* in self-defense, because nice people *don't* kill people!), "The Happiness Patrol" seems a much more relevant and much more inventive adventure. Though a recent *Cinefantastique* review noted the serial's debt to Harlan Ellison's *A Boy and His Dog* (1975), particularly in its conceit of having the Terra Alpha inhabitants wear painted-on faces to mask their unhappiness, the same critique can be made of virtually any *Doctor Who* serial. So many of the Doctor's television adventures take their source inspiration from literary and filmic antecedents, so the "copying" of plot details is not that troubling in "The Happiness Patrol." On the contrary, this serial moves ahead with a self-assured flair, and the social commentary is enjoyable and pointed.

The speculation that people's moods will one day be subject to government regulation is certainly the ultimate extension of the political correctness doctrine the U.S. sees today. According to the P.C. police, we must all watch what we say and how we express our ideas, lest we offend others. "The Happiness Patrol" says that eventually we will have to be happy at all times, lest we offend others with our bad attitudes. It is a pretty good conceit for a *Doctor Who* story, and as usual it is ahead of its time. It is told within the venue of the old *Doctor Who* standby, the "revolution" story (i.e., the *Time Machine* template) in the sense that it is about repression of free will (Eloi) by an overreaching bureaucracy (Morlocks).

"The Happiness Patrol" is worth watching today just to see Ace's reaction to all of these "happy" laws. As perhaps the surliest and ill-tempered of the Doctor's companions, she is an inspired choice to send to a world of perpetual happiness.

154. "Silver Nemesis" Written by Kevin Clarke; Directed by Christopher Clough; Designed by John Asbridge; Parts I—IV; Airdates: November 23, 30, December 7, 1988

SYNOPSIS: In November 1988, members of the Nazi Fourth Reich fight it out with a Cyberman vanguard for control of a mysterious asteroid called "the Silver Nemesis." Also involved in the quest for this object is the Lady Peinforte, who has traveled forward in time from the year 1638. Predictably, the Doctor and Ace also become enmeshed in the hunt; the Doctor, as usual, knows more about the battle than he is letting on. The Doctor reveals that he was the one who launched the asteroid into space in 1638, and that the statue inside the asteroid is made of a living metal called Validium. This valuable substance was created by Omega and Rassilon as a sort of ultimate defense. It should never have been allowed to leave Gallifrey in the first place, but it did. The Doctor encountered the Validium on Earth in 1638, split the material into three pieces and sent the Nemesis statue into space. Unfortunately, it is now returning...

GUEST CAST: DeFlores (Anton Diffring); Lady Peinforte (Fiona Walker); Richard Maynarde (Gerard Murphy); Mathematician (Leslie French); Karl (Metin Yenal); Security Guard (Martyn Read); Cyber Leader (David Banks); Jazz Quartet (Courtney Pine, Adrian Reid Ernest Mothle, Frank Tontoh); Cyber Lieutenant (Mark Hardy); Skinheads (Chris Chering, Symond Lawes); Cyberman (Brian Orrell); Mrs. Remington (Dobres Gray)

COMMENTARY: "Silver Nemesis" was broadcast on November 23, 1988, exactly 25 years after the premiere broadcast of "An Unearthly Child." It brings back a popular villain, the Cybermen, and offers a new template that could have led the series into its next 25 years had fate taken a different turn. Despite this exciting new idea, the majority of "Silver Nemesis" is muddled and confused. It is not a great serial because it lacks forward momentum and a clear, linear story.

Like "Remembrance of the Daleks," "Silver Nemesis" is overcomplicated. How did the Doctor become involved with Lady Peinforte and Validium in the first place? Why does Peinforte recognize the Doctor in his current incarnation? Does this mean that they met in 1638, but after the events of "Time and the Rani," McCoy's first story? Was the Peinforte encounter a recent one by the Doctor's standards? The back story to "Silver Nemesis" must have taken place sometime before Ace was introduced in "Dragonfire," so Mel would have been the Doctor's companion during that adventure...but again, none of this is made clear. How did the Validium get from Gallifrey to Earth in the first place? Did the Doctor steal it? Did another Time Lord steal it? Did Lady Peinforte, a woman of some resources, manage to steal it? Why does Lady Peinforte "merge" with the statue at the end of the story? How is this the union accomplished, and what does it mean? Is the Silver Nemesis just another plot device, exactly like the Hand of Omega from

"Remembrance of the Daleks"? These are just a few of the questions that are left unanswered in the serial. Like many latter-day *Doctor Who* serials, "Silver Nemesis" does not make even a modicum of sense.

More disturbingly, "Silver Nemesis" recycles the conclusion of "Remembrance of the Daleks." A Time Lord weapon is again involved (the Hand of Omega/Validium) and the Doctor's most evil opponents want to possess it (Daleks/Cybermen). The Doctor lets them believe they have won the prize (in both stories!) but the Time Lord tool ends up destroying the villain instead. Skaro is destroyed in "Remembrance of the Daleks" and the Cyberman fleet is obliterated in "Silver Nemesis." Both serials are action-packed adventures with plenty of pyrotechnics and splendidly choreographed fights as well. Ace dispatches the villains with primitive means in both "Remembrance of the Daleks" and "Silver Nemesis." In the Dalek story, she uses an augmented baseball bat. In the Cybermen story, she uses a slingshot and gold coins to blast the bad guys to smithereens. In both stories, the Doctor is responsible for mass destruction (Skaro/Cyberman fleet). This new type of *Doctor Who* story could be referred to as the "Time Lord weapon" template since Gallifreyan technology is the object of interest in both serials.

Although the last appearance of the Cybermen has some strong moments, "Silver Nemesis" also suffers from a lack of continuity with earlier *Who* adventures. This story takes place in 1988, only two years after Mondas almost destroyed the Earth in "The Tenth Planet." Despite this amazing incident, Earth in "Silver Nemesis" appears completely unchanged. No one mentions the invasion, and there is no sign of destruction or new technologies. Is this not the era of space travel seen in stories such as "Ambassadors of Death" and "The Android Invasion"? Shouldn't Earth technology be somewhat more advanced? As usual, Nathan-Turner's team has forgotten *Doctor Who* history and offered a completely incongruous serial. "Silver Nemesis" is baffling because it appears to exist in an alternate dimension, but no one ever even suggests it *could* be an alternate dimension.

"Silver Nemesis" features one great scene. As the Doctor, the Cyberleader and Lady Peinforte stand around the Silver Nemesis, Peinforte threatens to reveal the Doctor's secrets to Ace and the Cyberman. She recalls "the Old Time," and the Doctor's role in strange and unnatural events in Earth's distant past. To what does she refer? What is the Doctor's secret? Peinforte suggests he is more than a Time Lord, but what exactly is his true nature? This scene is part of a continuing effort to make the Doctor more mysterious, and less familiar to long-time viewers. The implication is that he is a figure of great importance in time and space, perhaps more important even than Rassilon or Omega. This idea could have been successfully mined for years, had *Doctor Who* continued. Finally, an inventive plot twist under the Nathan-Turner regime!

Ace's destiny is also suggested in "Silver Nemesis." While in Windsor Castle to retrieve a piece of the Validium, the Doctor and Ace see a beautiful painting on a staircase. It is a painting of Ace in seventeenth century garb. When Ace asks about it, the Doctor says simply that it "hasn't happened yet"— suggesting that he is familiar with all of time, and the fates of those he encounters. This fits into the theory that the Doctor is not just a random traveler, but a force of nature who is always ready to activate a secret plan that saves the galaxy from evil.

"Silver Nemesis" has been released on videotape with a great behind-the-scenes video, *The Making of Silver Nemesis*. It features interviews with stunt coordinators, actors, guest performers, John Nathan-Turner and the director. It follows days of rehearsal and location shooting on "Silver Nemesis" and covers the battle scene between the Nazis and the Cybermen. There are also a few shots from a Tom Baker rehearsal on the serial "The Talons of Weng Chiang."

155. "The Greatest Show in the Galaxy" Written by Stephen Wyatt; Directed by Alan Wareing; Designed by David Laskey; Parts I — IV; Airdates: December 14, 21, 28, 1988, January 4, 1989

SYNOPSIS: After a commercial advertising Festival Time at the Psychic Circus, the Doctor and Ace decide to pay a visit to the greatest show in the galaxy. Unfortunately, the circus is not a place of entertainment, but horror. It is overseen by the robed and masked Gods of Ragnarok, creatures who thrive on the energy of bread and circuses. They must be entertained, and they then eat up the vitality of their entertainers. They order the Doctor to entertain them or die, so the Doctor must give the performance of his life.

Episode #155, "The Greatest Show in the Galaxy," was novelized for Target Books by *Doctor Who* writer Stephen Wyatt.

GUEST CAST: Capt. Cook (T.P. McKenna); Mags (Jessica Martin); Bellboy (Christopher Guard); Flowerchild (Dee Sadler); Chief Clown (Ian Reddington); Morgana (Debora Manshi) Nord, Vandal of the Roads (Daniel Peacock); Whiz Kid (Giano Sammarco); Stallholder (Peggy Mount); Bus Conductor Robot (Dean Hollingsworth); Clown Robots (Patrick Ford, Alan Heap, Paul Sadler, Philip Sadler)

COMMENTARY: Stephen Wyatt, the author of the brilliant "Paradise Towers," returns with another triumph in "The Greatest Show in the Galaxy." It opens with a funny idea perfectly executed: a junk mail robot lands in the TARDIS. After a few jokes about the ubiquitous nature of junk mail, the story then proceeds to explore several classic horror elements (i.e., evil clowns) in rather inventive fashion. At its heart, "The Greatest Show in the Galaxy" owes a debt to the "Daemons" prototype because again Earth legends (the Gods of Ragnarok) are discovered to be evil extraterrestrials. Still, the circus atmosphere of "The Greatest Show in the Galaxy" makes it one of *Doctor Who*'s most unique and memorable latter-day serials. It is horrific in a surreal manner. Horror elements had not been so much in evidence in *Doctor Who* since the days of Tom Baker.

"The Greatest Show in the Galaxy" is also notably strong on character interaction and development. Fortunately, it steers clear of *Doctor Who* historical errors and snafus, a problem which plagued "Remembrance of the Daleks" and "Silver Nemesis." Aldred's Ace comes off particularly well in this story as she has to confront her fear of clowns and her genuine impression that circuses are creepy. She overcomes her fear and saves the Doctor's life in the climax. Despite the predictable conclusion, this is still a refreshing serial in terms of its treatment of the Doctor's companion. Usually companions do not expose their inner feelings. Instead, they serve merely as props to be captured and rescued. Not so with Ace. She loudly conveys her attitude about everything and in the process brings a breath of fresh air to the series.

The Doctor reveals more of his enigmatic history in "The Greatest Show in the Galaxy." He has encountered the evil Gods of Ragnarok before, but this time he is ready for them. Again, the Doctor is seen to be someone with the gift of prophecy or foreknowledge. At the beginning of the story, he is seen juggling *before* the junk mail arrives to herald the circus. He knew that his juggling skills would soon be necessary in a confrontation with an old enemy — but how did he know? These questions are positively tantalizing, and they contribute to the new feeling of mystery that permeates the latter half of McCoy's era. There is definitely a palpable sense that the series was building to a shocking revelation about the Doctor's true nature.

For a place that is ostensibly such fun, the circus has long been a site for terror. *Doctor Who* follows in the long tradition of horror films by exploiting this disturbing location. An early entry in this long line of circus horror was Tod Browning's disturbing *Freaks* (1932). Much later, Tobe Hooper's film *The Funhouse* (1981) also explored the dark underside of carnivals. The horror-satire *Killer Klowns from Outer Space* (1988), which premiered the same year as "The Greatest Show in the Galaxy," also featured evil clowns. *Doctor Who* shares a common belief with all of these filmic horrors, that the circus is fun only on the surface. Underneath the veneer of fun lives something incredibly evil. Other sci-fi series which have visited the circus are *The Fantastic Journey* (in the 1977 episode "The Funhouse") and *Star Trek: Voyager*. In the *Voyager* tale "The Thaw," Kate Mulgrew's Capt. Janeway had to escape from a world controlled by an alien clown (Michael McKean).

With "The Greatest Show in the Galaxy," Season 25 ended on a high note. Thanks to the efforts of Nathan-Turner and story editor Andrew Cartmel, an admirable new aura of mystery had been added. For a series that had lasted a quarter of a century, a new wrinkle like this seems truly revolutionary. One can only wish that the series had survived longer, and the conceit of the Doctor as an elemental force of nature could have been allowed to develop further.

SEASON 26

156. "Battlefield" Written by Ben Aaronovitch; Directed by Michael Kerringan; Designed by Martin Collins; Parts I—IV; Airdates: September 6, 13, 20, 27, 1989

SYNOPSIS: The TARDIS lands in the English town of Cadbury in 1989. The Doctor is surprised to discover that a UNIT convoy has broken down near the Lake of the High King, or Vortigern's Lake. UNIT is attacked by the evil knights of Mordred, whose goal is to find the magic sword Excalibur and destroy King Arthur. Mordred wants the Doctor dead since he believes the Doctor to be Merlin the Wizard. Behind Mordred's authority is his evil mother, Morgaine Le Fay. The Doctor becomes involved when he determines that in one of his future incarnations, he will indeed *be* Merlin. The Brigadier returns from retirement and learns from the Doctor that none of this should be occurring on Earth at all. The Arthurian characters are from another reality, a parallel dimension! The situation escalates when Morgaine conjures a beast called "The Destroyer" to ravage the planet.

GUEST CAST: Brigadier Lethbridge-Stewart (Nicholas Courtney); Morgaine (Jean Marsh); Brigadier Winifred Bambera (Angela Bruce); Mordred (Christopher Bowen); Ancelyn (Marcus Gilbert); Peter Warmsley (James Ellis); The Destroyer (Marek Anton); Major Husak (Paul Tomany); Shou Yuing (Ling Tai); Doris (Angela Douglas); Pat Rowlinson (Noel Collins); Elizabeth Rowlinson (June Bland); Sgt. Zbrigniev (Robert Jezek); Pilot Lavel (Dorota Rae); Knight (Stefan Schwartz)

COMMENTARY: "Battlefield" is yet another example of *Doctor Who*'s infinitely elastic format. The series can incorporate outer space adventures, the myth of Atlantis, time travel and now, in its twenty-sixth year, Arthurian legend. It is interesting that the fictional tales of Arthur and Camelot are revealed in *Doctor Who* not to be extraterrestrial in origin (nor from the Land of Fiction as seen in "The Mind Robber") but from an alternate dimension which co-exists with ours. In one sense perhaps, "Battlefield" is another adjustment of that serviceable story template, the "Daemons" prototype. Here it is not an extraterrestrial force responsible for human myth, but the inhabitants of a parallel world. Still, the "Daemons" aspect is oblique enough that "Battlefield" seems original.

"Battlefield" features Nicholas Courtney's last *Who* appearance. This delightful performer again plays the beloved role of Brigadier Lethbridge-Stewart, this time called out of retirement for one last glorious adventure alongside his Time

Lord friend. Courtney's presence in this story makes him one of the few actors to have worked with six of the eight incarnations of the Time Lord: He worked with William Hartnell in "The Dalek Masterplan" and "The Three Doctors" and with Patrick Troughton in "The Web of Fear," "The Invasion," "The Three Doctors" and "The Five Doctors." He worked with Jon Pertwee throughout Seasons 7 through 11, and with Tom Baker in "The Terror of the Zygons." He twice met Peter Davison, in "Mawdryn Undead" and "The Five Doctors." Now he develops his own chemistry with Sylvester McCoy in "Battlefield." Colin Baker's short-lived sixth incarnation is the only version of the Doctor that the resourceful Brigadier never encountered. One can only imagine what the stolid Brigadier would have thought of that Doctor's fashion taste. "Battlefield" is also the last adventure to feature UNIT, last seen briefly in the 1983 celebratory story "The Five Doctors." The UNIT of "Battlefield" is a sad organization since it features no familiar faces. Liz Shaw, Jo Grant, Capt. Yates and Sgt. Benton are all missed.

Actress Jean Marsh also makes her last appearance. She had twice before appeared opposite Hartnell (in "The Crusades" and "The Dalek Masterplan"). By appearing in both the first and last season of *Who*, one can safely state that Marsh performances bookend the 26-year series. In "Battlefield," she plays an evil queen, the same role she had essayed in *Willow* (1987).

"Battlefield" raises questions about the true nature of the Doctor. Viewers know that in one of his future incarnations he will enter an alternate universe and serve King Arthur as the wizard Merlin. How this will come to pass is left uncertain. It is clear, however, that this sequence of events must occur before the Doctor's villainous last incarnation (the Valeyard of "The Trial of the Time Lord"). The Doctor's ambiguous nature and his interference in the society of another world forms the heart of "Battlefield"'s drama.

There are other nice touches in "Battlefield." That lovely old yellow roadster Bessie returns for the first time since "The Five Doctors," and there are plenty of swordfights and battle scenes. Refreshingly, the costume for the Destroyer beast is a good one (much more imposing than the Tetrap in "Time and the Rani," for instance) and there is even a hint of a relationship between the Doctor and Morgaine Le Fay. Perhaps the most interesting element is the meeting of Ace and the Brigadier. They are very different companions from very different times, and yet they both play much the same kind of role. They bring humor and action to the series, and they are both staunch protectors of the Doctor. Their similarities far outweigh their differences, yet there is a noticeable disdain between the Brigadier and Ace.

Unfortunately, "Battlefield" is not great *Doctor Who*. The Arthurian overlay is a fantastic idea, but perhaps too much time is spent on fireworks. The Doctor's final speech to Jean Marsh about nuclear destruction elevates the story above the average, and makes this a memorable, if not top-flight, serial.

157. "Ghost Light" Written by Marc Platt; Directed by Alan Wareing; Designed by Nick Somerville; Parts I — III; Airdates: October 4, 11, 18, 1989

SYNOPSIS: The Doctor takes Ace to Perivale Village, her home town, to confront her worst fear: the haunted house called Gabriel Chase. Inside the house, an ancient evil is awakening, and the inhabitants all hide strange secrets. In the basement, the Doctor and Ace discover a spaceship. It arrived millions of years ago, with a powerful entity known as "Light" aboard. This "Light" was a surveyor of all life, and it took samples of Earth species, but something went wrong and the ship was commandeered by a criminal, Josiah Smith. He used the ship's technology for his own evil purposes. His plan now is to assassinate Queen Victoria and restore the glory of the British Empire! However, "Light" is awaking. Light refuses to believe he is on Earth because so much has changed since he catalogued it. All life, he decides, must be frozen as it is.

Marc Platt's "Ghost Light," episode #157, has been released on videotape by BBC/CBS-Fox Home Video, so *Doctor Who* fans can rewind, go back, and rewind again to unlock the secrets of this complicated episode.

GUEST CAST: Josiah Smith (Ian Hogg); Mrs. Pritchard (Sylvia Sims); Redvers Fenn-Cooper (Michael Cochrane); Control (Sharon Duce); Gwendoline (Katharine Schlesinger); Reverend Ernest Matthews (John Nettleton); Nimrod (Carl Forgione); Mrs. Grose (Brenda Kempner); Inspector Mackenzie (Frank Windsor); Light (John Hallam)

COMMENTARY: "Ghost Light" is one of weakest adventures in *Doctor Who* history. It is a hodgepodge of previously visited story ideas and overall an incomprehensible, convoluted mess. The notion that an alien criminal has broken free of his jail and is roaming free on Earth is reminiscent of Cessair Diplos in "The Stones of Blood." Like Diplos, Smith has unearthly powers. The presence of Nimrod, a Neanderthal man, in Victorian society recalls the abduction of primitive Earthlings by the Urbankans in "Four to Doomsday." The evil "Light" with his compulsion to catalogue the specimens of Earth revisits the characteristics of the Sontaran Styre in "The Sontaran Experiment." The story's very context, that of a haunted house and the dark secrets within it, replays the same ideas so successfully expressed in the Brontë–esque drama "Black Orchid." More troubling than all of this repetition is the fact that large portions of the story make no sense.

"Ghost Light" is unintelligible dramatically. What are the alien husks in the basement? At one point, Josiah suggests they are bodies that he has shed. If this is the case, how can they move by themselves? Are they living husks? Do they still possess an element of life? Why do these husks wear tuxedos? The next problem is Light himself. Why is he frightened of evolution? Why does he so easily believe the Doctor's lies about his performance and so obligingly commit suicide? Where does the ability to turn people into statues or primordial soup come from? Who is "Control"? If she is a Neanderthal like Nimrod and a "control" for Light's experiment, how does she overcome generations of evolution and become a proper Victorian lady by the end of the story? Why does the Doctor allow her to watch over the criminal Smith at the end of the story instead of insisting that he be taken to the authorities? Why is Josiah Smith frightened of light? What is the "light" in the snuff box? Why is the snuff box radioactive? Why is Cooper insane (again, this is a kind of reference to Cranleigh in "Black Orchid" who went to the Amazon and came back crazy). What generates the radioactive white light in the snuff box? How has Josiah Smith's desk drawer been transformed into a cryogenic freeze unit? Why do the serving women in Gabriel Chase at times act human and at other instances like robots? Why do the inhabitants of a Victorian house possess late-twentieth century hand guns? Has Josiah Smith time-traveled? If he can time travel, why doesn't he leave the house and his jailer (Light) behind in Victorian England? What does Smith think he can accomplish by assassinating the Queen? This plot strand is painfully reminiscent of the Master's lame plan to prevent the signing of the Magna Carta in "The King's Demons." These are essential questions if one is to understand this adventure. "Ghost Light"'s dramatic narrative is so muddled, so confused that it is impossible to make any sense of it. If it is not the worst written *Who* serial, then it is certainly the most poorly executed.

The central conceit of "Ghost Light" recalls *The Outer Limits* episode "The Guests" in which a group of humans were trapped in a Victorian mansion with an alien brain. "The Guests" is frightening and executed in superb fashion. It is a stylish black-and-white foray into horror which uses the conventions of horror films (high and low angles, shadowy photography) to convey Gothic-style terror. By contrast, "Ghost Light" is unstylish and nonsensical. It is only frightening in so far that it was produced at all. If ever a *Doctor Who* story needed revision, "Ghost Light" is it.

At the core of "Ghost Light" is the commendable notion that one must always face his/her darkest fear. The Doctor forces Ace to re-experience the feelings of dread she felt at Gabriel Chase as a child and conquer them. Unfortunately, this story strand is lost amidst the nonsense. "Ghost Light" seems to think that a *Doctor Who* story can be cobbled together out of elements that had been previously successful on the series. Familiar set pieces and story notions are all there but these ingredients do not form a cohesive narrative. In fairness to "Ghost Light," this was a problem that was becoming more prominent on *Doctor Who* by the episode. The narrative in "Silver Nemesis," "Remembrance of the Daleks" and "The Curse of Fenric" is nearly as confused as the one in "Ghost Light." Even in the dull, uninventive low of the Peter Davison era, the stories still made sense. Overnight, *Doc-*

tor Who forgot how to tell concise stories. "Ghost Light" is a nadir of the 26- year-old series.

"Ghost Light" is available on videocassette.

158. "The Curse of Fenric" Written by Ian Briggs; Directed by Nicholas Mallett; Designed by David Laskey; Parts I—IV; Airdates: October 25, November 1, 15, 18, 1989

SYNOPSIS: During World War II, monstrous creatures burst from the waters of Maiden's Point. The Doctor tells Ace that the nearby church is built on old Viking graves, and that "evil was once buried" there. When a blind scientist translates the runestones carved by ninth century Vikings, the evil awakens. Seventeen centuries ago, the Doctor and the evil entity met on a battlefield. The Doctor carved a chess set out of bones in the Arabian desert, and challenged Evil to a game. The Doctor won, and he trapped evil in the shadow dimensions. Evil was put in a sacred bottle and kept there for generations. After a while, the Doctor lost track of it. The bottle ended up in the Orient until Vikings raided Asia in the ninth century and took the bottle as booty. They never made it home. They all died at Maiden's Point, victims of the evil they had captured. The bottle has been hidden under the church ever since, with the evil entity called Fenric trapped inside. Since then, Fenric has grown in strength. It has summoned a horrible blood-sucking creature called a Haemovore from Earth's distant future. That Haemovore, "The Ancient One," has been turning people into vampires.

GUEST CAST: Dr. Judson (Dinsdale Landon); Commander Millington (Alfred Lynch); Jean (Joanne Kenny); Phyllis (Joanne Bell); Soring (Tomek Bork); Sgt. Prozorov (Peter Czajkowski); Reverend Mr. Wainright (Nicholas Parsons); Capt. Bates (Steven Rimkus); Sgt. Leigh (Marcus Hutton); Ms. Hardaker (Janet Henfrey); Nurse Crane (Anne Reid); Petrossian (Mark Conrad); Perkins (Christine Anholt); Baby (Aaron Handley)

COMMENTARY: What can be said about a *Doctor Who* story that on one hand seems incomprehensible and muddled and yet at other times is so emotionally raw, so powerful that it provokes gasps? "The Curse of Fenric" somehow accommodates both reactions. Like "Silver Nemesis" and "Ghost Light," its story strands are needlessly complicated. Unlike those stories, however, it has a powerful climax that reveals much about the Doctor and Ace.

Generations ago, the Doctor played Evil in a game of chess (*à la* Ingmar Bergman's *The Seventh Seal*). The Doctor won and sent Evil back to the shadow regions. After hundreds of years, the evil has returned to take over the Earth. This is a good framework, yet it is needlessly complicated by weird, disparate elements. For instance, why include a strange British officer who mimics in detail the regalia of the Nazis? Why include a cruel nurse for the handicapped, blind professor? Why introduce Haemovores from the future? These elements only undermine the crucial battle between the Doctor and Fenric, his opposite in "evil." Even Ace's personal story (about a little baby who will grow up to become her mother) is hopelessly pinioned amongst unsuccessful and confusing elements. "The Curse of Fenric" has much to praise in it, but narrative clarity is not one of its strengths. "The Curse of Fenric" is every bit as muddled and cluttered as "Ghost Light."

A few things rescue "The Curse of Fenric" from the trash heap of failed *Doctor Who* serials. The first such moment occurs near the end of the story when the Haemovores attack. The Doctor states that Haemovores can be stopped by faith. Faith, however, is not defined in religious terms. It is defined, rather boldly, as a total belief in anything. One Russian soldier holds off the vampires with his firm belief in Marxism. Ace uses her faith in and love for the Doctor to hold back the evil beasts. This is a great reinterpretation of the meaning of faith, and it explains the "real" reason why crucifixes and other religious symbols can successfully defeat vampires. They are not significant as symbols of Christianity, but as symbols of pure, unwavering human trust. This secular reinterpretation of "faith" is one of *Doctor Who*'s most ambitious ideas.

Another good moment occurs when the Doctor admits to Ace the reasons why he chose to travel with her in the first place. He knew she would lead him back to the evil he once conquered. This is a shock to Ace, and the Doctor is cruel in revealing this fact. He insults Ace and makes her feel terrible, but he must, otherwise Ace would continue to have "faith" in him and hold the "good" Haemovore back from the evil Fenric. It is obvious, however, that these things hurt the Doctor as much as Ace. It is a powerful moment between friends, and Aldred and McCoy handle it well.

"The Curse of Fenric" requires Ace to save a baby who turns out to be her mother. Throughout the tale, she grows closer to the baby, and at the end when she learns little Audrey is her mother, she confronts her feelings of hatred for her. This is another heartfelt, *real* moment between the Doctor and his troubled young companion, and it elevates the serial above its confused story. When Ace jumps into the water of Maiden's Point and cleanses herself of her hatred, it is a cathartic moment.

Ace also becomes angry with the Doctor and accuses him of playing games with fate. She is proven quite correct. The Doctor's ancient history and his lifelong duel with Evil is revealed for the first time. The image of the Doctor on a desert plain, carving chess pieces out of bone is an evocative vision, and the question is raised: Doctor Who? Is he a messiah? Is he mankind's savior? Is he the elemental force of "good" just as Fenric is obviously "evil?" The events of "The Curse of Fenric" put the long journey of the Doctor into a completely new perspective. It seems he has not been aimlessly wandering the universe after all. He has purposefully been journeying to stop evil. Is this why the TARDIS never goes to its programmed destination? Is it secretly programmed to hunt out evil and preserve the universe from it? It is fascinating food for thought. "The Curse of Fenric" also successfully retcons "Dragonfire." Now it is revealed that the Doctor went to Svartos to find Ace!

"The Curse of Fenric" successfully pays homage to horror classics such as *Night of the Living Dead* (1968) and *The Evil Dead* (1983) by featuring bloodthirsty Haemovore villains. They shamble across the church grounds, killing and maiming all who stand against them. "The Curse of Fenric" is also surprisingly similar to the 1979 John Carpenter film *The Fog*. In that story, a 100-year-old curse caused evil monsters to rise from the sea and exact vengeance on the living. As in *The Fog*, much of the action in "The Curse of Fenric" takes place inside a besieged church.

"The Curse of Fenric" is a popular serial, perhaps because it delves so deeply into the relationship between Ace and the Doctor. Although it has great moments, "The Curse of Fenric" seems to have been produced at the wrong time. *Doctor Who* stories of this era are confusing. "The Curse of Fenric" is worth watching if only for the last 15 minutes. The friendship between the Doctor and Ace and the chemistry between McCoy and Aldred has never been more tangible.

"The Curse of Fenric" is available on videocassette.

159. "Survival" Written by Rona Munro; Directed by Alan Wareing; Designed by Nick Somerville; Parts I — III; Airdates: November 22, 29, December 6, 1989

SYNOPSIS: The Doctor and Ace return to Perivale, her hometown, where four teenagers have recently disappeared without a trace. In a playground, Ace picks up a black cat while swinging on a swing. Suddenly, a humanoid/feline creature materializes on horseback and chases her. Ace runs but the beast-woman catches up with her, and they are both transported to a distant world of mauve skies and fiery volcanos. Still pursued by this cat creature, Ace ducks into the woods, where she encounters her friend Tryla and the other missing teens. They quickly inform her that on this planet, cats hunt people. Fortunately for Ace, it is not long before the Doctor transports himself to this strange world as well. Immediately upon arriving, the Doctor is captured and led through a village of the catmen. He is brought into a tent and shown to the Master! The Doctor reveals another bit of disturbing news: The planet is disintegrating rapidly! Even worse, both the Master and Ace are slowly transforming into feral cat people.

GUEST CAST: The Master (Anthony Ainley); Paterson (Julian Holloway); Karra (Lisa Bowerman); Harvey (Norman Page); Len (Gareth Hale); Mitch (Will Barton); Shreela (Sakuntala Rarnanee); Derek (David John); Stuart (Sean Oliver); Angie (Kate Eaton); Woman (Kathleen Bidmead)

COMMENTARY: The final *Doctor Who* serial ever telecast by the BBC is titled, ironically, "Survival." While it is infinitely more clear in writing and direction than previous serials such as "Ghost Light" and "The Curse of Fenric," it is a weak knock-off of *Planet of the Apes* (1968). In this case, the Doctor and his friends discover a world ruled by intelligent felines instead of super-smart simians. The felines hunt them on horseback. A new wrinkle is added in that anyone exposed to the atmosphere of the cheetah world is turned into a cat creature, but even that innovation is not enough to propel this serial to success. It is reminiscent of the human-to-beast transformations in H.G. Wells' 1896 novel *The Island of Dr. Moreau*.

The first moment of value in "Survival" occurs when the Doctor reminds Ace of her humanity and brings her back from the brink of bestiality. The second moment of thematic importance occurs when the Doctor conquers his own animalistic instincts on the cheetah world, and refuses to kill the Master. Unfortunately, even these moments of high drama seem derivative. Many years earlier, in the *Star Trek* story "Arena," Capt. Kirk refused to kill his opponent in much the same circumstances as those seen at the climax of "Survival."

Ainley makes his last appearance as the Master in "Survival" and at the end of the serial it appears he is killed on the dying cheetah world. This is no real indication of the character's death, however, since he also appeared to die in the numismaton flames of Sarn in the Davison serial "Planet of Fire." The next *Doctor Who* production, a 1996 telemovie starring Paul McGann as the Doctor, began with Sylvester McCoy transporting the ashes of the dead Master, so it is possible that "Survival" does represent a kind of death for the character.

The notion that cats are agents of evil has long been part of human mythology, and "Survival" plays on that belief. Supernatural cats also played roles in the *Star Trek* episodes "Assignment: Earth" and "Catspaw." Significantly, the cat was also the chosen symbol of the sixth incarnation of the Doctor. He wore a cat pin on his lapel and had fabric cat outlines sewed into the inside of his colorful jacket. It appears that a love of felines did not survive into his seventh incarnation.

"Survival" ends the 26-year journey of *Doctor Who* on the BBC. Unfortunately, the end of the series leaves several important plot threads dangling. Ace's odyssey has been left unfinished. In "Silver Nemesis" it is revealed she will eventually go back and time and play some role of importance to the Royal Family of England. Viewers never get to see that prophecy come to fruition. Also left incomplete is McCoy's dangerous new interpretation of the Doctor as brooding planner and elemental force of nature. Today it seems that the questions raised by "Silver Nemesis" and "The Curse of Fenric" will never be answered. The Fox 1996 movie reverted back to the previous "Time Lord" characterization of the Doctor that had been in evidence in the '70s and early '80s.

As for McCoy, he only appeared as the Doctor one more time, in the Paul McGann telemovie. He was in the first several scenes before the character regenerated.

Today, McCoy's interpretation of the Doctor is quite popular. Since he was the last actor to play the Doctor on television, his face has appeared on virtually all of the novels in *Doctor Who*'s "New Adventure" series. It is difficult to assess his era because it is such a turbulent one. The slapstick comedy of "Time and the Rani" and other early stories like "Delta and the Bannermen" gave way to muddled tales like "Ghost Light" and "The Curse of Fenric." This is not to say that McCoy is not effective in the role. On the contrary, it is his focused portrayal of the Doctor that keeps many a story from crashing and burning. In his era, "Paradise Towers," "Dragonfire," "The Greatest Show in the Galaxy," "Remembrance of the Daleks," "Battlefield" and "Silver Nemesis" are enjoyable, solid adventures. "Ghost Light" and "Time and the Rani" are wretched. The other stories ("Survival," "The Happiness Patrol," "The Curse of Fenric" and "Delta and the Bannermen") fall somewhere in between. When considering the McCoy era, there is a sense of acute disappointment. *Doctor Who* was leading to some interesting revelations and it should have been allowed to continue in that direction. McCoy and Aldred were a great team, and one wishes they could have continued for least another three years of adventures together. They had the potential to be the best team ever on *Doctor Who*.

"Survival" is available on videocassette.

PART IV

THE *DOCTOR WHO* SPIN-OFFS

Films

So great was the popularity of Terry Nation's Daleks following the broadcast of the "The Daleks" in late 1963 and early 1964 that plans were immediately initiated to feature the villainous "mobile dustbins" in a series of *Doctor Who* feature films. Since Dalekmania was sweeping England, it was logical to assume that any Dalek movie would be a safe bet from a financial standpoint. All those children buying up toy Daleks, Dalek comic books and causing *Doctor Who*'s ratings to spike could also coerce their parents into buying movie tickets. The greater intent, however, was to export the films to the U.S. and introduce the burgeoning Dalek phenomenon to the unconverted in the former British colony. It was hoped that legions of American children would be as mesmerized by the merciless mutants as their London counterparts had been.

The rights to produce a Dalek film were purchased from originator Terry Nation and the BBC by writer-producer Milton Subotsky and his partner, financier Max J. Rosenberg. Together, these gentlemen formed the brain trust of AARU. Later, their efforts would result in the creation of Amicus Productions, a fledgling competitor to Hammer Films. Over the years, Subotsky and Rosenberg produced several horror-oriented movies of high quality including *Dr. Terror's House of Horrors* (1964), *The House That Dripped Blood* (1971), which co-starred *Doctor Who* lead Jon Pertwee, *Tales From the Crypt* (1972) and *At The Earth's Core* (1976). The Daleks films represent some of the earliest efforts of this enterprising duo, as well as the embryo of Amicus. Although today Subotsky's and Rosenberg's work is not viewed with much fondness by *Doctor Who* fans, it is important to recall that in 1965 television programs rarely made the jump to the big screen. This is easily forgotten in the era of *Mission: Impossible* (1996), *The Fugitive* (1993), *The Saint* (1997), *The Avengers* (1998), *Lost in Space* (1998), *The X Files* (1998) and other blockbuster films based on television programs. In fact, *Batman* (1966) was one of the only American television series in the '60s which made the jump from network television to feature film. Seen in this light, Subotsky and Rosenberg might reasonably be called "ahead of their time" for seeing the possibility of profit in popular television, although Hammer Studios had already adapted the *Quatermass* series to film in the '50s. Still, Subotsky and Rosenberg made some excellent casting decisions. First and foremost, actor Peter Cushing was chosen to portray the title character in *Doctor Who and the Daleks*. With intelligent and witty portrayals of Van Helsing and Dr. Frankenstein behind him, the horror movie superstar was nothing less than an inspired decision. Who better to face off against the evil Daleks than the man who had repeatedly defeated Dracula? Nonetheless, AARU Films alienated many *Doctor Who* fans by changing some of the most important background details of the series.

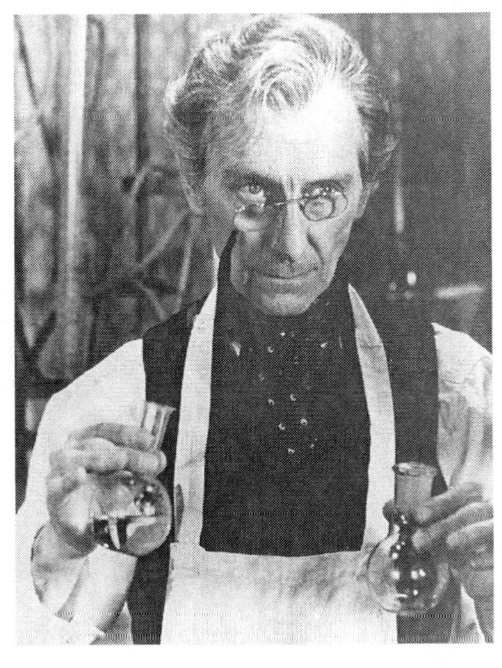

Horror star Peter Cushing (shown here in Hammer's 1957 *Curse of Frankenstein*) played "Doctor Who" in the AARU productions *Doctor Who and the Daleks* (1965) and *Daleks Invasion Earth 2150 A.D.* (1966).

It was decided by Subotsky and Rosenberg that the first Daleks film would be a remake of the serial that had introduced them to the world, "The Daleks." Adapting this story from Terry Nation's serial was no easy task. The producers had to introduce not only the Daleks and their enemies the Thals, they also had to present the main characters of the series, the TARDIS and the Doctor himself. In an effort to make their product more easily understood by the uninitiated, the AARU duo decided to streamline many of these details. In the series *Doctor Who,* the Doctor was a self-proclaimed "exile" from another, unnamed civilization. Rosenberg and Subotsky determined that this was a character element that would *not* translate easily or smoothly to the big screen. It was too complex, and it would take away time from the confrontation on Skaro. Accordingly, the Doctor became an English scientist named Doctor Who, not an alien of unknown origin. He was no longer a renegade adventurer in time but instead a doddery old inventor. His time machine was still called TARDIS, but now there was to be no explanation for the fact that the craft resembled a police box. Hence there was no mention of the failing "chameleon circuit" that the Doctor had noted in "An Unearthly Child" on television. Also, the vessel was referred to in the film as TARDIS, not *the* TARDIS, as in the series.

Other cosmetic changes were made. Susan was introduced as a girl of ten, a precocious child rather than the alluring teenager so memorably portrayed by television's Carole Ann Ford. Barbara changed too: She became the Doctor's older granddaughter. She was no longer a self-confident teacher, but rather a helpless damsel in distress. *Doctor Who and The Daleks* thus began with Barbara's boyfriend Ian arriving at the Who household for a visit. After a few moments of slapstick comedy, courtesy of Ian's bumbling, the Who family was off in TARDIS to the planet Skaro. As these changes make plain, no amount of retconning can explain this feature film or its sequel. It fits in a dissimilar universe from the series.

In 1965, expectations for *Doctor Who and the Daleks* were high. A U.S. comic book company called Dell adapted the film on the assumption that it would leave American children clamoring for ancillary merchandise. Unfortunately, *Doctor Who and the Daleks* went down poorly when it premiered in the United States. Even though the film did considerably better in Great Britain than the States, British fans were upset by its frequent divergences from the television series. In other words, those who bothered to see the film did not like what they saw.

Although *Doctor Who and the Daleks* made nary a box office ripple in America when it premiered there, the producers at AARU were already at work on the second feature in an envisioned trilogy. The story this time was taken from the tenth *Doctor Who* television adventure, "The Dalek Invasion of Earth," again written by Dalek creator Nation. The title of the new movie became *Daleks: Invasion Earth, 2150 A.D.* There were more changes to the *Doctor Who* universe in this 1966 follow-up. The Doctor was no longer accompanied by Ian and Barbara. Instead, his niece Louise and a police officer named Tom Campbell traveled alongside the Doctor and Susan in TARDIS. In the television version of this story, Susan stayed behind to marry a resistance fighter named David. Since Susan was clearly prepubescent in the film version, this angle was dropped. *Daleks: Invasion Earth* was also ignored in America, and the Daleks never captured the imagination of sci-fi fans in the States. In many cities, *Daleks: Invasion Earth* played on a double bill with *Night of the Living Dead.* It was that George Romero classic, not the second *Doctor Who* film, that went on to achieve legendary status.

With two American box office failures behind them, Subotsky and Rosenberg never produced the third film in their proposed trilogy. It was to have been based on Terry Nation's serial "The Chase." It was perhaps fortunate that they dropped plans for a movie based on this feature because "The Chase," though exciting on television, seemed to lack big screen appeal with its mindless cavorting backwards and forwards through time. The best aspect of the serial on television was the touching departure of companions Ian and Barbara. Since these characters had already been shuffled out of the movie series by the advent of the second feature, a film version of "The Chase" could have had no such emotional finale. It would have simply been more phantasmagoria with the Daleks.

Amicus Productions collapsed from internal strife in 1976 and the era of *Doctor Who* on the big screen had ended a rather dismal failure. Today, both movies are available on videocassette via Republic Pictures and Lumiere Pictures. They can be purchased at any Media Play outlet for $8.99.

Dr. Who and the Daleks Screenplay by Milton Subotsky; Directed by Gordon Flemyng; Produced by Milton Subotsky and Max J. Rosenberg; Running time: 80 minutes; Released 1965

Critical Reception

"...a diverting science fiction fantasy for all ages... Not only has this movie a sound moral but also a quaint Flash Gordon charm because of its fanciful sets. Cushing...is properly whimsical, and Gordon Flemyng's amiable direction wisely avoids camp."
—Kevin Thomas, *The Los Angeles Times*, January 10, 1969

"Like the American *Star Trek* teleseries, at its best it [the television series] featured interesting ideas rather than action, which this film fails to do."
—Phil Hardy, *The Film Encyclopedia: Science Fiction*, William Morrow and Company, Inc., New York, 1984

"This crudely made children's film remake of the early TV story in which the Daleks made their debut is of interest mainly to *Doctor Who* completists wishing to see Cushing in the role, which he never played on TV; though inferior to its original, it is at least superior to the even more tepid film sequel..."
—James Gunn, *The New Encyclopedia of Science Fiction*, Viking Penguin Inc., 1988, page 347

"Fun; a bit juvenile, but not bad. Cushing is great."
Jeff Rovin, *A Pictorial History of Science Fiction Films*, 1975, page 214

"Quaint, minimally imaginative, low budget science fiction."
—Donald C. Willis, *Horror & Science Fiction Films: A Checklist*, The Scarecrow Press, Inc., Metuchen, N.J., 1972, page 135

"Jammed full of far-fetched gadgets, equipment and scientific mumbo-jumbo, along with the horrible presence of the Daleks..."
—James Robert Parish and Michael R. Pitts, *The Great Science Fiction Pictures*, The Scarecrow Press, Inc., Metuchen, N.J., 1977, page 106

Credits

Regal Films International Limited Presents an AARU Production

CAST: Doctor Who (Peter Cushing); Ian Chesterton (Roy Castle); Barbara (Jennie Linden); Susan (Roberta Tovey); Alydon (Barrie Ingham); Temmosus (Geoffrey Toone); Gannatus (Michael Codes); Antodus (John Bown); Dyoni (Yvonne Antrobus); Elyon (Mark Peterson); Dalek Operators (Bruno Castaganoli, Michael Dillon, Robert Jewell, Brian Hands, Eric McKay, Kevin Manser, Ian Saunders, Gerard Taylor); Thals (Ken Garady, Martin Grace, Nicholas Head, Jack Waters, Bruce Wells, Gary Wyler, Sharon Young)

CREW: Based on the BBC Television Serial by Terry Nation; Director of Photography: John Wilcox, B.S.C.; Art Director: Bill Constable; Editor: Oswald Haffenrichter; Production Manager: Ted Lloyd; Assistant Director: Anthony Waye; Camera Operator: David Harcourt; Sound Recordist: Buster Ambler; Continuity: Pamela Davies; Wardrobe: Jackie Cummins; Makeup: Jill Carpenter; Hairdresser: Henry Montsash; Camera Grip: Ray Jones; Sound Editors: Roy Hyde, Tom Priestley; Associate Art Director: Ken Ryan; Set Decorator: Scott Slimon; Construction Manager: Bill Waldron; Sound Supervisor: John Cox; Special Effects: Ted Samuels; Special Electronic Effects: Les Hillman; Music Conducted and Composed by Malcolm Lockyer; Electronic Music: Barry Gray; Executive Producer: Joe

Vegoda; Filmed in Techniscope, Technicolor. Filmed at Shepperton Studios, Middlesex, England.

SYNOPSIS: It is a quiet night at the Who household in London. Doctor Who and his granddaughters Susan and Barbara are enjoying some quiet reading time in the living room. Barbara's boyfriend Ian drops in and introduces himself. Ian is obviously nervous about meeting his girlfriend's grandfather, and he ends up sitting on the box of candy he has brought for Barbara. Hoping to make the best of an awkward situation, Doctor Who shows Ian to the backyard where his invention, TARDIS, stands. Inside this police box is a cluttered laboratory and control room which the Doctor claims is capable of traveling through time and space. When Barbara boards TARDIS and leaps into Ian's arm, he inadvertently hits the red control pole and TARDIS transports itself to a new, unknown destination.

The sojourners arrive in a dead, petrified forest. Ian immediately wants to go home but the Doctor and Susan wish to take a look around. The young girl spies an advanced city in a clearing beyond the green-hued jungle. Ian again insists that they should leave, and the group acquiesces. Inside TARDIS, they all hear someone pounding on the door, but the scanner shows nobody outside. The Doctor discovers that a fault has developed in TARDIS' fluid link. They cannot leave this world until they locate a supply of mercury! Ian, Barbara, Susan and Doctor Who leave TARDIS and find that someone has left them a box with medicine tubes inside. They put it in the TARDIS and head to the city.

The Earthlings soon discover that the city is inhabited by evil beings called Daleks. The Daleks live in mobile armor suits to protect themselves from the radiation of Skaro. When Doctor Who realizes that he and his friends have been exposed to radioactive contamination, Susan is allowed to return to TARDIS to pick up the anti-radiation drug left for them by the Daleks' ancestral enemies, the Thals. Susan returns and gives the medicine to her friends. The Daleks discover the medicine cannot help them leave their metallic prisons, and they plot to kill all the Thals. The Daleks then offer to give the starving, humanoid Thals a supply of food, but the Thals must come to the Dalek city to claim it. Meanwhile, Doctor Who and his friends escape from their prison cell. They arrive just in time to warn the Thals of the ambush. Only one Thal is killed, and the rest flee to the petrified forest with Doctor Who and his family.

Since the Daleks now possess the Doctor's fluid link, which he reveals he broke on purpose so they could stay to investigate the city, the Earthlings have no choice but to stay and fight the Daleks with the pacifist Thals. While the Doctor and the Thals use reflective material to jam Dalek scanners, Ian and Barbara invade the city through a cavern. Doctor Who and the Thals manage to destroy the Daleks before the monsters can detonate another neutron bomb. With the Daleks powerless in their deactivated city, Doctor Who, Susan, Ian and Barbara return to TARDIS with the fluid link.

Doctor Who takes his friends home. When Ian opens the police box door, he discovers something has gone wrong. A Roman legion is approaching fast.

COMMENTARY: *Doctor Who and the Daleks* is by no means a great film, but neither is it the disaster that many fans have described. The picture is surprisingly strong the areas of production value and directorial flair. It is only in the character and story development that the picture fails to impress.

The production values in *Doctor Who and the Daleks* are superb. The Daleks have never looked better, not even in 26 years of *Doctor Who* on television. Indeed, the monsters have been improved radically from their first appearance in "The Daleks" in 1963. Instead of being a dull tank grey, the Daleks in *Doctor Who and the Daleks* are molded in radiant hues of red, blue, black and gold. They also have bigger, shinier flashers on the sides of their heads, and their arms can retract and extend to a degree never seen before or since on the television show. Additionally, some Daleks in the film are equipped with silver mechanical claws or grips rather than the standard, unintentionally amusing toilet plunger–like arms so visible in the teleseries. The eyestalk has also been notably improved as well. A Dalek's iris is seen to open and close in at least one key sequence (in the Dalek jail cell). These modifications to Raymond Cusick's design are most welcome, and they make the Daleks seem rather more believable than previously.

The art and scenic direction in this AARU production are also quite good. The film features two superb matte paintings. The first depicts an ominous-looking mountain leading to the rear entrance of the Dalek city. This image is seamlessly blended with the live action footage of Ian, Barbara and two Thals climbing the lower part of the mountain (the part of the hill built inside the studio). The second painting represents a chasm found inside the Dalek cavern. In another nice special effect for the time, a Thal torch plunges down the ravine towards the tiny, snaking river at the bottom, giving the drop a true sense of depth.

The petrified Skaro forest built inside the studio is also eerie. It comes complete with boiling swamps and pools, fog banks, dead trees and sand dunes. This locale is made all the more otherworldly by the fact that it is always seen in a strong green-blue hue. The entrance to the Dalek city is built to full-scale inside the studio, and it too is impressive. It even features a breakaway mountain that reveals another layer of the insidious Dalek technology planted beneath the rock.

There are a few visual disappointments in *Doctor Who and the Daleks.* The Thals are brought to life in a thoroughly uninspiring manner. The actors wear copper-colored Beatles wigs and dabs of blue eyeliner, and they sport painted arched, black eyebrows. The Thal skin also has a soft pink tint to it. In their open mustard vests, skin-tight slacks and Peter Pan–style pointed "fairy" shoes, the Thals come across today as rather fey, effeminate creations. It is clear, however, that their fundamentally "soft" design was inspired by the equally fanciful appearance of the Eloi in *The Time Machine.*

The other disappointment in the film is the interior of TARDIS. In the television series, the control room of the Doctor's time machine is elegant and simple. A central control console with a transparent, undulating time rotor sits in the middle of a barren room, surrounded only by white walls marked with round indentations (called "roundels" in fan fiction). In *Doctor Who and the Daleks,* the time machine interior is depicted as a huge, messy laboratory. There are wires and tubes flowing every which way and weird, disconcerting devices are seen hanging from all the black walls. It is a cluttered area with no real sense of purpose, design or elegance. These two production flaws are comparatively small, however, considering the fine lighting accomplishments and interesting alien sets.

Gordon Flemyng directs competently, and even stylistically at times. The long, slow pan from Susan and Barbara to the Doctor which opens the film represents a great visual joke. The movie begins tight on a shot of a book entitled *Physics for the Inquiring Mind.* The camera pulls back to reveal that Susan, a young girl, is reading this rather adult, intellectual text. The camera then pans to Barbara. She is reading an equally adult book entitled *Science.* The camera shifts again to the oldest persona in this troika, the Doctor. Unexpectedly, he is reading not some complicated science book but the *Dan Dare* comic strip! It is a good visual joke which immediately reveals Susan's and Barbara's intellect and the Doctor's fanciful side. It is a great, accomplished way to begin the film because the foundations of the characters are established without any dialogue or exposition.

Flemyng also captures the otherworldly action on Skaro in frightening, effective fashion. He uses shadows and P.O.V. shots to trace Susan's lonely journey from the Dalek city to TARDIS. There are also quick cuts of something that seems inhuman edited into this chase sequence. Of course, the "inhuman" thing turns out to be a peaceful Thal, Alydon, but Flemyng nonetheless manages to milk tension from the chase. The director also frequently shoots the Daleks from absurdly low angles, from the floor (or even *under* the floor). Of course, this makes the Daleks seem huge and menacing (when in fact they are not much taller than Susan!).

It is the shallowness of the main characters, unfortunately, that ultimately sinks *Doctor Who and the Daleks.* Peter Cushing is a wonderful actor, but he shows none of William Hartnell's attitude or charisma in the role of the Doctor. Instead of being a cantankerous, intellectual fumbler, Cushing portrays the Doctor as a kindly old man. He could be anybody's grandfather. In other words, there is nothing special or interesting about his portrayal of Doctor Who. Jenny Linden's Barbara is equally uninspired. She is a typical '50s sci-fi heroine. She is beautiful, she screams, and she frequently requires rescue. She also dutifully worries about her man, Ian Chesterton. Linden's Barbara carries none of the self-confidence, intelligence or regal qualities which made Jacqueline Hill's schoolteacher such a special and memorable companion on television. Roberta Tovey's Susan is fine. She is so different in concept than Carole Ann Ford's Susan Foreman that any comparison in performance would be fruitless. Tovey is a small child in *Doctor Who and the Daleks,* and there is nothing "unearthly" about her whatsoever. As a performer, Tovey is more than competent, and she projects boundless enthusiasm for the role.

Of all the characters, the revised Ian Chesterton suffers the most. The screenplay has made him a jerk and a fool, and Roy Castle portrays him in that manner. In *Doctor Who and the Daleks* Ian sits down on a box of chocolates, bumbles his way around Skaro and shows cowardice at every possible opportunity. He is given a tedious slapstick scene to perform, some weak schtick with a Dalek door that slams shut whenever he approaches it. Castle is competent with this foray into humor, but the slapstick nature of the joke has no place in *Doctor Who*. It is moronic. The producers apparently thought that this slapstick comedy would appeal to children. On the contrary, smart kids resent this kind of character in science fiction films. They prefer believable heroes who treat problems in a serious, responsible fashion. What fun is it to run out on the playground and pretend to be a jerky bumbler? In this case, William Russell's Ian Chesterton is much better a role model for children than Roy Castle's comic interpretation of the action hero.

It is hard to judge how effective Milton Subotksy's screenplay is because it so slavishly follows the details of "The Daleks." Because of this repetition, the *Time Machine* template has never been more obvious in *Doctor Who* history than it is in *Doctor Who and the Daleks*. Perhaps it is because for the first time *Doctor Who* is in color, like the George Pal film, and on the same big screen. For whatever reason, the story of *Doctor Who and the Daleks* seems awfully derivative of other material. It holds few surprises or new ideas. The film is also broader and less detailed than the television serial. This is perhaps understandable since it has a significantly shorter running time. It is a fact that films must move along more quickly and skim over minor characters who in a long television production might be worthy of more complexity. There is just no time to stop in *Doctor Who and the Daleks* and ponder on the character moments of minor characters like Temmosus or Alydon. As a result, the film is not a very dense one either thematically or narratively. About the only thing it accomplishes with real flair is a sense of place. The otherworldly Skaro is a memorable locale that it captures with style.

Doctor Who and the Daleks also features a strong musical score that is positively rousing at times. It is less electronic and moody than the television series theme and more orchestral. Malcolm Lockyer's and Barry Gray's (*Space: 1999*, *U.F.O.*) main composition sounds like a grand march, and it captures the weight of this encounter with the Daleks. Other than these qualities, the film is interesting only in that it ends in Ancient Rome. In essence this climax forecasts the serial "The Romans" as the next adventure in Doctor's Who time travels! The film's final moments also hint that this big screen version of the Doctor cannot control his time machine very well either, since he has set a course for the twentieth century and ended up in 64 B.C. or so!

Perhaps the best way to approach *Doctor Who and the Daleks* is to distance oneself from the television series altogether. This film diverges from the character and central situation of the program so drastically that the film seems infuriating if one tries to view it as "one" with the BBC show. Taken on its own terms, *Doctor Who and the Daleks* is not a bad adventure. It is not great science fiction but it is an enjoyable romp to an interesting alien planet.

Daleks: Invasion Earth, 2150 A.D. (a.k.a. *Doctor Who: Daleks Invasion Earth, 2150 A.D.*); Screenplay by Milton Subotsky; Directed by Gordon Flemyng; Produced by Milton Subotsky and Max J. Rosenberg; Running time: 80 minutes; Released 1966

Critical Reception

"...a story devoid of dramatic tension or science... The greatest ineptness of the screenplay is its failure to give Dr. Who, here played as a doddery old gent by Cushing, anything at all to do."

—James Gunn, *The New Encyclopedia of Science Fiction*, 1988, page 296

"This version was not nearly as good as the first, its production values were scantier and there was an excess of comedy."

—James Robert Parish and Michael R. Pitts, *The Great Science Fiction Pictures*, 1977, page 80

"...features inexplicably mobile Daleks, considerably more action and far better direction than its predecessor. It's more fun than the first, but the sheer length and relative simplicity of both films make them less than satisfying."

—Kyle Ylinen, *Sci Fi Universe*, #3, November 1994, page 77

"Flemyng directs carelessly and the result, like the earlier film, is far inferior to the BBC's teleseries."

—Phil Hardy, *The Film Encyclopedia: Science Fiction*, 1984, page 250

"Both adventures are lively entertainment and had each been more expert in the technical and script capacity, the result would have been far more satisfying."

—Jeff Rovin, *A Pictorial History of Science Fiction Films*, 1975, page 154

Credits

An AARU Production

CAST: Doctor Who (Peter Cushing); Tom Campbell (Bernard Cribbins); David (Ray Brooks); Wyler (Andrew Keir); Susan (Roberta Tovey); Louise (Jill Curzon); Wells (Roger Avon); Roboman (Geoffrey Cheshire); Conway (Keith Marsh); Brockley (Philip Madoc); Leader Robomen (Steve Peters); Thompson (Eddie Powell); Dortmun (Godfrey Quigley); Man on Bicycle (Peter Reynolds); Man With Carrier Bag (Bernard Spear); Young Woman (Sheila Steafel); Old Woman (Eileen Way); Craddock (Kenneth Watson); Robber (John Wreford); Leader Dalek Operator (Robert Jewell)

CREW: Based on the BBC. Television Serial by Terry Nation; Additional Material by David Whitaker; Director of Photography: John Wilcox, B.S.C.; Art Director: George Provis; Editor: Ann Chegwidden; Production Manager: Ted Wallis; Assistant Director: Anthony Waye; Camera Operator: David Harcourt; Sound Recordist: A. Ambler; Continuity: Pamela Davies; Wardrobe Supervisor: Jackie Cummings; Makeup: Bunty Phillips; Hairdresser: Bobbie Smith; Special Effects: Ted Samuels; Unit Manager: Tony Wallis; Construction Manager: Bill Waldron; Set Decorator: Maurice Pelling; Camera Grip: Ray Jones; Sound Editor: John Poyner; Sound Supervisor: John Cox; Music Conducted and Composed by John McGuffie; Electronic Music by Barry Gray; Executive Producer: Joe Vegoda; Filmed in Techniscope, Technicolor

SYNOPSIS: Officer Tom Campbell, a London cop on the beat, watches as a jewelry shop is robbed. He is attacked by one of the thieves and unable to prevent the crime. He runs to a police box to report the transgression, but it is no ordinary police box at all. It is TARDIS, the time-space machine of Doctor Who and his family. Inside TARDIS, Doctor Who, Susan and the Doctor's niece Louise tend to Campbell's injury. Doctor Who soon announces that they have arrived in the year 2150 A.D.

The travelers disembark and discover that London has been almost destroyed. A girder falls and nearly hits Susan. It brings rubble raining down on TARDIS. Campbell and Doctor Who head to a nearby warehouse to find a crowbar while Louise tends to Susan's ankle injury. Before long, Susan and Louise are escorted away from the landing site by a grungy-looking man who claims he is trying to help them. When Doctor Who and Tom return, they are surrounded by armed Robomen. A Dalek ascends from the Thames. The Daleks, whom Doctor Who thought vanquished on Skaro, have taken over the Earth! Tom and Doctor Who are led to a Dalek spaceship while Louise and Susan meet with the human resistance forces. Susan is shocked to hear a Dalek voice ordering the unconditional surrender of London over the radio. She too thought the Dalek evil destroyed.

Self-proclaimed masters of the world, the Daleks are enforcing a strange new plan. They have begun mining in Bedfordshire. Their goal is to remove the Earth's magnetic core and replace it with a giant rocket engine. They will then pilot the planet Earth to the vicinity of Skaro and conquer the Thals.

Doctor Who escapes with Tom from the Dalek holding cell by using his comb to break the magnetic seal on the jail door. He is then captured by the Daleks again. Craddock, Doctor Who and Tom have passed an intelligence test and are to be turned into the zombie-like Robomen. They are rescued from this fate when the Resistance attacks the saucer. Louise boards the craft to find her uncle, but he has already been freed by the human resistance fighter, David. Louise finds Tom, who has been hiding out by mimicking Robomen, and together they hide in the Dalek saucer as it makes for Bedfordshire. When the craft lands there, Louise and Tom escape through the disposal tube and find themselves once again on *terra firma*.

Susan and another member of the resistance, Wyler, also head for Bedfordshire. After their truck is destroyed by the Dalek saucer they make for the woods on foot. They find a small cottage inhabited by two poverty-stricken women. These women turn them over to the Daleks for a few scraps of food. Susan and Wyler are then taken to Bedfordshire to work in the giant mining operation. Doctor Who also ends up at the mine. After escaping the duplicitous black marketeer Brockley, the Doctor meets up with his friends and determines the way to stop the Daleks. The bomb the Daleks plan to drop in the magnetic core of Earth must be diverted from its path. Tom tends to this problem while Doctor Who is taken by the Daleks to their control center.

Doctor Who makes a break and runs to the Roboman control unit. He orders all Robomen to attack the Daleks! Revolution erupts as the zombified humans pummel the Daleks. Tom prevents the bomb from piercing the core and escapes with the rest of the human workers before the mine explodes. The magnetic forces unleashed pull the Daleks and their spaceship violently to the ground. The Dalek saucer explodes and the world is once again free. In gratitude, Doctor Who returns Tom Campbell to the twentieth century just moments before the jewelry robbery. This time, Campbell is successful in apprehending the criminals.

COMMENTARY: One of *Doctor Who*'s darkest and most successful early television serials is transformed into a lightweight, directionless adventure in the sequel adventure to *Doctor Who and the Daleks*, the slow-moving *Daleks: Invasion Earth 2150 A.D.* The Technicolor veneer of the production works as much against the story as for it, and once again the main characters are defined only in the blandest of possible terms.

"The Dalek Invasion of Earth" was a great, historic *Doctor Who* adventure. It was shot in grainy black-and-white and it had a documentary-style, authentic look which critic John Baxter and many others lauded. In the film version of Nation's story, all of those documentary, grainy qualities are completely obliterated. Technicolor infinitely reduces the believability and stark quality of the story. "The Dalek Invasion of Earth" also used hand-held cameras to extend the grainy, shaky quality of the adventure. That too is gone in the film.

On the other hand, there is no doubt that the climax of *Daleks: Invasion Earth* is far better visualized than the serial's conclusion. On television, stock footage of various explosions was cobbled together to suggest the destruction of the mine in Bedfordshire. In the film, the Daleks are pulled through walls, down mine shafts and into the ground. Then their ship hovers unsteadily and crashes violently to the ground, resulting in an incredible fireball. This is a far better special effects finish to the proceedings, but in the end it is just sound and fury representing nothing. Without the documentary, horrific tone of the original television show, these great visual effects are just icing on a less-than-satisfactory cake.

The art direction of *Doctor Who and the Daleks* was one of that film's greatest strengths. George Provis does a satisfactory job of following up on that success in the sequel. The ruins of London are convincing, although again Technicolor ruins the feeling that we are looking at a huge desolated vista instead of an in-studio painted backdrop. The Robomen costumes are flashier than the show's uniform, and the Mine Control room is an impressive set worthy of a James Bond film. The control area is lined with multiple ramps so the Daleks can slide in to the various pieces of hi-tech equipment. All of these touches are fine, but again they do nothing to motivate the story or the bland characters. One has to wonder what paralyzed Gordon Flemyng since he competently directed the first film. Here there are plenty of fiery stunts and action scenes, but their staging is static and less inventive than those in the last picture. Also far more stagy is his *mise en scène*, particularly in dialogue-heavy London interior sequences. Additionally, the famous shot of the Dalek ascending from the Thames is botched in *Daleks: Invasion Earth*. The camera does not find the wily Dalek until his dome and upper neck are already well out of the water. The surprise of this appearance and the thrill of something unknown creeping up from underwater is completely lost. The television show did it better.

On the character front, things are equally gloomy. Bernard Cribbins plays Tom Campbell. He is another pale replacement for the original Ian Chesterton (actor William Russell). Unfortunately, Milton Subotsky's screenplay requires Cribbins to suffer through the same kind of slapstick comedy routines that sunk Roy Castle's Ian in *Doctor Who and the Daleks*. Here Cribbins' Tom Campbell dresses up as a Roboman and has trouble matching their robot-like actions during a march.

Once again, the slapstick sequence is jarring because of its inappropriate placement. The comedy occurs right after the resistance attack on the Dalek saucer fails! Is this a genuine opportunity for humor?

Jill Curzon plays the Barbara surrogate "Louise" in *Daleks: Invasion Earth*. The talents of this actress are impossible to judge because the script gives her no part to play whatsoever. It provides Louise no memorable characteristics, no unique viewpoint — nothing at all, in fact. She is a pretty face amidst all the action, but no more. Roberta Tovey's "Susan" is also written in far less interesting terms than in the previous film, perhaps because the character spends the bulk of the film separated from her grandfather.

Minor characters from "The Dalek Invasion of Earth" also return in the film remake, but they are barely recognizable. Craddock, Wyler, David and Dortmun all recur but they represent nothing in this film other than "resistance" fighters. Wyler (if he is indeed supposed to be Tyler from the serial) has lost the cutthroat mentality which made his character so interesting in the serial. David, without Susan to romance, comes off as just a good-looking resistance stud. Even Dortmun's role is significantly reduced. He rolls out into the street, heaves bombs at the Daleks and is destroyed by the blast from one of his own bombs. What happened to the noble self-sacrifice of the serial, when Dortmun gave his life so Barbara could survive? Like Louise, these characters are given no individual flourishes or distinction.

Peter Cushing returns to play Doctor Who but he is just as bland as he was in the previous film. In this movie, Cushing has even less to do than before. Damningly, Doctor Who does nothing to advance the plot in *Daleks: Invasion Earth*.

The film tells its story in a slow, dull fashion, resulting in a kind of Cliff's Notes version of the television serial. The women in the woods return. They were so memorable in the television show because they were dirty and pitiful and duplicitous. They collaborated with the Daleks just for scraps of bread. In the movie, the women in the woods are given sarcastic lines and depicted more as evil witches than as pathetic people trying to survive in a terrible world. Ironically, the role of the Black Marketeer is made more effective in the film version. Brockley is played by Philip Madoc (of "The War Games," "Brain of Morbius," "The Power of Kroll" and *Space: 1999*) as a complete S.O.B. He is concerned only with his own skin and the accumulation of wealth. For some reason, this character comes off better on the big screen, perhaps because there is no distracting "Slyther" to interrupt his scenes. The moment when Brockley runs into a shed and is exterminated by a squad of Daleks is one of the most rewarding in the film.

Other sequences from the television show have been completely discarded. There is no Dalek Slyther creature, no London Bridge chase with a wheelchair, no reference to Big Ben's chimes sounding once again through the city, no unearthing of the TARDIS at the conclusion, and no sequence in which a man must face his zombified, Roboman brother. Without these important sequences, *Daleks: Invasion Earth* is clearly "The Daleks Invasion of Earth"–lite.

Of the two AARU motion pictures, the sequel is clearly the weaker. *Doctor*

The two AARU films have been released on videotape by Lumiere and Republic Pictures.

Who and the Daleks was a self-contained adventure in a relatively unified terrain — the surface of Skaro. *Daleks: Invasion Earth* feels like a lot of action set pieces that do not fit well together. The plot does not move forward in a linear fashion; scenes are strung together in incoherent, unfocused fashion. This film should have had a grander scope than *Doctor Who and the Daleks* with its bigger visual effects and giant tapestry, but it comes off as a far less memorable adventure. Even at a sparse running time of 80 minutes, it is tedious.

The Movies That Never Existed

Despite AARU's failed attempt to win the hearts and minds of *Doctor Who* fans in America and Great Britain with their duo of *Doctor Who* films, many producers, writers and directors over the last 30 years have attempted to get their own *Doctor Who* film off the ground. The first *Doctor Who* "movie that was never made" is the Milton Subotsky-Max J. Rosenberg adaptation of the Season Two serial "The Chase," yet another Dalek-centered adventure written by Terry Nation. This project fell through when *Doctor Who and the Daleks* and *Daleks: Invasion Earth, 2150 A.D.* tanked at U.S. box offices. Dalekmania, it seemed, was less than the universal phenomenon that the producers had predicted. Instead of starring in a motion picture event based on "The Chase," *Doctor Who and the Daleks* lead actor Peter Cushing went on to have another brush with science fiction history: In 1977 he played Grand Moff Tarkin in *Star Wars*. It is for that landmark film, not for his twin portrayals of Doctor Who, that Cushing is most warmly remembered today in science fiction circles.

The second failed attempt to bring the Time Lord to the silver screen came nearly a decade later. When Tom Baker assumed the role of the Doctor from Jon Pertwee in the mid-'70s, he was accompanied by Ian Marter as UNIT doctor Harry Sullivan. Together with Elisabeth Sladen's widely loved Sarah Jane Smith, these two performers oversaw another era of incredible popularity. Amazingly, a series that was over a decade old had managed to bounce back into the spotlight. Even more rewardingly, all the brouhaha was not centered around a villain like the Daleks, but rather on Tom Baker's quirky, charismatic portrayal of the lead character. *Doctor Who*, as an entity separate from the accursed Daleks, was blooming again. Reflecting this new public acceptance, the Season 12 serial "The Ark In Space" was watched by a whopping 14 million viewers in Great Britain. This was the highest rating for a serial in *Doctor Who*'s history. Naturally, the notion of a new *Doctor Who* feature film began to hatch in the minds of the series stars even while Amicus Productions collapsed. Marter and Baker co-authored an original script featuring the fourth incarnation of the Doctor. This new project was called *Doctor Who Meets Scratchman*. Baker talked about his plans for the film in a 1975 issue of *Sci Fi Monthly*, a popular British periodical about science fiction television:

> There have been two *Doctor Who* films in the past, both rather poor... There are many dangers in transporting a television series onto the big screen...a lot of things that you could get away with on the small screen wouldn't wash in the cinema. There will be quite a bit of special effects work, but I think that, like the TV series, the film's success will depend on the Doctor's character.[1]

Production moved forward on *Doctor Who Meets Scratchman* and veteran horror actor Vincent Price was rumored to have been cast as the villainous "Scratchman." Unfortunately, Marter's stint as a regular on the *Doctor Who* series ended after one season, although he returned as a guest star twice in Season 13 ("The Terror of the Zygons" and "The Android Invasion"). For undisclosed reasons, the film Marter and Baker scripted was never produced, though the two actors remained friends for many years. Later in the 1980s, Marter wrote several novelizations of *Doctor Who* television adventures, but the script for *Doctor Who Meets Scratchman* has never been novelized. Sadly, Marter died of a diabetes-induced heart attack in 1986 and his pet project has never seen the light of day.

In the early 1980s, talk of a *Doctor Who* movie began anew when the first batch of Tom Baker–era stories met with success in syndication all across the United States. When Baker left the role, interested Hollywood producers tucked tail and ran, quite understandably. Baker's personal popularity was the invigorating factor that had spawned all the renewed interest in *Doctor Who*. Though Peter Davison would soon find his niche on the series, to Americans he was to Tom Baker what Roger Moore was to Sean Connery...a decent replacement perhaps, but hardly the brilliant original.

It was not until 1988 that rumors started to fly fast and loose in fan circles about a new *Doctor Who* movie. *Starlog* #130 (May 1988) announced that *Starcrash* femme fatale Caroline Munro had already been cast as Cora, a Gallifreyan TARDIS engineer. In an interview with Steve Swires, Munro described the role this way:

> Cora won't be running about in tiny bikinis... She will be a strong, opinionated lady who won't stand for any nonsense. But she'll also have a vulnerable side, so the audience can feel sympathy for her.[2]

The role of the Doctor in the new film, however, was still up for grabs. The company that would be producing the movie, an outfit called Coast-to-Coast, had purchased the rights from BBC Worldwide and they were still looking for the right actor to fill the shoes of Hartnell, Troughton, Pertwee, Baker and the rest. During this time, producers Peter Litten and George Dugdale also went to *Doctor Who* fan conventions (with Caroline Munro in tow) to promote their new film, which they insisted was moving along well in pre-production.[3] Dugdale and Litten commissioned author Mark Ezra to write the screenplay of this new adventure which was titled simply *Doctor Who—The Movie*. The script was later rewritten by Johnny Byrne, the author of "Keeper of Traken," "Arc of Infinity" and "Warriors of the Deep." Names mentioned in connection to the role of the Time Lord included Colin Baker, Dudley Moore, Denholm Elliott, Alan Rickman, Richard O'Brien, John Cleese and Donald Sutherland. By 1989, Sylvester McCoy's name had also been added to that rapidly expanding list. At this time, rumors also began to surface which suggested the Doctor would be portrayed as an alcoholic or as a sex-obsessed womanizer. Adding to the confusion, Caroline Munro fell by the wayside by early 1990. This was a terrible shame because Munro is so well-loved by science fiction fans for her roles in *Star Crash* (1978), *The Spy Who Loved Me* (1977) and *The Golden Voyage of Sinbad* (1974), in which she starred with Tom Baker. It was also devastating because Munro had asserted to Steve Swires, again in *Starlog* #130, that she believed her role in the *Doctor Who* film would be the pinnacle of her acting career.

Despite contradictory rumors, reports of new actors playing the Doctor, and multiple rewrites, there was a greater impetus than ever to produce a film since *Doctor Who* had been put on hiatus by the BBC in 1989, apparently so the series could be produced independently. Of course, the series did not continue. Now fans were not getting their *Doctor Who* on the television set *or* on the movie screen. Separately from this unofficial series cancellation, the *Doctor Who* movie continued to stall. Johnny Byrne rewrote his screenplay several times and it was known variously as *Doctor Who—Time Lord*, and *Doctor Who—The Last of the Time Lords*.[4] Ironically, Byrne had written an episode of *Space: 1999* called "Last of the Psychons." He apparently carried the title idea to his work on *Doctor Who*.

The thirtieth anniversary of *Doctor Who* came and went in 1993 and there was no *Doctor Who* motion picture and no significant television celebration or revival. It was a dismal year for *Doctor Who* fans. In 1994, it looked like things might improve. Science fiction legend Leonard Nimoy became interested in directing a *Doctor Who* feature film. Denny Martin Flinn, who had co-written *Star Trek VI: The Undiscovered Country* with Nicholas Meyer, wrote a script for a big-budget science fiction adventure movie to be called *Dr. Who*. In conjunction with Coast-to-Coast Films, now known as Lumiere Pictures, plans went ahead for a new film starring *Remington Steele* lead Pierce Brosnan as the Doctor. This was shortly before Brosnan inherited the mantle of another pop culture icon, James Bond, and began principal photography on *Goldeneye* (1995). Nimoy's and Flinn's version, like many before it, failed to materialize. This time the cause was a legal one. The motion picture rights for *Doctor Who* reverted to the BBC in 1994 according to the terms of the original contract. This reversion of rights is currently the focus of a lawsuit brought by Lumiere Pictures against the BBC.

Pierce Brosnan, who played *Remington Steele* and Agent 007 in *Goldeneye* (1995) and *Tomorrow Never Dies* (1997), was Denny Martin Flinn's choice to play the Time Lord in a Lumiere Pictures *Doctor Who* feature film that was never made.

Instead of a feature film, a 1996 *Doctor Who* telemovie for the Fox Network and BBC starring Paul McGann was finally produced. It aired in America in May 1996. *Doctor Who* on the big screen was, sadly, something that would not be seen any time soon. All this wrangling certainly makes one appreciate the early if flawed efforts of AARU Productions all the more. At least Milton Subotsky and Max J. Rosenberg managed to make to make two pictures instead of promising fans the universe and giving them only dashed hopes.

The non-fiction work *The Nth Doctor* (1997) by *Doctor Who* expert Jean-Marc Lofficier details the failed *Doctor Who* movie attempts from 1987 to 1996. This excellent work is packed with outlines of rejected scripts and in-depth interviews with authors Johnny Byrne, Denny Martin Flinn and the like. It also "retconns" the events in these scripts to fit within the *Doctor Who* television series continuity. This author highly recommends *The Nth Doctor* to any *Doctor Who* fan or scholar looking to learn more about the last decade's worth of problems in transforming the Time Lord television series into a movie franchise.

Television Shows

K-9 and Company: A Girl's Best Friend Written by Terence Dudley; Directed by John Black; Produced by John Nathan-Turner; Airdate: December 28, 1981

When fans protested the dismissal of K-9 from *Doctor Who* in Season 18, producer John Nathan-Turner realized that perhaps the mothballing of the cybernetic pub was premature. He set about immediately to rectify the situation by producing a pilot for a new series to be entitled *K-9 and Company*. Elisabeth Sladen returned to the Whoniverse after approximately five years pursuing other roles to once again portray journalist Sarah Jane Smith. John Leeson was also rehired to voice the beloved robot pet. The 50-minute program aired on December 28, 1981, but it was not a success in the ratings. The program was rerun once on the BBC in 1982 and sold to hundreds of PBS stations in the United States shortly thereafter. It has thus been seen by many *Doctor Who* fans. The spin-off is now available on videocassette. The adventure was novelized by teleplay writer Terence Dudley for Target Books in 1987.

CREDITS

CAST: Sarah Jane Smith (Elisabeth Sladen); K-9 (John Leeson); Brendan Richards (Ian Sears); George Tracey (Colin Jeavons); Commander Pollock (Bill Fraser); Peter Tracey (Sean Chapman); Lavinia (Mary Wimbush); Baker (Linda Polan); Howard Baker (Neville Barber;) Sgt. Wilson (Nigel Gregory); Tobias (John Quarmby); Lilly Gregson (Gillian Martell); Carter (Stephen Oxley)

CREW: Producer: John Nathan-Turner; Set Designer Nigel Jones; Special Effects Design: Mat Irvine; Music: Peter Howell

SYNOPSIS: Many years after her journeys with the Doctor, successful journalist Sarah Jane Smith returns to the British Isles. Upon her arrival at the small town of Morton Harwood and the home of her Aunt Lavinia, Sarah discovers that the Time Lord has sent her a very interesting gift. She pries open a large crate and out rolls a charming, cybernetic dog, K-9 Mark III! The dog immediately identifies the reporter as its new "mistress."

K-9 has arrived just in time to help Sarah solve a mystery in the superstitious village. Aunt Lavinia apparently believed that there was an evil cult in Morton Harwood. This assertion is buttressed by the fact that Lavinia has disappeared without a trace. Has she departed Harwood for America, and if so, why? With the help of crusty old Commander Pollock, Lavinia's business partner, Sarah and K-9 discover the activity of a local Druidic cult. The cult has sinister plans for Brendan, Lavinia's young ward. Sarah and K-9 must protect the young man from becoming a sacrifice to the pagan Goddess Hecate.

***Doctor Who* (1996) (a.k.a. "The Enemy Within")** Written by Matthew Jacobs; Directed by Geoffrey Sax; Designed by Richard Hodulin & Fran Rosati; Airdate: May 14, 1996

It took many years to get launched, but a new *Doctor Who* television movie was finally produced in 1996. Philip Segal, a lifelong *Doctor Who* fan, first approached the BBC about obtaining the rights to the television series as early as 1993, the thirtieth anniversary of *Who*. Although Steven Spielberg and Amblin Entertainment were originally named in connection with Segal's bid to produce a new television movie with the BBC, ultimately it was Universal who backed the project.

The telefilm *Doctor Who*, known in fan circles as "The Enemy Within," features the last performance by Sylvester McCoy as the seventh incarnation of the Doctor. As the film opens, there is no sign or mention of previous companion Ace (actress Sophie Aldred). McCoy appears only in the first ten minutes of the film before regenerating into the new lead, Paul McGann (*Withnail and I*, *Alien*[3]). In some senses, the handing of the baton from McCoy to McGann makes this two-hour project perhaps "too" official. With McCoy's diminutive Doctor in evidence, it is obvious that "The Enemy Within" must be construed as a legitimate continuation of the events of the long-running BBC series. Any new series or film, therefore, will have to account for the eighth incarnation of the Doctor. If Paul McGann is unavailable or unwilling to resume his role as the Doctor, there will be problems. Will there be another regeneration, after only one adventure for the eighth Doctor? Will the McGann incarnation simply be ignored? Recast? Or will McCoy be hired again as the seventh Doctor, this time only to regenerate into yet another new lead actor? "The Enemy Within" has actually put the *Doctor Who* galaxy in more disarray than the initial series cancellation in 1989.

Although Paul McGann received high praise from fans for his portrayal of the Time Lord, the film itself was only a modest success with aficionados. Most fans did not approve of the kiss between the Doctor and new companion Grace, or the off-handed revelation that the Doctor may have some human ancestry. Equally disturbing was the fact that the new Doctor had a tendency to reveal to his friends the events of their future. This was a character trait never seen in the other incarnations, and directly in contrast with the "don't rewrite history" dictates of Hartnell. Fans also found the two-hour movie to be perhaps too dark. Above all other complaints, this one must have been the most galling to producer Philip Segal since in the late 1980s many fans had complained that the series had become too comical. Some *Doctor Who* fans, it seems, can rival Trekkies in their nitpicking ways.

Outside *Doctor Who* fandom, the McGann feature did surprisingly well. It attracted nine million viewers when it aired in Great Britain, a million more watchers than in America! With dismal ratings in the United States, both Fox and Universal have strayed away from producing a new series. *Doctor Who* is as dead in the water in 1996 as it was in 1989.

To date, the *Doctor Who* television movie has not been rerun on television nor released on videocassette.

Credits

CAST: The Doctor (Paul McGann); The Doctor (Sylvester McCoy); The Master (Eric Roberts); Dr. Grace Holloway (Daphne Ashbrook); Chang Lee (Yee Jee Tso); The Old Master (Gordon Tipple); Prof. Wagg (David Hurtubise); Gareth (Jeremy Badick); Salinger (John Novak); Miranda (Eliza Roberts); Curtis (Dolores Drake); Wheeler (Catherine Lough); Dr. Swift (Michael David Simms); Pete (William Sasson); Ted (Joel Wirkunen); TV Anchor (Mi-Jung Lee); TV Anchor (Joanna Piros); Cop (Bill Croft); Gangsters (Darryl Avon, Byron Lawson, Johnn Mam, Paul Wu)

CREW: Producers: Alex Beaton, Matthew Jacobs, Philip Seagal, Peter Ware, Jo Wright; Editor: Patrick Lusser, Daria Ellerman; Music: Ron Grainer, John Debney, Louis Febre, John Sponsler; Cinematography: Glen MacPherson; Costume Design: Jori Woodman; Visual Effects: Eric Alba, Tony Dow, Mariush Kushniruk, Northwest Imaging & FX; Art Director: Bridget McGuire; Special Effects Designer: Gary Paller; Assistant Directors: Patrick Leung, David Klohn; Casting: Trish Robinson, James Forsyth, Beth Ayer, John Hubbard; Set Decorator: Cynthia Lewis; Script Supervisor: Jessica Clothier; Camera Operators: George Fox, Randall Platt, Nick Watson; Makeup: Joann Fowler; Hairstyles: Julie McHaffie; Sound: Jacqueline Christianini, Gordon W. Anderson; Stunt Coordinators: Fred Ferron, J. Manaro; Stunt Double for the Doctor: Charles Andre; Stunt Double for Grace: Dawn Stouffer; Stunt Double for Chang Lee: Micheal Crest Jo

SYNOPSIS: The seventh incarnation of the Doctor is on an urgent mission to deliver the remains of the renegade called the Master to Gallifrey and the Time Lord High Council. The TARDIS malfunctions and the TARDIS crashlands in San Francisco. It is the last night of 1999.

The Master rejuvenates and escapes from the Doctor's time-space capsule. The Doctor ventures out in the American city to pursue the Master, but he is shot by terrestrial gang members. He is taken to emergency surgery at a metropolitan hospital and operated on by beautiful cardiologist Grace Holloway. She is shocked to discover that her patient has two hearts! She is even more shocked when he regenerates into a brand new, younger form. The Doctor and Grace become friends, and not a moment too soon. The Master has asserted his hypnotic influence over a San Franciscan named Chang Lee. With Lee's help, the Master plans to use the TARDIS to seize the Doctor's remaining regenerations. Unfortunately, by accessing the Eye of Harmony inside the magnificent TARDIS, the Master also threatens to destroy the stability of Earth himself.

The Doctor and Dr. Holloway must face the Master before the start of the new millennium, or all human life on Earth could be destroyed. At the same time, Holloway and the Doctor begin to explore a relationship that is perhaps more than platonic.

Radio Adaptations

In America, *Star Wars* fans were thrilled when National Public Radio produced a detailed, multi-part radio production of their favorite outer space saga in the early '80s. However, the George Lucas epic was not the first sci-fi legend to be translated from a visual medium to radio. *Doctor Who* had already been down that route as far back as 1976 when Tom Baker and Elisabeth Sladen reprised their roles as the Doctor and Sarah in a 20-minute production called "The Time Machine." Written by Bernard Venables, it aired under the aegis of the Radio 4 educational program entitled "Exploration Earth."

The ultimate intention of "The Time Machine" was similar to Sydney Newman's original purpose in creating the series back in the '60s: to illuminate the mysteries of science for curious youngsters. The story was filled with geographical details about the prehistoric days of planet Earth. The *Doctor Who* aspect of the adventure was incorporated because it was felt that all the facts and educational information would go down better if there was also a fun, fantastical element to the show. In addition, *Doctor Who* was riding high on the new popularity of Baker's fourth incarnation. Anything featuring *Doctor Who* during those golden days of the mid-'70s was guaranteed a huge audience.

"The Time Machine" involved the Doctor's attempts to battle the evil Megron in Earth's distant past. Megron hoped to prevent the birth of the human race and thereby cause anarchy to reign throughout Earth's long history. Sarah and the Doctor managed to defeat Megron and save the Earth from the alien plot.

"The Time Machine" was a very short adventure buttressed by the considerable vocal talents of Sladen and Baker. It was not the ultimate *Doctor Who* radio adventure, but it certainly laid the groundwork for further forays into the medium. A second drama called "Slipback" reached the British airwaves on BBC Radio 4 almost ten years later, in the summer of 1985. By then, it was not necessary to tie the *Doctor Who* format into an ongoing educational program time slot, and as a result the serial's running time was not nearly as short. The 66-minute program was written by *Doctor Who* story editor Eric Saward and it starred Colin Baker, Nicola Bryant and television guest star Valentine Dyall (the Black Guardian in the episodes "Mawdryn Undead," "Terminus" and "Enlightenment"). "Slipback" was aired during the series' 18-month hiatus, so this audio adventure was like manna from heaven for fans. It was a substitute for the missing Season 23.

"Slipback's" narrative concerned a deadly temporal event called a time eclipse. The TARDIS landed unexpectedly on a space probe called the Vipod Mor under command of the strange Capt. Slarn. Peri and the Doctor encountered not only a schizoid ship's computer, but an illicit attempt to control time travel. The Doctor was actually brought to the Vipod Mor so his knowledge of time travel could be absorbed by a hidden enemy.

Fan response to this adventure was unusually positive, although there were purists who felt it strayed too far into comedic terrain. Others felt it was impossible to fit "Slipback" into *Doctor Who* series continuity because it conflicted with some events seen in "Terminus" and "The Two Doctors." To this author's knowledge, there has not yet been any retconning of "Slipback" to fit it squarely into *Doctor Who* history, even though it is a solid addition to the short era of sixth Doctor Colin Baker.

The script for "Slipback" was later novelized by Eric Saward. The radio program itself has never been broadcast in the United States but it has become available to fans on this side of the Atlantic via a BBC Enterprises release. "Slipback" is featured on a two-tape set with the 1977 record album "Genesis of the Daleks," which featured narration from Tom Baker.

It was not until 1993, when *Doctor Who* fans hit another dry spell following the cancellation of the series, that another radio production was produced. "The Paradise of Death" was a five-segment serial written by former *Who* producer and director Barry Letts. "The Paradise of Death" was set in the era of the third Doctor, and the events of the adventure took place between those dramatized in "The Time Warrior" and "Invasion of the Dinosaurs." Pertwee, Sladen and Courtney all resumed their 1970s series roles for the drama, which was set at Spaceworld Theme Park. Recalling *Westworld* and *Jurassic Park*, "The Paradise of Death" revealed that were devious goings-on at a new, technologically unprecedented amusement park. In this case, aliens were controlling Spaceworld in a scheme to gain a foothold on the entire planet. It was only after many trials and cliffhangers, as well as the introduction of a comedic character named Jeremy Fitzoliver, that the Doctor was able to foil the plans of the villainous Tragen. Letts novelized his adventure for Virgin Books in 1994.

"The Paradise of Death" was amazingly well-done and it captured the spirit of the Jon Pertwee era vividly. It was so popular that Barry Letts penned another radio drama in 1996, "The Ghost of N-Space." It too featured Pertwee's third Doctor, but it was an outer space rather than earthbound adventure. "The Ghost of N-Space" marked the final performance by Pertwee as the Time Lord.

There have been persistent rumblings since "The Ghost of N-Space" that another radio adventure is forthcoming from Eric Saward. Rumor has it that this adventure would star Tom Baker's fourth incarnation and feature the origins of the villainous Cybermen. Baker has gone on record stating he would perform the drama only if it broke new ground for his character and did not merely rehash past glories. As of this writing, the adventure has not yet been produced.

Stage Adaptations

Although radio personality Howard Stern has anointed himself the King of All Media, it is clear that *Doctor Who* has an equal right to wear that particular crown. There is seemingly no limit to the number of media *Doctor Who* has conquered in its 36-year history. The series has been seen on television, translated to film, transcribed in print (comic books and novels), produced on radio and even reproduced on stage. The last accomplishment is perhaps the greatest of all when one considers the somewhat limited nature of theatrical productions. Can anyone seriously imagine a live, stage version of *Battlestar Galactica*, *Babylon 5* or *Star Trek*? Since each of those programs depends so heavily on optical special effects, they would not translate well or believably to this venue. On the other hand, the purview of *Doctor Who* has always been literate storytelling, not effects. In that regard, *Doctor Who* is perfect for the theater.

The first stage production concerning the universe of *Doctor Who* premiered at the Wyndham Theater in London in 1965[5]. The production was directed by Gillian Howell and written by two *Doctor Who* legends: Terry Nation and original story editor David Whitaker. Ironically, the play did not feature even a token appearance by the Doctor. Instead, the production revolved around the nefarious Daleks. (The year 1965 was the height of Dalekmania.) The story concerned the journey of the starship *Starfinder* and its encounter with the Daleks on Skaro. As in "The Dead Planet," the Thals were involved in the goings-on. The plot focused on the attempts of a sinister Earthman to revive the Daleks in the year 2179. By that time, the script revealed, the Daleks had been dead for almost half a century. Troughton's first serial "The Power of the Daleks" would repeat many elements of this plot, specifically the revival of dormant Daleks. Also of interest to continuity buffs was the fact that the story was set in 2179. If the Daleks had been dead for half a century, that would put the events of "The Daleks" in 2129. That date, however, conflicts with evidence given in "The Dalek Invasion of Earth." In that Terry Nation serial, William Hartnell recalled the adventure in "The Daleks" as taking place "millions of years" in the future.

Doctor Who's second theatrical venture also featured the Daleks. This time, however, the Doctor was also around. "Doctor Who and the Daleks in Seven Keys to Doomsday" appeared on the scene in December 1974 and ran well into Spring of 1975. Trevor Martin played the fourth incarnation of the Doctor and he was accompanied by two new companions: Jenny and Jimmy. Jenny was played by Wendy Padbury, the actress who had dramatized the role of young Zoe Herriott in the 1969 season of *Doctor Who*. Interestingly, this play was staged before Tom Baker had taken over the role of the Doctor in "Robot," so Trevor Martin has the distinction of being the only other actor besides Tom Baker to have played an "original" version of the fourth incarnation of the Time Lord.

Directed by Mick Hughes and written by frequent *Who* scribe Terrance Dicks, "Doctor Who and the Daleks in Seven Keys to Doomsday" reused the quest concept, a plot device visited in *Doctor Who*'s first season adventure "The Keys of Marinus" by Nation and later seen again in Season 16's "The Key to Time Saga." In the play, the Doctor, Jenny and Jimmy sought to collect the all-important "Seven Crystals of All Power." To collect these valuable stones, they had to fight creatures called Clawrentulars as well as the inevitable Daleks. At the end of the story, the Doctor booby-trapped the seven segments of the Crystal and then turned them over to the Daleks. Of course, the Daleks and the crystals were then destroyed. Much of the adventure throughout the play occurred on a planet called Karn; Dicks later set the Season 13 serial "The Brain of Morbius" on the planet Karn. Although the name was the same, the inhabitants of the world had changed by the latter serial.

The third play to be derived from *Doctor Who* is perhaps only peripherally related to the series. Actor Richard Franklin, who portrayed UNIT officer Yates in the Pertwee era, co-wrote, directed and produced a 1984 play called "Recall UNIT" for the Edinburgh Theater Festival. The work was almost exclusively comedic, but it nonetheless highlighted the talents of John Levene (Sgt. Benton) as well as voiceovers by Nicholas Courtney as Brigadier Lethbridge-Stewart. As in all *Doctor Who* stage productions, the Daleks also made an appearance.

The final *Doctor Who* foray into the world of staged drama is perhaps the grandest of all. "Doctor Who — The Ultimate Adventure" first appeared in March 1989, just months before *Doctor Who*'s last season began on the BBC. "The Ultimate Adventure" had a successful run before it closed in August of the same year. The adventure was penned by Terrance Dicks and directed by Carole Todd. Jon Pertwee played the Doctor, making him the first television actor and "legitimate" Doctor to make the jump from video to stage. The story concerned the Doctor's investigation of mysterious political unrest among the superpowers of Earth. A dark force had begun kidnapping American officials in an attempt to provoke an all-out war. The culprits are revealed by play's end to be the Cybermen and, again, the Daleks.

With some minimal rewriting to accommodate his more flamboyant incarnation, Colin Baker assumed the role of the Doctor midway through the play's run. The play is remembered best for another piece of performer trivia. For one performance, David Banks played the Doctor when Jon Pertwee was too ill to go on. Banks had played a Cyberleader in many episodes of *Doctor Who*, including "Earthshock," "The Five Doctors" and "Silver Nemesis." This makes the list of actors to play the Doctor even longer. By 1997, the Time Lord had been depicted by Hartnell, Cushing, Troughton, Pertwee, Trevor Martin, Tom Baker, Davison, Richard Hurndall (in "The Five Doctors"), Colin Baker, Michael Jayston (in "The Trial of the Time Lord"), McCoy, David Banks and McGann.

Videos

Doctor Who has exploded onto the home video market with astonishing success. Beyond the release of over 85 *Doctor Who* serials, the BBC has also unveiled a bevy of documentary tapes which reveal much about *Doctor Who*'s long and complex history. "The Hartnell Years" is a look at the bygone era of the first Doctor and it features footage from lost serials such as "The Crusades" and "The Celestial Toymaker." "The Troughton Years" is similarly detailed and it highlights surviving sequences from "The Abominable Snowmen" and "The Enemy of the World."

"The Jon Pertwee Years" remembers the age of the third Doctor with footage from "Mind of Evil," "Invasion of the Dinosaurs" and "Frontier in Space." Other tapes in this informative series include "The Tom Baker Years" and "The Colin Baker Years."

Beloved *Doctor Who* villains have also found a place in the home video spotlight. "Daleks — The Early Years" highlights two full episodes from the lost classic

"The Dalek Masterplan" starring Hartnell and Peter Purves, as well as a half-hour from "The Evil of the Daleks" starring Troughton and Frazer Hines. The tape is hosted by Peter Davison and also features clips from *Daleks: Invasion Earth*, outtakes from "The Five Doctors" and footage from "The Dalek Masterplan" cut to the song "I'm Going to Spend My Christmas with a Dalek." John Scott Martin, Raymond Cusick and Roy Skelton are interviewed.

"Cybermen — The Early Years" is similarly styled. Host Colin Baker reveals clips from the destroyed serial "The Tenth Planet" as well as two episodes each from the serials "The Moonbase" and "The Wheel in Space." "Tomb of the Cybermen" director Morris Barry, Roy Skelton and Wendy "Zoe" Padbury are interviewed.

The thirtieth anniversary special "More Than 30 Years in the TARDIS" is also currently available on videotape and it too reveals behind-the-scenes information about *Doctor Who*. Each of these documentaries can be purchased in the United States.

Colin Baker's most dramatic *Doctor Who* episode, "Vengeance on Varos," is among the many episodes released in America by BBC/CBS-Fox Home Video.

Outside these official BBC productions, there are many other exciting *Doctor Who* videos with which the intrepid fan can expand the boundaries of his or her horizons. Republic and Lumiere pictures have released *Doctor Who and the Daleks* (1965) and its sequel *Daleks: Invasion Earth* (1966) for those in the mood to revisit the era of Dalekmania. Other, unofficial documentaries include "I Was a Doctor Who Monster," a behind-the-scenes video presented by host Sylvester McCoy, and "The Doctors — 30 Years of Time Travel and Beyond," a documentary released by Mastervision which shows home movies made on the sets of "The Smugglers" and "The Abominable Snowmen." Reeltime Corporation has a fascinating group of documentaries in a series called "The Myth Makers." In each tape, a *Doctor Who* celebrity is profiled by Nicholas Briggs. The series has thus far profiled Sylvester McCoy, Caroline John, Louise Jameson, Colin Baker, Anneke Willis and dozens more. The "Myth Maker" tapes cover the full span of topics relating to these actors, not just their experiences on *Doctor Who*. It is an interesting collection of documentaries about actors whom *Doctor Who* fans have loved for over 30 years.

"The Trial of the Time Lord" saga was released on videotape in 1993 in a boxed set that looked like the Doctor's TARDIS.

In 1988, Reeltime also produced a 30-minute direct-to-video product entitled "War Time." Starring John Levene (Sgt. Benton), this was a fictional adventure about the UNIT officer and the tumultuous past which haunts him. Written by Andy Lane and Helen Stirling and directed by Keith Barnfather, "Wartime" also features Michael Wisher ("Davros") and interviewer Nicholas Briggs in supporting roles. Of even greater interest is Bill Baggs' epic video series *The Stranger*.

Who Is *The Stranger*?

In 1991, an enterprising individual named Bill Baggs saw a burgeoning new market in the world of direct-to-video films and he seized the opportunity to make his personal dreams a reality. An aspiring filmmaker and lifelong *Doctor Who* fan, the ambitious Baggs had watched with sympathy as his fellow *Who* aficionados suffered from the lack of new television *Who*. The fans had been in dire straits since the cancellation of the series in 1989, and they desperately wanted new *Doctor Who* serials. Even the high-quality "new adventures" published by Virgin Books could not appease that appetite. Baggs decided that he would step up to the plate himself and produce brand new *Doctor Who* adventures. He would then sell these new stories direct to the video market. Besides fulfilling fan desires and making a profit, this formula would permit Baggs to direct and produce films, his lifelong fantasy! It was a perfect plan in all respects.

Unfortunately, Baggs soon found that the BBC was satisfied with the status quo. The corporation was making a tidy profit merely by releasing old *Doctor Who* serials on videotape. Hence there was no need to produce any new, expensive drama. Not to be dissuaded, Baggs decided that his plan was still a sound one. He raised the money for the first film and came up with a new concept which would not use BBC–owned, copyrighted *Doctor Who* characters and concepts. Yet the final product would be similar enough to the adventures of the Time Lord that it would still appeal to starving *Doctor Who* fans. Thus was born the BBV production called *The Stranger*.

Writer Christian Darkin soon wrote the premiere installment of the new direct-to-video series called *The Stranger and Miss Brown*. "Summoned by Shadows" concerned a world-weary time traveler's epic journey across the wasteland of a distant world. Together with his companion Ms. Brown, the Stranger battled an evil, soul-stealing clown before the story ended in a thunderclap of action and revelations. "Summoned by Shadows" starred Colin Baker, the sixth incarnation of *Doctor Who*, and Nicola Bryant, the actress who had once been Perpigillium Brown. The two performers played subdued variations of the popular characters they had created on *Doctor Who* in the mid-'80s. Although Bryant was called "Miss Brown," she was never identified specifically as Peri. Nor was the enigmatic "Stranger" ever called "the Doctor" or highlighted as a Time Lord. The similarities to canon characters were nonetheless obvious to *Doctor Who* fans looking for similarities. It was as if the aborted era of the sixth Doctor had suddenly, finally been given the opportunity to conclude in an honorable, thoughtful manner. For the most part, *Doctor Who* fans were thrilled.

"Summoned by Shadows" was successful enough to warrant a video sequel called "More Than a Messiah" (1992). Sophie Aldred, who portrayed the beloved companion Ace in the last two televised seasons of *Doctor Who*, joined Baker and Bryant on their second outing. In only the flimsiest of costumes, the gorgeous Aldred dramatized a character called simply "Girl." This time the story took place on Majus 17, a holiday planet terrorized by alien wildlife. Baggs again produced and directed the otherworldly adventure.

"More Than a Messiah" was a second success for Baggs as well as a critical success for the actors who participated in the project. Colin Baker in particular had never been so well-accepted by fans. It was clear that a new empire, one only tangentially related to *Doctor Who*, had been born.

Since 1992, "More Than a Messiah" has been followed up by numerous sequels in the *Stranger* series. The first was called "In Memory Alone," a February 1993 release. The Nicholas Briggs written story concerned a ghostly railway station and a woman who seemed to be eternally waiting for transport out of the otherworldly limbo. The next sequel was 1994's "The Terror Game." This adventure strayed greatly from *Doctor Who* archetypes and revealed that the Stranger was actually named Solomon. He was not a renegade Time Lord, but a terrorist caught in the war between the Protectorate and the Preceptors. At one point before the start of "Summoned by Shadows," he was captured by the Protectorate and forced to forget his identity. The *Stranger* series thus began to draw on the formats of other famous series such as *Blake's 7*, which also began with a brainwashed terrorist learning his identity, and *The Prisoner*.

"The Terror Game" was followed by "Breach of the Peace" (1994) and "Eye of the Beholder" (1995). The final installment of the series, appropriately called "The Final Mission," was also released in 1995 and it starred David Troughton ("Curse of Peladon") and Elisabeth Sladen, Sarah of Seasons 11 through 14. This adventure revealed even more about the Stranger's dark, non-corporeal past. Colin Baker had now played the Stranger longer than he had played the Doctor on the BBC!

As the direct-to-video *Stranger* series progressed into the mid-'90s, the characters truly evolved from mere *Doctor Who* knock-offs into nicely detailed, interesting personalities. Although "The Stranger and Miss Brown" had begun as an attempt to continue the adventures of a certain Time Lord called the Doctor, it became a unique science fiction vision on its own terms. Baggs' potential opportunity had become a reality and all those *Doctor Who* fans who had once cried over the demise of the sixth Doctor and his friend Peri had something new and exciting to satisfy them.

While simultaneously producing *The Stranger*, Bill Baggs and BBV Productions unveiled further productions. In 1993, *The Airzone Solution* was made. This non-*Stranger* story about a nefarious corporation and its ecologically dangerous plans starred Peter Davison, Sylvester McCoy, Colin Baker, Jon Pertwee and Nicola Bryant. Another *Who* spin-off series soon sprang from the mind of Bill Baggs, this one featuring Caroline John in her 1970-71 series role as Dr. Liz Shaw. The cast of the new direct-to-video series also includes Louise Jameson, Leela of Seasons 14 and 15. This time the action revolves around an organization called P.R.O.B.E. (Preternatural Research Bureau) and its investigation of the occult. Caroline John and Louise Jameson uncovered dark mysteries and supernatural happenstance in *The Devil of Winterbourne*, which guest-starred Peter Davison, and *Zero Imperative* (1994), with Colin Baker, Jon Pertwee and Sylvester McCoy. Both ventures were directed, as usual, by the intrepid Baggs.

Other fans have followed the example of Baggs and created *Doctor Who*–inspired adventures such as *Shakedown* (1995), which concerned a Sontaran invasion of a space yacht, and *Downtime* (1995), about the return of the Yeti. Again, actors from the original series reprised their roles from *Doctor Who*. Although not all of these productions are of the highest quality, they are made with love and commitment. By making their own spin-offs of *Doctor Who*, series fans have taken the future into their own hands. No longer content just to write fan stories or settle for reruns, the *Doctor Who* fans are a bold lot who will build the Time Lord's video future, one way or another.

Books

Adaptations of Television Scripts

Doctor Who's numerous adventures in the land of fiction began in the '60s. Dalekmania was sweeping Great Britain like wildfire in 1964, and so it was decided that three "test" *Doctor Who* books could gauge the appeal of the product in print. Published by Frederick Muller Ltd. in 1964, the first of these novels was *Doctor Who and the Daleks* by David Whitaker. Whitaker adopted an unusual stylistic stance and wrote the entire novel from the viewpoint of companion Ian Chesterton. The events of the story were presented in the first-person throughout, as if Ian were keeping a diary or sharing his impressions with another person. This is one of the only *Doctor Who* adaptations to use the first-person approach. Also of interest in the adaptation of "The Daleks" is Whitaker's creation of an Emperor Dalek in a transparent glass armor suit. No such Dalek had appeared in the television version "The Daleks," but an Emperor Dalek recurred in "Power of the Daleks" and "Remembrance of the Daleks." Whitaker also wrote *Doctor Who and the Crusaders*, an adaptation of a popular early historical serial. The final book in the first trilogy was *Doctor Who and the Zarbi*, Bill Strutton's adaptation of his own "The Web Planet."

These introductory adventures proved that there was a market for *Doctor Who* stories in print. Target Books picked up the license and began novelizing serials at a rapid pace in the early '70s.

The classic William Hartnell era episode "The Massacre" was novelized for Target Books by *Doctor Who* writer John Lucarotti.

One thing that sets the *Doctor Who* novelizations apart is that they are written by authors who worked on the series. The *Star Trek* log series was penned by James Blish and the *Space: 1999* adaptations by E.C. Tubb and John Rankine—respected authors all, but none were involved with those television series beyond their adaptation assignments. Penned by series experts, many of the *Doctor Who* novelizations showed unexpected insight and flair. The adventure "The Gunfighters" was written by Donald Cotton. It was not presented as a standard adaptation of the series, but as an adventure recounted by Doc Holliday on his deathbed. Similarly, Donald Cotton's "The Myth Makers" told of the Doctor's intervention in the Trojan War from Homer's perspective, replete with Homeric prose. "The Romans" was another funny Cotton adaptation, recounted in a collection of translated Latin extracts. Included in the novelization of "The Romans" was Nero's hysterical "Ode to Barbara," Letters from Legionary (Second Class) Ascaris and selections of Jottings from Nero's Scrapbook. It was a most entertaining, witty and unexpected manner in which to retell *Doctor Who* adventures.

In 1980, Tom Baker's fourth incarnation of the Doctor made quite a splash in the U.S. Accordingly, Pinnacle Books received special permission from W.H. Allen and & Co., Ltd. (the parent company of Target Books) to publish and sell *Doctor Who* novels in America. The books were designed with brand new covers and a new *Doctor Who* logo. At the start of each of the ten books released in the series was a funny, well-written introduction to the series by author and genre personality Harlan Ellison. These books also described the Doctor and his companions in brief paragraphs before the text proper of the adventure, giving American newcomers time to adjust to the presence of Jo Grant or the third Doctor, characters

In America, Pinnacle Books published a set of ten *Doctor Who* novelizations. "Genesis of the Daleks" was adapted by Terrance Dicks. Note the different *Doctor Who* logo on the cover. It was never used during the series.

they had never seen on television. The books in the Pinnacle *Doctor Who* series are *Doctor Who and the Day of the Daleks* by Terrance Dicks, *Doctor Who and the Doomsday Weapon* by Malcolm Hulke (based on "Colony in Space"), *Doctor Who and the Dinosaur Invasion* by Hulke (based on "Invasion of the Dinosaurs"), *Doctor Who and the Genesis of the Daleks* by Dicks, *Doctor Who and the Revenge of the Cybermen* by Dicks, *Doctor Who and the Loch Ness Monster* by Dicks (based on "Terror of the Zygons"), *Doctor Who and the Talons of Weng-Chiang* by Dicks, *Doctor Who and the Masque of Mandragora* by Philip Hinchcliffe, *Doctor Who and the Android Invasion* by Dicks and *Doctor Who and the Seeds of Doom* by Hinchcliffe. These adventures sold well in the United States, but Target would soon distribute their versions in America and Pinnacle had no place in the market.

By the end of *Doctor Who*'s run in 1989, almost all of the television serials had been adapted by Target Books with some notable exceptions. Terry Nation's Dalek stories "The Chase," "The Dalek Masterplan" and "Mission to the Unknown" were owned by the author, and he did not grant permission for novelizations to be written. Also held up by this restriction were the early Troughton stories "The Power of the Daleks" and "The Evil of the Daleks." Similarly, "Shada," "The Pirate Planet" and "City of Death" were owned by one-time series story editor Douglas Adams. He also refused Target permission to let someone write novelizations of his work, and he was presumably uninterested in doing it himself. Otherwise, the entire 26-year span of *Doctor Who* could be read by the avid fan. In the days before *Doctor Who*'s availability on videocassette, this was the only way to relive the early adventures.

In 1986, a second *Doctor Who* novel series was initiated by Target Books. This cycle was called "The Companions of Doctor Who." Within this progression were three adventures. The first was *Harry Sullivan's War* by Harry Sullivan himself, Ian Marter. The second was *Turlough and the Earthlink Dilemma* by *Blake's 7* fan and scholar Tony Attwood and with a foreword by actor Mark Strickson. The last in the companion series was Terence Dudley's adaptation of his teleplay for *K-9 and Company*. By the publication of this story, K-9 had already been the subject of several *Doctor Who* children's stories from Arrow Books. *K-9 and the Beast of Vega, K-9 and the Missing Planet, K-9 and the Time Trap* and *K-9 and the Zeta Rescue,* all by author Dave Martin, featured the new adventures of everyone's favorite mechanical puppy. Amazingly, no books were written in Target's "Companion" series that featured the Doctor's female companions, even though Susan Foreman's life on post–Dalek Earth would have made for excellent reading. Nyssa's adventures tending to the wounded on "Terminus" would also have been inspiring material for a novel, but no other authors thought so.

Also released by Target in the late '80s were a set of *Doctor Who* stories based on the unproduced Season 23. These were stories that were called off when the series was forced to go on hiatus by BBC executive Michael Grade. These serials featured Colin Baker's sixth incarnation of the Doctor and his companion Peri. Novels in this series are *The Nightmare Fair* by Graham Williams, *Mission to Magnus* by Philip Martin and *The Ultimate Evil* by Wally Daly.

By the early 1990s, Virgin Books had won the contract to produce further *Doctor Who* books. Amazingly, some of the restrictions concerning the early Dalek stories were lifted and *Who* fan and historian John Peel set about writing adaptations of "The Power of the Daleks" and "The Dalek Masterplan." These novels were nearly twice as long as the 125–145 page Target adaptations and they often strayed from the personification of the characters as seen on the television series. Still, they were serious and quite good. Peel recently graduated from the Whouniverse and penned the novelization of the movie *The Avengers* (1998).

In 1996, BBC Books released a novelization of the McGann telefilm called simply *Doctor Who: The Novel of the Film.* It was written by Gary Russell, and for some reason the cover art featured the *Doctor Who* logo from the Pertwee era. The book also carried the amusing tag-line "He's Back...and it's about time!"

New Fiction

Virgin Books forever won the hearts of *Doctor Who* fans by initiating a new series called "The New Adventures of Doctor Who" in 1991. Peter Darvill-Evans oversaw the project and netted the best *Doctor Who* writing talent available to give the new progression of adventures the authentic feel of the series. The first four books were released under the group title "Tymeworm" and each installment name was followed by an individual subtitle. The four adventures describe the Doctor's pursuit of the time travelling Goddess of Ishtar. He follows the evil creature from ancient Mesopotamia to Nazi Germany, to an encounter at the edge of known space, and finally to a final showdown inside his own psyche. *Timewrym: Genesis* was written by John Peel, *Timewyrm: Exodus* by Terrance Dicks, *Timewyrm: Apocalypse* by Nigel Robinson and *Timewyrm: Revelation* by Paul Cornell.

The second published serial in "The New Adventures," titled "Cat's Cradle," is a three-part saga about the implosion of the telepathic TARDIS. The Doctor and Ace find themselves in a huge alien city filled with evil mental projections. The fail-safe mechanism of the TARDIS assumes the projection of a cat and guides the two heroes safely through the dangers of the city to save the ship. To repair and replenish itself, however, the TARDIS must be allowed to travel to certain unusual planets throughout the galaxy. During these adventures, the Doctor and Ace have no choice but to go where the TARDIS leads them. The books in this series are *Cat's Cradle: Time's Crucible* by Marc Platt, the author of "Ghost Light," *Cat's Cradle: Warhead* by Andrew Cartmel, series story editor from 1987–89, and *Cat's Cradle: Witchmark* by Andrew Hunt.

Following the lengthy "Timewyrm" and "Cat's Cradle" epics, *Doctor Who*'s "New Adventures" shifted to single tales. *Nightshade* by the *Stranger* contributor Mark Gatiss saw the Doctor return to Earth in the 1960s and face an ancient evil in a story reminiscent of "The Awakening." *Love and War* by Paul Cornell introduced a new companion, archaeologist Bernice Summerfield, a character reportedly based on actress Emma Thompson. Ace and the Doctor have a falling-out in this book, and Ace leaves the Doctor's company. Thus, Ace is the first companion to meet the Doctor on television but leave him in a book! In later books it is learned that Ace has gone off to fight in the Great Dalek War.

There are dozens of books in this long-lasting "New Adventures" cycle including *Transit* by Ben Aaronovitch, author of "Remembrance of the Daleks," *The Highest Science* by Gareth Roberts, *The Pit* by Neil Penswick and *Deceit* by Darvill-Evans, which sees (surprise!) the return of a more rough and callous Ace to the *Doctor Who* adventures. Also in the "New Adventure" cycle are *Iceberg* by Cyber-Leader and one-time Doctor (on stage) David Banks, the Larry Niven–like epic *Lucifer Rising* by Andy Lane and Jim Mortimore, *Theatre of War* by Justin Richards, the voodoo-obsessed *White Darkness* by David McIntee, *Shadowmind* by Christopher Bulis and *Birthright* by Nigel Robinson. The Silurians return in *Blood Heat.*

Not surprisingly, familiar *Doctor Who* story elements and characters appear throughout all of the New Adventures, including the Land of Fiction in Steve Lyon's *Conundrum*; UNIT in *No Future* by Paul Cornell; Brian Hayle's Peladon, Alpha Centauri and Ice Warriors in *Legacy* by Gary Russell; and even Victorian England (the setting of "The Talons of Weng-Chiang") in *All-Consuming Fire* by Andy Lane. Other titles include *Tragedy Day, Just War, The Left Handed Hummingbird, Dimension Riders, Strange England, St. Anthony's Fire, Parasite, Warlock, Infinite Requiem, Human Nature, Original Sin, Sky Pirates, Zamper, Toy Soldiers, Head Games, The God Engine, Christmas on a Rational Planet, Return of the Living Dead, The Death of Art, Damaged Goods, Bad Therapy, So Vile a Sin, Lungbarrow* and *The Dying Days. Happy Endings*, the fiftieth "New Adventure" title, finds companion Benny being married inside Saul, the psychic church first encountered in *Timewrym: Revelations.* The story is a celebration that reunites many of the characters seen throughout the "New Adventures."

"The New Adventures" are for the most part competently written, thought-provoking adventures true to the spirit of late '80s *Doctor Who.* Since they primarily feature the seventh incarnation of the Time Lord, appreciation of the "New Adventures" is heightened if one likes Ace and Sylvester McCoy's diminutive

Doctor. If one does not enjoy these characters, stay away from the series. Since much time in these novels is spent, some might say wasted, on a character who has never even been seen on the series, Bernice "Benny" Summerfield, some purists may find "The New Adventures" hard to relate to. The *Doctor Who* "new" novels are frequently compared to the Pocket Books *Star Trek* line and they share many of the same strengths and faults. Characters do not always sound like themselves, writing style fluctuates and *deus ex machina* solutions rule the day. The best novels tend to be those written by old hands like Terrance Dicks. To this day, many fans fiercely debate whether the "New Adventures" should be considered "canon."

In 1994, Virgin Books introduced another line of *Doctor Who* books to supplant the "New Adventures." This time, Darvill-Evan's replacement editor Rebecca Levene decided the writers would not be limited to recounting the heretofore unknown adventures of the seventh Doctor, Ace and "Benny." Instead, scribes were free to feature any incarnation of the Doctor they wished. Accordingly, "The Missing Adventures" are frequently more interesting to read for those longtime *Doctor Who* fans who favor Tom Baker, Troughton, Pertwee, Davison, Colin Baker or Hartnell over McCoy. *Lords of the Storm* by David McIntee is a Sontaran adventure featuring Turlough and Davison's incarnation. *The Sands of Time* by Justin Richards is a sequel to "The Pyramids of Mars" with Tegan and the Davison Doctor again. *The Eye of the Giant* is by Christopher Bulis and it stars Mike Yates and the Pertwee incarnation of the Time Lord. *The Well-Mannered War* by Gareth Roberts features Tom Baker's Doctor, Lalla Ward's Romana and K-9. David McIntee's second "Missing Adventure," *The Dark Path,* stars Troughton's Doctor, Jamie and Victoria. Other titles in the series include *Millennial Rites*, which finds Colin Baker's sixth Doctor encountering the Great Intelligence and Anne Travers in 1999, *Invasion of the Cat People* with the second Doctor, Polly and Ben, *Sorcerer's Apprentice*, a Hartnell–era story featuring Susan, Ian and Barbara, and *System Shock*, a tale of CD-ROM revenge and a fiendish plot to corrupt the Internet in 1990s London. It features the fourth Doctor, Sarah and Harry Sullivan.

Many authors who contributed to "The New Adventures" returned for the "Missing Adventures," and so there are a variety of in-jokes and insider references to other adventures. This "homage" actually detracts from many stories. Tone is a problem too. It is hard to imagine the Hartnell or Troughton incarnations of the Doctor in '90s style sci-fi imaginings. Somehow the tone is not right. In 1997 it was announced that "The Missing Adventures" would end, and many in the publishing industry speculated that BBC Books would soon take back the rights to the series from Virgin Books and begin publishing their own line of *Doctor Who* adventures.

Nonfiction

The Doctor has thrived not only in new fictional adventures, but also in a wide array of nonfiction works. Not surprisingly, most of the authors who contributed "New Adventures" and "Missing Adventures" were also the force behind

In the early 1980s, several quiz books were written for Target Books by *Doctor Who* fan Nigel Robinson.

so many of the new nonfiction books. Perhaps the best place to start a review of "nonfiction" is not with these works, however, but with the landmark text *The Making of Doctor Who* by Malcolm Hulke and Terrance Dicks. Released in 1972 by Piccolo Books, this book was an exhaustive look behind the scenes of *Doctor Who*. Since it was written by former writers for the series, *The Making of Doctor Who* was especially valuable in describing how a BBC program was produced.

The next milestone came about in 1981. Jean-Marc Lofficier wrote *The Doctor Who Programme Guide, Volume I*, which featured capsule plot summaries of each serial from "An Unearthly Child" to "Logopolis." The second half of the work was completed almost a decade later, after *Doctor Who*'s cancellation. Lofficier's works are a critical starting place for any *Doctor Who* scholar; they note episode titles, novelization titles, authors and writers' credits. Since publishing these works, Lofficier has not been absent from the world of *Doctor Who*. He also wrote *Doctor Who: The Terrestrial Index* (1991) for Target Books. This work was important because of the chapter entitled "The History of Mankind According to *Doctor Who*." It is the author's exhaustive and inspirational attempt to retconn all the events of the *Doctor Who* universe into one taut, logical narrative. To Lofficier's credit, he makes everything fit together almost seamlessly...except the destruction of Atlantis! *The Terrestrial Index* also covers *Doctor Who* ancillary tie-ins such as games, novels, short stories and the like. In 1997, Lofficier published *The Nth Doctor*

(Virgin Books), a fascinating behind-the-scenes story about the *Doctor Who* film projects from 1987—1997 that were never made. This book reviews the scripts, assigns them Whovian-style titles, interviews figures such as scribes Johnny Byrne and Denny Martin Flinn, and notes how these scripts fit the flavor of the Whoniverse. It is a solid, well-written piece of research that delves into a hitherto unexplored realm of *Doctor Who*'s history.

Authors David J. Howe, Mark Stammers and Stephen Walker also found a niche detailing various *Doctor Who* time periods. They authored *The First Doctor Handbook*, *The Third Doctor Handbook*, *The Fourth Doctor Handbook*, *The Fifth Doctor Handbook* and *The Sixth Doctor Handbook*. Each work traces the evolution of an era, remembers important companions, charts television ratings and explores the background of individual stories. At the time of this writing, the duo were working on *The Second Doctor Handbook*. Howe, Stammers and Walker have also written *Doctor Who–The Sixties* and *Doctor Who–The Seventies*. Perhaps the most infamous work of Howe and Stammers, however, is *Doctor Who–The Companions*, a deluxe, oversized text which offers information on every companion from Ian and Barbara through Bernice Summerfield. This work is notorious because it features the nude photograph of Katy Manning (Jo Grant) draped across a Dalek. Howe has also penned *Timeframe–The 30th Anniversary Book and Illustrated History*.

Other nonfiction works include a 1983 release from W.H. Allen, *Doctor Who: A Celebration—Two Decades Through Time and Space*. Written by Peter Haining, this text features interviews with Verity Lambert, Terrance Dicks, Barry Letts and each of the first five actors to play the Doctor. There are chapters devoted to Gallifrey, the Master and K-9. Also included in Haining's work is a capsule behind-the-scenes blurb for each story from "An Unearthly Child" to "The King's Demons." On the biography side of nonfiction, there is Jessica Carney's work *Who's There? The Life and Career of William Hartnell*. This book is written from a special viewpoint since Carney is Hartnell's granddaughter. Sophie Aldred and Mike Trucker have also written an account of Aldred's days on the *Doctor Who* series, called *Ace in the Hole*.

If all of this is not enough for the avid *Doctor Who* reader, there is also *The Discontinuity Guide* by Paul Cornell, Martin Day and Keith Topping. Introduced by Terrance Dicks, this work painstakingly catalogues all of the goofs, bloopers and blunders throughout the 26 years *Doctor Who* appeared on television. For those in the mood to look rather than read, there is *The Doctor Who Art of Andrew Skilliter*, a beautiful book filled with fantastic landscapes, alien creatures and outer space vistas...all with a *Doctor Who* theme.

Role-Playing Games

Sometimes reading about *Doctor Who* history or discovering new printed adventures is simply not enough for the intrepid fan. Sometimes, one wants to jump

Ian Marsh and Peter Darvill-Evans' *Time Lord* role-playing game let the avid *Doctor Who* fan participate in new galactic adventures.

right into the TARDIS and join the Time Lord for an adventure in time and space. Accordingly, there are have been two different *Doctor Who* role-playing games available over the last ten years. The first was released by FASA in the mid-'80s. FASA had already created *Star Trek* and James Bond–oriented role playing games, so *Doctor Who* was a natural choice. In the mid-'80s, middle school and high school students in America were endlessly fascinated by "Dungeons and Dragons," "Top Secret" and the like, so the market for role-playing games boomed. The FASA *Doctor Who* starter package cost $15 in the United States in 1987 and came complete with three informational notebooks: "The Time Traveler's Handbook," "The TARDIS Operator's Manual" and "The Visitor's Guide to Gallifrey." Approximately a half-dozen adventure modules were released with the FASA Game.

The second *Doctor Who* role-playing game was created by Ian Marsh and "New Adventures" editor Peter Darvill-Evans in 1991. Called "Time Lord," this game manual (published by Virgin Books) provided the components for fans to create a *Doctor Who* role-playing game. The abilities of all seven incarnations of the Doctor, as well as all of his 29 companions, were included in the book with various ratings in typical role-playing categories such as Knowledge, Determination, Iron Constitution et al. Perhaps less traditional were categories such as Pseudoscience, Transmat, Hypnotism, Cryptanalysis and Musicianship. A section of "Time Lord" also featured information on the TARDIS control room, the dematerialization circuit and the like. The book came complete with one ready-made "Time Lord" adventure called "The Templar Throne."

"Time Lord" also made some rather fannish boasts about its legitimacy to "true" *Doctor Who* lore. The writers did not consider Kamelion or Katarina to be "legitimate" companions and thus these two were left from the game. The writers also notified their audience that the Brigadier Lethbridge-Stewart would only be referred to as The Brigadier Lethbridge Stewart (minus the hyphen) to conform with early *Doctor Who* stories. Even with this fetish for accuracy, "Time Lord" failed on the American market, probably because role-playing games had run out of steam by the 1990s.

Comics

In Great Britain in the 1960s, children found great enjoyment in reading comic books based on popular genre television series. Competing high-quality magazines featured strips of many television adventures such as *The Avengers*, *Supercar*, *Quatermass*, *Space: 1999* and *U.F.O.* Not surprisingly, *Doctor Who* has been a figure in British comic book lore for over 30 years. The mysterious Doctor appeared first in the November 1964 issue of the British mag *TV Comic*. *Doctor Who* was introduced as a black-and-white strip penned by a ten-year veteran in comic book art and former artist on the *Fireball XL-5* strip, Neville Main. Main was only allowed to use the likeness of Hartnell from the BBC series, so television companions Ian, Barbara and Susan were not seen in the adaptation. Instead, the Doctor's human grandchildren John and Gillian were presented in issue #674. They met their time-traveling grandfather and started a long journey in the TARDIS with him. Artist Bill Mevin began Year 2 on the *TV Comic* series, but was quickly superseded by artist John Canning. He drew the comic for five years, until the beginning of the Jon Pertwee era.

Not long after *TV Comic*'s *Doctor Who* comic began, rival *TV Century 21* unveiled "The Daleks" by Terry Nation and David Whitaker. Drawn by Richard Jennings, this comic exclusively featured the Daleks and their development on Skaro. Since the Daleks were not appearing in the *Doctor Who* strip, *TV Comic* introduced a Dalek knock-off race called "The Trods." In 1966, *TV Comic* acquired the rights to use the Daleks and the Trods were killed off. The comic officially became known as *Doctor Who and the Daleks*, and it starred the Patrick Troughton incarnation of the Doctor. After just 22 issues, the rights to use the Daleks were withdrawn by Nation and the comic strip returned to its original name, *Doctor Who*. With the absence of the Daleks, a new heavy was needed in the comic book and so *TV Comic* negotiated with Kit Pedler and Gerry Davis to use the Cybermen. Accordingly, the Cybermen (in their "Tenth Planet" garb) appeared in virtually every issue for over a year.

Also in 1966, an American company called Dell adapted the screenplay of AARU's *Doctor Who and the Daleks*. This was a special one-shot comic by Dick Giordano and Sal Trapani, designed to coincide with the release of the film in the States. Like the film that inspired it, the comic did not do particularly well on the market.

Back in England, some changes were made to *TV Comic*'s running *Doctor Who* series. Grandchildren John and Gillian were sent off to Galactic University and the Doctor went to Scotland to pick up Jamie McCrimmon, the first companion from the television series to be featured in the strip. By March 1969, Jamie had disappeared. After Issue #916, the Doctor was exiled to Earth following the events of "The War Games." Amazingly, the comic continued to use the Troughton likeness and it offered a few months of stories that found Troughton's Doctor living out his exile peaceably on Earth until he was abducted by Time Lords and forced to regenerate.

The first issue of Marvel's *Doctor Who* Classic Comics was published in 1992. It revisited the many comic book triumphs of the Time Lord since the 1960s.

In 1970, the Jon Pertwee era began both on television and in comics. In May 1970, Caroline John's Liz Shaw was introduced to the strip, only to disappear again by August. In February 1971, the *Doctor Who* comic strip moved to a new magazine called *Countdown*. The artists on the book were Harry Lindfield and Frank Langford. Shortly thereafter, *Countdown* became *TV Action in Countdown* and then *TV Action*. By 1974, *Doctor Who* was featured again in a comic magazine called *TV Comic*.

In 1979, Marvel Comics produced *Doctor Who Weekly* in the United Kingdom. With artwork by Dave Gibbons, this publication had a magazine style layout like Charlton's *Space: 1999* book or Marvel's own *Planet of the Apes* mag. Each issue featured stories about the series by fan Jeremy Bentham and episode synopses by Gordon Blows. When Tom Baker's incarnation of *Doctor Who* became popular in the United States, it was decided to export Marvel's *Doctor Who* comic to America as well. In the States, *Doctor Who—A Marvel Premiere* issue #57 premiered with Tom Baker stories; by 1984, *Doctor Who* had an official Marvel magazine in the states. Unfortunately, the magazine started to lose money in 1986 and was cancelled. At that point, the British version was frequently exported to the States.

Back in England, Peter Davison's Doctor had been featured for the first time in February 1982. The comic also introduced a character who would become quite popular with fans, Abslom Daak—Dalek Killer! So well-received was this character that he returned in some "New Adventure" novels in the early 1990s. By 1984, Colin Baker's Doctor was featured in the Marvel comic. In November 1987, Sylvester McCoy's became the star. Ace joined the cast of the comic book in 1990, following the cancellation of the series on BBC television.

In 1992, Marvel unveiled *Doctor Who Classic Comics*. This new book recycled material from the William Hartnell scripts of the 1960s all the way to the days of Sylvester McCoy. The comic was cancelled in 1994 after recycling a great deal of material and offering new articles.

PART V

THE *DOCTOR WHO* FAN MATRIX

Internet Sites

The Internet is a great new forum in which the adventurous *Doctor Who* fan can expound at length upon the television series, count the faults of the recent telemovie or review fan fiction...and then be ruthlessly shot down by other fans! In seriousness, if one can adjust to the fact that all responses on the Internet will not be as polite or as well considered as the message you just posted, the Internet is a vast resource. Essentially, *Doctor Who*'s presence on the World Wide Web falls into five categories. Each category is unique, and each one caters to a different crowd within fandom.

First, there are service- and merchandise-oriented sites where fans can purchase videotapes, T-shirts and other *Doctor Who* items. These are the sites where people can drop much money if they are so inclined. In the rapidly expanding commercial world of *Doctor Who*, there is as much memorabilia as there are traveling companions! Of special interest to that fan looking to spend some hard-earned cash is the *800 TREKKER* www site where not only *Doctor Who,* but *Star Trek*, *Star Wars*, *Mystery Science Theater 3000* and *The Stranger* merchandise is offered at affordable prices. The *Doctor Who* merchandise currently available consists of TARDIS key rings, trading card sets, videotape releases, novels, posters, ties and CDs like the Timelords' rock 'n' roll album *Doctorin' the Tardis.* There is even a blue five-foot-tall video shelf built to resemble the TARDIS. The price tag for that little treasure is over $200. Other Internet sites that fit into the "merchandise" category are *The Doctor Who Collectors' Source*, specializing in videotapes and novels, *The Who Shop* and *The Sci-Fi Network Website*. It should be carefully noted that in most cases a credit card number is required to complete a monetary deal at these sites, so *caveat emptor*! Just because a site is noted in this survey does not mean that this author endorses it.

The second category of *Doctor Who* Internet locations includes those sites devoted to the series as a whole. These pages offer episode guides, serial airdates, cast information and notable dates in *Doctor Who* history. Among these general information sites are *The Doctor Who Fan Network, The Doctor Who Program Guide* (compiled by Matthew Newton), *The Doctor Who Dynamic Ranking Web Page, The Exospace Page, Outpost Gallifrey, Doctor Who Background and Setting, Gonad-o-Vision Doctor Who Episode Guide, Doctor Who in Detail, The Braxiatel Collection* from Ian Truskett, *The Ultimate Guide to Doctor Who* and even the juicy *Dr. Who's Canonical List of Sluts*, which rates the sex appeal of the Doctor's various companions from 1963 to 1983[1]. There are more specialized information sites as well. There are obituary sites for legends such as Terry Nation and Jon Pertwee and *The Complete Episodes/Clips/Etc. List* by Andrew Cloninger, which has late-breaking information about rediscovered missing serials or pieces of *Doctor Who* film recovered by fans. Perhaps the best place for a newbie to begin a *Doctor Who* conversation is within America Online Services. In the sci-fi television section there is a folder devoted to *Doctor Who*. Within this forum there is a message board for each incarnation of the rascally Time Lord, from Hartnell to McGann. New boards about other topics, like the 1996 telemovie, the K-9 spin-off and the book *The Nth Doctor* also pop up frequently. For those willing to jump in head first, there are also *Doctor Who* chat rooms such as *Tardis Live!* and newsgroup forums such as rec.arts.drwho.

The third style of Internet site is one which is devoted lovingly and solely to one particular character or actor in the *Doctor Who* universe. Whether one is a fan of Mel Bush and Bonnie Langford or of Zoe Herriott and Wendy Padbury, it is safe to assume that somewhere on the information superhighway there is a *Who* page catering to that special interest. Titles of these sites include *Tegan's Worldwide Admirers, The Mel Bush Internet Fan Club Web Page, The Ben Jackson Page, Elisabeth Sladen Information Network* and *The Unofficial Peter Davison Worship Page* by Jennifer Wade. These sites post images of the actors and actresses, list their roles outside *Doctor Who* and discuss their popularity within the *Who* universe.

The fourth type of Internet location is perhaps the most interesting of all. These areas sport unauthorized *Doctor Who* fan fiction. Essentially, they are cyber-fanzines. Since fan tastes are wildly divergent, some of these sites are rather racy and sexually explicit. These fan sites include *The Doctor Who Fiction List, The Net Adventures of Doctor Who, Splink!*, Lori Grenci's adult *Warm Gallifreyen Nights* and *Don't Shoot the Pianist*, named after an episode in the serial "The Gunfighters." As is always the case with fan fiction, the stories in these fiction sites range from the exquisite to the excruciating. In this category also are role-playing and strategic gaming sites such as *The Doctor Who Role Playing Mailing List* and *The Doctor Who Role Playing Site.*

The fifth and last category of *Doctor Who* sites comprises those net pages where fans can download pictures from the series, musical and vocal excerpts from various episodes, or images from things related to all things *Doctor Who*. These sites include *K-9's Kennel, Doctor Who Pictures, The Doctor Who Image Archive, Doctor Who: The Key to Time* by Aussie Brigitte Jellinek[8] and *The Umpteenth Doctor's Picture Gallery* by Chance Chandler.

The Internet unites *Doctor Who* fans from all over the world, presents new adventures through fan fiction, enables devotees to buy memorabilia, and is a valuable resource for people wishing to learn more about the series. With all these uses, the Internet is more helpful than Matrix of the Time Lords, and less frequently inhabited by evil renegades from other galaxies as well. Although this is just a cursory survey of *Doctor Who* Internet sites, the helpful thing about so many pages is that they offer "links" to other locations of equal interest. It is safe to say that an intrepid Time Lord could devote more than one regeneration to exploring *Doctor Who* fan activity on the net.

Fan Clubs

Science fiction "fandom" is an interesting phenomenon of the latter half of the twentieth century. Who among us could have predicted in 1966 that thousands of people would be flocking to *Star Trek* conventions in 1998? Who could have foreseen that 20 years after its cancellation, *Space: 1999* fans would still be lobbying for the return of a series which, sadly, most people in America do not even remember? Or that *Battlestar Galactica*, a one-season wonder in 1978, would be experiencing a resurgence of popularity in the United States in the late 1990s with new toys, new models and new novels littering the marketplace? Why do people become "fans" of science fiction programming in the first place? What are the qualities of a certain television series or film series (as is the case with *Star Wars*) which manage to evoke so much loyalty and dedication in people?

Some have suggested the answer to that final question lies squarely with the great days of one's childhood and the concurrent, later-in-life nostalgia for those days. *Battlestar Galactica*, *Star Wars* and *Space: 1999* all represent a piece of 1970s American pop culture, and many fans today were children when they watched these series originally. The shows remind them of those bygone days of disco music, Apollo flights and *The Hardy Boys*. For adults, fandom is simply a commitment or connection to a production that a viewer fell in love with years ago. *Doctor Who* fans are thus obsessed with the continued production of a program that has raised many generations of children in Great Britain. In this sense, *Doctor Who* is not just a cult in England, it is a national institution, a tradition. It is perhaps not quite the same in the United States.

On this side of the Atlantic, *Doctor Who* is a "cult" show seen only by those people fortunate enough to catch the series in the late '70s in syndication, or later on PBS.

Like all science fiction fans, *Doctor Who* fans come in every shape and size. Some *Who* fans have even turned their love of the series into thriving careers. John Peel, an original organizer of the *Doctor Who* Appreciation Society in Great Britain in the 1970s, has become a top-selling novelist thanks to *Doctor Who*. Other founders of the club (Gary Russell, Gordon Blews, Jeremy Bentham and Keith Barnfather) have also turned a love of their favorite series into new books, magazine articles

Two Jon Pertwee era *Doctor Who* fanzines written by *Doctor Who* fans Stephen James Walker and Jeremy Bentham.

and other projects. And, of course, Bill Baggs and Nicholas Briggs have made their dreams come true, actually mingling with and directing *Doctor Who* performers on the sets of direct-to-video productions such as *The Stranger*, *The Devil of Winterbourne* and *The Airzone Solution*. In the '80s, aspiring writer Jean Airey took her love for *Star Trek* and *Doctor Who* and combined them in a 1985 New Media Books publication called *The Doctor and the Enterprise*. She also became a freelance interviewer for *Starlog* magazine and associated with the likes of stars Sylvester McCoy, Bonnie Langford and others. Airey's love for *Doctor Who* transmuted into a career! These *Doctor Who* fans could be considered a rather talented, committed bunch.

Fan activity regarding *Doctor Who* is not limited to writing novels and fanzines or producing videos such as *Downtime* and *Shakedown*. There are hundreds of *Doctor Who* fan sites on the Internet and dozens of *Doctor Who* fan clubs around the world. Prominent among these fan organizations are the *Doctor Who* Appreciation Society, the Prydonians of Prynceton, the Australasian *Doctor Who* Fan Club, the New Zealand *Doctor Who* Fan Club, the *Doctor Who* Fan Club of America, the *Doctor Who* Information Network of Canada, the John Levene Fan Club, the *Doctor Who* Fan Club of America, the High Council of Gallifrey, the Patrick Troughton Appreciation Society, American Fans of Jon Pertwee, the Friends of Tom Baker, Companions of *Doctor Who* and the Who Is Colin Baker Fan Club of America. Whew! Each *Doctor Who* club formed during the last 20 years has offered typical "fan" fare such as new stories, interviews with actors and newsletters such as "Lint from the Technicolor Wonder Cozzie," "The Time/Space Visualizer," "TARDIS," "The Troughton Recorder" and "The Pyrdonian Renegade."

Fan Jean Airey's *The Doctor and the Enterprise,* published by New Media Books in 1985, combined the universes of *Star Trek* and *Doctor Who* in one exciting adventure.

In America, *Doctor Who* fandom reached its peak perhaps in the mid to late 1980s. Circa 1985-86, *Doctor Who* stars were frequently invited to *Star Trek* conventions and many *Doctor Who* conventions were held all over the continent. Some of the more notable American festivals included Miami Con 1984 (which featured John Nathan-Turner and many series stars) and Infinicon 86 (which featured Patrick Troughton, Caroline Munro and Peter Davison). Today the picture is not quite so bright and *Doctor Who* fandom in the United States is much less a factor than *The X Files, Star Wars* or even *Battlestar Galactica.* There are too many products out there competing for attention today, and older shows like *Who* and *1999* are not getting the air time nor exposure they did in the early '80s. The new *Doctor Who* movie was virtually ignored by American viewers despite the fact that it was heavily advertised during episodes of Fox's *The X Files.* One would deduce that the *X Files*' large viewership would include many *Doctor Who* fans. Apparently that was not the case.

Though there are still many *Doctor Who* fan clubs and Internet sites in America, all is not rosy in the world of *Doctor Who* in 1998. Like *Star Trek* fans who have had to contend with new generations and spin-offs, *Doctor Who* fandom has had to deal with significant internal schisms. A large percentage of fans favor the series in its serious '60s and mid-'70s style. Others prefer the Douglas Adams humor of the late '70s and early '80s. For some fans, Tom Baker *is* the Doctor and everyone else is a poor substitute. For some, Sylvester McCoy oversaw the worst era in the show's history; for others he is far and away their favorite incarnation of the Time Lord. To some fans, Nathan-Turner is a hero, to others he is the man responsible for *Doctor Who*'s slip in quality. Opinion is equally divided about other topics. Are the "New Adventures" canon? Is "Benny" canon? Should American producers like Philip Segal be allowed to write the next chapter in *Doctor Who*'s heretofore British history? These are just a few of the questions which have splintered *Doctor Who* fandom and made it a less powerful voice in the return of *Doctor Who* than it could be. For instance, why no organized campaign to get *Doctor Who* aired on the Sci-Fi Channel? Or Bravo? Or even Nickelodeon?

Janet Fielding, who played Tegan Jovanka, at an American *Doctor Who* convention.

Shaun Lyon, of the Time Meddlers of Los Angeles and Gallifrey, wrote an open letter to the United States fans on the Internet in 1997 declaring that *Doctor Who* fandom across the continent is starting to dwindle. Lyon blames this fact not on time passing, or the advent of new epics like *Babylon* 5, but on a lack of communication and coordination among America's various *Doctor Who* clubs. Lyon proposes a central committee whose duty would be to communicate all fan news about conventions, the Internet and upcoming events.

Despite *Doctor Who*'s declining popularity in America, it continues to be immensely popular in Great Britain and in other countries throughout the world. The best thing that could happen to revive *Who* fandom in the States would be a complete airing of the series on The Sci-Fi Channel, or a new series aired on Fox, UPN or the WB Network. It is clear that *Doctor Who* can only succeed in the twenty-first century if new generations of fans are exposed to it. Although there are many video releases, a young fan is unlikely to purchase a video for a series he has never seen. And what if that youngster picks up "The Pirate Planet" or "Ghost Light" instead of "The Robots of Death" or "The Tomb of the Cybermen"? It is clear that Americans must be introduced to the Doctor on the free medium of television, where a "habit" can be formed cheaply.

Epilogue: Time Is Relative

Although no new television series has been produced since the *Doctor Who* telefilm in 1996, the universe of the Time Lord has continued to thrive. BBC/CBS-Fox releases several serials a year on video and over 85 serials are already on the shelves. The Internet is a kind of lively Time Lord Matrix for communicative fans, and it continues to be inundated with *Doctor Who* websites and pages. In bookstores there are the inevitable *The New Adventures* and *The Missing Adventures* from Virgin Books. There are also frequent articles about the series in genre magazines such as *Dreamwatch*, *Starlog*, *TV Zone*, *Sci-Fi Universe* and *Cinefantastique*. There is even an official *Doctor Who Magazine* with a regular column by John Nathan-Turner and contributions from Tom Baker.

Of course, the one thing all *Doctor Who* fans desire most is a new series or

Over the years, *Doctor Who* has remained a topic of interest in British and American genre magazines.

feature film. Reading about *Doctor Who* in comic books or in new novels is a great pastime, to be sure, but this aging video franchise requires a new product if it is to move into the twenty-first century. Bill Baggs, Nicholas Briggs and other intrepid fans continue to employ *Doctor Who* actors in new direct-to-video adventures, but even these fine efforts to perpetuate the legend cannot really be considered "canon" *Doctor Who*.

Any new series or film version of *Doctor Who* will raise several questions. Is the McGann movie to be considered canon? If so, then McGann should star in a new film or series. If it is not considered canon, then who will play the Doctor? Will he be incarnation #9 or a revamp of incarnation #8?

On the other hand, a new movie or television series need not be a continuation of the BBC series at all. It could be a complete revamp. The legend of the Doctor could begin again, from the very beginning. There could be new companions, new theories about Time Lords and new interpretations of classic villains such as the Cybermen and the Daleks. It would be a wondrous rebirth, and an opportunity to correct some of the niggling continuity errors that have plagued the series.

Another possibility is that there will be no new *Doctor Who* at all. This alternative seems entirely unlikely since the series boasts 110 million fans in over 60 countries worldwide. The Doctor is simply too interesting a character to languish in the never-never land of hiatus. Yet the ratings failure of the McGann epic in America gives viewers reason to pause. Is the era of the Doctor on television over at last? The low ratings in the U.S. prove that audiences are not so large in the States as one might have thought.

Perhaps *Doctor Who*'s legacy is not what it will bring to audiences in the future, but what its 26 years on the air have already brought. *Doctor Who* offered intelligent television science fiction in the early '60s, when such a thing was rare. Its impact on later programs, particularly *Star Trek: The Next Generation*, was significant. It is the longest-running sci-fi television show in history, and it has been seen all over the world.

What could a new series possibly add to that list of accomplishments? A love for *Doctor Who* has already inspired a new generation of filmmakers and writers, including Bill Baggs, Nicholas Briggs and Ben Aaronovitch. Perhaps in years to come it will be these adventurous souls who bring us new adventures and new television programs, visions far more ambitious and wonderful than anything hinted at in the first 30 years of *Doctor Who*. If they do infuse the new millennium with exciting new science fiction visions, then *Doctor Who* will have been the training ground for the technicians and architects of our future.

Doctor Who and *Star Trek* are both over 30 years old. Both series have seen beloved actors and characters depart. Both series have lived so long that recent episodes conflict with data from earlier stories. Is there a point where the burden of history is too much to bear? When creativity is stymied by the need to fit continuity? Do these once grand visions become tied so inexorably to their own convoluted mythologies that they degenerate into soap opera? These are the questions both franchises must face as they move into the twenty-first century. If *Doctor Who*'s best days are in the past, then fans must take heart in the fact that the series lived so long and spawned so many descendants. The genre conventions of the '50s, the *Quatermass* saga and other sci-fi tropes found a new outlet in *Doctor Who* too. The series paved the way for future genre programming, so in a sense the Doctor's mission is accomplished.

In the final moments of "The War Games," Zoe asks Patrick Troughton's Doctor if they will ever meet again. With a sad smile, he replies, "Time is relative." Through the magic of VCRs, comics and books, fans can make that statement a reality. They can travel back to Zoe's first meeting with the Doctor, or to her last. In that sense, viewers will encounter their favorite Time Lord long into the future, whether it is in rerun, new home video releases or even a new series.

As usual, the Doctor was right. Time is relative, and this funny old television series done on the cheap has had more lives than a Time Lord!

APPENDIX A

Doctor Who Production Codes

Like all British television productions, *Doctor Who* serials are noted in the BBC library by individual identification codes. In America, production codes are frequently numerical. For example, the first episode of a program's fourth season might be listed as show 401, the second as 402, and so on. For *Doctor Who*, however, serials are represented not by numbers but by sequential alphabetical listings. It is by these sequences that the episodes are most often referenced in books such as Jean-Marc Lofficier's *Programme Guide*. Unfortunately, *Doctor Who* ran so long that the BBC went through the alphabet seven times trying to catalogue it! Thus various serials are referred to by such cryptic codes as 4F, 7C and AAA. The result is that when reading *Doctor Who* nonfiction books, one frequently has to laboriously decode these alphabetical sequences to guess which specific episode the author is writing about.

In this book, a simple 1—159 sequence was used to prevent this sort of confusion. For completists, however, a list of "official" *Doctor Who* production codes is provided below. (An asterisk after a title indicates a serial that has been released on videotape.)

Serial No./Episode Title	*BBC Code*
1. "An Unearthly Child"*	A
2. "The Daleks"*	B
3. "The Edge of Destruction"	C
4. "Marco Polo"	D
5. "The Keys of Marinus"	E
6. "The Aztecs"*	F
7. "The Sensorites"	G
8. "The Reign of Terror"	H
9. "Planet of Giants"	J
10. "The Dalek Invasion of Earth"*	K
11. "The Rescue"*	L
12. "The Romans"*	M
13. "The Web Planet"*	N
14. "The Crusades"	P
15. "The Space Museum"	Q
16. "The Chase"*	R
17. "The Time Meddler"	S
18. "Galaxy Four"	T
19. "Mission to the Unknown"	T/A
20. "The Myth Makers"	U
21. "The Dalek Masterplan"	V
22. "The Massacre"	W
23. "The Ark"*	Y
24. "The Celestial Toymaker"	X

Serial No./Episode Title	*BBC Code*
25. "The Gunfighters"	Z
26. "The Savages"	AA
27. "The War Machines"*	BB
28. "The Smugglers"	CC
29. "The Tenth Planet"	DD
30. "The Power of the Daleks"	EE
31. "The Highlanders"	FF
32. "The Underwater Menace"	GG
33. "The Moonbase"	HH
34. "The Macra Terror"	JJ
35. "The Faceless Ones"	KK
36. "The Evil of the Daleks"	LL
37. "The Tomb of the Cybermen"*	MM
38. "The Abominable Snowmen"	NN
39. "The Ice Warriors"	OO
40. "The Enemy of the World"	PP
41. "The Web of Fear"	QQ
42. "Fury from the Deep"	RR
43. "The Wheel in Space"	SS
44. "The Dominators"*	TT
45. "The Mind Robber"*	UU
46. "The Invasion"*	V
47. "The Krotons"*	WW
48. "The Seeds of Death"*	XX
49. "The Space Pirates"	YY
50. "The War Games"*	ZZ
51. "Spearhead from Space"*	AAA
52. "Doctor Who and the Silurians"*	BBB
53. "Ambassadors of Death"	CCC
54. "Inferno"*	DDD
55. "Terror of the Autons"*	EEE
56. "The Mind of Evil"	FFF
57. "The Claws of Axos"*	GGG
58. "Colony in Space"*	HHH
59. "The Daemons"*	JJJ
60. "Day of the Daleks"*	KKK
61. "The Curse of Peladon"*	MMM
62. "The Sea Devils"*	LLL
63. "The Mutants"	NNN
64. "The Time Monster"	OOO
65. "The Three Doctors"*	RRR
66. "The Carnival of Monsters"*	PPP
67. "Frontier In Space"*	QQQ
68. "Planet of the Daleks"	SSS
69. "The Green Death"*	TTT
70. "The Time Warrior"*	UUU
71. "Invasion of the Dinosaurs"	WWW
72. "Death to the Daleks"*	XXX
73. "The Monster of Peladon"*	YYY
74. "Planet of the Spiders"*	ZZZ
75. "Robot"*	4A
76. "The Ark in Space"*	4C
77. "The Sontaran Experiment"*	4B
78. "Genesis of the Daleks"*	4E
79. "Revenge of the Cybermen"*	4D
80. "Terror of the Zygons"*	4F
81. "Planet of Evil"*	4H
82. "The Pyramids of Mars"*	4G
83. "The Android Invasion"*	4J
84. "The Brain of Morbius"*	4K
85. "The Seeds of Doom"*	4L
86. "The Masque of Mandragora"*	4M
87. "The Hand of Fear"*	4N
88. "The Deadly Assassin"*	4P
89. "The Face of Evil"	4Q
90. "The Robots of Death"*	4R
91. "The Talons of Weng-Chiang"*	4S
92. "Horror of Fang Rock"*	4V
93. "The Invisible Enemy"	4T
94. "Image of the Fendahl"*	4X
95. "The Sunmakers"	4W
96. "Underworld"	4Y
97. "The Invasion of Time"	4Z
98. "The Ribos Operation"*	5A
99. "The Pirate Planet"*	5B
100. "The Stones of Blood"*	5C
101. "The Androids of Tara"*	5D
102. "The Power of Kroll"*	5E
103. "The Armageddon Factor"*	5F
104. "Destiny of the Daleks"*	5J
105. "City of Death"*	5H
106. "The Creature from the Pit"	5G
107. "Nightmare of Eden"*	5K
108. "The Horns of Nimon"	5L
109. "Shada"*	5M
110. "The Leisure Hive"*	5N
111. "Meglos"	5Q
112. "Full Circle"*	5R
113. "State of Decay"*	5P
114. "Warrior's Gate"*	5S
115. "The Keeper of Traken"*	5T
116. "Logopolis"*	5V
117. "Castrovalva"*	5Z
118. "Four to Doomsday"	5W
119. "Kinda"*	5Y
120. "The Visitation"*	5X
121. "Black Orchid"*	6A
122. "Earthshock"*	6B
123. "Time Flight"	6C
124. "Arc of Infinity"*	6E
125. "Snakedance"*	6D
126. "Mawdryn Undead"*	6F
127. "Terminus"*	6G
128. "Enlightenment"*	6H
129. "The King's Demons"*	6J
130. "The Five Doctors"*	6K
131. "Warriors of the Deep"*	6L
132. "The Awakening"*	6M
133. "Frontios"*	6N
134. "Resurrection of the Daleks"*	6P
135. "Planet of Fire"*	6Q
136. "The Caves of Androzani"*	6R

Serial No./Episode Title	*BBC Code*
137. "The Twin Dilemma"*	6S
138. "Attack of the Cybermen"	6T
139. "Vengeance on Varos"*	6V
140. "Mark of the Rani"*	6X
141. "The Two Doctors"*	6W
142. "Timelash"*	6Y
143. "Revelation of the Daleks"	6Z
144. "The Mysterious Planet"*	7A
145. "Mindwarp"*	7B
146. "Terror of the Vervoids"*	7C1
147. "The Ultimate Foe"*	7C2
148. "Time and the Rani"*	7D
149. "Paradise Towers"*	7E
150. "Delta and the Bannermen"	7F
151. "Dragonfire"*	7G
152. "Remembrance of the Daleks"*	7H
153. "The Happiness Patrol"*	7L
154. "Silver Nemesis"*	7K
155. "The Greatest Show in the Galaxy"	7J
156. "Battlefield"*	7N
157. "Ghost Light"*	7O
158. "The Curse of Fenric"*	7M
159. "Survival"*	7P

APPENDIX B

Recommended Viewing

Throughout this text, the author has noted similarities between *Doctor Who* and other science fiction television productions and films. It is always easier to spot such similarities with one's own eyes rather than trust a description by someone who may or may not have a specific agenda in mind. For that reason, the author has provided below a chart of recommended viewing which might afford the curious *Doctor Who* viewer a better grasp of the series' antecedents and descendents.

For some viewers, this will reveal *Doctor Who*'s enormous influence on other programs and vice versa, and for others it may just be an entertaining way to see *Doctor Who* or other favorites in a new light.

First watch	Then watch	Look for
Doctor Who "Tomb of the Cybermen"	*Star Trek: The Next Generation* "The Best of Both Worlds"	similarities between Borg and Cybermen
Doctor Who "Vengeance on Varos" "Mindwarp"	*Star Trek: The Next Generation* "The Last Outpost," "Captain's Holiday" "The Price"	similarities between Sil and the Ferengi
Doctor Who "City of Death"	*Star Trek: The Next Generation* "All Good Things"	scenes at the dawn of Man
Doctor Who "The Silurians" "The Sea Devils"	*Star Trek: Voyager* "Distant Origins"	treatment of a race evolved from dinosaurs
Doctor Who "The Ark in Space"	*Alien, Aliens*	central situation, depiction of aliens, resolution
Doctor Who "Warriors of the Deep"	*Deep Star Six, Leviathan*	setting, characters

First watch	Then watch	Look for
The Time Machine	*Doctor Who* "The Daleks"	Overall dynamic: Thals = Eloi Daleks = Morlocks Doctor = H.G. Wells
Quatermass and The Pit	*Doctor Who* "The Daemons" "Image of the Fendahl" "The Talons of Weng-Chiang"	Overall dynamic: Use of myth, legends
Phantom of the Opera	*Doctor Who* "The Caves of Androzani"	Sharez Jek as a Phantom surrogate
Doctor Who "The War Games"	*Star Trek: Voyager* "The Killing Ground"	same plot

APPENDIX C

The 20 Best Episodes of *Doctor Who*

As the length of this reference guide indicates, *Doctor Who* has an enormously detailed and complex history. For those readers who would like to begin a further exploration of the series but are overwhelmed by the scope of such a task, the author has listed his personal choices for the 20 best *Doctor Who* serials. These serials are all available on videocassette. They have been chosen not only for their high quality, but also because they exhibit the quintessential characteristics of *Doctor Who*. This list does not take into account incomplete or destroyed serials.

For those interested in determining which "era" is best, Tom Baker's era scored six of the top 20, Hartnell's scored four, Troughton's scored three, Davison's and Pertwee's each scored two, and Colin Baker's and McCoy's each scored one. "The Three Doctors," which also made the list, features the first three incarnations of the Doctor.

In descending order by rank, the 20 best episodes are as follows:

1. "The Tomb of the Cybermen" (Patrick Troughton)
2. "The Aztecs" (William Hartnell)
3. "The Robots of Death" (Tom Baker)
4. "Genesis of the Daleks" (Tom Baker)
5. "City of Death" (Tom Baker)
6. "The Dalek Invasion of Earth" (William Hartnell)
7. "Doctor Who and the Silurians" (Jon Pertwee)
8. "The Mind Robber" (Patrick Troughton)
9. "The Three Doctors" (Pertwee, Troughton, Hartnell)
10. "Black Orchid" (Peter Davison)
11. "The War Games" (Patrick Troughton)
12. "The Ark in Space" (Tom Baker)
13. "Vengeance on Varos" (Colin Baker)
14. "Carnival of Monsters" (Jon Pertwee)
15. "The Stones of Blood" (Tom Baker)

16. "The Daleks" (William Hartnell)
17. "Mawdryn Undead" (Peter Davison)
18. "Paradise Towers" (Sylvester McCoy)
19. "The Talons of Weng-Chiang" (Tom Baker)
20. "The Romans" (William Hartnell)

NOTES

Introduction

1. Mortimer, Ellen. *Starlog*, Issue #23: "*Doctor Who,* "Britain's Time Traveler Arrives in the Colonies." June 1979, page 35.

2. Blocher, Karen Funk, and Teresa Murray, *Starlog*, Issue #167: "A Time Lord's Times." June 1991, page 53.

Part I: The History

1. Caruba, David. *Starlog*, Issue #116: "Creating *Doctor Who*." March 1987, page 42.

2. *Ibid*, page 42.

3. *TV Zone*, Issue #41: "*Doctor Who* Death." April 1993, page 7.

4. Kirkpatrick, Richard, and Koukol, David. *Epilog*, Issue #12: "*Doctor Who*—Seasons 14–26." November 1991, page 25.

5. Haining, Peter. *Doctor Who—A Celebration, Two Decades Through Time and Space*. W.H. Allen, London, 1983, page 173.

6. Pixley, Andrew. *Time Screen*, Issue #21: "British Telefantasy in Comics." Spring 1995, page 6.

7. Haining, page 25.

8. Nazzaro, Joe. *TV Zone*, Special #17: "In the Beginning." Pages 30–31.

9. 1972 Purple Records Limited. "Who is the Doctor?" Words by Maciver, produced and arranged by Rupert Hine. Erie Music Ltd.

10. Peel, John. *Fantasy Empire*, Issue #9. "*Doctor Who* 9th Season Guide." March 1984, page 44.

11. Haining, page 62.

12. Hirsch, David. *Starlog*, Issue #47: "The Return of *Doctor Who*." June 1981, page 53.

13. Nazzaro, Joe. *Starlog*, Issue #197: "Forever the Doctor." December 1993, page 50.

14. Pirani, Adam. *Starlog*, Issue #83: "On the Set of "Resurrection of the Daleks." June 1984, page 34.

15. Howe, David J., Mark Stammers, and Stephen James Walker. *Doctor Who—The Handbook: The Sixth Doctor*. Virgin Publishing, London, 1991, page 227.

16. *Ibid*, page 194.

17. *Ibid*, page 200.

18. Kirkpatrick, Richard, and Koukol, David. *Epilog* Issue #12: "*Doctor Who*—Seasons 14–26." November 1991, page 25.

19. O'Neill, Patrick Daniel. *Starlog*, Issue #113: "*Doctor Who* Tours U.S. During Hiatus." December 1986, page 11.

20. O'Neill, Patrick Daniel. *Starlog*, Issue #118: "*Doctor Who* Renewed Without Baker." May 1987, page 9.

21. Biodrowski, Steve. *Cinefantastique* Volume 30, Number 4: "Dr. Who? Sylvester McCoy, That's Who!" August 1998, page 62.

22. *TV Zone*, Issue #2: "The Fate of *Doctor Who*." December 1989, page 4.

23. Kirkpatrick, Richard, and Koukol, David. *Epilog* Issue #12: "*Doctor Who*—Seasons 14–26." November 1991, page 24.

24. Anchors, William E. *Epilog*, Issue #41: "*Doctor Who* 30th Anniversary." April 1994, page 5.

25. *Ibid*, page 6.

26. *Dreamwatch*, Issue #15: "Philip Segal/*Doctor Who*." November 1995, page 15.

Part II: Curriculum Vitae

1. Nazzaro, Joe. *Starlog*, Issue #197: "Forever the Doctor." December 1993, page 51.

2. Javna, John. *The Best of Science Fiction TV*. Harmony Books, New York, 1987, page 30.

Part III: The Series

1. Richardson, David. *TV Zone*, Issue #41: "Mark Eden: From Tibet to the Village." April 1993, page 10.

2. Baxter, John. *Science Fiction in the Cinema—A Complete Critical Review of SF films from A TRIP TO THE MOON (1902) to 2001: A SPACE ODYSSEY*. Paperback Library, New York, 1970, page 186.

3. *TV Zone*, Issue #41: "*Doctor Who* Death." April 1993, page 7.

4. Egan, Thomas. *Fantasy Empire*, Issue #9. "Bundles from Britain." March 1984, page 5.

5. Vincent-Rudzki, Jan. *TV Zone:* "Tomb Exhumed." August 1992, pages 18–19.

6. O'Neill, Patrick Daniel. *Starlog,* Issue #111: "Nicholas Courtney." October 1986, page 35.

7. *Ibid*, page 35.

8. Blocher, Karen Funk, and Teresa Murray. *Starlog*, Issue #167: "A Time Lord's Times." June 1991, page 50.

9. Peel, John. *Fantasy Empire*, Issue #9. "*Doctor Who* 9th Season Guide." March 1984, page 51.

10. Mount, Paul. *Space and Time*: "Invasion of the Dinosaurs." Reproduced by arrangement with BBC TV.

11. Hopkins, Gary. *Space and Time*: "Invasion of the Dinosaurs." Reproduced by arrangement with BBC TV.

12. Airey, Jean, and Haldeman, Laurie. *Starlog*, Issue #124: "Harry Sullivan's Travels." November 1987, page 85.

13. Towey, Ian. *Dreamwatch*, Issue #15: "A Journey to the Dark Side: *Doctor Who*'s 'Pyramids of Mars.'" November 1995, page 18.

14. Airey, Jean, and Laurie Haldeman. *Starlog*, Issue #115: "Tom Baker—The Curious Heart of *Doctor Who*. " December 1987, page 47.

15. Barbee, Larry S. *Starlog*, Issue #170: "The Lost *Doctor Who*." September 1991, page 63.

16. Airey, Jean, and Laurie Haldeman. *Starlog*, Issue #143: "Dog Days." September 1991, page 42.

17. *Ibid*, "Tom Baker," page 47.

18. Lofficier, Jean-Marc. *The Nth Doctor*. Virgin Publishing, London, 1997, page 4.

19. Attwood, Tony. *The Companions of Doctor Who — Turlough and the Earthlink Dilemma*. Target, London, 1986, page 7.

20. Howe, David J.; Stammers, Mark; and Walker, Stephen James. *Doctor Who — The Handbook: The Sixth Doctor*. Virgin Publishing, London, 1991, page 64.

Part IV: Doctor Who Spin Offs

1. Andres, Donald. *Sci-Fi Monthly*. "The TV Sci-Fi Interview: Tom Baker British Television's *Doctor Who*! Talking to a Time Lord." 1976, page 6.

2. Swires, Steven. *Starlog*, Issue #130: "Caroline Munro, Starting Over." May 1988, page 57.

3. *TV Zone*, Issue #3: "Who to Believe." February 1990, page 3.

4. Lofficier, Jean-Marc. *The Nth Doctor*. Virgin Publishing, London, 1997, page 79.

5. Lofficier, Jean-Marc. *Doctor Who — The Terrestrial Index*. Virgin Publishing, London, 1991, page 123.

Part V: The Doctor Who Fan Matrix

1. Maloni, Kelly, Ben Greenman, Kristin Miller, and Jeff Hearn. *Net Trek — Your Guide to Trek Life in Cyberspace*. Michael Wolff, New York, 1995, page 318.

2. Maloni, Greenman, Miller, and Hearn, page 319.

Bibliography

Fiction

Attwood, Tony. *The Companions of Doctor Who—Turlough and the Earthlink Dilemma.* London: Target, 1986.
Baker, Pip, and Jane Baker. *Doctor Who—The Ultimate Foe.* London: Target, 1988.
_____, and _____. *Doctor Who—Time and the Rani.* London: Target, 1988.
Bidmead, Christopher H. *Doctor Who—Frontios.* London: Target, 1984.
Black, Ian Stuart. *Doctor Who—The War Machines.* London: Target, 1988.
Briggs, Ian. *Doctor Who—Dragonfire.* London: Target, 1989.
Clegg, Barbara. *Doctor Who—Enlightenment.* London: Target, 1984.
Cotton, Donald. *Doctor Who—The Gunfighters.* London: Target, 1985.
_____. *Doctor Who—The Myth Makers.* London: Target, 1985.
_____. *Doctor Who—The Romans.* London: Target, 1987.
Davis, Gerry. *Doctor Who and the Tenth Planet.* London: Target, 1976.
_____. *Doctor Who—The Highlanders.* London: Target, 1984.
Davis, Glyn. *Doctor Who—The Space Museum.* London: Target, 1987.
Dicks, Terrance. *Doctor Who—Ambassadors of Death.* London: Target, 1987.
_____. *Doctor Who and the Abominable Snowmen.* Target: London, 1974.
_____. *Doctor Who and the Android Invasion.* Los Angeles: Pinnacle, 1980.
_____. *Doctor Who and the Carnival of Monsters.* London: Target, 1977.
_____. *Doctor Who and the Day of the Daleks.* Los Angeles: Pinnacle, 1979.
_____. *Doctor Who and the Destiny of the Daleks.* London: Target, 1979.
_____. *Doctor Who and the Face of Evil.* London: Target, 1978.
_____. *Doctor Who and the Genesis of the Daleks.* Los Angeles: Pinnacle, 1979.
_____. *Doctor Who and the Horror of Fang Rock.* London: Target, 1978.
_____. *Doctor Who and the Invasion of Time.* London: Target, 1979.
_____. *Doctor Who and the Invisible Enemy.* London: Target, 1979
_____. *Doctor Who and the Keeper of Traken.* London: Target, 1982.
_____. *Doctor Who and the Loch Ness Monster.* Los Angeles: Pinnacle, 1979.
_____. *Doctor Who and the Monster of Peladon.* London: Target, 1980.
_____. *Doctor Who and the Mutants.* London: Target, 1977.
_____. *Doctor Who and the Nightmare of Eden.* London: Target, 1980.
_____. *Doctor Who and the Planet of Evil.* London: Target, 1977.
_____. *Doctor Who and the Planet of the Daleks.* London: Target, 1976.
_____. *Doctor Who and the Revenge of the Cybermen.* Los Angeles: Pinnacle, 1979.
_____. *Doctor Who and the Sea Devils.* London: Target, 1974.
_____. *Doctor Who and the Sunmakers.* London: Target, 1982.

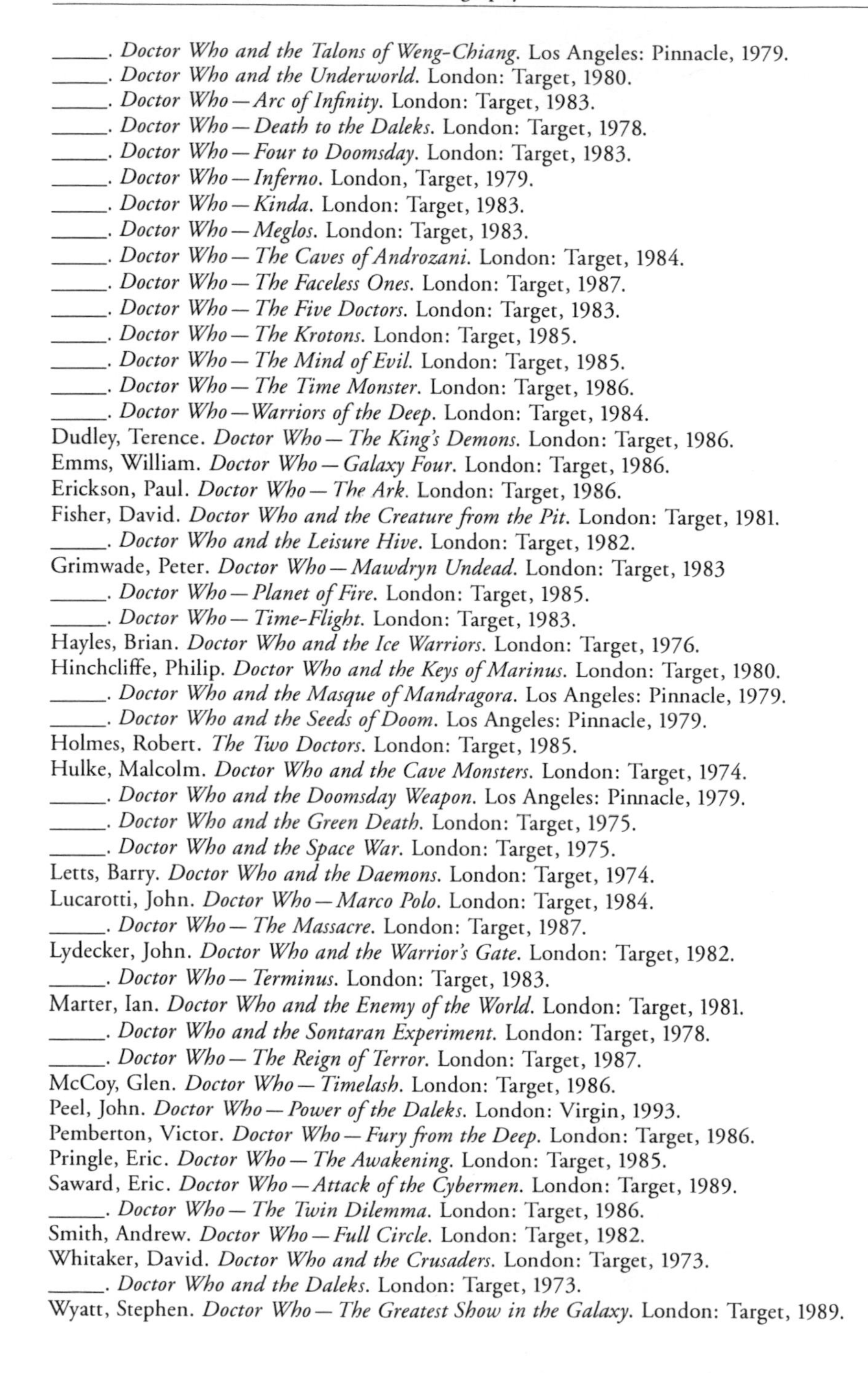

_____. *Doctor Who and the Talons of Weng-Chiang.* Los Angeles: Pinnacle, 1979.
_____. *Doctor Who and the Underworld.* London: Target, 1980.
_____. *Doctor Who—Arc of Infinity.* London: Target, 1983.
_____. *Doctor Who—Death to the Daleks.* London: Target, 1978.
_____. *Doctor Who—Four to Doomsday.* London: Target, 1983.
_____. *Doctor Who—Inferno.* London, Target, 1979.
_____. *Doctor Who—Kinda.* London: Target, 1983.
_____. *Doctor Who—Meglos.* London: Target, 1983.
_____. *Doctor Who—The Caves of Androzani.* London: Target, 1984.
_____. *Doctor Who—The Faceless Ones.* London: Target, 1987.
_____. *Doctor Who—The Five Doctors.* London: Target, 1983.
_____. *Doctor Who—The Krotons.* London: Target, 1985.
_____. *Doctor Who—The Mind of Evil.* London: Target, 1985.
_____. *Doctor Who—The Time Monster.* London: Target, 1986.
_____. *Doctor Who—Warriors of the Deep.* London: Target, 1984.
Dudley, Terence. *Doctor Who—The King's Demons.* London: Target, 1986.
Emms, William. *Doctor Who—Galaxy Four.* London: Target, 1986.
Erickson, Paul. *Doctor Who—The Ark.* London: Target, 1986.
Fisher, David. *Doctor Who and the Creature from the Pit.* London: Target, 1981.
_____. *Doctor Who and the Leisure Hive.* London: Target, 1982.
Grimwade, Peter. *Doctor Who—Mawdryn Undead.* London: Target, 1983
_____. *Doctor Who—Planet of Fire.* London: Target, 1985.
_____. *Doctor Who—Time-Flight.* London: Target, 1983.
Hayles, Brian. *Doctor Who and the Ice Warriors.* London: Target, 1976.
Hinchcliffe, Philip. *Doctor Who and the Keys of Marinus.* London: Target, 1980.
_____. *Doctor Who and the Masque of Mandragora.* Los Angeles: Pinnacle, 1979.
_____. *Doctor Who and the Seeds of Doom.* Los Angeles: Pinnacle, 1979.
Holmes, Robert. *The Two Doctors.* London: Target, 1985.
Hulke, Malcolm. *Doctor Who and the Cave Monsters.* London: Target, 1974.
_____. *Doctor Who and the Doomsday Weapon.* Los Angeles: Pinnacle, 1979.
_____. *Doctor Who and the Green Death.* London: Target, 1975.
_____. *Doctor Who and the Space War.* London: Target, 1975.
Letts, Barry. *Doctor Who and the Daemons.* London: Target, 1974.
Lucarotti, John. *Doctor Who—Marco Polo.* London: Target, 1984.
_____. *Doctor Who—The Massacre.* London: Target, 1987.
Lydecker, John. *Doctor Who and the Warrior's Gate.* London: Target, 1982.
_____. *Doctor Who—Terminus.* London: Target, 1983.
Marter, Ian. *Doctor Who and the Enemy of the World.* London: Target, 1981.
_____. *Doctor Who and the Sontaran Experiment.* London: Target, 1978.
_____. *Doctor Who—The Reign of Terror.* London: Target, 1987.
McCoy, Glen. *Doctor Who—Timelash.* London: Target, 1986.
Peel, John. *Doctor Who—Power of the Daleks.* London: Virgin, 1993.
Pemberton, Victor. *Doctor Who—Fury from the Deep.* London: Target, 1986.
Pringle, Eric. *Doctor Who—The Awakening.* London: Target, 1985.
Saward, Eric. *Doctor Who—Attack of the Cybermen.* London: Target, 1989.
_____. *Doctor Who—The Twin Dilemma.* London: Target, 1986.
Smith, Andrew. *Doctor Who—Full Circle.* London: Target, 1982.
Whitaker, David. *Doctor Who and the Crusaders.* London: Target, 1973.
_____. *Doctor Who and the Daleks.* London: Target, 1973.
Wyatt, Stephen. *Doctor Who—The Greatest Show in the Galaxy.* London: Target, 1989.

Nonfiction

Baxter, John. *Science Fiction in the Cinema—A Complete Critical Review of SF films from A TRIP TO THE MOON (1902) to 2001: A SPACE ODYSSEY.* New York: Paperback Library, 1970.

Gerani, Gary, and Schulman, Paul. *Fantastic Television: A Pictorial History of Sci-Fi, the Unusual and the Fantastic.* New York: Harmony, 1977.

Howe, David J.; Stammers, Mark; Walker, Stephen James. *Doctor Who—The Handbook: The Sixth Doctor.* London: Virgin, 1991.

Javna, John. *The Best of Science Fiction TV.* New York: Harmony, 1987.

Lofficier, Jean-Marc. *The Nth Doctor.* London: Virgin, 1997.

_____. *Doctor Who—The Programme Guide, Volume 1: The Programmes.* London: Target, 1981.

_____. *Doctor Who—The Terrestrial Index.* London: Virgin, 1991.

Maloni, Kelly; Ben Greenman, Kristin Miller, and Jeff Hearn. *Net Trek—Your Guide to Trek Life in Cyberspace.* New York: Michael Wolff, 1995.

Marsh, Ian, and Peter Darvill-Evans. *Time Lord: Create Your Own Adventures in Time and Space.* London: Virgin, 1991.

Muir, John. *Exploring Space: 1999.* Jefferson, N.C.: McFarland, 1997.

Robinson, Nigel. *The Second Doctor Who Quiz Book.* Target: London, 1983.

_____. *The Third Doctor Who Quiz Book.* London: Target, 1985.

Stanley, John. *Revenge of the Creature Features Movie Guide,* 3d rev. ed. Pacifica, Calif.: Creatures at Large Press, 1988.

White, Patrick J. *The Complete Mission: Impossible Dossier.* New York: Avon, 1991.

Zicree, Mark Scott. *The Twilight Zone Companion.* New York: Bantam, 1982.

Periodicals

Ackerman, Forrest J. "The Four Faces of Doctor Who." *Famous Monsters of Filmland,* Issue #55, July 1979, pages 18–79.

Airey, Jean. "New *Doctor Who* Companion." *Starlog,* Issue #113, December 1986, page 10.

Airey, Jean and Laurie Haldeman. "Dog Days." *Starlog,* Issue #143, September 1991, pages 20–22; 42.

_____, and _____. "Harry Sullivan's Travels." *Starlog,* Issue #124, November 1987, pages 84–85.

_____, and _____. "Tom Baker—The Curious Heart of *Doctor Who.*" *Starlog,* Issue #115, December 1987, pages 45–49.

Anchors, William E. "*Doctor Who* 30th Anniversary." *Epilog,* Issue #41, April 1994, pages 5–6.

Andres, Donald. "The TV Sci-Fi Interview: Tom Baker British Television's *Doctor Who*! Talking to a Time Lord. *Sci-Fi Monthly,* Issue #5, 1976, page 6.

Barbee, Larry S. "The Lost *Doctor Who.*" *Starlog,* Issue #170, September 1991, page 63.

Biodrowski, Steve. "Dr. Who? Sylvester McCoy, that's who!" *Cinefantastique,* Volume 30, Number 4, August 1998, page 62.

Blocher, Karen Funk & Murray, Teresa. "A Time Lord's Times." *Starlog,* Issue #167, June 1991, pages 49–53.

Caruba, David. "Creating *Doctor Who.*" *Starlog,* Issue #116, March 1987, pages 42–43; 64.

"*Doctor Who* Death." *TV Zone,* Issue #41, April 1993, page 7.

Egan, Thomas. "Bundles from Britain." *Fantasy Empire,* Issue #9, March 1984, pages 5–6.

Evans, Andrew. "Who '92." *Starburst,* Special Issue #14, Yearbook 1992/93, pages 25–30.

"The Fate of *Doctor Who. TV Zone*, Issue #2, December 1989, page 4.
Frankcombe, Mark. "Sarah Sutton An Interview with an Indispensable Companion." *Fantasy Enterprises*, Issue #1, November 1986, pages 20–25.
Hirsch, David. "The Return of *Doctor Who*." *Starlog*, Issue #47, June 1981, page 53.
Hopkins, Gary. "Invasion of the Dinosaurs." *Space and Time*, Reproduced by arrangement with BBC TV.
_____. "Peter Davison: An Interview with the New Doctor." *Fantasy Empire*, Issue #9, March 1984, pages 59–62.
Kirkpatrick, Richard and Koukol, David. "*Doctor Who*—Seasons 1–13." *Epilog*, Issue #11, October, 1991, pages 29–54.
_____, and _____. "*Doctor Who*— Seasons 14–26." *Epilog*, Issue #12, November, 1991, pages 4–26.
Martin, Andrew. "Great Powers in *Who*." *TV Zone* Special #4, March 1992, pages 48–51.
Molesworth, Richard. "More than 30 Years in the Making." *Dreamwatch*, Issue #2, November 1994, pages 14–15.
Mortimer, Ellen. "*Doctor Who*, Britain's Time Traveler Arrives in the Colonies." *Starlog*, Issue #23, June 1979, pages 34–43.
Mount, Paul. "Invasion of the Dinosaurs." *Space and Time*, Reproduced by arrangement with BBC TV.
Nazzaro, Joe. "Directing the Unfinished "Shada." *TV Zone*, Issue #33, August 1992, pages 12–14.
_____. "Forever the Doctor." *Starlog*, Issue #197, December 1993, page 50.
_____. "In the Beginning." *TV Zone*, Special #17, June 1995, Pages 30–35.
O'Neill, Patrick Daniel. "*Doctor Who* Renewed without Baker." *Starlog*, Issue #118, May 1987, page 9.
_____. "*Doctor Who* Tours U.S. During Hiatus." *Starlog*, Issue #113, December 1986, page 11.
_____. "John Nathan-Turner Producing *Doctor Who*." *Starlog*, Issue #82, May 1984, pages 30–37.
_____. "Nicholas Courtney." *Starlog*, Issue #111, October 1986, pages 34–35; 71.
_____. "Who is He This Time?" *Starlog*, Issue #134, September 1988, pages 32–34.
Peel, John. "9th Season Guide." *Fantasy Empire*, Issue #9, March 1984, pages 43–54.
"Philip Segal/*Doctor Who*." *Dreamwatch*, Issue #15, November 1995, page 15.
Pirani, Adam. "On the set of "Resurrection of the Daleks." *Starlog*, Issue #83, June 1984, pages 33–34.
Pixley, Andrew. "British Telefantasy in Comics." *Time Screen*, Issue #21, Spring 1995, pages 4–38.
Richardson, David. "Mark Eden: From Tibet to the Village." *TV Zone*, Issue #41, April 1993, pages 8–11.
Swires, Steven. "Caroline Munro, Starting Over." *Starlog*, Issue #130, May 1988, pages 57–60; 94.
Towey, Ian. "A Journey to the Dark Side: *Doctor Who*'s "Pyramids of Mars." *Dreamwatch*, Issue #15, November 1995, page 18.
Vincent-Rudzki, Jan. "Tomb Exhumed." *TV Zone*, Issue #30, August 1992, pages 16–19.
"Who to Believe." *TV Zone*, Issue #3, February 1990, page 3.
Wood, Greme, and Leonard Andrew. "Sylvester McCoy on *Who*." *TV Zone* Special #4, March 1992, pages 5–7.

VIDEOGRAPHY

The Television Serials

All videos in this section are available from BBC/CBS-Fox Video.

"The Android Invasion." 1975. Director: Barry Letts. Writer: Terry Nation. Starring Tom Baker.
"The Androids of Tara." 1978. Director: Michael Hayes. Writer: David Fisher. Starring Tom Baker.
"The Ark in Space." 1975. Director: Rodney Bennett. Writer: Robert Holmes. Starring Tom Baker.
"The Armageddon Factor." 1979. Director: Michael Hayes. Writer: Bob Baker, Dave Martin. Starring Tom Baker.
"The Aztecs." 1964. Director: John Crockett. Writer: John Lucarotti. Starring William Hartnell.
"Battlefield." 1987. Director: Michael Kerrigan. Writer: Ben Aaronovitch. Starring Sylvester McCoy.
"Black Orchid." 1982. Director: Ron Jones. Writer: Terence Dudley. Starring Peter Davison.
"The Brain of Morbius." 1976. Director: Christopher Barry. Writer: Terrance Dicks. Starring Tom Baker.
"Carnival of Monsters." 1973. Director: Barry Letts. Writer: Robert Holmes. Starring Jon Pertwee.
"Castrovalva." 1982. Director: Fiona Cumming. Writer: Christopher H. Bidmead. Starring Peter Davison.
"The Caves of Androzani." 1984. Director: Graeme Harper. Writer: Robert Holmes. Starring Peter Davison.
"The Chase." 1965. Director: Richard Martin. Writer: Terry Nation. Starring William Hartnell.
"City of Death." 1979. Director: Michael Hayes. Writer: Douglas Adams, Graham Williams. Starring Tom Baker.
"The Claws of Axos." 1971. Director: Michael Ferguson. Writer: Bob Baker, Dave Martin. Starring Jon Pertwee.
"The Curse of Fenric." 1989. Director: Nicholas Mallett. Writer: Ian Briggs. Starring Sylvester McCoy.
"The Curse of Peladon." 1972. Director: Lennie Mayne. Writer: Brian Hayles. Starring Jon Pertwee.
"The Daemons." 1971. Director: Christopher Barry. Writer: Guy Leopold. Starring Jon Pertwee.

"The Dalek Invasion of Earth." 1964. Director: Richard Martin. Writer: Terry Nation. Starring William Hartnell.
"The Daleks." 1963. Director: Christopher Barry. Writer: Terry Nation. Starring William Hartnell.
"Day of the Daleks." 1972. Director: Paul Bernard. Writer: Louis Marks. Starring Jon Pertwee.
"The Deadly Assassin." 1976. Director: David Maloney. Writer: Robert Holmes. Starring Tom Baker.
"Death to the Daleks." 1974. Director: Michael Briant. Writer: Terry Nation. Starring Jon Pertwee.
"Destiny of the Daleks." 1979. Director Ken Grieve. Writer: Terry Nation. Starring Tom Baker.
"Doctor Who and the Silurians." 1970. Director: Timothy Combe; Writer: Malcolm Hulke. Starring Jon Pertwee.
"The Dominators." 1968. Director: Morris Barry. Writer: Norman Ashby. Starring Patrick Troughton.
"Dragonfire." 1987. Director: Chris Clough. Writer: Ian Briggs. Starring Sylvester McCoy.
"Earthshock." 1982. Director: Peter Grimwade. Writer: Eric Saward. Starring Peter Davison.
"The Five Doctors." 1983. Director: Peter Moffatt. Writer: Terrance Dicks. Starring Peter Davison, Jon Pertwee, Patrick Troughton, Richard Hurndall.
"Frontier In Space." 1973. Director: Paul Bernard. Writer: Malcolm Hulke. Starring Jon Pertwee.
"Genesis of the Daleks." 1975. Director: David Maloney. Writer: Terry Nation. Starring Tom Baker.
"Ghost Light." 1989. Director: Alan Wareing. Writer: Marc Platt. Starring Sylvester McCoy.
"The Hand of Fear" 1976. Director: Lennie Mayne. Writer: Bob Baker and Dave Martin. Starring Tom Baker.
"The Happiness Patrol." 1987. Director: Chris Clough. Writer: Graeme Curry. Starring Sylvester McCoy.
"Image of the Fendahl." 1977. Director: George Spenton-Foster. Writer: Chris Boucher. Starring Tom Baker.
"Inferno." 1970. Director: Douglas Camfield. Writer: Don Houghton. Starring Jon Pertwee.
"The Invasion." 1968. Director: Douglas Camfield. Writer: Derrick Sherwin. Starring Patrick Troughton.
"The King's Demons." 1983. Director Tony Virgo. Writer: Terence Dudley. Starring Peter Davison.
"The Krotons." 1969. Director: David Maloney. Writer: Robert Holmes. Starring Patrick Troughton.
"The Leisure Hive." 1980. Director: Lovett Bickford. Writer: David Fisher. Starring Tom Baker.
"Logopolis." 1981. Director: Peter Grimwade. Writer: Christopher H. Bidmead. Starring Tom Baker.
"The Mark of the Rani." 1985. Director: Sarah Hellings. Writers: Pip and Jane Baker. Starring Colin Baker.
"The Masque of Mandragora." 1976. Director: Rodney Bennett. Writer: Louis Marks. Starring Tom Baker.
"Mawdryn Undead." 1983. Director: Peter Moffatt. Writer: Peter Grimwade. Starring Peter Davison.
"The Mind Robber." 1968. Director: David Maloney. Writer: Peter Ling. Starring Patrick Troughton.

"Paradise Towers." 1987. Director: Nicholas Mallett. Writer: Stephen Wyatt. Starring Sylvester McCoy.
"The Pirate Planet." 1978. Director: Pennant Robert. Writer: Douglas Adams. Starring Tom Baker.
"Planet of Evil." 1975. Director: David Maloney. Writer: Louis Marks. Starring Tom Baker.
"Planet of the Spiders." 1974. Director: Barry Letts. Writer: Robert Sloman. Starring Jon Pertwee.
"The Power of Kroll." 1979. Director: Norman Stewart. Writer: Robert Holmes. Starring Tom Baker.
"The Pyramids of Mars." 1975. Director: Paddy Russell. Writer: Stephen Harris. Starring Tom Baker.
"Remembrance of the Daleks." 1988. Director: Andrew Morgan. Writer: Ben Aaronovitch. Starring Sylvester McCoy.
"The Rescue." 1965. Director: Christopher Barry. Writer: David Whitaker. Starring William Hartnell.
"Resurrection of the Daleks." 1984. Director: Matthew Robinson. Writer: Eric Saward. Starring Peter Davison.
"The Ribos Operation." 1978. Director: George-Spenton Foster. Writer: Robert Holmes. Starring Tom Baker.
"Robot." 1974-75. Director: Christopher Barry. Writer: Terrance Dicks. Starring Tom Baker.
"The Robots of Death." 1977. Director: Michael Briant. Writer: Chris Boucher. Starring Tom Baker.
"The Romans." 1965. Director: Christopher Barry. Writer: Dennis Spooner. Starring William Hartnell.
"The Seeds of Death." 1969. Director: Michael Ferguson. Writer: Brian Hayles. Starring Patrick Troughton.
"Silver Nemesis." 1988. Director: Christopher Clough. Writer: Kevin Clarke. Starring Sylvester McCoy.
"Snakedance." 1983. Director: Fiona Cumming. Writer: Christopher Bailey. Starring Peter Davison.
"The Sontaran Experiment." 1975. Director: Rodney Bennett. Writers: Bob Baker and Dave Martin. Starring Tom Baker.
"Spearhead from Space." 1970. Director: Derek Martinus. Writer: Robert Holmes. Starring Jon Pertwee.
"The Stones of Blood." 1978. Director: Darrol Blake. Writer: David Fisher. Starring Tom Baker.
"Survival." 1989. Director: Alan Wareing. Writer: Rona Munro. Starring Sylvester McCoy.
"The Talons of Weng Chiang." 1977. Director: David Maloney. Writer: Robert Holmes. Starring Tom Baker.
"The Terror of the Autons." 1971. Director: Barry Letts. Writer: Robert Holmes. Starring Jon Pertwee.
"The Three Doctors." 1973. Director: Lennie Mayne. Writers: Bob Baker, Dave Martin. Starring Jon Pertwee, Patrick Troughton, William Hartnell.
"Time and the Rani." 1987. Director: Andrew Morgan. Writers: Pip and Jane Baker. Starring Sylvester McCoy.
"The Time Warrior." 1974. Director: Alan Bromly. Writer: Robert Holmes. Starring Jon Pertwee.
"The Tomb of the Cybermen." 1967. Director: Morris Barry. Writers: Gerry Davis, Kit Pedler. Starring Patrick Troughton.
"The Trial of the Time Lord." 1986. Directors: Nicholas Mallett, Ron Jones, Chris Clough. Writers: Robert Holmes, Philip Martin, Pip and Jane Baker. Starring Colin Baker.

"The Twin Dilemma." 1984. Director: Peter Moffatt. Writer: Anthony Steven. Starring Colin Baker.

"The Two Doctors." 1985. Director: Peter Moffatt. Writer: Robert Holmes. Starring Colin Baker and Patrick Troughton.

"An Unearthly Child." 1963. Director: Waris Hussein. Writers: Anthony Coburn and C.E. Webber. Starring William Hartnell.

"Vengeance on Varos." 1985. Director: Ron Jones. Writer: Philip Martin. Starring Colin Baker.

"The Visitation." 1982. Director: Peter Moffatt. Writer: Eric Saward. Starring Peter Davison.

"Warriors of the Deep." 1984. Director: Pennant Roberts. Writer: Johnny Byrne. Starring Peter Davison.

"The War Games." 1969. Director: David Maloney. Writers: Terrance Dicks, Malcolm Hulke. Starring Patrick Troughton.

"The Web Planet." 1965. Director: Richard Martin. Writer: Bill Strutton. Starring William Hartnell.

The Feature Films

Daleks: Invasion Earth, 2150 A.D.. 1966. Director: Gordon Flemyng. Writer: Milton Subotsky. Starring Peter Cushing. An AARU Production. Released on videotape through Republic Pictures and Lumiere Pictures.

Doctor Who and the Daleks. 1965. Director: Gordon Flemyng. Writer: Milton Subotsky. Starring Peter Cushing. An AARU Production. Released on videotape through Republic Pictures and Lumiere Pictures.

Index